MW00651199

FOUNDATION PRESS EDITORIAL BOARD

SAUL LEVMORE
DIRECTING EDITOR
William B. Graham Distinguished Service Professor of Law and
Former Dean of the Law School
University of Chicago

GUY-URIEL E. CHARLES
Charles J. Ogletree Jr. Professor of Law
Harvard Law School

NORA FREEMAN ENGSTROM
Ernest W. McFarland Professor of Law
Stanford Law School

DANIEL A. FARBER
Sho Sato Professor of Law
University of California at Berkeley

HEATHER K. GERKEN
Dean and the Sol & Lillian Goldman Professor of Law
Yale University

SAMUEL ISSACHAROFF
Bonnie and Richard Reiss Professor of Constitutional Law
New York University

HAROLD HONGJU KOH
Sterling Professor of International Law and
Former Dean of the Law School
Yale University

THOMAS W. MERRILL
Charles Evans Hughes Professor of Law
Columbia University

ROBERT L. RABIN
A. Calder Mackay Professor of Law
Stanford University

HILLARY A. SALE
Agnes Williams Sesquicentennial Professor of Law
Associate Dean for Strategy, and Professor of Management
Georgetown University

UNIVERSITY CASEBOOK SERIES®

PRACTICING BIOETHICS LAW

SECOND EDITION

LESLIE C. GRIFFIN
William S. Boyd Professor of Law
University of Nevada, Las Vegas Boyd School of Law

JOAN H. KRAUSE
Dan K. Moore Distinguished Professor of Law
University of North Carolina School of Law

FOUNDATION
PRESS

The publisher is not engaged in rendering legal or other professional advice, and this publication is not a substitute for the advice of an attorney. If you require legal or other expert advice, you should seek the services of a competent attorney or other professional.

University Casebook Series is a trademark registered in the U.S. Patent and Trademark Office.

© 2016 LEG, Inc. d/b/a West Academic
© 2021 LEG, Inc. d/b/a West Academic
444 Cedar Street, Suite 700
St. Paul, MN 55101
1-877-888-1330

Printed in the United States of America

ISBN: 978-1-68328-817-6

For Mikaela Barbara Saver

ACKNOWLEDGMENTS

We thank Catherine Galvez, Victor Kang, Erica Smit and Whitney Short, all UNLV Boyd School of Law students and now alumni, and Matt Geenen and Sabrina Shah, students at the UNC School of Law, for excellent research assistance, and Mayara Cueto-Diaz for her careful preparation of the manuscript. We are grateful to Staci Herr, Executive Editor, Foundation Press, and Tessa M. Boury, Senior Acquisitions Editor at Foundation Press, for their confidence in the project and their wise recommendations throughout the process of two editions. Special thanks go to Richard Saver, Arch T. Allen Distinguished Professor of Law at the UNC School of Law, for his excellent advice and suggestions about the content of the book.

We would also like to thank the authors and copyright holders of the following works, who permitted their inclusion in this book:

Barnard, Noel, Throw Me a Bone Marrow Transplant: Peripheral Blood Stem Cells and the National Organ Transplant Act, 13 North Carolina Journal of Law & Technology 387, 396–98, copyright © 2012. Reprinted with the permission of the author and North Carolina Journal of Law & Technology;

Brandt, Allan M., Racism and Research: The Case of the Tuskegee Syphilis Study, 8 Hastings Center Report 21, copyright © 1978. Reprinted with the permission of the Hastings Center Report;

Diamond, Nicholas J., The Flaws of Stem Cell Legislation: Sherley, Brustle, and Future Policy Challenges Posed by Induced Pluripotent Stem Cells, 14 Minnesota Journal of Law, Science & Technology 259, 265–67, copyright © 2013. Reprinted with the permission of the author and Minnesota Journal of Law, Science & Technology;

Healy, Kieran & Kimberly D. Krawiec, Custom, Contract, and Kidney Exchange, 62 Duke Law Journal 645, copyright © 2012. Reprinted with the permission of the authors;

Hoffman, Sharona, Regulating Clinical Research, 31 Capital University Law Review 71, copyright © 2003. Reprinted with the permission of the author;

Javitt, Gail H., Take Another Little Piece of My Heart: Regulating the Research Use of Human Biospecimens, 41 Journal of Law, Medicine & Ethics 424, copyright © 2013. Reprinted with the permission of the author and the Journal of Law, Medicine & Ethics;

Meisel, Alan, Canterbury v. Spence: The Inadvertent Landmark Case, in Health Law & Bioethics: Cases in Context, edited by Sandra H. Johnson et al., copyright © 2009. Reprinted with the permission of Wolters Kluwer Law & Business;

Robertson, John, Paid Organ Donations and the Constitutionality of NOTA, 40 Hastings Constitutional Law Quarterly 221, copyright ©

2013. Reprinted with the permission of the author and Hastings Constitutional Law Quarterly;

Saver, Richard S., Is It Really All About the Money? Reconsidering Non-Financial Interests in Medical Research, 40 Journal of Law, Medicine & Ethics 467, copyright © 2012. Reprinted with the permission of the author and the Journal of Law, Medicine & Ethics;

Sawicki, Nadia N., The Conscience Defense to Malpractice, 108 California Law Review 1255, copyright © 2020. Reprinted with the permission of the author;

Scannell, Kate, Book Review Essay: The Immortal Life of Henrietta Lacks, Rebecca Skloot, 31 Journal of Legal Medicine 493, copyright © 2010. Reprinted with the permission of the Journal of Legal Medicine;

Sepper, Elizabeth, Taking Conscience Seriously, 98 Virginia Law Review 1501, copyright © 2012. Reprinted with the permission of the author and Virginia Law Review.

INTRODUCTION

Welcome to *Practicing Bioethics Law*. This book is designed to work in conjunction with its Casebook Companion website, http://practicing bioethicslaw.com/resources.asp. The book provides basic readings in the field of bioethics law, including court cases, statutes, administrative regulations, briefs, and law review and other academic articles. The website provides practice documents, videos, pictures, scientific materials and other information that is too complex to include in a traditional casebook. We combined the book and the website so that you could learn how to practice bioethics law at the same time that you are beginning to understand the theory and content of bioethics law.

You should think of the website as a supplement and consult it whenever you are reading the casebook. Both the book and the website are divided into seven chapters; the website sections correspond to the book's sections. Throughout the book, there are boxes instructing you to go to the website to gain additional information about a subject. The website is especially useful for acquiring the scientific background that is so important to bioethics law.

Go to the website to see . . .

The book also includes numerous practice exercises, which are also flagged by boxes in the text. You should work through all these exercises in preparation for class discussions. The casebook is based on a theory of active and engaged learning. Don't settle for just understanding the facts or holding of a case. Your job as a lawyer is to figure out how to make the existing law work for your client. The practice exercises are designed to test your understanding of the concepts you are learning. You should expect to spend significant time developing detailed answers to the practice questions. You will probably contribute and learn more from class discussions if you have wrestled with the problems and tried to develop good solutions for them.

Practice Exercise: Go to the website and follow the link to read . . . how would you represent your client?

Bioethics law is a broad and expanding field that offers numerous possibilities for legal careers. The book is designed to introduce you to a range of jobs available to you so that you can start to think about what area of the law you would like to practice. Lawyers work in hospitals, litigate cases, propose and produce legislation, engage in administrative proceedings, protect intellectual property, defend the rights of patients, and push the law in new directions. We hope the readings and practice exercises will give you an idea of the interesting career possibilities open to you.

Changes in science and technology regularly challenge existing bioethics law. For that reason, every chapter has a final section entitled

"Looking Ahead." This section identifies the cutting edge issues that bioethicists now confront. The topics in this section also provide a good source of ideas for research papers for students who are taking a paper-writing seminar.

The field of biomedical ethics, a sub-discipline of bioethics that focuses on medicine, provides the theoretical background for the ethical component of this book. Biomedical ethics has been commonly organized around four foundational principles: autonomy, non-maleficence, beneficence and justice. The principle of autonomy focuses on the patient's right to make her own choices about medical care and treatment. The principle of non-maleficence is based on the old maxim *primum non nocere*, meaning that the first rule for medical professionals is to do no harm. The principle of beneficence requires medical personnel not only to avoid harm to patients, but also to further their patients' best interests. The principle of justice requires that each person receive her due. In the medical setting, the principle of justice usually focuses on the fair distribution of medical resources. Beauchamp & Childress, Principles of Biomedical Ethics (2021). You should regularly think about these principles as you consider the ethical aspects of the subjects studied in this book. If you want to gain further information about any bioethical question, be sure to consult the valuable 6-volume encyclopedia, Bruce Jennings, ed., Bioethics (Macmillan 2014).

As a lawyer, you will need to figure out how the law interacts with and responds to these principles as well as developments in medicine and science. This is not an easy task. During the 1970s, when the first case in this book, *In the Matter of Karen Quinlan*, was decided, homicide laws were generally interpreted to prohibit families from discontinuing medical treatment for their incompetent loved ones. Judges, lawyers, families and patients had to reckon with how to reconcile the principle of patient autonomy with criminal law and medical technology that allowed patients in persistent vegetative states to live indefinitely while attached to life-supporting machinery. Today, states debate whether physician-assisted suicide should be legal, and some countries allow voluntary euthanasia.

This book and the accompanying website provide you with the tools to address such questions. Chapter 1 addresses the law and ethics of death and dying. Chapter 2 examines how the law protects patients and research subjects through the mechanism of informed consent. Chapter 3 explores reproductive privacy and parenthood through the lens of abortion, surrogate motherhood, and adoptive parenthood. Chapter 4 focuses on the principle of justice: asking how health care and organs should be distributed in a just manner. Chapter 5 asks whether health care professionals have conscience rights to refuse treatment. Chapter 6 examines the property interests in bioethics by looking at patent law and research profits. Finally, Chapter 7 addresses the new frontier created by the study of the brain and the developing field of neuroethics.

For readability, we removed most citations from the readings and provided ellipses only where lengthy segments of text were omitted. We kept citations in some documents when the citation 1) identified important cases that were the basis of the ruling; 2) introduced non-legal material into the discussion or 3) helped readers to understand how lawyers cite and introduce legal and non-legal information into legal briefs, pleadings, and other documents.

Updates to the book's materials will also be provided on the website.

SUMMARY OF CONTENTS

TABLE OF CONTENTS

TABLE OF CASES

The principal cases are in bold type.

UNIVERSITY CASEBOOK SERIES®

PRACTICING BIOETHICS LAW

SECOND EDITION

CHAPTER 1

DEATH: RESOLVING BIOMEDICAL ETHICS THROUGH CONSTITUTIONAL LAW

Introduction. Ethics is the systematic reflection on individual and social morality. As a field of study, it seeks to identify the best norms for human social life. Bioethics focuses on how biological and other scientific discoveries impact the moral life and how those discoveries can be used to promote human well-being. The field of biomedical ethics, a sub-discipline of bioethics that focuses on medicine, has been commonly organized around four foundational principles: autonomy, non-maleficence, beneficence, and justice. The principle of autonomy focuses on the patient's right to make her own choices about medical care and treatment. The principle of non-maleficence is based on the old maxim *primum non nocere*, meaning the first rule for medical professionals is to do no harm. The principle of beneficence requires medical personnel not only to avoid harm to patients, but also to further their patients' best interests. The principle of justice requires that each person receive her due. In the medical setting, the principle of justice usually focuses on the fair distribution of medical resources. Beauchamp & Childress, Principles of Biomedical Ethics (2021).

Law has a different set of standards. One goal includes establishing norms that prevent harm and allow people to live together in peace. Criminal law, for example, identifies crimes for which individuals can be prosecuted and then punished by the government. Homicide laws that prohibit killing another person are leading examples of criminal laws.

State laws generally identify the unlawful killing of another human being as criminal homicide. N.J. Stat. Ann. § 2A:113–1 (West 2014). Criminal law and biomedical ethics came into potential conflict after twenty-one-year-old Karen Ann Quinlan passed out at a party and stopped breathing. Although Quinlan's parents, Joseph and Julia Quinlan, initially held out hope for Karen's recovery, eventually Karen was diagnosed as being in a persistent vegetative state (PVS). That meant that while Karen was still alive, she was unconscious and incapable of ever regaining consciousness. As a result, her parents asked their daughter's medical caretakers to remove Karen from the respirator that helped her breathe.

The Quinlans were devout Roman Catholics who had consulted with their parish priest before deciding that removing the respirator was the

right thing to do. Karen's physician, Dr. Robert Morse, however, refused to discontinue treatment because he thought it violated his medical and professional ethics as a doctor. Moreover, hospital authorities worried that New Jersey homicide law prohibited removing Quinlan from the respirator, and state prosecutors were interested in enforcing the criminal laws. When the parties could not resolve their dispute, they turned to the New Jersey courts. See Sandra H. Johnson, Quinlan and Cruzan: Beyond the Symbols, in Health Law & Bioethics: Cases in Context (S.H. Johnson et al. eds., 2009).

Quinlan is illustrative of many developments in biomedical ethics and law. Technology kept Karen alive and diagnosed her persistent vegetative state. The Quinlans held a strong moral belief that disconnecting Karen was consistent with her wishes and their own Catholic faith. The doctors feared legal and professional sanction for ending a human life. State prosecutors needed and wanted to enforce New Jersey homicide law.

In those circumstances, the New Jersey courts stepped in to resolve the problem. As you read the following two *Quinlan* cases from New Jersey, decide if you think the judges did a good job in the difficult circumstances of the case. In particular, do you agree that Joseph Quinlan was the appropriate guardian and decision-maker for his daughter? Do you find the trial court or the New Jersey Supreme Court more persuasive on the question of Joseph Quinlan's guardianship? Do you think Karen would have agreed with her parents' decision to terminate her life support? Do you agree that removing a patient from a respirator is not homicide? Or are you surprised that removing a patient from a respirator was once considered a possible homicide?

A. *QUINLAN*: REMOVING THE RESPIRATOR

In the Matter of Karen Quinlan, an Alleged Incompetent

Superior Court of New Jersey, Chancery Division, 1975.
137 N.J. Super. 227, 348 A.2d 801.

■ MUIR, J.S.C.

In his initial pleading Joseph Quinlan, father of 21-year-old Karen Ann Quinlan, seeks, on grounds of mental incompetency, to be appointed the guardian of the person and property of his daughter. He alleges her 'vital processes are artificially sustained via the extraordinary means of a mechanical MA–1 Respirator.' He imprecates the court grant 'the express power of authorizing the discontinuance of all extraordinary means of sustaining the vital processes of his daughter.'

By a pleading amendment he also seeks to restrain the Morris County Prosecutor, Karen Quinlan's attending and treating physicians and St. Clare's Hospital from interfering with the exercise of the

authorization sought, and to enjoin the prosecutor from prosecuting for homicide when the authorization sought is effected.

The court, pursuant to R. 4:26–2, appointed Daniel Coburn, Esq., guardian ad litem.

At the pretrial conference held on the return date of an order to show cause issued with the amended pleading, the State of New Jersey through the Attorney General intervened.

Plaintiff initially asserted that Karen Quinlan is legally and medically dead but altered this position prior to trial by admitting she is not dead 'according to any legal standard recognized by the State of New Jersey.'

It is stipulated by all parties that Karen Ann Quinlan is unfit and unable to manage her own affairs.

The court's findings of fact are as hereinafter set forth: . . .

On the night of April 15, 1975 friends of Karen summoned the local police and emergency rescue squad, and she was taken to Newton Memorial Hospital. The precise events leading up to her admission to Newton Memorial Hospital are unclear. She apparently ceased breathing for at least two 15-minute periods. Mouth-to-mouth resuscitation was applied by her friends the first time and by a police respirator the second time. The exact amount of time she was without spontaneous respiration is unknown.

Upon her admission to Newton Memorial urine and blood tests were administered which indicated the presence of quinine, aspirin, barbiturates in normal range and traces of valium and librium. The drugs found present were indicated by Dr. Robert Morse, the neurologist in charge of her care at St. Clare's, to be in the therapeutic range, and the quinine consistent with mixing in drinks like soda water. . . .

Karen was transferred to the Intensive Care Unit (I.C.U.) of St. Clare's Hospital, under the care of Dr. Morse. At the time of her transfer she was still unconscious, still on a respirator; a catheter was inserted into her bladder and a tracheostomy had been performed. . . .

Dr. Morse testified concerning the treatment of Karen at St. Clare's. He averred she receives oral feedings since intravenous feeding is insufficient to sustain her. She is fed a high caloric nutrient called 'Vivenex,' which she receives through a small nasal gastro tube inserted in her gastro-intestinal system. He asserts this is necessary to keep her 'viable.' She has apparently lost considerable weight, being described as emaciated by most of the examining experts, who also indicate her weight condition to be good under the circumstances.

There is constant threat of infection, according to Dr. Morse. Antibiotics are administered to thwart potential infection, with tests constantly being made to keep a check on this threat. The hospital records indicate specialists consulted with respect to the cleaning,

utilization and operation of the urethral catheter and with respect to the treatment and care of decubiti (lesions commonly known as bed sores) generated by her continuous repose.

The day-by-day charts, entitled 'Vital Signs,' kept by nurses who give her 24-hour care, indicate, in part, the following:

1. Her color was generally pale, her skin warm, she was almost constantly suffering from diaphoresis (sweating), many times profusely but occasionally moderately or not at all;

2. There was always a reaction to painful stimuli, she responded decerebrately to pain, she sometimes would grimace as if in pain, which would be followed by increased rigidity of her arms and legs;

3. There would be periodic contractions and spasms, periodic yawning, periodic movements of spastic nature;

4. Pupils were sometimes dilated, sometimes normal, but almost always sluggish to light;

5. Body waste disposal through the urethral catheter and the bowel was indicated to occur;

6. Feedings of Vivinex were given alternately with water on various nurses shifts;

7. The nurses were constantly moving, positioning and bathing her;

8. Body rashes occurred at times; decubiti were treated with heat lamps on occasions;

9. Sometimes she would trigger and assist the respirator; other times she would go for periods without triggering it at all;

10. Her extremities remained rigid with contraction of them being described as severe at times;

11. On May 7 nurses indicated she blinked her eyes two times when asked to and appeared responsive by moving her eyes when talked to, but there is no further evidence of this type [sic] reaction thereafter.

Dr. Javed indicated that efforts were made to wean or remove Karen from the respirator. The hospital records support this. Dr. Javed testified that for weaning to be successful, the patient must have a stable respiratory pattern. Karen was taken off the respirator for short periods of time. Each time, her respiratory rate, rate of breathing, went up and the volume of air intake would decrease. He indicated her breathing rate would more than double in intensity while her 'tidal volume' or air intake would drop 50%. The longest period of time she was off the respirator was one-half hour. He further indicated that during removal from the respirator her pO2 dropped. He stated that the respiratory problem is secondary to the neurological problem, and without improvement in the latter she cannot be removed from the respirator since she would be unable to maintain her vital processes without its assistance.

Dr. Morse's hospital notes indicate there is no neurological improvement from the time of her admission to St. Clare's to date. He testified that Karen changed from a sleeping comatose condition to a sleep-awake type comatose condition but described this as normal in comatose patients and not any indication of improvement. During the awake cycle she is still unconscious. . . .

Dr. Morse reflected carefully in his testimony on Karen's prognosis. He described her condition as a chronic or 'persistent vegetative state'. Dr. Fred Plum, a creator of the phrase, describes its significance by indicating the brain as working in two ways:

> We have an internal vegetative regulation which controls body temperature, which controls breathing, which controls to a considerable degree blood pressure, which controls to some degree heart rate, which controls chewing, swallowing and which controls sleeping and waking. We have a more highly developed brain, which is uniquely human, which controls our relation to the outside world, our capacity to talk, to see, to feel, to sing, to think. . . . Brain death necessarily must mean the death of both of these functions of the brain, vegetatiive [sic] and the sapient. Therefore, the presence of any function which is regulated or governed or controlled by the deeper parts of the brain which in layman's terms might be considered purely vegetative would mean that the brain is not biologically dead.

Dr. Morse, in reflecting on the prognosis, notes Karen's absence of awareness of anything or anyone around her. In response to a direct question he noted she is not suffering from locked-in syndrome in which a patient is conscious but so totally paralyzed that communications can be made only through a complex system of eye or eyelid movements.

Dr. Morse states Karen Quinlan will not return to a level of cognitive function (i.e., that she will be able to say 'Mr. Coburn I'm glad you are my guardian.') What level or plateau she will reach is unknown. He does not know of any course of treatment that can be given and cannot see how her condition can be reversed, but is unwilling to say she is in an irreversible state or condition. He indicated there is a possibility of recovery but that level is unknown, particularly due to the absence of pre-hospital history. . . .

The decision to request removal of their daughter from the respirator, understandably came tortuously, arduously to the Quinlans. At the outset they authorized Dr. Morse to do everything he could to keep her alive, believing she would recover. They participated in a constant vigil over her with other family members. They were in constant contact with the doctors, particularly Dr. Morse, receiving day-by-day reports concerning her prognosis which, as time passed, became more and more pessimistic and more and more discouraging to them.

Mrs. Quinlan and the children were the first to conclude Karen should be removed from the respirator. Mrs. Quinlan, working at the local parish church, had ongoing talks with Father Trapasso, who supported her conclusion and indicated that it was a permissible practice within the tenets of Roman Catholic teachings.

Mr. Quinlan was slower in making his decision. His hope for recovery continued despite the disheartening medical reports. Neither his wife nor Father Trapasso made any attempt to influence him. A conflict existed between letting her natural body function control her life and the hope for recovery. Precisely when he came to a decision is not clear. By his testimony he indicated early September, but he signed a release to the hospital dated July 31, 1975, hereafter referred to, which makes it reasonably inferrable [sic] that the decision was made in July. Once having made the decision, he sought Father Trapasso's encouragement, which he received.

Father Trapasso based his support of the position taken by the Quinlans on the traditional, moral precepts of the Roman Catholic faith and upon a declaration, designated an Allocutio, by Pope Pius XII made on November 24, 1957. . . .

The Quinlans on July 31, 1975 signed the following:

> We authorize and direct Doctor Morse to discontinue all extraordinary measures, including the use of a respirator for our daughter Karen Quinlan.
>
> We acknowledge that the above named physician has thoroughly discussed the above with us and that the consequences have been fully explained to us. Therefore, we hereby RELEASE from any and all liability the above named physician, associates and assistants of his choice, Saint Clare's Hospital and its agents and employees.

The Quinlans, upon signing the release, considered the matter decided. Dr. Morse, however, felt he could not and would not agree to the cessation of the respirator assistance. He testified—characterizing the issue of extraordinary treatment and the termination of it as something brought up suddenly in July—that he advised the Quinlans prior to the time of the release that he wanted to check into the matter further before giving his approval. After checking on other medical case histories he concluded that to terminate the respirator would be a substantial deviation from medical tradition, that it involved ascertaining 'quality of life,' and that he would not do so.

Karen Quinlan is quoted as saying she never wanted to be kept alive by extraordinary means. The statements attributed to her by her mother, sister and a friend are indicated to have been made essentially in relation to instances where close friends or relatives were terminally ill. In one instance an aunt, in great pain, was terminally ill from cancer. In another instance the father of a girl friend was dying under like circumstances.

In a third circumstance a close family friend was dying of a brain tumor. Mrs. Quinlan testified that her daughter was very full of life, that she loved life and did not want to be kept alive in any way she would not enjoy life to the fullest. . . .

The judicial conscience and morality involved in considering whether the court should authorize Karen Quinlan's removal from the respirator are inextricably involved with the nature of medical science and the role of the physician in our society and his duty to his patient. . . .

There is a duty to continue the life-assisting apparatus, if, within the treating physician's opinion, it should be done. Here Dr. Morse has refused to concur in the removal of Karen from the respirator. It is his considered position that medical tradition does not justify that act. There is no mention, in the doctor's refusal, of concern over criminal liability, and the court concludes that such is not the basis for his determination. It is significant that Dr. Morse, a man who demonstrated strong empathy and compassion, a man who has directed care that impressed all the experts, is unwilling to direct Karen's removal from the respirator.

The assertion that Karen would elect, if competent, to terminate the respirator requires careful examination.

She made these statements at the age of 20. In the words of her mother, she was full of life. She made them under circumstances where another person was suffering, suffering in at least one instance from severe pain. While perhaps it is not too significant, there is no evidence she is now in pain. Dr. Morse describes her reacting no noxious stimuli-pain-as reflex but not indicative that she is sensing the pain as a functioning human being does. The reaction is described as stereotyped, and her reflexes show no adjustment that would indicate she mentally experiences pain.

The conversations with her mother and friends were theoretical ones. She was not personally involved. They were not made under the solemn and sobering fact that death is a distinct choice. Karen Quinlan, while she was in complete control of her mental faculties to reason out the staggering magnitude of the decision not to be 'kept alive,' did not make a decision. This is not the situation of a 'living will' which is based upon a concept of informed consent.

While the repetition of the conversations indicates an awareness of the problems of terminal illness, the elements involved—the vigor of youth that espouses the theoretical good and righteousness, the absence of being presented the question as it applied to her—are not persuasive to establish a probative weight sufficient to persuade this court that Karen Quinlan would elect her own removal from the respirator.

The breadth of the power to act and protect Karen's interests is, I conclude, controlled by a judicial conscience and morality which dictate that the determination whether or not Karen Ann Quinlan be removed from the respirator is to be left to the treating physician. It is a medical

decision, not a judicial one. I am satisfied that it may be concurred in by the parents but not governed by them. This is so because there is always the dilemma of whether it is the conscious being's relief or the unconscious being's welfare that governs the parental motivation. . . .

A significant amount of the legal presentation to the court has involved whether the act of removing Karen from the respirator constitutes an affirmative act, or could be considered an act of omission. An intricate discussion on semantics and form is not required since the substance of the sought-for authorization would result in the taking of the life of Karen Quinlan when the law of the State indicates that such an authorization would be a homicide. . . .

V

Joseph Quinlan applies to be appointed guardian ad litem of his daughter's person and property. Karen Quinlan is incompetent and unfit and unable to govern herself as to manage her affairs. As next of kin Mr. Quinlan qualifies to be her guardian, unless it is shown his appointment would be contrary to Karen's best interest. The guardian ad litem opposes his appointment.

The responsibility of the guardian over property is to manage the business affairs of the incompetent. There is no reason why Mr. Quinlan should not serve in this capacity.

The responsibility of the guardian over the person of the incompetent is to make the decisions, in this instance, that relate to her welfare, insofar as those decisions are within the person's control. I have ruled that it is a medical decision whether or not Karen should be removed from the respirator. Just as that decision is a medical one, the continued care and treatment of Karen is a medical one. There will be, however, from time to time medical decisions relating to further treatment that will require a guardian's counsel, advice and concurrence. This is reflected by the testimony of Dr. Morse.

Mr. Quinlan impressed me as a very sincere, moral, ethical and religious person. He very obviously anguished over his decision to terminate what he considers the extraordinary care of his daughter. That anguish would be continued and magnified by the inner conflicts he would have if he were required to concur in the day-by-day decisions on the future care and treatment of his daughter. These conflicts would have to offset his decision-making processes. I, therefore, find it more appropriate and in Karen's interests if another is appointed.

For the same reasons, I do not feel Mrs. Quinlan should be appointed.

Daniel Coburn, esq., who has acted on Karen's behalf throughout this proceeding, is appointed the guardian of her person. Both guardians shall serve without bond in accordance with law and the rules of court, after qualification.

Judgment should be submitted accordingly.

NOTES AND QUESTIONS

1. *Physician vs. Patient Autonomy.* Do you agree with the trial court's deference to Dr. Morse, notably its statement "[t]here is a duty to continue the life-assisting apparatus, if, within the treating physician's opinion, it should be done. . . . [T]he determination whether or not Karen Ann Quinlan be removed from the respirator is to be left to the treating physician. It is a medical decision, not a judicial one."? Is that assertion consistent with any of the four biomedical principles of autonomy, non-maleficence, beneficence, or justice?

2. *Guardianship.* The trial judge also wrote that the medical decision "may be concurred in by the parents, but not governed by them. This is so because there is always the dilemma of whether it is the conscious being's relief or the unconscious being's welfare that governs the parental motivation." Do you agree that parents waver between their own relief and the welfare of their children? Does this uncertainty about parental motivation confirm that Joseph Quinlan should not have been the guardian for his daughter? Do you agree with the trial judge that Joseph would be too anguished to provide good decisions for Karen? What about Karen's mother? Were Karen's physicians better protectors of her well-being than her parents?

3. *Burden of Proof.* Do you believe that Karen's reported statements about not wanting to be kept alive provided enough evidence to discontinue the respirator? Do you believe her family and friends accurately reported her wishes? Should evidence of a person's attitude toward living in a PVS be necessary before treatment is discontinued, or is it acceptable for courts to assume that no reasonable person would want to continue treatment while in a PVS with no hope of recovery? Do you know how you would want to be treated in Karen's situation? Are your friends and family aware of your opinion?

4. *New Jersey Supreme Court.* Did the New Jersey Supreme Court—in the opinion below—do a better job resolving the Quinlan controversy? Do you agree with the privacy rationale identified in the court's opinion, or do you think the court should have made more reference to the principle of autonomy? Does the U.S. Constitution support a principle of medical autonomy? How does privacy in the death context compare with an individual's right to make decisions about contraception or abortion?

In the Matter of Karen Quinlan, an Alleged Incompetent

Supreme Court of New Jersey, 1976.
70 N.J. 10, 355 A.2d 647.

■ HUGHES, C.J.

This brings us to a consideration of the constitutional and legal issues underlying the foregoing determinations.

CONSTITUTIONAL AND LEGAL ISSUES

I. The Free Exercise of Religion

We think the contention as to interference with religious beliefs or rights may be considered and dealt with without extended discussion, given the acceptance of distinctions so clear and simple in their precedential definition as to be dispositive on their face.

Simply stated, the right to religious beliefs is absolute but conduct in pursuance thereof is not wholly immune from governmental restraint. . . . [R]anged against the State's interest in the preservation of life, the impingement of religious belief, much less religious 'neutrality' as here, does not reflect a constitutional question, in the circumstances at least of the case presently before the Court. Moreover, like the trial court, we do not recognize an independent parental right of religious freedom to support the relief requested. . . .

III. The Right of Privacy

It is the issue of the constitutional right of privacy that has given us most concern, in the exceptional circumstances of this case. Here a loving parent, qua parent and raising the rights of his incompetent and profoundly damaged daughter, probably irreversibly doomed to no more than a biologically vegetative remnant of life, is before the court. He seeks authorization to abandon specialized technological procedures which can only maintain for a time a body having no potential for resumption or continuance of other than a 'vegetative' existence.

We have no doubt, in these unhappy circumstances, that if Karen were herself miraculously lucid for an interval (not altering the existing prognosis of the condition to which she would soon return) and perceptive of her irreversible condition, she could effectively decide upon discontinuance of the life-support apparatus, even if it meant the prospect of natural death. To this extent we may distinguish *Heston*, supra, which concerned a severely injured young woman (Delores Heston), whose life depended on surgery and blood transfusion; and who was in such extreme shock that she was unable to express an informed choice (although the Court apparently considered the case as if the patient's own religious decision to resist transfusion were at stake), but most importantly a patient apparently salvable to long life and vibrant health;—a situation not at all like the present case.

We have no hesitancy in deciding, in the instant diametrically opposite case, that no external compelling interest of the State could compel Karen to endure the unendurable, only to vegetate a few measurable months with no realistic possibility of returning to any semblance of cognitive or sapient life. We perceive no thread of logic distinguishing between such a choice on Karen's part and a similar choice which, under the evidence in this case, could be made by a competent patient terminally ill, riddled by cancer and suffering great pain; such a patient would not be resuscitated or put on a respirator in the example

described by Dr. Korein, and a fortiori would not be kept against his will on a respirator.

Although the Constitution does not explicitly mention a right of privacy, Supreme Court decisions have recognized that a right of personal privacy exists and that certain areas of privacy are guaranteed under the Constitution. Eisenstadt v. Baird, 405 U.S. 438, 92 S. Ct. 1029, 31 L.Ed.2d 349 (1972); Stanley v. Georgia, 394 U.S. 557, 89 S. Ct. 1243, 22 L.Ed.2d 542 (1969). The Court has interdicted judicial intrusion into many aspects of personal decision, sometimes basing this restraint upon the conception of a limitation of judicial interest and responsibility, such as with regard to contraception and its relationship to family life and decision. Griswold v. Connecticut, 381 U.S. 479, 85 S. Ct. 1678, 14 L.Ed.2d 510 (1965).

The Court in Griswold found the unwritten constitutional right of privacy to exist in the penumbra of specific guarantees of the Bill of Rights "formed by emanations from those guarantees that help give them life and substance." 381 U.S. at 484, 85 S. Ct. at 1681, 14 L.Ed.2d at 514. Presumably this right is broad enough to encompass a patient's decision to decline medical treatment under certain circumstances, in much the same way as it is broad enough to encompass a woman's decision to terminate pregnancy under certain conditions. Roe v. Wade, 410 U.S. 113, 153, 93 S. Ct. 705, 727, 35 L.Ed.2d 147, 177 (1973).

Nor is such right of privacy forgotten in the New Jersey Constitution. N.J.Const. (1947), Art. I, par. 1.

The claimed interests of the State in this case are essentially the preservation and sanctity of human life and defense of the right of the physician to administer medical treatment according to his best judgment. In this case the doctors say that removing Karen from the respirator will conflict with their professional judgment. The plaintiff answers that Karen's present treatment serves only a maintenance function; that the respirator cannot cure or improve her condition but at best can only prolong her inevitable slow deterioration and death; and that the interests of the patient, as seen by her surrogate, the guardian, must be evaluated by the court as predominant, even in the face of an opinion Contra by the present attending physicians. Plaintiff's distinction is significant. The nature of Karen's care and the realistic chances of her recovery are quite unlike those of the patients discussed in many of the cases where treatments were ordered. In many of those cases the medical procedure required (usually a transfusion) constituted a minimal bodily invasion and the chances of recovery and return to functioning life were very good. We think that the State's interest Contra weakens and the individual's right to privacy grows as the degree of bodily invasion increases and the prognosis dims. Ultimately there comes a point at which the individual's rights overcome the State interest. It is for that reason that we believe Karen's choice, if she were competent to make it, would be vindicated by the law. Her prognosis is extremely

poor,—she will never resume cognitive life. And the bodily invasion is very great,—she requires 24 hour intensive nursing care, antibiotics, the assistance of a respirator, a catheter and feeding tube.

Our affirmation of Karen's independent right of choice, however, would ordinarily be based upon her competency to assert it. The sad truth, however, is that she is grossly incompetent and we cannot discern her supposed choice based on the testimony of her previous conversations with friends, where such testimony is without sufficient probative weight. Nevertheless we have concluded that Karen's right of privacy may be asserted on her behalf by her guardian under the peculiar circumstances here present.

If a putative decision by Karen to permit this non-cognitive, vegetative existence to terminate by natural forces is regarded as a valuable incident of her right of privacy, as we believe it to be, then it should not be discarded solely on the basis that her condition prevents her conscious exercise of the choice. The only practical way to prevent destruction of the right is to permit the guardian and family of Karen to render their best judgment, subject to the qualifications hereinafter stated, as to whether she would exercise it in these circumstances. If their conclusion is in the affirmative this decision should be accepted by a society the overwhelming majority of whose members would, we think, in similar circumstances, exercise such a choice in the same way for themselves or for those closest to them. It is for this reason that we determine that Karen's right of privacy may be asserted in her behalf, in this respect, by her guardian and family under the particular circumstances presented by this record.

IV. The Medical Factor

. . . We glean from the record here that physicians distinguish between curing the ill and comforting and easing the dying; that they refuse to treat the curable as if they were dying or ought to die, and that they have sometimes refused to treat the hopeless and dying as if they were curable. In this sense, as we were reminded by the testimony of Drs. Korein and Diamond, many of them have refused to inflict an undesired prolongation of the process of dying on a patient in irreversible condition when it is clear that such 'therapy' offers neither human nor humane benefit. We think these attitudes represent a balanced implementation of a profoundly realistic perspective on the meaning of life and death and that they respect the whole Judeo-Christian tradition of regard for human life. No less would they seem consistent with the moral matrix of medicine, 'to heal,' very much in the sense of the endless mission of the law, 'to do justice.'

Yet this balance, we feel, is particularly difficult to perceive and apply in the context of the development by advanced technology of sophisticated and artificial life-sustaining devices. For those possibly curable, such devices are of great value, and, as ordinary medical procedures, are essential. Consequently, as pointed out by Dr. Diamond,

they are necessary because of the ethic of medical practice. But in light of the situation in the present case (while the record here is somewhat hazy in distinguishing between 'ordinary' and 'extraordinary' measures), one would have to think that the use of the same respirator or like support could be considered 'ordinary' in the context of the possibly curable patient but 'extraordinary' in the context of the forced sustaining by cardio-respiratory processes of an irreversibly doomed patient. And this dilemma is sharpened in the face of the malpractice and criminal action threat which we have mentioned. . . .

Nevertheless, there must be a way to free physicians, in the pursuit of their healing vocation, from possible contamination by self-interest or self-protection concerns which would inhibit their independent medical judgments for the well-being of their dying patients. We would hope that this opinion might be serviceable to some degree in ameliorating the professional problems under discussion.

A technique aimed at the underlying difficulty (though in a somewhat broader context) is described by Dr. Karen Teel, a pediatrician and a director of Pediatric Education, who writes in the Baylor Law Review under the title 'The Physician's Dilemma: A Doctor's View: What The Law Should Be.' Dr. Teel recalls:

> Physicians, by virtue of their responsibility for medical judgments are, partly by choice and partly by default, charged with the responsibility of making ethical judgments which we are sometimes ill-equipped to make. We are not always morally and legally authorized to make them. The physician is thereby assuming a civil and criminal liability that, as often as not, he does not even realize as a factor in his decision. There is little or no dialogue in this whole process. The physician assumes that the judgment is called for and, in good faith, he acts. Someone must and it has been the physician who has assumed the responsibility and the risk.
>
> I suggest that it would be more appropriate to provide a regular forum for more input and dialogue in individual situations and to allow the responsibility of these judgments to be shared. Many hospitals have established an Ethics Committee composed of physicians, social workers, attorneys, and theologians, * * * which serves to review the individual circumstances of ethical dilemma and which has provided much in the way of assistance and safeguards for patients and their medical caretakers. Generally, the authority of these committees is primarily restricted to the hospital setting and their official status is more that of an advisory body than of an enforcing body.
>
> The concept of an Ethics Committee which has this kind of organization and is readily accessible to those persons rendering medical care to patients, would be, I think, the most promising

direction for further study at this point. (This would allow) some much needed dialogue regarding these issues and (force) the point of exploring all of the options for a particular patient. It diffuses the responsibility for making these judgments. Many physicians, in many circumstances, would welcome this sharing of responsibility. I believe that such an entity could lend itself well to an assumption of a legal status which would allow courses of action not now undertaken because of the concern for liability. (27 Baylor L. Rev. 6, 8–9 (1975)).

The most appealing factor in the technique suggested by Dr. Teel seems to us to be the diffusion of professional responsibility for decision, comparable in a way to the value of multi-judge courts in finally resolving on appeal difficult questions of law. Moreover, such a system would be protective to the hospital as well as the doctor in screening out, so to speak, a case which might be contaminated by less than worthy motivations of family or physician. In the real world and in relationship to the momentous decision contemplated, the value of additional views and diverse knowledge is apparent. . . .

V. Alleged Criminal Liability

Having concluded that there is a right of privacy that might permit termination of treatment in the circumstances of this case, we turn to consider the relationship of the exercise of that right to the criminal law. We are aware that such termination of treatment would accelerate Karen's death. The County Prosecutor and the Attorney General maintain that there would be criminal liability for such acceleration. Under the statutes of this State, the unlawful killing of another human being is criminal homicide. N.J.S.A. 2A:113–1, 2, 5. We conclude that there would be no criminal homicide in the circumstances of this case. We believe, first, that the ensuing death would not be homicide but rather expiration from existing natural causes. Secondly, even if it were to be regarded as homicide, it would not be unlawful.

These conclusions rest upon definitional and constitutional bases. The termination of treatment pursuant to the right of privacy is, within the limitations of this case, *ipsa facto* lawful. Thus, a death resulting from such an act would not come within the scope of the homicide statutes proscribing only the unlawful killing of another. There is a real and in this case determinative distinction between the unlawful taking of the life of another and the ending of artificial life-support systems as a matter of self-determination.

Furthermore, the exercise of a constitutional right such as we have here found is protected from criminal prosecution. See Stanley v. Georgia, supra, 394 U.S. at 559, 89 S. Ct. at 1245, 22 L.Ed.2d at 546. We do not question the State's undoubted power to punish the taking of human life, but that power does not encompass individuals terminating medical treatment pursuant to their right of privacy. See id. at 568, 89 S. Ct. at 1250, 22 L.Ed.2d at 551. The constitutional protection extends to

third parties whose action is necessary to effectuate the exercise of that right where the individuals themselves would not be subject to prosecution or the third parties are charged as accessories to an act which could not be a crime. Eisenstadt v. Baird, supra, 405 U.S. at 445–46, 92 S. Ct. at 1034–35, 31 L.Ed.2d at 357–58; Griswold v. Connecticut, supra, 381 U.S. at 481, 85 S. Ct. at 1679–80, 14 L.Ed.2d at 512–13. And, under the circumstances of this case, these same principles would apply to and negate a valid prosecution for attempted suicide were there still such a crime in this State.[9]

VI. The Guardianship of the Person

. . . The trial court was apparently convinced of the high character of Joseph Quinlan and his general suitability as guardian under other circumstances, describing him as 'very sincere, moral, ethical and religious.' The court felt, however, that the obligation to concur in the medical care and treatment of his daughter would be a source of anguish to him and would distort his 'decision-making processes.' We disagree, for we sense from the whole record before us that while Mr. Quinlan feels a natural grief, and understandably sorrows because of the tragedy which has befallen his daughter, his strength of purpose and character far outweighs these sentiments and qualifies him eminently for guardianship of the person as well as the property of his daughter. Hence we discern no valid reason to overrule the statutory intendment of perference [sic] to the next of kin.

DECLARATORY RELIEF

We thus arrive at the formulation of the declaratory relief which we have concluded is appropriate to this case. Some time has passed since Karen's physical and mental condition was described to the Court. At that time her continuing deterioration was plainly projected. Since the record has not been expanded we assume that she is now even more fragile and nearer to death than she was then. Since her present treating physicians may give reconsideration to her present posture in the light of this opinion, and since we are transferring to the plaintiff as guardian the choice of the attending physician and therefore other physicians may be in charge of the case who may take a different view from that of the present attending physicians, we herewith declare the following affirmative relief on behalf of the plaintiff. Upon the concurrence of the guardian and family of Karen, should the responsible attending

[9] An attempt to commit suicide was an indictable offense at common law and as such was indictable in this State as a common law misdemeanor. 1 Schlosser, Criminal Laws of New Jersey s 12.5 (3d ed. 1970); See N.J.S.A. 2A:85–1. The legislature towngraded [sic] the offense in 1957 to the status of a disorderly persons offense, which is not a 'crime' under our law. N.J.S.A. 2A:170–25.6. And in 1971, the legislature repealed all criminal sanctions for attempted suicide. N.J.S.A. 2A:85–5.1. Provision is now made for temporary hospitalization of persons making such an attempt. N.J.S.A. 30:4–26.3a. We note that under the proposed New Jersey Penal Code (Oct. 1971) there is no provision for criminal punishment of attempted suicide. See Commentary, s 2C:11–6. There is, however, an independent offense of 'aiding suicide.' s 2C:11–6b. This provision, if enacted, would not be incriminatory in circumstances similar to those presented in this case.

physicians conclude that there is no reasonable possibility of Karen's ever emerging from her present comatose condition to a cognitive, sapient state and that the life-support apparatus now being administered to Karen should be discontinued, they shall consult with the hospital 'Ethics Committee' or like body of the institution in which Karen is then hospitalized. If that consultative body agrees that there is no reasonable possibility of Karen's ever emerging from her present comatose condition to a cognitive, sapient state, the present life-support system may be withdrawn and said action shall be without any civil or criminal liability therefor on the part of any participant, whether guardian, physician, hospital or others.[10] We herewith specifically so hold.

CONCLUSION

We therefore remand this record to the trial court to implement (without further testimonial hearing) the following decisions:

1. To discharge, with the thanks of the Court for his service, the present guardian of the person of Karen Quinlan, Thomas R. Curtin, Esquire, a member of the Bar and an officer of the court.

2. To appoint Joseph Quinlan as guardian of the person of Karen Quinlan with full power to make decisions with regard to the identity of her treating physicians.

We repeat for the sake of emphasis and clarity that upon the concurrence of the guardian and family of Karen, should the responsible attending physicians conclude that there is no reasonable possibility of Karen's ever emerging from her present comatose condition to a cognitive, sapient state and that the life-support apparatus now being administered to Karen should be discontinued, they shall consult with the hospital 'Ethics Committee' or like body of the institution in which Karen is then hospitalized. If that consultative body agrees that there is no reasonable possibility of Karen's ever emerging from her present comatose condition to a cognitive, sapient state, the present life-support system may be withdrawn and said action shall be without any civil or criminal liability therefor on the part of any participant, whether guardian, physician, hospital or others.

By the above ruling we do not intend to be understood as implying that a proceeding for judicial declaratory relief is necessarily required for the implementation of comparable decisions in the field of medical practice.

Modified and remanded.

---

[10] The declaratory relief we here award is not intended to imply that the principles enunciated in this case might not be applicable in divers other types of terminal medical situations such as those described by Drs. Korein and Diamond, Supra, not necessarily involving the hopeless loss of cognitive or sapient life.

NOTES AND QUESTIONS

1. *Principles.* Did any of the four biomedical principles of autonomy, non-maleficence, beneficence, or justice appear in the decision? Was the New Jersey Supreme Court correct that the moral command of medicine "to heal" could not be applied in Karen's case? What about the physician's duty to "do no harm" to patients? Was that obligation violated by the court's decision? Does the principle of non-maleficence provide a reason why doctors should never discontinue medical treatment?

2. *Free Exercise.* The New Jersey Supreme Court quickly dismissed the argument that the Quinlans had a First Amendment free exercise of religion right to refuse treatment on Karen's behalf. Free exercise law has frequently wavered between the competing ideas that religious citizens must obey the law and that religious citizens should be exempt from the law if it violates their conscience. See generally Employment Division v. Smith, 494 U.S. 872 (1990) and Wisconsin v. Yoder, 406 U.S. 205 (1972).

The court refers to the case of Delores Heston, a 22-year-old Jehovah's Witness who was seriously injured in a car accident and was unable to consent to treatment. Jehovah's Witnesses refuse whole blood transfusions because they believe they are forbidden by scriptural passages, including Genesis 9:4, Leviticus 17:12, Deuteronomy 12:23–25, and Acts 15:28–29. Jehovah's Witnesses believe that receiving a whole blood transfusion jeopardizes their everlasting life with God. Heston's mother argued in court that surgery should not be undertaken because it involved whole blood transfusions. The court ordered the surgery to proceed. John F. Kennedy Memorial Hospital v. Heston, 58 N.J. 576 (1971).

Courts have regularly ordered transfusions for children of Jehovah's Witnesses while allowing adults to refuse treatment. Is this a sensible rule? Is there any good legal argument that parents must be allowed to follow their religious beliefs in deciding how to treat their children?

3. *Privacy.* Although bioethicists emphasize autonomy for patients, the New Jersey Supreme Court relied upon the U.S. Supreme Court's doctrine of privacy to conclude that the constitutional right of privacy protected the decision to remove Karen from a respirator. What is the difference between privacy and autonomy? Do you agree that privacy is the appropriate legal category to name the right protected in *Quinlan*? Why are cases about abortion and contraception (*Roe* and *Griswold*) related to the right to refuse medical treatment?

4. *Extraordinary/Ordinary Means.* Bioethical tradition frequently distinguished ordinary from extraordinary medical treatment. The words had several meanings. From the doctor's perspective, "ordinary" meant the standard care or treatment and "extraordinary" meant an unusual or exceptional treatment. From the bioethicist's perspective: however, "ordinary" treatment was morally required for the patient while "extraordinary" was not. "[E]xcessive expense, excessive pain, excessive difficulty or other inconvenience, and no reasonable or 'proportionate' hope of benefit [are] criteria for deciding that a treatment is 'extraordinary' in the context of a particular patient in particular circumstances." Editorial,

Ordinary and Extraordinary Means, 7 J. Med. Ethics 55 (1981). Recently, ethicists and bioethicists have started to use the term "disproportionate care" instead of the more traditional "extraordinary care" term. According to the Ethical and Religious Directives for Catholic Health Care Services, "disproportionate means are those that in the patient's judgment do not offer a reasonable hope of benefit or entail an excessive burden, or impose excessive expense on the family or the community." How would you determine whether a treatment option "do[es] not offer a reasonable hope of benefit?" What would constitute an excessive burden? Who should be able to decide these questions? Trent Horn, What is "Extraordinary" Care? Oct. 18, 2018, https://www.catholic.com/magazine/online-edition/what-is-extraordinary-care. Do you think staying on a respirator in Karen's circumstances was ordinary, extraordinary or disproportionate? Is her opinion or her doctor's opinion more important in assessing what is ordinary care?

5. *Ethics Committees.* The New Jersey Supreme Court seemed to place a lot of faith in hospital ethics committees, suggesting that they could help doctors make difficult decisions and take some burdens off patients. According to the American Medical Association, an ethics committee "is advisory in nature and confined exclusively to ethical matters, and that the size and availability of the committee should be consistent with the needs of the institution. Procedures followed by the ethics committee should comply with institutional and ethical policies on confidentiality, and any denominational health care institutions should publicize the fact that particular religious beliefs are to be taken into consideration in a committee's recommendations." Danielle Chaet, AMA Code of Medical Ethics' Opinions on Ethics Committees and Consultations, AMA Journal of Ethics, May 2016. The *Quinlan* case was influential in providing the first major impetus for the creation of hospital ethics committees. Soon, hospitals and medical centers in other states followed suit in creating their own advisory ethics committees. George Annas & Michael Grodin, Hospital Ethics Committees, Consultants, and Courts, AMA Journal of Ethics, May 2016, https://journalofethics.ama-assn.org/article/hospital-ethics-committees-consultants-and-courts/2016-05.

> **Practice Exercise: Go to** the website and follow the link to read more about ethics committees. Then, design your own ethics committee: Who will serve on the committee? How long are the appointments? What are the qualifications? Do decisions have to be unanimous or a majority vote? What happens if the committee cannot reach a decision? How long will a committee have to decide in emergency and non-emergency situations? Is there an appeals process?

Why did the New Jersey Supreme Court mention a role for the hospital ethics committee in the final circumstances of Karen's case? According to the opinion, what involvement did the hospital ethics committee have to play in the final decision about Karen's treatment? Do you think ethics committees

can be useful today, or do they provide merely another level of bureaucracy in difficult circumstances?

6. *Homicide.* Are you surprised that some people thought removing a patient from a respirator was homicide? Do you think the New Jersey Supreme Court should have ordered the hospital to keep Karen connected because removing a respirator was homicide? Why is the removal of the respirator not considered homicide? Is it because the patient dies as a result of a natural cause? Is it because refusing treatment is a constitutional right that cannot be prosecuted? Both?

The court observed that attempted suicide is no longer a crime in New Jersey. Why not? In the past, if a competent person refused a respirator, should it have been viewed criminally as attempted suicide? Do you think attempted suicide should be criminalized today?

Why did the court emphasize that Karen had "no realistic possibility of returning to any semblance of cognitive or sapient life?" If there had been some possibility, however slight, that Karen could recover, would removing the respirator be grounds for a prosecution for homicide? Consider a patient with 1% chance of recovery of cognitive or sapient life. Should the respirator be removed? A patient with 5%? 10%? 25%? 49%? 51%? 75%? Does the patient's quality of life have anything to do with your assessment, or should quality of life never be considered in making determinations about refusal of treatment?

7. *COVID-19 and the New York State Task Force on Life and Law.* On January 21, 2020, the U.S. Centers for Disease Control and Prevention (CDC) made the first travel-related diagnosis of novel coronavirus (2019-nCoV) in the United States. Soon after, the World Health Organization (WHO) declared the virus, which had already seen outbreaks in China, Japan, South Korea, and Thailand, a Public Health Emergency of International Concern (PHEIC) and declared a global health emergency. Within weeks of the outbreak, health care providers and government officials began to voice concern over the lack of personal protective equipment (PPE), and more alarmingly, the lack of ventilators available for patients. Because COVID-19 is a respiratory virus that attacks the lungs, the virus can make it very difficult for some patients to breathe. For these patients, ventilators are critical to their care and survival. Prior to the emergence of COVID-19, it is estimated that 70%–80% of the U.S.'s ventilator supply was already being used to treat patients suffering from other respiratory illnesses such as flu and cancer. As early as March 2020, medical providers were worried the U.S. would reach a point where ventilators would need to be rationed. Ethicists and health care providers were now faced with a question few had ever imagined having to

> **Go to** the website to read the WHO's statement regarding the outbreak of the novel coronavirus (2019-nCoV) and read the full report on Ventilator Allocation published by the New York State Task Force on Life and the Law and the New York State Department of Health.

address outside a medical ethics classroom—Who gets a ventilator during a shortage?

Governor Mario Cuomo created the New York State Task Force on Life and Law in 1985 to advise the state on ethically complex public-policy issues. In 2015, the task force published a two-hundred-and-seventy-two-page report on ventilator allocation during a pandemic. The report, which had taken eight years to produce, recommends a system centered on "exclusion criteria," mortality risk assessment, and period time trials. The Task Force cited concerns with using non-clinical, subjective, approaches such as distribution based on a first-come-first-serve basis, randomizing allocation, and prioritizing patients meeting certain social criteria. Instead, the Task Force developed adult, pediatric, and neonatal guidelines based on an ethical framework and evidence-based clinical data to support the goal of saving the most lives during a pandemic.

Ultimately, the Task Force determined there are five components underlying the ethical framework: 1) duty to care, 2) duty to steward resources, 3) duty to plan, 4) distributive justice, and 5) transparency. Each decision to receive or continue care is made by a triage officer or triage committee that does not have any direct contact with the patient. This is done to ensure decisions do not conflict with a clinician's duty of care and decisions are made based on objective, rather than subjective, criteria.

New York's adult protocols consist of three steps:

1) Exclusion Criteria: a patient is screened for exclusion criteria and if the patient has a medical condition on the exclusion list, the patient is ineligible for ventilator therapy. Instead, alternative therapies are utilized. The purpose of applying exclusion criteria is to identify patients with a short life expectancy irrespective of their current acute illness, so patients most likely to survive ventilator therapy are prioritized.

2) Mortality Risk Assessment: a patient's mortality risk is assessed based on a Sequential Organ Failure Assessment (SOFA) score. SOFA scores measure function in six key organs and systems: lungs, liver, brain, kidneys, blood clotting, and blood pressure.

3) Time Trials: periodic clinical assessments are conducted after a patient receives ventilator therapy for 48 hours and again at 120 hours. SOFA scores are continually assessed and changes in the patient's clinical presentation are compared to results from the patient's prior assessments. Periodic evaluations are necessary to determine whether the therapy is effective, while allowing for efficient and equitable distribution of ventilators.

New York State Task Force on Life and the Law and New York State Department of Health, Ventilator Allocation Guidelines (2015).

Do you think the study adequately addresses disparities in health care for at-risk and disadvantaged populations? Are there any additional ethical frameworks you would include? Any you would exclude? Is a subjective or

objective approach better when dealing with resource allocation? Why? For additional guidance, see https://www.hhs.gov/sites/default/files/optimizing-ventilator-use-during-covid19-pandemic.pdf.

Many hospitals turned to ethics committees to make these decisions, hoping to shield treating clinicians from having to make these determinations on their own. See I. Glenn Cohen, Andrew M. Crespo & Douglas B. White, Potential Legal Liability for Withdrawing or Withholding Ventilators During COVID-19: Assessing the Risks and Identifying Needed Reforms, 323 JAMA 1901 (2020).

8. *Nancy Beth Cruzan*. Karen Quinlan lived for nine years after the respirator was turned off. Her parents did not want to remove Karen from artificial nutrition and hydration. During those years, Nancy Beth Cruzan was seriously injured in a car accident when she was 25 years old. Immediately after the accident, doctors performed a gastrostomy to place a feeding tube in Nancy's stomach. Doctors later decided that, like Karen, Nancy was in a persistent vegetative state (PVS) from which her expert witnesses testified she would not recover. As in *Quinlan*: however, many people believed that recovery could be possible and criticized the Cruzans when they made the decision to disconnect Nancy's feeding tube. Is nutrition morally, medically, and legally different from respiration? Is a feeding tube ordinary or extraordinary means?

Like the Quinlans, the Cruzans also faced the possibility that the law would view the removal of nutrition as a homicide. After the hospital refused to comply with the Cruzans' wishes to remove nutrition, the family went to court. Although a Missouri trial court granted the parents' request, the Missouri Supreme Court ruled there was not clear and convincing evidence that Nancy would want the treatment to be discontinued and denied the parents' attempt to disconnect.

After the loss in the Missouri Supreme Court, the Cruzans' lawyer filed the following petition for certiorari with the United States Supreme Court. In these legal circumstances, the petitioner's first job is to persuade the Court to hear the case and then to present her case and questions in a manner that will pull the Court toward her position. Is the following petition persuasive that the Court should hear the case? Is it persuasive that the Cruzans should win the case? How could the petition have been improved? How well drafted was the Question Presented to the Court, namely "Whether a state's interest in life, codified in the state 'living will act,' can override all constitutional privacy, liberty and equal protection rights of an incompetent person to reject medical treatment."?

A primary reason that the Court grants certiorari is to resolve an important question on which the lower courts have issued conflicting rulings. Does the petition persuade you that the state courts disagreed about the constitutional right to refuse medical treatment?

B. *CRUZAN*: DISCONTINUING NUTRITION AND HYDRATION

Cruzan v. Director of Missouri Department of Health

Supreme Court of the United States, No. 88–1503, October Term, 1988.
Petition for Writ of Certiorari to the Missouri Supreme Court.
1989 WL 1174083 (U.S.).

Petition

QUESTION PRESENTED

As the result of a car accident more than five years ago, Nancy Cruzan is an incompetent person in a persistent vegetative state without hope of ever recovering cognitive interaction with the world around her. She can live indefinitely in this state. She is kept alive by means of a surgically implanted gastrostomy tube which artificially provides her fluid and nutrition. The question presented is:

Whether a state's interest in life, codified in the state "living will act", can override all constitutional privacy, liberty and equal protection rights of an incompetent person to reject medical treatment.

The petitioners Nancy Beth Cruzan by her natural parents and co-guardians Lester and Joyce Cruzan respectfully pray that a writ of certiorari issue to review the judgment and opinion of the Missouri Supreme Court in this case.

JURISDICTION

The Circuit Court for Jasper County, Probate Division, entered its judgment on July 27, 1988, upholding petitioners' constitutional right to terminate artificial life support. On November 16, 1988, the Missouri Supreme Court reversed the trial court. Thereafter, on December 13, 1988, the Missouri Supreme Court denied a timely petition for rehearing. The jurisdiction of this Court is invoked under 28 U.S.C. § 1257(3).

CONSTITUTIONAL AND STATUTORY PROVISIONS INVOLVED

The Constitution of the United States provides in pertinent part:

AMENDMENT I

Congress shall make no law respecting an establishment of religion, or prohibiting the free exercise thereof; or abridging the freedom of speech, or of the press; or the right of the people peaceably to assemble, and to petition the Government for a redress of grievances.

AMENDMENT IV

The right of the people to be secure in their persons, houses, papers, and effects, against unreasonable searches and seizures, shall not be violated, and no Warrants shall issue, but upon probable cause,

supported by Oath or affirmation, and particularly describing the place to be searched, and the persons or things to be seized.

AMENDMENT V

No person shall be held to answer for a capital, or otherwise infamous crime, unless on a presentment or indictment of a Grand Jury, except in cases arising in the land or naval forces, or in the Militia, when in actual service in time of War or public danger; nor shall any person be subject for the same offence to be twice put in jeopardy of life or limb; nor shall be compelled in any criminal case to be a witness against himself, nor be deprived of life, liberty, or property, without due process of law; nor shall private property be taken for public use, without just compensation.

AMENDMENT IX

The enumeration in the Constitution, of certain rights, shall not be construed to deny or disparage others retained by the people.

AMENDMENT XIV, SECTION 1

All persons born or naturalized in the United States, and subject to the jurisdiction thereof, are citizens of the United States and of the State wherein they reside. No State shall make or enforce any law which shall abridge the privileges or immunities of citizens of the United States; nor shall any State deprive any person of life, liberty, or property, without due process of law; nor deny to any person within its jurisdiction the equal protection of the laws.

The Missouri Life Support Declarations Act, 25 V.A.M.S. § 459.0100(3) (6); 459.015: 459.055(5), provides in pertinent part:

> 'Death-prolonging procedure,' any medical procedure or intervention which, when applied to a patient, would serve only to prolong artificially the dying process and where, in the judgment of the attending physician pursuant to usual and customary medical standards, death will occur within a short time whether or not such procedure or intervention is utilized. Death-prolonging procedure shall not include . . . any procedure to provide nutrition or hydration;
>
> 'Terminal condition,' an incurable or irreversible condition which, in the opinion of the attending physician, is such that death will occur within a short time regardless of the application of medical procedures.
>
> . . . I have the primary right to make my own decisions concerning treatment that might unduly prolong the dying process . . . It is not my intent to authorize affirmative or deliberate acts or omissions to shorten my life rather only to permit the natural process of dying.

> . . . Sections 459.010 to 459.055 do not condone, authorize or approve mercy killing or euthanasia nor permit any affirmative or deliberate act or omission to shorten or end life.

STATEMENT

A. Nancy Cruzan's Condition

Nancy Cruzan lies in a Missouri state rehabilitation hospital in a persistent vegetative state ("PVS"). PVS is a type of permanent unconsciousness or coma in which all cognitive functioning is gone but in which the brain stem continues to function to some degree. Nancy breathes on her own and she has periods of wakefulness (with her eyes open) and reflexive sleep/wake cycles, but she is unaware of herself or her environment. Her eyes when open move randomly in all directions, but they do not track objects or persons or respond to the environment around her. There is no hope that Nancy will ever recover from her state and be restored to any cognitive functioning. She is completely dependent on others for care. Her body is stiff and so severely contracted that her fingernails cut into her wrists. Her face is red, puffy and swollen, and she drools on herself. She is missing teeth. Her bathing, oral care and personal feminine hygiene, including menses, are cared for by others. She must be turned every few hours to prevent bedsores.

Nancy's condition was caused by the severe injuries she sustained when she was thrown from her car in an automobile accident early in the morning of January 11, 1983. The state trooper who arrived first at the scene examined Nancy and believed her dead. Although emergency personnel arriving later were able to restore signs of life, Nancy never regained consciousness after the accident. Four weeks after the accident, when hope still existed for recovery, both her father and her then husband provided separate written consent to allow the hospital to have a gastrostomy tube surgically implanted in Nancy's stomach. The gastrostomy tube is the sole means by which Nancy has received fluids and nutrition since she was moved to the Missouri state rehabilitation hospital on October 19, 1983. Nancy Cruzan was 25 years old on the day of her accident and she is 31 today. Doctors believe she has a normal life expectancy.

B. Proceedings in the Lower Courts

In the summer of 1987 Nancy's natural parents, Joe and Joyce Cruzan, who are also her court-appointed guardians, determined that hope no longer existed for recovery and that Nancy would not want the continued gastrostomy feeding. They requested the state rehabilitation hospital at Mt. Vernon, Missouri to stop the artificial feeding. The hospital administrator told the Cruzans that he could not authorize such action without a court order. Similarly, the probate judge overseeing Nancy's guardianship told the Cruzans that they did not have a right to transfer her to a private hospital or to take Nancy home to carry out her wishes without court authorization. On October 23. 1987, therefore, the

Cruzans filed a declaratory judgment action in probate court on Nancy's behalf. The petition sought a declaration that Nancy had a common law right to be free from unwanted medical treatment and a state and federal constitutional right to privacy which protected her right to refuse unwanted medical treatment.

After a bench trial, the trial court concluded that Nancy's "lifestyle and other statements to family and friends suggest that she would not wish to continue her present existence without hope as it is." The trial court also held that Nancy has a fundamental right to liberty, found in both the Due Process Clause of the Fourteenth Amendment and in the Missouri Constitution, to be free from unwanted medical treatment. It further ruled that to deny Nancy's parents the right to carry out her will would deny Nancy her federal constitutional right to equal protection of the laws. Finally, the trial court ruled that if the Missouri "living will act" were construed to bar the exercise of Nancy Cruzan's right to decline further treatment, then the act violated Nancy's federal constitutional rights.

The Missouri Attorney General appealed directly to the Missouri Supreme Court. That court, in a sharply divided 4–3 decision, reversed the trial court. Using a balancing test, the majority concluded that Missouri's strong interest in life outweighed any constitutional or common law right to refuse medical treatment retained by an incompetent person like Nancy Cruzan.[1] The majority rejected the decision of the New Jersey Supreme Court in *In re Quinlan* and similar rulings from other state supreme courts which held that PVS patients retain constitutional rights. It charged that those courts improperly discounted the state's interest in life by making inappropriate judgments about the quality of a life for a PVS patient. In Missouri the state's interest is not in the quality of life, but "in life: that interest is unqualified."

The majority found the basis for Missouri's strong interest in life, in large part, in Missouri's "living will" act. Life Support Declarations Act, Mo. Rev. Stat. 459.010, *et seq*. The Missouri legislature modeled the Missouri living will act on the Uniform Rights of the Terminally Ill Act, but it made several changes to the Uniform Act which dramatically limited the use of living wills in Missouri. For example, the legislature added language which removed artificial nutrition and hydration from the list of medical procedures that a person could choose to forgo through use of the living will. The majority in Cruzan held that the limitations grafted onto the Uniform living will act by the Missouri legislature evidenced a strong Missouri public policy in favor of life.[2] It ruled that the trial court erred in finding the living will act unconstitutional.

---

1 The majority opinion described Nancy's constitutional rights as encompassing the " 'right to liberty,' 'the right to privacy,' 'equal protection and due process.' "

2 Judge Welliver in his dissent charged that the legislature in placing the limitations on the living well [sic] had perpetrated a "fraud on Missourians who believe we have been given a

The majority could find no constitutional rights retained by an incompetent person like Nancy Cruzan sufficient to override this strong state policy interest in life. It held that federal privacy rights would not extend to a person in Nancy's condition, based on its reading of *Bowers v. Hardwick,* 478 U.S. 186 (1986).[3] Moreover, the majority stated that even if incompetent persons did retain federal constitutional rights to refuse unwanted medical treatment, such treatment could be stopped only if it caused physical pain. It noted that a PVS patient like Nancy Cruzan is not capable of experiencing pain. It also held that supplying fluids and nutrition through a gastrostomy tube is not "heroically invasive" medical treatment that can be stopped in any event; it is merely ordinary care.[4] The majority held that Nancy Cruzan retains no interest in stopping unwanted gastrostomy feeding which can outweigh the general interest of the state of Missouri in her life.[5]

The majority opinion provoked three separate dissents. Judge Welliver found the Missouri living will act, on its face, contrary to an individual's federal privacy right to control fundamental decisions about his own body. Specifically, Judge Welliver found it constitutionally impermissible to exclude surgically supplied fluids and nutrition from the list of medical treatments that a person may choose to forgo. Judge Higgins likewise found that the majority improperly employed the living will statute so that it could ignore the court's "responsibilities to Nancy Cruzan under the Constitution."

Judge Blackmar reasoned that decisions about medical treatment for family members are properly left to the family, without interference by the state. He also found the absolutist characterization of Missouri's interest in life simply wrong on at least two grounds: (1) "The very existence of capital punishment" suggests that "some lives are not worth preserving," and (2) the living will statute "in fact allows and encourages the preplanned termination of life."

Nancy Cruzan and her parents filed a timely petition for rehearing, which a divided court denied by a 4–3 vote. The rehearing denial again provoked extensive dissent.

---

right to execute a living will, and die naturally, respectfully, and in peace." He argued that the living will act violates the federal privacy and liberty rights of Missourians.

[3] The majority also held that the state right to privacy in the Missouri constitution did not extend to medical treatment decisions. This ruling is of course not a basis for appeal to this Court.

[4] The majority also stated that even if Nancy's gastrostomy feeding could be considered medical treatment, the statements she made to her roommate prior to the accident, standing alone, were not specific enough to constitute informed consent. Therefore, it reasoned that those statements were also not sufficient to prove Nancy's intent to be free from continued treatment. Judge Higgins strongly objected to this finding, charging that the majority had launched upon the "inexcusable exercise" of ignoring the trial court findings of facts and adopting its own facts to fit its conclusions.

[5] The majority also held that, as guardians, the Cruzans had no power to withdraw treatment. Instead, a guardian in Missouri is required, after Cruzan, to provide all possible medical treatment to an incompetent ward without option or discretion.

REASONS FOR GRANTING THE PETITION

Unfortunately, Nancy Cruzan's case is not unique. Thousands of people lie in hospitals across the United States in the persistent vegetative state without hope of ever recovering. The number will only increase. The highest state courts of Arizona and Massachusetts have ruled that such patients retain a federal constitutional right to refuse medical treatment, including artificially supplied fluids and nutrition. Missouri and Washington high courts have ruled to the contrary. This sharp conflict between the highest courts of four states warrants immediate review.

I. The Decision Below Conflicts With Decisions of Other State Supreme Courts

The Missouri Supreme Court cited over 50 cases from 16 different states and admitted that " 'nearly unanimously" the various courts of sister states have ruled in favor of an incompetent patient's constitutional right to refuse various forms of medical treatment.[6] Four of those decisions came from state supreme courts that have directly addressed whether an incompetent patient, even though he can no longer communicate his wishes, retains the federal constitutional right to stop artificially supplied fluids and nutrition and die with dignity.[7]

In *Rasmussen v. Fleming,* 741 P.2d 674 (Ariz. 1987), the Supreme Court of Arizona held that a PVS patient retains a "fundamental" federal right to refuse medical treatment, anchored "within the constitutionally protected zone of privacy."[8] The Arizona court succinctly defined the

---

[6] *See, e.g., In re Quinlan,* 355 A.2d 647, 663–64 (N.J.). *cert. denied,* 429 U.S. 922 (1976) (PVS patient has a constitutional right to privacy that encompasses removal of medical treatment, here a respirator; the "only practical way to prevent destruction of the right is to permit the guardian and family of Karen to render their best judgment"); *In re L.H.R.,* 321 S.E.2d 716, 723 (Ga. 1984) (family is appropriate party to make determination of medical treatment for an incompetent adult in PVS without hope of recovery); *In re Torres,* 357 N.W.2d 332, 339–41 (Minn. 1984) (guardian has the power, acting in the best interests of a comatose ward, to exercise the constitutional right to privacy of that ward and order removal of a respirator); *see also Corbett v. D'Alessandro,* 487 So.2d 368 (Fla. App.), *review denied,* 492 So.2d 1331 (Fla. 1986) (PVS patient has a federal constitutional right to privacy which requires removal of feeding tube when requested by her husband); *In re Drabick,* 245 Cal. Rptr. 840, 854–55 (Cal. Ct. App. 1988), *review denied* (Cal. July 28, 1988), *cert. denied,* 109 S. Ct. 399 (1988) (incompetent patient in PVS has a federal constitutional right to removal of a feeding tube; "it is possible for others to make a decision that reflects his interest more closely than would a purely technological decision to do whatever is possible").

[7] *Rasmussen v. Fleming,* 741 P.2d 674 (Ariz. 1987); *Brophy v. New England Sinai Hospital, Inc.,* 497 N.E.2d 626 (Mass. 1986); *Cruzan v. Harmon,* 760 S.W.2d 408 (Mo. 1988); *In re Grant,* 747 P.2d 445 (Wash. 1987), *modified.* 757 P.2d 534 (Wash. 1988). Only one federal court has addressed this issue *(Gray by Gray v. Romeo,* 697 F. Supp. 580 (D.R.I. 1988.) That court held that an incompetent person retains the federal constitutional right to refuse artificial tube feeding. The case was not appealed.

[8] In *Rasmussen,* the guardian sought an order empowering him to remove a nasogastric feeding tube and to, place "Do Not Resuscitate" and "Do Not Hospitalize notations on the chart of his ward, Mildred Rasmussen, a PVS patient. Mrs. Rasmussen died during the pendency of the appeal and it was unclear whether she had the feeding tube inserted at the time or, not. The court chose to decide the case as one presenting novel issues capable of repetition yet evading review. The court found that Mildred Rasmussen also retained a common law state constitutional right to refuse unwanted medical treatment.

modern day dilemma: "Medical technology has effectively created a twilight zone of suspended animation where death commences while life, in some form continues;" not surprisingly, some people when caught in such a dilemma choose "a plan of medical treatment that allows nature to take its course and permits them to die with dignity."

Mildred Rasmussen left behind no indication of her intent. The Arizona Supreme Court held that she nonetheless retained the federal constitutional right to have decisions made which reflected her interests as closely as possible. That interest is determined by a guardian, not the state.

In Arizona, like in Missouri, this constitutional right of the incompetent is not unfettered, but must be balanced against the countervailing state interest in preserving life before unwanted medical treatment can be removed. But the Arizona court concluded that the state interest in life weakens where the "treatment at issue 'serves only to prolong a life inflicted with an incurable condition.' " The court held that the state interest in life therefore could not override a PVS patient's federal constitutional right to have unwanted medical treatment in the form of fluids and nutrition through a nasogastric tube stopped.

The decision of the Supreme Judicial Court of Massachusetts is in accord with *Rasmussen*. *Brophy v. New England Sinai Hospital, Inc.*, 497 N.E.2d 626 (Mass. 1986). In *Brophy,* the court held that a PVS patient retains the federal constitutional right to privacy, which can be exercised by his wife, to direct removal of gastrostomy feeding in accordance with his prior expressed wishes.[9] It held that the federal Constitution prohibits the state from controlling such decisions: "It is antithetical to our scheme of ordered liberty and to our respect for the autonomy of the individual for the State to make decisions regarding the individual's quality of life."[10]

The majority opinion in *Cruzan* is in direct conflict with *Rasmussen* and *Brophy*. The *Cruzan* majority held that incompetent persons in Missouri do not retain the federal right to privacy to refuse unwanted medical treatment. Indeed, the majority set up a balancing test in Missouri in such a fashion that the state interest in life will always overcome an incompetent person's interest in his own life.

On one side of the balance, the majority drastically reduced any rights an incompetent person retains. Guardians after *Cruzan* must now provide all possible forms of medical treatment that can prolong life

---

[9] The court also found that Paul Brophy retained a common law right to refuse treatment.

[10] One other state supreme court has recognized the federal privacy right to reject artificial gastrostomy feeding, although it appeared to base its decision on state law grounds. *See McConnell v. Beverly Enterprises-Connecticut, Inc.*, 209 Conn. 692 (1989) (the Connecticut living will statute, which embodies the recognized federal constitutional right to privacy as well as the common law right to self-determination, allowed a family to obtain removal of artificial feeding for PVS patient in accordance with prior expressed wishes); *see also In re Gardner*, 534 A.2d 947 (Maine 1987) (PVS patient has a common law right to autonomy that allowed removal of artificial feeding in accordance with prior wishes).

without option or discretion. Family members and doctors no longer retain *any* interest or control of medical treatments for their loved ones and patients.[11] And after *Cruzan,* no incompetent patient in Missouri, regardless of any expressions of intent, can refuse gastrostomy feeding. The majority determined that gastrostomy feeding was not medical treatment, but ordinary care which all patients must accept.

Balanced against these whittled down rights of incompetent persons the majority erected a state interest in life so overpowering that it will always justify state infringement of the rights of an incompetent person. The majority stated that medical treatment can be removed if it constitutes a "burden" to the patient. But the majority determined that only treatment that caused physical pain constituted a burden. Since a PVS patient like Nancy by definition cannot experience pain, *no* treatment can ever constitute a burden to a PVS patient. A PVS patient will always lose on this issue alone. Moreover, the majority held that Missouri's interest in life is "unqualified." The Arizona and Massachusetts high courts held that the state's interest in life weakens for a patient in PVS, where the medical treatment serves only to prolong a life inflicted with an incurable condition. *See, e.g., Rasmussen,* 741 P.2d at 684. By contrast, the *Cruzan* majority held that Missouri's interest in life *strengthens* when a person deteriorates to a PVS, because medical treatment can sustain the body for a substantial time. With this lopsided balancing test the majority opinion in essence has placed Missouri's interest in an incompetent person's life above that person's interest in his own life in all situations.

The Washington Supreme Court has taken an approach similar to Missouri. *In re Grant,* 747 P.2d 445 (Wash. 1987), *modified,* 757 P.2d 534 (1988) involved Barbara Grant, a 22-year-old woman afflicted with a progressive neurologic illness called Batten's disease. She was in the final throes of the disease, without hope of recovery, but not yet in a PVS. She had never been competent. Barbara's mother, also her legal guardian, sought an order forbidding the state hospital from using various forms of life-prolonging treatment on Barbara as her condition deteriorated. The court initially ruled in a 5–4 decision that Barbara had a federal constitutional right to privacy, which could be exercised through her mother, to prohibit the use of all forms of medical treatment, including artificial feeding through a surgically implanted tube. Subsequently, Justice Durham removed her name from the majority opinion and joined the opinion of Justice Andre, concurring in part and dissenting in part. This change affected the decision of the court solely

[11] In fact, the majority left open only one narrow option for an incompetent person. An incompetent person may retain the federal constitutional rights to have decisions made about medical treatment that reflect his interest only if, prior to incompetency, he executed a living will or other unspecified "formalities" that provide in advance clear and convincing evidence of his intent. But it is obvious that few persons, particularly youthful accident victims like Nancy Cruzan, will execute such advance directives. All persons who do not execute such directives, whatever they might be, lose the federal constitutional right to privacy in Missouri.

on the issue of artificial feeding. Thus, the Washington Supreme Court held that a lifelong incompetent patient retains the federal right to privacy, which can be exercised by her family, to refuse unwanted medical treatment in the form of a respirator, intubation, CPR and a defibrillator. But that incompetent person is denied the federal privacy right to refuse surgical insertion of a gastrostomy tube or to demand removal of that tube once surgically implanted.[12]

A comparison of the holdings of these state courts reveals that the federal constitutional rights of incompetent persons to have treatment discontinued depends upon the state in which the patient is hospitalized. The Arizona court held that an incompetent person who never expressed her wishes still retains the federal privacy right to have a guardian make choices about medical treatment that reflect the incompetent's best interests. Both the Arizona and the Massachusetts courts held that the federal privacy right extends to refusing artificial provision of fluids and nutrition. By contrast the *Cruzan* majority held that, without a living will or other express prior directives regarding intent, an incompetent patient loses all constitutional rights. Further, even express directives would not protect the federal right of a patient like Nancy Cruzan to discontinue artificial feeding through a gastrostomy tube, which is considered basic patient care in Missouri that must be administered to all incompetent patients. There is no federal right in Missouri to refuse surgical insertion of a gastrostomy tube or to request removal of such a tube.

Nancy Cruzan is constitutionally entitled to a decision about her medical treatment that most closely reflects her interests. Such a fundamental decision, which is best made by the guardians and family after a hearing to determine proper motives, should not depend on the state of residence. The conflict between the majority opinion in *Cruzan* and the high courts of Arizona and Massachusetts that recognized the federal constitutional right of incompetent persons to refuse medical treatment requires immediate review by this Court.

2. The Decision Below Conflicts With Decisions of This Court

This Court has long protected individuals against governmental invasions of the body. *Skinner v. Oklahoma*, 316 U.S. 535, 541–43 (1942) (state prohibited from controlling, by sterilization, which convicts might reproduce because reproduction is "one of the basic civil rights of man"); *Rochin v. California*, 342 U.S. 165, 172 (1952); *Scherber v. California*, 384 U.S. 757, 772 (1966) ("The integrity of an individual's person is a cherished value of our society"); *see Olmstead v. United States*, 277 U.S. 438, 478 1928) (Brandeis, J., dissenting) ("The makers of our

[12] In *In re O'Connor*, 534 N.Y.S.2d 886, 892 (C.A.N.Y 1988), the New York high court held that a 77-year-old woman suffering from severe brain damage had no common law right to refuse medical treatment unless she left behind clear and convincing proof of "a firm and settled commitment" to terminate life support under the particular circumstances present.

Constitution . . . conferred, as against the government, the right to be let alone—the most comprehensive of rights and the right most valued by civilized men"). It has likewise long recognized and protected an individual's right to self-determination, which allows a person to control decisions made about his own body. *See, e.g., Union Pacific Ry. Co. v. Botsford*, 141 U.S. 250, 251 (1891) ("No right is held more sacred . . . than the right of every individual to the possession and control of his own person.").

This right has been characterized as a liberty interest protected by the Due Process Clause of the Fourteenth Amendment and more recently as a privacy right which springs from the penumbra of personal freedoms created by the Bill of Rights. *See Roe v. Wade*, 410 U.S. 113 (1973); *Griswold v. Connecticut*, 381 U.S. 479, 485 (1965). However characterized, the right should extend to protect individuals from invasive medical treatment forced on them by the state. *See, e.g., Eisenstadt v. Baird*, 405 U.S. 438, 453 (1972) ([I]f "the right of privacy means anything, it is the right of the *individual*, married or single, to be free from unwanted governmental intrusions into matters so fundamentally affecting a person as the decision whether to bear or beget a child.") (emphasis in original). *Doe v. Bolton*, 410 U.S. 179, 213 (1973) (Douglas, J., concurring) ("*the freedom to care for one's health and person*" is constitutionally protected) (emphasis in original).

This Court has not directly addressed whether a person has a constitutional right to refuse life-prolonging medical technology. Yet it is difficult to conceive of a right more implicit in our concept of liberty or more deeply ingrained in our constitutional tradition than the right of each individual to make decisions concerning the integrity of the body without interference from the state. The four judge majority in *Cruzan*, nonetheless, concluded that federal privacy rights would not extend to Nancy Cruzan. The majority based its denial of federal right, solely on a narrow interpretation of *Bowers v. Hardwick*, 478 U.S. 186 (1986). The reliance in Bowers is misplaced. In *Bowers* this Court held that the right of privacy did not extend to protect "the right of homosexuals to engage in acts of sodomy." The Court found that the "right" to engage in sodomy bore no "resemblance" to the protected fundamental rights such as marriage, family and procreation. Those rights, which are entitled to "heightened judicial protection," fall into the category of "fundamental liberties" so " 'implicit in the concept of ordered liberty,' such that 'neither liberty nor justice would exist if [they] were sacrificed' " and as "liberties that are 'deeply rooted in this Nation's history and tradition.' " *Id.* at 192 (citations omitted). The Court found that sodomy was not such a right. *Id.* The right to be free from state ordered medical procedures, however, is indeed the type of right long cherished by this Court. Such a right bears little resemblance to consensual sodomy.

Moreover, there is clearly no basis in the decisions of this Court to discriminate against incompetent persons with regard to these

fundamental constitutional rights. In Missouri today, if an accident renders a person unable to voice his decisions about medical treatment, the state dictates that that person must receive all medical treatment possible. The constitutional interest of the incompetent person, however, is not in literally voicing choices; it is in ensuring that he receives treatment that reflects his interest and desires. *See, e.g., Brophy,* 497 N.E.2d at 634 (the right to withdraw treatment must extend to incompetents as well as competents "because the value of human dignity extends to both"); *Drabick,* 245 Cal. Rptr. at 854–55 (it is "possible for others to make a decision that reflects [the incompetent's] interests more closely than would a purely technological decision to do whatever is possible. . . .").

The majority in *Cruzan* has ruled that an incompetent person simply loses the federal constitutional right to have choices made about medical treatment that reflect his interest. This holding is a direct infringement on the equal protection, privacy and liberty rights of an incompetent person, Moreover, the Missouri living will act which supports such a denial is, as the trial court found, constitutionally invalid on its face. The majority decision has left incompetent persons and their families without medical treatment options and stripped of constitutional rights protected by other state courts and long guaranteed by this Court. It has led Missouri to the edge of the slippery slope of state ordered medical treatment. Immediate review by this Court is warranted.

3. This Case Presents Questions of Critical National Importance

New techniques and machines have created wonderful and beneficial technological advances in medical care. Unfortunately, they have also created a dark side to medical treatment where people, trapped and helpless, are subject to the "ultimate horror not of death but . . . of being maintained in limbo, in a sterile room, by machines controlled by strangers." Whether people are deprived of their constitutional rights and sentenced to such a fate depends now totally on their state of residence. A tenuous 4–3 majority of the Missouri Supreme Court has denied incompetent persons in Missouri the right to a natural death with dignity, free from unwanted technological interference, in favor of a broad rule that all steps technologically possible to prolong life for incompetent persons must be taken. More states will face these issues,[13] and without guidance from this Court, will simply add to the confusing patchwork of constitutional rights accorded incompetent patients. Families across the United States will be faced with the horrible, yet real, prospect that the only way to carry out the wishes of their now medically incompetent loved one is to move the loved one to a state which honors

---

[13] Other states have recently or will soon, face these issues. For example, the Supreme Court of Illinois recently heard arguments in the case of *In re Sidney Greenspan,* No. 67903, which involved the constitutional right to remove artificial feeding from an elderly man in a PVS.

the constitutional rights of incompetents. Incompetent persons without families will obviously have no ability to move.

The states need guidance. Because the proper resolution of these issues depends essentially upon the nature and strength of an individual's federal constitutional rights, that guidance must come from this Court, not the state courts or state legislatures. Indeed, as in Missouri, the state legislature may be the very group seeking to deprive incompetent persons of federal rights. As Judge Welliver argued persuasively in dissent, the Missouri living will act is constitutionally invalid on its face. Other legislation proposed in the Missouri legislature is even more offensive to constitutional sensibilities.[14]

If an incompetent patient like Nancy Cruzan is not entitled to refuse medical care which she would refuse if she could speak, then the majority has succeeded in elevating the state's interest in a patient's life above the individual's interest in her own life. The *Cruzan* majority has ignored Nancy Cruzan's intent and the wishes of her family and ruled that all steps technologically possible must be taken to prolong the lives of incompetent patients. Review of this broad ruling by this Court is vital to determine whether individual medical treatment should be a decision for patients, families and their doctors, or for the states.

CONCLUSION

The petition for a writ of certiorari should be granted.

NOTES AND QUESTIONS

1. *Question Presented.* Was the petitioner effective in urging the Court to grant cert. by phrasing the question presented in the following manner: "Whether a state's interest in life, codified in the state 'living will act,' can override all constitutional privacy, liberty and equal protection rights of an incompetent person to reject medical treatment?" How would you have drafted the question presented?

2. *Statement.* Was the two-paragraph statement of Nancy Cruzan's condition effective in presenting her situation to the Court? Was Nancy's situation presented sympathetically enough, or would you have included more facts about her medical situation and quality of life?

3. *Missouri Ruling.* According to the petition, the Missouri Supreme Court ruled 4–3 against Cruzan. What were the arguments on both sides? Why did the Missouri court decline to follow *Quinlan* and rule on Cruzan's behalf? Why did the majority conclude the state had an "unqualified" interest in Nancy's life?

Presumably the closeness of the vote in Missouri (4–3) and the arguments of the three dissenters strengthened the petitioner's argument that the U.S. Supreme Court should hear the case. Did the petition do a good

---

[14] Recently drafted Missouri Senate Bill No. 371 proposes to make it a criminal violation for any person to withdraw or withhold fluids and nutrition in any form from any person in Missouri, competent or not, regardless of that person's intent.

job of arguing the validity of the dissenters' approach to *Cruzan*? As footnote 2 states, "Judge Welliver in his dissent charged that the legislature in placing the limitations on the living will had perpetrated a 'fraud on Missourians who believe we have been given a right to execute a living will, and to die naturally, respectably, and in peace.'" Can you tell why Judge Welliver thought the living will statute was fraudulent and unconstitutional?

Dissenting Judge Blackmar reasoned that contrary to the majority's belief in the state's absolute interest in life, the living will statute "in fact allows and encourages the preplanned termination of life." Why is the preplanned termination of life not considered a homicide? Should living wills really allow the preplanned termination of life?

4. *Other States.* In order to demonstrate there was a split of opinion in courts around the country that justified the Court's granting review of their case, the petitioner summarized other state laws. What did the petition say about the relevance of *Quinlan*? How did Missouri law differ from the laws of Arizona, Massachusetts and Washington? As you review the different state precedents, be sure to identify the specific factual circumstances of each case and the precise question that each state court reviewed. How many of the state plaintiffs were similarly situated to Nancy Cruzan?

5. *Supreme Court.* The U.S. Supreme Court granted the cert. petition to hear Cruzan's case, but then ruled for the state of Missouri on the merits. What is the holding of *Cruzan*? Can you tell from the ruling if patients possess any constitutional rights? How many legal protections for patients can you identify in the decision? Are they consistent with the principles of biomedical ethics? Is *Cruzan* consistent with *Quinlan*?

Cruzan v. Director, Missouri Department of Health

Supreme Court of the United States, 1988.
497 U.S. 261, 110 S.Ct. 2841.

■ REHNQUIST, C.J., delivered the opinion of the Court, in which WHITE, O'CONNOR, SCALIA, and KENNEDY, JJ., joined. O'CONNOR, J. and SCALIA, J. filed concurring opinions. BRENNAN, J., filed a dissenting opinion, in which MARSHALL and BLACKMUN, JJ., joined. STEVENS, J., filed a dissenting opinion.

■ CHIEF JUSTICE REHNQUIST delivered the opinion of the Court.

. . . . We granted certiorari to consider the question whether Cruzan has a right under the United States Constitution which would require the hospital to withdraw life-sustaining treatment from her under these circumstances.

At common law, even the touching of one person by another without consent and without legal justification was a battery. Before the turn of the century, this Court observed that "[n]o right is held more sacred, or is more carefully guarded, by the common law, than the right of every individual to the possession and control of his own person, free from all

restraint or interference of others, unless by clear and unquestionable authority of law." This notion of bodily integrity has been embodied in the requirement that informed consent is generally required for medical treatment. Justice Cardozo, while on the Court of Appeals of New York, aptly described this doctrine: "Every human being of adult years and sound mind has a right to determine what shall be done with his own body; and a surgeon who performs an operation without his patient's consent commits an assault, for which he is liable in damages." *Schloendorff v. Society of New York Hospital,* 211 N.Y. 125, 129–30, 105 N.E. 92, 93 (1914). The informed consent doctrine has become firmly entrenched in American tort law.

The logical corollary of the doctrine of informed consent is that the patient generally possesses the right not to consent, that is, to refuse treatment. Until about 15 years ago and the seminal decision in *In re Quinlan,* 70 N.J. 10, 355 A.2d 647, cert. denied *sub nom. Garger v. New Jersey,* 429 U.S. 922, 97 S. Ct. 319, 50 L.Ed.2d 289 (1976), the number of right-to-refuse-treatment decisions was relatively few. Most of the earlier cases involved patients who refused medical treatment forbidden by their religious beliefs, thus implicating First Amendment rights as well as common-law rights of self-determination. More recently, however, with the advance of medical technology capable of sustaining life well past the point where natural forces would have brought certain death in earlier times, cases involving the right to refuse life-sustaining treatment have burgeoned. . . .

As these cases demonstrate, the common-law doctrine of informed consent is viewed as generally encompassing the right of a competent individual to refuse medical treatment. Beyond that, these cases demonstrate both similarity and diversity in their approaches to decision of what all agree is a perplexing question with unusually strong moral and ethical overtones. State courts have available to them for decision a number of sources—state constitutions, statutes, and common law—which are not available to us. In this Court, the question is simply and starkly whether the United States Constitution prohibits Missouri from choosing the rule of decision which it did. This is the first case in which we have been squarely presented with the issue whether the United States Constitution grants what is in common parlance referred to as a "right to die. . . ." [I]n deciding "a question of such magnitude and importance . . . it is the [better] part of wisdom not to attempt, by any general statement, to cover every possible phase of the subject."

The Fourteenth Amendment provides that no State shall "deprive any person of life, liberty, or property, without due process of law." The principle that a competent person has a constitutionally protected liberty interest in refusing unwanted medical treatment may be inferred from our prior decisions. In *Jacobson v. Massachusetts,* 197 U.S. 11, 24–30, 25 S. Ct. 358, 360–61, 49 L.Ed. 643 (1905), for instance, the Court balanced an individual's liberty interest in declining an unwanted smallpox

vaccine against the State's interest in preventing disease. Decisions prior to the incorporation of the Fourth Amendment into the Fourteenth Amendment analyzed searches and seizures involving the body under the Due Process Clause and were thought to implicate substantial liberty interests.

Just this Term, in the course of holding that a State's procedures for administering antipsychotic medication to prisoners were sufficient to satisfy due process concerns, we recognized that prisoners possess "a significant liberty interest in avoiding the unwanted administration of antipsychotic drugs under the Due Process Clause of the Fourteenth Amendment." Still other cases support the recognition of a general liberty interest in refusing medical treatment.

But determining that a person has a "liberty interest" under the Due Process Clause does not end the inquiry;[7] "whether respondent's constitutional rights have been violated must be determined by balancing his liberty interests against the relevant state interests."

Petitioners insist that under the general holdings of our cases, the forced administration of life-sustaining medical treatment, and even of artificially delivered food and water essential to life, would implicate a competent person's liberty interest. Although we think the logic of the cases discussed above would embrace such a liberty interest, the dramatic consequences involved in refusal of such treatment would inform the inquiry as to whether the deprivation of that interest is constitutionally permissible. But for purposes of this case, we assume that the United States Constitution would grant a competent person a constitutionally protected right to refuse lifesaving hydration and nutrition.

Petitioners go on to assert that an incompetent person should possess the same right in this respect as is possessed by a competent person. . . . The difficulty with petitioners' claim is that in a sense it begs the question: An incompetent person is not able to make an informed and voluntary choice to exercise a hypothetical right to refuse treatment or any other right. Such a "right" must be exercised for her, if at all, by some sort of surrogate. Here, Missouri has in effect recognized that under certain circumstances a surrogate may act for the patient in electing to have hydration and nutrition withdrawn in such a way as to cause death, but it has established a procedural safeguard to assure that the action of the surrogate conforms as best it may to the wishes expressed by the patient while competent. Missouri requires that evidence of the incompetent's wishes as to the withdrawal of treatment be proved by clear and convincing evidence. The question, then, is whether the United

[7] Although many state courts have held that a right to refuse treatment is encompassed by a generalized constitutional right of privacy, we have never so held. We believe this issue is more properly analyzed in terms of a Fourteenth Amendment liberty interest. See *Bowers v. Hardwick*, 478 U.S. 186, 194–95, 106 S. Ct. 2841, 2846, 92 L.Ed.2d 140 (1986).

States Constitution forbids the establishment of this procedural requirement by the State. We hold that it does not.

Whether or not Missouri's clear and convincing evidence requirement comports with the United States Constitution depends in part on what interests the State may properly seek to protect in this situation. Missouri relies on its interest in the protection and preservation of human life, and there can be no gainsaying this interest. As a general matter, the States—indeed, all civilized nations—demonstrate their commitment to life by treating homicide as a serious crime. Moreover, the majority of States in this country have laws imposing criminal penalties on one who assists another to commit suicide. We do not think a State is required to remain neutral in the face of an informed and voluntary decision by a physically able adult to starve to death.

But in the context presented here, a State has more particular interests at stake. The choice between life and death is a deeply personal decision of obvious and overwhelming finality. We believe Missouri may legitimately seek to safeguard the personal element of this choice through the imposition of heightened evidentiary requirements. It cannot be disputed that the Due Process Clause protects an interest in life as well as an interest in refusing life-sustaining medical treatment. Not all incompetent patients will have loved ones available to serve as surrogate decisionmakers. And even where family members are present, "[t]here will, of course, be some unfortunate situations in which family members will not act to protect a patient." A State is entitled to guard against potential abuses in such situations. Similarly, a State is entitled to consider that a judicial proceeding to make a determination regarding an incompetent's wishes may very well not be an adversarial one, with the added guarantee of accurate factfinding that the adversary process brings with it. Finally, we think a State may properly decline to make judgments about the "quality" of life that a particular individual may enjoy, and simply assert an unqualified interest in the preservation of human life to be weighed against the constitutionally protected interests of the individual.

In our view, Missouri has permissibly sought to advance these interests through the adoption of a "clear and convincing" standard of proof to govern such proceedings. "The function of a standard of proof, as that concept is embodied in the Due Process Clause and in the realm of factfinding, is to 'instruct the factfinder concerning the degree of confidence our society thinks he should have in the correctness of factual conclusions for a particular type of adjudication.'" "This Court has mandated an intermediate standard of proof—'clear and convincing evidence'—when the individual interests at stake in a state proceeding are both 'particularly important' and 'more substantial than mere loss of money.'" Thus, such a standard has been required in deportation proceedings, in denaturalization proceedings, in civil commitment

proceedings, and in proceedings for the termination of parental rights. Further, this level of proof, "or an even higher one, has traditionally been imposed in cases involving allegations of civil fraud, and in a variety of other kinds of civil cases involving such issues as . . . lost wills, oral contracts to make bequests, and the like."

We think it self-evident that the interests at stake in the instant proceedings are more substantial, both on an individual and societal level, than those involved in a run-of-the-mine civil dispute. But not only does the standard of proof reflect the importance of a particular adjudication, it also serves as "a societal judgment about how the risk of error should be distributed between the litigants." The more stringent the burden of proof a party must bear, the more that party bears the risk of an erroneous decision. We believe that Missouri may permissibly place an increased risk of an erroneous decision on those seeking to terminate an incompetent individual's life-sustaining treatment. An erroneous decision not to terminate results in a maintenance of the status quo; the possibility of subsequent developments such as advancements in medical science, the discovery of new evidence regarding the patient's intent, changes in the law, or simply the unexpected death of the patient despite the administration of life-sustaining treatment at least create the potential that a wrong decision will eventually be corrected or its impact mitigated. An erroneous decision to withdraw life-sustaining treatment, however, is not susceptible of correction. In *Santosky,* one of the factors which led the Court to require proof by clear and convincing evidence in a proceeding to terminate parental rights was that a decision in such a case was final and irrevocable. *Santosky, supra,* 445 U.S. at 759, 102 S. Ct., at 1397–98. The same must surely be said of the decision to discontinue hydration and nutrition of a patient such as Nancy Cruzan, which all agree will result in her death.

It is also worth noting that most, if not all, States simply forbid oral testimony entirely in determining the wishes of parties in transactions which, while important, simply do not have the consequences that a decision to terminate a person's life does. At common law and by statute in most States, the parol evidence rule prevents the variations of the terms of a written contract by oral testimony. The statute of frauds makes unenforceable oral contracts to leave property by will, and statutes regulating the making of wills universally require that those instruments be in writing. There is no doubt that statutes requiring wills to be in writing, and statutes of frauds which require that a contract to make a will be in writing, on occasion frustrate the effectuation of the intent of a particular decedent, just as Missouri's requirement of proof in this case may have frustrated the effectuation of the not-fully-expressed desires of Nancy Cruzan. But the Constitution does not require general rules to work faultlessly; no general rule can.

In sum, we conclude that a State may apply a clear and convincing evidence standard in proceedings where a guardian seeks to discontinue

nutrition and hydration of a person diagnosed to be in a persistent vegetative state. We note that many courts which have adopted some sort of substituted judgment procedure in situations like this, whether they limit consideration of evidence to the prior expressed wishes of the incompetent individual, or whether they allow more general proof of what the individual's decision would have been, require a clear and convincing standard of proof for such evidence.

The Supreme Court of Missouri held that in this case the testimony adduced at trial did not amount to clear and convincing proof of the patient's desire to have hydration and nutrition withdrawn. In so doing, it reversed a decision of the Missouri trial court which had found that the evidence "suggest[ed]" Nancy Cruzan would not have desired to continue such measures, but which had not adopted the standard of "clear and convincing evidence" enunciated by the Supreme Court. The testimony adduced at trial consisted primarily of Nancy Cruzan's statements made to a housemate about a year before her accident that she would not want to live should she face life as a "vegetable," and other observations to the same effect. The observations did not deal in terms with withdrawal of medical treatment or of hydration and nutrition. We cannot say that the Supreme Court of Missouri committed constitutional error in reaching the conclusion that it did.

Petitioners alternatively contend that Missouri must accept the "substituted judgment" of close family members even in the absence of substantial proof that their views reflect the views of the patient. They rely primarily upon our decisions in *Michael H. v. Gerald D.,* 491 U.S. 110, 109 S. Ct. 2333, 105 L.Ed.2d 91 (1989), and *Parham v. J.R.,* 442 U.S. 584, 99 S. Ct. 2493, 61 L.Ed.2d 101 (1979). But we do not think these cases support their claim. In *Michael H.,* we *upheld* the constitutionality of California's favored treatment of traditional family relationships; such a holding may not be turned around into a constitutional requirement that a State *must* recognize the primacy of those relationships in a situation like this. And in *Parham,* where the patient was a minor, we also *upheld* the constitutionality of a state scheme in which parents made certain decisions for mentally ill minors. Here again petitioners would seek to turn a decision which allowed a State to rely on family decisionmaking into a constitutional requirement that the State recognize such decisionmaking. But constitutional law does not work that way.

No doubt is engendered by anything in this record but that Nancy Cruzan's mother and father are loving and caring parents. If the State were required by the United States Constitution to repose a right of "substituted judgment" with anyone, the Cruzans would surely qualify. But we do not think the Due Process Clause requires the State to repose judgment on these matters with anyone but the patient herself. Close family members may have a strong feeling—a feeling not at all ignoble or unworthy, but not entirely disinterested, either—that they do not wish

to witness the continuation of the life of a loved one which they regard as hopeless, meaningless, and even degrading. But there is no automatic assurance that the view of close family members will necessarily be the same as the patient's would have been had she been confronted with the prospect of her situation while competent. All of the reasons previously discussed for allowing Missouri to require clear and convincing evidence of the patient's wishes lead us to conclude that the State may choose to defer only to those wishes, rather than confide the decision to close family members.[12]

The judgment of the Supreme Court of Missouri is

Affirmed.

■ JUSTICE O'CONNOR, concurring.

.... I also write separately to emphasize that the Court does not today decide the issue whether a State must also give effect to the decisions of a surrogate decisionmaker. In my view, such a duty may well be constitutionally required to protect the patient's liberty interest in refusing medical treatment. Few individuals provide explicit oral or written instructions regarding their intent to refuse medical treatment should they become incompetent. States which decline to consider any evidence other than such instructions may frequently fail to honor a patient's intent. Such failures might be avoided if the State considered an equally probative source of evidence: the patient's appointment of a proxy to make health care decisions on her behalf. Delegating the authority to make medical decisions to a family member or friend is becoming a common method of planning for the future. Several States have recognized the practical wisdom of such a procedure by enacting durable power of attorney statutes that specifically authorize an individual to appoint a surrogate to make medical treatment decisions. Some state courts have suggested that an agent appointed pursuant to a general durable power of attorney statute would also be empowered to make health care decisions on behalf of the patient. Other States allow an individual to designate a proxy to carry out the intent of a living will. These procedures for surrogate decisionmaking, which appear to be rapidly gaining in acceptance, may be a valuable additional safeguard of the patient's interest in directing his medical care. Moreover, as patients are likely to select a family member as a surrogate, giving effect to a proxy's decisions may also protect the "freedom of personal choice in matters of . . . family life."

Today's decision, holding only that the Constitution permits a State to require clear and convincing evidence of Nancy Cruzan's desire to have artificial hydration and nutrition withdrawn, does not preclude a future determination that the Constitution requires the States to implement the

---

[12] We are not faced in this case with the question whether a State might be required to defer to the decision of a surrogate if competent and probative evidence established that the patient herself had expressed a desire that the decision to terminate life-sustaining treatment be made for her by that individual.

decisions of a patient's duly appointed surrogate. Nor does it prevent States from developing other approaches for protecting an incompetent individual's liberty interest in refusing medical treatment. As is evident from the Court's survey of state court decisions, no national consensus has yet emerged on the best solution for this difficult and sensitive problem. Today we decide only that one State's practice does not violate the Constitution; the more challenging task of crafting appropriate procedures for safeguarding incompetents' liberty interests is entrusted to the "laboratory" of the States, in the first instance.

■ JUSTICE SCALIA, concurring.

The various opinions in this case portray quite clearly the difficult, indeed agonizing, questions that are presented by the constantly increasing power of science to keep the human body alive for longer than any reasonable person would want to inhabit it. The States have begun to grapple with these problems through legislation. I am concerned, from the tenor of today's opinions, that we are poised to confuse that enterprise as successfully as we have confused the enterprise of legislating concerning abortion—requiring it to be conducted against a background of federal constitutional imperatives that are unknown because they are being newly crafted from Term to Term. That would be a great misfortune.

While I agree with the Court's analysis today, and therefore join in its opinion, I would have preferred that we announce, clearly and promptly, that the federal courts have no business in this field; that American law has always accorded the State the power to prevent, by force if necessary, suicide—including suicide by refusing to take appropriate measures necessary to preserve one's life; that the point at which life becomes "worthless," and the point at which the means necessary to preserve it become "extraordinary" or "inappropriate," are neither set forth in the Constitution nor known to the nine Justices of this Court any better than they are known to nine people picked at random from the Kansas City telephone directory; and hence, that even when it *is* demonstrated by clear and convincing evidence that a patient no longer wishes certain measures to be taken to preserve his or her life, it is up to the citizens of Missouri to decide, through their elected representatives, whether that wish will be honored. It is quite impossible (because the Constitution says nothing about the matter) that those citizens will decide upon a line less lawful than the one we would choose; and it is unlikely (because we know no more about "life and death" than they do) that they will decide upon a line less reasonable. . . .

What I have said above is not meant to suggest that I would think it desirable, if we were sure that Nancy Cruzan wanted to die, to keep her alive by the means at issue here. I assert only that the Constitution has nothing to say about the subject. To raise up a constitutional right here we would have to create out of nothing (for it exists neither in text nor tradition) some constitutional principle whereby, although the State may

insist that an individual come in out of the cold and eat food, it may not insist that he take medicine; and although it may pump his stomach empty of poison he has ingested, it may not fill his stomach with food he has failed to ingest. Are there, then, no reasonable and humane limits that ought not to be exceeded in requiring an individual to preserve his own life? There obviously are, but they are not set forth in the Due Process Clause. What assures us that those limits will not be exceeded is the same constitutional guarantee that is the source of most of our protection—what protects us, for example, from being assessed a tax of 100% of our income above the subsistence level, from being forbidden to drive cars, or from being required to send our children to school for 10 hours a day, none of which horribles are categorically prohibited by the Constitution. Our salvation is the Equal Protection Clause, which requires the democratic majority to accept for themselves and their loved ones what they impose on you and me. This Court need not, and has no authority to, inject itself into every field of human activity where irrationality and oppression may theoretically occur, and if it tries to do so it will destroy itself.

■ JUSTICE BRENNAN, with whom JUSTICE MARSHALL and JUSTICE BLACKMUN join, dissenting.

. . . . Because I believe that Nancy Cruzan has a fundamental right to be free of unwanted artificial nutrition and hydration, which right is not outweighed by any interests of the State, and because I find that the improperly biased procedural obstacles imposed by the Missouri Supreme Court impermissibly burden that right, I respectfully dissent. Nancy Cruzan is entitled to choose to die with dignity. . . .

II

B

Although the right to be free of unwanted medical intervention, like other constitutionally protected interests, may not be absolute, no state interest could outweigh the rights of an individual in Nancy Cruzan's position. Whatever a State's possible interests in mandating life-support treatment under other circumstances, there is no good to be obtained here by Missouri's insistence that Nancy Cruzan remain on life-support systems if it is indeed her wish not to do so. Missouri does not claim, nor could it, that society as a whole will be benefited by Nancy's receiving medical treatment. No third party's situation will be improved and no harm to others will be averted.

The only state interest asserted here is a general interest in the preservation of life. But the State has no legitimate general interest in someone's life, completely abstracted from the interest of the person living that life, that could outweigh the person's choice to avoid medical treatment. "[T]he regulation of constitutionally protected decisions . . . must be predicated on legitimate state concerns *other than* disagreement with the choice the individual has made. . . . Otherwise, the interest in

liberty protected by the Due Process Clause would be a nullity." Thus, the State's general interest in life must accede to Nancy Cruzan's particularized and intense interest in self-determination in her choice of medical treatment. There is simply nothing legitimately within the State's purview to be gained by superseding her decision. . . .

III

This is not to say that the State has no legitimate interests to assert here. As the majority recognizes, Missouri has a *parens patriae* interest in providing Nancy Cruzan, now incompetent, with as accurate as possible a determination of how she would exercise her rights under these circumstances. Second, if and when it is determined that Nancy Cruzan would want to continue treatment, the State may legitimately assert an interest in providing that treatment. But *until* Nancy's wishes have been determined, the only state interest that may be asserted is an interest in safeguarding the accuracy of that determination.

Accuracy, therefore, must be our touchstone. Missouri may constitutionally impose only those procedural requirements that serve to enhance the accuracy of a determination of Nancy Cruzan's wishes or are at least consistent with an accurate determination. The Missouri "safeguard" that the Court upholds today does not meet that standard. The determination needed in this context is whether the incompetent person would choose to live in a persistent vegetative state on life support or to avoid this medical treatment. Missouri's rule of decision imposes a markedly asymmetrical evidentiary burden. Only evidence of specific statements of treatment choice made by the patient when competent is admissible to support a finding that the patient, now in a persistent vegetative state, would wish to avoid further medical treatment. Moreover, this evidence must be clear and convincing. No proof is required to support a finding that the incompetent person would wish to continue treatment. . . .

D

Finally, I cannot agree with the majority that where it is not possible to determine what choice an incompetent patient would make, a State's role as *parens patriae* permits the State automatically to make that choice itself. Under fair rules of evidence, it is improbable that a court could not determine what the patient's choice would be. Under the rule of decision adopted by Missouri and upheld today by this Court, such occasions might be numerous. But in neither case does it follow that it is constitutionally acceptable for the State invariably to assume the role of deciding for the patient. A State's legitimate interest in safeguarding a patient's choice cannot be furthered by simply appropriating it.

The majority justifies its position by arguing that, while close family members may have a strong feeling about the question, "there is no automatic assurance that the view of close family members will necessarily be the same as the patient's would have been had she been

confronted with the prospect of her situation while competent." I cannot quarrel with this observation. But it leads only to another question: Is there any reason to suppose that a State is *more* likely to make the choice that the patient would have made than someone who knew the patient intimately? To ask this is to answer it. . . .

I respectfully dissent.

■ JUSTICE STEVENS, dissenting.

. . . . In my view, the Constitution requires the State to care for Nancy Cruzan's life in a way that gives appropriate respect to her own best interests.

III

These considerations cast into stark relief the injustice, and unconstitutionality, of Missouri's treatment of Nancy Beth Cruzan. Nancy Cruzan's death, when it comes, cannot be an historic act of heroism; it will inevitably be the consequence of her tragic accident. But Nancy Cruzan's interest in life, no less than that of any other person, includes an interest in how she will be thought of after her death by those whose opinions mattered to her. There can be no doubt that her life made her dear to her family and to others. How she dies will affect how that life is remembered. The trial court's order authorizing Nancy's parents to cease their daughter's treatment would have permitted the family that cares for Nancy to bring to a close her tragedy and her death. Missouri's objection to that order subordinates Nancy's body, her family, and the lasting significance of her life to the State's own interests. The decision we review thereby interferes with constitutional interests of the highest order.

To be constitutionally permissible, Missouri's intrusion upon these fundamental liberties must, at a minimum, bear a reasonable relationship to a legitimate state end. Missouri asserts that its policy is related to a state interest in the protection of life. In my view, however, it is an effort to define life, rather than to protect it, that is the heart of Missouri's policy. Missouri insists, without regard to Nancy Cruzan's own interests, upon equating her life with the biological persistence of her bodily functions. Nancy Cruzan, it must be remembered, is not now simply incompetent. She is in a persistent vegetative state and has been so for seven years. The trial court found, and no party contested, that Nancy has no possibility of recovery and no consciousness.

It seems to me that the Court errs insofar as it characterizes this case as involving "judgments about the 'quality' of life that a particular individual may enjoy." Nancy Cruzan is obviously "*alive*" in a physiological sense. But for patients like Nancy Cruzan, who have no consciousness and no chance of recovery, there is a serious question as to whether the mere persistence of their bodies is "*life*" as that word is commonly understood, or as it is used in both the Constitution and the Declaration of Independence. The State's unflagging determination to

perpetuate Nancy Cruzan's physical existence is comprehensible only as an effort to define life's meaning, not as an attempt to preserve its sanctity. . . .

In short, there is no reasonable ground for believing that Nancy Beth Cruzan has any *personal* interest in the perpetuation of what the State has decided is her life. As I have already suggested, it would be possible to hypothesize such an interest on the basis of theological or philosophical conjecture. But even to posit such a basis for the State's action is to condemn it. It is not within the province of secular government to circumscribe the liberties of the people by regulations designed wholly for the purpose of establishing a sectarian definition of life.

My disagreement with the Court is thus unrelated to its endorsement of the clear and convincing standard of proof for cases of this kind. Indeed, I agree that the controlling facts must be established with unmistakable clarity. The critical question, however, is not how to prove the controlling facts but rather what proven facts should be controlling. In my view, the constitutional answer is clear: The best interests of the individual, especially when buttressed by the interests of all related third parties, must prevail over any general state policy that simply ignores those interests. Indeed, the only apparent *secular* basis for the State's interest in life is the policy's persuasive impact upon people other than Nancy and her family. Yet, "[a]lthough the State may properly perform a teaching function," and although that teaching may foster respect for the sanctity of life, the State may not pursue its project by infringing constitutionally protected interests for "*symbolic* effect." The failure of Missouri's policy to heed the interests of a dying individual with respect to matters so private is ample evidence of the policy's illegitimacy.

I respectfully dissent.

NOTES AND QUESTIONS

1. *Informed Consent.* In a famous case from 1914 where a patient complained that surgeons had operated on her without her consent, Judge Cardozo of the New York Court of Appeals wrote: "Every human being of adult years and sound mind has a right to determine what shall be done with his own body; and a surgeon who performs an operation without his patient's consent, commits an assault, for which he is liable in damages." Schloendorff v. Soc'y of N.Y. Hosp., 105 N.E. 92, 93 (1914). In *Cruzan*, the Supreme Court acknowledged the doctrine of informed consent as an important part of American tort law and tradition, and recognized the "logical corollary of the doctrine of informed consent is that the patient generally possesses the right not to consent, that is, to refuse treatment." Does the Court conclude that there is a constitutional right to informed consent, or is consent always a matter of state common law or statute?

2. *Liberty Interest.* Note that in footnote 7 of the opinion, the Chief Justice asserts that the right to refuse treatment is best understood as a

liberty interest, not a *privacy* interest. What is the difference? Recall that the Court's privacy line of cases started with Griswold v. Connecticut, 381 U.S. 479 (1965), which held that the right to marital privacy is broad enough to include contraceptive use, and culminated in Roe v. Wade, 410 U.S. 113 (1973), which held that the right to privacy protects a woman's right to terminate her pregnancy by abortion. Then-Justice Rehnquist was one of two dissenters in *Roe v. Wade*. Do you think that explains why the Court chose liberty over privacy in *Cruzan*? What do you think the result of the case would have been if the Court had decided that the right to refuse medical treatment is a protected *privacy* interest? If Cruzan had the privacy right to terminate her own pregnancy, why didn't she enjoy an even stronger privacy right to refuse nutrition and hydration?

Should the New Jersey Supreme Court have written about Karen Quinlan's liberty interest instead of her right to privacy in refusing medical treatment? Does the Court *hold* that patients possess a liberty interest when it writes "[t]he principle that a competent person has a constitutionally protected liberty interest in refusing unwanted medical treatment may be *inferred* from our prior decisions?" Is inferring the same as recognizing or holding?

3. *Balancing Test.* Why and how should the individual's liberty be weighed against the state's interests? The Court cited Jacobson v. Massachusetts, 197 U.S. 11, 24–30 (1905), in which the Court upheld the state's right to require Jacobson to receive a smallpox vaccination, against his will, because of the state's interests in public safety and health.

> **Practice Exercise:** Write down the list of Missouri's interests and Nancy Cruzan's interests. How would you balance them against one another?

Did you agree with the majority that the state's interests justified the clear and convincing evidence standard? Or did Justice William Brennan persuade you that "no state interest could outweigh the rights of an individual in Nancy Cruzan's position. . . . [T]he State has no legitimate general interest in someone's life, completely abstracted from the interest of the person living that life, that could outweigh the person's choice to avoid medical treatment"? Justice John Paul Stevens wrote "there is no reasonable ground for believing that Nancy Beth Cruzan has any *personal* interest in the perpetuation of what the State has decided is her life." Is that an accurate statement of Cruzan's interests and Missouri's interests?

4. *Substituted Judgment.* The Cruzans proposed an alternative argument that "Missouri must accept the 'substituted judgment' of close family members even in the absence of substantial proof that their views reflect the views of the patient." Would this be a good legal standard for patients, or would it give too much freedom to family members to make decisions that would harm the patient? In what ways is a "substituted judgment" rule better than a "clear and convincing evidence" standard? Why does the Court reject the argument that the state must respect the family's decision as a matter of constitutional law?

5. *Clear and Convincing Evidence.* After the Supreme Court remanded the case, two new witnesses who had worked with Nancy Cruzan, while her name was Nancy Davis, came forward to testify about her wishes about medical treatment, and the trial judge granted the Cruzans' request to disconnect the feeding tube. See Sandra H. Johnson, Quinlan and Cruzan: Beyond the Symbols, in Health Law & Bioethics: Cases in Context 66 (S.H. Johnson et al. eds., 2009). Why was this clear and convincing evidence? Are you skeptical whether the clear and convincing standard was met in this case? The Court upheld, but did not mandate, Missouri's use of the clear and convincing evidence standard to resolve such disputes. Is that an appropriate evidentiary standard? Is it too high a threshold for patients reasonably to meet? Too low a threshold to safeguard this paramount interest? What other standard might be preferable?

> **Practice Exercise:** Write down the exact evidence you would need to establish by clear and convincing evidence that Nancy Cruzan's treatment should be discontinued.

An 18-year-old who had never talked about life and death and suffered an accident like Cruzan's could presumably never meet the clear and convincing evidence standard. Is there a point at which keeping that person alive becomes unconstitutional? Is this why a substituted judgment standard is preferable? Should parents be automatically authorized to make a decision on behalf of their children?

6. *Courts and Legislatures.* Do you agree with Justice Scalia's argument that the federal courts have no business in this field? If so, how should legislatures address the problems of death and dying? Should all states adopt Missouri's clear and convincing standard? Does Scalia's reasoning free states to pass statutes implementing the substituted-judgment rule?

7. *Surrogate Decision-Makers.* According to Chief Justice Rehnquist's opinion, the Court did not face the question "whether a State might be required to defer to the decision of a surrogate if competent and probative evidence established that the patient herself had expressed a desire that the decision to terminate life-sustaining treatment be made for her by that individual." States usually handle these issues by allowing individuals to appoint a health care agent or medical power of attorney. Justice Sandra Day O'Connor

> wr[o]te separately to emphasize that the Court does not today decide the issue whether a State must also give effect to the decisions of a surrogate decisionmaker. In my view, such a duty may well be constitutionally required to protect the patient's liberty interest in refusing medical treatment. Today's decision, holding only that the Constitution permits a State to require clear and convincing evidence of Nancy Cruzan's desire to have artificial hydration and nutrition withdrawn, does not preclude a future determination that the Constitution requires the States to implement the decisions of a patient's duly appointed surrogate.

Do you think there is a constitutional right to have your surrogate decision-maker's decision enforced on your behalf?

Go to the website and learn how to create durable powers of attorney and living wills in Missouri.

Post-*Cruzan*, what is the best way to ensure that medical personnel follow your medical wishes? Which of the Missouri forms would you urge future clients to adopt, the living will or the durable power of attorney? Is there any way that you would change those forms? Is anything about the forms "fraudulent" or "unconstitutional" as Judge Welliver argued about the Missouri living will law in *Cruzan*? Do they leave anything out? Are courts constitutionally required to enforce these directives?

A recent development in end-of-life planning has been the POLST (Physician Orders for Life-Sustaining Treatment) form. The POLST document is a standardized and portable medical order carried by the patient that proves that a discussion between a medical provider and a patient with a serious or terminal illness has taken place. A POLST form allows emergency medical services to provide specific procedures and treatment options that the patient has decided beforehand with his or her medical provider. One important difference between a POLST form and a document such as an advance directive is that the POLST form can be used by the entire community of medical service providers. This means that the form is recognized and acted upon by first responders, emergency medical service providers, nursing homes, physicians, nurses, and anyone else in the health care field. This makes POLST highly versatile.

Go to the website to see a sample California POLST form.

The POLST approach favors extensive conversation between physicians and patients, who together choose a course of treatment for the seriously ill patient. Unlike a living will or a health care power of attorney, the POLST form contains actionable medical orders that determine what treatment the patient will receive. Go to POLST's website, https://polst.org/programs-in-your-state/, to see if your state has adopted POLST as a resource for dying patients. Notice that POLST is available only for patients who are very ill; healthy individuals still need advance directives such as health care powers of attorney or living wills.

Practice Exercise: How would a case like Terri Schiavo's be handled in your state if she became seriously injured without a living will or health care power of attorney? Try to figure out in particular: 1) the effect of not having an advance directive, 2) your state's order of surrogate decision-makers and 3) the standards governing their decisions. Start with the website.

In 1990, Terri Schiavo suffered cardiac arrest due to an unexplained potassium disorder in her body. Her husband, Michael Schiavo, immediately called for medical assistance. Terri never recovered and

remained in a persistent vegetative state for eight years until her husband requested discontinuance of treatment. Terri's parents resisted Michael's request, filing numerous lawsuits seeking their appointment as guardians in place of Michael so that they could keep their daughter alive. In re Guardianship of Schiavo, No. 90–2908GD–003, 2000 WL 34546715 (Fla. Cir. Ct. Feb. 11, 2000) aff'd, 780 So. 2d 176 (Fla. Dist. Ct. App. 2001). State and federal courts repeatedly upheld Michael's legal right to make medical decisions on behalf of his wife.

Schiavo's case arose in Florida. If an incapacitated person lacks any advance directive, Florida law allows health care decisions to be made by individuals in the following order of priority:

> (a) The judicially appointed guardian of the patient or the guardian advocate of the person having a developmental disability as defined in s. 393.063, who has been authorized to consent to medical treatment, if such guardian has previously been appointed; however, this paragraph shall not be construed to require such appointment before a treatment decision can be made under this subsection;
>
> (b) The patient's spouse;
>
> (c) An adult child of the patient, or if the patient has more than one adult child, a majority of the adult children who are reasonably available for consultation;
>
> (d) A parent of the patient;
>
> (e) The adult sibling of the patient or, if the patient has more than one sibling, a majority of the adult siblings who are reasonably available for consultation;
>
> (f) An adult relative of the patient who has exhibited special care and concern for the patient and who has maintained regular contact with the patient and who is familiar with the patient's activities, health, and religious or moral beliefs; or
>
> (g) A close friend of the patient.
>
> (h) A clinical social worker licensed pursuant to chapter 491, or who is a graduate of a court-approved guardianship program. Such a proxy must be selected by the provider's bioethics committee and must not be employed by the provider. If the provider does not have a bioethics committee, then such a proxy may be chosen through an arrangement with the bioethics committee of another provider. The proxy will be notified that, upon request, the provider shall make available a second physician, not involved in the patient's care to assist the proxy in evaluating treatment. Decisions to withhold or withdraw life-prolonging procedures will be reviewed by the facility's bioethics committee. Documentation of efforts to locate proxies from prior classes must be recorded in the patient record.

Fla. Stat. Ann. § 765.401 (West). Florida case law required the surrogate to satisfy the following conditions:

> 1) The surrogate must be satisfied that the patient executed any document knowingly, willingly and without undue influence and that the evidence of the patient's oral declaration is reliable;
>
> 2) The surrogate must be assured that the patient does not have a reasonable probability of recovering competency so that the right could be exercised directly by the patient; and
>
> 3) The surrogate must take care to assure that any limitations or conditions expressed either orally or in the written declaration have been carefully considered and satisfied.

In re Guardianship of Schiavo, No. 90–2908GD–003, 2000 WL 34546715, *5–6 (Fla. Cir. Ct. Feb. 11, 2000) aff'd, 780 So. 2d 176 (Fla. Dist. Ct. App. 2001). Are your state's rules any different?

C. *GLUCKSBERG*: ASSISTANCE IN SUICIDE

The Next Lawsuit. Post-*Cruzan*, terminally ill patients challenged laws prohibiting assisted suicide, which existed in every state in 1996. The challengers made two constitutional arguments to invalidate the assisted suicide laws. First, they argued that the Fourteenth Amendment's Due Process Clause included a right to privacy large enough to include assistance in dying. That argument relied on *Quinlan* and *Cruzan* as well as the abortion and contraceptive privacy cases—*Roe*, *Griswold*, and *Eisenstadt*—relied upon by the New Jersey Supreme Court in *Quinlan*. Second, the patients argued that denying them assistance in dying violated the Equal Protection Clause of the Fourteenth Amendment. If terminally ill patients could refuse treatment under *Cruzan*, thus ending their lives, the challengers argued, then there was no rational basis to refuse aid in dying to other terminally ill patients. The results would be the same: both groups were terminally ill and both would die, but only one would be denied its treatment of choice.

> **Go to** the website and read the Glucksberg Complaint and the Quill Complaint. Read the complaints carefully. Compare and contrast them. Do you think one is more effective than the other? If so, why? Write in any edits that you think need to be made. We will discuss these in detail in class.

Getting to the Supreme Court. The Washington patients won in the Washington district court and the Ninth Circuit. The district court ruled that competent, terminally ill adults have a due process right to physician-assisted suicide and an equal protection right to be treated similarly to terminally ill patients who refuse treatment. Compassion in Dying v. Washington, 850 F. Supp. 1454 (W.D. Wash. 1994). After a panel of the Ninth Circuit reversed the district court's ruling, the *en banc* court affirmed the district court, ruling that the Fourteenth Amendment includes "a constitutionally-protected liberty interest in *determining the time and manner of one's own death*, an interest that must be weighed

against the state's legitimate and countervailing interests, especially those that relate to the preservation of human life." Compassion in Dying v. Washington, 79 F.3d 790 (9th Cir. 1996) (emphasis added). On the facts of the case, the court ruled that the interests were balanced in favor of the patients.

How do you assess the Ninth Circuit's characterization of the constitutional right at issue, a liberty interest in determining the time and manner of one's own death? Would you have preferred the court to use the wording that there is a constitutionally-protected right to die? A right to die with dignity? A right to a physician's assistance in committing suicide if one is terminally ill? A right to commit suicide?

In New York, the district court rejected the plaintiffs' equal protection claim, ruling that it was "hardly unreasonable or irrational for the State to recognize a difference between allowing nature to take its course, even in the most severe situations, and intentionally using an artificial death-producing device." Quill v. Koppell, 870 F. Supp. 78, 84 (S.D.N.Y. 1994). The Second Circuit reversed with the argument:

> Withdrawal of life support requires physicians or those acting at their direction physically to remove equipment and, often, to administer palliative drugs which may themselves contribute to death. *The ending of life by these means is nothing more nor less than assisted suicide.* It simply cannot be said that those mentally competent, terminally-ill persons who seek to hasten death but whose treatment does not include life support are treated equally.

Quill v. Vacco, 80 F.3d 716, 729 (2d Cir. 1996) (emphasis added). The court then concluded that the government's classification was irrational, asking "what interest can the state possibly have in requiring the prolongation of a life that is all but ended? Surely, the state's interest lessens as the potential for life diminishes [citing *Quinlan*]." Id. The Court then granted cert. in *Glucksberg*, 518 U.S. 1057 (1996), as well as *Vacco*, 518 U.S. 1055 (1996).

Amicus Briefs. Following are excerpts from two friend-of-the-court, "amicus" briefs that were filed in the Supreme Court in connection with *Glucksberg* and *Vacco*, one by the American Medical Association on behalf of the Petitioner, State of Washington, and one by a group of prominent philosophers on behalf of the patients.

Amicus briefs usually provide additional factual background or legal arguments that help the Court decide the case. Which brief has better legal arguments? Which has better ethical arguments? What is the connection between the philosophers' philosophical claims and their legal ones? Who has a better understanding of the practice of medicine? Of patients' needs? Do you think the Supreme Court Justices would be more impressed by a brief from the American Medical Association or from prominent philosophy professors?

Try to identify the most persuasive aspects of each brief. If you were arguing this case, what other amici would you have sought out? Another way of thinking about that question is to ask what additional factual information or legal argument would be valuable to the parties or to the Court.

Washington v. Glucksberg, Brief of the AMA

Supreme Court of the United States, No. 96–110, October Term, 1996.
On Writ of Certiorari to the United States Court of Appeals for the Ninth Circuit.
United States Supreme Court Amicus Brief of the American Medical Association, the American Nurses Association, and the American Psychiatric Association in Support of Petitioners.
Filed November 12, 1996.
1996 WL 656263.

INTRODUCTION AND INTEREST OF AMICI

The right to control one's medical treatment is among the most important rights that the law affords each person. The associations of health care professionals that are submitting this brief strongly support the recognition and enforcement of that right. Health care professionals are committed to their ethical and legal obligations to honor patient requests to withhold or withdraw unwanted life-prolonging treatment and to provide patients with all medication necessary to alleviate physical pain, even in circumstances where such medication might hasten death. Through these means, patients can avoid entrapment in a prolonged, painful, or overly medicalized dying process.

The decision below, however, takes the unprecedented step of announcing a constitutional right to control the timing and manner of one's death through the use of physician-assisted suicide. The court of appeals would confer upon health care professionals the awesome responsibility of deciding who, among the many patients who would request physician-assisted suicide, are eligible to obtain the assistance of a physician in killing themselves. The power to assist in intentionally taking the life of a patient is antithetical to the central mission of healing that guides both medicine and nursing. It is a power that most health care professionals do not want and could not control. Once established, the right to physician-assisted suicide would create profound danger for many ill persons with undiagnosed depression and inadequately treated pain, for whom physician-assisted suicide rather than good palliative care could become the norm. At greatest risk would be those with the least access to palliative care—the poor, the elderly, and members of minority groups.

The American Medical Association ("AMA"), the American Nurses Association ("ANA"), the American Psychiatric Association ("APA"), and 43 other national specialty and state medical societies that are submitting this brief represent hundreds of thousands of health care professionals who care each day for millions of Americans. Our members

have deep compassion for those who are suffering the pain and torment of chronic or terminal illness. We have learned much in recent years about palliative care. Our experience is that a desire for physician-assisted suicide does not persist in patients who receive good palliative care.

Amici acknowledge that many patients today do not receive proper treatment for their pain, depression, or psychological distress. Nevertheless, physician-assisted suicide is not the right answer to the problem of inadequate care. Although for some patients it might appear compassionate intentionally to cause death, institutionalizing physician-assisted suicide as a medical treatment would put many more patients at serious risk for unwanted and unnecessary death. Rather than recognize a right to physician-assisted suicide, our society instead should recognize the urgent necessity of extending to all patients the palliative care they need and redouble our efforts to provide such care to all.

To explain more fully the bases for amici's position, we begin with a discussion of important aspects of caring for seriously ill patients who request physician-assisted suicide that were misapprehended by the court below.

HEALTH CARE BACKGROUND

The core of the Ninth Circuit's opinion is its view that each individual has a fundamental liberty interest "in choosing the timing and manner of one's death." While the phrase is superficially appealing, it belies the sad reality that none of us has the power completely to control the circumstances of our death. Illness, itself only one potential cause of death, comes unbidden and with unpredictable effect. The Ninth Circuit's argument thus rests, at bottom, on an unrealistic assumption about our ability to control death.

At the same time, the Ninth Circuit overlooked the degree to which—without resorting to physician-assisted suicide—patients already can control aspects of the dying process. By recognizing patients' rights to refuse unwanted medical treatment or to have such treatment withdrawn, and by providing adequate pain relief, the health care professions have the capacity to prevent a prolonged and painful dying process. While much more remains to be done to ensure that all patients have access to good palliative care and effective advance care planning, experience to date shows that properly trained health care professionals can effectively meet their patients' needs for compassionate end-of-life care without acceding to requests for suicide.

A. Commitment To Patient Autonomy

The health care professions' ethical commitment to the principle of patient autonomy plays a vital role in providing patients with the ability to control their course of treatment. This commitment is expressed, for example, in Opinion 2.20 of the AMA Code of Medical Ethics. Opinion 2.20 provides, in part, that "[t]he principle of patient autonomy requires

that physicians respect the decision to forgo life-sustaining treatment of a patient who possesses decisionmaking capacity." AMA Council on Ethical and Judicial Affairs, Code of Medical Ethics: Current Opinions § 2.20; *see also* ANA, Code for Nurses with Interpretive Statements § 1.1 (patients "have the moral right to determine what will be done with their own person" and "to accept, refuse, or terminate treatment without coercion").

Opinion 2.20 has great significance for patients near the end of life. To those who fear unwanted medical intervention in the dying process, the message of Opinion 2.20 is that a patient need not accept, and physicians must not impose, a medical treatment that the patient does not want. As a practical matter, this means that a patient can refuse not only mechanical interventions such as respirators, feeding tubes, or dialysis, but also chemotherapy, antibiotics, or any other treatment that would have the effect of prolonging the patient's life. Through such means, persons suffering from chronic diseases (such as multiple sclerosis or amyotrophic lateral sclerosis) as well as terminal diseases can plan with their physicians which life-sustaining treatment to accept.

Opinion 2.20 unequivocally establishes that "[p]hysicians have an obligation to relieve pain and suffering and to promote the dignity and autonomy of dying patients in their care" and, significantly, that this obligation "includes providing palliative treatment even though it may foreseeably hasten death." Although criticized by the Ninth Circuit as illogical, the recognition that physicians should provide patients pain medication sufficient to ease their pain, even where that may serve to hasten death, is vital to ensuring that no patient suffer from physical pain.

The principle of patient autonomy, however, has never been understood to give patients the right to every procedure or treatment they might demand. For example, physicians need not provide futile treatment—that is, treatment that has no reasonable chance of helping the patient. Code of Medical Ethics § 2.035. Similarly, physicians should not provide patients with treatments that are known to be ineffective or harmful. Such limitations are important. If a patient may demand and receive anything from a health care professional, individuals who practice the healing arts will cease being professionals.

B. Physician-Assisted Suicide

Long viewed as outside the realm of legitimate health care, physician-assisted suicide occurs "when a physician facilitates a patient's death by providing the necessary means and/or information to enable the patient to perform the life-ending act." Code of Medical Ethics § 2.211; AMA Council on Ethical and Judicial Affairs, Physician-Assisted Suicide, 10 Issues in L. & Med. 91, 92 (1994). The practice involves physicians intentionally providing patients with the means for suicide, such as prescribing barbiturates in an amount certain to cause death and for the

purpose of causing death. *See, e.g.*, Quill, Death and Dignity: A Case of Individualized Decision Making, 324 New Eng. J. Med. 691 (1991).

The ethical prohibition against physician-assisted suicide is a cornerstone of medical ethics. Its roots are as ancient as the Hippocratic Oath that a physician "will neither give a deadly drug to anybody if asked for it, nor . . . make a suggestion to this effect," and the merits of the ban have been debated repeatedly in this nation since the late nineteenth century. Most recently, the AMA has reexamined and reaffirmed the ethical prohibition against physician-assisted suicide in 1977, 1988, 1991, 1993, and 1996.[2] Physician-assisted suicide remains "fundamentally incompatible with the physician's role as healer, would be difficult or impossible to control, and would pose serious societal risks." Code of Medical Ethics § 2.211. Other health care professions have similar tenets. Physicians and nurses have the ability to respond sensitively to the concerns of seriously ill and dying patients and can meet their patients' needs without acceding to requests for suicide.

C. Requests for Physician-Assisted Suicide

The Ninth Circuit's decision rests in substantial part on the assumption that there are a "growing number of terminally ill patients who die protracted and painful deaths," and who, absent physician-assisted suicide, are condemned to face "unmitigated torture" before they die. Implicit in the court's holding are the views that those who request suicide do so to avoid excruciating pain, and that health care professionals can do nothing compassionate in response other than to assist in suicide. The court cited no evidence to support these views. In fact, available information demonstrates that these views are misguided.

1. There is no evidence that increasing numbers of patients are dying in severe pain. To the contrary, "[t]he potential for management of pain has recently improved, both through the development of better techniques and through enhanced care delivery through hospice and palliative care efforts." AMA Council on Scientific Affairs, Good Care of the Dying Patient, 275 JAMA 474, 475 (1996). The pain of most terminally ill patients can be controlled throughout the dying process without heavy sedation or anesthesia. *Id.*; *see, e.g.*, Byock, Consciously Walking the Fine Line: Thoughts on a Hospice Response to Assisted Suicide and Euthanasia, 9 J. Pall. Care 25, 26 (1993); Foley, The Relationship of Pain and Symptom Management to Patient Requests for Physician-Assisted Suicide, 6 J. Pain & Symp. Mgmt. 289 (1991); Levy, Pharmacologic Treatment of Cancer Pain, 335 New Eng. J. Med. 1124 (1996). For a very few patients, however, sedation to a sleep-like state may be necessary in the last days or weeks of life to prevent the patient from experiencing severe pain. N.Y. State Task Force, When Death Is

---

[2] AMA Council on Scientific Affairs, Good Care of the Dying Patient, 275 JAMA 474, 477 (1996). Most recently, in the aftermath of the decision below, the AMA's House of Delegates in June 1996 overwhelmingly endorsed a recommendation to affirm the ban on physician-assisted suicide.

Sought: Assisted Suicide and Euthanasia in the Medical Context 40 & n.21 (1994). Notably, when pain medication is properly administered, for most patients the risk of respiratory depression that hastens death is minimal. N.Y. State Task Force at 162.

Given the increasing ability to control pain, it is not surprising that, contrary to the Ninth Circuit's assumption, the demand for physician-assisted suicide does not come principally from those seeking relief from physical pain. A recent study of such requests in Washington State found that "neither severe pain nor dyspnea was a common patient concern, suggesting that intolerable physical symptoms are not the reason most patients request physician-assisted suicide or euthanasia." Back et al., Physician-Assisted Suicide and Euthanasia in Washington State, 275 JAMA 919, 924 (1996). This finding is consistent with a report from Compassion-in-Dying, *see* Preston & Mero, Observations Concerning Terminally Ill Patients Who Choose Suicide, 4 J. Pharm. Care & Pain Symp. Control 183, 187 (1996) ("[i]n no patient was pain the primary reason for suicide"); with other studies of patients and physicians, *see* Emanuel et al., Euthanasia and Physician-Assisted Suicide: Attitudes and Experiences of Oncology Patients, Oncologists, and the Public, 347 Lancet 1805, 1809 & nn.6, 12 (1996) ("[p]atients experiencing pain were not inclined to euthanasia or physician-assisted suicide"); as well as with studies of Holland's experience, *see* Van der Maas et al., Euthanasia and Other Medical Decisions Concerning the End of Life, 338 Lancet 669, 672 (1991) (relief from pain was mentioned as a factor in fewer than half of cases, and was the sole factor in only five percent of cases).

This is not to say that all patients have access to and actually receive adequate pain relief and good palliative care. They do not. The delivery of such care is "grossly inadequate" today, and efforts to make such care universally available have not yet succeeded. N.Y. State Task Force at 43–47; Connors et al., A Controlled Trial to Improve Care for Seriously Ill Hospitalized Patients, 274 JAMA 1591 (1995). There are many obstacles to the delivery of adequate pain management. These include a lack of professional training and knowledge, misconceptions about the risks of addiction and respiratory depression associated with pain medication, inadequate communication (reflecting both inadequate attention from health care professionals and undue reluctance of patients and their families to use pain relief medication), and concern over criminal or licensure actions against the prescribing physicians. N.Y. State Task Force at 44–47; AMA Council, 275 JAMA at 476. Of further concern, individuals treated at centers that serve predominantly minority patients are more likely than others to receive inadequate pain treatment; the same is true for elderly and female patients. N.Y. State Task Force at 44 & n.37. Yet for "many patients, pain and suffering could be alleviated using medications and techniques that have been widely publicized and require only modest resources." *Id.* at 35. There is, in short, compelling evidence of the need to ensure that all patients have

access to quality palliative care, but not of any need for physician-assisted suicide in order to control pain.

2. Most patients that request suicide do so out of concerns that, in the future, their pain may become intolerable, they may suffer a loss of dignity and become dependent upon others, or they will excessively burden their families. Back et al., 275 JAMA at 921; Emanuel et al., 347 Lancet at 1807. The suffering that such concerns may cause is real. But if the anticipatory and existential nature of that suffering is recognized and addressed, it can often effectively be alleviated. Foley, 6 J. Pain & Symp. Mgmt. at 289–90; N.Y. State Task Force at x, 181.

Concerns about future loss of control, loss of dignity, or pain frequently can be met by reassuring the patient of a continuing commitment to attentive comfort care and by assisting the patient to confront an underlying and unspoken fear of death. "Many patients and physicians displace anxieties about death onto the circumstances of dying: pain, dependence, loss of dignity, and the unpleasant side effects of medical treatments. Focusing on or becoming enraged at the process distracts from the fear of death itself." Hendin, Suicide, Assisted Suicide, and Euthanasia: Lessons from the Dutch Experience, Summary of Testimony Presented to House Subcommittee on the Constitution 1 (1996). A full approach to palliative care addresses spiritual and existential feelings as well as personal and social burdens, using a team approach that draws on social workers and pastors as well as physicians and nurses. Clinicians with experience assisting dying patients to confront such concerns report that the desire for death passes, and that patients say they have found unexpected meaning in their lives that makes their final days worth living. *E.g.*, Cundiff, Euthanasia Is Not the Answer 29–39 (1992).

The anxieties that can accompany serious illness are often complicated, however, by the onset of depression. Depression is the single factor found to be a significant predictor of the desire for death. Emanuel et al., 347 Lancet at 1809; Chochinov et al., Desire for Death in the Terminally Ill, 152 Am. J. Psych. 1185, 1190 (1995). In one study of 44 terminally ill patients, all but one of the eleven patients with "clinical depressive illness" expressed some wish for death, while none of the remaining 33 expressed such a wish. Brown et al., Is it Normal for Terminally Ill Patients to Desire Death?, 143 Am. J. Psych. 208, 210 (1986); *see also* Conwell & Caine, Rational Suicide and the Right to Die: Reality and Myth, 325 New Eng. J. Med. 1100, 1101 (1991) ("of 44 patients in the later stages of cancer, only 3 had considered suicide, and each of them had a severe clinical depression"); AMA Council, 275 JAMA at 475; Chochinov et al., 152 Am. J. Psych. 1185. In this regard, those with terminal or chronic illness are no different than others who express suicidal wishes. Most who commit suicide suffer from depression or some other diagnosable psychiatric illness, which generally is treatable.

Hendin, Suicide and the Request for Suicide: Meaning and Motivation, 35 Duq. L. Rev. 285, 285 (1996); N.Y. State Task Force at 13, 180.

It is clear that "a substantial proportion of terminally ill patients who express a desire to die could potentially benefit from a trial of treatment for depression." Chochinov et al., 152 Am. J. Psych. at 1190. For example, "[t]he elderly appear to be more prone than younger victims to take their lives during the type of acute depressive episode that responds most effectively to available, modern treatments." Conwell & Caine, 325 New Eng. J. Med. at 1101. Nevertheless, most physicians fail to recognize depression, thereby precluding the opportunity for effective treatment. *Id.* at 1101–02.

3. The demand for physician-assisted suicide among the terminally ill is thus best understood not as a necessary response to untreatable pain uniquely felt by the dying, but in the broader context of requests for suicide generally. "Among all suicides, only two percent to four percent are terminally ill." N.Y. State Task Force at 12. Moreover, while severe chronic or terminal illness is a risk factor for suicide, "only a small percentage of terminally ill or severely ill patients attempt or commit suicide." *Id.* at 9, 13. And those patients are similar to physically healthy individuals who contemplate suicide—they "are usually suffering from a treatable mental illness, most commonly depression." *Id.*

Thus, contrary to the Ninth Circuit's most basic premise, terminal illness does not present a special case for physician-assisted suicide. Patients with chronic or terminal illness who seek physician-assisted suicide are typically depressed or anticipating extreme suffering. Their needs and concerns are ones that health care professionals can meet with compassionate care. There may be, even in a system that provides optimal palliative care to all patients, individuals whose pain may not be treatable absent sedation and whose wish for physician-assisted suicide to avoid sedation is sincere. But the number of such individuals is likely to be very small, and the social cost of accommodating their preference for physician-assisted suicide over sedation and withdrawal of treatment is likely to be high. For reasons that follow, even if physician-assisted suicide were thought appropriate for such patients, no one can predict with any confidence that physician-assisted suicide, if authorized by the state, could reliably be limited to them.

D. The Inherent Difficulty In Regulating Physician-Assisted Suicide

Proponents of physician-assisted suicide agree that lines must be drawn between categories of individuals for whom physician-assisted suicide is to be deemed acceptable or unacceptable. The Ninth Circuit permitted physician-assisted suicide for those with a "terminal illness." In Vacco v. Quill, No. 95–1858, the Second Circuit purported to restrict physician-assisted suicide narrowly to those who were "in the final stages of terminal illness." Both courts expressly limited their holdings to the provision of physician-assisted suicide but the Ninth Circuit candidly

expressed its doubt that any reasonable distinction could be maintained between physician-assisted suicide and voluntary euthanasia. The "critical line," the Ninth Circuit stated, was between the "voluntary and involuntary termination of an individual's life."

The Ninth Circuit declared that "while there is always room for error in any human endeavor, we believe that sufficient protections can and will be developed by the various states." As two commenters note, however: "Where? Which state has done so? In its 153-page opinion, not once does the Ninth Circuit attempt to show how this might be accomplished." Callahan & White, The Legalization of Physician-Assisted Suicide: Creating a Regulatory Potemkin Village, 30 U. Rich. L. Rev. 1, 83 (1996). Existing rules limiting physician-assisted suicide are not being followed today. AMA Bd. of Trustees, Euthanasia/Physician-Assisted Suicide: Lessons in the Dutch Experience, 10 Issues in L. & Med. 81 (1994). For example, the study of euthanasia and physician-assisted suicide commissioned by the Dutch government showed that approximately one in four cases of euthanasia did not qualify as voluntary under the guidelines. Van der Maas et al., 338 Lancet at 671; Kass & Lund, Physician-Assisted Suicide, Medical Ethics and the Future of the Medical Profession, 35 Duq. L. Rev. 395, 412–13 & nn.29–30 (1996). Different social circumstances in the United States make effective regulation even less likely here than in Holland. *See* AMA Bd. of Trustees, 10 Issues in L. & Med. at 88–89. Difficulties inherent in the regulation of physician-assisted suicide suggest that even strenuous efforts to regulate such a practice will not succeed.

1. One proposed restriction is to limit physician-assisted suicide to those in the last stages of a terminal illness. An initial difficulty arises, however, in identifying the eligible class. Available evidence suggests "that physicians' predictions of expected remaining life are generally inaccurate." Callahan & White, 30 U. Rich. L. Rev. at 46 & n.202. For example, while admission to hospice is contingent on a diagnosis of six or fewer months to live, a recent study showed that 15 percent of hospice patients survived longer than six months and eight percent survived longer than one year. Christakis & Escarce, Survival of Medicare Patients after Enrollment in Hospice Programs, 335 New Eng. J. Med. 172 (1996); see Lynn et al., Defining the "Terminally Ill": Insights from SUPPORT, 35 Duq. L. Rev. 311 (1996). Life expectancy is thus inherently problematic as a criterion for establishing eligibility to exercise a constitutional right.

The lack of clear-cut lines between those who are terminally ill and those who are in the last stages of a terminal illness suggests that any attempt to limit the availability of physician-assisted suicide to the latter would be arbitrary. But the same is true for the line between the terminally ill and the chronically ill. No one can confidently say that the degree of pain or suffering experienced by a person in the last stages of a terminal disease is greater than that experienced by someone at an

earlier stage of terminal illness, or by someone who is chronically ill. Moreover, if the pain or suffering is thought to be irremediable, then the longer the patient's life expectancy, logically the more pain and suffering awaits the patient. Kamisar, Against Assisted Suicide—Even a Very Limited Form, 72 U. Det. Mercy L. Rev. 735, 737, 740–41 (1995). There would thus be little to prevent expansion of physician-assisted suicide beyond the confines of the last stages of terminal illness.

The experience in the Netherlands illustrates the difficulty of hewing to particular guidelines. Physician-assisted suicide and euthanasia remain unlawful but are not prosecuted if performed by a physician in accordance with established procedures. Keown, "Some Reflections on Euthanasia in the Netherlands," in Euthanasia, Clinical Practice and the Law 193, 197 (Gormally ed., 1994). In one recent, much-discussed case, a physician, who assisted in the suicide of a physically healthy, 50-year-old woman who sought death in the aftermath of the death of her two sons, was acquitted by a three-judge court in Assen of charges that he had violated the Dutch procedures. The Assen case is significant in that it "marked Dutch acceptance of depressed suicidal patients as eligible for assisted suicide or euthanasia," Hendin, Seduced by Death: Doctors, Patients, and the Dutch Cure, 10 Issues in L. & Med. 123, 129 (1994), and thereby demonstrated the difficulty of restricting the availability of physician-assisted suicide even to those with a physical illness.

2. There are also formidable obstacles to restricting physician-assisted suicide only to those patients who voluntarily request it. First, the fact that many patients do not receive adequate pain relief or suffer from undiagnosed and untreated depression puts undue pressure on them to seek physician-assisted suicide. A substantial percentage of elderly patients suffer mental confusion that also routinely goes undiagnosed. Francis et al., A Prospective Study of Delirium in Hospitalized Elderly, 263 JAMA 1097 (1990). Moreover, poor and minority individuals are at the greatest risk for receiving inadequate care and thus may feel the greatest pressure to request physician-assisted suicide.

Pressure to contain health care costs exacerbates the problem. Even if, as one would expect, health care insurers would consciously seek to avoid suggesting to patients or physicians that they consider financial costs in making a decision to hasten death, the continuing pressure to reduce costs can only constrain the availability and quality of palliative care and support services that patients and families need. Wolf, Physician-Assisted Suicide in the Context of Managed Care, 35 Duq. L. Rev. 455 (1996). These limitations on the availability of proper care clearly can place pressure on patients to express a wish for suicide that they might not otherwise feel. As the Chief of the Pain Service at Memorial Sloan-Kettering Cancer Center reports, "[w]e commonly see

[requests for physician-assisted suicide] dissolve with adequate control of pain and other symptoms." Foley, 6 J. Pain & Symp. Mgmt. at 290.

Providers willing to comply with requests for suicide may be among those least sensitive to the impact of these pressures and least familiar with alternative responses to their patients' needs. A recent study shows that support for physician-assisted suicide was highest among those health care professionals least knowledgeable about pain symptom management and least capable (due to emotional exhaustion) of empathizing with the patient. Portenoy et al., Determinants of the Willingness to Endorse Assisted Suicide: A Survey of Physicians, Nurses, and Social Workers,—Psychosomatics—(forthcoming April 1997); *see also* Bachman et al., Attitudes of Michigan Physicians and the Public toward Legalizing Physician-Assisted Suicide and Voluntary Euthanasia, 334 New Eng. J. Med. 303, 308 (1996) ("doctors who had the least contact with terminally ill patients were the most likely to support the legalization of assisted suicide"). There is thus added reason to doubt that patients seeking physician-assisted suicide would receive adequate palliative care before such a request is granted.

Second, separating the wishes of the patient from those of the family is extremely problematic. One of the most common reasons why patients request suicide is to spare their families and loved ones the burdens and expense of caring for them. *See, e.g.*, Blendon et al., Should Physicians Aid their Patients in Dying?, 267 JAMA 2658, 2660–61 (1992); Emanuel, Cost Savings at the End of Life: What Do the Data Show?, 275 JAMA 1907 (1996). But to what extent are these feelings the result of the family's expectations? In one recent study, families of elderly, terminally ill patients were significantly more likely than the patients themselves to express support for physician-assisted suicide. Koenig et al., Attitudes of Elderly Patients and Their Families toward Physician-Assisted Suicide, 156 Arch. Int. Med. 2240, 2244 (1996). Families, especially when confronted with the expense and burden of caring for a terminally ill family member, may be beset with conflicting feelings about hastening a family member's death, as recent cases vividly illustrate. *E.g.*, "Countdown to a Suicide," The New York Times, Dec. 20, 1995, at A–20 (Delury case). Even those family members consciously committed to preserving their loved one's sense of dignity and autonomy may needlessly acquiesce in or encourage a suicide that could be avoided by assuring the patient that, in their eyes, illness has not compromised his or her dignity. Byock, "Physician-Assisted Suicide Is Not an Acceptable Practice for Physicians," in Physician-Assisted Suicide: Ethical Positions, Medical Practices, and Public Policy Options (Weir ed., forthcoming May 1997).

Third, experience to date provides little basis for confidence that health care professionals can reliably determine whether patients have provided truly informed consent for assisted suicide. Frank, sensitive, and extended conversations between physicians and patients are

presumptively antecedents to such a determination. Such conversations would be infinitely more complex than any that regularly occur today. For example, ineffective communication remains a major obstacle to achieving pain management, American Pain Society Quality of Care Committee, Quality Improvement Guidelines for the Treatment of Acute Pain and Cancer Pain, 274 JAMA 1874, 1874 (1995), even though pain relief is plainly a goal shared by both health care professionals and patients. And despite their importance, discussions about advance care planning are rare and poorly handled, which hampers effective and responsive end-of-life care. Emanuel, "Advance Directives," in Principles and Practice of Supportive Oncology (Berger et al. eds., forthcoming 1996).

The well-established phenomena of transference and countertransference further complicate the problem of relying upon physicians and nurses to identify voluntary requests. Miles, Physicians and Their Patients' Suicides, 271 JAMA 1786 (1994). Particularly when caring for chronically ill, dying, or suicidal patients, caregivers often have "difficulty tolerating such patients' dependency." *Id.* at 1786 (footnote omitted). Their "feelings of frustration and inadequacy occasioned by irreversible medical problems" sometimes lead them "to withdraw from such patients or see them as hopelessly or rationally suicidal" when in fact they are not, which "in turn may precipitate suicides." *Id.* As one physician with extensive experience caring for dying patients has observed, "[o]nly because I knew that I could not and would not kill my patients was I able to enter most fully and intimately into caring for them as they lay dying." Miles, quoted in Kass & Lund, 35 Duq. L. Rev. at 418.

Health care professionals also experience great frustration at not being able to offer the patient a cure. For some, the ability to offer the patient the "treatment" of assisted suicide may provide a sense of "mastery over the disease and the accompanying feelings of helplessness." Hendin, Seduced by Death, 10 Issues in L. & Med. at 129. This may cause health care professionals or a patient's family to endorse and reinforce requests for suicide more readily than the patient's own ambivalent feelings would warrant. Miles, 271 JAMA at 1786. Published accounts of physician-assisted suicide reveal that even those physicians who consciously seek only to implement a patient's voluntary request overlook ways in which their recommendation and support of physician-assisted suicide reinforced the patient's decision for death and left unexamined indications that the patient really did not want to die. Hendin, Selling Death and Dignity, 25 Hast. Ctr. Rep. 19 (1995); Hendin, Seduced by Death, 10 Issues in L. & Med. at 125–29.

3. The obstacles to identifying and restricting physician-assisted suicide to those patients who meet criteria of terminality and voluntariness are not likely to be overcome simply by devoting more resources to oversight of treatment decisions. Indeed, the unprecedented intrusion into the physician-patient relationship needed independently

to regulate such treatment decisions would be fundamentally inconsistent with the private nature of health care treatment, and all too likely to undermine what progress has been made in decisions to withdraw or withhold life-sustaining treatment and to use effective pain control. Callahan & White, 30 U. Rich. L. Rev. at 67, 80.

Transforming physician-assisted suicide into a medical procedure would create momentum in favor of its use that regulation could not reverse. Were physician-assisted suicide to become a legitimate medical option, then a decision not to select that option would make many patients feel responsible for their own suffering and for the burden they impose on others. Once a patient can choose physician-assisted suicide, it is but a short step to ask a patient why he or she has not done so. Indeed, it seems likely the patient would feel pressure to revisit the question repeatedly, perhaps every day. Many patients thus will "experience—and be helped [by their families or physicians] to experience—their right to choose physician-assisted death as a duty to do so." Kass & Lund, 35 Duq. L. Rev. at 407.

SUMMARY OF ARGUMENT

In announcing that the Due Process Clause affords every individual "a liberty interest in choosing the timing and manner of one's death" (Pet. App. A–21), the Ninth Court was moved by the condition of the individual patients seeking judicial relief. The court of appeals failed, however, to examine the broader context in which these patients acted and the circumstances of many other patients who will be affected by its judgment. It also failed to articulate a persuasive constitutional or moral basis for invalidating these longstanding laws. The ancient prohibition on physician-assisted suicide reflects a deeply rooted antipathy to the intentional taking of human life, even when described as "mercy killing." None of the decisions of this Court cited below establishes a basis in the Constitution for invalidating state laws that maintain this prohibition.

Moreover, even if a liberty interest in committing suicide were recognized, the interests of states in adhering to the prohibition against physician assistance have grown, if anything, stronger in recent years. Advances in palliative care make it possible to control most patients' pain without resort to heavy sedation, and further improvements in the provision of appropriate pain relief and compassionate end-of-life care will happen. In acting precipitously to declare a constitutional right to physician-assisted suicide, the Ninth Circuit's judgment may slow the momentum of such efforts. This Court should refrain from a constitutional ruling that "may be fraught with serious consequences to the nation." New State Ice Co. v. Liebmann, 285 U.S. 262, 311 (1932) (Brandeis, J., dissenting).

ARGUMENT

THIS COURT'S DUE PROCESS JURISPRUDENCE DOES NOT PROVIDE A BASIS FOR FINDING A CONSTITUTIONAL LIBERTY INTEREST IN OBTAINING A PHYSICIAN'S ASSISTANCE TO COMMIT SUICIDE

As a constitutional matter, neither this Court's jurisprudence nor any other legal principle supports the inference of a novel and potentially harmful right to physician-assisted suicide. The prohibition against physician-assisted suicide serves a vital social function that, once lost, will result in incalculable and severe damage to patients and to the health care profession.

A. The Individual's Fourteenth Amendment Liberty Interest In Refusing Medical Treatment Does Not Encompass The Right To Physician Assistance In Committing Suicide.

In finding a liberty interest in controlling the timing and manner of one's death, the Ninth Circuit relied initially upon this Court's decision in Cruzan v. Director, Missouri Department of Health, 497 U.S. 261 (1990). The Cruzan case concerned the plight of Nancy Cruzan, who, at the age of 25, suffered an automobile accident that left her permanently unconscious, existing in what is termed a persistent vegetative state. She was kept alive by means of a surgically implanted feeding tube for six years after the accident, during which time she never regained consciousness. 497 U.S. at 266. When it became clear that Nancy's condition would never improve, her parents, seeking to implement the treatment decision they believed she would have made, sought to discontinue life support functions. *Id.* at 268.

Cruzan thus presented the Court with the profoundly difficult question of whether and in what manner a state could refuse to honor the request of an incompetent patient's surrogate that life support functions be discontinued. In a careful and narrowly drawn opinion, the Court suggested that "the forced administration of life-sustaining medical treatment, and even of artificially-delivered food and water essential to life, would implicate a competent person's liberty interest," but that "the dramatic consequences involved in refusal of such treatment would inform the inquiry as to whether the deprivation of that interest is constitutionally permissible." *Id.* at 279. The Court then upheld the State of Missouri's requirement that an incompetent patient's wish to cease treatment be proved by clear and convincing evidence. *Id.* at 280–82.

The liberty interest discussed in Cruzan is grounded in the common law protection afforded to every person to refuse unwanted medical treatment. *Id.* at 269–70. Medical treatment performed without the patient's consent historically has been treated as a battery, excusable only in emergency circumstances. *Id.* at 270; Keeton et al., Prosser and

Keeton on the Law of Torts 39–42, 190 (5th ed. 1984); Winters v. Miller, 446 F.2d 65, 68 (2d Cir.), cert. denied, 404 U.S. 985 (1971). The right to refuse treatment is the "logical corollary" of the prohibition against medical treatment without the patient's informed consent. Cruzan, 497 U.S. at 270. These principles constitute fundamental tenets of the health care professions and are readily embraced by amici as a matter of both common law and constitutional right.

Physician-assisted suicide does not involve the imposition of treatment against the patient's will. It involves instead the furnishing of assistance that is (at least in theory) desired by the patient. Thus, the rationale that unwanted medical treatment can be refused because it amounts to a common law assault and battery provides no legal or logical basis for finding a right to physician-assisted suicide.

In other contexts, courts, including this one, have been reluctant to find a right to obtain medical treatment. *See* New York State Ophthalmological Soc'y v. Bowen, 854 F.2d 1379, 1389–92 (D.C. Cir. 1988), cert. denied, 490 U.S. 1098 (1989); *cf.* United States v. Rutherford, 442 U.S. 544 (1979) (terminally ill cancer patients not entitled to a drug that has not been approved by the Food and Drug Administration). Amici believe there should be constitutional protection for the "freedom to determine the course of [one's] own treatment." Cruzan, 497 U.S. at 289 (O'Connor, J., concurring). The assistance sought in this case, however, is to a procedure that neither state law nor the medical profession has ever considered to be a legitimate medical treatment. It would be particularly ironic, therefore, if the first "treatment" to which patients were held to have a constitutional right were physician-assisted suicide.

The Ninth Circuit also relied upon broader linguistic formulations of the sources of the right to refuse treatment, such as the "right to be let alone," Olmstead v. United States, 277 U.S. 438, 478 (1928) (Brandeis, J., dissenting), or the right of every adult "to determine what shall be done with his own body." Schloendorff v. Society of New York Hosp., 105 N.E. 92, 93 (N.Y. 1914) (Cardozo, J.). These formulations are rightly looked to as indicative of the importance and centrality of the autonomy principle. But the paradox of invoking autonomy as justification for killing oneself has long been noted. And in practice, the principle has never been interpreted as sweepingly as the Ninth Circuit proposes. Cruzan itself alluded to the limits of the autonomy principle, noting that the consequences of a particular procedure "would inform the inquiry" as to whether treatment can be refused. 497 U.S. at 279. This Court has repeatedly recognized other limits as well. For example, laws prohibiting prostitution or use of illicit drugs, or mandating vaccinations or blood tests, have never been considered constitutionally infirm. *See, e.g.*, Washington v. Harper, 494 U.S. 210, 221–22 (1990) (state may administer antipsychotic medicine to mentally ill prisoner over his objection); Jacobson v. Massachusetts, 197 U.S. 11, 24–30 (1905) (state may require vaccinations because Fourteenth Amendment "does not

import an absolute right" to be "wholly freed from restraint"); Schmerber v. California, 384 U.S. 757 (1966) (police may perform alcohol-blood test of suspect over his objection); Breithaupt v. Abram, 352 U.S. 432, 439 (1957) (same); *cf.* Employment Div. v. Smith, 494 U.S. 872, 878 (1990) (state may prohibit use of peyote even as part of religious ritual). Accordingly, the principle of bodily integrity, while of central and vital importance, does not in itself justify a constitutional right to physician-assisted suicide.

B. Physician-Assisted Suicide Lies Outside The Continuum Of Liberty Interests That This Court Has Previously Recognized As Constitutionally Protected.

1. The Ninth Circuit also relied more broadly on the balance of this Court's due process jurisprudence. Heightened judicial protection is provided for some rights that have no textual support in the Constitution if they are "implicit in the concept of ordered liberty," such that "neither liberty nor justice would exist if they were sacrificed." Palko v. Connecticut, 302 U.S. 319, 325–26 (1937). These liberties, which are "deeply rooted in this Nation's history and tradition," Moore v. City of East Cleveland, 431 U.S. 494, 503 (1977) (footnote omitted), may be located on a "rational continuum which, broadly speaking, includes a freedom from all substantial arbitrary impositions and purposeless restraints. . . ." Poe v. Ullman, 367 U.S. 497, 543 (1961) (Harlan, J., dissenting).

Asserted rights that are absent from both the text of the Constitution and the traditions of our nation lie at the furthest edge of the continuum. Moore, 431 U.S. at 503. And the constitutional stature of conduct that has long been prohibited by state law is even more tenuous. Physician-assisted suicide is not a right that our society historically has protected against state interference. Both suicide and attempted suicide were unlawful under the Common Law of England and the laws of the colonies. *See* 4 Blackstone, Commentaries on the Laws of England 89 (1978); Marzen et al., Suicide: A Constitutional Right?, 24 Duq. L. Rev. 1, 56–57 (1985). Although all states have chosen to decriminalize both suicide and attempted suicide, 35 states continue to proscribe assisting in another's suicide, and eight other states prohibit it as a common law crime. 2 Meisel, The Right to Die § 18.17, at 478 Table 18–1 (2d ed. 1995). This long-standing governmental and societal antipathy to aiding in a suicide, while perhaps not conclusive, counsels strongly against finding the liberty interest urged by respondents here.

2. Nevertheless, the Ninth Circuit identified a right to physician-assisted suicide by relying heavily upon Planned Parenthood v. Casey, 505 U.S. 833 (1992). In Casey, the Court reaffirmed that women have a constitutionally protected liberty interest in obtaining an abortion that states may not unduly burden. 505 U.S. at 869. In so holding, the Court stated that abortion was akin to "personal decisions relating to marriage, . . . child rearing, and education," which involve "the most intimate and

personal choices a person may make in a lifetime, choices central to personal dignity and autonomy," and which are "central to the liberty protected by the Fourteenth Amendment." *Id.* at 851. The Court further stated that "[a]t the heart of liberty is the right to define one's own concept of existence, of meaning, of the universe, and of the mystery of human life." *Id.* From this, the Ninth Circuit concluded that a right to physician-assisted suicide falls within the ambit of personal liberty protected by the Fourteenth Amendment.

Casey and this Court's other substantive due process decisions should not be read so broadly. First, whatever interpretation the quoted language may bear in the abstract, its meaning ought not be understood apart from its context. Casey narrowly reaffirmed an existing liberty interest principally on grounds of stare decisis. And while the more sweeping argument that the Due Process Clause creates a broad realm of autonomy in making personal choices has been made to the Court on a number of occasions, the Court has never embraced this principle in this open-ended form. *See, e.g.*, Cruzan, 497 U.S. at 279 n.7. Presumably this is because, read broadly, the quoted language would encompass not simply the decisions of the terminally ill, but a broad range of decisions, including any person's choice to terminate his or her life at any time. *See* Pet. App. A–28 to A–29. Thus, for example, a depressed 25-year-old, who has not received appropriate psychiatric treatment, would have a liberty interest in obtaining assistance in committing suicide. As discussed above, such a right has never been recognized by this Court, by any courts at common law, or indeed, by respondents.

Second, as a factual matter, a woman's right to choose to have an abortion differs materially from a patient's right to physician-assisted suicide. In the physician-assisted suicide context, the procedure at issue has no life-or health-promoting benefits whatsoever; its sole function is to achieve the death of the patient. In the abortion context, however, the procedure itself is medical and cannot be performed by an unqualified person without extreme risk of permanently injuring or killing the woman. It is instructive in this regard to recall the Court's recognition in Roe v. Wade, 410 U.S. 113, 163–64 (1973), that the state has a compelling interest in preserving the fetus once the fetus is viable. Neither Roe nor Casey authorizes any person to assist in killing an independent human life.

Third, Casey rests in substantial measure on the recognition that undue obstacles to obtaining an abortion, by restricting a woman's "ability to control [her] reproductive li[fe]," compromise her "ability to participate equally in the economic and social life of the Nation." Casey, 505 U.S. at 856. Preserving the right of choice prevents the state from imposing "its own vision of women's role" in society. *Id.* at 852. The Court's explicit recognition of this dimension of the right to choice makes clear that the Roe and Casey decisions must be understood as grounded in part on the need to afford women liberty to participate in society equal

to that of men. Others of this Court's privacy decisions have also served to invalidate similar discriminatory legislation. No comparable rationale applies to physician-assisted suicide.

Finally, in contrast to other liberty interests previously recognized by this Court, the liberty interest asserted here is unique in that the state concededly has compelling reasons to prohibit its exercise by most who would seek to invoke it. To begin with, the right to control the timing and manner of one's death is not limited to "physician-assisted suicide" for "terminally ill competent adults who wish to hasten their deaths with medication prescribed by their physicians." Pet. App. A–113 to A–114. The Ninth Circuit acknowledged that this formulation of the right was only a starting point, and that the right was likely to be broadened over time. Without resolving the issue, the Ninth Circuit signaled that it was likely in the future to invalidate any proposed distinction between physician-assisted suicide and voluntary euthanasia for patients who could not carry out a suicide themselves. Pet. App. A–100 to A–101. And, while the Ninth Circuit did not directly acknowledge the problematic nature of restricting the right only to the terminally ill, the court did admit that, in its view, the critical dividing line was between voluntary and involuntary termination of life. *Id.* at A–100 & n.120. This admission reflects the fact that profound suffering that can prompt a request for suicide arises not simply in the terminally ill but in the chronically ill and physically healthy as well. *E.g.*, Kamisar, 72 U. Det. Mercy L. Rev. at 739.

At the same time, the Ninth Circuit recognized that physician-assisted suicide was unjustifiable for many people, and proposed to rely on states and the medical profession to develop procedural safeguards to prevent individuals that did not meet criteria from receiving assistance in committing suicide. Admission of the need for extensive regulation and safeguards to prevent most who would seek to exercise this right from doing so is, however, strong reason to doubt that any such right can fairly be viewed as "implicit in the concept of ordered liberty." Palko, 302 U.S. at 325–26. It is inconsistent with the nature of a fundamental right that its exercise is so troubling and susceptible to abuse that extensive state regulation and proscription is justifiable. The admitted need for extensive state regulation also illustrates why, far from being an essentially "private" matter, physician-assisted suicide is a public act with wide-ranging and profound consequences for families, health care professionals, and society.

C. States Have Strong Interests In Prohibiting Physicians And Nurses From Assisting In Suicides.

Because all agree that the states have strong interests in regulating life-and-death decisionmaking, the salient question is where the Constitution permits the state to draw the line. Amici urge the Court to permit states to prohibit physician-assisted suicide outright. This approach is supported by at least three strong state interests.

1. First, states have an overwhelming interest in avoiding preventable suicides. For many reasons, a state could reasonably conclude that, once physician-assisted suicide is permitted for any class of patients, the number of patients committing suicide with the assistance of a physician will substantially increase no matter how narrowly the initial restrictions are drawn, and will involve patients in circumstances far removed from those surrounding the respondents.

To begin with, states could justifiably conclude that relatively few, if any, patients would ever legitimately meet the kind of strict criteria that a state might seek to impose in lieu of banning physician-assisted suicide out-right. Most terminally ill patients do not raise the issue of physician-assisted suicide and, given advances in palliative care, it is unlikely that the needs of those who do raise the issue cannot be met through other means.

States could also reasonably conclude, however, that restrictions intended to limit physician-assisted suicide to a narrow class of patients would not work. The demand for physician-assisted suicide principally comes not from the patients in actual and untreatable pain at the very end of life, but from those, whether healthy, chronically ill, or terminally ill, who are depressed, or who fear future pain, loss of dignity, or unduly burdening their families. Once physician-assisted suicide becomes available, many patients whose needs could have been met through appropriate palliative care will instead be directed toward physician-assisted suicide. States could further conclude that the many pressures on patients that may lead to consideration of suicide would, if suicide were officially blessed as a medical treatment, exert powerful pressure on patients to accept suicide more as a duty than as a right.

In this regard, the requirement that such requests be deemed voluntary by one or more physicians is not likely to provide an effective safeguard. For example, terminally ill patients typically are highly dependent upon, and vulnerable to influence by, the very individuals—family and physician—who often have conflicting feelings about pursuing treatment options that could reduce the patient's desire for suicide. To pursue alternatives is to increase the likelihood of extending the patient's life and, necessarily, the obligation of caring for the patient. The family may, entirely unconsciously but nevertheless powerfully, find such an outcome acutely burdensome and therefore subtly encourage the patient to accept death and thereby promote the patient's interest in suicide. The physician is typically in no position to discern the operation of such pressures, and may have his or her own reasons for not attending to them. Absent the kind of due process safeguards that attend decisions by the state to terminate life, which are antithetical to the privacy of the physician-patient relationship, there is little likelihood that an inappropriate exercise of physician-assisted suicide will ever come to light. *Cf.* Bowen v. American Hosp. Ass'n, 476 U.S. 610 (1986).

States also have a strong interest in drawing a defensible line. The one they now rely upon is well established in the common law and medical ethics. For example, although the provision of medication in doses strong enough to relieve pain typically will not bring about a patient's death, such a result can occur. As long as the physician's intent is to ease the patient's pain and not to cause death, the administration of such medication is ethical and fully consistent with a physician's role as healer. Indeed, the provision of such medication is in principle no different than the provision of chemotherapy that is intended to heal but could have the unintended effect of hastening death.

Although the Ninth Circuit criticized this doctrine of double effect, the doctrine's reliance upon intent is solidly grounded in principles of law and morality. The Ninth Circuit proposed no better alternative, and tacitly admitted that its own line was flawed. Once physician-assisted suicide is recognized, how can the right to voluntary euthanasia be denied to those who lack the physical ability to administer the life-ending drug to themselves? And once such a right is recognized for those who are terminally ill, how can it be denied to those who, chronically ill or irremediably depressed, claim to be suffering comparably unendurable pain? Even the ultimate stopping point proposed by the Ninth Circuit—between voluntary and involuntary patient requests (*id.*)—is not secure. It rests on a determination of patient intent that is at least as problematic as the determination of physician intent. Thus, not only does the Ninth Circuit's line lack any basis in the common law, it is as vulnerable to the Ninth Circuit's own analysis as is the line states draw today.

2. Second, states can argue strongly that abandoning the prohibition on physician-assisted suicide will undermine efforts to expand the provision of palliative care to all patients. Although such efforts would not end if physician-assisted suicide were permitted, the prohibition on physician-assisted suicide provides health care professionals with a tremendous incentive to improve and expand the availability of palliative care. Permitting physician-assisted suicide would also jeopardize the hard-won advances firmly to establish for all patients a right not only to have unwanted medical treatment withheld or withdrawn but also to receive pain medication sufficient to ease pain, even if that would hasten the patient's death. The widespread acceptance of these rights by health care professionals, courts, legislatures, and the public depended upon the recognition and acceptance of the distinction between these rights and physician-assisted suicide. *See generally* 2 Meisel § 18.18, at 479–85. If that important boundary is lost, much support for withholding and withdrawing treatment or providing ample pain medication may be lost as well.

3. Finally, states have a strong interest in avoiding the damage to the health care professions and their ability to serve patients that would flow from an abandonment of the prohibition against physician-assisted

suicide. *E.g.*, Semler v. Oregon State Bd. of Dental Examiners, 294 U.S. 608, 612–13 (1935) (state's strong interest in "maintenance of professional standards" permits it to enforce "a general rule even though in particular instances there might be no actual" harm); Ohralik v. Ohio State Bar Ass'n, 436 U.S. 447, 460 (1978) (state interest in "maintaining standards among members of the licensed professions" is "particularly strong"); Shapero v. Kentucky Bar Ass'n, 486 U.S. 466, 485 (1988) (O'Connor, J., dissenting) (state "should have considerable latitude to ban" conduct that "undermines the substantial government interest in promoting the high ethical standards" of a profession). Health care professionals have long understood that with the right to practice comes enormous responsibility. Patients come to physicians and nurses at times of greatest need and vulnerability, depending on them to respond to their needs capably and faithfully. Many patients may understandably wonder, finding themselves badly injured and in the care of a physician they do not know but whose license permits him or her to assist in taking the lives of patients, whether that physician will truly act only to preserve their lives. Will they be confident, as they watch a physician draw a dose of morphine, that the physician is committed only to easing their pain and not to taking their lives? *See* Kass & Lund, 35 Duq. L. Rev. at 408. The ban on physician-assisted suicide helps ensure that patients will never lose the trust that must exist for the relationships between health care professionals and patients to flourish.

CONCLUSION

For the reasons stated above, the judgment of the court of appeals should be reversed.

Washington v. Glucksberg, Philosophers' Brief

Supreme Court of the United States, No. 96–110, October Term, 1996.
On Writ of Certiorari to the United States Court of Appeals for the Ninth Circuit.

Vacco v. Quill, Philosophers' Brief

Supreme Court of the United States, No. 95–1858, October Term, 1996.
On Writ of Certiorari to the United States Court of Appeals for the Second Circuit.
United States Supreme Court Amicus Brief for Ronald Dworkin, Thomas Nagel, Robert Nozick, John Rawls, Thomas Scanlon, and Judith Jarvis Thomson in Support of Respondents.
Filed December 10, 1996.
1996 WL 708956.

INTEREST OF THE AMICI CURIAE

Amici are six moral and political philosophers who differ on many issues of public morality and policy. They are united, however, in their conviction that respect for fundamental principles of liberty and justice, as well as for the American constitutional tradition, requires that the decisions of the Courts of Appeals be affirmed.

INTRODUCTION AND SUMMARY OF ARGUMENT

These cases do not invite or require the Court to make moral, ethical or religious judgments about how people should approach or confront their death or about when it is ethically appropriate to hasten one's own death or to ask others for help in doing so. On the contrary, they ask the Court to recognize that individuals have a constitutionally protected interest in making those grave judgments for themselves, free from the imposition of any religious or philosophical orthodoxy by court or legislature. States have a constitutionally legitimate interest in protecting individuals from irrational, ill-informed, pressured or unstable decisions to hasten their own death. To that end, states may regulate and limit the assistance that doctors may give individuals who express a wish to die. But states may not deny people in the position of the patient-plaintiffs in these cases the opportunity to demonstrate, through whatever reasonable procedures the state might institute-even procedures that err on the side of caution-that their decision to die is indeed informed, stable, and fully free. Denying that opportunity to terminally-ill patients who are in agonizing pain or otherwise doomed to an existence they regard as intolerable could only be justified on the basis of a religious or ethical conviction about the value or meaning of life itself. Our Constitution forbids government to impose such convictions on its citizens.

Petitioners and the amici who support them offer two contradictory arguments. Some deny that the patient-plaintiffs have any constitutionally protected liberty interest in hastening their own deaths.[2] But that liberty interest flows directly from this Court's previous decisions. It flows from the right of people to make their own decisions about matters "involving the most intimate and personal choices a person may make in a lifetime, choices central to personal dignity and autonomy." *Planned Parenthood v. Casey,* 505 U.S. 833, 851 (1992).

The Solicitor General, urging reversal in support of Petitioners, recognizes that the patient-plaintiffs do have a constitutional liberty interest at stake in these cases. *See* Brief for the United States as Amicus Curiae Supporting Petitioners at 12, *Washington v. Vacco* [hereinafter Brief for the United States] ("The term 'liberty' in the Due Process Clause . . . is broad enough to encompass an interest on the part of terminally ill, mentally competent adults in obtaining relief from the kind of suffering experienced by the plaintiffs in this case, which includes not only severe physical pain, but also the despair and distress that comes from physical deterioration and the inability to control basic bodily functions."); *see also id.* at 13 ("*Cruzan* . . . supports the conclusion that

---

[2] *See, e.g.,* Brief for the Petitioners at 25–33, *Washington v. Glucksberg*; Brief for Petitioners Vacco and Pataki at 19–20, *Vacco v. Quill;* Brief Amici Curiae of the United States Catholic Conference, New York Catholic Conference, et al. in Support of Petitioners at 7–21, *Washington v. Glucksberg*; Brief for the Institute for Public Affairs of the Union of Orthodox Jewish Congregations of America and the Rabbinical Council of America as Amici Curiae in Support of Petitioners at 5–13, *Vacco v. Quill and Washington v. Glucksberg.*

a liberty interest is at stake in this case."). The Solicitor General nevertheless argues that Washington and New York properly ignored this profound interest when they required the patient-plaintiffs to live on in circumstances they found intolerable. He argues that a state may simply declare that it is unable to devise a regulatory scheme that would adequately protect patients whose desire to die might be ill-informed or unstable or foolish or not fully free, and that a state may therefore fall back on a blanket prohibition. This Court has never accepted that patently dangerous rationale for denying protection altogether to a conceded fundamental constitutional interest. It would be a serious mistake to do so now. If that rationale were accepted, an interest acknowledged to be constitutionally protected would be rendered empty.

ARGUMENT

I. THE LIBERTY INTEREST ASSERTED HERE IS PROTECTED BY THE DUE PROCESS CLAUSE

The Due Process Clause of the Fourteenth Amendment protects the liberty interest asserted by the patient-plaintiffs here.

Certain decisions are momentous in their impact on the character of a person's life-decisions about religious faith, political and moral allegiance, marriage, procreation and death, for example. Such deeply personal decisions pose controversial questions about how and why human life has value. In a free society, individuals must be allowed to make those decisions for themselves, out of their own faith, conscience and convictions. This Court has insisted, in a variety of contexts and circumstances, that this great freedom is among those protected by the Due Process Clause as essential to a community of "ordered liberty." *Palko v. Connecticut,* 302 U.S. 319, 325 (1937). In its recent decision in *Planned Parenthood v. Casey,* 505 U.S. 833, 851 (1992), the Court offered a paradigmatic statement of that principle:

> matters[ ] involving the most intimate and personal choices a person may make in a lifetime, choices central to a person's dignity and autonomy, are central to the liberty protected by the Fourteenth Amendment.

That declaration reflects an idea underlying many of our basic constitutional protections.[3] As the Court explained in *West Virginia State Board of Education v. Barnette,* 319 U.S. 624, 642 (1943):

[3] In *Cohen v. California,* 403 U.S. 15, 24 (1971), for example, this Court held that the First Amendment guarantee of free speech and expression derives from "the belief that no other approach would comport with the premise of individual dignity and choice upon which our political system rests." Interpreting the religion clauses of the First Amendment, this Court has explained that "[t]he victory for freedom of thought recorded in our Bill of Rights recognizes that in the domain of conscience there is a moral power higher than the State." *Girouard v. United States,* 328 U.S. 61, 68 (1946). And, in a number of Due Process cases, this Court has protected this conception of autonomy by carving out a sphere of personal family life that is immune from government intrusion. *See, e.g., Cleveland Bd. of Educ. v. LeFleur,* 414 U.S. 632, 639 (1974) ("This Court has long recognized that freedom of personal choice in matters of marriage and family life is one of the liberties protected by the Due Process Clause of the Fourteenth

> If there is any fixed star in our constitutional constellation, it is that no official . . . can prescribe what shall be orthodox in politics, nationalism, religion, or other matters of opinion or force citizens to confess by word or act their faith therein.

A person's interest in following his own convictions at the end of life is so central a part of the more general right to make "intimate and personal choices" for himself that a failure to protect that particular interest would undermine the general right altogether. Death is, for each of us, among the most significant events of life. As the Chief Justice said in *Cruzan v. Missouri,* 497 U.S. 261, 281 (1990), "[t]he choice between life and death is a deeply personal decision of obvious and overwhelming finality." Most of us see death—whatever we think will follow it—as the final act of life's drama, and we want that last act to reflect our own convictions, those we have tried to live by, not the convictions of others forced on us in our most vulnerable moment.

Different people, of different religious and ethical beliefs, embrace very different convictions about which way of dying confirms and which contradicts the value of their lives. Some fight against death with every weapon their doctors can devise. Others will do nothing to hasten death even if they pray it will come soon. Still others, including the patient-plaintiffs in these cases, want to end their lives when they think that living on, in the only way they can, would disfigure rather than enhance the lives they had created. Some people make the latter choice not just to escape pain. Even if it were possible to eliminate all pain for a dying patient—and frequently that is not possible—that would not end or even much alleviate the anguish some would feel at remaining alive, but intubated, helpless and often sedated near oblivion.

None of these dramatically different attitudes about the meaning of death can be dismissed as irrational. None should be imposed, either by the pressure of doctors or relatives or by the fiat of government, on people who reject it. Just as it would be intolerable for government to dictate that doctors never be permitted to try to keep someone alive as long as possible, when that is what the patient wishes, so it is intolerable for government to dictate that doctors may never, under any circumstances,

---

Amendment."); *Eisenstadt v. Baird,* 405 U.S. 438, 453 (1973) (recognizing right "to be free from unwarranted governmental intrusion into matters so fundamentally affecting a person as the decision to bear and beget a child"); *Skinner v. Oklahoma,* 316 U.S. 535, 541 (1942) (holding unconstitutional a state statute requiring the sterilization of individuals convicted of three offenses, in large part because the state's actions unwarrantedly intruded on marriage and procreation, "one of the basic civil rights of man"); *Loving v. Virginia,* 388 U.S. 1, 12 (1967) (striking down the criminal prohibition of interracial marriages as an infringement of the right to marry and holding that "[t]he freedom to marry has long been recognized as one of the vital personal rights essential to the orderly pursuit of happiness by free men"). These decisions recognize as constitutionally immune from state intrusion that realm in which individuals make "intimate and personal" decisions that define the very character of their lives. *See* Charles Fried, *Right and Wrong* 14647 (1978) ("What a person is, what he wants, the determination of his life plan, of his concept of the good, are the most intimate expressions of self-determination, and by asserting a person's responsibility for the results of this self-determination, we give substance to the concept of liberty.").

help someone to die who believes that further life means only degradation. The Constitution insists that people must be free to make these deeply personal decisions for themselves and must not be forced to end their lives in a way that appalls them, just because that is what some majority thinks proper.

II. THIS COURT'S DECISIONS IN *CASEY* AND *CRUZAN* COMPEL RECOGNITION OF A LIBERTY INTEREST HERE

A. *Casey* Supports the Liberty Interest Asserted Here

In *Casey,* this Court, in holding that a State cannot constitutionally proscribe abortion in all cases, reiterated that the Constitution protects a sphere of autonomy in which individuals must be permitted to make certain decisions for themselves. The Court began its analysis by pointing out that "[a]t the heart of liberty is the right to define one's own concept of existence, of meaning, of the universe, and of the mystery of human life." 505 U.S. at 851. Choices flowing out of these conceptions, on matters "involving the most intimate and personal choices a person may make in a lifetime, choices central to personal dignity and autonomy, are central to the liberty protected by the Fourteenth Amendment." *Id.* "Beliefs about these matters," the Court continued, "could not define the attributes of personhood were they formed under compulsion of the State." *Id.*

In language pertinent to the liberty interest asserted here, the Court explained why decisions about abortion fall within this category of "personal and intimate" decisions. A decision whether or not to have an abortion, "originat[ing] within the zone of conscience and belief," involves conduct in which "the liberty of the woman is at stake in a sense unique to the human condition and so unique to the law." *Id.* at 852. As such, the decision necessarily involves the very "destiny of the woman" and is inevitably "shaped to a large extent on her own conception of her spiritual imperatives and her place in society." *Id.* Precisely because of these characteristics of the decision, "the State is [not] entitled to proscribe [abortion] in all instances." *Id.* Rather, to allow a total prohibition on abortion would be to permit a state to impose one conception of the meaning and value of human existence on all individuals. This the Constitution forbids.

The Solicitor General nevertheless argues that the right to abortion could be supported on grounds other than this autonomy principle, grounds that would not apply here. He argues, for example, that the abortion right might flow from the great burden an unwanted child imposes on its mother's life. But whether or not abortion rights could be defended on such grounds, they were not the grounds on which this Court in fact relied. To the contrary, the Court explained at length that the right flows from the constitutional protection accorded all individuals to "define one's own concept of existence, of meaning, of the universe, and of the mystery of human life." *Casey,* 505 U.S. at 851.

The analysis in *Casey* compels the conclusion that the patient-plaintiffs have a liberty interest in this case that a state cannot burden with a blanket prohibition. Like a woman's decision whether to have an abortion, a decision to die involves one's very "destiny" and inevitably will be "shaped to a large extent on [one's] own conception of [one's] spiritual imperatives and [one's] place in society." *Id.* at 852. Just as a blanket prohibition on abortion would involve the improper imposition of one conception of the meaning and value of human existence on all individuals, so too would a blanket prohibition on assisted suicide. The liberty interest asserted here cannot be rejected without undermining the rationale of *Casey*. Indeed, the lower court opinions in the Washington case expressly recognized the parallel between the liberty interest in *Casey* and the interest asserted here. *See Compassion in Dying v. Washington,* 79 F.3d 790, 801 (9th Cir.1996) (en banc) ("In deciding right-to-die cases, we are guided by the Court's approach to the abortion cases. *Casey* in particular provides a powerful precedent, for in that case the Court had the opportunity to evaluate its past decisions and to determine whether to adhere to its original judgment."), *aff'g,* 850 F. Supp. 1454, 1459 (W.D. Wash.1994) ("[T]he reasoning in *Casey* [is] highly instructive and almost prescriptive . . ."). This Court should do the same.

B. *Cruzan* Supports the Liberty Interest Asserted Here

We agree with the Solicitor General that this Court's decision in "*Cruzan* . . . supports the conclusion that a liberty interest is at stake in this case." Petitioners, however, insist that the present cases can be distinguished because the right at issue in *Cruzan* was limited to a right to reject an unwanted invasion of one's body. But this Court repeatedly has held that in appropriate circumstances a state may require individuals to accept unwanted invasions of the body. *See, e.g., Schmerber v. California,* 384 U.S. 757 (1966) (extraction of blood sample from individual suspected of driving while intoxicated, notwithstanding defendant's objection, does not violate privilege against self-incrimination or other constitutional rights); *Jacobson v. Massachusetts,* 197 U.S. 11 (1905) (upholding compulsory vaccination for smallpox as reasonable regulation for protection of public health). The liberty interest at stake in *Cruzan* was a more profound one. If a competent patient has a constitutional right to refuse life-sustaining treatment, then, the Court implied, the state could not override that right. The regulations upheld in *Cruzan* were designed only to ensure that the individual's wishes were ascertained correctly. Thus, if *Cruzan* implies a right of competent patients to refuse life-sustaining treatment, that implication must be understood as resting not simply on a right to refuse bodily invasions but on the more profound right to refuse medical intervention when what is at stake is a momentous personal decision, such as the timing and manner of one's death. In her concurrence, Justice O'Connor expressly recognized that the right at issue involved a "deeply personal decision"

that is "inextricably intertwined" with our notion of "self-determination." 497 U.S. at 287–89.

Cruzan also supports the proposition that a state may not burden a terminally ill patient's liberty interest in determining the time and manner of his death by prohibiting doctors from terminating life support. Seeking to distinguish *Cruzan,* Petitioners insist that a state may nevertheless burden that right in a different way by forbidding doctors to assist in the suicide of patients who are not on life-support machinery. They argue that doctors who remove life support are only allowing a natural process to end in death whereas doctors who prescribe lethal drugs are intervening to cause death. So, according to this argument, a state has an independent justification for forbidding doctors to assist in suicide that it does not have for forbidding them to remove life support. In the former case though not the latter, it is said, the state forbids an act of killing that is morally much more problematic than merely letting a patient die.

This argument is based on a misunderstanding of the pertinent moral principles. It is certainly true that when a patient does not wish to die, different acts, each of which foreseeably results in his death, nevertheless have very different moral status. When several patients need organ transplants and organs are scarce, for example, it is morally permissible for a doctor to deny an organ to one patient, even though he will die without it, in order to give it to another. But it is certainly not permissible for a doctor to kill one patient in order to use his organs to save another. The morally significant difference between those two acts is *not,* however, that killing is a positive act and not providing an organ is a mere omission, or that killing someone is worse than merely allowing a "natural" process to result in death. It would be equally impermissible for a doctor to let an injured patient bleed to death, or to refuse antibiotics to a patient with pneumonia—in each case the doctor would have allowed death to result from a "natural" process—in order to make his organs available for transplant to others. A doctor violates his patient's rights regardless of whether the doctor acts or refrains from acting, against the patient's wishes, in a way that is designed to cause death.

When a competent patient does want to die, the moral situation is obviously different, because then it makes no sense to appeal to the patient's right not to be killed as a reason why an act designed to cause his death is impermissible. From the patient's point of view, there is no morally pertinent difference between a doctor's terminating treatment that keeps him alive, if that is what he wishes, and a doctor's helping him to end his own life by providing lethal pills he may take himself, when ready, if that is what he wishes—except that the latter may be quicker and more humane. Nor is that a pertinent difference from the doctor's point of view. If and when it is permissible for him to act with death in view, it does not matter which of those two means he and his patient choose. If it is permissible for a doctor deliberately to withdraw medical

treatment in order to allow death to result from a natural process, then it is equally permissible for him to help his patient hasten his own death more actively, if that is the patient's express wish.

It is true that some doctors asked to terminate life support are reluctant and do so only in deference to a patient's right to compel them to remove unwanted invasions of his body. But other doctors, who believe that their most fundamental professional duty is to act in the patient's interests and that, in certain circumstances, it is in their patient's best interests to die, participate willingly in such decisions: they terminate life support to cause death because they know that is what their patient wants. *Cruzan* implied that a state may not absolutely prohibit a doctor from deliberately causing death, at the patient's request, in that way and for that reason. If so, then a state may not prohibit doctors from deliberately using more direct and often more humane means to the same end when that is what a patient prefers. The fact that failing to provide life sustaining treatment may be regarded as "only letting nature take its course" is no more morally significant in this context, when the patient wishes to die, than in the other, when he wishes to live. Whether a doctor turns off a respirator in accordance with the patient's request or prescribes pills that a patient may take when he is ready to kill himself, the doctor acts with the same intention: to help the patient die.

The two situations do differ in one important respect. Since patients have a right not to have life support machinery attached to their bodies, they have, in principle, a right to compel its removal. But that is not true in the case of assisted suicide: patients in certain circumstances have a right that the state not forbid doctors to assist in their deaths, but they have no right to compel a doctor to assist them. The right in question, that is, is only a right to the help of a willing doctor.

III. STATE INTERESTS DO NOT JUSTIFY A CATEGORICAL PROHIBITION ON ALL ASSISTED SUICIDE

The Solicitor General concedes that "a competent, terminally ill adult has a constitutionally cognizable liberty interest in avoiding the kind of suffering experienced by the plaintiffs in this case." He agrees that this interest extends not only to avoiding pain, but to avoiding an existence the patient believes to be one of intolerable indignity or incapacity as well. *Id.* at 12. The Solicitor General argues, however, that states nevertheless have the right to "override" this liberty interest altogether, because a state could reasonably conclude that allowing doctors to assist in suicide, even under the most stringent regulations and procedures that could be devised, would unreasonably endanger the lives of a number of patients who might ask for death in circumstances when it is plainly not in their interests to die or when their consent has been improperly obtained.

This argument is unpersuasive, however, for at least three reasons. *First,* in *Cruzan,* this Court noted that its various decisions supported the recognition of a general liberty interest in refusing medical

treatment, even when such refusal could result in death. 497 U.S. at 278–79. The various risks described by the Solicitor General apply equally to those situations. For instance, a patient kept alive only by an elaborate and disabling life support system might well become depressed, and doctors might be equally uncertain whether the depression is curable: such a patient might decide for death only because he has been advised that he will die soon anyway or that he will never live free of the burdensome apparatus, and either diagnosis might conceivably be mistaken. Relatives or doctors might subtly or crudely influence that decision, and state provision for the decision may (to the same degree in this case as if it allowed assisted suicide) be thought to encourage it.

Yet there has been no suggestion that states are incapable of addressing such dangers through regulation. In fact, quite the opposite is true. In *McKay v. Bergstedt,* 106 Nev. 808, 801 P.2d 617 (1990), for example, the Nevada Supreme Court held that "competent adult patients desiring to refuse or discontinue medical treatment" must be examined by two non-attending physicians to determine whether the patient is mentally competent, understands his prognosis and treatment options, and appears free of coercion or pressure in making his decision. *Id.* at 827–28, 801 P.2d at 630. *See also id.* (in the case of terminally-ill patients with natural life expectancy of less than six months, patient's right of self-determination shall be deemed to prevail over state interests, whereas non-terminal patient's decision to terminate life-support systems must first be weighed against relevant state interests by trial judge); *In re Farrell,* 108 N.J. 335, 354, 529 A.2d 404, 413 (1987) (terminally-ill patient requesting termination of life-support must be determined to be competent and properly informed about prognosis, available treatment options and risks, and to have made decision voluntarily and without coercion). Those protocols served to guard against precisely the dangers that the Solicitor General raises. The case law contains no suggestion that such protocols are inevitably insufficient to prevent deaths that should have been prevented.

Indeed, the risks of mistake are overall greater in the case of terminating life support. *Cruzan* implied that a state must allow individuals to make such decisions through an advance directive stipulating either that life support be terminated (or not initiated) in described circumstances when the individual was no longer competent to make such a decision himself, or that a designated proxy be allowed to make that decision. All the risks just described are present when the decision is made through or pursuant to such an advance directive, and a grave further risk is added: that the directive, though still in force, no longer represents the wishes of the patient. The patient might have changed his mind before he became incompetent, though he did not change the directive, or his proxy may make a decision that the patient would not have made himself if still competent. In *Cruzan,* this Court held that a state may limit these risks through reasonable regulation. It

did not hold—or even suggest—that a state may avoid them through a blanket prohibition that, in effect, the liberty interest altogether.

Second, nothing in the record supports the conclusion that no system of rules and regulations could adequately reduce the risk of mistake. As discussed above, the experience of states in adjudicating requests to have life-sustaining treatment removed indicates the opposite.[4] The Solicitor General has provided no persuasive reason why the same sort of procedures could not be applied effectively in the case of a competent individual's request for physician-assisted suicide.

Indeed, several very detailed schemes for regulating physician-assisted suicide have been submitted to the voters of some states[5] and one has been enacted.[6] In addition, concerned groups, including a group of distinguished professors of law and other professionals, have drafted and defended such schemes. *See, e.g.,* Charles H. Baron, *et. al., A Model State Act to Authorize and Regulate Physician-Assisted Suicide,* 33 Harv. J. Legis. 1 (1996). Such draft statutes propose a variety of protections and review procedures designed to insure against mistakes, and neither Washington nor New York attempted to show that such schemes would be porous or ineffective. Nor does the Solicitor General's brief: it relies instead mainly on flat and conclusory statements. It cites a New York Task Force report, written before the proposals just described were

[4] When state protocols are observed, sometimes the patient is permitted to die and sometimes not. *See, e.g., In re Tavel,* 661 A.2d 1061 (Del.1995) (affirming finding that petitioner-daughter had proven by clear and convincing evidence that incompetent patient would want life support systems removed); *In re Martin,* 450 Mich. 204, 538 N.W.2d 399 (1995) (holding that wife's testimony and affidavit did not constitute clear and convincing evidence of incompetent patient's pre-injury decision to decline life-sustaining medical treatment in patient's present circumstances); *DiGrella v. Elston,* 858 S.W.2d 698, 710 (Ky.1993) ("If the attending physician, the hospital or nursing home ethics committee where the patient resides, and the legal guardian or next of kin all agree and document the patient's wishes and condition, and if no one disputes their decision, no court order is required to proceed to carry out [an incompetent] patient's wishes"); *Mack v. Mack,* 329 Md. 188, 618 A.2d 744 (1993) (holding that wife failed to provide clear and convincing evidence that incompetent husband would want life support removed); *In re Doe,* 411 Mass. 512, 583 N.E.2d 1263 (applying doctrine of substituted judgment and holding that evidence supported finding that, if incompetent patient were capable of making a choice, she would remove life support).

[5] For example, 46% of California voters supported Proposition 161, which would have legalized physician-assisted suicide, in November 1992. The measure was a proposed amendment to Cal. Penal Code § 401 (1992) which currently makes assisted suicide a felony. Those who did not vote for the measure cited mainly religious reasons or concerns that the proposed law was flawed because it lacked safeguards against abuse and needed more restrictions that might be easily added, such as a waiting period and a psychological examination. Alison C. Hall, *To Die With Dignity: Comparing Physician-Assisted Suicide in the United States, Japan, and the Netherlands,* 74 Wash. U.L.Q. 803, 817 n.84 (1996).

[6] In November 1994, Oregon voters approved the Oregon Death With Dignity Act through voter initiative, legalizing physician-assisted suicide under limited circumstances. Oregon Death With Dignity Act, Or. Rev. Stat. §§ 127.800–.827 (1995). Under the Oregon Act, a capable adult resident of the state, who has been determined by the attending physician and consulting physician to be suffering from a terminal disease, and who has voluntarily expressed his or her wish to die, may make a written request for medication for the purpose of ending his life in a human and dignified manner in accordance with [the provisions of the Act]. Or. Rev. Stat. § 127.805 (1995). The Act provides specific definitions of essential terms such as "incapable" and "terminal disease." The Act also provides numerous other regulations designed to safeguard the integrity of the process.

drafted, whose findings have been widely disputed and were implicitly rejected in the opinion of the Second Circuit below. *See generally Quill v. Vacco,* 80 F.3d 716 (2d Cir.1996). The weakness of the Solicitor General's argument is signaled by his strong reliance on the experience in the Netherlands which, in effect, allows assisted suicide pursuant to published guidelines. Brief for the United States at 23–24. The Dutch guidelines are more permissive than the proposed and model American statutes, however. The Solicitor General deems the Dutch practice of ending the lives of people like neo-nates who cannot consent particularly noteworthy, for example, but that practice could easily and effectively be made illegal by any state regulatory scheme without violating the Constitution.

The Solicitor General's argument would perhaps have more force if the question before the Court were simply whether a state has any rational basis for an absolute prohibition; if that were the question, then it might be enough to call attention to risks a state might well deem not worth running. But, as the Solicitor General concedes, the question here is a very different one: whether a state has interests sufficiently compelling to allow it to take the extraordinary step of altogether refusing the exercise of a liberty interest of constitutional dimension. In those circumstances, the burden is plainly on the state to demonstrate that the risk of mistakes is very high, and that no alternative to complete prohibition would adequately and effectively reduce those risks. Neither of the Petitioners has made such a showing.

Nor could they. The burden of proof on any state attempting to show this would be very high. Consider, for example, the burden a state would have to meet to show that it was entitled altogether to ban public speeches in favor of unpopular causes because it could not guarantee, either by regulations short of an outright ban or by increased police protection, that such speeches would not provoke a riot that would result in serious injury or death to an innocent party. Or that it was entitled to deny those accused of crime the procedural rights that the Constitution guarantees, such as the right to a jury trial, because the security risk those rights would impose on the community would be too great. One can posit extreme circumstances in which some such argument would succeed. *See, e.g., Korematsu v. United States,* 323 U.S. 214 (1944) (permitting United States to detain individuals of Japanese ancestry during wartime). But these circumstances would be extreme indeed, and the *Korematsu* ruling has been widely and severely criticized.

Third, it is doubtful whether the risks the Solicitor General cites are even of the right character to serve as justification for an absolute prohibition on the exercise of an important liberty interest. The risks fall into two groups. The first is the risk of medical mistake, including a misdiagnosis of competence or terminal illness. To be sure, no scheme of regulation, no matter how rigorous, can altogether guarantee that medical mistakes will not be made. But the Constitution does not allow

a state to deny patients a great variety of important choices, for which informed consent is properly deemed necessary, just because the information on which the consent is given may, in spite of the most strenuous efforts to avoid mistake, be wrong. Again, these identical risks are present in decisions to terminate life support, yet they do not justify an absolute prohibition on the exercise of the right.

The second group consists of risks that a patient will be unduly influenced by considerations that the state might deem it not in his best interests to be swayed by, for example, the feelings and views of close family members. But what a patient regards as proper grounds for such a decision normally reflects exactly the judgments of personal ethics—of why his life is important and what affects its value—that patients have a crucial liberty interest in deciding for themselves. Even people who are dying have a right to hear and, if they wish, act on what others might wish to tell or suggest or even hint to them, and it would be dangerous to suppose that a state may prevent this on the ground that it knows better than its citizens when they should be moved by or yield to particular advice or suggestion in the exercise of their right to make fateful personal decisions for themselves. It is not a good reply that some people may not decide as they really wish—as they would decide, for example, if free from the "pressure" of others. That possibility could hardly justify the most serious pressure of all—the criminal law which tells them that they may not decide for death if they need the help of a doctor in dying, no matter how firmly they wish it.

There is a fundamental infirmity in the Solicitor General's argument. He asserts that a state may reasonably judge that the risk of "mistake" to some persons justifies a prohibition that not only risks but insures and even aims at what would undoubtedly be a vastly greater number of "mistakes" of the opposite kind—preventing many thousands of competent people who think that it disfigures their lives to continue living, in the only way left to them, from escaping that—to them—terrible injury. A state grievously and irreversibly harms such people when it prohibits that escape. The Solicitor General's argument may seem plausible to those who do not agree that individuals are harmed by being forced to live on in pain and what they regard as indignity. But many other people plainly do think that such individuals are harmed, and a state may not take one side in that essentially ethical or religious controversy as its justification for denying a crucial liberty.

Of course, a state has important interests that justify regulating physician-assisted suicide. It may be legitimate for a state to deny an opportunity for assisted suicide when it acts in what it reasonably judges to be the best interests of the potential suicide, and when its judgment on that issue does not rest on contested judgments about "matters involving the most intimate and personal choices a person may make in a lifetime, choices central to personal dignity and autonomy." *Casey*, 505 U.S. at 851. A state might assert, for example, that people who are not

terminally ill, but who have formed a desire to die, are, as a group, very likely later to be grateful if they are prevented from taking their own lives. It might then claim that it is legitimate, out of concern for such people, to deny any of them a doctor's assistance. This Court need not decide now the extent to which such paternalistic interests might override an individual's liberty interest. No one can plausibly claim, however—and it is noteworthy that neither Petitioners nor the Solicitor General does claim—that any such prohibition could serve the interests of any significant number of terminally ill patients. On the contrary, any paternalistic justification for an absolute prohibition of assistance to such patients would of necessity appeal to a widely contested religious or ethical conviction many of them, including the patient-plaintiffs, reject. Allowing *that* justification to prevail would vitiate the liberty interest.

Even in the case of terminally ill patients, a state has a right to take all reasonable measures to insure that a patient requesting such assistance has made an informed, competent, stable and uncoerced decision. It is plainly legitimate for a state to establish procedures through which professional and administrative judgments can be made about these matters, and to forbid doctors to assist in suicide when its reasonable procedures have not been satisfied. States may be permitted considerable leeway in designing such procedures. They may be permitted, within reason, to err on what they take to be the side of caution. But they may not use the bare possibility of error as justification for refusing to establish any procedures at all and relying instead on a flat prohibition.

CONCLUSION

Each individual has a right to make the "most intimate and personal choices central to personal dignity and autonomy." That right encompasses the right to exercise some control over the time and manner of one's death.

The patient-plaintiffs in these cases were all mentally competent individuals in the final phase of terminal illness and died within months of filing their claims. Jane Doe described how her advanced cancer made even the most basic bodily functions such as swallowing, coughing, and yawning extremely painful and that it was "not possible for [her] to reduce [her] pain to an acceptable level of comfort and to retain an alert state." Faced with such circumstances, she sought to be able to "discuss freely with [her] treating physician [her] intention of hastening [her] death through the consumption of drugs prescribed for that purpose." *Quill v. Vacco,* 80 F.2d 716, 720 (2d Cir.1996) (quoting declaration of Jane Doe). George A. Kingsley, in advanced stages of AIDS which included, among other hardships, the attachment of a tube to an artery in his chest which made even routine functions burdensome and the development of lesions on his brain, sought advice from his doctors regarding prescriptions which could hasten his impending death. *Id.* Jane Roe, suffering from cancer since 1988, had been almost completely bed-ridden

since 1993 and experienced constant pain which could not be alleviated by medication. After undergoing counseling for herself and her family, she desired to hasten her death by taking prescription drugs. *Compassion in Dying v. Washington,* 850 F. Supp. 1454, 1456 (1994). John Doe, who had experienced numerous AIDS-related ailments since 1991, was "especially cognizant of the suffering imposed by a lingering terminal illness because he was the primary caregiver for his long-term companion who died of AIDS" and sought prescription drugs from his physician to hasten his own death after entering the terminal phase of AIDS. *Id.* at 1456–57. James Poe suffered from emphysema which caused him "a constant sensation of suffocating" as well as a cardiac condition which caused severe leg pain. Connected to an oxygen tank at all times but unable to calm the panic reaction associated with his feeling of suffocation even with regular doses of morphine, Mr. Poe sought physician-assisted suicide. *Id.* at 1457.

A state may not deny the liberty claimed by the patient-plaintiffs in these cases without providing them an opportunity to demonstrate, in whatever way the state might reasonably think wise and necessary, that the conviction they expressed for an early death is competent, rational, informed, stable and uncoerced.

Affirming the decisions by the Courts of Appeals would establish nothing more than that there is such a constitutionally protected right in principle. It would establish only that some individuals, whose decisions for suicide plainly cannot be dismissed as irrational or foolish or premature, must be accorded a reasonable opportunity to show that their decision for death is informed and free. It is not necessary to decide precisely which patients are entitled to that opportunity. If, on the other hand, this Court reverses the decisions below, its decision could only be justified by the momentous proposition—a proposition flatly in conflict with the spirit and letter of the Court's past decisions—that an American citizen does not, after all, have the right, even in principle, to live and die in the light of his own religious and ethical beliefs, his own convictions about why his life is valuable and where its value lies.

NOTES AND QUESTIONS

1. *Factual Information.* Identify the most important factual information about medical care that you learned from the amicus briefs. Did the AMA provide information about physician-assisted suicide that should be relevant to the Court's decision? Did the philosophers provide any factual information in their brief?

2. *Philosophy.* Did the AMA do a good job of defending the biomedical ethical principle of autonomy? Did the philosophers do a good job of defending the biomedical ethical principle of autonomy? Which brief offered a better understanding of patient autonomy?

How did philosophical or ethical reasoning affect the legal argument of the briefs? Do you agree with the Philosophers' Brief that:

> [t]hese cases do not invite or require the Court to make moral, ethical or religious judgments about how people should approach or confront their death or about when it is ethically appropriate to hasten one's own death or to ask others for help in doing so. On the contrary, they ask the Court to recognize that individuals have a constitutionally protected interest in making those grave judgments for themselves, free from the imposition of any religious or philosophical orthodoxy by court or legislature.

Or did the physicians get the better of the ethical argument when they wrote the "ethical prohibition against physician-assisted suicide is a cornerstone of medical ethics" that should not be defeated in this case?

3. *Legal Arguments.* Which brief is more persuasive on the meaning of the Due Process Clause? The Equal Protection Clause? Did the Court accept all the AMA's arguments and reject all the philosophers' arguments in the following opinion? Are you surprised that the decision was unanimous? Are the concurrences more persuasive than the opinion of the Court?

Washington v. Glucksberg

Supreme Court of the United States, 1997.
521 U.S. 702, 117 S.Ct. 2258.

■ REHNQUIST, C.J., delivered the opinion of the Court, in which O'CONNOR, SCALIA, KENNEDY, and THOMAS, JJ., joined. O'CONNOR, J., filed a concurring opinion, in which GINSBURG and BREYER, JJ., joined in part, STEVENS, J., SOUTER, J., GINSBURG, J., and BREYER, J., filed opinions concurring in the judgment.

■ CHIEF JUSTICE REHNQUIST delivered the opinion of the Court.

The question presented in this case is whether Washington's prohibition against "caus[ing]" or "aid[ing]" a suicide offends the Fourteenth Amendment to the United States Constitution. We hold that it does not.

It has always been a crime to assist a suicide in the State of Washington. In 1854, Washington's first Territorial Legislature outlawed "assisting another in the commission of self-murder." Today, Washington law provides: "A person is guilty of promoting a suicide attempt when he knowingly causes or aids another person to attempt suicide." Wash. Rev. Code § 9A.36.060(1) (1994). "Promoting a suicide attempt" is a felony, punishable by up to five years' imprisonment and up to a $10,000 fine. §§ 9A.36.060(2) and 9A.20.021(1)(c). At the same time, Washington's Natural Death Act, enacted in 1979, states that the "withholding or withdrawal of life-sustaining treatment" at a patient's direction "shall not, for any purpose, constitute a suicide." Wash. Rev. Code § 70.122.070(1).

Petitioners in this case are the State of Washington and its Attorney General. Respondents Harold Glucksberg, M.D., Abigail Halperin, M.D.,

Thomas A. Preston, M.D., and Peter Shalit, M.D., are physicians who practice in Washington. These doctors occasionally treat terminally ill, suffering patients, and declare that they would assist these patients in ending their lives if not for Washington's assisted-suicide ban. In January 1994, respondents, along with three gravely ill, pseudonymous plaintiffs who have since died and Compassion in Dying, a nonprofit organization that counsels people considering physician-assisted suicide, sued in the United States District Court, seeking a declaration that Wash. Rev. Code § 9A.36.060(1) (1994) is, on its face, unconstitutional.

The plaintiffs asserted "the existence of a liberty interest protected by the Fourteenth Amendment which extends to a personal choice by a mentally competent, terminally ill adult to commit physician-assisted suicide." Relying primarily on *Planned Parenthood of Southeastern Pa. v. Casey,* 505 U.S. 833, 112 S. Ct. 2791, 120 L.Ed.2d 674 (1992), and *Cruzan v. Director, Mo. Dept. of Health,* 497 U.S. 261, 110 S. Ct. 2841, 111 L.Ed.2d 224 (1990), the District Court agreed, and concluded that Washington's assisted-suicide ban is unconstitutional because it "places an undue burden on the exercise of [that] constitutionally protected liberty interest." The District Court also decided that the Washington statute violated the Equal Protection Clause's requirement that " 'all persons similarly situated . . . be treated alike.' "

A panel of the Court of Appeals for the Ninth Circuit reversed, emphasizing that "[i]n the two hundred and five years of our existence no constitutional right to aid in killing oneself has ever been asserted and upheld by a court of final jurisdiction." The Ninth Circuit reheard the case en banc, reversed the panel's decision, and affirmed the District Court. Like the District Court, the en banc Court of Appeals emphasized our *Casey* and *Cruzan* decisions. The court also discussed what it described as "historical" and "current societal attitudes" toward suicide and assisted suicide, and concluded that "the Constitution encompasses a due process liberty interest in controlling the time and manner of one's death—that there is, in short, a constitutionally-recognized 'right to die.' " After "[w]eighing and then balancing" this interest against Washington's various interests, the court held that the State's assisted-suicide ban was unconstitutional "as applied to terminally ill competent adults who wish to hasten their deaths with medication prescribed by their physicians." The court did not reach the District Court's equal protection holding. We granted certiorari, and now reverse.

I

We begin, as we do in all due process cases, by examining our Nation's history, legal traditions, and practices. In almost every State—indeed, in almost every western democracy—it is a crime to assist a suicide. The States' assisted-suicide bans are not innovations. Rather, they are longstanding expressions of the States' commitment to the protection and preservation of all human life. Indeed, opposition to and condemnation of suicide—and, therefore, of assisting suicide—are

consistent and enduring themes of our philosophical, legal, and cultural heritages.

More specifically, for over 700 years, the Anglo-American common-law tradition has punished or otherwise disapproved of both suicide and assisting suicide. . . .

For the most part, the early American Colonies adopted the common-law approach. For example, . . . Virginia also required ignominious burial for suicides, and their estates were forfeit to the Crown.

Over time, however, the American Colonies abolished these harsh common-law penalties. William Penn abandoned the criminal-forfeiture sanction in Pennsylvania in 1701, and the other Colonies (and later, the other States) eventually followed this example. . . . [T]his change reflected the growing consensus that it was unfair to punish the suicide's family for his wrongdoing. . . .

That suicide remained a grievous, though nonfelonious, wrong is confirmed by the fact that colonial and early state legislatures and courts did not retreat from prohibiting assisting suicide. Swift, in his early 19th-century treatise on the laws of Connecticut, stated that "[i]f one counsels another to commit suicide, and the other by reason of the advice kills himself, the advisor is guilty of murder as principal." This was the well-established common-law view, as was the similar principle that the consent of a homicide victim is "wholly immaterial to the guilt of the person who cause[d] [his death]." And the prohibitions against assisting suicide never contained exceptions for those who were near death. Rather, "[t]he life of those to whom life ha[d] become a burden—of those who [were] hopelessly diseased or fatally wounded—nay, even the lives of criminals condemned to death, [were] under the protection of the law, equally as the lives of those who [were] in the full tide of life's enjoyment, and anxious to continue to live."

The earliest American statute explicitly to outlaw assisting suicide was enacted in New York in 1828, and many of the new States and Territories followed New York's example. . . . By the time the Fourteenth Amendment was ratified, it was a crime in most States to assist a suicide. . . .

Though deeply rooted, the States' assisted-suicide bans have in recent years been reexamined and, generally, reaffirmed. Because of advances in medicine and technology, Americans today are increasingly likely to die in institutions, from chronic illnesses. Public concern and democratic action are therefore sharply focused on how best to protect dignity and independence at the end of life, with the result that there have been many significant changes in state laws and in the attitudes these laws reflect. Many States, for example, now permit "living wills," surrogate health-care decisionmaking, and the withdrawal or refusal of life-sustaining medical treatment. At the same time, however, voters and

legislators continue for the most part to reaffirm their States' prohibitions on assisting suicide.

The Washington statute at issue in this case, Wash. Rev. Code § 9A.36.060 (1994), was enacted in 1975 as part of a revision of that State's criminal code. Four years later, Washington passed its Natural Death Act, which specifically stated that the "withholding or withdrawal of life-sustaining treatment . . . shall not, for any purpose, constitute a suicide" and that "[n]othing in this chapter shall be construed to condone, authorize, or approve mercy killing. . . ." In 1991, Washington voters rejected a ballot initiative which, had it passed, would have permitted a form of physician-assisted suicide. Washington then added a provision to the Natural Death Act expressly excluding physician-assisted suicide. 1992 Wash. Laws, ch. 98, § 10; Wash. Rev. Code § 70.122.100 (1994).

California voters rejected an assisted-suicide initiative similar to Washington's in 1993. On the other hand, in 1994, voters in Oregon enacted, also through ballot initiative, that State's "Death With Dignity Act," which legalized physician-assisted suicide for competent, terminally ill adults. Since the Oregon vote, many proposals to legalize assisted-suicide have been and continue to be introduced in the States' legislatures, but none has been enacted. And just last year, Iowa and Rhode Island joined the overwhelming majority of States explicitly prohibiting assisted suicide. Also, on April 30, 1997, President Clinton signed the Federal Assisted Suicide Funding Restriction Act of 1997, which prohibits the use of federal funds in support of physician-assisted suicide.

Thus, the States are currently engaged in serious, thoughtful examinations of physician-assisted suicide and other similar issues. For example, New York State's Task Force on Life and the Law—an ongoing, blue-ribbon commission composed of doctors, ethicists, lawyers, religious leaders, and interested laymen—was convened in 1984 and commissioned with "a broad mandate to recommend public policy on issues raised by medical advances." Over the past decade, the Task Force has recommended laws relating to end-of-life decisions, surrogate pregnancy, and organ donation. After studying physician-assisted suicide, however, the Task Force unanimously concluded that "[l]egalizing assisted suicide and euthanasia would pose profound risks to many individuals who are ill and vulnerable. . . . [T]he potential dangers of this dramatic change in public policy would outweigh any benefit that might be achieved."

Attitudes toward suicide itself have changed since Bracton, but our laws have consistently condemned, and continue to prohibit, assisting suicide. Despite changes in medical technology and notwithstanding an increased emphasis on the importance of end-of-life decisionmaking, we have not retreated from this prohibition. Against this backdrop of history, tradition, and practice, we now turn to respondents' constitutional claim.

II

. . . Our established method of substantive-due-process analysis has two primary features: First, we have regularly observed that the Due Process Clause specially protects those fundamental rights and liberties which are, objectively, "deeply rooted in this Nation's history and tradition," and "implicit in the concept of ordered liberty," such that "neither liberty nor justice would exist if they were sacrificed." Second, we have required in substantive-due-process cases a "careful description" of the asserted fundamental liberty interest. Our Nation's history, legal traditions, and practices thus provide the crucial "guideposts for responsible decisionmaking," that direct and restrain our exposition of the Due Process Clause. As we stated recently in *Flores*, the Fourteenth Amendment "forbids the government to infringe . . . 'fundamental' liberty interests *at all,* no matter what process is provided, unless the infringement is narrowly tailored to serve a compelling state interest."

Turning to the claim at issue here, the Court of Appeals stated that "[p]roperly analyzed, the first issue to be resolved is whether there is a liberty interest in determining the time and manner of one's death," or, in other words, "[i]s there a right to die?" Similarly, respondents assert a "liberty to choose how to die" and a right to "control of one's final days," and describe the asserted liberty as "the right to choose a humane, dignified death," and "the liberty to shape death." As noted above, we have a tradition of carefully formulating the interest at stake in substantive-due-process cases. For example, although *Cruzan* is often described as a "right to die" case, we were, in fact, more precise: We assumed that the Constitution granted competent persons a "constitutionally protected right to refuse lifesaving hydration and nutrition." The Washington statute at issue in this case prohibits "aid[ing] another person to attempt suicide," and, thus, the question before us is whether the "liberty" specially protected by the Due Process Clause includes a right to commit suicide which itself includes a right to assistance in doing so.

We now inquire whether this asserted right has any place in our Nation's traditions. Here, as discussed *supra,* we are confronted with a consistent and almost universal tradition that has long rejected the asserted right, and continues explicitly to reject it today, even for terminally ill, mentally competent adults. To hold for respondents, we would have to reverse centuries of legal doctrine and practice, and strike down the considered policy choice of almost every State. . . .

Respondents contend that in *Cruzan* we "acknowledged that competent, dying persons have the right to direct the removal of life-sustaining medical treatment and thus hasten death," and that "the constitutional principle behind recognizing the patient's liberty to direct the withdrawal of artificial life support applies at least as strongly to the choice to hasten impending death by consuming lethal medication." Similarly, the Court of Appeals concluded that "*Cruzan,* by recognizing a

liberty interest that includes the refusal of artificial provision of life-sustaining food and water, necessarily recognize[d] a liberty interest in hastening one's own death."

The right assumed in *Cruzan*, however, was not simply deduced from abstract concepts of personal autonomy. Given the common-law rule that forced medication was a battery, and the long legal tradition protecting the decision to refuse unwanted medical treatment, our assumption was entirely consistent with this Nation's history and constitutional traditions. The decision to commit suicide with the assistance of another may be just as personal and profound as the decision to refuse unwanted medical treatment, but it has never enjoyed similar legal protection. Indeed, the two acts are widely and reasonably regarded as quite distinct. In *Cruzan* itself, we recognized that most States outlawed assisted suicide—and even more do today—and we certainly gave no intimation that the right to refuse unwanted medical treatment could be some-how transmuted into a right to assistance in committing suicide.

The history of the law's treatment of assisted suicide in this country has been and continues to be one of the rejection of nearly all efforts to permit it. That being the case, our decisions lead us to conclude that the asserted "right" to assistance in committing suicide is not a fundamental liberty interest protected by the Due Process Clause. The Constitution also requires, however, that Washington's assisted-suicide ban be rationally related to legitimate government interests. This requirement is unquestionably met here. . . .[20]

Finally, the State may fear that permitting assisted suicide will start it down the path to voluntary and perhaps even involuntary euthanasia. The Court of Appeals struck down Washington's assisted-suicide ban only "as applied to competent, terminally ill adults who wish to hasten their deaths by obtaining medication prescribed by their doctors." Washington insists, however, that the impact of the court's decision will not and cannot be so limited. If suicide is protected as a matter of constitutional right, it is argued, "every man and woman in the United States must enjoy it." . . . Thus, it turns out that what is couched as a limited right to "physician-assisted suicide" is likely, in effect, a much broader license, which could prove extremely difficult to police and contain. Washington's ban on assisting suicide prevents such erosion.

This concern is further supported by evidence about the practice of euthanasia in the Netherlands. The Dutch government's own study revealed that in 1990, there were 2,300 cases of voluntary euthanasia (defined as "the deliberate termination of another's life at his request"), 400 cases of assisted suicide, and more than 1,000 cases of euthanasia without an explicit request. In addition to these latter 1,000 cases, the

[20] The court identified and discussed six state interests: (1) preserving life; (2) preventing suicide; (3) avoiding the involvement of third parties and use of arbitrary, unfair, or undue influence; (4) protecting family members and loved ones; (5) protecting the integrity of the medical profession; and (6) avoiding future movement toward euthanasia and other abuses.

study found an additional 4,941 cases where physicians administered lethal morphine overdoses without the patients' explicit consent. This study suggests that, despite the existence of various reporting procedures, euthanasia in the Netherlands has not been limited to competent, terminally ill adults who are enduring physical suffering, and that regulation of the practice may not have prevented abuses in cases involving vulnerable persons, including severely disabled neonates and elderly persons suffering from dementia. The New York Task Force, citing the Dutch experience, observed that "assisted suicide and euthanasia are closely linked," and concluded that the "risk of . . . abuse is neither speculative nor distant." . . .

We need not weigh exactingly the relative strengths of these various interests. They are unquestionably important and legitimate, and Washington's ban on assisted suicide is at least reasonably related to their promotion and protection. We therefore hold that Wash. Rev. Code § 9A.36.060(1) (1994) does not violate the Fourteenth Amendment, either on its face or "as applied to competent, terminally ill adults who wish to hasten their deaths by obtaining medication prescribed by their doctors."

Throughout the Nation, Americans are engaged in an earnest and profound debate about the morality, legality, and practicality of physician-assisted suicide. Our holding permits this debate to continue, as it should in a democratic society. The decision of the en banc Court of Appeals is reversed, and the case is remanded for further proceedings consistent with this opinion.

It is so ordered. . . .

■ JUSTICE O'CONNOR, concurring.

. . . . I join the Court's opinions because I agree that there is no generalized right to "commit suicide." But respondents urge us to address the narrower question whether a mentally competent person who is experiencing great suffering has a constitutionally cognizable interest in controlling the circumstances of his or her imminent death. I see no need to reach that question in the context of the facial challenges to the New York and Washington laws at issue here. . . . The parties and *amici* agree that in these States a patient who is suffering from a terminal illness and who is experiencing great pain has no legal barriers to obtaining medication, from qualified physicians, to alleviate that suffering, even to the point of causing unconsciousness and hastening death. In this light, even assuming that we would recognize such an interest, I agree that the State's interests in protecting those who are not truly competent or facing imminent death, or those whose decisions to hasten death would not truly be voluntary, are sufficiently weighty to justify a prohibition against physician-assisted suicide. . . .

In sum, there is no need to address the question whether suffering patients have a constitutionally cognizable interest in obtaining relief from the suffering that they may experience in the last days of their lives.

There is no dispute that dying patients in Washington and New York can obtain palliative care, even when doing so would hasten their deaths. The difficulty in defining terminal illness and the risk that a dying patient's request for assistance in ending his or her life might not be truly voluntary justifies the prohibitions on assisted suicide we uphold here.

■ JUSTICE STEVENS, concurring in the judgments.

.... But just as our conclusion that capital punishment is not always unconstitutional did not preclude later decisions holding that it is sometimes impermissibly cruel, so is it equally clear that a decision upholding a general statutory prohibition of assisted suicide does not mean that every possible application of the statute would be valid. A State, like Washington, that has authorized the death penalty, and thereby has concluded that the sanctity of human life does not require that it always be preserved, must acknowledge that there are situations in which an interest in hastening death is legitimate. Indeed, not only is that interest sometimes legitimate, I am also convinced that there are times when it is entitled to constitutional protection.

II

... I insist that the source of Nancy Cruzan's right to refuse treatment was not just a common-law rule. Rather, this right is an aspect of a far broader and more basic concept of freedom that is even older than the common law. This freedom embraces not merely a person's right to refuse a particular kind of unwanted treatment, but also her interest in dignity, and in determining the character of the memories that will survive long after her death. In recognizing that the State's interests did not outweigh Nancy Cruzan's liberty interest in refusing medical treatment, *Cruzan* rested not simply on the common-law right to refuse medical treatment, but—at least implicitly—on the even more fundamental right to make this "deeply personal decision."

Thus, the common-law right to protection from battery, which included the right to refuse medical treatment in most circumstances, did not mark "the outer limits of the substantive sphere of liberty" that supported the Cruzan family's decision to hasten Nancy's death. Those limits have never been precisely defined. They are generally identified by the importance and character of the decision confronted by the individual. Whatever the outer limits of the concept may be, it definitely includes protection for matters "central to personal dignity and autonomy."

The *Cruzan* case demonstrated that some state intrusions on the right to decide how death will be encountered are also intolerable. The now-deceased plaintiffs in this action may in fact have had a liberty interest even stronger than Nancy Cruzan's because, not only were they terminally ill, they were suffering constant and severe pain. Avoiding intolerable pain and the indignity of living one's final days incapacitated and in agony is certainly "[a]t the heart of [the] liberty . . . to define one's

own concept of existence, of meaning, of the universe, and of the mystery of human life.

While I agree with the Court that *Cruzan* does not decide the issue presented by these cases, *Cruzan* did give recognition, not just to vague, unbridled notions of autonomy, but to the more specific interest in making decisions about how to confront an imminent death. Although there is no absolute right to physician-assisted suicide, *Cruzan* makes it clear that some individuals who no longer have the option of deciding whether to live or to die because they are already on the threshold of death have a constitutionally protected interest that may outweigh the State's interest in preserving life at all costs. The liberty interest at stake in a case like this differs from, and is stronger than, both the common-law right to refuse medical treatment and the unbridled interest in deciding whether to live or die. It is an interest in deciding how, rather than whether, a critical threshold shall be crossed.

III

. . . Many terminally ill people find their lives meaningful even if filled with pain or dependence on others. Some find value in living through suffering; some have an abiding desire to witness particular events in their families' lives; many believe it a sin to hasten death. Individuals of different religious faiths make different judgments and choices about whether to live on under such circumstances. There are those who will want to continue aggressive treatment; those who would prefer terminal sedation; and those who will seek withdrawal from life-support systems and death by gradual starvation and dehydration. Although as a general matter the State's interest in the contributions each person may make to society outweighs the person's interest in ending her life, this interest does not have the same force for a terminally ill patient faced not with the choice of whether to live, only of how to die. Allowing the individual, rather than the State, to make judgments "about the 'quality' of life that a particular individual may enjoy," does not mean that the lives of terminally ill, disabled people have less value than the lives of those who are healthy. Rather, it gives proper recognition to the individual's interest in choosing a final chapter that accords with her life story, rather than one that demeans her values and poisons memories of her. *See* Brief for Bioethicists as *Amici Curiae* 11; *see also* R. Dworkin, Life's Dominion 213 (1993) ("Whether it is in someone's best interests that his life end in one way rather than another depends on so much else that is special about him—about the shape and character of his life and his own sense of his integrity and critical interests—that no uniform collective decision can possibly hope to serve everyone even decently").

■ JUSTICE BREYER, concurring in the judgments. . . .

I do not agree, however, with the Court's formulation of that claimed "liberty" interest. The Court describes it as a "right to commit suicide with another's assistance." But I would not reject the respondents' claim without considering a different formulation, for which our legal tradition

may provide greater support. That formulation would use words roughly like a "right to die with dignity." But irrespective of the exact words used, at its core would lie personal control over the manner of death, professional medical assistance, and the avoidance of unnecessary and severe physical suffering-combined. . . .

I do not believe, however, that this Court need or now should decide whether or a not such a right is "fundamental." That is because, in my view, the avoidance of severe physical pain (connected with death) would have to constitute an essential part of any successful claim and because, as Justice O'CONNOR points out, the laws before us do not *force* a dying person to undergo that kind of pain. Rather, the laws of New York and of Washington do not prohibit doctors from providing patients with drugs sufficient to control pain despite the risk that those drugs themselves will kill. And under these circumstances the laws of New York and Washington would overcome any remaining significant interests and would be justified, regardless.

Vacco v. Quill

Supreme Court of the United States, 1997.
521 U.S. 793, 117 S.Ct. 2293.

■ CHIEF JUSTICE REHNQUIST delivered the opinion of the Court.

In New York, as in most States, it is a crime to aid another to commit or attempt suicide, but patients may refuse even lifesaving medical treatment. The question presented by this case is whether New York's prohibition on assisting suicide therefore violates the Equal Protection Clause of the Fourteenth Amendment. We hold that it does not.

Petitioners are various New York public officials. Respondents Timothy E. Quill, Samuel C. Klagsbrun, and Howard A. Grossman are physicians who practice in New York. They assert that although it would be "consistent with the standards of [their] medical practice[s]" to prescribe lethal medication for "mentally competent, terminally ill patients" who are suffering great pain and desire a doctor's help in taking their own lives, they are deterred from doing so by New York's ban on assisting suicide. Respondents, and three gravely ill patients who have since died, sued the State's Attorney General in the United States District Court. They urged that because New York permits a competent person to refuse life-sustaining medical treatment, and because the refusal of such treatment is "essentially the same thing" as physician-assisted suicide, New York's assisted-suicide ban violates the Equal Protection Clause. . . .

New York's statutes outlawing assisting suicide affect and address matters of profound significance to all New Yorkers alike. They neither infringe fundamental rights nor involve suspect classifications. These laws are therefore entitled to a "strong presumption of validity."

On their faces, neither New York's ban on assisting suicide nor its statutes permitting patients to refuse medical treatment treat anyone differently from anyone else or draw any distinctions between persons. *Everyone,* regardless of physical condition, is entitled, if competent, to refuse unwanted lifesaving medical treatment; *no one* is permitted to assist a suicide. Generally speaking, laws that apply evenhandedly to all "unquestionably comply" with the Equal Protection Clause. . . .

Unlike the Court of Appeals, we think the distinction between assisting suicide and withdrawing life-sustaining treatment, a distinction widely recognized and endorsed in the medical profession[6] and in our legal traditions, is both important and logical; it is certainly rational.

The distinction comports with fundamental legal principles of causation and intent. First, when a patient refuses life-sustaining medical treatment, he dies from an underlying fatal disease or pathology; but if a patient ingests lethal medication prescribed by a physician, he is killed by that medication.

Furthermore, a physician who withdraws, or honors a patient's refusal to begin, life-sustaining medical treatment purposefully intends, or may so intend, only to respect his patient's wishes and "to cease doing useless and futile or degrading things to the patient when [the patient] no longer stands to benefit from them." The same is true when a doctor provides aggressive palliative care; in some cases, painkilling drugs may hasten a patient's death, but the physician's purpose and intent is, or may be, only to ease his patient's pain. A doctor who assists a suicide, however, "must, necessarily and indubitably, intend primarily that the patient be made dead." Similarly, a patient who commits suicide with a doctor's aid necessarily has the specific intent to end his or her own life, while a patient who refuses or discontinues treatment might not.

The law has long used actors' intent or purpose to distinguish between two acts that may have the same result. *See, e.g., United States v. Bailey,* 444 U.S. 394, 403–06, 100 S. Ct. 624, 631–33, 62 L.Ed.2d 575 (1980) ("[T]he . . . common law of homicide often distinguishes . . . between a person who knows that another person will be killed as the result of his conduct and a person who acts with the specific purpose of taking another's life."); *Morissette v. United States,* 342 U.S. 246, 250, 72 S. Ct. 240, 243, 96 L.Ed. 288 (1952) (distinctions based on intent are "universal and persistent in mature systems of law."); M. Hale, 1 Pleas of the Crown 412 (1847) ("If A. with an intent to prevent a gangrene beginning in his hand doth without any advice cut off his hand, by which he dies, he is not thereby *felo de se* for tho it was a voluntary act, yet it

---

[6] The American Medical Association emphasizes the "fundamental difference between refusing life-sustaining treatment and demanding a life-ending treatment."; Brief for American Medical Association et al. as *Amici Curiae* 18–25. Of course, as respondents' lawsuit demonstrates, there are differences of opinion within the medical profession on this question. *See* New York Task Force, *supra,* at 104–09.

was not with an intent to kill himself."). Put differently, the law distinguishes actions taken "because of" a given end from actions taken "in spite of" their unintended but foreseen consequences. *Feeney,* 442 U.S. at 279, 99 S. Ct. at 2296; *Compassion in Dying v. Washington,* 79 F.3d 790, 858 (C.A.9 1996) (Kleinfeld, J., dissenting) ("When General Eisenhower ordered American soldiers onto the beaches of Normandy, he knew that he was sending many American soldiers to certain death. . . . His purpose, though, was to . . . liberate Europe from the Nazis.").

Given these general principles, it is not surprising that many courts, including New York courts, have carefully distinguished refusing life-sustaining treatment from suicide. In fact, the first state-court decision explicitly to authorize withdrawing lifesaving treatment noted the "real distinction between the self-infliction of deadly harm and a self-determination against artificial life support." *In re Quinlan,* 70 N.J. 10, 43, 52, and n.9, 355 A.2d 647, 665, 670, and n.9, cert. denied *sub nom. Garger v. New Jersey,* 429 U.S. 922, 97 S. Ct. 319, 50 L.Ed.2d 289 (1976).

Similarly, the overwhelming majority of state legislatures have drawn a clear line between assisting suicide and withdrawing or permitting the refusal of unwanted lifesaving medical treatment by prohibiting the former and permitting the latter. And "nearly all states expressly disapprove of suicide and assisted suicide either in statutes dealing with durable powers of attorney in health-care situations, or in 'living will' statutes." Thus, even as the States move to protect and promote patients' dignity at the end of life, they remain opposed to physician-assisted suicide. . . .

This Court has also recognized, at least implicitly, the distinction between letting a patient die and making that patient die. In *Cruzan v. Director, Mo. Dept. of Health,* 497 U.S. 261, 278, 110 S. Ct. 2841, 2851, 111 L.Ed.2d 224 (1990), we concluded that "[t]he principle that a competent person has a constitutionally protected liberty interest in refusing unwanted medical treatment may be inferred from our prior decisions," and we assumed the existence of such a right for purposes of that case. But our assumption of a right to refuse treatment was grounded not, as the Court of Appeals supposed, on the proposition that patients have a general and abstract "right to hasten death," but on well-established, traditional rights to bodily integrity and freedom from unwanted touching. In fact, we observed that "the majority of States in this country have laws imposing criminal penalties on one who assists another to commit suicide." *Cruzan* therefore provides no support for the notion that refusing life-sustaining medical treatment is "nothing more nor less than suicide."

For all these reasons, we disagree with respondents' claim that the distinction between refusing lifesaving medical treatment and assisted suicide is "arbitrary" and "irrational."[11] Granted, in some cases, the line

[11] Respondents also argue that the State irrationally distinguishes between physician-assisted suicide and "terminal sedation," a process respondents characterize as "induc[ing]

between the two may not be clear, but certainty is not required, even were it possible. Logic and contemporary practice support New York's judgment that the two acts are different, and New York may therefore, consistent with the Constitution, treat them differently. By permitting everyone to refuse unwanted medical treatment while prohibiting anyone from assisting a suicide, New York law follows a longstanding and rational distinction.

The judgment of the Court of Appeals is reversed.

It is so ordered.

■ JUSTICE STEVENS, concurring in the judgments.

. . . . In New York, a doctor must respect a competent person's decision to refuse or to discontinue medical treatment even though death will thereby ensue, but the same doctor would be guilty of a felony if she provided her patient assistance in committing suicide. Today we hold that the Equal Protection Clause is not violated by the resulting disparate treatment of two classes of terminally ill people who may have the same interest in hastening death. I agree that the distinction between permitting death to ensue from an underlying fatal disease and causing it to occur by the administration of medication or other means provides a constitutionally sufficient basis for the State's classification. Unlike the Court, however, I am not persuaded that in all cases there will in fact be a significant difference between the intent of the physicians, the patients, or the families in the two situations.

There may be little distinction between the intent of a terminally ill patient who decides to remove her life support and one who seeks the assistance of a doctor in ending her life; in both situations, the patient is seeking to hasten a certain, impending death. The doctor's intent might also be the same in prescribing lethal medication as it is in terminating life support. A doctor who fails to administer medical treatment to one who is dying from a disease could be doing so with an intent to harm or kill that patient. Conversely, a doctor who prescribes lethal medication does not necessarily intend the patient's death—rather that doctor may seek simply to ease the patient's suffering and to comply with her wishes. The illusory character of any differences in intent or causation is confirmed by the fact that the American Medical Association unequivocally endorses the practice of terminal sedation—the administration of sufficient dosages of pain-killing medication to

---

barbiturate coma and then starv[ing] the person to death." Petitioners insist, however, that " '[a]lthough proponents of physician-assisted suicide and euthanasia contend that terminal sedation is covert physician-assisted suicide or euthanasia, the concept of sedating pharmacotherapy is based on informed consent and the principle of double effect.' " Just as a State may prohibit assisting suicide while permitting patients to refuse unwanted lifesaving treatment, it may permit palliative care related to that refusal, which may have the foreseen but unintended "double effect" of hastening the patient's death. *See* New York Task Force, When Death is Sought, *supra* n.6, at 163 ("It is widely recognized that the provision of pain medication is ethically and professionally acceptable even when the treatment may hasten the patient's death, if the medication is intended to alleviate pain and severe discomfort, not to cause death.").

terminally ill patients to protect them from excruciating pain even when it is clear that the time of death will be advanced. The purpose of terminal sedation is to ease the suffering of the patient and comply with her wishes, and the actual cause of death is the administration of heavy doses of lethal sedatives. This same intent and causation may exist when a doctor complies with a patient's request for lethal medication to hasten her death.

Thus, although the differences the majority notes in causation and intent between terminating life support and assisting in suicide support the Court's rejection of the respondents' facial challenge, these distinctions may be inapplicable to particular terminally ill patients and their doctors. Our holding today in *Vacco v. Quill,* 521 U.S. 793, 117 S. Ct. 2293, 138 L.Ed. 834, that the Equal Protection Clause is not violated by New York's classification, just like our holding in *Washington v. Glucksberg* that the Washington statute is not invalid on its face, does not foreclose the possibility that some applications of the New York statute may impose an intolerable intrusion on the patient's freedom.

There remains room for vigorous debate about the outcome of particular cases that are not necessarily resolved by the opinions announced today. How such cases may be decided will depend on their specific facts. In my judgment, however, it is clear that the so-called "unqualified interest in the preservation of human life," *Cruzan,* 497 U.S. at 282, 110 S. Ct. at 2853; 521 U.S. at 728, 117 S. Ct. at 2272, is not itself sufficient to outweigh the interest in liberty that may justify the only possible means of preserving a dying patient's dignity and alleviating her intolerable suffering.

NOTES AND QUESTIONS

1. *History vs. Technology*. The Chief Justice relied heavily upon American history and tradition to decide the Constitution does not protect a right to physician-assisted suicide. Do you agree with the idea that history is the best source for understanding what due process rights the Constitution protects? Or did the Court fail to understand that advances in science and technology require the courts to adapt the law to new circumstances, as the New Jersey Supreme Court did in *Quinlan*?

Alexander Morgan Capron describes three stages of development in life-support law and policy. In stage one, in the mid-1960s, a Harvard Medical School committee published an influential definition of "brain death" that allowed some patients to be removed from life support. In the second stage, which includes *Quinlan* and *Cruzan,* policies were developed that gave patients more choice about their medical situation. Capron explains that stage three involves medical aid-in-dying, which is now legal in nine states and in other countries. Looking Back at Withdrawal of Life-Support Law and Policy to See what Lies Ahead for Medical Aid-in-Dying, Yale J. Biol. Med. 2019 Dec. 92(4): 781–91. Does the experience of stages one and two give you insight into what should happen in stage three? How do you see life-support

law evolving in the future, and what modern socio-cultural factors could play a role in this evolution?

2. Cruzan. Do you agree with the Chief Justice's interpretation of *Cruzan*? According to the Chief, "although *Cruzan* is often described as a 'right to die' case, we were, in fact, more precise: We assumed that the Constitution granted competent persons a 'constitutionally protected right to refuse lifesaving hydration and nutrition.'" Was that the holding of *Cruzan*? At the oral argument, Washington's attorney told the Court that "even if you find the existence of a liberty interest, that the same important state interests that were present in *Cruzan* are present in this case and would justify the statute nonetheless." Oral Argument, Washington v. Glucksberg, 1997 WL 13671 at *5–6. Did the Court agree?

3. *Autonomy.* What did the Court say about the bioethical principle of autonomy? Do you agree with the Chief Justice that the

> right assumed in *Cruzan*, however, was not simply deduced from abstract concepts of personal autonomy. Given the common-law rule that forced medication was a battery, and the long legal tradition protecting the decision to refuse unwanted medical treatment, our assumption was entirely consistent with this Nation's history and constitutional traditions. The decision to commit suicide with the assistance of another may be just as personal and profound as the decision to refuse unwanted medical treatment, but it has never enjoyed similar legal protection.

Does this mean that the Constitution doesn't protect personal autonomy?

At the oral argument, Solicitor General Walter Dellinger urged the Court to recognize "that a person states a cognizable liberty interest when he or she alleges that the state is imposing severe pain and suffering or has adopted a rule which prevents someone from the only means of relieving that pain and suffering." Dellinger described this as a "narrow liberty interest" and rejected the Ninth Circuit's idea that there is a "general liberty interest in dying." Oral Argument, Washington v. Glucksberg, 1997 WL 13671 at *18. Did the Court adopt the SG's definition of liberty interest?

4. *Euthanasia.* What is the difference between physician-assisted suicide (PAS) and voluntary euthanasia? Do you agree that legalizing PAS inevitably leads to voluntary euthanasia? Involuntary euthanasia? If the Court had found a constitutional right to PAS, would it have had to find a constitutional right to voluntary euthanasia? Do you agree that American history supports a right to refuse treatment but not a right to assistance in dying? Do you think there is any way *Cruzan* could have been interpreted to authorize PAS?

What lessons did you draw from the Netherlands' experience with euthanasia? What lessons did the Court draw from the experience? The AMA brief referred to a physician in the Netherlands who "assisted in the suicide of a physically healthy, 50-year-old woman who sought death in the aftermath of the death of her two sons, [and] was acquitted by a three-judge court in Assen of charges that he had violated the Dutch procedures." What legal lessons do you draw from that story?

Belgium, the Netherlands and Luxembourg have all legalized euthanasia as well as physician-assisted suicide. In the Netherlands, in 2010 there were 3,667 euthanasia deaths and 192 PAS deaths, and in 2012, 4,003 euthanasia deaths and 185 PAS death. Alex Schadenberg, Netherlands 2012 Euthanasia Report: Sharp Increase In Euthanasia Deaths, Euthanasia Prevention Coalition (Sept. 24, 2013), at http://alexschadenberg.blogspot.com/2013/09/netherlands-euthanasia-report-indicates.html. What conclusions do you draw from this evidence that euthanasia numbers are much higher than PAS numbers in countries where both are legal? In China, assisted suicide and euthanasia are illegal. Japan has no law on euthanasia, but PAS is illegal. New Zealand permitted PAS in 2020.

In 2013, Marc and Eddy Verbessem, 45-year-old deaf twins from Belgium, opted for euthanasia after they learned they were going blind and feared they would be unable to communicate with one another. Their brother Dirk told reporters that his brothers' lives "had become insufferable . . . my brothers trudged from one disease to another. They were really worn out." Marc and Eddy Verbessem, Deaf Belgian Twins, Euthanized After Starting to Turn Blind, The Huffington Post, Jan. 14, 2013, at http://www.huffingtonpost.com/2013/01/14/marc-eddy-verbessem-belgium-euthanasia_n_2472320.html. In February 2014, the Belgian Parliament approved extending its euthanasia law to include terminally ill children who experience "constant and unbearable suffering" and show a "capacity of discernment." Dan Bilefsky, Belgium Close to Allowing Euthanasia for Ill Minors, N.Y. Times, Feb. 14, 2014, at A4. Do you find the idea of euthanasia for children "morally repugnant"? Id. What about the twin brothers choosing death?

5. *Killing and Letting Die.* In rejecting the equal protection argument in *Vacco*, the Court concluded that the traditional difference between killing a patient and letting a patient die warranted treating terminally ill patients who refuse treatment differently from terminally ill patients who desire assistance in dying. In contrast, the philosophers had argued in their amicus brief that the distinction was "based on a misunderstanding of the pertinent moral principles." If a patient does not want to die, the philosophers explained, the doctor would be equally wrong to kill the patient or to let him bleed to death; the killing v. letting die distinction would be meaningless. "When a competent patient does want to die," they conclude,

> the moral situation is obviously different, because then it makes no sense to appeal to the patient's right not to be killed as a reason why an act designed to cause his death is impermissible. From the patient's point of view, there is no morally pertinent difference between a doctor's terminating treatment that keeps him alive, if that is what he wishes, and a doctor's helping him to end his own life by providing lethal pills he may take himself, when ready, if that is what he wishes—except that the latter may be quicker and more humane. Nor is that a pertinent difference from the doctor's point of view. If and when it is permissible for him to act with death in view, it does not matter which of those two means he and his patient choose. If it is permissible for a doctor deliberately to withdraw medical treatment in order to allow death to result from

> a natural process, then it is equally permissible for him to help his patient hasten his own death more actively, if that is the patient's express wish.

Brief for Ronald Dworkin et al., 11–12. What does this disagreement teach you about the differences between philosophical and legal argument? Between bioethics and constitutional law?

6. *Principle of Double Effect.* In rejecting the equal protection argument in *Vacco*, the Court acknowledged the medical practice of terminal sedation but distinguished it from PAS. What is terminal sedation? The Court's distinction was based on the principle of double effect. According to that principle, which is usually attributed to medieval theologian St. Thomas Aquinas, actions sometimes have two effects, one good and one bad. If the bad effect is foreseen, but unintended, the act may be undertaken. According to opponents of PAS, in terminal sedation, the intended goal and the good effect are to ease pain. The unintended, foreseen and bad effect is to hasten death. Therefore, terminal sedation is moral. In PAS, however, the intent is to kill, which is morally prohibited.

The Court cited a New York Task Force that concluded: "It is widely recognized that the provision of pain medication is ethically and professionally acceptable even when the treatment may hasten the patient's death, if the medication is intended to alleviate pain and severe discomfort, not to cause death." Do you agree that this is a significant moral difference that supports a legal difference between terminal sedation and PAS?

7. *Doctors' Ethics.* Would the ethics of the medical profession be completely undermined if doctors participated in physician-assisted suicide? In euthanasia? Are there any circumstances in which doctors are morally justified in hastening the end of their patients' lives? After Hurricane Katrina hit New Orleans in 2005, Memorial Medical Center lost power and doctors faced difficult choices about how to care for patients in dangerous conditions. According to one description of the hurricane,

> Four days into the ordeal, Dr. Ewing Cook, who'd previously survived two heart attacks, struggled to reach the eighth-floor intensive-care unit, where he examined a patient with advanced cancer. Convinced that she was close to death and that he couldn't possibly make it up the stairs again, he asked the nurse to raise her dosage of morphine. "There's no question I hastened her demise," he later said. Cook allegedly spoke with [surgeon Anna] Pou about injecting patients with morphine and the sedative Versed, and she wrote prescriptions for substantial amounts of morphine, which, despite the chaos, were filled by the hospital pharmacy. (Whether her intent was to relieve pain or end life remains in dispute.) Meanwhile, the pulmonologist John Thiele apparently injected several category-three patients with morphine and Versed. Knowing that he would soon evacuate, he felt he could not "justify hanging a morphine drip and praying it didn't run out after everyone left and before the patient died."

Amanda Schaffer, The Moral Dilemmas of Doctors During Disaster, The New Yorker, Sept. 12, 2013, at http://www.newyorker.com/tech/elements/the-moral-dilemmas-of-doctors-during-disaster; see generally Sheri Fink, Five Days at Memorial: Life and Death in a Storm-Ravaged Hospital (2013). How do you assess the ethics of these doctors' conduct? Was their action justified by the principle of double effect? Is what they did any different from the normal conduct of doctors described in *Vacco*? Does it matter if some of the patients who received the morphine "were apparently not on the verge of death or even in terrible pain"? Id. A special grand jury ruled that Louisiana should not indict the doctors for murder. Do you agree? See Sherwin B. Nuland, Critical Conditions, N.Y. Times, Sept. 5, 2013, at BR20 (reviewing Fink, Five Days at Memorial).

8. *Next Lawsuit.* The concurrences suggest that some as-applied challenges to assisted suicide laws may succeed. Read carefully and decide who the ideal client in an as-applied challenge to the assisted suicide laws would be. Take time to write out your complaint with the description of your client(s). Remember the lessons you learned about drafting good complaints from the complaints filed in *Glucksberg* and *Vacco.*

9. *PAS by Court Decision.* Post-*Glucksberg*, after litigation by a terminally ill patient who challenged the constitutionality of assisted suicide laws under the Montana Constitution, the Montana Supreme Court ruled, without reaching the constitutional issues, that state homicide laws allow a consent defense to PAS. Thus the state consent statute "would shield physicians from homicide liability if, with the patients' consent, the physicians provide aid in dying to terminally ill, mentally competent patients." Baxter v. State, 224 P.3d 1211 (Mont. 2009). Although consent defenses are usually against public policy "when defendants directly commit blatantly aggressive, peace-breaching acts against another party," the court ruled, no such policy reason barred the consent defense when physicians aid patients in dying. The court observed, however, that in PAS physicians are not directly involved in the patient's death, but "only provide a means by which a terminally ill patient *himself* can give effect to his life-ending decision." Why shouldn't physicians be able to directly aid patients to end their lives if the patients consent?

> In 2014, 29-year-old Brittany Maynard publicized her decision to move to Oregon to use PAS. **Go to** the website and watch the three videos that she and her family prepared. What is your reaction to the videos?

A New Mexico judge ruled that a state resident, who suffered from uterine cancer and wanted the peace of mind of having aid in dying available, was entitled to relief under the New Mexico Constitution. "This Court cannot envision a right more fundamental, more private or more integral to the liberty, safety and happiness of a New Mexican than the right of a competent, terminally ill patient to choose aid in dying," the judge wrote. Morris v. Brandenberg, No. D–202–CV 2012–02909 (N.M. 2d Jud. Dist. Jan. 13, 2014). Would your home state's constitution support similar relief?

10. *PAS by Initiative and Legislation.* As the Court notes, Oregon became the first state to legalize PAS in 1994 by ballot measure. Washington State voters passed a similar initiative in 2008. Then the Vermont legislature legalized PAS in May 2013.

Nine states—California, Colorado, Hawaii, Maine, New Jersey, New Mexico, Oregon, Vermont, and Washington—and the District of Columbia now have physician aid-in-dying legislation, often called death with dignity. What would you want to know about that legislation in order to use it or help someone else use it? Death with Dignity Acts, https://www.deathwithdignity.org/learn/death-with-dignity-acts/. What do you think of the following Oregon statistics, https://www.deathwithdignity.org/oregon-death-with-dignity-act-annual-reports/?

Go to the website and read the Oregon Doctors' Checklist. Does the checklist address all your concerns about PAS?

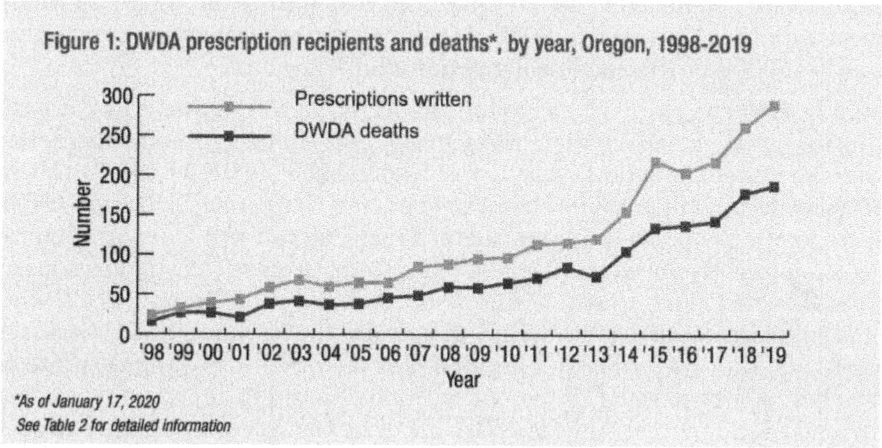

Figure 1: DWDA prescription recipients and deaths*, by year, Oregon, 1998-2019

**As of January 17, 2020*
See Table 2 for detailed information

Do these state laws go too far or not far enough? Would you legalize euthanasia along with physician-assisted suicide?

If your PAS statute applied only to terminally-ill individuals, would a non-terminally-ill patient have an equal protection and/or due process challenge to the PAS law? How would you draft that complaint?

11. *End of Life Care.* In September 2014 the Institute of Medicine (IOM), now called the National Academy of Medicine, released a comprehensive report called Dying in America: Improving Quality and Honoring Individual Preferences Near the End of Life, https://pubmed.ncbi.nlm.nih.gov/25927121/. Given what you have learned in this chapter, can IOM's recommendations address current legal concerns about death and dying? How would you implement these reforms in our current health care system? The health care system's treatment of death and dying will be examined in more detail in Chapter 4.

Practice Exercise: Draft the legislation that you think would best legalize PAS. What safeguards, if any, would you include? Would there be waiting periods? Would there be age and residency limitations? Would your law apply only to the terminally ill? How does it compare to the Oregon, Washington and Vermont laws on the website?

Rodney Knoepfle went to a Montana hospital. He had a long medical history of heart trouble, chronic pain and a number of hip and lumbar surgeries. He filled out a Do Not Resuscitate/Do Not Intubate (DNR/DNI) order when he checked into the hospital. He was given a blue armband to mark this status, and his medical records showed the DNR/DNI. Nonetheless, the hospital resuscitated him when he got into medical trouble, and he died two years later after never getting back into healthy shape. Are you surprised that a jury awarded him $209,000 in medical costs and $200,000 for mental and physical pain and suffering? Did he suffer wrongful prolongation of life? Jury Awards $400,000 in "Wrongful Prolongation of Life" Lawsuit, Physician's Weekly, Jan. 5, 2021, https://www.physiciansweekly.com/jury-awards-400000-in-wrongful-prolongation-of-life-lawsuit/.

12. *Right to Live.* This chapter has focused on terminally ill patients' right to die. What about their right to live? In Abigail Alliance for Better Access to Developmental Drugs v. von Eschenbach, 495 F.3d 695 (D.C. Cir. 2007), terminally ill patients sued the Food and Drug Administration (FDA) seeking greater access to experimental drugs. As you will learn in Chapter 2, FDA approval of new drugs is a long and slow process that requires many levels of testing. The *Abigail* plaintiffs argued that the FDA's rules allowing occasional access to experimental drugs for the terminally ill were too restrictive. They filed a lawsuit arguing that the Due Process Clause protects "the right of a terminally ill patient with no remaining approved treatment options to decide, in consultation with his or her own doctor, whether to seek access to investigational medications that the [FDA] concedes are safe and promising enough for substantial human testing." Id. at 701.

Do any of the cases in this chapter support a judgment for Abigail Alliance? Are you surprised that the D.C. Circuit ruled against the terminally ill plaintiffs? We examine *Abigail Alliance* in more detail in Chapter 2.

So far we have seen the progression of the law of death and dying from *Quinlan* to *Cruzan, Glucksberg* and post-*Glucksberg* case law and legislation. Can you predict what the *next* lawsuits will involve? Stop and identify the most pressing concerns in this area. How is today's technology different from that available in the case of Karen Quinlan? In the next section we consider a basic question fundamental to this chapter: how do we know if someone is really dead or dying?

D. LOOKING AHEAD: CAN WE BE SURE ABOUT BRAIN DEATH AND VEGETATIVE STATES?

1. BRAIN DEATH

Karen Ann Quinlan and Nancy Beth Cruzan were in vegetative states. They were not brain dead. Brain death occurs when a person irreversibly loses all functions of the brain, including brain stem reflexes such as pupillary response, absence of ocular movement, and absence of a respiratory drive. Patients suffering from brain death are unable to regulate their heartbeat or breathing without assistance. In contrast, patients in a vegetative state have brain stem activity, including basic reflexes such as blinking and some physical response to painful stimuli. Additionally, many patients in a vegetative state are able to regulate their heartbeat and breathing without assistance, although Karen Quinlan initially was not. According to the Uniform Determination of Death Act (1981), which proposed a standard later adopted by all fifty states, death is defined as "irreversible cessation of circulatory and respiratory functions" or "irreversible cessation of all functions of the entire brain, including the brain stem." Thus, all fifty states define brain death as legal death even if the heart continues to beat.

Doctors run extensive tests on patients before declaring them brain dead, including an apnea test that adds carbon dioxide to the patient's blood. A person with a functioning brain stem tries to breathe in response to the carbon dioxide. "If the patient tries to breathe, you abort the test immediately and say the patient is not brain-dead." See Benedict Carey & Denise Grady, At Issue in 2 Wrenching Cases: What to Do After the Brain Dies, N.Y. Times, Jan. 10, 2014, at A1.

New Jersey and New York order health care personnel to take account of the family's religious and moral commitments in dealing with brain death. New Jersey law, for example, provides that "[t]he death of an individual shall not be declared upon the basis of neurological criteria . . . when the licensed physician authorized to declare death, has reason to believe, on the basis of information in the individual's available medical records, or information provided by a member of the individual's family or any other person knowledgeable about the individual's personal religious beliefs that such a declaration would violate the personal religious beliefs of the individual. In these cases, death shall be declared, and the time of death fixed, solely upon the basis of cardio-respiratory criteria . . . ." N.J. Stat. § 26:6A–5 (2020); Lawrence O. Gostin, Legal and Ethical Responsibilities Following Brain Death: The McMath and Muñoz Cases, 311 JAMA 903 (2014).

Recent cases have raised two difficult questions about brain death and vegetative states. First, are there circumstances in which brain-dead patients should be kept "alive?" Second, is the category of vegetative state clear enough that medical care can be legitimately refused for people in that condition? In What is the Difference Between Coma, Minimally Conscious State, Persistent Vegetative State, and Brain Death?, Dr. James P. Kelly explains that in a coma, "[p]atients cannot be awakened, are unresponsive to stimuli such as pain, sound, or touch, and do not experience sleep-wake cycles." In a minimally conscious state, "patients are intermittently aware of their surrounding and may respond to commands." In a persistent vegetative state, "patients exhibit no signs of perception and communication or awareness of self. . .patients may be able to breathe on their own and open their eyes, experience sleep-wake cycles, grind their teeth, thrash, or make facial movements." With brain death, there is "coma; a permanent cessation of activity in the brain and brainstem,. . .; and no ability to generate a breath." Their hearts, however, may continue to beat. Brain & Life, Dec. 2017/Jan. 2018, https://www.brainandlife.org/articles/what-is-the-difference-between-coma-minimally-conscious-state-persistent/. What difference do these situations make for patient treatment?

> **Go to** the website and review the summary of IOM's recommendations.

How do you assess the fact that brain dead patients have bodies that may continue to function, as with the heartbeat, even though they are brain dead? Do you agree that "the evidence now clearly shows that brain death is not equivalent to the death of the human organism. We therefore face a choice: either we stop removing vital organs from brain dead patients, or we accept that it is not wrong to kill an innocent human who has irreversibly lost consciousness." Peter Singer, The Challenge of Brain Death for the Sanctity of Life Ethic, Ethics & Bioethics 2018, 8 (3–4), 153.

2. BRAIN DEATH AND PATIENT AUTONOMY

Late in 2013, two different scenarios raised questions about brain death and patient autonomy.

Case I. In Oakland, California, Jahi McMath, a thirteen-year-old girl, "died" after developing unexpected complications during a tonsillectomy. Although doctors declared Jahi brain dead due to lack of brain stem activity, Jahi's parents wanted to continue the ventilator and feeding tube that kept their daughter "alive." The McMaths believed Jahi was alive because her heart was beating; they hoped she would recover and sometimes described her as just "asleep."

Did hospital officials have an obligation to comply with the parents' wishes in this case? Does the case law that you read in this chapter resolve the question of what happens when patients want to continue (not discontinue) care that doctors deem futile? Do you agree with many

bioethicists who argued that doctors must not treat dead patients? As Professor Arthur Caplan explained, "You can't really feed a corpse." See Liz Szabo, Ethicists Criticize Treatment of Teen, Texas Patient, USA Today Jan. 10, 2014, at ARC.

The McMath family was able to move Jahi to an undisclosed private location in New Jersey that offered to treat her. Although her body continued to deteriorate, mechanical assistance kept her heart and lungs moving until her death in 2018 from complications associated with liver failure. The Alameda County Coroner's Office issued an official death certificate for Jahi in January 2014. Jahi's family fought to have that determination reversed and her official date of death listed as June 22, 2018. Was the New Jersey facility that Jahi was moved to in 2014 mistreating a corpse? Or is it a good idea that New Jersey law accommodated the McMaths' religious belief that Jahi was not dead? Is your answer affected by the cost of keeping Jahi alive, or who paid those costs? Does it influence your thinking that fewer transplant organs would be available if individuals were kept alive post-brain death? Do you think care for Jahi used resources that should have gone to other patients? Do you think the situation developed the way it did because there was not good communication between doctors and the patient's family? How much do you think Jahi's treatment was affected by racism? Do you agree that "It is possible to acknowledge the history of racist medical practices that underlie the mistrust that many African Americans feel toward the U.S. health care system *and* to acknowledge that McMath's family believed that race was a factor in the disrespect they felt without assigning racist intentions to the hospital personnel in McMath's case"? Yolonda Wilson, Jahi McMath, Race and Bioethics, Hastings Center, July 19, 2018, https://www.thehastingscenter.org/jahi-mcmath-race-bioethics/.

> **Go to** the website and watch the videos of Jahi McMath. Do they prove she was alive at the time they were taken?

Case II. In Texas, Marlise Muñoz passed out at her home from a blood clot and was declared brain dead at the hospital. Muñoz was fourteen weeks pregnant. Both Muñoz and her husband Erick were emergency medical technicians who had discussed their wishes about medical treatment with one another. Marlise, however, did not have an advance directive. Erick Muñoz requested that the ventilator be removed so that he could bury his wife. The hospital authorities, however, cited a Texas law (the Texas Advance Directives Act) holding that "a person may not withdraw or withhold life-sustaining treatment . . . from a pregnant patient." V.T.C.A., Health & Safety Code § 166.049.

The Texas judge ruled that Section 166.049 did not apply to Marlise Muñoz because of the definition of death in Section 671.001 of the same statute, which states: "If artificial means of support preclude a determination that a person's spontaneous respiratory and circulatory functions have ceased, the person is dead when, in the announced opinion of a physician, according to ordinary standards of medical practice, there is irreversible cessation of all spontaneous brain function. Death occurs when the relevant functions cease." Therefore, the judge ruled, the pregnancy section did not apply because Mrs. Muñoz was dead. See Judgment, Muñoz v. John Peter Smith Hospital, No. 096–270080–14, 96th Jud. Dist., Tarrant County, Texas, Jan. 24, 2014. The judge ordered Muñoz removed from the ventilator and "all other 'life-sustaining' treatment." The hospital removed the ventilator in response to the court's order.

> **Practice Exercise:** Draft a complaint for Erick Muñoz about the hospital's refusal to remove the ventilator. Keep in mind the lessons you learned about writing a good complaint from the right-to-die complaints at the beginning of this chapter. **Go to** the website, read the Muñoz affidavit, and incorporate it into your complaint.

Because the judge's ruling was based on the statute, he did not reach Muñoz's constitutional complaints that the statutory pregnancy exception violated the right to privacy and the right to equal protection. Abortion case law protects a woman's right to abort a non-viable fetus; is the pregnancy exception in the Texas statute (and similar ones in other states) unconstitutional if applied pre-viability? Should the case have turned out differently if the fetus were at twenty-eight weeks or more in development? Or did the judge misinterpret the Texas statute by not protecting all fetal life? Whose life is entitled to "life-sustaining treatment?" According to a 2019 study, 38 states identify pregnancy as a condition that affects advance directives and/or surrogate decisionmaking for incapacitated women. Erin S. DeMartino et al., US State Regulation of Decisions for Pregnant Women Without Decisional Capacity, 321 JAMA 1629 (2019).

While Muñoz's lawsuit was unfolding, a Canadian woman, Robyn Benson, who was twenty-two weeks pregnant, suffered a brain hemorrhage and was declared brain dead. Her husband, Dylan, kept her on life support for almost eight weeks after she was declared brain dead until their son, Iver, was delivered by cesarean section. Robyn died the next day after delivery. Iver went home after several months in intensive care. Ian Austen, Brain-Dead, a Canadian Woman Remains a Silent Partner Awaiting Birth, N.Y. Times, Feb. 7, 2014, at A7; Paula Newton, Brain-dead Canadian Woman Dies After Son's Birth, CNN (Feb. 12, 2014), at http://www.cnn.com/2014/02/11/health/canada-brain-dead-pregnant-woman/.

What do these controversies tell us about the concept of brain death? Do they show that the concept of brain death is inadequate and must be rejected? Do you agree with Professors Miller and Truog that "no bioethics commentary on cases involving 'brain death' is intellectually acceptable in the absence of acknowledging that there is vigorous controversy in the field over the determination of death and the status of those diagnosed as 'brain dead'?" Franklin G. Miller & Robert D. Truog, Bioethics and the Dogma of "Brain Death," Bioethics Forum Blog (Feb. 3, 2014), https://www.thehastingscenter.org/bioethics-and-the-dogma-of-brain-death/.

Criticisms of the brain death standard include its

> [i]nadequacies in the philosophical rationale for the concept that the unifying functioning of the body has been lost with loss of brain functioning, combined with a concern that biologically, there is still a sense that the body is alive, often long after brain death occurs. Wound healing can continue to occur, most organs continue to function for some period, hormonal and body-temperature regulation may be maintained. It has been reported that a child's growth can continue. And as the Munõz [and Benson] case[s] demonstrates, a pregnancy can be maintained even after the pregnant woman has met the neurologic criteria for death.

David C. Magnus et al., Perspective: Accepting Brain Death, 370(10) N. Eng. J. Med. 891 (Mar. 6, 2014). Are those weaknesses reasons to abandon brain death, or do you agree with the authors that "[g]iven the brain's importance in determining who we are and its crucial role in driving the activity of bodily organs and systems, it is not surprising that loss of cortical and brain-stem function should be equated with death?" Id. Whose opinion on the brain is the most important—that of the patient, the patient's family, or the doctors?

3. VEGETATIVE STATES AND MINIMAL CONSCIOUSNESS

Many things can happen to a patient who suffers acute brain injury. See the chart below for a list of the different paths that the brain may take, which range from death to recovery.

As the chart suggests, unlike patients in a persistent (lasting more than one month) or permanent (after three to twelve months, depending on the injury) vegetative state (PVS), patients in a minimally conscious state (MCS) have some hope of recovery. PVS patients are in a "state of 'wakeful unresponsiveness' in which the eyes are open, but there is no awareness of self or others. Patients who are vegetative do not have cognitive or higher brain functions, such as the ability to think and reason. But they do have autonomic ones, such as the direction of cardiac and respiratory function and sleep-wake cycles, which originate in the brain stem." Joseph J. Fins, Brain Injury: Neuroscience and Neuroethics,

in Hastings Center Bioethics Briefing (Sept. 21, 2015), https://www.thehastingscenter.org/briefingbook/the-vegetative-and-minimally-conscious-states/. In contrast, as the name suggests, MCS is a "state of consciousness. MCS patients demonstrate unequivocal but fluctuating evidence of awareness of self and the environment." Some patients have emerged from MCS to be able to relate and communicate with others. Id. Terry Wallis was in a nursing home for nineteen years before emerging to consciousness; Don Herbert began speaking after nine years. Both had likely been diagnosed to be in PVS when they were probably in MCS. Id.

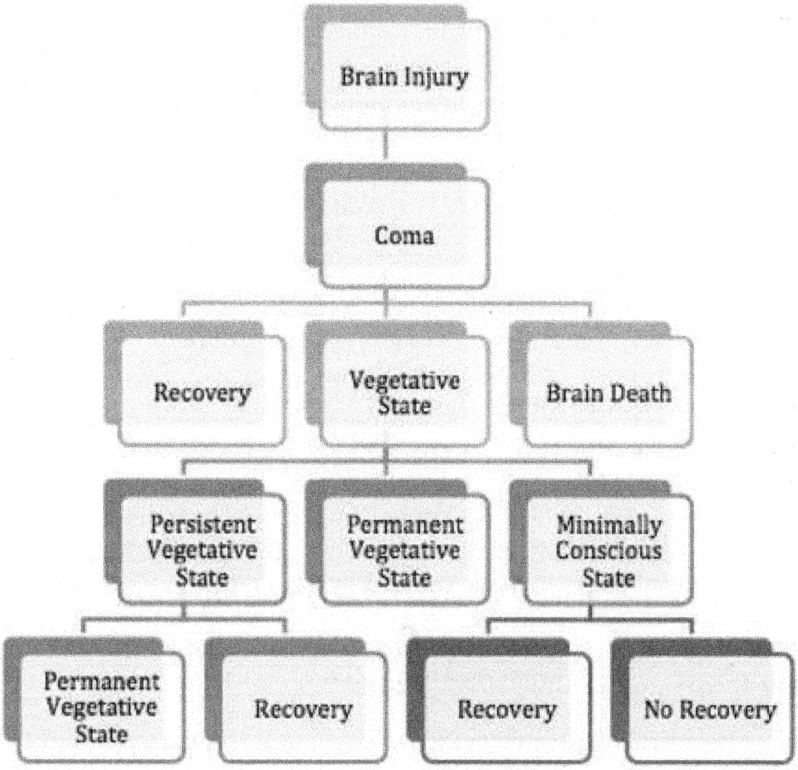

Is it possible that legal attention to the right to refuse treatment for Karen Ann Quinlan and Nancy Beth Cruzan, and the right to die for many others, has undermined an equally important "right to care?" Until recently, the only way to confirm a PVS was through an autopsy. Now new technologies like Functional Magnetic Resonance Imaging (fMRI), which we study in Chapter 7, can help us understand patients' conditions while they are alive. Should growing awareness of the MCS change the direction of bioethics law? Is the first step more careful diagnosis of the PVS and MCS to make sure that patients with any chance of recovery are treated? See Damian Cruse et al., Bedside Detection of Awareness in the Vegetative State: A Cohort Study, 378 Lancet 2088 (Dec. 17/24/31, 2011); Joseph J. Fins, Disorders of Consciousness and Disordered Care:

Families, Caregivers, and Narratives of Necessity, 2013:94 Archives of Phys. Med. & Rehab. 1934 (2013). Are there any constitutional arguments that support a right to care? Are there any constitutional arguments that support a right to live, a concept discussed in the *Abigail Alliance* case at the end of Section C?

Imagine that the Quinlan and Cruzan cases happened today and parents argued that their children should be removed from treatment because they were in persistent vegetative states. Should the parents' requests be denied because of the information we now have about minimally conscious states? Does the state have greater interest in keeping patients alive today than it did in the 1970s and 1980s because of what we know about the brain?

In Chapter 2, we examine the role of informed consent in the protection of patients and human subjects.

CHAPTER 2

INFORMED CONSENT: LEGAL PROTECTION OF PATIENTS AND HUMAN SUBJECTS

Introduction. In Chapter 1, we learned about the importance of consent to American tort and constitutional law. In *Cruzan*, Chief Justice Rehnquist described the history of consent law in the following words:

> At common law, even the touching of one person by another without consent and without legal justification was a battery. Before the turn of the century, this Court observed that "[n]o right is held more sacred, or is more carefully guarded, by the common law, than the right of every individual to the possession and control of his own person, free from all restraint or interference of others, unless by clear and unquestionable authority of law." This notion of bodily integrity has been embodied in the requirement that informed consent is generally required for medical treatment. Justice Cardozo, while on the Court of Appeals of New York, aptly described this doctrine: "Every human being of adult years and sound mind has a right to determine what shall be done with his own body; and a surgeon who performs an operation without his patient's consent commits an assault, for which he is liable in damages." *Schloendorff v. Society of New York Hospital,* 211 N.Y. 125, 129–130, 105 N.E. 92, 93 (1914). The informed consent doctrine has become firmly entrenched in American tort law.

Cruzan v. Dir., Mo. Dep't of Health, 497 U.S. 261, 267 (1990). We also learned that consent protects the bioethical principle of autonomy, the patient's right to make her own choices about medical care and treatment. *Quinlan* and *Cruzan* were landmark cases precisely because they involved incompetent patients who could not consent to treatment for themselves.

In this chapter, we learn more details about consent and the different contexts in which *informed consent* is necessary. Informed consent is a process by which patients give their permission for medical interventions, both in the treatment and research contexts. The law requires not only that patients give their consent, but also that such consent be *informed:* patients must be provided with all relevant information (such as risks and benefits) before being asked to agree. We build on our knowledge of patients and informed consent to focus on the subject of research on human subjects. Our area of legal practice shifts as well. At the beginning of the chapter, in Section A, we consider old tort

and constitutional law cases that are relevant to the subject of consent. From there we move to regulatory subjects as we consider which administrative systems and regulations best protect informed consent. Much of our focus will be on the meaning of consent in the context of research on human subjects.

Unfortunately, the history of human medicine and research includes many terrible episodes where lack of consent was linked to the victimization of vulnerable individuals. Most notorious is the history of Nazi experimentation, which we consider in Section B below. The Nazi experiments were part of a broader eugenics movement that aimed to improve or eliminate those deemed inferior, including the mentally retarded, criminals, gays and lesbians, Jews, and other vulnerable minorities. The eugenics movement was also influential in the United States, where beginning in the early twentieth century, thirty-five states passed laws allowing sterilization of prisoners and persons deemed mentally deficient. The laws reflected elite and popular opinion that criminality and mental illness were inherited traits.

The first case in this chapter, *Canterbury v. Spence*, establishes the standard for informed consent pertaining to treating patients. It is followed by *Buck v. Bell*, a case that demonstrates what occurs when there is no informed consent standard. *Buck* is a 1927 Supreme Court opinion that upheld the involuntary sterilization of Carrie Buck, a "feeble-minded" young woman. In *Buck*, Justice Oliver Wendell Holmes, one of the most respected Justices in Supreme Court history, upheld the sterilization in a brief opinion that included the offhand remark "[t]hree generations of imbeciles are enough." The "three generations" remark reflected the belief that sterilization would prevent the hereditary passage of negative physical and character traits to subsequent generations. See Paul A. Lombardo, Three Generations, No Imbeciles: Eugenics, the Supreme Court, and *Buck v. Bell* (2008). After considering *Canterbury*, *Buck*, and its legacy, Section A1 concludes with a report on recent sterilizations of women prisoners in California.

American history also includes terrible examples of exploitation of research subjects. Section A2 considers the exploitation of African American men with syphilis in Tuskegee, Alabama. It was the discovery of the Tuskegee experiments, where informed consent was never given, that led to the development of Institutional Review Boards (IRBs), which are considered in Section B. The current status of IRBs can help you decide if informed consent is better protected today than it was in 1927.

A. THE HISTORICAL RECORD

1. THE STANDARD FOR INFORMED CONSENT

Canterbury v. Spence

United States Court of Appeals, District of Colombia, 1972.
150 U.S. App. D.C. 263, 464 F.2d 772.

■ SPOTTSWOOD W. ROBINSON, III, CIRCUIT JUDGE.

I.

. . . The record we review tells a depressing tale. A youth troubled only by back pain submitted to an operation without being informed of a risk of paralysis incidental thereto. A day after the operation he fell from his hospital bed after having been left without assistance while voiding. A few hours after the fall, the lower half of his body was paralyzed, and he had to be operated on again. Despite extensive medical care, he has never been what he was before. Instead of the back pain, even years later, he hobbled about on crutches, a victim of paralysis of the bowels and urinary incontinence. In a very real sense this lawsuit is an understandable search for reasons.

At the time of the events which gave rise to this litigation, appellant was nineteen years of age, a clerk-typist employed by the Federal Bureau of Investigation. In December, 1958, he began to experience severe pain between his shoulder blades.

Dr. Spence examined appellant in his office at some length but found nothing amiss. On Dr. Spence's advice appellant was x-rayed, but the films did not identify any abnormality. Dr. Spence then recommended that appellant undergo a myelogram—a procedure in which dye is injected into the spinal column and traced to find evidence of disease or other disorder—at the Washington Hospital Center.

Appellant entered the hospital on February 4, 1959. The myelogram revealed a "filling defect" in the region of the fourth thoracic vertebra. Since a myelogram often does no more than pinpoint the location of an aberration, surgery may be necessary to discover the cause. Dr. Spence told appellant that he would have to undergo a laminectomy—the excision of the posterior arch of the vertebra—to correct what he suspected was a ruptured disc. Appellant did not raise any objection to the proposed operation nor did he probe into its exact nature.

Appellant explained to Dr. Spence that his mother was a widow of slender financial means living in Cyclone, West Virginia, and that she could be reached through a neighbor's telephone. Appellant called his mother the day after the myelogram was performed and, failing to contact her, left Dr. Spence's telephone number with the neighbor. When Mrs. Canterbury returned the call, Dr. Spence told her that the surgery was occasioned by a suspected ruptured disc. Mrs. Canterbury then

asked if the recommended operation was serious and Dr. Spence replied "not anymore than any other operation." . . .

Dr. Spence performed the laminectomy on February 11 at the Washington Hospital Center. Mrs. Canterbury traveled to Washington, arriving on that date but after the operation was over, and signed a consent form at the hospital. The laminectomy revealed several anomalies: a spinal cord that was swollen and unable to pulsate, an accumulation of large tortuous and dilated veins, and a complete absence of epidural fat which normally surrounds the spine. A thin hypodermic needle was inserted into the spinal cord to aspirate any cysts which might have been present, but no fluid emerged. In suturing the wound, Dr. Spence attempted to relieve the pressure on the spinal cord by enlarging the dura—the outer protective wall of the spinal cord—at the area of swelling.

For approximately the first day after the operation appellant recuperated normally, but then suffered a fall and an almost immediate setback. . . .

Several hours later, appellant began to complain that he could not move his legs and that he was having trouble breathing; paralysis seems to have been virtually total from the waist down. Dr. Spence was notified on the night of February 12, and he rushed to the hospital. Mrs. Canterbury signed another consent form and appellant was again taken into the operating room. The surgical wound was reopened and Dr. Spense [sic] created a gusset to allow the spinal cord greater room in which to pulsate.

Appellant's control over his muscles improved somewhat after the second operation but he was unable to void properly. As a result of this condition, he came under the care of a urologist while still in the hospital. In April, following a cystoscopic examination, appellant was operated on for removal of bladder stones, and in May was released from the hospital. He reentered the hospital the following August for a 10-day period, apparently because of his urologic problems. For several years after his discharge he was under the care of several specialists, and at all times was under the care of a urologist. At the time of the trial in April, 1968, appellant required crutches to walk, still suffered from urinal incontinence and paralysis of the bowels, and wore a penile clamp. . . .

II.

Appellant filed suit in the District Court on March 7, 1963, four years after the laminectomy and approximately two years after he attained his majority. The complaint stated several causes of action against each defendant. Against Dr. Spence it alleged, among other things, negligence in the performance of the laminectomy and failure to inform him beforehand of the risk involved. Against the hospital the complaint charged negligent post-operative care in permitting appellant to remain unattended after the laminectomy, in failing to provide a nurse or orderly

to assist him at the time of his fall, and in failing to maintain a side rail on his bed. The answers denied the allegations of negligence and defended on the ground that the suit was barred by the statute of limitations. . . .

At the close of appellant's case in chief, each defendant moved for a directed verdict and the trial judge granted both motions. . . .

The judge did not allude specifically to the alleged breach of duty by Dr. Spence to divulge the possible consequences of the laminectomy.

We reverse. The testimony of appellant and his mother that Dr. Spence did not reveal the risk of paralysis from the laminectomy made out a prima facie case of violation of the physician's duty to disclose which Dr. Spence's explanation did not negate as a matter of law. . . .

III.

Suits charging failure by a physician adequately to disclose the risks and alternatives of proposed treatment are not innovations in American law. They date back a good half-century, and in the last decade they have multiplied rapidly. There is, nonetheless, disagreement among the courts and the commentators on many major questions, and there is no precedent of our own directly in point. . . .

The root premise is the concept, fundamental in American jurisprudence, that "every human being of adult years and sound mind has a right to determine what shall be done with his own body. . . ." True consent to what happens to one's self is the informed exercise of a choice, and that entails an opportunity to evaluate knowledgeably the options available and the risks attendant upon each. The average patient has little or no understanding of the medical arts, and ordinarily has only his physician to whom he can look for enlightenment with which to reach an intelligent decision. From these almost axiomatic considerations springs the need, and in turn the requirement, of a reasonable divulgence by physician to patient to make such a decision possible. . . .

The context in which the duty of risk-disclosure arises is invariably the occasion for decision as to whether a particular treatment procedure is to be undertaken. To the physician, whose training enables a self-satisfying evaluation, the answer may seem clear, but it is the prerogative of the patient, not the physician, to determine for himself the direction in which his interests seem to lie. To enable the patient to chart his course understandably, some familiarity with the therapeutic alternatives and their hazards becomes essential. . . .

[W]e ourselves have found "in the fiducial qualities of [the physician-patient] relationship the physician's duty to reveal to the patient that which in his best interests it is important that he should know." We now find, as a part of the physician's overall obligation to the patient, a similar duty of reasonable disclosure of the choices with respect to proposed therapy and the dangers inherently and potentially involved. . . .

It is well established that the physician must seek and secure his patient's consent before commencing an operation or other course of treatment. . . . And it is evident that it is normally impossible to obtain a consent worthy of the name unless the physician first elucidates the options and the perils for the patient's edification. . . .

IV.

The majority of courts dealing with the problem have made the duty depend on whether it was the custom of physicians practicing in the community to make the particular disclosure to the patient. If so, the physician may be held liable for an unreasonable and injurious failure to divulge, but there can be no recovery unless the omission forsakes a practice prevalent in the profession. . . .

There are, in our view, formidable obstacles to acceptance of the notion that the physician's obligation to disclose is either germinated or limited by medical practice. To begin with, the reality of any discernible custom reflecting a professional consensus on communication of option and risk information to patients is open to serious doubt. . . .

Nor can we ignore the fact that to bind the disclosure obligation to medical usage is to arrogate the decision on revelation to the physician alone. Respect for the patient's right of self-determination on particular therapy demands a standard set by law for physicians rather than one which physicians may or may not impose upon themselves. . . .

We hold that the standard measuring performance of that duty by physicians, as by others, is conduct which is reasonable under the circumstances.

V.

Once the circumstances give rise to a duty on the physician's part to inform his patient, the next inquiry is the scope of the disclosure the physician is legally obliged to make. . . .

In our view, the patient's right of self-decision shapes the boundaries of the duty to reveal. That right can be effectively exercised only if the patient possesses enough information to enable an intelligent choice. The scope of the physician's communications to the patient, then, must be measured by the patient's need, and that need is the information material to the decision. Thus the test for determining whether a particular peril must be divulged is its materiality to the patient's decision: all risks potentially affecting the decision must be unmasked. . . .

[T]he physician's liability for nondisclosure is to be determined on the basis of foresight, not hindsight; no less than any other aspect of negligence, the issue on nondisclosure must be approached from the viewpoint of the reasonableness of the physician's divulgence in terms of what he knows or should know to be the patient's informational needs. If, but only if, the fact-finder can say that the physician's communication

was unreasonably inadequate is an imposition of liability legally or morally justified. . . .

The scope of the standard is not subjective as to either the physician or the patient; it remains objective with due regard for the patient's informational needs and with suitable leeway for the physician's situation. In broad outline, we agree that "[a] risk is thus material when a reasonable person, in what the physician knows or should know to be the patient's position, would be likely to attach significance to the risk or cluster of risks in deciding whether or not to forego the proposed therapy."

The topics importantly demanding a communication of information are the inherent and potential hazards of the proposed treatment, the alternatives to that treatment, if any, and the results likely if the patient remains untreated. The factors contributing significance to the dangerousness of a medical technique are, of course, the incidence of injury and the degree of the harm threatened. . . .

VII.

An unrevealed risk that should have been made known must materialize, for otherwise the omission, however unpardonable, is legally without consequence. Occurrence of the risk must be harmful to the patient, for negligence unrelated to injury is nonactionable. And, as in malpractice actions generally, there must be a causal relationship between the physician's failure to adequately divulge and damage to the patient.

A causal connection exists when, but only when, disclosure of significant risks incidental to treatment would have resulted in a decision against it. . . . The more difficult question is whether the factual issue on causality calls for an objective or a subjective determination. . . .

Better it is, we believe, to resolve the causality issue on an objective basis: in terms of what a prudent person in the patient's position would have decided if suitably informed of all perils bearing significance. If adequate disclosure could reasonably be expected to have caused that person to decline the treatment because of the revelation of the kind of risk or danger that resulted in harm, causation is shown, but otherwise not. The patient's testimony is relevant on that score of course but it would not threaten to dominate the findings. . . .

X.

This brings us to the remaining question, . . . whether appellant's evidence was of such caliber as to require a submission to the jury. . . . [T]he evidence was clearly sufficient to raise an issue as to whether Dr. Spence's obligation to disclose information on risks was reassonably [sic] met or was excused by the surrounding circumstances. Appellant testified that Dr. Spence revealed to him nothing suggesting a hazard associated with the laminectomy. His mother testified that, in response to her specific inquiry, Dr. Spence informed her that the laminectomy

was no more serious than any other operation. When, at trial, it developed from Dr. Spence's testimony that paralysis can be expected in one percent of laminectomies, it became the jury's responsibility to decide whether that peril was of sufficient magnitude to bring the disclosure duty into play. . . .

Reversed and remanded for a new trial.

NOTES AND QUESTIONS

1. *Patient Standard.* Why is it the "prerogative of the patient, not the physician, to determine for himself the direction in which his interests seem to be"? For many years tort law informed consent lawsuits were governed by the standard of how a reasonable physician would behave, and what the "custom" of physicians was. The professional standard is still the standard in about half of jurisdictions. See, e.g., Studdert et al., Geographic Variation in Informed Consent Law: Two Standards for Disclosure of Treatment Risks, 4 J. Empirical Leg. Stud. 103 (2007) (finding that twenty-five states use the physician standard, twenty-three use the patient standard, and Colorado and Georgia are not classified as either.). Why is the patient's decision about treatment favored over the knowledge of the physician in this case? What should Dr. Spence have told Canterbury in order to satisfy the demands of informed consent? Criticism of the doctrine as overly focused on physician information disclosure rather than on patient understanding has led some to advocate for a "shared decisionmaking" standard as a way to enhance informed consent. James F. Childress & Marcia Day Childress, What Does the Evolution From Informed Consent to Shared Decision Making Teach Us About Authority in Health Care?, 22 AMA J. Ethics E423 (2020).

2. *Foresight, Not Hindsight.* What does the court mean when it says that the physician's judgment must be assessed according to foresight, not hindsight? What information is available from foresight in this case? What is obvious in hindsight?

3. *Subjective or Objective.* What does the court mean when it says that the "scope of the standard is not subjective as to either the physician or the patient; it remains objective with due regard for the patient's informational needs and with suitable leeway for the physician's situation"? What is the difference between a subjective and an objective standard on these facts? Does the objective standard focus on Canterbury or on a reasonable patient? Whose interests are likely to be protected or excluded by each standard?

4. *Causal Relationship.* What does the court mean when it says "there must be a causal relationship between the physician's failure to adequately divulge an[y] damage to the patient"? How could Canterbury prove causation in this case?

5. *COVID Consent.* In the early days of the COVID-19 pandemic, many hospitals abandoned elective procedures to avoid the spread of the virus and to preserve hospital resources for an anticipated influx of COVID patients. Others continued to do some non-elective procedures, in addition to necessary emergency procedures. While the normal informed consent process requires a doctor to detail the many different outcomes, the possible

dangers associated with the procedure, and other necessary information, during the pandemic informed consent may also require disclosure of information relating to the possibility of contracting COVID-19 while in the hospital. This practice has been criticized, as there is always an inherent risk of contracting illness from surgery or other procedures while hospitalized—a risk already noted in many informed consent forms. Should the risks of pandemic diseases be addressed separately, or subsumed under current warnings regarding hospital-acquired infections? For a sample COVID informed consent form relating to plastic surgery, see https://www.plasticsurgery.org/documents/medical-professionals/COVID19-Informed-Consent.pdf.

6. *Elements of Informed Consent.* According to Professor Meisel, *Canterbury* identifies the "mainstay of informed consent: the source of a doctor's duty to provide information to a patient; the standard by which the adequacy of disclosure is to be measured; the requisite causal nexus between inadequate disclosure and the patient's injury; the type of injury that will support recovery; the physician's privilege to withhold information; the role of expert testimony in establishing the inadequacy of disclosure and causation; and the nature of the cause of action for inadequate disclosure, necessary to establish the appropriate statute of limitations and evidentiary rules. . . ." Alan Meisel, Canterbury v. Spence: The Inadvertent Landmark Case in Health Law & Bioethics: Cases in Context (S.H. Johnson et al. eds. 2009). Do you understand what all these elements entail? Consider how much you understand of how the case worked in practice before you read the following excerpt from Professor Meisel.

Canterbury v. Spence: The Inadvertent Landmark Case

Alan Meisel, 2009.
Health Law & Bioethics: Cases in Context, 9, 17–18, 21–22.

Theory of the Case

Canterbury's case was fraught with problems from the outset. The fundamental problem was the issue of what caused Canterbury's paralysis. Was it the very condition for which he sought treatment from Dr. Spence—the pain between his shoulder blades? Was it something that happened during the first surgery, the laminectomy, which was intended to treat this pain? Was it the fall from bed, and if so, was that because the doctors' orders were unclear, inadequate, or conflicting, or because the nurses (who were employees of the hospital, not of the doctors) did not carry them out correctly? Was it instead the second surgery immediately after the fall? Or was it some combination of these?

Closely related to the causation problem was the issue of negligence. Even if the cause of the paralysis was something one of the defendants did, the law said that neither Dr. Spence nor the hospital could be held liable unless what they did was negligent. To establish this, Davis (Canterbury's lawyer) had to show that their conduct failed to meet the

standard of care—what a reasonable physician of similar training, education, and experience would have done under the circumstances. To complicate matters even more, in most American jurisdictions at that time (D.C. among them), the locality rule required the plaintiff to establish what a reasonable physician in that locality would do, and that required the testimony of an expert witness—another physician from that locality. Unlike today, when it is a relatively simple matter to hire a professional expert witness, in the 1960s and 1970s the "conspiracy of silence" still reigned in many jurisdictions. Getting a doctor to testify against a peer—especially a doctor from the same locality, and perhaps the same hospital staff, same neighborhood, same church, or same country club—was nigh unto impossible.

Because of these difficulties, Davis also advanced legal theories focusing on Canterbury's lack of consent to treatment. One theory was fairly straightforward: Canterbury was, by the law of that time, a minor because he was under the age of 21. Consequently, his consent was not legally valid, and parental consent was necessary. It is clear Dr. Spence did not obtain consent from Canterbury's mother before the surgery. But even if legally valid consent to the laminectomy had not been obtained, the one-year statute of limitations on a battery cause of action—the theory that would have had to be pursued for lack of consent—had run by the time the complaint was filed.

However, because the statute of limitations had not yet run on a negligence cause of action, in addition to filing claims for garden variety negligence Davis gambled that he could also bring an action for lack of informed consent, couched in the language of negligence—which, while well-accepted today, was somewhat unusual at that time. . . .

What Was He Told and When Was He Told It?

Informed consent is a classic "he said, she said" issue. After the fact the patient invariably will say, "the doctor didn't tell me what could go wrong, and if he had, I never would have agreed to that." In contrast, the doctor invariably will say, "I told him that could go wrong, and he said he'd take his chances." As time has gone by and doctors and their lawyers have realized the legal risks of inadequate disclosure, they have devised written forms (the so-called "informed consent forms" widely used today) ostensibly to document that the patient was told exactly what those risks would entail. Some doctors have been surprised to learn that a signed consent form only establishes that the patient signed the form, but not that he really was provided with material information (or that he understood it—which is yet another complexity of the law and practice of informed consent). . . .

The Opinion

There must have been something in the air in 1972, for that was the year that informed consent came into its own—not just in the *Canterbury* decision, but in major opinions from the California and Rhode Island

Supreme Courts as well. For whatever reason, Judge Robinson seized on the issue and devoted all but five paragraphs of his 21-page opinion to the discussion of informed consent. In the end, the Court of Appeals recognized a cause of action for inadequate disclosure and held that it sounded in negligence, not battery, and therefore was not barred by the statute of limitations.

The core holding of *Canterbury* is that the fiduciary nature of the doctor-patient relationship imposes an affirmative obligation on physicians to disclose information about proposed treatment to patients. The scope of the information that must be disclosed is that which a reasonable person—not the patient in question—would find material to making a decision whether to undergo or forgo the proposed treatment, including information about the risks of treatment, the benefits of treatment, and alternative treatments. The scope of disclosure is most definitely not governed by the professional custom of physicians, for to do so would be completely inconsistent with the ethical underpinnings of informed consent—the patient's right to determine for himself his own medical interests (and, it might be added, because evidence of such a professional custom is completely lacking). The failure to fulfill this obligation constitutes professional negligence and—if it would lead a reasonable person in the patient's situation to undergo treatment and if that treatment causes physical harm to the patient—is the basis for an award of damages to the patient to compensate for his injuries. . . .

Now that you know the standard for informed consent, consider how that standard would have made a difference in the following case.

2. STERILIZATION

Buck v. Bell

Supreme Court of Appeals of Virginia, 1925.
143 Va. 310, 130 S.E. 516.

■ WEST, J., delivered the opinion of the Court.

Carrie Buck, by R. G. Shelton, her guardian and next friend, complains of a judgment of the Circuit Court of Amherst county by which Dr. J. H. Bell, Superintendent of the State Colony for Epileptics and Feeble-Minded, was ordered to perform on her the operation of salpingectomy, for the purpose of rendering her sexually sterile. See part of the Virginia sterilization act copied in the margin.[1]

---

[1] The Virginia sterilization act (Acts 1924, chap. 394, p. 569) reads, in part, as follows: 'Whereas, both the health of the individual patient and the welfare of society may be promoted in certain cases by the sterilization of mental defectives under careful safeguard and by competent and conscientious authority; and

After requiring the service of a copy of the petition and notice of the time and place when the special board of directors will hear and act on the petition upon the inmate and her guardian, and, if the inmate be an infant, upon the living parents, and giving the inmate the right to be represented by counsel, the act further provides:

> 'The said special board may deny the prayer of the said petition, or if the said special board shall find that the said inmate is insane, idiotic, imbecile, feeble-minded, or epileptic, and by the laws of heredity is the probable potential parent of socially inadequate offspring likewise afflicted, that the said inmate may be sexually sterilized without detriment to his or her general health, and that the welfare of the inmate and of society will be promoted by such sterilization, the said special board may order the said superintendent to perform or to have performed by some competent physician to be named in such order upon the said inmate, after not less than thirty days from the date of such order, the operation of vasectomy if a male or of salpingectomy if a female; provided that nothing in this act shall be construed to authorize the operation of castration nor the removal of sound organs from the body.'

The statute then provides that the special board, the superintendent, the inmate or his committee, guardian or next friend, may appeal from the order of the board to the circuit court, and that any

---

'Whereas, such sterilization may be effected in males by the operation of vasectomy and in females by the operation of salpingectomy, both of which said operations may be performed without serious pain or substantial danger to the life of the patient; and

'Whereas, the Commonwealth has in custodial care and in supporting in various State institutions many defective persons who if now discharged or paroled would likely become by the propagation of their kind a menace to society, but who if incapable of procreating might properly and safely be discharged or paroled and become self-supporting with benefit both to themselves and to society; and

'Whereas, human experience has demonstrated that heredity plays an important part in the transmission of insanity, idiocy, imbecility, epilepsy and crime; now, therefore,

'1. Be it enacted by the General Assembly of Virginia, That whenever the Superintendent of the Western State Hospital, or of the Eastern State Hospital, or of the Southwestern State Hospital, or of the Central State Hospital, or of the State Colony for Epileptics and Feeble-Minded, shall be of opinion that it is for the best interests of the patients and of society that any inmate of the institution under his care should be sexually sterilized, such superintendent is hereby authorized to perform, or cause to be performed by some capable physician or surgeon, the operation of sterilization on any such patient confined in such institution afflicted with hereditary forms of insanity that are recurrent, idiocy, imbecility, feeble-mindedness or epilepsy; provided that such superintendent shall have first complied with the requirements of this act.

'2. Such superintendent shall first present to the special board of directors of his hospital or colony a petition stating the facts of the case and the grounds of his opinion, verified by his affidavit to the best of his knowledge and belief, and praying that an order may be entered by said board requiring him to perform or have performed by some competent physician to be designated by him in his said petition or by said board in its order, upon the inmate of his institution named in such petition, the operation of vasectomy if upon a male and of salpingectomy if upon a female.'

party to such appeal in the circuit court may apply to the Supreme Court of Appeals for an appeal from the final order therein.

On the 23rd day of January, 1924, Carrie Buck was adjudged to be feeble-minded within the meaning of the Virginia statute, and committed to the State Colony for Epileptics and Feeble-Minded. On September 10, 1924, A. S. Priddy, then Superintendent of the Colony, presented to the special board of directors his petition praying for an order that Carrie Buck be sexually sterilized by the surgical operation known as salpingectomy. The hearing was conducted strictly in accordance with the provisions of the statute, and, upon the evidence introduced before them, the board entered the order prayed for. From this order an appeal was taken by Carrie Buck and R. G. Shelton, her guardian and next friend, to the Circuit Court of Amherst county. Upon the record and evidence introduced at the trial in the circuit court, the judgment complained of was entered, from which this appeal was allowed.

These facts, among others, appear from the evidence:

The operation of salpingectomy is the cutting of the fallopian tubes between the ovaries and the womb, and the tying of the ends next to the womb. The ovaries are left intact and continue to function. The operation of vasectomy consists of the cutting down of a small tube which runs from the testicle, without interference with the testicle. These operations do not impair the general health, or affect the mental or moral status of the patient, or interfere with his, or her, sexual desires or enjoyment. They simply prevent reproduction. In the hands of a skilled surgeon, they are 100 per cent successful in results.

At the time Carrie Buck was committed to the State Colony for Epileptics and Feeble-Minded, she was seventeen years old and the mother of an illegitimate child of defective mentality. She had the mind of a child nine years old, and her mother had theretofore been committed to the same Colony as a feeble-minded person. Carrie Buck, by the laws of heredity, is the probable potential parent of socially inadequate offspring, likewise affected as she is. Unless sterilized by surgical operation, she must be kept in the custodial care of the Colony for thirty years, until she is sterilized by nature, during which time she will be a charge upon the State. If sterilized under the law, she could be given her liberty and secure a good home, under supervision, without injury to society. Her welfare and that of society would be promoted by such sterilization.

The appellant contends that the judgment is void because the Virginia sterilization act is repugnant to the provisions of the State and Federal Constitution (Const. Va., Art. 1, secs. 9, 11; Const. U.S. Amends. 8, 14) in that—

(a) It does not provide due process of law;

(b) It imposes a cruel and unusual punishment; and

(c) It denies the appellant and other inmates of the State Colony the equal protection of the law.

1. An adjudication by an impartial tribunal vested with lawful jurisdiction to hear and determine the questions involved, after reasonable notice to the parties interested and an opportunity for them to be heard, fulfills all the requirements of due process of law. . . .

There is no controversy as to the legality or regularity of the proceedings by which appellant was adjudged to be feeble-minded and committed to the State Colony.

The statute under review clearly vests the special board of directors of the State Colony for Epileptics and Feeble-Minded, after notice according to law, with jurisdiction to hear and determine the prayer of any petition filed by the Superintendent of the Colony for the sexual sterilization of an inmate thereof.

In the instant case, the proceeding was strictly in conformity with the statute. The Superintendent of the Colony, having first served a copy of the petition and a notice of the time and place it would be presented on the inmate, her guardian and her mother, her father being dead, presented to the special board of directors of the Colony his petition, stating the facts of the case and the grounds of his opinion, verified by his affidavit and praying that an order be entered by the board requiring him, or some other competent physician, to perform upon Carrie Buck the operation of salpingectomy. Upon a later day, fixed by the board, the board proceeded in the presence of the inmate, her guardian and her attorney, to hear and consider the petition and evidence offered in support of and against the petition, and entered its final order, from which the inmate appealed to the circuit court and subsequently to this court.

The act complies with the requirements of due process of law.

2. The contention that the statute imposes cruel and unusual punishment cannot be sustained.

The act is not a penal statute. The purpose of the legislature was not to punish but to protect the class of socially inadequate citizens named therein from themselves, and to promote the welfare of society by mitigating race degeneracy and raising the average standard of intelligence of the people of the State.

The evidence shows that the operation, practically speaking, is harmless and 100 per cent safe, and in most cases relieves the patient from further confinement in the Colony. . . .

3. Does the statute deny to appellant and other inmates of the State Colony the equal protection of the law? This question must be answered in the negative.

It is not controverted that the State may, in proper cases, by due process of law, take into custody and deprive the insane, the feeble-

minded and other defective citizens of the liberty which is otherwise guaranteed them by the Constitution.

The right to enact such laws rests in the police power, which the States did not surrender when they entered the Federal Union, and the exercise of that power the Virginia Constitution provides shall never be abridged.

Where the police power conflicts with the Constitution, the latter is supreme, but the courts will not restrain the exercise of such power, except where the conflict is clear and plain.

. . . Disregarding other classes of mental defectives, upon whom the statute operates, the purpose of the act is to promote the welfare and prevent procreation by those who have been, or may hereafter be, judicially ascertained to be feeble-minded and are inmates of the State Colony for Epileptics and Feeble-Minded. The status of a feeble-minded person, who comes under the operation of the sterilization act, is not fixed until such patient, after judicial commitment to the Colony, shall have undergone expert observation for at least two months and been subjected to the Binet Simon measuring scale of intelligence, or some other approved test of mentality, and found to be feeble-minded. Code 1919, sec. 1083.

Code, section 1078, designates those who have not been adjudged to be feeble-minded as persons 'supposed to be feeble-minded.' The sterilization act has no reference to the latter class except in so far as they may be legally ascertained to belong to the former and are committed to the Colony. It cannot be said, as contended, that the act divides a natural class of persons into two and arbitrarily provides different rules for the government of each. The two classes existed before the passage of the sterilization act. The female inmate, unlike the woman on the outside, was already deprived of the power of procreation by segregation, and must remain so confined until sterilized by nature, unless it is ascertained that her welfare and the welfare of society will be promoted by her sterilization under the act. There can be no discrimination against the inmates of the Colony, since the woman on the outside, if in fact feeble-minded, can, by the process of commitment and afterwards a sterilization hearing, be sterilized under the act.

Appellants rely upon *Smith v. Board of Examiners of Feeble-Minded, Epileptics, etc.*, 85 N.J. Law, 46, 88 Atl. 963. The New Jersey act provided for the sterilization of epileptics who were 'inmates confined in the several charitable institutions in the counties and State.' The court held the act unconstitutional because the statute arbitrarily created two classes and applied the statutory remedy to that one of the classes to which it had the least application, and therefore denied Smith, who was an inmate of a charitable institution, the equal protection of the laws. The right to sterilize did not, as in Virginia, depend upon whether the welfare of the patient would be promoted by the operation. For the

reasons given in discussing the Virginia act, we decline to follow the New Jersey case.

The Indiana act was held invalid in *Williams v. Smith*, 190 Ind. 526, 131 N.E. 2, because it denied the appellee due process of law.

We have found no case involving similar statutes where the court has held that the State is without power to enact such laws, provided it be exercised through a statute which affords due process of law and equal protection of the laws to those affected by it.

For the foregoing reasons, we are of the opinion that the Virginia sterilization act is based upon a reasonable classification and is a valid enactment under the State and Federal Constitutions.

Affirmed.

NOTES AND QUESTIONS

1. *State Sterilization Laws.* Indiana was the first state to pass a eugenic sterilization law in 1907. Washington and California followed in 1909. Sterilization laws were perceived to correct two problems. First, they were seen as a cure for irregular sexual activities such as masturbation or prostitution. Second, because of the belief that criminality and immorality were hereditary, sterilization was thought to put an end to the birth of "defective" human beings. See Alexandra Minna Stern, From Legislation to Lived Experience: Eugenic Sterilization in California and Indiana, 1907–1979," 95–116, A Century of Eugenics in America: From the Indiana Experiment to the Human Genome Era (Paul A. Lombardo ed., 2011); Lombardo, Three Generations, No Imbeciles, *supra*.

The Indiana law authorized a committee composed of a physician, two board members, and two surgeons to decide whether any "criminals, idiots, rapists and imbeciles" held in state institutions should be sterilized because "procreation is inadvisable and there is no probability of improvement of the mental condition of the inmate." In Williams v. Smith, 131 N.E. 2 (Ind. 1921), which is cited in the Virginia case, the Indiana Supreme Court ruled that the statute denied Warren Wallace Smith due process of law; "the prisoner has no opportunity to cross-examine the experts who decide that this operation should be performed upon him. He has no chance to bring experts to show that it should not be performed; nor has he a chance to controvert the scientific question that he is of a class designated in the statute." Id.

Did Virginia learn a lesson from Indiana and, therefore, draft a law that satisfied due process by including hearings and appeals? Is there anything in the Virginia statute that makes you think it violated due process? Can you make the argument that the statute violated substantive due process but not procedural due process? What is the difference between substantive and procedural due process?

2. *State Arguments.* State authorities argued that, in contrast to New Jersey, Virginia's law protected liberty because it allowed Buck and others, once sterilized, to return to the community instead of remaining in colonies

for the feebleminded. Do you agree? Is there any way in which the sterilization laws protected or promoted Buck's well-being?

3. *Test Case.* Pro-eugenics reformers carefully drafted the Virginia law to ensure the law's survival and then engineered a test case to assure the law's constitutionality. Once they realized that Carrie Buck, an unmarried seventeen-year-old, had given birth to Vivian Buck immediately before being institutionalized at the Virginia Colony for Epileptics and Feeble-minded, where her mother, Emma, was already in residence, they had found their ideal plaintiff. The three generations could be used to illustrate the heredity of imbecility, feeblemindedness or other disorders. Lombardo, Three Generations, No Imbeciles, *supra*.

The pro-eugenics advocates chose attorney Irving Whitehead to represent Buck. Whitehead was an advocate of sterilization who had served on the Colony's board and was a childhood friend of Dr. Priddy, the head of the colony. Id. at 106. At trial, Whitehead did little to cross-examine the state's witnesses and rested his case without calling any witnesses on Buck's behalf. The state's expert witnesses testified that all three generations of Bucks—including six-month-old Vivian—demonstrated abnormal and feebleminded development. Later school records indicated that Vivian, who died at age nine, was an honor student. How does this information affect your assessment of the Virginia Supreme Court's opinion?

4. *Due Process.* Is there any way to protect due process in the context of sterilization? Do you agree with how the United States Supreme Court decided the case, as reprinted below?

Buck v. Bell

Supreme Court of the United States, 1927.
274 U.S. 200, 47 S.Ct. 584.

■ MR. JUSTICE HOLMES delivered the opinion of the Court. MR. JUSTICE BUTLER dissenting.

This is a writ of error to review a judgment of the Supreme Court of Appeals of the State of Virginia, affirming a judgment of the Circuit Court of Amherst County, by which the defendant in error, the superintendent of the State Colony for Epileptics and Feeble Minded, was ordered to perform the operation of salpingectomy upon Carrie Buck, the plaintiff in error, for the purpose of making her sterile. The case comes here upon the contention that the statute authorizing the judgment is void under the Fourteenth Amendment as denying to the plaintiff in error due process of law and the equal protection of the laws.

Carrie Buck is a feeble-minded white woman who was committed to the State Colony above mentioned in due form. She is the daughter of a feeble-minded mother in the same institution, and the mother of an illegitimate feeble-minded child. She was eighteen years old at the time of the trial of her case in the Circuit Court in the latter part of 1924. An Act of Virginia approved March 20, 1924 (Laws 1924, c. 394) recites that the health of the patient and the welfare of society may be promoted in

certain cases by the sterilization of mental defectives, under careful safeguard, etc.; that the sterilization may be effected in males by vasectomy and in females by salpingectomy, without serious pain or substantial danger to life; that the Commonwealth is supporting in various institutions many defective persons who if now discharged would become a menace but if incapable of procreating might be discharged with safety and become self-supporting with benefit to themselves and to society; and that experience has shown that heredity plays an important part in the transmission of insanity, imbecility, etc. The statute then enacts that whenever the superintendent of certain institutions including the above named State Colony shall be of opinion that it is for the best interest of the patients and of society that an inmate under his care should be sexually sterilized, he may have the operation performed upon any patient afflicted with hereditary forms of insanity, imbecility, etc., on complying with the very careful provisions by which the act protects the patients from possible abuse.

The superintendent first presents a petition to the special board of directors of his hospital or colony, stating the facts and the grounds for his opinion, verified by affidavit. Notice of the petition and of the time and place of the hearing in the institution is to be served upon the inmate, and also upon his guardian, and if there is no guardian the superintendent is to apply to the Circuit Court of the County to appoint one. If the inmate is a minor notice also is to be given to his parents, if any, with a copy of the petition. The board is to see to it that the inmate may attend the hearings if desired by him or his guardian. The evidence is all to be reduced to writing, and after the board has made its order for or against the operation, the superintendent, or the inmate, or his guardian, may appeal to the Circuit Court of the County. The Circuit Court may consider the record of the board and the evidence before it and such other admissible evidence as may be offered, and may affirm, revise, or reverse the order of the board and enter such order as it deems just. Finally any party may apply to the Supreme Court of Appeals, which, if it grants the appeal, is to hear the case upon the record of the trial in the Circuit Court and may enter such order as it thinks the Circuit Court should have entered. There can be no doubt that so far as procedure is concerned the rights of the patient are most carefully considered, and as every step in this case was taken in scrupulous compliance with the statute and after months of observation, there is no doubt that in that respect the plaintiff in error has had due process at law.

The attack is not upon the procedure but upon the substantive law. It seems to be contended that in no circumstances could such an order be justified. It certainly is contended that the order cannot be justified upon the existing grounds. The judgment finds the facts that have been recited and that Carrie Buck 'is the probable potential parent of socially inadequate offspring, likewise afflicted, that she may be sexually sterilized without detriment to her general health and that her welfare

and that of society will be promoted by her sterilization,' and thereupon makes the order. In view of the general declarations of the Legislature and the specific findings of the Court obviously we cannot say as matter of law that the grounds do not exist, and if they exist they justify the result. We have seen more than once that the public welfare may call upon the best citizens for their lives. It would be strange if it could not call upon those who already sap the strength of the State for these lesser sacrifices, often not felt to be such by those concerned, in order to prevent our being swamped with incompetence. It is better for all the world, if instead of waiting to execute degenerate offspring for crime, or to let them starve for their imbecility, society can prevent those who are manifestly unfit from continuing their kind. The principle that sustains compulsory vaccination is broad enough to cover cutting the Fallopian tubes. Jacobson v. Massachusetts, 197 U.S. 11. Three generations of imbeciles are enough.

But, it is said, however it might be if this reasoning were applied generally, it fails when it is confined to the small number who are in the institutions named and is not applied to the multitudes outside. It is the usual last resort of constitutional arguments to point out shortcomings of this sort. But the answer is that the law does all that is needed when it does all that it can, indicates a policy, applies it to all within the lines, and seeks to bring within the lines all similarly situated so far and so fast as its means allow. Of course so far as the operations enable those who otherwise must be kept confined to be returned to the world, and thus open the asylum to others, the equality aimed at will be more nearly reached.

Judgment affirmed.

■ MR. JUSTICE BUTLER dissents.

NOTES AND QUESTIONS

1. *Holmes' Opinion.* Do you agree with Justice Holmes? If so, why? If not, what do you find objectionable about his argument?

2. *Jacobson.* Justice Holmes cited another Court case, *Jacobson v. Massachusetts*, which upheld mandatory smallpox vaccination. Do you agree that the "principle that sustains compulsory vaccination is broad enough to cover cutting the Fallopian tubes?" Does *Buck* follow from *Jacobson*? In a COVID case ruling in favor of a religious groups' challenge to COVID-related restrictions on their worship, Justice Gorsuch asked how the Court had "mistaken this Court's modest decision in *Jacobson* for a towering authority that overshadows the Constitution during a pandemic." Roman Catholic Diocese of Brooklyn v. Cuomo, ___ U.S. ___, 141 S.Ct. 63, 71 (2020). What does that

> **Practice Exercise:** Go back through the excerpted opinion and highlight any sentences or phrases that you find objectionable. Then, explain why you disagree with them.

statement tell you about the connection between the state's public health powers and religious freedom?

3. *Recusal.* Chief Justice William Howard Taft was a supporter of the eugenics movement. He offered his name to eugenics organizations and provided an introduction and endorsement to a prominent pro-eugenics book. See Lombardo, Three Generations, No Imbeciles, *supra.* Justice Holmes had also been an advocate of eugenics. Should the Justices have been recused from this case? Did they let their pro-eugenics views blind them to the situation of Carrie Buck?

> **Go to** the website and watch the YouTube video as an example of how eugenics impacted legislation. (*Buck v. Bell* is mentioned at 4:30–6:04.)

Why do you think Justice Butler dissented from the opinion? Is it possible that the Roman Catholic Justice opposed sterilization because his church taught it was always immoral? If so, would that mean that the Justice was improperly influenced by his religious beliefs? See id. at 172 (evidence is inconclusive whether Butler dissented for religious reasons).

4. *Bioethics.* How does the study of bioethics relate to eugenics? Do you think issues raised by eugenics may have led to bioethics?

5. *Rape.* Buck reported that she became pregnant with Vivian after Clarence Garland, a nephew of her foster parents, raped her. How does this fact affect your assessment of the case? Id. Given the Supreme Court's reasoning, would the case have come out differently if Buck's rape had been submitted into the evidence at trial?

6. *Reproductive Freedom Exercise.* Draft an alternative opinion that acknowledges that reproductive freedom is a fundamental right. Would the case have turned out differently with such a right in place, or would the state have been able to prove that it had compelling reasons to sterilize Carrie Buck?

7. *Skinner*. In Skinner v. Oklahoma, 316 U.S. 535 (1942), the Court ruled that Oklahoma's Habitual Criminal Sterilization Act, which allowed criminals convicted two or more times for felonies involving moral turpitude to be sterilized, violated the Equal Protection Clause. The Court based its ruling upon the fact that the law allowed sterilization for felonies involving larceny, but not embezzlement. Because those two offenses were basically of the "same quality," it violated equal protection for the state to sterilize for one crime but not the other.

Buck v. Bell was not overruled even though the Court ruled that strict scrutiny applied in cases involving a fundamental right of procreation. Did the government have a compelling interest in sterilizing Carrie Buck? Can you distinguish *Skinner* from *Buck*? Justice Douglas' opinion for the Court, as well as concurrences by Chief Justice Stone and Justice Jackson, all distinguished *Buck v. Bell* from *Skinner* and found it unnecessary to overrule the sterilization precedent.

Acknowledging Justice Holmes' comment that it "is the usual last resort of constitutional arguments to point out shortcomings of this [equal protection] sort," Justice Douglas wrote that in *Skinner*, the "embezzlers are forever free," while the larcenists were imprisoned. In contrast, in *Buck* "the operations enable those who otherwise must be kept confined to be returned to the world, and thus open the asylum to others, the equality aimed at will be more nearly reached." Therefore, there was an equal protection violation in *Skinner* but not *Buck*. Does that argument make sense to you?

Chief Justice Stone distinguished the two cases on the grounds that while Skinner "was given a hearing to ascertain whether sterilization would be detrimental to his health, he was given none to discover whether his criminal tendencies are of an inheritable type. Undoubtedly a state may, after appropriate inquiry, constitutionally interfere with the personal liberty of the individual to prevent the transmission by inheritance of his socially injurious tendencies. Buck v. Bell, 274 U.S. 200." Are you surprised that, even by 1942, Supreme Court Justices accepted that courts could hold hearings about inheritable criminal tendencies? Skinner v. State of Okl. ex rel. Williamson, 316 U.S. 535, 544 (1942).

Justice Robert Jackson, who on May 2, 1945, became chief prosecutor for the United States at the Nuremberg trials of Nazi war criminals, wrote the following comparison of the two cases:

> I also think the present plan to sterilize the individual in pursuit of a eugenic plan to eliminate from the race characteristics that are only vaguely identified and which in our present state of knowledge are uncertain as to transmissibility presents other constitutional questions of gravity. This Court has sustained such an experiment with respect to an imbecile, a person with definite and observable characteristics where the condition had persisted through three generations and afforded grounds for the belief that it was transmissible and would continue to manifest itself in generations to come. *Buck v. Bell*, 274 U.S. 200.

Skinner v. State of Okl. ex rel. Williamson, 316 U.S. 535, 546 (1942) What do you think of Justice Jackson's analysis?

8. *Modern Medicine*. Do you think advances in modern medicine could lead to a new eugenics movement? If so, what would that movement look like? How do you think bioethics and the law could deal with it? Some commentators see a link between discussions of population control, eugenics, and reproductive justice. Caitlin Fendley, Eugenics is Trending. That's a Problem, Wash. Post, Feb. 17, 2020, www.washingtonpost.com/outlook/2020/02/17/eugenics-is-trending-thats-problem/. Scotland has already considered this issue. See Calum Mackellar, Eugenic Policies of the Past Teach Sobering Lessons, Scotsman Aug. 24, 2014, at http://www.scotsman.com/news/eugenic-policies-of-the-past-teach-sobering-lessons–1–3486562 (suggesting that developments in genetics will lead to new eugenics concerns). What do you think of Justice Clarence Thomas's argument that the "use of abortion to achieve eugenic goals is not merely hypothetical." Box v. Planned

Parenthood of Indiana & Kentucky, Inc., ___ U.S. ___, ___, 139 S.Ct. 1780, 1783 (2019). How can abortion be used eugenically?

9. *California's Sterilization Laws*. In 1909, California became the third state to pass a sterilization law. California's law applied broadly to the feebleminded, inmates, patients, and eventually to those "afflicted with mental disease which may have been inherited and is likely to be transmitted to descendants, the various degrees of feeblemindedness, those suffering from perversion or marked departures from normal mentality or from disease of a syphilitic nature." How was California's law different from the Virginia law?

According to Professor Stern, California's sterilization law was unique in 1) not providing any legal mechanisms or hearings to protect patients, 2) requiring no notification to a guardian and 3) never facing *any* serious legal challenge such as occurred in Indiana and Virginia. Therefore, for seventy years, California led the country in sterilizations—"more than 20,000 surgeries, or one-third of all those nationwide." (Virginia was second with 8,000.) See Alexandra Minna Stern, "From Legislation to Lived Experience: Eugenic Sterilization in California and Indiana, 1907–1979," 99–101, A Century of Eugenics in America: From the Indiana Experiment to the Human Genome Era (Paul A. Lombardo ed., 2011).

Stern also noted "the disproportionate number of operations carried out on those with Spanish surnames." Id. at 109. Does this history explain the recent experience of California prisoners described below?

10. *Sterilization Rates*. Rates of sterilization declined across the states during the 1950s. Why do you think that happened? See Stern, *supra* (new attitudes toward mental health and mental retardation and the growth of mental health agencies reversed the sterilization trend). Yet Indiana's law was not officially repealed until 1974 and California's until 1979.

11. *Compensation*. Should individuals who were sterilized by the states receive compensation for their injuries? See Katherine A. West, Following in North Carolina's Footsteps: California's Challenge in Compensating Its Victims of Compulsory Sterilization, 53 Santa Clara L. Rev. 301, 302 (2013) (recommending that California follow North Carolina's suggestion of offering $50,000 per person and estimating there are from 225 to 497 living survivors of the state's policy).

Does the next reading suggest that California officials still do not understand the dangers of eugenics and sterilization?

Sterilization of Female Inmates

California State Auditor, 2014.
Report 2013–120.

Summary

Results in Brief

The California Department of Corrections and Rehabilitation (Corrections) oversees the inmate population of the State's 33 adult

prisons. During our eight-year audit period—which we defined as fiscal years 2005–06 through 2012–13—four of these prisons housed substantially all of the female inmates: California Institution for Women, Central California Women's Facility, Folsom Women's Facility, and Valley State Prison for Women (Valley). Valley no longer houses women since its conversion to a men's prison in January 2013. For much of our audit period, Corrections' role in providing inmates with medical care was not significant; the more substantial role was played by California Correctional Health Care Services (Receiver's Office) under the direction of a federal court-appointed receiver. A receiver took control of prison medical care in 2006 and will retain control until the court finds that Corrections can maintain a constitutionally adequate prison medical care system.

From fiscal years 2005–06 through 2012–13, 144 female inmates were sterilized by a procedure known as a bilateral tubal ligation. The last of these female inmate sterilizations occurred in 2011. Although various surgical procedures may result in a female's sterilization, bilateral tubal ligations are generally surgical procedures that are performed for the sole purpose of sterilization, and state regulations impose certain requirements that must be met before such a procedure is performed. However, the state entities responsible for providing medical care to these inmates—Corrections[1] and the Receiver's Office—sometimes failed to ensure that inmates' consent for sterilization was lawfully obtained. Overall, we noted that 39 inmates[2] were sterilized following deficiencies in the informed consent process. We found two types of deficiencies. First, we found no evidence that the inmate's physician—the individual who would perform the procedure in a hospital or an alternate physician—signed the consent form as required by state regulations. Second, we noted potential violations of the required waiting period between when the inmate consented to the procedure and when the sterilization surgery actually took place. Some inmates were sterilized following violations of both of these requirements. Although neither Corrections nor employees of the Receiver's Office actually performed the sterilization procedures, we concluded that they had a responsibility to ensure that the informed consent requirements were followed in those instances when their employees obtained inmates' consent, which was the case for at least 19 of the 39 inmates. Either the

[1] Corrections was responsible for inmate health care between July 1, 2005, and the appointment of the first federal receiver, effective April 2006. During this time period, 15 inmates had tubal ligation procedures, and based on available and potentially incomplete medical records, documentation for at least four of these inmates demonstrated potential violations of informed consent requirements.

[2] The true number of inmates for whom Corrections or the Receiver's Office did not ensure that lawful consent was obtained before sterilization may be higher. For example, one hospital destroyed seven inmate medical records in accordance with its records retention policy. Five of these seven inmates consented to the sterilization procedure while in prison, and it is unclear—based on available records—whether physicians signed the sterilization consent forms just prior to surgery.

remaining 20 inmates signed their consent to be sterilized at a physical location other than a prison or the Receiver's Office had difficulty determining whether the individual who obtained consent was an employee.

Lawful consent is represented by key steps as defined by the California Code of Regulations, Title 22 (Title 22). For example, the physician or an alternate physician must sign the consent form just before performing the surgery, and a waiting period is required after the patient signs the consent form. The missing physicians' signatures on some of the inmates' consent forms are especially concerning because of what the physician signature certifies: that the required waiting period has been satisfied and that the patient appears mentally competent and understands the lasting effects of sterilization. The physician is the last check in the informed consent process and provides the patient with the final opportunity to change her mind.

All the bilateral tubal ligations we reviewed were performed at general acute care hospitals rather than in prison medical facilities. A lawyer for the Receiver's Office stated that the specific provisions of Title 22 do not apply to prison employees, because Title 22 applies only to general acute care hospitals. Nevertheless, because employees of the Receiver's Office played a significant role in these 19 inmates' care and in obtaining their consent to be sterilized, our legal counsel advised us that a court would likely find that the Receiver's Office had a responsibility to ensure that consent was lawfully obtained from these inmates in accordance with Title 22.

Although the consent forms we were able to review demonstrated that each female inmate signed a consent form, we have concerns about whether the female inmates undergoing bilateral tubal ligations received adequate counseling about their decision to be sterilized. Despite a Receiver's Office policy that prison medical staff must use progress notes—a term for documenting information made in an inmate's medical record—to summarize discussions with inmates, in no instance did we find a female inmate whose progress notes adequately reflected that she had been counseled about her decision to be sterilized. The lack of notes in the inmates' medical records regarding informed consent and sterilization made it impossible for us to reach a conclusion as to the quality and content of the consultations between prison medical staff and inmates. We were also unable to conclude whether inmates received educational materials, whether prison medical staff answered inmates' questions, or whether these staff provided the inmates with all of the necessary information to make such a sensitive and life-changing decision as sterilization.

The Receiver's Office also failed to ensure that the prison medical staff under its direction followed state regulations requiring specific approvals for bilateral tubal ligation procedures, including approvals by two committees made up of high-ranking prison medical staff and

medical executives from the Receiver's Office. The failure to obtain the necessary approvals was systemic; all but one of the 144 bilateral tubal ligation procedures lacked the necessary approvals. Overall, our file review demonstrated that prison medical staff infrequently requested approval to sterilize inmates, and when they did, it was not always clear that these requests were approved. In many cases, prison medical staff simply requested approval for other medical procedures—such as cesarean sections at hospitals—and did not indicate that the inmate was also to be sterilized.

Since January 2010, when the Receiver's Office asserts it became aware of the sterilization procedures—following allegations by a legal advocacy group—its medical claims data show that the number of female inmates who have undergone bilateral tubal ligations and other medical procedures that result in sterilization has greatly decreased. In addition, since that time we found that the Receiver's Office has better adhered to its processes for reviewing medical services for necessity and for obtaining required approvals for medical services. Nevertheless, because the function of approving a medical procedure has been and remains separate from the process for scheduling the procedure at a general acute care hospital or other community medical facility, the opportunity still exists for inmates to receive medical services that are not authorized. Until the Receiver's Office ensures that medical scheduling is driven by authorized requests for service, it risks subjecting inmates to potentially unnecessary medical procedures and cannot demonstrate that it is in full control of the medical care inmates receive.

Recommendations

To ensure that the necessary education and disciplinary action can be taken, the Receiver's Office should report to the California Department of Public Health, which licenses general acute care hospitals, and the Medical Board of California, which licenses physicians, the names of all hospitals and physicians associated with inmates' bilateral tubal ligations during fiscal years 2005–06 through 2012–13 for which consent was unlawfully obtained. The Receiver's Office should make these referrals as soon as is practicable.

To ensure that it can better monitor how its medical staff and contractors adhere to the informed consent requirements of Title 22, sections 70707.1 through 70707.7, the Receiver's Office should develop a plan by August 2014 to implement a process by December 2014 that would include the following:

- Providing additional training to prison medical staff regarding Title 22 requirements for obtaining informed consent for sterilization procedures, including the applicable forms and mandatory waiting period requirements, to ensure that consent is lawfully obtained.

- Developing checklists or other tools that prison medical staff can use to ensure that medical procedures are not scheduled until after the applicable waiting periods for sterilization have been satisfied.
- Periodically reviewing, on a consistent basis, a sample of cases in which inmates received treatment resulting in sterilization at general acute care hospitals, to ensure that all informed consent requirements were satisfied.
- Until such time as the Receiver's Office implements a process for obtaining inmate consent for sterilization under Title 22 that complies with all aspects of the regulations, it should discontinue its practice of facilitating an inmate's consent for sterilization in the prison and allow the general acute care hospital to obtain an inmate's consent.

To improve the quality of the information prison medical staff document in inmate medical records, the Receiver's Office should do the following:

- Train its entire prison medical staff on its policy in the inmate medical procedures related to appropriate documentation in inmates' medical records. This training should be completed by December 31, 2014.
- Either develop or incorporate into an existing process a means by which it evaluates prison medical staffs' documentation in inmate medical records and retrains prison medical staff as necessary. The Receiver's Office should develop and implement this process by June 30, 2015.

To ensure that inmates receive only medical services that are authorized through its utilization management process, the Receiver's Office should do the following:

- Develop processes by August 31, 2014, such that a procedure that may result in sterilization is not scheduled unless the procedure is approved at the necessary level of the utilization management process.
- By October 31, 2014, train its scheduling staff to verify that the appropriate utilization management approvals are documented before they schedule a procedure that may result in sterilization.

Agency Comments

In its response to the audit, the Receiver's Office generally agreed with the report's factual findings, but noted that it reached conclusions about its duty to ensure compliance with the sterilization and consent procedures set forth in Title 22 that differ from the report. Nevertheless, the Receiver's Office pledged to implement all of the recommendations.

NOTES AND QUESTIONS

1. *Recommendations.* How do you assess the recommendations provided in this report? How would you administer them to make sure the standards were enforced?

2. *Prison Officials' Role in Sterilization.* Is it appropriate for prison officials to recommend sterilization to prisoners? According to one prisoner, Christina Cordero, 34, who spent two years in prison for auto theft, "As soon as [the prison doctor] found out that I had five kids, he suggested that I look into getting it done. The closer I got to my due date, the more he talked about it, ... He made me feel like a bad mother if I didn't do it." Corey G. Johnson, Female Inmates Sterilized in California Prisons Without Approval, Reveal, Jul. 7, 2013, at https://revealnews.org/article/female-inmates-sterilized-in-california-prisons-without-approval/; Corey G. Johnson, California Female Inmates Sterilized Illegally, Desert Sun, Jun. 21, 2014, at http://www.desertsun.com/story/news/nation/2014/06/20/california-female-inmates-sterilized/11034317/.

> **Practice Exercise:** Write out the full policy that you think the California prison system should adopt for sterilizations. How would informed consent be protected? What administrative procedures need to be in place to protect against abuse? Should sterilization of prisoners be legal under some circumstances or should it be completely banned? How do sterilizations relate to transgendered prisoners?

A Tennessee judge offered to remove 30 days from prisoners' sentences if they were sterilized. Male inmates would get permanent vasectomies, while women would get temporary birth control implants. 38 males and 32 females agreed to the procedure. The judge said, "I hope to encourage them to take personal responsibility and give them a chance, when they do get out, to not to be burdened with children. This gives them a chance to get on their feet and make something of themselves." Nick Thieme, A Tennessee Jail Is Offering Vasectomies for Reduced Prison Time: That's Wildly Unethical, Slate, Jul. 21, 2017, https://slate.com/technology/2017/07/tennessee-jails-vasectomy-plan-is-wildly-unethical.html. Do you agree with the judge?

3. *Equal Opportunities.* Do you agree with the prison official who said sterilization is "an empowerment issue for female inmates, providing them the same options as women on the outside?" Id.

4. *Informed Consent.* Can a woman in labor give informed consent to a sterilization? See id. (Professor Dorothy Roberts explains "courts have concluded that soliciting approval for sterilization during labor is coercive because pain and discomfort can impair a woman's ability to weigh the decision. . . . No woman should give consent on the operating table.").

5. *Reading Proficiency for Consent.* Investigators found that most of the women tested at less than a high school level of reading proficiency, and a third of them below the sixth-grade level. What level of reading proficiency does it take to give informed consent to a sterilization? Corey G. Johnson,

Female Prison Inmates Sterilized Illegally, California Audit Confirms, Reveal, Jun. 19, 2014, at https://revealnews.org/article/female-prison-inmates-sterilized-illegally-california-audit-confirms/.

6. *Potential Claims*. What lawsuits would you file on behalf of the California prisoners? What remedies would you seek? How can courts provide a remedy for sterilization?

7. *State Interests*. The prison doctor who performed the sterilizations told reporters "he provided an important service to poor women who faced health risks in future pregnancies because of past cesarean sections." When he learned that the state had paid $147,460 in fees to sterilization doctors, he commented, "Over a 10-year period, that isn't a huge amount of money . . . compared to what you save in welfare paying for these unwanted children—as they procreated more." Johnson, Female Inmates Sterilized in California Prisons Without Approval, *supra*. What interest does the state have in the number of children that a woman bears? That a woman prisoner bears?

8. *Eugenics*. Does the prison episode demonstrate that eugenics is still part of California culture despite the repeal of the twentieth-century eugenics laws? Should eugenics and sterilization always be prohibited?

> **Practice Exercise:** Draft the model legislation that you think California should adopt. Then go to the website and compare your legislation with the bill that California adopted.

9. *Sterilization Legislation*. In response to the discovery of prison sterilizations, state legislators introduced a bill, SB 1135, to provide a proper policy on sterilization in state prisons. Governor Jerry Brown signed legislation banning sterilization as a means of birth control for the state's prisoners. Corey G. Johnson, California Bans Coerced Sterilization of Female Inmates, Reveal, Sept. 26, 2014, https://revealnews.org/article-legacy/california-bans-coerced-sterilization-of-female-inmates/. Is that the best approach to sterilization?

In California, the investigation showed that Mexican American women were sterilized disproportionately to their numbers in the population. See Roque Planas, Mexican Americans Sterilized Disproportionately In California Institutions, Study Says, Jun. 9, 2013, at http://www.huffingtonpost.com/2013/06/05/mexican-americans-sterilized_n_3390305.html. Are you surprised that discrimination occurred in the prison setting? Would you expect minorities to be treatment poorly in other places where informed consent is important, e.g., when they are patients or research subjects?

Native American women were also victims of sterilization. At least 25% of Native American women were sterilized after family planning legislation passed in 1970. In 1977, chief tribal judge Marie Sanchez told the United Nations that those women "were targets of the 'modern form' of genocide—sterilization." Brianna Theobald, A 1970 Law Led to the Mass Sterilization of Native American Women: That History Still Matters, Time, Nov. 28, 2019, https://time.com/5737080/native-american-sterilization-history/.

In the next section, we examine the long and troubling legacy of such racism in medical research.

3. RACISM AND RESEARCH

Racism and Research: The Case of the Tuskegee Syphilis Study

Allan M. Brandt, 1978.
8 Hastings Center Report 21–29.

In 1932 the U.S. Public Health Service (USPHS) initiated an experiment in Macon County, Alabama, to determine the natural course of untreated, latent syphilis in black males. The test comprised 400 syphilitic men, as well as 200 uninfected men who served as controls. The first published report of the study appeared in 1936 with subsequent papers issued every four to six years, through the 1960s. When penicillin became widely available by the early 1950s as the preferred treatment for syphilis, the men did not receive therapy. In fact on several occasions, the USPHS actually sought to prevent treatment. Moreover, a committee at the federally operated Center for Disease Control decided in 1969 that the study should be continued. Only in 1972, when accounts of the study first appeared in the national press, did the Department of Health, Education and Welfare halt the experiment. At that time seventy-four of the test subjects were still alive; at least twenty-eight, but perhaps more than 100, had died directly from advanced syphilitic lesions. In August 1972, HEW appointed an investigatory panel which issued a report the following year. The panel found the study to have been "ethically unjustified," and argued that penicillin should have been provided to the men. . . .

Racism and Medical Opinion

A brief review of the prevailing scientific thought regarding race and heredity in the early twentieth century is fundamental for an understanding of the Tuskegee Study. By the turn of the century, Darwinism had provided a new rationale for American racism. Essentially primitive peoples, it was argued, could not be assimilated into a complex, white civilization. Scientists speculated that in the struggle for survival the Negro in America was doomed. Particularly prone to disease, vice, and crime, black Americans could not be helped by education or philanthropy. Social Darwinists analyzed census data to predict the virtual extinction of the Negro in the twentieth century, for they believed the Negro race in America was in the throes of a degenerative evolutionary process.

The medical profession supported these findings of late nineteenth- and early twentieth-century anthropologists, ethnologists, and biologists. Physicians studying the effects of emancipation on health concluded almost universally that freedom had caused the "mental, moral, and

physical deterioration of the black population." They substantiated this argument by citing examples in the comparative anatomy of the black and white races. As Dr. W. T. English wrote: "A careful inspection reveals the body of the negro a mass of minor defects and imperfections from the crown of the head to the soles of the feet." Cranial structures, wide nasal apertures, receding chins, projecting jaws, all typed the Negro as the lowest species in the Darwinian hierarchy. . . .

According to these physicians, lust and immorality, unstable families, and reversion to barbaric tendencies made blacks especially prone to venereal diseases. One doctor estimated that over 50 percent of all Negroes over the age of twenty-five were syphilitic. Virtually free of disease as slaves, they were now overwhelmed by it, according to informed medical opinion. Moreover, doctors believed that treatment for venereal disease among blacks was impossible, particularly because in its latent stage the symptoms of syphilis become quiescent . . .

The Origins of the Experiment

In 1929, under a grant from the Julius Rosenwald Fund, the USPHS conducted studies in the rural South to determine the prevalence of syphilis among blacks and explore the possibilities for mass treatment. The USPHS found Macon County, Alabama, in which the town of Tuskegee is located, to have the highest syphilis rate of the six counties surveyed. The Rosenwald Study concluded that mass treatment could be successfully implemented among rural blacks. Although it is doubtful that the necessary funds would have been allocated even in the best economic conditions, after the economy collapsed in 1929, the findings were ignored. It is, however, ironic that the Tuskegee Study came to be based on findings of the Rosenwald Study that demonstrated the possibilities of mass treatment.

Three years later, in 1932, Dr. Taliaferro Clark, Chief of the USPHS Venereal Disease Division and author of the Rosenwald Study report, decided that conditions in Macon County merited renewed attention. Clark believed the high prevalence of syphilis offered an "unusual opportunity" for observation. From its inception, the USPHS regarded the Tuskegee Study as a classic "study in nature," rather than an experiment. As long as syphilis was so prevalent in Macon and most of the blacks went untreated throughout life, it seemed only natural to Clark that it would be valuable to observe the consequences. He described it as a "ready-made situation." Surgeon General H. S. Cumming wrote to R.R. Moton, Director of the Tuskegee Institute:

> The recent syphilis control demonstration carried out in Macon County, with the financial assistance of the Julius Rosenwald Fund, revealed the presence of an unusually high rate in this county and, what is more remarkable, the fact that 99 per cent of this group was entirely without previous treatment. This combination, together with the expected cooperation of your hospital, offers an unparalleled opportunity for carrying on this

> piece of scientific research which probably cannot be duplicated anywhere else in the world.

Although no formal protocol appears to have been written, several letters of Clark and Cumming suggest what the USPHS hoped to find. Clark indicated that it would be important to see how disease affected the daily lives of the men:

> The results of these studies of case records suggest the desirability of making a further study of the effect of untreated syphilis on the human economy among people now living and engaged in their daily pursuits.

It also seems that the USPHS believed the experiment might demonstrate that antisyphilitic treatment was unnecessary. As Cumming noted: "It is expected the results of this study may have a marked bearing on the treatment, or conversely the non-necessity of treatment, of cases of latent syphilis."

The immediate source of Cumming's hypothesis appears to have been the famous Oslo Study of untreated syphilis. Between 1890 and 1910, Professor C. Boeck, the chief of the Oslo Venereal Clinic, withheld treatment from almost two thousand patients infected with syphilis. He was convinced that therapies then available, primarily mercurial ointment, were of no value. When arsenic therapy became widely available by 1910, after Paul Ehrlich's historic discovery of "606," the study was abandoned. E. Bruusgaard, Boeck's successor, conducted a follow-up study of 473 of the untreated patients from 1925 to 1927. He found that 27.9 percent of these patients had undergone a "spontaneous cure," and now manifested no symptoms of the disease. Moreover, he estimated that as many as 70 percent of all syphilitics went through life without inconvenience from the disease. His study, however, clearly acknowledged the dangers of untreated syphilis for the remaining 30 percent.

Thus every major textbook of syphilis at the time of the Tuskegee Study's inception strongly advocated treating syphilis even in its latent stages, which follow the initial inflammatory reaction. In discussing the Oslo Study, Dr. J.E. Moore, one of the nation's leading venereologists wrote, "This summary of Bruusgaard's study is by no means intended to suggest that syphilis be allowed to pass untreated." If a complete cure could not be effected, at least the most devastating effects of the disease could be avoided. Although the standard therapies of the time, arsenical compounds and bismuth injection, involved certain dangers because of their toxicity, the alternatives were much worse. As the Oslo Study had shown, untreated syphilis could lead to cardiovascular disease, insanity, and premature death. . . . "Another compelling reason for treatment," noted Moore, "exists in the fact that every patient with latent syphilis may be, and perhaps is, infectious for others." In 1932, the year in which the Tuskegee Study began, the USPHS sponsored and published a paper

by Moore and six other syphilis experts that strongly argued for treating latent syphilis.

The Oslo Study, therefore, could not have provided justification for the USPHS to undertake a study that did not entail treatment. Rather, the suppositions that conditions in Tuskegee existed "naturally" and that the men would not be treated anyway provided the experiment's rationale. In turn, these two assumptions rested on the prevailing medical attitudes concerning blacks, sex, and disease. For example, Clark explained the prevalence of venereal disease in Macon County by emphasizing promiscuity among blacks:

> This state of affairs is due to the paucity of doctors, rather low intelligence of the Negro population in this section, depressed economic conditions, and the very common promiscuous sex relations of this population group which not only contribute to the spread of syphilis but also contribute to the prevailing indifference with regard to treatment.

In fact, Moore, who had written so persuasively in favor of treating latent syphilis, suggested that existing knowledge did not apply to Negroes. Although he had called the Oslo Study "a never-to-be-repeated human experiment," he served as an expert consultant to the Tuskegee Study:

> I think that such a study as you have contemplated would be of immense value. It will be necessary of course in the consideration of the results to evaluate the special factors introduced by a selection of the material from negro males. Syphilis in the negro is in many respects almost a different disease from syphilis in the white.

Dr. O. C. Wenger, chief of the federally operated venereal disease clinic at Hot Springs, Arkansas, praised Moore's judgment, adding, "This study will emphasize those differences." On another occasion he advised Clark, "We must remember we are dealing with a group of people who are illiterate, have no conception of time, and whose personal history is always indefinite."

The doctors who devised and directed the Tuskegee Study accepted the mainstream assumptions regarding blacks and venereal disease. The premise that blacks, promiscuous and lustful, would not seek or continue treatment, shaped the study. A test of untreated syphilis seemed "natural" because the USPHS presumed the men would never be treated; the Tuskegee Study made that a self-fulfilling prophecy. . . .

The HEW Final Report

HEW finally formed the Tuskegee Syphilis Study Ad Hoc Advisory Panel on August 28, 1972, in response to criticism that the press descriptions of the experiment had triggered. The panel, composed of nine members, five of them black, concentrated on two issues. First, was the study justified in 1932 and had the men given their informed consent?

Second, should penicillin have been provided when it became available in the early 1950s? The panel was also charged with determining if the study should be terminated and assessing current policies regarding experimentation with human subjects. The group issued their report in June 1973.

By focusing on the issues of penicillin therapy and informed consent, the *Final Report* and the investigation betrayed a basic misunderstanding of the experiment's purposes and design. The HEW report implied that the failure to provide penicillin constituted the study's major ethical misjudgment; implicit was the assumption that no adequate therapy existed prior to penicillin. Nonetheless medical authorities firmly believed in the efficacy of arsenotherapy for treating syphilis at the time of the experiment's inception in 1932. The panel further failed to recognize that the entire study had been predicated on nontreatment. Provision of effective medication would have violated the rationale of the experiment-to study the natural course of the disease until death. On several occasions, in fact, the USPHS had prevented the men from receiving proper treatment. Indeed, there is no evidence that the USPHS ever considered providing penicillin.

The other focus of the *Final Report*—informed consent—also served to obscure the historical facts of the experiment. In light of the deceptions and exploitations which the experiment perpetrated, it is an understatement to declare, as the *Report* did, that the experiment was "ethically unjustified," because it failed to obtain informed consent from the subjects. The *Final Report's* statement, "Submitting voluntarily is not informed consent," indicated that the panel believed that the men had volunteered *for the experiment*. The records in the National Archives make clear that the men did not submit voluntarily to an experiment; they were told and they believed that they were getting free treatment from expert government doctors for a serious disease. The failure of the HEW *Final Report* to expose this critical fact—that the USPHS lied to the subjects—calls into question the thoroughness and credibility of their investigation.

Failure to place the study in a historical context also made it impossible for the investigation to deal with the essentially racist nature of the experiment. The panel treated the study as an aberration, well-intentioned but misguided. Moreover, concern that the *Final Report* might be viewed as a critique of human experimentation in general seems to have severely limited the scope of the inquiry. The *Final Report* is quick to remind the reader on two occasions: "The position of the Panel must not be construed to be a general repudiation of scientific research with human subjects." The *Report* assures us that a better-designed experiment could have been justified:

> It is possible that a scientific study in 1932 of untreated syphilis, properly conceived with a clear protocol and conducted with suitable subjects who fully understood the implications of their

> involvement, might have been justified in the pre-penicillin era. This is especially true when one considers the uncertain nature of the results of treatment of late latent syphilis and the highly toxic nature of therapeutic agents then available.

This statement is questionable in view of the proven dangers of untreated syphilis known in 1932.

Since the publication of the HEW *Final Report,* a defense of the Tuskegee Study has emerged. These arguments, most clearly articulated by Dr. R.H. Kampmeier in the *Southern Medical Journal,* center on the limited knowledge of effective therapy for latent syphilis when the experiment began. Kampmeier argues that by 1950, penicillin would have been of no value for these men. Others have suggested that the men were fortunate to have been spared the highly toxic treatments of the earlier period. Moreover, even these contemporary defenses assume that the men never would have been treated anyway. As Dr. Charles Barnett of Stanford University wrote in 1974, "The lack of treatment was not contrived by the USPHS but was an established fact of which they proposed to take advantage." Several doctors who participated in the study continued to justify the experiment. Dr. J. R. Heller, who on one occasion had referred to the test subjects as the "Ethiopian population," told reporters in 1972:

> I don't see why they should be shocked or horrified. There was no racial side to this. It just happened to be in a black community. I feel this was a perfectly straightforward study, perfectly ethics, with controls. Part of our mission as physicians is to find out what happens to individuals with disease and without disease.

These apologies, as well as the HEW *Final Report,* ignore many of the essential ethical issues which the study poses. The Tuskegee Study reveals the persistence of beliefs within the medical profession about the nature of blacks, sex, and disease—beliefs that had tragic repercussions long after their alleged "scientific" bases were known to be incorrect. Most strikingly, the entire health of a community was jeopardized by leaving a communicable disease untreated. There can be little doubt that the Tuskegee researchers regarded their subjects as less than human. As a result, the ethical canons of experimenting on human subjects were completely disregarded.

The study also raises significant questions about professional self-regulation and scientific bureaucracy. Once the USPHS decided to extend the experiment in the summer of 1933, it was unlikely that the test would be halted short of the men's deaths. The experiment was widely reported for forty years without evoking any significant protest within the medical community. Nor did any bureaucratic mechanism exist within the government for the periodic reassessment of the Tuskegee experiment's ethics and scientific value. The USPHS sent physicians to Tuskegee every several years to check on the study's progress, but never subjected

the morality or usefulness of the experiment to serious scrutiny. Only the press accounts of 1972 finally punctured the continued rationalizations of the USPHS and brought the study to an end. Even the HEW investigation was compromised by fear that it would be considered a threat to future human experimentation.

In retrospect the Tuskegee Study revealed more about the pathology of racism than it did about the pathology of syphilis; more about the nature of scientific inquiry than the nature of the disease process. The injustice committed by the experiment went well beyond the facts outlined in the press and the HEW *Final Report*. The degree of deception and damages have been seriously underestimated. As this history of the study suggests, the notion that science is a value-free discipline must be rejected. The need for greater vigilance in assessing the specific ways in which social values and attitudes affect professional behavior is clearly indicated.

NOTES AND QUESTIONS

1. *Tuskegee*. Was there any positive justification for the Tuskegee study, as its defenders suggest? Write a list of the positive aspects of the study.

2. *Ethical Violations*. After writing your list, consider the following ethical problems with Tuskegee identified in Carol A. Heintzelman, The Tuskegee Syphilis Study and Its Implications for the 21st Century, 10(4) The New Social Worker (Fall 2003):

> **Practice Exercise:** Write a list of the ethical violations or problems you can identify with the study and compare it to your list from Question 1.

a. *Deception in Recruiting*: "It was never explained to the subjects that the survey was designed to detect syphilis. The term 'bad blood,' which was a local colloquialism for everything from anemia to leukemia, was used by the doctors and never defined for the subjects. Subjects were never told they had syphilis, the course of the disease, or treatment. The treatment presented consisted of spinal taps, which were described as 'spinal shots.' "

b. *Withholding of Treatment for Research Purposes*: "researchers judged that the benefits of nontreatment outweighed the benefits of treatment." The researchers thought there might be toxic reaction to penicillin (such as fever, angina, or ruptured blood vessels), and were not sure if penicillin could do anything for patients in an advanced stage of syphilis. What do you think of the researchers' concerns that it might be ineffective to give penicillin to the Tuskegee men?

c. *Failure to Report*. Alabama had a state law dating from 1927 that required that state agencies be notified about venereal

diseases. Would such notification have protected the men's *wives* from infection?

d. *No Accurate Records* were kept.

e. *Stereotypes about African Americans* underlay the whole study.

f. *Medical Blindness.* Publications about the Tuskegee study existed for forty years without the ethics of the study being challenged by any medical researchers.

g. *Legacy of Distrust in the African American Community* persists today.

3. *Compensation.* Each survivor received a settlement of $40,000. Was that adequate to compensate for his damages? How would you compare the damages in the Tuskegee case with damages for sterilized individuals like Carrie Buck?

4. *Researchers' Contributions.* How important is it to you whether the Tuskegee men were infected with syphilis by the researchers? Is a study of men already afflicted with syphilis less troubling than one in which researchers infect the research subjects?

While researching Tuskegee, Professor Susan M. Reverby discovered the files of United States Public Health Service Dr. John C. Cutler at the University of Pittsburgh Archives. The papers showed that Cutler, with the support of U.S. health agencies, had conducted a study in Guatemala from 1946–1948. Susan M. Reverby, "Normal Exposure" and Inoculation Syphilis: A PHS "Tuskegee" Doctor in Guatemala, 1946–1948, 23 (1) J. of Pol. Hist. 6 (2011). According to Reverby, Guatemala differed from Tuskegee "in two majors [sic] ways: government doctors *did infect* people with syphilis (and gonorrhea and chancroid and then *did treat* them with penicillin." Id. at 9. In contrast to Tuskegee, where researchers wanted to watch the development of syphilis in already-infected individuals, in Guatemala the doctors wanted to test individual response to exposure and then determine if immediate treatment could stop the course of the disease. The researchers sent already-infected prostitutes into prisons to infect prisoners. They also infected prostitutes so they could infect the prisoners, and then, when the prisoners were slow to contract the disease, expanded the research population to non-prisoners and sought new, direct means of infection. No consent was ever requested or given to the study.

Reverby's research about Guatemala was confirmed by a U.S. government report, *Ethically Impossible.* According to the government's report, there was "no documentation of informed consent for study enrollment, any indication that subjects understood they were participating in research, or enumeration of incentives received by specific subjects for participation." In 2010 President Barack Obama apologized to the government and people of Guatemala for the experiments. How do you assess the ethics of Guatemala compared to the ethics of Tuskegee?

Go to the website and learn about the apology.

5. *Social Benefit.* According to Professor Reverby, "Cutler and his colleagues thought they might be making a great contribution to understanding this dreadful disease. Caught at the beginning of a paradigm shift in the disease's impact on humans—for penicillin was just then making its scourge seem less frightening—they believed they were doing the right thing even while acknowledging the risks and discussing the ethical edge they crossed. This should never be forgotten." Susan M. Reverby, Still "Ethically Impossible?" The Presidential Commission's Report on the STD Inoculation Studies in Guatemala, Bioethics Forum, Hastings Center, Sept. 22, 2011. Does Reverby's comment make you more or less sympathetic to Dr. Cutler and his fellow researchers? What lessons do you draw from Tuskegee?

6. *HeLa.* Does the following story of Henrietta Lacks confirm that American medical research is infected by racism?

Book Review Essay: The Immortal Life of Henrietta Lacks, Rebecca Skloot

Kate Scannell.
31 Journal of Legal Medicine 493 (2010).

ENCOUNTERING HENRIETTA LACKS

. . . I first "encountered" Henrietta Lacks in the early 1980s—more than three decades after she had died from cervical cancer in 1951. I had been asked to assist a fellow researcher with his experiment, by concocting various broths and "prepping" the cells he would require. Eager to avoid the tedium of my own research project, I dutifully assembled the requisite ingredients and glassware. And, as he had recommended, I met with "The Guy" who oversaw our cell cultures so I could learn how to handle them properly.

"These are HeLa cells," he informed me as he gently handed over a culture bottle on which was scrawled various numbers and initials. He explained that the cells were from an "eternal" human lineage—faithfully and perpetually reproducing for decades, generously providing researchers around the world with a standardized and plentiful supply of cells for experimental purposes.

His astounding description left me awestruck. I had been taught that all human cells were programmed to die—it was part of the natural order. What unique biophysical property did these undying cells possess? What separated these immortal cells from claims of the divine?

"The Guy" couldn't answer these questions. But he did offer that the cells had been so-named with the initials of the woman from whom they'd been taken: "Henrietta Lacks."

The following hour or so that I spent under a sterile hood prepping those HeLa cells affected me deeply. And though mesmerized by the cells' disembodied immortality, I was more powerfully preoccupied with their personification. I became intensely curious about Henrietta Lacks—the person whom those cells survived. Regrettably, however, I could find no

illuminating information about her in the medical texts available to me back then.

"... ON THE BANKS OF THE RIVER OF DEATH"

It is now 2010 and, sorting through the new arrivals at my local bookstore, I stumble upon *The Immortal Life of Henrietta Lacks* by Rebecca Skloot. On its dust jacket is an arresting photograph of a beautiful and clear-eyed woman who seems to be looking straight through time, to the precise moment in which I look at her. The cover text underneath the book's title reads: "Doctors took her cells without asking. Those cells never died. They launched a medical revolution and a multi-million dollar industry. More than twenty years later, her children found out. Their lives would never be the same."

I purchase the book and read it in one day. And, although made newly aware of many vital details that characterize Henrietta's life, still, I keenly feel her abiding absence. Indeed, having left no words or first-person narrative of her own, her story is wholly reconstructed through the second-hand accounts of family members and doctors. In the end, she remains—immortally—without a voice that we hear, without an identity of her own making.

Tellingly, even Henrietta's name was often misrepresented or confused within various medical and lay publications about HeLa cells. She died without an obituary and was buried in an unmarked grave.

In 1999, the book's author visits Henrietta's birthplace in Virginia—located off Route 360, "just past Difficult Creek on the banks of the River of Death." There Skloot hopes to find and interview any family members still living in the mile-long subsection of the area known as "Lacks Town." She drives past an unpainted shack that marks its entry and soon encounters Cootie, Henrietta's first cousin. He tells Skloot: "Everybody in Lacks Town kin to Henrietta, but she been gone so long, even her memory pretty much dead now. . . . Everything about Henrietta dead except them cells." Ten years later, when Skloot revisits the town where Henrietta grew up tending gardens and "planting tobacco behind mule-drawn plows," it is virtually gone and "it felt like everything related to Henrietta's history was vanishing."

The historical invisibility of women, blacks, and impoverished Americans is a figurative "river of death" that courses throughout this book. It is not only Henrietta's life which is submerged, but also the lives of her community and family members. A profoundly heartbreaking example of this involves Elsie, one of Henrietta's two daughters, who was committed with the problematic diagnosis of "idiocy" to the Crownsville State Hospital—known formerly as the Hospital for the Negro Insane. In 1955, four years after Henrietta's death and at the age of fifteen, Elsie died in that gruesome asylum all alone and unbeknownst to her sister, Deborah, through whom much of Henrietta's story is told.

In 2001, the author accompanies Deborah to Crownsville to fulfill her promise to help "figure[e] out what happened to Elsie." They meet a hospital director who informs them that most of the medical records from that time period had been contaminated by asbestos and "carted away in bags and buried." Still, because of some personal "habit of collecting potentially historic documents" he is able to locate an autopsy report and photograph of Elsie that he stored in a closet near his desk. In that photograph, Elsie "stares somewhere just below the camera, crying, her face misshapen and barely recognizable" and she "appears to be screaming" while her "head is twisted unnaturally to the left, chin raised and held in place by a large pair of white hands." In the end, the "picture" of Elsie we are left holding is one of terrible deafening silence, literalized by hands around her small throat.

RESEARCH QUESTIONS LEFT UNANSWERED

The medical research establishment figures prominently in this book, primarily in the ways it regarded Henrietta Lacks and HeLa cells. With a mostly even hand, Skloot holds up a lens through which she views the doctors and researchers who populated not only the hospitals and research labs where Henrietta and her cells resided but also the urgent medical questions that were left unanswered for the Lacks family.

Yet, for this reader, it is the brief side-trip to Crownsville that provides the most vividly distilled impression about the research establishment. Skloot, while trying to learn what happened to Elsie, uncovers troubling information about ostensibly covert research activities at Crownsville. The hospital director shares his private trove of documents and newspaper clippings with Skloot, allowing her to determine that, while Elsie was at Crownsville, "scientists often conducted research on patients there without consent." Research sometimes included the insertion of "metal probes into patients' brains" or pneumoencephalography—a painful (and now archaic) procedure in which holes are drilled through a person's skull, and spinal fluid is replaced with air in order to obtain clearer X-ray images of the brain. The hospital director evaluates the data at his disposal and makes a calculated guess that Elsie had been studied.

As affecting as they are, still, these haunting images and alarming reports concerning Elsie and Crownsville do not take center stage under the hot lights cast upon the research establishment. For that, we are transported to Baltimore; it is 1951, and Henrietta Lacks is seeking medical care for cervical cancer at John Hopkins Hospital—a charity hospital with a segregated ward for black patients. Before she receives caustic radium treatment, two "dime-sized" samples of her cervical tissue are removed, allegedly without her permission. The samples are given to George Gey, a tissue-culture scientist who for years has struggled to develop a continuously reproducing human cell line that could facilitate and advance cancer research.

As it turns out, Henrietta would die several months later, at 31 years of age. Her cancerous cells, however, would survive her and proliferate wildly in Gey's lab, "with mythological intensity." He would freely distribute them to scientists throughout the world, who, in turn, would often make amazing medical discoveries. Over time, for-profit cell banks and biotech companies would enter the picture and launch a "multimillion-dollar" industry from a "dime"-sized sample of Henrietta's cervix.

Meanwhile, Henrietta's children would struggle financially—some of them unable to afford basic health care—and they would not even learn about their mother's scientific legacy for decades to come. When first contacted by John Hopkins officials in 1973, they come to understand that the doctors want to test them for cancer, so they willingly comply with blood sampling. As Henrietta's husband later recounts: "They said they got my wife and she part alive. . . . They been doin' experiments on her and they wanted to test my children see if they got that cancer killed their mother." But, as the family grimly discovers, there's been an abysmal misunderstanding—in fact, the doctors only wanted the family's samples in order to conduct further HeLa cell experimentation. This painful revelation arrives as a shock for Deborah, who for days had been phoning Hopkins for her "cancer results," anxiously dreading that she may have inherited her mother's fatal disease.

The family's formidable distrust of researchers and doctors only expands when in 1976, reading an article in *Rolling Stone* magazine, they also learn about massive commercial profiteering from HeLa cells. As Deborah remarks, "if our mother cells done so much for medicine, how come her family can't afford to see no doctors? Don't make no sense. People got rich off my mother without us even knowin' about them takin' her cells, now we don't get a dime."

A SPECIMEN'S RED TOENAILS

And yet, above all else, it is the doctors' casual disregard and thudding incuriosity about the family's interest in their mother as a person and human being that destroys any last vestige of their trust. When Skloot makes her initial phone contact with Deborah and proposes writing a book about her mother, Deborah eagerly responds that such a book would be "great." Only one year old when Henrietta died, Deborah has tired of everyone's focus on her mother as though she were just some dehumanized assortment of cells. "Everything always about just the cells and don't even worry about her name and was HeLa even a person." She asks, "You know what I really want? I want to know, what did my mother smell like? For all my life I just don't know anything, not even the little common things, like what color she like? Did she like to dance?"

For decades, no researchers inform or consult with the Lacks family about the nature and scope of their experimentation with Henrietta's cells. Instead, popular media bombard the Lacks siblings with disturbing and weirdly evocative depictions of their mother, whose early death left

them with few memories of her. Deborah sees "a *Newsweek* article called PEOPLE-PLANTS that said that scientists had crossed Henrietta Lacks's cells with tobacco cells" which leads her to fear "they'd created a human plant-monster that was half her mother, half tobacco." Hearing that scientists had used HeLa cells to study viruses like AIDS and Ebola, Deborah imagines "her mother eternally suffering the symptoms of each disease: bone-crushing pain, bleeding eyes, suffocation." She is horrified to read that some people have even tried to kill HeLa cells.

Even while Henrietta lay dying a painful and agonizing death in the hospital, doctors write in the medical record: "Henrietta is still a miserable specimen." Later, during Henrietta's autopsy, one of Gey's assistants charged with collecting additional pathology samples gasps when she suddenly notes that "Henrietta's toenails were covered in chipped bright red polish." Recounting that episode years later, the assistant explains: "I nearly fainted. I thought, *Oh jeez, she's a real person.* I started imagining her sitting in the bathroom painting those toenails, and it hit me for the first time that those cells we'd been working with all this time and sending all over the world, they came from a live woman. I'd never thought of it that way."

A STORY MANY-STORIED

This story is many-storied—not only about "HeLa cells and Henrietta Lacks, but of Henrietta's family—particularly Deborah—and their life-long struggle to make peace with the existence of those cells, and the science that made them possible." Their colossal struggle intimately involves issues of race, gender, poverty, class, and health care inequality. It raises substantial questions about medical practice and research ethics, about societal care of the mentally ill, about the moral conduct of journalistic inquiry into other peoples' lives. It ignites legal and ethical debates about tissue ownership and the commercialization of human biological materials.

When the struggle is fueled by depersonalization and dehumanization of Henrietta Lacks and her family, we also wrestle with great philosophical disturbances; at this level, the book sounds a cautionary note about the valorization of medical and scientific "objectivity." We see how claims to such objectivity can actually derive from the denial of someone's subjectivity. How the "progress" of scientific research can depend upon dehumanizing the body and its parts which hauntingly reside as "specimens" within the freezers of commercial biobanks and unregulated storage facilities scattered throughout the country.

But underneath all of this—stripped bare of scientific mind, of political and ideological counsel, of celestial advisement and legal consideration, of professional belonging and identity—I would have to say that the book tells a remarkably simple story infused with a very old theme. In essence, the story is a fiercely human tale about the importance of seeing one another in the clarifying light of each other's unique and

radiant mortal being. We are reminded that this sometimes requires faith and forgiveness, the acute notice of a corpse's painted toenails, or a road trip to Crownsville. But, always, it requires a basic respect for persons that calls on us to seek each other out with curiosity and compassion, rejecting utilitarian yardsticks to measure our humanity or the value of others' lives. There is a moral to the story, and it is fully captured by Elie Wiesel in the book's epigraph:

> We must not see *any* person as an abstraction.
> Instead, we must see in every person a universe with its own secrets,
> With its own treasures, with its own sources of anguish,
> And with some measure of triumph.

NOTES AND QUESTIONS

1. *Public Access.* After European scientists published the genome of the HeLa cells and made it available for download (thus making public genetic information about Henrietta's relatives) the National Institutes of Health entered into an agreement with Lacks' family. The family receives no financial compensation, but the genome data are stored in NIH databases, where researchers can apply for access. Two members of the Lacks family will be members of the NIH committee that decides who gets access. See Carl Zimmer, A Family Consents to a Medical Gift, 62 Years Later, N.Y. Times, Aug. 7, 2013, at A1. Is this a satisfactory resolution of Henrietta's case? We examine the rules and standards governing tissue donation below in Section B.

HeLa cells are being used in research into vaccines against COVID-19. One writer has argued, "Now, the extraordinary events of 2020—the #BlackLivesMatter movement for racial justice, and the unequal toll of COVID-19 on communities of colour—are compelling scientists to reckon with past injustices." Editorial, Henrietta Lacks: Science Must Right A Historical Wrong, Nature, Sept. 1, 2020, https://www.nature.com/articles/d41586-020-02494-z. How could bioethics contribute to that goal to close the gap? Some people have called for a ban on the use of HeLa cells. Others, including Lacks's family members, have wanted attention paid to the memory of the real woman, Henrietta Lacks. Nature magazine argued that a "step must be to acknowledge and undo the disparities that are baked into basic research—because the systemic racism that existed when Lacks's cells were taken still exists today." Id. Some scientists donate money to the Lacks Foundation whenever they use the cells. "To give back now, researchers should not only study why the disease is more prevalent and severe among Black people, but also help to implement solutions to close the gap." Do you agree that "From the very start of the pandemic, elderly, disabled, and chronically ill people heard the

> **Develop** a distribution policy for the COVID vaccine. Who should get it first? Who should get it last? What factors enter into your reasoning? What would be inappropriate factors to consider?

unusually clear message that we are less worthy of saving, that our lives are worth less"? Andrew Pulrang, What I've Learned As a Disabled Person From the COVID-19 Pandemic, Forbes, Dec. 28, 2020, https://www.forbes.com/sites/andrewpulrang/2021/12/28/what-ive-learned-as-a-disabled-person-from-the-covid-19-pandemic/?

2. *Societal Benefit.* Do you think it matters how much benefit HeLa cells provided for society? Did the ethical violations outweigh the positive results?

3. *Compensation.* Was Henrietta's family justly compensated? What do you consider when deciding this? How does this compensation compare to the compensation offered for Tuskegee survivors or victims of sterilization?

4. *Prevention.* What institutions and procedures could prevent the abuses involved in Tuskegee, Guatemala, and HeLa? In the next section we study in detail the standards and mechanisms that developed to protect research with human subjects. For research in the United States, the most important standard has been the Common Rule, and the most important mechanism has been the Institutional Review Board (IRB), both of which emerged in response to Tuskegee.

B. SETTING STANDARDS FOR RESEARCH WITH HUMAN SUBJECTS

1. *Historical Background.* The protection of human subjects has gone through numerous stages since World War II. Dr. Fischer describes the following seven stages of development. See Bernard A. Fischer IV, A Summary of Important Documents in the Field of Research Ethics, 32 (1) Schizophrenia Bull. 69 (2005).

> **a.** *The Nuremberg Code.* Nazi scientists and doctors who had experimented with human beings were prosecuted for war crimes during the Nuremberg Trials. In 1947, the Nuremberg Military Tribunal issued a 10-point code focused on the idea that human participation in research must be *voluntary*.
>
> **b.** *The Declarations of Geneva and Helsinki.* Again in response to the abuses of the Second World War, the World Medical Association issued a code of medical ethics in 1949 (the *Declaration of Geneva*) and then a more detailed code in 1953 (the *Declaration of Helsinki*). Both declarations emphasize that the health of the patient must be the doctor's first consideration. The declarations also expanded protections for voluntary participation in research and informed consent.
>
> **c.** *The Beecher Paper.* Harvard Professor Henry K. Beecher was concerned about American research that violated the rights of human subjects and in 1966 published "Ethics and Clinical Research" in the *New England Journal of Medicine.* Beecher demonstrated that some studies pursued scientific knowledge at the expense of human health. Mentally retarded

children were infected with hepatitis, for example, even though there was *no* possible benefit to them from the inoculation.

d. *The Vancouver Group* was a group of medical journal editors who agreed that authors must disclose conflicts of interest and certify that their research complied with the *Declaration of Helsinki.*

e. *The Belmont Report.* The U.S. Department of Health, Education and Welfare established the National Commission for the Protection of Human Subjects of Biomedical and Behavioral Research in 1974. In 1979 the commission released the Belmont Report, which identified the fundamental ethical principles that must guide all research with human subjects. "The commission concluded that the primary principles underlying ethical research with human beings are respect for persons, beneficence, and justice. The methods used to recognize these principles are informed consent, risk/benefit analysis, and appropriate selection of patients." Id. at 72.

f. *The Common Rule.* The National Research Act of 1974 established a specific set of guidelines to protect informed consent. The Common Rule establishes the standards that must be met in research with human subjects; it governs sixteen federal agencies and researchers who receive federal funding. Most research involves federal funding and so the Common Rule is widely applied. Clinical trials that involve treatments other than drugs and devices, such as surgery or bone marrow transplants, are not regulated by the Food and Drug Administration (FDA) and are subject to Department of Health and Human Services (DHHS) regulation only if they are "conducted, supported or otherwise subject to regulation by any federal department or agency." 45 C.F.R. § 46.101.

2. *Clinical Trials.* According to the National Institutes of Health, most research involving human subjects takes place in clinical trials. "Clinical research is medical research that involves people like you. When you volunteer to take part in clinical research, you help doctors and researchers learn more about disease and improve health care for people in the future. Clinical research includes all research that involves people." See NIH Clinical Trials and You, at https://www.nih.gov/health-information/nih-clinical-research-trials-you/basics. Clinical research usually begins in the scientist's laboratory, where he or she searches for promising treatments for diseases. Potential treatments are first tested in animals for safety and effectiveness. If a drug succeeds in animals, the researcher sends a request for permission to study the drug in humans (called an Investigational New Drug (IND) application) to the Food and Drug Administration (FDA). See Christine Grady, Clinical Trials, Hastings Center Bioethics Briefings, Sept. 21, 2015, https://www.the

hastingscenter.org/briefingbook/clinical-trials/. The research on human subjects proceeds in the following stages:

- **Phase I trials**: Researchers test a drug or treatment in a small group of people (20–80) for the first time. The purpose is to study the drug or treatment to learn about safety and identify side effects.
- **Phase II trials**: The new drug or treatment is given to a larger group of people (100–300) to determine its effectiveness and to further study its safety.
- **Phase III trials**: The new drug or treatment is given to large groups of people (1,000–3,000) to confirm its effectiveness, monitor side effects, compare it with standard or similar treatments, and collect information that will allow the new drug or treatment to be used safely.
- **Phase IV trials**: After a drug is approved by the FDA and made available to the public, researchers track its safety in the general population, seeking more information about a drug or treatment's benefits, and optimal use.

Go to the website and review one of the Phase I consent forms (Phase I(A) or Phase I(B)). Would you participate in this study? Why or why not? Do you prefer the sample language of form Phase I(C)? Consider the definition of Phase I above. Phase I is the first time that a drug has been tested in human beings. Why do you think Phase I studies are usually conducted on healthy volunteers? Are patients who suffer from the disease to be targeted by the drug or healthy volunteers better candidates for Phase I? Does anyone who participates in a Phase I study receive benefit from her participation?

NIH Clinical Trials and You, at https://www.nih.gov/health-information/nih-clinical-research-trials-you/basics.

The "gold standard" for research with human subjects is the randomized control trial (RCT), which seeks to determine whether one treatment is equivalent to or superior to another. Participants are randomized—assigned by chance, usually by a computer program—to either the experimental treatment or the control treatment. The control group receives either a placebo and/or the standard treatment for the illness. In a single-blind study, the participants don't know which group they're in.

Practice Exercise: Think of a disease that is important to you, and then use the website to see if there are clinical trials about that disease in which you might be willing to participate.

In a double-blind study, neither the researchers nor the participants know which group the subjects are in. Grady, *supra*.

The researchers write a protocol explaining their proposed study, which goes to an institution's Institutional Review Board (IRB) for review. We study the details of IRBs in the following sections.

1. INTRODUCTION TO THE IRB

Regulating Clinical Research: Informed Consent, Privacy, and IRBs

Sharona Hoffman.
31 Capital University Law Review 71 (2003).

II. A Historical Overview of Research Abuses and the Development of Research Regulations

During World War II, the Nazis conducted large-scale, experiments on concentration camp prisoners that were designed not only to gather medical data, but also to torture and kill the subjects. In some camps, German doctors infected numerous healthy inmates with yellow fever, smallpox, typhus, cholera, and diphtheria germs that caused hundreds of them to die. In other camps Nazi physicians conducted experiments relating to high altitude, malaria, freezing, mustard gas, bone transplantation, sea water, sterilization, and incendiary bombs. The full scope and ghastliness of the Nazi medical experimentation was revealed and documented during the Nuremberg Trials after World War II.

In the United States, medical research was conducted for many decades without any regulatory oversight. Perhaps not surprisingly, in an environment devoid of regulation and monitoring, an alarming number of research abuses occurred in this country as well. In the early 1950s, nearly one hundred percent of participants in Phase I clinical trials, the first and riskiest phase of human research studies, were prisoners. In Ohio, for example, live cancer cells were introduced into both forearms of many prisoners. Two weeks after the injection, the affected area of one arm would be surgically removed for study, while the malignant cells were left in the other forearm for further observation. At the Ionia State Hospital in Michigan, at least 142 inmates were recruited for secret CIA psychological experiments. As late as 1969, eighty-five percent of new medications were still tested on prisoners.

Research abuses in the decades following WWII were not limited to the prison environment but also involved other vulnerable populations. For example, patients at the Jewish Chronic Disease Hospital in Brooklyn had live cancer cells injected under their skin, and retarded children in the Willowbrook State School on Staten Island were infected with a mild strain of hepatitis. The experiments were done without the subjects' knowledge or consent.

In 1972, news of the notorious Tuskegee syphilis study highlighted the problem of mistreatment of medical research subjects in the United States. The Tuskegee study, whose participants were all African-American men, was conducted from 1932 until the beginning of the 1970s and sought to analyze the natural progression of untreated syphilis. The researchers, therefore, did not provide patients with penicillin, an antibiotic that is a fully effective cure for syphilis and was widely available as early as 1953. The subjects, who believed they were receiving adequate care, continued to suffer unnecessarily from the debilitating effects of the disease.

The federal government finally responded to publicity concerning research abuses by promulgating oversight regulations. The FDA and the National Institutes of Health (NIH) developed internal policy guidelines in 1966 and 1971, respectively, and these became federal regulations in 1974. The National Commission for the Protection of Human Subjects in Biomedical and Behavioral Research was established through the National Research Act of 1974 and operated for four years, until 1978. Pursuant to the Commission's recommendations, the federal regulations underwent revision in 1981, and they have remained in effect since then.

III. The Federal Regulations that Govern IRBs and Informed Consent

A. What Is Regulated?

Research studies, generally termed "clinical trials," for the development of new drugs and devices are regulated by the FDA. Medications that are the focus of study in clinical trials are called investigational new drugs (INDs). Clinical trials that involve treatments other than drugs and devices, such as surgery or bone marrow transplants, are not regulated by the FDA and are subject to DHHS regulation only if they are "conducted, supported or otherwise subject to regulation by any federal department or agency."

B. IRBs

Research that is conducted, supported, or regulated by DHHS, the FDA, or another federal agency must be reviewed by an IRB. An IRB is a committee designated by an institution to provide initial approval and periodic monitoring for biomedical research studies. The IRB's primary purpose is to protect the rights and welfare of human subjects. The IRB reviews a document known as the "protocol" for each proposed clinical trial, which describes the objectives of the research, its procedures, eligibility requirements for participants, the number of subjects to be tested, and other details. The material submitted to the IRB also includes a document known as the "informed consent" form, which is given to all potential enrollees in order to provide them with a detailed explanation of the clinical trial and an opportunity to agree to participation in the study. After the IRB approves the informed consent form, all those who

wish to become human subjects must sign a copy of the document, affirming the voluntariness of their choice.

The structure and duties of IRBs are governed by the DHHS and FDA regulations. Each IRB must be composed of at least five members with diverse cultural and ethnic backgrounds, and both men and women should be included. At least one member of the IRB should be a person whose principal concerns are in the scientific realm, and one individual's expertise should be nonscientific (e.g. a lawyer or minister). Furthermore, to enhance its objectivity, each IRB must include at least one member who is not otherwise affiliated with the research facility and who has no immediate family members affiliated with the entity. According to DHHS's Office for Protection from Research Risks (OPRR), now renamed the Office for Human Research Protection (OHRP), eighty-six percent of IRB members in 1995 were affiliated with academic research institutions as full-time faculty (56%), clinical and research staff (18%), and administrators (6%). Academic institutions do not compensate IRB members for their work, and thus these individuals must volunteer their time without receiving payment or relief from other job duties.

Unless an expedited review is conducted, research protocols must be reviewed at IRB meetings at which a majority of members are present, including a member whose expertise is nonscientific. Decisions concerning approval of each study are made by majority vote.

The IRB may approve, disapprove, or require modifications to the proposed research activities. Investigators must be given written notification of the IRB's decisions, and IRBs are required to monitor the clinical trials they approve at intervals of at least once a year, or more frequently, depending on the severity of the risks entailed. This periodic monitoring is known as "continuing review."

Before approving a clinical trial, the IRB must ensure that specific criteria are met. These include: (1) risks to participants are minimized; (2) risks to subjects are reasonable in light of anticipated benefits; and (3) selection of participants is equitable, and the protocol is sensitive to the particularized problems of research involving vulnerable populations, such as children, prisoners, pregnant women, mentally disabled individuals, or economically or educationally deprived persons.

C. Informed Consent

The contents of informed consent forms are also governed by the federal regulations. The informed consent document must be written in language that is accessible to subjects. Informed consent may not include language that waives any of the subject's rights or releases the institution or research personnel from liability for negligence. The regulations further require that informed consent be obtained in writing from each enrollee, though they allow for certain exceptions.

The regulations specify certain data that must be featured on the informed consent document. This information includes a description of

the research, an explanation of risks, benefits, and alternatives, a discussion of confidentiality, a list of contact people, and a statement that participation is voluntary and may be discontinued at any time.

D. Research Involving Only Existing Medical Records Or Tissue Samples

In some cases investigators conduct research that does not involve treatment of any human subject. Instead, the research entails the study of existing medical records or tissue samples. For example, researchers might want to determine whether patients who have a particular type of cancer suffered certain symptoms before their diagnosis and might attempt to make that determination through an examination of their recorded medical histories. Investigators are not required to obtain informed consent from subjects for such research if the information is publicly available or if the researcher will record the data in a way that will make it impossible for subjects to be identified.

> **Practice Exercise:** Create your own IRB and see if it complies with federal regulations. Describe how you will create your IRB, who will serve on it, and what procedures you will follow. The regulations are on the website.

> **Go to** the website after your IRB is formed and review two different research protocols: (1) SUPPORT Trial; and (2) Yale Tissue. After reviewing these protocols, would you vote to approve them? Why or why not?

In addition, the regulations provide that an IRB may waive informed consent requirements if it finds "[t]hat the research presents no more than minimal risk of harm to subjects and involves no procedures for which written consent is normally required outside of the research context." Accordingly, in limited circumstances in which subject welfare will not be compromised, this provision could allow for the use of identifiable medical records without subject consent.

Practice Experience

You have been asked to start an IRB at your hospital and, once the IRB is started, to review a research protocol to see if it complies with federal regulations. Professor Hoffman's article summarized some of the regulations and procedures governing IRBs, which are usually referred to as the "Common Rule." Parts of the Common Rule are reprinted below so you can practice working in a regulatory context.

To ensure that patients understand the consent form, it is essential—according to Professor Hoffman's article—to make the medical and legal terms intellectually accessible to laypersons.

After many years, the Common Rule was amended to include the following language, which became applicable in 2019.

The Common Rule for the Protection of Human Subjects

45 CFR Part 690.

45 C.F.R. § 690.101 To what does this policy apply?

(a) Except as detailed in § 690.104, this policy applies to all research involving human subjects conducted, supported, or otherwise subject to regulation by any Federal department or agency that takes appropriate administrative action to make the policy applicable to such research. This includes research conducted by Federal civilian employees or military personnel, except that each department or agency head may adopt such procedural modifications as may be appropriate from an administrative standpoint. It also includes research conducted, supported, or otherwise subject to regulation by the Federal Government outside the United States. Institutions that are engaged in research described in this paragraph and institutional review boards (IRBs) reviewing research that is subject to this policy must comply with this policy.

45 C.F.R. § 690.104 Exempt research.

(a) Unless otherwise required by law or by department or agency heads, research activities in which the only involvement of human subjects will be in one or more of the categories in paragraph (d) of this section are exempt from the requirements of this policy, except that such activities must comply with the requirements of this section and as specified in each category.

(d) Except as described in paragraph (a) of this section, the following categories of human subjects research are exempt from this policy:

(1) Research, conducted in established or commonly accepted educational settings, that specifically involves normal educational practices that are not likely to adversely impact students' opportunity to learn required educational content or the assessment of educators who provide instruction. This includes most research on regular and special education instructional strategies, and research on the effectiveness of or the comparison among instructional techniques, curricula, or classroom management methods.

(2) Research that only includes interactions involving educational tests (cognitive, diagnostic, aptitude, achievement), survey procedures, interview procedures, or observation of public behavior (including visual or auditory recording) if at least one of the following criteria is met:

(i) The information obtained is recorded by the investigator in such a manner that the identity of the human subjects cannot

readily be ascertained, directly or through identifiers linked to the subjects;

(ii) Any disclosure of the human subjects' responses outside the research would not reasonably place the subjects at risk of criminal or civil liability or be damaging to the subjects' financial standing, employability, educational advancement, or reputation; or

(iii) The information obtained is recorded by the investigator in such a manner that the identity of the human subjects can readily be ascertained, directly or through identifiers linked to the subjects, and an IRB conducts a limited IRB review to make the determination required by § 690.111(a)(7).

(3) (i) Research involving benign behavioral interventions in conjunction with the collection of information from an adult subject through verbal or written responses (including data entry) or audiovisual recording if the subject prospectively agrees to the intervention and information collection and at least one of the following criteria is met:

(A) The information obtained is recorded by the investigator in such a manner that the identity of the human subjects cannot readily be ascertained, directly or through identifiers linked to the subjects;

(B) Any disclosure of the human subjects' responses outside the research would not reasonably place the subjects at risk of criminal or civil liability or be damaging to the subjects' financial standing, employability, educational advancement, or reputation; or

(C) The information obtained is recorded by the investigator in such a manner that the identity of the human subjects can readily be ascertained, directly or through identifiers linked to the subjects, and an IRB conducts a limited IRB review to make the determination required by § 690.111(a)(7).

(ii) For the purpose of this provision, benign behavioral interventions are brief in duration, harmless, painless, not physically invasive, not likely to have a significant adverse lasting impact on the subjects, and the investigator has no reason to think the subjects will find the interventions offensive or embarrassing. Provided all such criteria are met, examples of such benign behavioral interventions would include having the subjects play an online game, having them solve puzzles under various noise conditions, or having them decide how to allocate a nominal amount of received cash between themselves and someone else.

(iii) If the research involves deceiving the subjects regarding the nature or purposes of the research, this exemption is not applicable unless the subject authorizes the deception through a prospective agreement to participate in research in circumstances in which the subject is informed that he or she will be unaware of or misled regarding the nature or purposes of the research.

(4) Secondary research for which consent is not required: Secondary research uses of identifiable private information or identifiable biospecimens, if at least one of the following criteria is met:

(i) The identifiable private information or identifiable biospecimens are publicly available;

(ii) Information, which may include information about biospecimens, is recorded by the investigator in such a manner that the identity of the human subjects cannot readily be ascertained directly or through identifiers linked to the subjects, the investigator does not contact the subjects, and the investigator will not re-identify subjects;

(iii) The research involves only information collection and analysis involving the investigator's use of identifiable health information when that use is regulated under 45 CFR parts 160 and 164, subparts A and E, for the purposes of "health care operations" or "research" as those terms are defined at 45 CFR 164.501 or for "public health activities and purposes" as described under 45 CFR 164.512(b); or

(iv) The research is conducted by, or on behalf of, a Federal department or agency using government-generated or government-collected information obtained for nonresearch activities, if the research generates identifiable private information that is or will be maintained on information technology that is subject to and in compliance with section 208(b) of the E-Government Act of 2002, 44 U.S.C. 3501 note, if all of the identifiable private information collected, used, or generated as part of the activity will be maintained in systems of records subject to the Privacy Act of 1974, 5 U.S.C. 552a, and, if applicable, the information used in the research was collected subject to the Paperwork Reduction Act of 1995, 44 U.S.C. 3501 et seq.

(5) Research and demonstration projects that are conducted or supported by a Federal department or agency, or otherwise subject to the approval of department or agency heads (or the approval of the heads of bureaus or other subordinate agencies that have been delegated authority to conduct the research and demonstration projects), and that are designed to study, evaluate, improve, or otherwise examine public benefit or service programs, including

procedures for obtaining benefits or services under those programs, possible changes in or alternatives to those programs or procedures, or possible changes in methods or levels of payment for benefits or services under those programs. Such projects include, but are not limited to, internal studies by Federal employees, and studies under contracts or consulting arrangements, cooperative agreements, or grants. Exempt projects also include waivers of otherwise mandatory requirements using authorities such as sections 1115 and 1115A of the Social Security Act, as amended.

(i) Each Federal department or agency conducting or supporting the research and demonstration projects must establish, on a publicly accessible Federal Web site or in such other manner as the department or agency head may determine, a list of the research and demonstration projects that the Federal department or agency conducts or supports under this provision. The research or demonstration project must be published on this list prior to commencing the research involving human subjects.

45 C.F.R. § 690.107 IRB membership.

(a) Each IRB shall have at least five members, with varying backgrounds to promote complete and adequate review of research activities commonly conducted by the institution. The IRB shall be sufficiently qualified through the experience and expertise of its members (professional competence), and the diversity of its members, including race, gender, and cultural backgrounds and sensitivity to such issues as community attitudes, to promote respect for its advice and counsel in safeguarding the rights and welfare of human subjects. The IRB shall be able to ascertain the acceptability of proposed research in terms of institutional commitments (including policies and resources) and regulations, applicable law, and standards of professional conduct and practice. The IRB shall therefore include persons knowledgeable in these areas. If an IRB regularly reviews research that involves a category of subjects that is vulnerable to coercion or undue influence, such as children, prisoners, individuals with impaired decision-making capacity, or economically or educationally disadvantaged persons, consideration shall be given to the inclusion of one or more individuals who are knowledgeable about and experienced in working with these categories of subjects.

(b) Each IRB shall include at least one member whose primary concerns are in scientific areas and at least one member whose primary concerns are in nonscientific areas.

(c) Each IRB shall include at least one member who is not otherwise affiliated with the institution and who is not part of the immediate family of a person who is affiliated with the institution.

(d) No IRB may have a member participate in the IRB's initial or continuing review of any project in which the member has a conflicting interest, except to provide information requested by the IRB.

(e) An IRB may, in its discretion, invite individuals with competence in special areas to assist in the review of issues that require expertise beyond or in addition to that available on the IRB. These individuals may not vote with the IRB.

45 C.F.R. § 690.111 Criteria for IRB approval of research.

(a) In order to approve research covered by this policy the IRB shall determine that all of the following requirements are satisfied:

(1) Risks to subjects are minimized:

(i) By using procedures that are consistent with sound research design and that do not unnecessarily expose subjects to risk, and

(ii) Whenever appropriate, by using procedures already being performed on the subjects for diagnostic or treatment purposes.

(2) Risks to subjects are reasonable in relation to anticipated benefits, if any, to subjects, and the importance of the knowledge that may reasonably be expected to result. In evaluating risks and benefits, the IRB should consider only those risks and benefits that may result from the research (as distinguished from risks and benefits of therapies subjects would receive even if not participating in the research). The IRB should not consider possible long-range effects of applying knowledge gained in the research (e.g., the possible effects of the research on public policy) as among those research risks that fall within the purview of its responsibility.

(3) Selection of subjects is equitable. In making this assessment the IRB should take into account the purposes of the research and the setting in which the research will be conducted. The IRB should be particularly cognizant of the special problems of research that involves a category of subjects who are vulnerable to coercion or undue influence, such as children, prisoners, individuals with impaired decision-making capacity, or economically or educationally disadvantaged persons.

(4) Informed consent will be sought from each prospective subject or the subject's legally authorized representative, in accordance with, and to the extent required by, § 690.116.

(5) Informed consent will be appropriately documented or appropriately waived in accordance with § 690.117.

(6) When appropriate, the research plan makes adequate provision for monitoring the data collected to ensure the safety of subjects.

(7) When appropriate, there are adequate provisions to protect the privacy of subjects and to maintain the confidentiality of data.

(b) When some or all of the subjects are likely to be vulnerable to coercion or undue influence, such as children, prisoners, individuals with impaired decision-making capacity, or economically or educationally disadvantaged persons, additional safeguards have been included in the study to protect the rights and welfare of these subjects.

45 C.F.R. § 690.116 General requirements for informed consent.

(b) Basic elements of informed consent. Except as provided in paragraph (d), (e), or (f) of this section, in seeking informed consent the following information shall be provided to each subject or the legally authorized representative:

(1) A statement that the study involves research, an explanation of the purposes of the research and the expected duration of the subject's participation, a description of the procedures to be followed, and identification of any procedures that are experimental;

(2) A description of any reasonably foreseeable risks or discomforts to the subject;

(3) A description of any benefits to the subject or to others that may reasonably be expected from the research;

(4) A disclosure of appropriate alternative procedures or courses of treatment, if any, that might be advantageous to the subject;

(5) A statement describing the extent, if any, to which confidentiality of records identifying the subject will be maintained;

(6) For research involving more than minimal risk, an explanation as to whether any compensation and an explanation as to whether any medical treatments are available if injury occurs and, if so, what they consist of, or where further information may be obtained;

(7) An explanation of whom to contact for answers to pertinent questions about the research and research subjects' rights, and whom to contact in the event of a research-related injury to the subject;

(8) A statement that participation is voluntary, refusal to participate will involve no penalty or loss of benefits to which the subject is otherwise entitled, and the subject may discontinue participation at any time without penalty or loss of benefits to which the subject is otherwise entitled; and

(9) One of the following statements about any research that involves the collection of identifiable private information or identifiable biospecimens:

(i) A statement that identifiers might be removed from the identifiable private information or identifiable biospecimens and that, after such removal, the information or biospecimens could be used for future research studies or distributed to another investigator for future research studies without

additional informed consent from the subject or the legally authorized representative, if this might be a possibility; or

(ii) A statement that the subject's information or biospecimens collected as part of the research, even if identifiers are removed, will not be used or distributed for future research studies.

(c) Additional elements of informed consent. Except as provided in paragraph (d), (e), or (f) of this section, one or more of the following elements of information, when appropriate, shall also be provided to each subject or the legally authorized representative:

(1) A statement that the particular treatment or procedure may involve risks to the subject (or to the embryo or fetus, if the subject is or may become pregnant) that are currently unforeseeable;

(2) Anticipated circumstances under which the subject's participation may be terminated by the investigator without regard to the subject's or the legally authorized representative's consent;

(3) Any additional costs to the subject that may result from participation in the research;

(4) The consequences of a subject's decision to withdraw from the research and procedures for orderly termination of participation by the subject;

(5) A statement that significant new findings developed during the course of the research that may relate to the subject's willingness to continue participation will be provided to the subject;

(6) The approximate number of subjects involved in the study;

(7) A statement that the subject's biospecimens (even if identifiers are removed) may be used for commercial profit and whether the subject will or will not share in this commercial profit;

(8) A statement regarding whether clinically relevant research results, including individual research results, will be disclosed to subjects, and if so, under what conditions; and

(9) For research involving biospecimens, whether the research will (if known) or might include whole genome sequencing (i.e., sequencing of a human germline or somatic specimen with the intent to generate the genome or exome sequence of that specimen).

(d) Elements of broad consent for the storage, maintenance, and secondary research use of identifiable private information or identifiable biospecimens. Broad consent for the storage, maintenance, and secondary research use of identifiable private information or identifiable biospecimens (collected for either research studies other than the proposed research or nonresearch purposes) is permitted as an alternative to the informed consent requirements in paragraphs (b) and (c) of this section. If the subject or the legally authorized representative

is asked to provide broad consent, the following shall be provided to each subject or the subject's legally authorized representative:

(1) The information required in paragraphs (b)(2), (b)(3), (b)(5), and (b)(8) and, when appropriate, (c)(7) and (9) of this section;

(2) A general description of the types of research that may be conducted with the identifiable private information or identifiable biospecimens. This description must include sufficient information such that a reasonable person would expect that the broad consent would permit the types of research conducted;

(3) A description of the identifiable private information or identifiable biospecimens that might be used in research, whether sharing of identifiable private information or identifiable biospecimens might occur, and the types of institutions or researchers that might conduct research with the identifiable private information or identifiable biospecimens;

(4) A description of the period of time that the identifiable private information or identifiable biospecimens may be stored and maintained (which period of time could be indefinite), and a description of the period of time that the identifiable private information or identifiable biospecimens may be used for research purposes (which period of time could be indefinite);

(5) Unless the subject or legally authorized representative will be provided details about specific research studies, a statement that they will not be informed of the details of any specific research studies that might be conducted using the subject's identifiable private information or identifiable biospecimens, including the purposes of the research, and that they might have chosen not to consent to some of those specific research studies;

(6) Unless it is known that clinically relevant research results, including individual research results, will be disclosed to the subject in all circumstances, a statement that such results may not be disclosed to the subject; and

(7) An explanation of whom to contact for answers to questions about the subject's rights and about storage and use of the subject's identifiable private information or identifiable biospecimens, and whom to contact in the event of a research-related harm.

45 C.F.R. § 690.117 Documentation of informed consent.

(a) Except as provided in paragraph (c) of this section, informed consent shall be documented by the use of a written informed consent form approved by the IRB and signed (including in an electronic format) by the subject or the subject's legally authorized representative. A written copy shall be given to the person signing the informed consent form.

The IRB system is designed to protect human subjects from exploitation and to assure they give informed consent. However, the system is not designed to prevent all the flawed incentives that may influence researchers and keep them from fully protecting research subjects. We identify the flawed incentives that mar research in the next section.

2. FLAWED INCENTIVES IN RESEARCH

Given what you just learned about informed consent, was there a failure of informed consent in the following case? Is it relevant to the case whether you think of plaintiff John Moore as a patient or as a research subject? Should the same standards that applied to patients like Jerry Canterbury in Section A apply to John Moore in this case?

Moore v. Regents of the University of California

Supreme Court of California, 1990.
51 Cal.3d 120, 793 P.2d 479.

I. INTRODUCTION

■ PANELLI, JUSTICE.

We granted review in this case to determine whether plaintiff has stated a cause of action against his physician and other defendants for using his cells in potentially lucrative medical research without his permission. Plaintiff alleges that his physician failed to disclose preexisting research and economic interests in the cells before obtaining consent to the medical procedures by which they were extracted. The superior court sustained all defendants' demurrers to the third amended complaint, and the Court of Appeal reversed. We hold that the complaint states a cause of action for breach of the physician's disclosure obligations, but not for conversion.

II. FACTS

. . . The plaintiff is John Moore (Moore), who underwent treatment for hairy-cell leukemia at the Medical Center of the University of California at Los Angeles (UCLA Medical Center). The five defendants are: (1) Dr. David W. Golde (Golde), a physician who attended Moore at UCLA Medical Center; (2) the Regents of the University of California (Regents), who own and operate the university; (3) Shirley G. Quan, a researcher employed by the Regents; (4) Genetics Institute, Inc. (Genetics Institute); and (5) Sandoz Pharmaceuticals Corporation and related entities (collectively Sandoz).

Moore first visited UCLA Medical Center on October 5, 1976, shortly after he learned that he had hairy-cell leukemia. After hospitalizing Moore and "withdr[awing] extensive amounts of blood, bone marrow aspirate, and other bodily substances," Golde confirmed that diagnosis. At this time all defendants, including Golde, were aware that "certain

blood products and blood components were of great value in a number of commercial and scientific efforts" and that access to a patient whose blood contained these substances would provide "competitive, commercial, and scientific advantages."

On October 8, 1976, Golde recommended that Moore's spleen be removed. Golde informed Moore "that he had reason to fear for his life, and that the proposed splenectomy operation . . . was necessary to slow down the progress of his disease." Based upon Golde's representations, Moore signed a written consent form authorizing the splenectomy.

Before the operation, Golde and Quan "formed the intent and made arrangements to obtain portions of [Moore's] spleen following its removal" and to take them to a separate research unit. Golde gave written instructions to this effect on October 18 and 19, 1976. These research activities "were not intended to have . . . any relation to [Moore's] medical . . . care." However, neither Golde nor Quan informed Moore of their plans to conduct this research or requested his permission. Surgeons at UCLA Medical Center, whom the complaint does not name as defendants, removed Moore's spleen on October 20, 1976.

Moore returned to the UCLA Medical Center several times between November 1976 and September 1983. He did so at Golde's direction and based upon representations "that such visits were necessary and required for his health and well-being, and based upon the trust inherent in and by virtue of the physician-patient relationship. . . ." On each of these visits Golde withdrew additional samples of "blood, blood serum, skin, bone marrow aspirate, and sperm." On each occasion Moore travelled to the UCLA Medical Center from his home in Seattle because he had been told that the procedures were to be performed only there and only under Golde's direction.

"In fact, [however,] throughout the period of time that [Moore] was under [Golde's] care and treatment, . . . the defendants were actively involved in a number of activities which they concealed from [Moore]. . . ." Specifically, defendants were conducting research on Moore's cells and planned to "benefit financially and competitively . . . [by exploiting the cells] and [their] exclusive access to [the cells] by virtue of [Golde's] on-going physician-patient relationship. . . ."

Sometime before August 1979, Golde established a cell line from Moore's T-lymphocytes. On January 30, 1981, the Regents applied for a patent on the cell line, listing Golde and Quan as inventors. "[B]y virtue of an established policy . . . , [the] Regents, Golde, and Quan would share in any royalties or profits . . . arising out of [the] patent." The patent issued on March 20, 1984, naming Golde and Quan as the inventors of the cell line and the Regents as the assignee of the patent.

The Regents' patent also covers various methods for using the cell line to produce lymphokines. Moore admits in his complaint that "the true clinical potential of each of the lymphokines . . . [is] difficult to

predict, [but] . . . competing commercial firms in these relevant fields have published reports in biotechnology industry periodicals predicting a potential market of approximately $3.01 Billion Dollars by the year 1990 for a whole range of [such lymphokines]. . . ."

With the Regents' assistance, Golde negotiated agreements for commercial development of the cell line and products to be derived from it. Under an agreement with Genetics Institute, Golde "became a paid consultant" and "acquired the rights to 75,000 shares of common stock." Genetics Institute also agreed to pay Golde and the Regents "at least $330,000 over three years, including a pro-rata share of [Golde's] salary and fringe benefits, in exchange for . . . exclusive access to the materials and research performed" on the cell line and products derived from it. On June 4, 1982, Sandoz "was added to the agreement," and compensation payable to Golde and the Regents was increased by $110,000. "[T]hroughout this period, . . . Quan spent as much as 70 [percent] of her time working for [the] Regents on research" related to the cell line.

Based upon these allegations, Moore attempted to state 13 causes of action.[4]

III. DISCUSSION

A. *Breach of Fiduciary Duty and Lack of Informed Consent*

Moore repeatedly alleges that Golde failed to disclose the extent of his research and economic interests in Moore's cells before obtaining consent to the medical procedures by which the cells were extracted. These allegations, in our view, state a cause of action against Golde for invading a legally protected interest of his patient. This cause of action can properly be characterized either as the breach of a fiduciary duty to disclose facts material to the patient's consent or, alternatively, as the performance of medical procedures without first having obtained the patient's informed consent. . . .

[We reach] the following conclusions: (1) a physician must disclose personal interests unrelated to the patient's health, whether research or economic, that may affect the physician's professional judgment; and (2) a physician's failure to disclose such interests may give rise to a cause of action for performing medical procedures without informed consent or breach of fiduciary duty.

To be sure, questions about the validity of a patient's consent to a procedure typically arise when the patient alleges that the physician failed to disclose medical risks, as in malpractice cases, and not when the patient alleges that the physician had a personal interest, as in this case.

[4] 1) "Conversion"; (2) "lack of informed consent"; (3) "breach of fiduciary duty"; (4) "fraud and deceit"; (5) "unjust enrichment"; (6) "quasi-contract"; (7) "bad faith breach of the implied covenant of good faith and fair dealing"; (8) "intentional infliction of emotional distress"; (9) "negligent misrepresentation"; (10) "intentional interference with prospective advantageous economic relationships"; (11) "slander of title"; (12) "accounting"; and (13) "declaratory relief."

The concept of informed consent, however, is broad enough to encompass the latter. "The scope of the physician's communication to the patient . . . must be measured by the patient's need, and that need is whatever information is material to the decision." . . .

It is important to note that no law prohibits a physician from conducting research in the same area in which he practices. Progress in medicine often depends upon physicians, such as those practicing at the university hospital where Moore received treatment, who conduct research while caring for their patients.

Yet a physician who treats a patient in whom he also has a research interest has potentially conflicting loyalties. This is because medical treatment decisions are made on the basis of proportionality—weighing the benefits *to the patient* against the risks *to the patient.* As another court has said, "the determination as to whether the burdens of treatment are worth enduring for any individual patient depends upon the facts unique in each case," and "the patient's interests and desires are the key ingredients of the decision-making process." A physician who adds his own research interests to this balance may be tempted to order a scientifically useful procedure or test that offers marginal, or no, benefits to the patient. The possibility that an interest extraneous to the patient's health has affected the physician's judgment is something that a reasonable patient would want to know in deciding whether to consent to a proposed course of treatment. It is material to the patient's decision and, thus, a prerequisite to informed consent.

Golde argues that the scientific use of cells that have already been removed cannot possibly affect the patient's medical interests. The argument is correct in one instance but not in another. If a physician has no plans to conduct research on a patient's cells at the time he recommends the medical procedure by which they are taken, then the patient's medical interests have not been impaired. In that instance the argument is correct. On the other hand, a physician who does have a preexisting research interest might, consciously or unconsciously, take that into consideration in recommending the procedure. In that instance the argument is incorrect: the physician's extraneous motivation may affect his judgment and is, thus, material to the patient's consent.

We acknowledge that there is a competing consideration. To require disclosure of research and economic interests may corrupt the patient's own judgment by distracting him from the requirements of his health. But California law does not grant physicians unlimited discretion to decide what to disclose. Instead, "it is the prerogative of the patient, not the physician, to determine for himself the direction in which he believes his interests lie." "Unlimited discretion in the physician is irreconcilable with the basic right of the patient to make the ultimate informed decision. . . ."

Accordingly, we hold that a physician who is seeking a patient's consent for a medical procedure must, in order to satisfy his fiduciary

duty and to obtain the patient's informed consent, disclose personal interests unrelated to the patient's health, whether research or economic, that may affect his medical judgment.

1. Dr. Golde

We turn now to the allegations of Moore's third amended complaint to determine whether he has stated such a cause of action. We first discuss the adequacy of Moore's allegations against Golde, based upon the physician's disclosures prior to the splenectomy.

Moore alleges that, prior to the surgical removal of his spleen, Golde "formed the intent and made arrangements to obtain portions of his spleen following its removal from [Moore] in connection with [his] desire to have regular and continuous access to, and possession of, [Moore's] unique and rare Blood and Bodily Substances." Moore was never informed prior to the splenectomy of Golde's "prior formed intent" to obtain a portion of his spleen. In our view, these allegations adequately show that Golde had an undisclosed research interest in Moore's cells at the time he sought Moore's consent to the splenectomy. Accordingly, Moore has stated a cause of action for breach of fiduciary duty, or lack of informed consent, based upon the disclosures accompanying that medical procedure.

We next discuss the adequacy of Golde's alleged disclosures regarding the postoperative takings of blood and other samples. In this context, Moore alleges that Golde "expressly, affirmatively and impliedly represented . . . that these withdrawals of his Blood and Bodily Substances were necessary and required for his health and well-being." However, Moore also alleges that Golde actively concealed his economic interest in Moore's cells during this time period. "[D]uring each of these visits . . ., and even when [Moore] inquired as to whether there was any possible or potential commercial or financial value or significance of his Blood and Bodily Substances, or whether the defendants had discovered anything . . . which was or might be . . . related to any scientific activity resulting in commercial or financial benefits . . ., the defendants repeatedly and affirmatively represented to [Moore] that there was no commercial or financial value to his Blood and Bodily Substances . . . and in fact actively discouraged such inquiries."

Moore admits in his complaint that defendants disclosed they "were engaged in strictly academic and purely scientific medical research. . . ." However, Golde's representation that he had no financial interest in this research became false, based upon the allegations, at least by May 1979, when he "began to investigate and initiate the procedures . . . for [obtaining] a patent" on the cell line developed from Moore's cells.

In these allegations, Moore plainly asserts that Golde concealed an economic interest in the postoperative procedures. Therefore, applying the principles already discussed, the allegations state a cause of action for breach of fiduciary duty or lack of informed consent. . . .

2. The Remaining Defendants

The Regents, Quan, Genetics Institute, and Sandoz are not physicians. In contrast to Golde, none of these defendants stood in a fiduciary relationship with Moore or had the duty to obtain Moore's informed consent to medical procedures. If any of these defendants is to be liable for breach of fiduciary duty or performing medical procedures without informed consent, it can only be on account of Golde's acts and on the basis of a recognized theory of secondary liability, such as respondeat superior. The procedural posture of this case, however, makes it unnecessary for us to address the sufficiency of Moore's secondary-liability allegations. . . .

NOTES AND QUESTIONS

1. *Informed Consent Law.* In Section A, we learned that in jurisdictions that follow *Canterbury*, tort law assesses informed consent from the perspective of the patient, not the doctor; with foresight, not hindsight; from an objective, not a subjective point of view; and requires causation as well as injury to the patient. Did the California Supreme Court apply the same standards of informed consent in *Moore*? What would an objective person in Moore's circumstances want to know about Golde's *research interests* in Moore? Could anyone predict with foresight that Moore's spleen would be valuable, or is that determination purely a matter of hindsight? Do you think Moore would have behaved any differently if Golde had informed him of his research interests in Moore's spleen? Does Moore really have any injuries for tort law to compensate? Does *Moore* give you additional reasons to prefer a patient-based standard of informed consent over one that relies on the physician's professional judgment of what should be disclosed?

2. How do you assess the argument that Dr. Golde owed Moore only the duty to inform him about his medical condition, and not about the benefits that would accrue to Golde through Golde's research on Moore's body parts?

3. Do you think the court was mistaken in allowing liability against Dr. Golde but not against the Regents, Quan, Genetics Institute and Sandoz? Do you think those individuals and institutions should be held accountable in some way, or did they act appropriately?

4. Professor Javitt argues that the court's reasoning was "flawed" because it "failed to distinguish between Moore as a patient and Moore as a research subject." According to Javitt:

> In failing to inform Moore that he planned to use the cells in research, Golde therefore committed a wrong to Moore the-research-subject independently of whatever duties he owed Moore as a patient. The court failed to acknowledge Moore's transition from patient to research subject, and therefore failed to consider the duties owed to Moore in that capacity. Had Golde not been his treating physician, or if he had had no inkling of the cells' potential research value at the time of the surgery, he would have been under

> no obligation, by the court's reasoning, to inform Moore of the value of his cells. Nor, by the court's reasoning, did Quan or UCLA have any duty to obtain Moore's consent to use his cells. The court's limited holding therefore does little to protect the interests of the vast majority of contributors of tissue samples.

Gail H. Javitt, Take Another Little Piece of My Heart: Regulating the Research Use of Human Biospecimens, 41 J.L. Med. & Ethics 424, 426 (2013). What standard can protect both patients and research subjects? Should researchers owe a fiduciary duty and a duty of informed consent to tissue donors?

5. The court observed that to "require disclosure of research and economic interests may corrupt the patient's own judgment by distracting him from the requirements of his health." Do you agree? If you were in John Moore's position and were informed by Dr. Golde about his research, would you have lost focus on your health?

6. *Conflicts of Interest.* When is a conflict of interest present between a doctor and a patient? Between a doctor and a research subject? Between an individual's interest as a patient and as a research subject? Between a researcher and a research subject? The court wrote that a

> physician who treats a patient in whom he also has a research interest has potentially conflicting loyalties. This is because medical treatment decisions are made on the basis of proportionality—weighing the benefits *to the patient* against the risks *to the patient*. As another court has said, "the determination as to whether the burdens of treatment are worth enduring for any individual patient depends upon the facts unique in each case," and "the patient's interests and desires are the key ingredients of the decision-making process." A physician who adds his own research interests to this balance may be tempted to order a scientifically useful procedure or test that offers marginal, or no, benefits to the patient. The possibility that an interest extraneous to the patient's health has affected the physician's judgment is something that a reasonable patient would want to know in deciding whether to consent to a proposed course of treatment. It is material to the patient's decision and, thus, a prerequisite to informed consent.

Would you describe a researcher's position differently?

Do you think that the types of disclosure and informed consent that we identified in Section B1 in the IRB context can solve all conflicts of interest? What do you think about the recommendations made by the Institute of Medicine (IOM) about conflicts of interest in the following report?

Conflict of Interest in Medical Research, Education, and Practice

Institute of Medicine (IOM) Report Brief, April 2009.

Collaborations between physicians or medical researchers and pharmaceutical, medical device, and biotechnology companies can

benefit society—most notably by promoting the discovery and development of new medications and medical devices that improve individual and public health. However, financial ties between medicine and industry may create conflicts of interest. Such conflicts present the risk of undue influence on professional judgments and thereby may jeopardize the integrity of scientific investigations, the objectivity of medical education, the quality of patient care, and the public's trust in medicine.

Recent news stories have documented troubling interactions between industry and physicians, researchers, and medical institutions. These situations, which could undermine public confidence in medicine, may include

- companies and academic investigators not publishing negative results from industry-sponsored clinical trials or delaying publication after trial completion;
- physicians and researchers failing to disclose substantial payments from pharmaceutical companies as required by universities, research sponsors, or medical journals; and
- settlements between federal prosecutors and medical device and pharmaceutical companies related to alleged illegal payments or gifts to physicians.

In an effort to prevent these types of situations, many academic medical centers, professional societies, medical journals, and other institutions have adopted stronger policies on conflict of interest.

In 2007, the Institute of Medicine (IOM) appointed the Committee on Conflict of Interest in Medical Research, Education, and Practice to examine conflicts of interest in medicine and to recommend steps to identify, limit, and manage conflicts of interest without negatively affecting constructive collaborations. The committee's report stresses the importance of preventing bias and mistrust rather than trying to remedy damage after it is discovered. This report specifically focuses on financial conflicts of interest involving pharmaceutical, medical device, and biotechnology companies.

DISCLOSING AND ASSESSING FINANCIAL RELATIONSHIPS

The committee recommends that medical institutions—including academic medical centers, professional societies, patient advocacy groups, and medical journals—establish conflict of interest policies that require disclosure and management of both individual and institutional financial ties to industry. Institutions should create conflict of interest committees to evaluate these ties. If necessary, a board-level committee should deal with conflicts of interest at the institutional level, which typically arise when research conducted within an institution could affect the value of an institution's investments or patents.

Disclosure of financial relationships with industry is an essential, though limited, first step in identifying and responding to conflicts of interest. Because current policies are highly variable and sometimes confusing, the committee recommends standardizing the content, format, and procedures for disclosing financial relationships physicians and researchers have with industry. Such standardization will provide institutions with specific information they need to assess the severity of conflicts and to determine whether the relationship needs to be eliminated or actively managed. It will also simplify requirements for physicians and researchers who must disclose information to multiple institutions. Physicians, researchers, academic medical centers, professional societies, consumer and patient advocacy groups, medical journals, accreditation and certification organizations, licensing boards, other government agencies, and organizations with experience in database development and management should be involved in developing uniform disclosure standards.

In addition to steps taken by the medical community, Congress should create a national reporting program that requires pharmaceutical, medical device, and biotechnology companies to make public all payments to physicians, researchers, health care institutions, professional societies, patient advocacy and disease groups, and providers of continuing medical education. Public reporting will enhance accountability by allowing academic medical centers, medical journals, and others to verify disclosures made to them by faculty members, article authors, and others.

IMPROVING CONFLICT OF INTEREST POLICIES IN MEDICAL RESEARCH, EDUCATION, AND PRACTICE

Although the committee recognizes that collaborations with industry can be beneficial, the committee recommends, as a general rule, that researchers should not conduct research involving human participants if they have a financial interest in the outcome of the research, for example, if they hold a patent on an intervention being tested in a clinical trial. The only exceptions should be if an individual's participation is judged to be essential for the safe and appropriate conduct of the research.

Financial relationships with industry are extensive in medical education. To reduce the risk for bias within the learning environment, academic medical centers and teaching hospitals should prohibit faculty from accepting gifts, making presentations that are controlled by industry, claiming authorship for ghost-written publications, and entering into consulting arrangements that are not governed by written contracts for expert services to be paid for at fair market value. Medical centers also should restrict visits by industry sales people and limit use of drug samples to patients who lack financial access to medications.

Many providers of accredited continuing medical education—a usual requirement for relicensure of physicians—receive the majority of their funding from industry. The report recommends a broad-based consensus

process to develop a new system for funding high-quality accredited continuing medical education that is free of industry influence. The committee recognizes that such a system may involve higher costs for physicians and require cost-cutting steps by education providers.

Acceptance of meals and gifts and other relationships with industry are also common among physicians who practice outside medical centers. Data suggest that these relationships may influence physicians to prescribe a company's medicines even when evidence indicates another drug would be more beneficial. Therefore, the committee recommends eliminating these problematic relationships between physicians and industry.

In addition, the committee recommends that community physicians should also follow the restrictions described previously regarding gifts, including meals, from companies; presentations or articles whose content is controlled by industry; meetings with sales representatives; and use of drug samples. Professional societies and health care facilities should adopt policies that reinforce this recommendation.

Clinical practice guidelines influence physician practice, quality measures, and insurance coverage decisions. Given this influence, clinical practice guidelines need to be developed with greater transparency and accountability. The committee recommends that professional societies and other groups that develop practice guidelines not accept direct industry funding for guideline development and generally exclude individuals with conflicts of interest from the panels that draft the guidelines. In addition, these groups should make public their conflict of interest policies, their funding sources, and any financial relationships panel members have with industry.

In order to promote the adoption of conflict of interest policies by institutions engaged in medical research, education, clinical care, or the development of practice guidelines, the report urges other organizations such as health insurers, accrediting bodies, and government agencies to develop incentives for policy change consistent with the recommendations in the committee's report. For example, health insurers and other organizations that use clinical practice guidelines should avoid using guidelines that were developed without strong conflict of interest protections.

The committee also recommends that the Department of Health and Human Services develop a research agenda to create a stronger evidence base for future conflict of interest policies. Such research should evaluate the impact of conflict of interest policies, including both desired outcomes and possible unwanted consequences.

CONCLUSION

Society traditionally has placed great trust in physicians and researchers, granting them the considerable leeway to regulate themselves. However, there is growing concern among lawmakers,

government agencies, and the public that extensive conflicts of interest in medicine require stronger measures. Responsible and reasonable conflict of interest policies and procedures will reduce the risk of bias and the loss of trust while avoiding undue burdens or harms and without damaging constructive collaborations with industry. Decisions about biomedical research, medical education, and patient care directly affect the public's health. The public needs to be able to trust that physicians' decisions are not inappropriately influenced by their financial relationships with industry.

NOTES AND QUESTIONS

1. *Disclosure.* What do you think of the report's recommendation that physicians and researchers disclose their financial relationships with industry? The report recommends "standardizing the content, format, and procedures for disclosing financial relationships physicians and researchers have with industry." How would you recommend that disclosure be standardized? Is there a certain format for disclosure you would recommend? What would the form say?

Can disclosure cure all conflicts of interest? Despite its emphasis on disclosure, the report recommends "as a general rule, that researchers should not conduct research involving human participants if they have a financial interest in the outcome of the research, for example, if they hold a patent on an intervention being tested in a clinical trial. The only exceptions should be if an individual's participation is judged to be essential for the safe and appropriate conduct of the research." Is this rule too strict? Would it wrongly keep all patent holders from research? How would such a standard have worked in *Moore* and the case of Henrietta Lacks? Why shouldn't these patent-holders conduct the research after full disclosure to the research subject?

2. *National Reporting Program: Sunshine.* The report recommends that Congress authorize a national reporting program "that requires pharmaceutical, medical device, and biotechnology companies to make public all payments to physicians, researchers, health care institutions, professional societies, patient advocacy and disease groups, and providers of continuing medical education." Do you agree that such a reporting program is necessary?

A section of the Affordable Care Act (ACA) called the Physician Payment Sunshine Act (PPSA) requires pharmaceutical, medical device and biologics manufacturers reimbursed by Medicaid or Medicare to disclose payments to teaching hospitals and physicians on a public website. That website is the Open Payments website, which is now operational and accessible to the public. Does this website promote transparency and disclosure? Do you think websites would provide any insight to patients? How would you design such a website? What format and information would be most helpful to patients? See Alison R. Hwong et al., A Systematic Review of State and Manufacturer Physician Payment Disclosure Websites: Implications for Implementation of the Sunshine Act, 42 J. L. Med. & Ethics 208 (2014).

Pharmaceutical companies and medical device makers paid $10.03 billion to doctors and teaching hospitals during 2019. The sum includes payments for consulting and speaking fees, travel, meals, entertainment, research grants, and ownership and investment interests. See The Facts About Open Payments Data (2019), https://openpaymentsdata.cms.gov/summary. How do you think consumers react to this information? While some may not like their doctors accepting money for consulting and trips, will others see it as a sign of their doctors' expertise?

Practice Exercise: Visit the website and see if you can find your doctor or a local doctor in the Open Payments system. Could you find any information about your own doctor? Can you imagine any circumstances in which you, or your friends and family, would consult this website? Could you glean any information regarding the quality of doctors from the site?

Professor Saver explains that the Sunshine Act's record has been "uneven," due in part to its "bumpy rollout" and the difficulty of presenting the financial information in the most accessible manner. He questions whether patients will really use the website. Nonetheless, "policymakers can more closely examine correlations between industry spending directed at individual physicians and their prescribing and referral decisions. Moreover, savvy counsel are recognizing that Sunshine Act information provides explosive evidence in private civil litigation and this Article explores the first wave of cases." Richard S. Saver, Deciphering the Sunshine Act: Transparency Regulation and Financial Conflicts in Health Care, 43:4 American Journal of Law and Medicine 303 (2017). If you were a savvy litigator, how would you use this information?

3. *Other Recommendations.* The IOM report also recommends, "[t]o reduce the risk for bias within the learning environment, academic medical centers and teaching hospitals should prohibit faculty from accepting gifts, making presentations that are controlled by industry, claiming authorship for ghost-written publications, and entering into consulting arrangements that are not governed by written contracts for expert services to be paid for at fair market value." Furthermore, the report advocates that meals and gifts and other relationships with industry not be allowed. Are these recommendations too strict?

4. *Researchers.* In another section of the report, IOM recommended that institutions use four criteria when assessing conflict of interest policies:

- Proportionality: Is the policy effective, efficient, and directed at the most important and most common conflicts?
- Transparency: Is the policy comprehensible and accessible to the individuals and institutions that may be affected by it?
- Accountability: Does the conflict of interest policy indicate who is responsible for monitoring, enforcing, and revising it?
- Fairness: Does the policy apply equally to all relevant groups within an institution and in different institutions?

Are these principles clear enough that they would provide enough guidance to you to draft a COI policy?

Professor Spece recommends direct disclosure of researcher conflicts of interest to participants in clinical trials. By "direct" disclosure, he means that researchers should reveal the source, amount and mechanism of their funding directly to the research subject, instead of indirectly (e.g., by the websites identified in Note 2). The mechanism of funding includes per capita payments to researchers. Would it influence your consent to participate in a clinical trial if you learned that your researcher earned a sum of money per capita, i.e., a payment for every individual enrolled? Do you agree that such detailed direct disclosure is a necessary part of informed consent? Roy G. Spece, Jr., Direct and Enhanced Disclosure of Researcher Financial Conflicts of Interest: The Role of Trust, 23 Health Matrix 409, 410–11 (2013).

Spece addressed the possibility that "strong empirical proof demonstrating the high likelihood of significant harm and little good resulting from direct disclosure might overcome a presumption in favor of subjects' individual rights to bodily integrity and autonomy in decision making." Id. at 411. Would you agree that this is possible, or argue instead that full and direct disclosure of financial conflicts of interest is an absolute requirement of informed consent? See id. at 412 ("currently there is no strong empirical proof of direct disclosure's effects on subjects' trust in their researchers that would overcome the presumption in favor of individual rights.")

What do you think of using "enhanced direct disclosure," which Spece illustrates in the following example:

> An example of an enhanced direct disclosure that might affect researcher-subject trust would be a requirement that subjects in studies funded on a per capita basis be told:
>
> This study is funded by Company X, which has paid Researcher Y $10,000 for each subject enrolled.
>
> [If true, add: "X and Y claim that these payments are not in excess of fair market value." If not true, add: "X and Y are not willing to state there are no excess payments."]
>
> This form of per capita funding (a set amount for each subject enrolled) risks payment to Y that exceeds the fair market value of resources, goods, and services supplied by Y to X. [If applicable, add: "especially when X and Y or those in similar positions refuse to state that there are no excess payments."].
>
> Excess payments present the risk of biasing, in favor of X, Y's decisions concerning the design of the research study, whether and when to enroll or keep each subject, and how to determine whether

> the data from the study demonstrate [the studied intervention] is safe and effective.

Id. at 413–14. Should such a description be added to every informed consent study you analyzed above? Does this discussion about financial conflicts lead you to conclude that the subjects of human research should be reimbursed for their participation in clinical trials?

> **Practice Exercise:** Draft a conflict of interest policy for a physician who conducts research on her patients at a teaching hospital. Did your policy include any non-financial interests, as Professor Saver argues in following reading?

Is It Really All About the Money? Reconsidering Non-Financial Interests in Medical Research

Richard S. Saver.
40 J.L. Med. & Ethics 467 (2012).

Introduction

Conflicts of interest have been reduced to *financial* conflicts. The National Institutes of Health's (NIH) new rules for managing conflicts of interest in medical research, the first major change to the regulations in over 15 years, address only financial ties. Although several commentators urged that the regulations also cover non-financial interests, the Department of Health and Human Services declined to do so. Similarly, the Institute of Medicine's (IOM) influential 2009 Conflict of Interest Report focuses almost exclusively on financial conflicts. Institutional policies at academic medical centers and guidance from professional bodies and medical journals also primarily emphasize financial ties. Even broadly worded rules are applied more readily to financial ties than non-financial interests, such as the regulations that restrict institutional review board (IRB) members with conflicting interests from participating in protocol reviews.

Concern about financial ties crowds out consideration of other influences that may bias research conduct. But why? This article argues that we under-prioritize non-financial interests at our peril. It questions whether the distinctions between financial and nonfinancial interests call for widely different responses and critically assesses the commonly offered justifications for disparate regulatory focus. . . .

I. Non-Financial Interests in Medical Research

Definitional Issues

Certain interests arise in medical research that are not directly associated with the investigator's professional judgment and conduct. These secondary interests, including financial gain and enhanced reputation, may conflict with or negatively impact the primary research goals of promoting unbiased investigations, advancing knowledge, and protecting subjects from unnecessary risk. Secondary interests can

compromise the design, conduct, and reporting of research, while also threatening subject safety and undermining public trust. Non-financial, secondary interests have sometimes been labeled "intrinsic conflicts of interest" or "intellectual conflicts of interest," among other terms. This article uses the simpler term "nonfinancial interest" in the broadest sense to cover any non-financial source of bias that can unduly influence primary research goals. The phrasing "conflict of interest" is intentionally avoided. Often the non-financial interests do not pose a stark conflict with primary research goals, but they can still present misaligned incentives problems.

Non-financial interests include considerations other than direct economic gain that investigators still highly value, such as career advancement. Recruiting subjects and completing published studies are essential to an academic researcher's retention, tenure, and promotion. Apart from simple career advancement, investigators may be swayed by the prospects of enhanced reputation, professional honors and prestige, access to power, and general "glory-seeking." Social relationships formed in the research process, ranging from collegial to competitive to hierarchical, also create pressures and can compromise the actions of investigators, journal editors, peer reviewers, and other key stakeholders. In addition, intellectual or political predispositions can bias research conduct. Even the investigator's sincere interest in helping subjects presents complicating effects, as this can lead to overly optimistic estimations about a study's benefits and make it difficult to concede that a clinical trial should be halted or changed. Also, ambition to advance medical knowledge, investigative zeal, and intellectual passion can undermine investigator objectivity and subject protection. Non-financial interests can likewise arise at the institutional level. For example, reputational concerns and the reluctance to antagonize powerful faculty investigators complicate academic medical centers' institutional oversight.

Prevalence and Degree of Influence

While not attracting the same degree of current scrutiny as financial ties, non-financial interests have long been identified as important determinants of research conduct. Norman Levinsky authored a widely cited "Sounding Board" column in the *New England Journal of Medicine* in 2002 warning that "[t]he potential nonfinancial conflict between the personal interests of investigators and those of subjects is inherent in all research involving human subjects, including that in which there is also a financial conflict." It is also worth remembering that financial interests did not figure prominently, if at all, in many of the notorious research scandals, such as the Tuskegee Syphilis Study and the injection of live cancer cells into elderly patients at the Jewish Chronic Disease Hospital, that led to enactment of the National Research Act of 1974 and the current regulatory scheme for protecting research subjects.

Even in the current era of big-dollar, industry-funded research, concerns continue to recur about non-financial interests compromising research conduct. For example, the Institute of Medicine has warned that researchers' desire to add publications to their curriculum vitas may result in limited value studies. Such investigations provide publication opportunities but do little to advance the state of general medical knowledge, needlessly exposing subjects to harm and requiring them to expend human capital for limited benefit to themselves or the larger research enterprise. Investigative zeal concerns arose following a recent *New England Journal of Medicine* study examining treatment for mild gestational diabetes during pregnancy, even though no financial conflicts were present. Critics alleged that the researchers put the interests of the protocol ahead of subject safety, resulting in a trial design that exposed control subjects to considerable risk of harm. Investigative zeal also played a central role in the controversies surrounding Dr. Thomas Starzl, a pioneer in transplantation research at the University of Pittsburgh. Starzl came under fire for aggressively switching research subjects to a new immunosuppressant drug, even though he had forsaken any financial interest in the study medication. Non-financial interests have also been associated with publication bias. A 2007 World Health Organization (WHO) review of breastfeeding studies found that, in some instances, positive results were more likely to be published than other data. Because there was no industry funding involved, any publication bias was likely due to non-financial considerations, such as the researchers' uncritical, and perhaps ideological, belief in the value of breastfeeding.

Unfortunately, the evidence base is underdeveloped concerning the prevalence and influence of nonfinancial interests. Some studies purport to show that financial ties exert more powerful bias effects than non-financial interests. However, these studies are limited in scope and number. Meanwhile, other investigations suggest that financial conflicts and certain non-financial interests, such as allegiance to a particular treatment approach, raise comparable concerns. Both are associated with quite similar bias effects, including failure to publish negative results and selection of less effective interventions to compare against the favored approach. More importantly, even with financial conflicts, no conclusive evidence causally links financial ties to negative effects as few systematic studies exist and the data remains subject to differing interpretation. As such, it may be premature to conclude that non-financial interests pose considerably less risk than financial conflicts. At the very least, dismissing non-financial interests as too weak to merit serious regulatory attention seems ill-advised.

Indeed, the indirect and circumstantial evidence suggest that non-financial interests raise misaligned incentives problems on a regularly recurring basis. A review of scientific misconduct incidents reported on HHS' Office of Research Integrity's website concluded that many of the

reported incidents of faked data and other troubling actions to alter study results rarely appeared to involve researchers with conflicting financial interests. Instead, the misconduct likely related to "the more mundane but omnipotent pressures on researchers to produce good results so they can get more grants, keep their jobs, and move upward on the ladder of academic success." Apart from empirical studies, many researchers also anecdotally report that non-financial interests are widespread and, at times, pose more risk than financial interests. For example, the editors of PLoS Medicine note that "professional affinities and rivalries . . . scientific or technological competition, religious beliefs, and political or ideological views are often the fuels for [academic] passions and for [research] careers . . . [and these] interests are perhaps even more potent than financial ones." David Korn, writing in the *Journal of the American Medical Association*, observes that nonfinancial interests "may more powerfully influence faculty behavior than any prospect of financial enrichment." Other commentators make similar claims.

II. Why Regulate Differently? . . .

Boundary Confusion

[One] explanation for the heightened emphasis on financial ties is the contention that financial interests can be separated from the larger problem of secondary interests generally in medical research. This carve-out potential supposedly allows for narrowly tailored, efficient regulation. HHS justified the revised NIH conflict of interest rules addressing only financial interests in part because "[w]hile we acknowledge that non-financial conflicts of interest can influence the scientific process, we chose to retain the focus of these regulations on [financial conflict of interests] because we believe this is a discrete area in which there is heightened need to strengthen management and oversight."

But, such line-drawing seems inaccurate and incomplete because of considerable boundary confusion. It may not be possible or effective to treat financial interests as a discrete area of regulation because it is not always clear where financial ties end and non-financial interests begin. Non-financial rewards can also result in financial gain. An investigator's enhanced academic reputation may be monetizeable as it translates into increased ability to attract research grants or improvements in salary. At the institutional level, the prestige and acclaim associated with productive research can be critical to an academic medical center's financial success in terms of securing new grants, donations, and industry funding.

The boundary problems run in the other direction as well. Financial ties can introduce relationships that ultimately bring primarily social, not economic, pressures into the mix, further blurring the distinction between financial and non-financial interests. For example, commentators urge, and many institutions have increasingly adopted, restrictions on even de minimis financial ties, such as small gifts from

pharmaceutical firms. Proponents of these restrictions point to social science and psychological studies that suggest a gift of any amount imposes on its recipient a sense of indebtedness and an inclination to want to reciprocate. Reciprocity and social obligation, in turn, can bias key stakeholders in the research endeavor in subtle yet powerful ways. According to this view, it is the largely social relationship created between recipient and industry donor, not the minimal economic interest implicated, that ultimately poses the most risk and therefore warrants regulatory concern. . . .

Boundary Confusion and the Gelsinger Case

The notorious research scandal involving the death of Jesse Gelsinger demonstrates how boundary confusion complicates regulatory response to secondary interests in medical research. The Gelsinger episode has been typically portrayed as a cautionary tale of financial interests run amok. But it may have been the underlying non-financial interests that actually presented the most serious problems. Gelsinger died while enrolled in a gene therapy study at the University of Pennsylvania (Penn). The clinical trial evaluated a risky procedure for infusing genetically altered viruses as treatment for a rare genetic disorder that compromises liver function. Disturbing improprieties were alleged, including failure to follow the protocol's eligibility criteria and non-disclosure of adverse events in prior animal studies. One of the co-investigators, James Wilson, had patents on some aspects of the procedure and Wilson and Penn had equity interests in the company, Genovo, Inc., that partially funded Penn's Institute for Human Gene Therapy. Genovo had rights to market, and therefore stood to profit, from development of treatments that might result from the research.

Critics questioned whether the lure of financial gain led to lax oversight and a rush to proceed with dangerous experimentation. At first, Wilson steadfastly maintained that monetary gain played little part in the questionable research decisions. Instead, he acknowledged investigative zeal, academic passion, and related non-financial pressures: "I don't think about how my doing this work is going to make me rich. It's about leadership and notoriety and accomplishment. Publishing in first-rate journals. That's what turns us on. You've got to be on the cutting edge and take risks if you're going to stay on top."

Wilson later published an article in 2009, a condition of the settlement for the resulting litigation, in which he explored "lessons learned" from the Gelsinger affair. In this article, Wilson acknowledged the possibility of bias due to the financial ties. Yet he also observed the great difficulty in carving out financial ties from non-financial interests:

> [A]cademic medicine is a competitive profession with the primary measure of success being recognition by your colleague of your research accomplishments . . . The quest for this recognition influences work plans, priorities and decisions, and is a requisite means to the ultimate goal of furthering science.

> Incorporating the incentive for personal financial gain into this complex dynamic is problematic specifically as it relates to the conduct of clinical trials. I learned it is very hard to convincingly uncouple drivers for academic success from the incentives derived from potential financial gain.

In fact, it is plausible that the Gelsinger scandal still would have occurred even if Wilson and Penn had disavowed any financial interests in the outcome of the study. Wilson had ceded large degrees of control over patient care decisions to his co-investigators, who did not have the same financial conflicts, and it has not been clearly established that Wilson made the decision allegedly to violate the protocol's eligibility criteria in enrolling Gelsinger. Meanwhile, co-investigator Dr. Mark Batshaw, who did not have Wilson's financial conflict, spent a great deal of his clinical career dealing with victims of the liver disease. His heavy investment in finding a cure may have compromised judgment and encouraged imprudent risk-taking for the sake of helping future patients. Even Jesse Gelsinger's father, Paul Gelsinger, who initiated the lawsuit against Wilson and Penn, "faults not only Wilson's financial stake but the blind spots that [co-investigator] Batshaw's passion to cure children born with OTCD [the rare liver disease] may have caused."

It is also not clear that Penn's limited ownership interest in Genovo fully explains the University's conduct. Penn's institutional review board and conflict of interest committee allegedly were lax in approving the protocol and not insisting upon stricter conditions for management of Wilson's financial conflicts. But Penn's investment in Genovo, when viewed relative to its overall financial portfolio, was not significant. Also, if members of the IRB or conflict of interest committee felt pressure to "go easy" on Wilson in their review, it may have been less about the financial implications for Penn and more about the inclination to give a wide berth to a powerful "star" investigator and professional colleague whose cutting-edge research brought prestige to the institution as a whole.

Despite all the attention the financial conflicts generated, "[t]here is no evidence that the financial interests of [Penn] and Wilson in the success of the research had any relation to Gelsinger's death." Yet the fallout from the Gelsinger episode has, as a regulatory matter, mostly increased oversight of financial interests. Following the Gelsinger episode, the Food and Drug Administration and NIH did tighten regulation of gene transfer studies generally, including increasing inspections and developing better systems for adverse event reporting. But as for managing secondary interests, the regulatory response largely concerned financial ties. HHS issued new guidance on financial interests and various professional associations revised their conflict of interest policies, largely concentrating on financial conflicts.

The disproportionate focus on financial conflicts is hard to reconcile with the actual facts of the Gelsinger affair. The Gelsinger episode

demonstrates how predominant attention to financial ties leads to oversimplification of very difficult regulatory challenges. If we really want to avoid another Gelsinger episode, additional regulatory effort needs to be directed more systematically and thoughtfully to the non-financial side of the equation. We should not take false comfort from vigor in regulating financial interests, as this may simply not be sufficient.

NOTES AND QUESTIONS

1. *Non-Financial Interests.* What are the non-financial interests identified by the article? Write a list of those interests. Then rank them in order of which ones would be most likely to influence a researcher. How many of those non-financial interests would influence researchers more than financial ones?

2. *History.* Professor Saver explains that Tuskegee, the Jewish Chronic Disease Hospital, and the Gelsinger episode were all influenced by non-financial interests. Think back to what you learned about the experiments at Tuskegee. What role did financial and non-financial interests play in setting the structure of the research study at Tuskegee? The study in Guatemala?

> **Practice Exercise:** How would you revise your conflict of interest policy in light of Professor Saver's article?

3. *Regulating Non-Financial Interests.* According to the article, NIH has focused on financial interests "because we believe this is a discrete area in which there is heightened need to strengthen management and oversight." Financial interests can be regulated through disclosure of the money paid to researchers and by the more detailed informed consent forms recommended by Professor Spece. Recall that Professor Spece proposed informed consent forms that state: "This study is funded by Company X, which has paid Researcher Y $10,000 for each subject enrolled."

How would non-financial interests be disclosed on an informed consent form? Should researchers explain to research subjects that their promotions depend upon the success of their research?

> **Practice Exercise:** Go to the website and read summaries of the five most recent cases of scientific misconduct investigated by the Office of Research Integrity. Can you tell if the researchers were influenced by financial or non-financial interests? Do you think ORI is a good mechanism to limit research misconduct?

4. *How Valuable are IRBs?* Do you think members of the Penn IRB who reviewed the gene therapy study would have been willing to disapprove protocols offered by well-known doctors who worked at Penn? From your experience designing an IRB and reading about the regulations governing them, do you think the IRB system can adequately address both financial and non-financial interests of researchers?

In an op-ed in *The New York Times*, University of Minnesota Medical Ethics Professor Carl Elliott criticized his school's "string of slow, festering research scandals," which included a psychiatrist's felony conviction and research disqualification for fraud, another psychiatrist's suspension for enrolling illiterate Hmong refugees in a study without their consent, and the suicide of a young man enrolled in a department of psychiatry research protocol. Elliott blamed the "antiquated bureaucratic apparatus" of IRBs for some of the problems. He argued that the current regulatory system is "essentially an honor code," not a "formal regulatory system," because IRB members never meet the research subjects but instead rely on the honesty and truthfulness of the researchers in reporting their results. Carl Elliott, The University of Minnesota's Medical Research Mess, N.Y. Times, May 26, 2015, at A19. Do you agree with Elliott's criticisms of IRBs?

> **Practice Exercise:** Professor Hoffman identified deficiencies in the IRB system. Can you add others based on your experience of reviewing protocols?

In the next section, we consider proposed reforms to the IRB system.

3. REFORMS OF THE SYSTEM

Regulating Clinical Research: Informed Consent, Privacy, and IRBs

Sharona Hoffman.
31 Capital University Law Review 71 (2003).

IV. Deficiencies In The Regulatory System

A. IRB Workloads

A 1998 statement issued by the Office of Inspector General of the U.S. Department of Health and Human Services (OIG) was highly critical of contemporary research oversight. The OIG stated that the enormous workloads of many IRBs currently prevent them from adequately performing their review functions. A follow-up report issued by the Office of Inspector General in April of 2000 concluded that in the intervening two years, only minimal progress had been made to diminish the workload pressures of IRBs. The number of initial reviews conducted by IRBs increased by an average of forty-two percent from 1993 to 1998, and some IRBs review up to 2,000 protocols per year. Some IRBs also receive 200 or more reports of adverse events each month concerning the clinical trials they oversee. An external review conducted at Johns Hopkins University after the death of a healthy human subject revealed that until June of 2001 a single IRB, meeting every two weeks, was responsible for the approval of 800 new protocols and the annual reviews they generated. The reviewers emphatically stated: "[w]e view this as grossly inadequate." As noted above, most IRB members have full time jobs on the faculties or staffs of research institutions, and are not paid for

their IRB services or relieved of other work duties. Consequently, the time members can spend on IRB work is limited, and IRBs generally meet only once or twice a month for a few hours.

OPRR expressed concern that the IRBs' work is also hampered by deficient expertise and resources. Some IRB members lack in-depth understanding of the federal regulations governing biomedical research, and IRBs do not have the space, privacy, and level of staff support necessary to perform their duties adequately. Small IRBs may have only one salaried staff member to coordinate all IRB activities and perform administrative tasks.

If IRBs become frequent defendants in lawsuits, the IRB system may be fundamentally threatened. Since IRBs rely heavily on the work of volunteers, they may find it difficult to recruit members in the future. Physicians who are concerned about potential liability may be very reluctant to offer their services to IRBs.

B. Flaws In The Informed Consent Process

An increasing volume of evidence indicates that the informed consent process is severely flawed in many cases. Often, human subjects either are given insufficient information or do not comprehend the data they receive.

The 1998 OIG statement was very critical of informed consent procedures. It noted, for example, that a 1995 Advisory Commission on Human Radiation Experiments found, after interviewing actual subjects that few realized they were involved in research, and many had little understanding of the informed consent forms they had signed.

Commonly, the problem is confusion about the differences between research and clinical treatment. While some research subjects are healthy volunteers who would not otherwise seek medical treatment, many are patients with particular illnesses who are recruited for clinical research by their treating physicians. These patients are vulnerable to a phenomenon known as the "therapeutic misconception." Because they are sick and are recruited for enrollment by their doctors, they become convinced that their research participation will be of definite medical benefit to them. These patients are therefore resistant to explanations that treatments involved in clinical trials are unproven and experimental, no matter how clearly and explicitly these explanations are given.

Numerous studies have focused on the issue of informed consent and have revealed very troubling evidence concerning the ability of research subjects to provide valid consent. In a labor-induction study with fifty-two participants, thirty-nine percent of the women were found to be unaware that they were participating in a research study although all had signed informed consent forms. Even those who realized they were research subjects often misunderstood essential aspects of the study and their role in it.

Several investigators asked fifty cancer patients to review a hypothetical consent form for participation in a placebo-controlled clinical trial. Subjects were asked to interpret four different statements in the consent form. Depending on the statement, the subjects provided incorrect answers twenty-six to fifty-four percent of the time.

In another survey, forty-seven percent of responding researchers indicated that they thought few of their subjects, enrolled in multinational studies in the 1980s, knew they were participating in controlled experiments, even though they had given written consent. In two additional studies, over three quarters of physicians who were questioned believed that subjects rarely understood all the data given to them.

The difficulty of obtaining informed consent is exacerbated by the fact that informed consent documents are generally written in language that is technical and sophisticated and consequently inappropriate for the intended audience. While many informed consent documents require a college level reading comprehension ability, the average American has only an eighth grade reading comprehension level. Rather than providing useful explanations for patients, the forms often serve to educate only the medically trained IRB members who review them.

The challenge of obtaining genuine consent from subjects has had grave consequences for some institutions. During 1998 and 1999, OPRR suspended federal research funding at Chicago's Rush-Presbyterian-St. Luke's Medical Center, the West Los Angeles VA Medical Center, Duke University Medical Center, the University of Illinois at Chicago, and six University of Colorado institutions, all of which are well-regarded research facilities. In January of 2000, research activities were suspended at the University of Pennsylvania and the University of Alabama at Birmingham. Prominent among the violations for which these entities were cited was the failure to obtain adequate informed consent from subjects.

[C]. Informed Consent Is Particularly Difficult To Obtain From Gravely Ill Patients

Genuine informed consent is particularly difficult to obtain when the patients at issue suffer from life-threatening diseases. The decision-making capacity of gravely ill patients is often compromised by the emotional trauma of their illnesses or by various social and familial pressures. Consequently, those who have the most to gain or lose from receiving experimental treatment are also those who are least able to provide meaningful informed consent.

Illness can be viewed as an "ontological assault" that undermines the patient's identity by "attacking the fundamental unity of mind and body." A patient suffering from multiple sclerosis described the experience of disease in these words:

> The most deeply held assumption of daily life is the assumption that I, personally, will continue to be alive and it is in light of this assumption that one engages in daily activities. The onset of illness, however, brings one concretely face-to-face with personal vulnerability. Thus, the person who is ill is unable readily to fit illness into the typified schema used to organize and interpret experience. One finds oneself preoccupied with the demands of the here and now, confined to the present moment, unable effectively to project into the future.

Commentators have noted that serious sickness creates in patients a strong desire to be cared for and to be free of the responsibility and stress of decision-making, as though they were once again children. Many scholars have noted that the thought processes of those suffering from prolonged or serious illnesses are often impaired and have urged that research protocols involving such patients be subject to heightened IRB scrutiny. One informed consent study found that as the seriousness of the illness increases, the ability of potential subjects to remember information relevant to their research participation decreases. Seriously ill patients may experience depression, extreme anxiety, rage, denial, or desperation to find a cure, all of which may cloud their judgment and hamper their ability to evaluate the benefits and risks of a clinical trial.

V. Recommendations

A. IRBs

It is clear that many IRBs inadequately perform their oversight functions. Their deficient performance, however, does not stem from deliberate misconduct or indifference towards the welfare of human subjects, but rather, from inadequate resources, unmanageable workloads, and, in some cases, insufficient expertise. Alleviating these problems is essential to enhancing protection for clinical trial participants.

An effective means of improving the functioning of IRBs would be the addition of more full-time, paid, professionals to their staffs. The size of the professional staff would vary in accordance with the workloads of the IRBs. The professional staff members should be charged with the review of all protocols that are submitted for initial approval, amendment, and continuing review to the IRB. One or two members of the IRB with relevant medical expertise should also read each protocol and provide comments to the staff. The professional staff should then provide written reports to the full IRB membership, summarizing the protocol and their recommendations. The IRB volunteers would be responsible for reading the reports, asking follow-up questions, and voting on whether to approve the protocol.

Under this system, each IRB member will not be required to read every page of every protocol, many of which are quite voluminous, and therefore IRB duties will become less burdensome. The system will also

expedite the review process so that investigators will not have to wait several months for approval of their submitted proposals. Finally, professional staffs would assure that each protocol actually receives a thorough and systematic initial review and continued monitoring, which many commentators have suggested does not always occur when these tasks are left exclusively in the hands of well-meaning, but overworked volunteers.

Additional funding would obviously be needed to support the hiring of adequate professional staffs. To obtain the necessary economic support, IRBs could charge commercial research sponsors for review of their protocols. Similarly, if the research is sponsored by a governmental entity, the sponsor could be required to add a fixed sum or a small percentage to its grant in order to support IRB activities. Nothing in the federal regulations prohibits the imposition of such charges.

NOTES AND QUESTIONS

1. *Overloaded IRBs*. Professor Hoffman's article discussed the fact that some IRBs are responsible for reviewing up to 2,000 protocols per year. When coupled with the statement that many IRBs meet twice per month, these IRBs would be responsible for reviewing over eighty new protocols each meeting. Even if each protocol took an average of fifteen minutes to approve or deny, the IRB would need to spend over twenty hours each meeting to review the new protocols. Given that many IRB members have full-time careers and serve as volunteers, do you think researchers should depend on this system and expect individuals to contribute this much time as a volunteer? Also, given that Professor Hoffman stated that most new protocols are quite voluminous, how long do you think it would take, on average, to adequately review each new protocol?

2. *Volunteers*. How extensive is the training you think necessary to become an IRB member? Did you know average citizens may apply to become IRB members? See Human Subjects Office, University of Iowa, Become an IRB Member, https://hso.research.uiowa.edu/become-irb-member. Who is likely to volunteer? Does the presence of volunteers affect the reliability of IRB decisions? The Iowa website mentions a "diverse membership." What would it mean for an IRB to have a diverse membership?

3. *Full-Time IRBs*. Do you agree with Professor Hoffman that IRBs should include full-time staff, which would alleviate the workload for the rest of the IRB? How would you recommend paying the full-time staff members (e.g., raising IRB fees for researchers, from the institution, etc.)?

4. *Rethink the Clinical Trial?* A more fundamental challenge comes from *The New York Times*: "do clinical trials even work? Or are the diseases of individuals so particular that testing experimental medicines in broad groups is doomed to create more frustration than knowledge?" Clifton Leaf, Op-Ed, Do Clinical Trials Work?, N.Y. Times, Jul. 14, 2013, at SR1. The author points out that 95% of drugs in initial clinical trials are not approved, that the subject populations of research do not match the characteristics of patients with the disease being studied, and that as the test population

increases in number from Phase I to Phase III, the percentage of drug effectiveness decreases. Id.; see also J.A. DiMasi et al., Trends in Risk Associated With New Drug Development: Success Rates for Investigational Drugs, 87:3 Nature 272 (March 2010) ("The clinical approval success rate in the United States was 16% for self-originated drugs (originating from the pharmaceutical company itself) during both the 1993–1998 and the 1999–2004 subperiods. For all compounds (including licensed-in and licensed-out drugs in addition to self-originated drugs), the clinical approval success rate for the entire study period was 19%."); J.A. DiMasi et al., Clinical Approval Success Rates for Investigational Cancer Drugs, 94:3 Nature 329 (September 2013) ("the estimated clinical approval success rate for cancer compounds was 13.4%").

Is there any replacement for the traditional clinical trial? What do you think of these suggestions?

> [D]esign small clinical trials and enroll only those who have the appropriate genetic or molecular signature; test[ ] up to a dozen drugs from multiple companies, phasing out those that don't appear to be working and subbing in others, without stopping the study. Part of the novelty lies in a statistical technique called Bayesian analysis that lets doctors quickly glean information about which therapies are working best.

Id. "It is important to maintain a philosophy of continual improvement with respect to clinical trials broadly and specifically with an aim towards optimizing every aspect of the research and development process." David B. Fogel, Factors Associated With Clinical Trials that Fail and Opportunities of Improving the Likelihood of Success: A Review, doi: 10.1016/j.conctc.2018.08.001. How would you recommend repeatedly improving clinical trials?

5. *COVID Changes.* In Spring 2020, the Office for Human Research Protections (OHRP) released guidance on conducting research in light of the COVID-19 pandemic. OHRP Guidance on COVID-19, Apr. 8, 2020, https://www.hhs.gov/ohrp/regulations-and-policy/guidance/ohrp-guidance-on-covid-19/index.html. For studies not involving COVID treatments, tests, or vaccines, the OHRP has highlighted the ability to make changes to approved research prior to IRB review and approval if the changes are necessary to eliminate apparent immediate hazards to the research subject—for example, eliminating unnecessary in-person visits or converting those visits to telephone or video calls. The changes must be reported to the IRB, but may be made without IRB approval. Similar guidance has been issued by the FDA for research governed by that agency. FDA Guidance on Conduct of Clinical Trials of Medical Products during COVID-19 Pandemic: Guidance for Industry, Investigators, and Institutional Review Boards, Mar., 2020 (updated Apr. 2, 2020), https://www.hhs.gov/ohrp/sites/default/files/fda-covid-guidance-2apr2020.pdf.

6. *Not Doing Enough for Patients?* Abigail Burroughs was battling cancer at age 21 when she ran out of conventional treatment options. She then worked hard to lobby people who could help "create wider access to

developmental cancer drugs and other drugs for serious life-threatening illnesses." Abigail died on June 9, 2001; however, Abigail Alliance, the organization founded by her father, remained to carry on her fight. The organization is dedicated to helping inform people about clinical trials and to work on getting drugs into the market more quickly.

Has the research system failed because it does not help those patients most in need, as Abigail Alliance suggested in the following case? This opinion should help you to review the entire IRB process that we have studied in this section as well as the constitutional law arguments that we learned in Chapter 1. Start to identify the key strengths and weaknesses of the system as you read the opinion.

Abigail Alliance for Better Access to Developmental Drugs v. von Eschenbach

United States Court of Appeals, District of Columbia Circuit, 2007.
495 F.3d 695.

■ GRIFFITH, CIRCUIT JUDGE:

This case presents the question whether the Constitution provides terminally ill patients a right of access to experimental drugs that have passed limited safety trials but have not been proven safe and effective. The district court held there is no such right. A divided panel of this Court held there is. Because we conclude that there is no fundamental right "deeply rooted in this Nation's history and tradition" of access to experimental drugs for the terminally ill, *see Washington v. Glucksberg*, we affirm the judgment of the district court.

I.

A.

The Abigail Alliance for Better Access to Developmental Drugs (the "Alliance") is an organization of terminally ill patients and their supporters that seeks expanded access to experimental drugs for the terminally ill. The Food, Drug, and Cosmetic Act ("FDCA" or "Act"), however, generally prohibits access to new drugs unless and until they have been approved by the Food and Drug Administration ("FDA"). *See* 21 U.S.C. § 355(a). Gaining FDA approval can be a long process. First, an experimental drug's sponsor (*e.g.*, a drug company) must submit an application for approval. Because no drug may be approved without a finding of "substantial evidence that the drug will have the effect it purports or is represented to have," an application must contain "full reports of investigations which have been made to show whether or not such drug is safe for use and whether such drug is effective in use." Such reports rely in large measure on clinical trials with human subjects.

But before a sponsor can even begin human testing, it must submit for the FDA's approval an investigational new drug application ("IND"). Once the application for human testing has been approved, several phases of clinical testing begin. The Alliance's amended complaint

alleges that this testing process is an extremely lengthy one, requiring nearly seven years for the average experimental drug.

Clinical testing for safety and effectiveness requires three or sometimes four phases. Phase I involves the initial introduction of a new drug into human subjects. A Phase I study usually consists of twenty to eighty subjects and is "designed to determine the metabolism and pharmacologic actions of the [new] drug in humans, the side effects associated with increasing doses, and, if possible, to gain early evidence on effectiveness." Although gathering data on effectiveness may be part of Phase I, its primary focus is to determine whether the drug is safe enough for continued human testing. Phase II studies are "well controlled" and "closely monitored" clinical trials of no more than several hundred subjects, used to evaluate both the "effectiveness of the drug for a particular indication" and its "common short-term side effects and risks."

Phase III studies are expanded clinical trials of several hundred to several thousand subjects designed to "gather . . . additional information about effectiveness and safety that is needed to evaluate the overall benefit-risk relationship of the drug and to provide an adequate basis for physician labeling." [In some circumstances, a Phase IV review is conducted, which "delineate[s] additional information about the drug's risks, benefits, and optimal use."] At any time during the clinical trials, a drug sponsor is required to notify the FDA of "[a]ny adverse experience associated with the use of the drug that is both serious and unexpected," and the FDA may order a "clinical hold" halting the trials if it determines that safety concerns so warrant. To guide the clinical testing process, Congress has directed the FDA to establish "[s]cientific advisory panels" to "provid[e] expert scientific advice and recommendations to the Secretary regarding a clinical investigation of a drug or the approval for marketing of a drug." These panels must include scientists from a variety of disciplines.

Terminally ill patients need not, however, always await the results of the clinical testing process. The FDA and Congress have created several programs designed to provide early access to promising experimental drugs when warranted. For example, under the "treatment IND" program, the FDA may approve use of an investigational drug by patients not part of the clinical trials for the treatment of "serious or immediately life-threatening disease[s]" if there exists "no comparable or satisfactory alternative drug or other therapy," if "[t]he drug is under investigation in a controlled clinical trial," and if the drug's sponsor "is actively pursuing marketing approval of the investigational drug with due diligence." The FDA reserves the right, however, to deny any treatment IND request if (1) the agency believes there is no "reasonable basis" to conclude that the drug is effective; or (2) granting the request "[w]ould . . . expose the patient [ ] . . . to an unreasonable and significant additional risk of illness or injury." Sponsors may not profit from any

approved treatment IND program and may only "recover costs of manufacture, research, development, and handling of the investigational drug."[4]

B.

Concluding that the FDA's current process for early access to new drugs was inadequate to meet the needs of its terminally ill members, the Alliance submitted its own proposals to the FDA. Those proposals culminated in a "citizen petition" to the FDA, *see* 21 C.F.R. § 10.25, arguing that there is a "different risk-benefit tradeoff facing patients who are terminally ill and who have no other treatment options." Although the Alliance agreed that "[e]xtensive marshalling of evidence regarding drug interactions, dose optimization, and the like" is "appropriate for new drugs to treat patients with other alternatives . . . these steps may well entail a delay that is fatal" for terminally ill patients. The Alliance contended that these patients "should have the ability to opt for a new treatment that has met a lower evidentiary hurdle with respect to safety and efficacy." The Alliance's proposal suggested that the FDA allow early access based upon "the risk of illness, injury, or death from the disease in the absence of the drug." Accordingly, the Alliance requested that the FDA promulgate new regulations that would allow sponsors to market experimental drugs, under some circumstances, after the completion of Phase I trials.

The FDA never responded to the Alliance's citizen petition, but did respond to the Alliance's earlier submissions. After noting that a number of senior FDA officials had reviewed those submissions, the agency concluded that the Alliance "raised several important questions about expanded access that we believe deserve further consideration," but questioned whether the specific proposal put forward by the Alliance "would have the intended desirable effects for patients." The officials concluded that the early access proposed by the Alliance "points to an area of significant range of opinion within the patient and provider communities about the standards that should be met before a drug is marketed." Although "some members of the cancer community have suggested that [the] FDA needs to maintain a strong clinical trial system as the basis of the approval of cancer drugs, . . . others, like [the Alliance],

---

[4] The FDA has several other regulatory programs designed to hasten research of the safety and effectiveness of drugs for terminally or severely ill patients and allow early access where scientifically and medically warranted. For example, under its "Fast Track" program, the agency has "established procedures designed to expedite the development, evaluation, and marketing of new therapies intended to treat persons with life-threatening and severely-debilitating illnesses, especially where no satisfactory alternative therapy exists." 21 C.F.R. § 312.80. Fast Track allows the FDA to waive its IND application requirement if it is "unnecessary or cannot be achieved," *id.* § 312.10, and even allows a waiver request to be made "[i]n an emergency . . . by telephone or other rapid communication," *id.* The "Accelerated Approval" program provides a truncated approval process for "certain new drug products that have been studied for their safety and effectiveness in treating serious or life-threatening illnesses and that provide meaningful therapeutic benefit to patients over existing treatments." *Id.* § 314.500. The FDA categorizes some new drugs, including nearly all cancer drugs, as "priority drugs" and seeks to accelerate their availability.

have criticized [the FDA] for relying too heavily on completing certain trials before approval." The FDA noted that "[i]n the realm of reviewing medical products to treat serious and life-threatening diseases, there is inevitable tension between early availability of products to patients, especially patients with refractory disease, and the need to obtain sufficient data to provide a reasonable expectation of benefit and lack of excessive harm."

Relying upon its experience exercising its scientific and medical judgment in creating its regulations for experimental drugs and, in certain circumstances, exceptions to those regulations for the terminally ill, the FDA noted that "a reasonably precise estimate of response rate" and "enough experience to detect serious adverse effects" are "critical" in determining when experimental drugs should be made available. For example, most experimental cancer drugs "have potentially lethal toxicity, with potentially large effects on a patient's remaining quality of life." Accordingly, "it does not serve patients well to make drugs too widely available before there is a reasonable assessment of such risks to guide patient decisions, and experience in managing them." The FDA concluded that accepting the Alliance's proposal "would upset the appropriate balance that [it is] seeking to maintain, by giving almost total weight to the goal of early availability and giving little recognition to the importance of marketing drugs with reasonable knowledge for patients and physicians of their likely clinical benefit and their toxicity."

Having thus been rejected by the FDA, the Alliance turned to the courts, arguing that the United States Constitution provides a right of access to experimental drugs for its members. In a complaint that mirrored much of its earlier submissions to the FDA, the Alliance argued that the FDA's lengthy clinical trials, combined with the "FDA's restrictions on pre-approval availability[,] amount to a death sentence for these [terminally ill] patients." Nor, the Alliance argues, are the FDA's exceptions to the clinical testing process sufficient to provide the terminally ill the access they need because they "are small, when they exist at all," and the ban on profits prevents many drug sponsors from participating.

"Terminally ill patients," in the Alliance's view, "are typically willing to assume risks. . . ." Before the district court, the Alliance argued that the Constitution guarantees them the right to do so. The district court rejected that argument, holding that "there is no constitutional right of access to unapproved drugs." A divided panel of this Court reversed, concluding that "where there are no alternative government-approved treatment options, a terminally ill, mentally competent adult patient's informed access to potentially life-saving investigational new drugs determined by the FDA after Phase I trials to be sufficiently safe for expanded human trials warrants protection under the Due Process Clause." We vacated that decision and granted rehearing *en banc*.

As framed by the Alliance, we now consider:

> Whether the liberty protected by the Due Process Clause embraces the right of a terminally ill patient with no remaining approved treatment options to decide, in consultation with his or her own doctor, whether to seek access to investigational medications that the [FDA] concedes are safe and promising enough for substantial human testing.

That is, we must determine whether terminally ill patients have a fundamental right to experimental drugs that have passed Phase I clinical testing. If such a right exists, the Alliance argues that both 21 C.F.R. § 312.34(b)(3) (preventing access to experimental drugs for terminally ill patients where there is insufficient evidence of effectiveness or where there is an unreasonable risk of injury) and 21 C.F.R. § 312.7 (prohibiting drug manufacturers from profiting on the sale of experimental drugs) must be subjected to strict scrutiny because they interfere with a fundamental constitutional right. We do not address the broader question of whether access to medicine might ever implicate fundamental rights.

II.

The Due Process Clause of the Fifth Amendment provides that "[n]o person shall be . . . deprived of life, liberty, or property, without due process of law." In *Glucksberg,* the Supreme Court described its "established method of substantive-due-process analysis" as having "two primary features."

> First, we have regularly observed that the Due Process Clause specially protects those fundamental rights and liberties which are, objectively, deeply rooted in this Nation's history and tradition and implicit in the concept of ordered liberty, such that neither liberty nor justice would exist if they were sacrificed. Second, we have required in substantive-due-process cases a careful description of the asserted fundamental liberty interest.

We will assume *arguendo* that the Alliance's description of its asserted right would satisfy *Glucksberg*'s "careful description" requirement. Looking to whether the Alliance has demonstrated that its right is deeply rooted in this Nation's history, tradition, and practices, the Alliance's claim for constitutional protection rests on two arguments: (1) that "common law and historical American practices have traditionally trusted individual doctors and their patients with almost complete autonomy to evaluate the efficacy of medical treatments"; and (2) that FDA policy is "inconsistent with the way that our legal tradition treats persons in all other life-threatening situations." More specifically, the Alliance argues that the concepts of self-defense, necessity, and interference with rescue are broad enough to demonstrate the existence of the fundamental right they seek-a right for "persons in mortal peril" to "try to save their own lives, even if the chosen means would otherwise be illegal or involve enormous risks."

A.

"We begin, as we do in all due process cases, by examining our Nation's history, legal traditions, and practices." The Alliance argues that its right can be found in our history and legal traditions because "the government never interfered with the judgment of individual doctors about the medical *efficacy* of particular drugs until 1962," *i.e.*, when major amendments were made to the Food, Drug, and Cosmetic Act. . . .

The Alliance has little to say, however, about our Nation's history of regulating the *safety* of drugs. The Alliance's effort to focus on efficacy regulation ignores one simple fact: it is unlawful for the Alliance to procure experimental drugs not only because they have not been proven effective, but because they have not been proven safe. Although the Alliance contends that it only wants drugs that "are safe and promising enough for substantial human testing," *i.e.*, drugs that have passed Phase I testing, current law bans access to an experimental drug on safety grounds until it has successfully completed all phases of testing. *See* 21 C.F.R. § 312.21(b) (requiring that Phase II studies examine "*common short-term side effects and risks*" of new drugs) (emphasis added); *id.* § 312.21(c) (requiring Phase III studies to "gather . . . additional information about effectiveness and *safety* that is needed to evaluate the overall benefit-risk relationship of the drug") (emphasis added). Thus, to succeed on its claim of a fundamental right of access for the terminally ill to experimental drugs, the Alliance must show not only that there is a tradition of access to drugs that have not yet been proven effective, but also a tradition of access to drugs that have not yet been proven safe.

. . . we conclude that our Nation has long expressed interest in drug regulation, calibrating its response in terms of the capabilities to determine the risks associated with both drug safety and efficacy.

Drug regulation in the United States began with the Colonies and States when the Colony of Virginia's legislature passed an act in 1736 that addressed the dispensing of more drugs than was "necessary or useful" because that practice had become "dangerous and intolerable." . . . By 1870, at least twenty-five states or territories had statutes regulating adulteration (impure drugs), and a few others had laws addressing poisons. In the early history of our Nation, we observe not a tradition of protecting a right of access to drugs, but rather governments responding to the risks of new compounds as they become aware of and able to address those risks. . . . In 1848, the Import Drug Act, ch. 70, 9 Stat. 237 (1848), banned "imported adulterated drugs" after a Congressional committee concluded that "this country had become the grand mart and receptacle of all the refuse [drug] merchandise . . ., not only from the European warehouses, but from the whole Eastern world." . . . Congress acted again when it passed the Biologics Controls Act of 1902, ch. 1378, 32 Stat. 728 (1902), in response to a series of deadly reactions to a tainted diphtheria vaccine that killed children in New

Jersey and Missouri. . . . Congress followed with the Pure Food and Drugs Act of 1906, which prohibited the manufacture of any drug that was "adulterated or misbranded."

The current regime of federal drug regulation began to take shape with the Food, Drug, and Cosmetic Act of 1938. The Act required that drug manufacturers provide proof that their products were safe before they could be marketed. The new Act also prohibited false therapeutic claims. . . .

We end our historical analysis where the Alliance would prefer it begin-with the 1962 Amendments to the FDCA. Undoubtedly, as the Alliance argues at length, Congress amended the FDCA in 1962 to explicitly require that the FDA only approve drugs deemed effective for public use. Thus, the Alliance argues that, prior to 1962, patients were free to make their own decisions whether a drug might be effective. But even assuming *arguendo* that efficacy regulation began in 1962, the Alliance's argument ignores our Nation's history of drug safety regulation described above. . . .

B.

The Alliance next turns to several common law doctrines, arguing that barring access to experimental drugs for terminally ill patients is "inconsistent with the way that our legal tradition treats persons in all other life-threatening situations." Specifically, the Alliance argues that three doctrines—(1) the doctrine of necessity; (2) the tort of intentional interference with rescue; and (3) the right to self-defense—each support the recognition of a right to self-preservation. Such a right to self-preservation, the Alliance believes, would permit "persons in mortal peril . . . to try to save their own lives, even if the chosen means would otherwise be illegal or involve enormous risks." Specifically, in this case, the Alliance believes that a right to self-preservation would give the terminally ill a constitutionally protected right of access to experimental drugs.

Looking first to the Alliance's necessity argument, the Alliance invokes the common law doctrine, which " 'traditionally covered the situation where physical forces beyond the actor's control rendered illegal conduct the lesser of two evils.' " . . . Nonetheless, the Supreme Court's analysis of the common law doctrine of necessity in *Oakland* leaves little room for the Alliance's argument that common law necessity could justify overriding the Food, Drug, and Cosmetic Act.

In *Oakland,* a group of patients seeking access to marijuana for medicinal purposes argued that "because necessity was a defense at common law, medical necessity should be read into the Controlled Substances Act." The Supreme Court rejected that argument because "[u]nder any conception of legal necessity, one principle is clear: The defense cannot succeed when the legislature itself has made a determination of values." Although the Court limited its analysis to the

statutory issue and did not address the defendant's constitutional arguments, the learning of *Oakland* is clear. Congress may limit or even eliminate a necessity defense that might otherwise be available. That is precisely what the FDCA has done. Congress has prohibited general access to experimental drugs, *see* 21 U.S.C. § 355(a), and has prescribed in detail how experimental drugs may be studied and used by the scientific and medical communities, *see id.* § 355(i). Given the Supreme Court's conclusion that the common law defense of necessity remains controversial and cannot override a value judgment already determined by the legislature, the common law doctrine of necessity provides little support to the Alliance's proposed right.

The Alliance next invokes the tort of intentional interference with lifesaving efforts, which the Restatement of Torts defines as "intentionally prevent[ing] a third person from giving to another aid *necessary* to his bodily security." But that is not this case. The Alliance seeks access to drugs that are experimental and have not been shown to be safe, let alone effective at (or "necessary" for) prolonging life. Indeed, the Alliance concedes that taking experimental drugs can "involve enormous risks." In essence, the Alliance insists on a constitutional right to assume any level of risk. It is difficult to see how a tort addressing interference with providing "necessary" aid would guarantee a constitutional right to override the collective judgment of the scientific and medical communities expressed through the FDA's clinical testing process. Thus, we cannot agree that the tort of intentional interference with rescue evidences a right of access to experimental drugs.

Finally, the Alliance looks to traditional self-defense principles to support its proposed constitutional right. The common law doctrine of self-defense provides that "[o]ne who is not the aggressor . . . is justified in using a reasonable amount of force against his adversary when he reasonably believes (a) that he is in immediate danger of unlawful bodily harm from his adversary and (b) that the use of such force is necessary to avoid this danger." Self-defense typically arises when a victim is being attacked by an aggressor and uses reasonable force to overcome immediate danger. The Alliance argues that self-defense permits victims to assume two types of risk: (1) the risk that the victim will kill the attacker; and (2) the risk that "[f]ighting back may dramatically increase the . . . harm" to the victim. So, the argument goes, if victims of crimes are allowed to assume these risks in defending their lives, terminally ill patients should also be allowed to assume the risk that an experimental drug may hasten their deaths.

That self-defense principles should be applied in the medical context is evidenced, the Alliance argues, by the Supreme Court's abortion jurisprudence. . . . *Roe* "recognized another, entirely separate right to abortion: a woman's right to abort a fetus *at any stage of a pregnancy* if doing so is necessary to preserve her life or health." "That right," the Alliance argues, "is grounded in traditional self-defense principles rather

than privacy. . . ." Applying that concept here, the Alliance argues that because its terminally ill members are in immediate danger of harm from cancer, they can use whatever medical means are necessary to defend themselves. Thus, they argue, even if a medical treatment might otherwise be prohibited by law, the doctrine of self-defense justifies access to that treatment, just as self-defense justifies an assault victim using physical force otherwise prohibited by law.

This analogy also fails because this case is not about using reasonable force to defend oneself (as in most cases involving self-defense), nor is it about access to life-saving medical treatment. This case is about whether there is a constitutional right to assume, in the Alliance's own words, "enormous risks," in pursuit of *potentially* life-saving drugs. Unlike the cases in which the doctrine of self-defense might properly be invoked, this case involves risk from drugs with no proven therapeutic effect, which at a minimum separates this example from the abortion "life of the mother" exception. Because terminally ill patients cannot fairly be characterized as using reasonable force to defend themselves when they take unproven and possibly unsafe drugs, the Alliance's desire that the terminally ill be free to assume the risk of experimental drugs cannot draw support from the doctrine of self-defense.

III.

Although it has not addressed the precise constitutional argument urged by the Alliance, we find it highly significant that the Supreme Court has rejected several similar challenges to the FDCA and related laws brought on statutory grounds. And other courts have rejected arguments that the Constitution provides an affirmative right of access to particular medical treatments reasonably prohibited by the Government.

In keeping with those decisions, we conclude that the Alliance has not provided evidence of a right to procure and use experimental drugs that is deeply rooted in our Nation's history and traditions. To the contrary, our Nation's history evidences increasing regulation of drugs as both the ability of government to address these risks has increased and the risks associated with drugs have become apparent. Similarly, our legal traditions of allowing a necessity defense, prohibiting intentional interference with rescue, and recognizing a right of self-defense cannot justify creating a constitutional right to assume any level of risk without regard to the scientific and medical judgment expressed through the clinical testing process.

IV.

Because the Alliance's claimed right is not fundamental, the Alliance's claim of a right of access to experimental drugs is subject only to rational basis scrutiny. . . . Applying the rational basis standard to the Alliance's complaint, we cannot say that the government's interest does

not bear a rational relation to a legitimate state interest. That conclusion is compelled by the Supreme Court's decision in *United States v. Rutherford,* 442 U.S. 544, 99 S.Ct. 2470, 61 L.Ed.2d 68 (1979). In that case, terminally ill patients sought to prevent the FDA from prohibiting access to the drug laetrile, even though the drug had not been approved for public use. In rejecting a challenge by terminally ill patients claiming that the FDCA's safety requirement did not apply to them, the Supreme Court held that "[f]or the terminally ill, as for anyone else, a drug is unsafe if its potential for inflicting death or physical injury is not offset by the possibility of therapeutic benefit." . . .

Although terminally ill patients desperately need curative treatments, as *Rutherford* holds, their deaths can certainly be hastened by the use of a potentially toxic drug with no proven therapeutic benefit. Thus, we must conclude that, prior to distribution of a drug outside of controlled studies, the Government has a rational basis for ensuring that there is a scientifically and medically acceptable level of knowledge about the risks and benefits of such a drug. We therefore hold that the FDA's policy of limiting access to investigational drugs is rationally related to the legitimate state interest of protecting patients, including the terminally ill, from potentially unsafe drugs with unknown therapeutic effects.

V.

For the foregoing reasons, the judgment of the district court is affirmed.

So ordered.

■ ROGERS, CIRCUIT JUDGE, with whom CHIEF JUDGE GINSBURG joins, dissenting:

Today, the court rejects the claim that terminally ill patients who have exhausted all government-approved treatment options have a fundamental right to access investigational new drugs. The court's opinion reflects a flawed conception of the right claimed by the Abigail Alliance for Better Access to Developmental Drugs and a stunning misunderstanding of the stakes. The court shifts the inquiry required by *Glucksberg,* by changing the nature of the right, by conflating the right with the deprivation, and by prematurely advancing countervailing government interests. The court fails to come to grips with the Nation's history and traditions, which reflect deep respect and protection for the right to preserve life, a corollary to the right to life enshrined in the Constitution. The court confuses this liberty interest with the manner in which the Alliance alleges that the liberty has been deprived, namely by denying terminally ill patients access to investigational medications under the narrow conditions described by the Alliance. The court conflates the inquiry as to whether a fundamental right exists at all with whether the government has demonstrated a compelling interest, when strictly scrutinized, rendering its restrictive policy constitutional.

These missteps lead the court to rely upon how rights and liberties have been limited and restricted—addressing regulations to prevent fraud in the sale of misbranded and adulterated medications or safety restrictions applicable to all medicines for any palliative purpose—which says little about the historic importance of the underlying right of a person to save her own life. Likewise, in its treatment of the common law doctrines of necessity, interference with rescue, and self defense, the court points to evolved limitations on those doctrines while ignoring the core concerns that animate them, namely the special importance of life and attempts to preserve it. That the ultimate protection of such varying attempts to save life is cabined by the precedents—regarding what constitutes "necessity," the related "necessity" of any aid being given to a third party, and the "reasonable" and "necessary" limitations on any force used in self-defense—does not suggest the absence of an underlying right to attempt to protect life, but rather the recognition of competing governmental interests that in various circumstances justify the deprivation of or a limitation upon the right. . . .

In the end, it is startling that the oft-limited rights to marry, to fornicate, to have children, to control the education and upbringing of children, to perform varied sexual acts in private, and to control one's own body even if it results in one's own death or the death of a fetus have all been deemed fundamental rights covered, although not always protected, by the Due Process Clause, but the right to try to save one's life is left out in the cold despite its textual anchor in the right to life. . . . It bears outlining the history and common law basis for the Alliance's claim in order to demonstrate, once again, that the history and traditions of this Nation support the right of a terminal patient, and not the government, to make this fundamentally personal choice involving her own life. Because judicial precedents and the historical record require strict scrutiny before upsetting rights of this magnitude, the FDA must demonstrate a compelling governmental interest before its policy restricting access can survive. Accordingly, I would remand the case to the district court to make the initial determination as to whether FDA has met its burden, and I respectfully dissent. . . .

III.

For these reasons, I have serious disagreements with the court's assessment of the Alliance's claim to a fundamental right protected by the Fifth Amendment to the Constitution. It is no more than tragic wordplay to suggest that the Alliance's liberty claim to potentially life prolonging medications, when no other government approved alternatives exist, does not involve a corollary to the right to life enshrined in the Fifth Amendment to the Constitution. Denying a terminally ill patient her only chance to survive without even a strict showing of governmental necessity presupposes a dangerous brand of paternalism. As the court phrases it, because "*[w]e* . . . cannot know until the clinical testing process has been completed that these drugs are

necessary," the terminally ill patient, informed by her physician, is denied a right to decide whether to bear those risks in an attempt to preserve her life. Such intervention is directly at odds with this Nation's history and traditions giving recognition to individual self-determination and autonomy where one's own life is at stake and should extend no further than the result in this case. Because the right of a terminally ill patient to access potentially life-saving investigational medications satisfies the *Glucksberg* test, I would remand this case for the district court to assess in the first instance whether there exists a compelling governmental interest, narrowly tailored, to overcome the Alliance's interest. Accordingly, I respectfully dissent.

NOTES AND QUESTIONS

1. *What Is the Fundamental Right Involved?* As we learned in Chapter 1 when we read *Glucksberg*, and as the majority and dissent insist here, substantive due process analysis requires that the claimed constitutional right be identified with specificity. The majority and dissent argue about the constitutional right alleged here by Abigail Alliance. How does the majority characterize the right? How does the dissent characterize it? Do you agree with the majority that there is no "right of access to experimental drugs that have passed limited safety trials but have not been proven safe and effective"? Do you agree with the dissent that the right to life is more fundamental than many other rights that the Supreme Court has recognized?

2. *Common Law.* Review the common law arguments about necessity, rescue and self-defense. Did you find those arguments persuasive here? Is any one of those arguments more persuasive than the others? How did the majority and the dissent disagree about the application of the common law in *Abigail Alliance*?

3. *Remand.* If the case had been remanded to apply strict scrutiny, as the dissent argued, what would have been the result in the district court? Could the government's arguments about not making these drugs available to terminally ill patients survive strict scrutiny?

4. *Bioethical Principles.* The dissent speaks frequently about protecting individual autonomy to make choices about staying alive. What bioethical principle, if any, guided the majority's reasoning? Is the dissent correct that the majority demonstrated "a dangerous brand of paternalism"?

5. *Canterbury.* The dissent referred to *Canterbury*, which we read at the beginning of this chapter. Which opinion is more faithful to *Canterbury*, the majority or the dissent? Is the lesson of *Canterbury* and this chapter that the Abigail Alliance deserves access to these drugs as long as they give full informed consent?

6. *Right to Try Laws.* The federal Right to Try Act, 21 USC §§ 360bbb–0a, was passed in May 2018. Unlike for drugs made available under FDA "compassionate use" provisions (now renamed "Expanded Access," *infra*), the FDA does not approve or deny right to try requests. It "recommends that patients first consult with their physician and that physicians consult with the sponsor of the investigational drug or biological product. The sponsor is in the best position to provide information about whether the drug or biological product meets the criteria to be considered an eligible investigational drug for use under the Right to Try Act." FDA, Right to Try, https://www.fda.gov/patients/learn-about-expanded-access-and-other-treatment-options/right-try. As of 2020, 41 states have passed right-to-try laws. The federal law applies to everyone, but you can also find out your state's laws identified at https://righttotry.org/in-your-state/.

> **Practice Exercise:** Draft a sample right to try law. Then go to the website and compare your version to the federal Right to Try Act. Would you make any changes to the proposed language? What would you tell a pharmaceutical manufacturer to do if confronted with a request?

In response to these concerns, the FDA has amended its own "Expanded Access" provisions to streamline the process. See Food & Drug Administration, Expanded Access, https://www.fda.gov/news-events/public-health-focus/expanded-access. Regardless of whether access is sought through the FDA process or the Right to Try avenue, however, patients cannot access experimental medications without the manufacturers' consent. Why might a manufacturer decline to make such drugs available outside of recognized clinical trials?

In the next section, we identify five issues that challenge the current system and that you can expect to confront in practice.

C. LOOKING AHEAD: IMPROVING CONSENT IN NEW CIRCUMSTANCES

1. CAN TECHNOLOGY IMPROVE INFORMED CONSENT?

Do you think informed consent is satisfied if every item of the following checklist is met?

1) that the subjects are not only patients and, to the extent to which they are patients, that their therapeutic interests, even if not incidental, will be subordinated to scientific interests;
2) that it is problematic and indeterminate whether their welfare will be better served by placing their medical fate in the hands of a physician rather than an investigator;
3) that in opting for the care of a physician they may be better or worse off and for such and such reasons;

4) that clinical research will allow doctors to penetrate the mysteries of medicine's uncertainties about which treatments are best, dangerous, or ineffective;
5) that clinical research may possibly be in the patient's immediate best interest, perhaps promise benefits in the future, or provide no benefit, particularly if the patient is assigned to a control (placebo) arm of a study;
6) that research is governed by a research protocol and a research question and, therefore, his or her interests and needs will yield to the claims of science; and
7) that physician-investigators will respect whatever decision the subject ultimately makes;
8) that much of this information should be included in a video shown at the beginning of the informed consent process;
9) that the video should explain the difference between research and therapy;
10) that the investigator or a research nurse should orally discuss all aspects of the clinical trial with the subject;
11) that participants will be quizzed on their understanding of the protocol;
12) that protocols should be adapted to an eighth grade reading level;
13) that every IRB should include an expert in reading comprehension and elementary education.

Hoffman, *supra*, at 88–89 (incorporating list of ideas suggested by Professor Jay Katz).

One study found that informed consent increased considerably if five communications strategies were followed: keep forms at an eighth-grade level; use larger font size (14), more white space, bulleting, bolding, and underlining; use graphic displays instead of text; add a verbal description of the project; and keep the form short.

Practice Exercise: Go to the website and watch the video on informed consent prepared by the National Institutes of Mental Health (NIMH). Do you think it is a good model of informed consent?

One study found that informed consent increased considerably if five communications strategies were followed:

— keep forms at an **eighth-grade** level;

— use larger **font size** (14), more white space, bulleting, bolding, and underlining;

— use **graphic displays** instead of text;

— add a **verbal description** of the project;

— and keep the form **SHORT**.

What do you think? See Alan R. Tait et al., Informing the Uninformed: Optimizing the Consent Message Using a Fractional Factorial Design, 167(7) JAMA Pediatr. 640–46 (2013).

> **Go to** the website and watch the four videos regarding the necessary education level of human subjects.

Are the videos at the appropriate education level for human subjects? Compare videos 1 and 2 with videos 3 and 4. Which ones do you think are more appropriate for adults? Would you give all adults the same video or would you change videos based on the human subject's socioeconomic status, education level, age, race, etc.?

Could you improve the presentation of any of the informed consent forms you studied in this chapter?

2. APOMEDIATED CLINICAL TRIALS

Professor O'Connor explains that we are entering a new age of "apomediated" research: "apomediation is envisioned as a more horizontal, peer-to-peer style of information exchange in which no single apomediary is essential to the process." Such research is distinct from traditional intermediary research, where the researcher controls the proposal and the choice of subjects. Instead, today, thanks to social media, patients can begin their own research. A patient interested in the connection between Vitamin D and genetic mutations, for example, can go online, contact other persons similarly interested in the disease, and upload and review her data without the help of a researcher. Dan O'Connor, The Apomediated World: Regulating Research When Social Media Has Changed Research, 41 J.L. Med. & Ethics 470 (2013).

In one case described by Professor O'Connor, one patient came up with the idea that ALS patients report their use of lithium online so that readers could determine whether lithium was a safe and effective treatment for ALS. In that situation, who is the researcher? Who needs protection as a human subject? Should there be any regulation at all of these patient-sponsored initiatives?

> **Practice Exercise:** Compare the PatientsLikeMe approach to research with the other companies listed on the website.

Numerous websites lend themselves to such uses by patients, including www.patientslikeme.com (makes money by selling patient information to companies that are developing products); http://diygenomics.net (brings tools and libraries together for small scale genomics labs for the process of sequence assembly); https://www.inspire.com (receives funding

by providing research for life science companies); and http://www.armyofwomen.org (focusing on breast cancer—receives funds from grants and donations).

Do you like this patient-started approach to research? Or would it be better if the researchers used these sites to contact people (see, e.g., http://trialx.com, http://bcpatientrecruitment.com/) instead of letting the research be decided by patients? Will people lose their privacy in a world of apomediated research? Or do most people understand how social media sites work and give up some privacy in order to enjoy the benefits?

Facebook changed its positive and negative news feeds to see how that input affected the tone of members' Facebook posts. Is this human subjects research that should be governed by the Common Rule? What do you think of applying the following ethical rule to Facebook: "If you're afraid to ask your subjects for their permission to conduct the research, there's probably a deeper ethical issue that must be considered?" Would ethical standards be met if Facebook had given people the option to opt into the research? What if it had debriefed them about the study only after it took place? Did Facebook members have a right to learn that they had been studied and what the results of the research showed? See Vindu Goel, As Data Overflows Online, Researchers Grapple With Ethics, N.Y. Times, Aug. 13, 2014, at B1.

3. INCIDENTAL FINDINGS

Incidental findings raise several bioethical concerns. The Presidential Commission for the Study of Bioethical Issues defined incidental findings as "findings that lie outside the aim of a test or procedure." Presidential Commission for the Study of Bioethical Issues, Bioethics Commission on Incidental Findings: Anticipate and Communicate, Dec. 12, 2013, at https://bioethicsarchive.georgetown.edu/pcsbi/node/3186.html. Generally, an incidental finding occurs when researchers are studying a participant for one issue and incidentally discover another issue. For example, a researcher conducts a memory study on a participant's brain and finds a brain tumor. See id. Does the researcher owe a duty to the participant to disclose the researcher's findings? Consider the following examples:

> **Go to** the website and read the IRB Primer on Incidental Findings.

> A research subject gives informed consent to undergo an MRI examination in connection with a study of brain hemorrhages. The researcher sees a brain tumor on the subject's MRI.
>
> A research subject gives informed consent to undergo an MRI examination in connection with a study of brain activity and intelligence. The researcher sees an unusually-shaped blip on the subject's MRI.

> A research subject gives informed consent to have her genome sequenced in order to participate in a study of multiple sclerosis. The researcher finds that the subject has the BRCA gene, which indicates susceptibility to breast cancer. Another subject in the same study has the gene associated with Alzheimer's disease.
>
> A research subject gives informed consent to undergo a CT scan in a study of the appendix. The CT scan reveals a polycystic liver.
>
> A research subject gives informed consent to be a control in an Alzheimer's imaging trial, and her scan reveals two brain aneurysms.
>
> A research subject gives informed consent to have his genome sequenced as part of a project to better diagnose syndromes of developmental delay, intellectual disability, and seizures. Researchers find the aorta weakening of Marfan syndrome.
>
> A research subject gives informed consent to have his genome sequenced to evaluate heart disease; researchers find he has myoclonus dystonia, a neuromuscular disease.
>
> A research subject who says she has normal hearing gives informed consent to have her genome sequenced in a study to investigate atherosclerosis. Researchers notice a deafness mutation.

Ricki Lewis, Incidental Findings from Genome Sequencing—Nuances and Caveats, Scientific American, Mar. 22, 2013, at http://blogs.scientificamerican.com/guest-blog/2013/03/22/incidental-findings-from-genome-sequencing-nuances-and-caveats/. Should researchers tell the subjects about the discoveries listed above? Some believe that incidental findings should not be reported unless there is "strong evidence of benefit." See Robert Green, et.al, ACMG Recommendations for Reporting of Incidental Findings in Clinical Exome and Genome Sequencing, American College of Medical Genetics and Genomics (2013). Others believe that "variations in any and all disease-associated genes could be medically useful and should be reported." Id.

These situations all involve incidental findings (IFs), "a finding concerning an individual research participant that has potential health or reproductive importance and is discovered in the course of conducting research but is beyond the aims of the study." Susan M. Wolf et al., The Law of Incidental Findings in Human Subjects Research: Establishing Researchers' Duties, 36 J.L. Med. & Ethics 361 (2008). Although scans and other imaging techniques made it possible for researchers to discover many IFs, the ability to sequence the human genome has expanded the scope of IFs. "In the context of genetic research, the question is how to deal with the dozens or hundreds of disparate IFs that can potentially be uncovered in any individual research participant's genetic material." Elizabeth R. Pike et al., Finding Fault? Exploring Legal Duties to Return

Incidental Findings in Genomic Research, 102 Geo. L.J. 795, 800 (2014). We examine genetic testing in Chapter 6.

Which IFs should be revealed to human subjects? What do you think of the following four approaches:

1. No return of incidental findings;
2. Return all genomic data without interpretation;
3. Return results consistent with a compendium put together by scientific consensus;
4. Return IFs only when they are analytically valid, have significant health implications, and are clinically actionable.

Id. What policy would you draft for incidental findings?

4. COMPASSION IN PUBLIC HEALTH EMERGENCIES

Should drugs that have not been tested on human beings ever be given to people outside a clinical trial? The FDA allows "compassionate use" for those with "a serious or immediately life-threatening disease or condition and no comparable or satisfactory therapeutic alternatives." What circumstances do you think are serious enough to warrant compassionate use?

Dr. Sam Brisbane, a Liberian doctor, died after contracting the Ebola virus. He remained at the hospital to help patients, with the Ebola present, even though he risked contracting it himself. He was unable to escape the virus due to inadequate supplies, infrastructure, and training in infection control. Dr. Brisbane decided to remain at the hospital and risk his life to save others' lives. See Josh Mugele & Chad Priest, A Good Death—Ebola and Sacrifice, 371 N. Eng. J. Med. 1185 (2014).

The Ebola outbreak in Western Africa tested the limits of the principle of compassionate use. Ebola is a disease that historically has not affected a lot of people, and rarely affects people in the United States; prior to the recent outbreak, probably fewer than 3000 people had been infected since 1976. Because of the extensive research procedures described in this chapter, bringing a successful drug to market usually costs millions of dollars; manufacturers can be expected to focus on drugs needed for large numbers of people. Because of the lack of private market interest in Ebola, the U.S. government offered $100 million to drug companies to work on Ebola vaccines and treatment in preparation for Ebola's possible use by terrorists. The products available in 2014 have not yet been tested on human subjects. See Richard Harris, Why Is There No Drug to Treat Ebola?, NPR, Morning Edition, Aug. 12, 2014, at http://www.npr.org/2014/08/12/339752974/why-is-there-no-drug-to-treat-ebola.

After a serious outbreak of Ebola in West Africa, stories emerged about four people connected with ZMapp, one of the products that is hoped to treat the disease. In Sierra Leone, a medical team from Doctors Without Borders and the World Health Organization decided not to give ZMapp to Doctor Sheik Umar Khan, a prominent doctor who led the fight against the Ebola outbreak in Sierra Leone. Dr. Khan was never asked whether he wanted the drug. He died on July 29, 2014. On the other hand, after their sponsoring organization requested doses of ZMapp from the manufacturer—Mapp Biopharmaceuticals—two white American missionaries received doses after their return to United States. A seventy-five-year-old Spanish priest also received a dose of the serum. Then the company ran out of product. No Africans received the first doses of the serum. See Andrew Pollack, Opting Against Ebola Drug for Ill African Doctor, N.Y. Times, Aug. 12, 2014, at A1; David Greene, Use of Experimental Ebola Serum Raises Ethical Questions, NPR, Morning Edition, Aug. 11, 2014, at http://www.npr.org/2014/08/11/339485891/use-of-experimental-ebola-serum-raises-ethical-questions.

Practice Exercise: Write down your ethical assessment of this situation before reviewing the comments below.

Do you agree with bioethicist Arthur Caplan that "it is very troubling that the only people known to have gotten the drug to date are two Americans and a Spaniard?" Arthur Caplan, Bioethicist: Ebola Treatment to West is Troubling, Bad Science, NBC News, Aug. 12, 2014, at http://www.nbcnews.com/storyline/ebola-virus-outbreak/bioethicist-ebola-treatment-west-troubling-bad-science-n178026. Does the situation demonstrate that racism persists in human subjects research?

Do you agree with the judgment of the doctors in Sierra Leone, who said they didn't give Dr. Khan a dose because they "feared stoking the considerable suspicion of Western medical institutions in the country?" Pollack, *supra*. Or do you agree with bioethicist Alta Charo's commentary:

> No one can say that the optics here are not troubling. That is you have a very small amount of a drug that might work and the only people who get it are the Americans. But you need to also remember that if we had given it to non-Americans first there would be equally bad optics of testing drugs on people from developing countries before we're willing to test it on ourselves, which has usually been the complaint in the past.

Greene, *supra*.

Coming Attractions Bridal and Formal (CABF), a bridal shop in Akron, Ohio, was visited by Texas nurse Amber Vinson. Before her visit, Nurse Vinson had treated a patient with the Ebola virus at a Dallas hospital. The hospital told medical personnel that they were free to travel and intermingle with people after the Ebola treatment. Vinson was

diagnosed with Ebola after she returned home. CABF was closed for cleaning and then closed permanently because of its reputational damage associated with Ebola. Should CABF be allowed to sue the hospital for a health care liability claim? A Texas court of appeals said yes because the hospital's duties as a health care provider were involved. "[W]e conclude CABF asserts an action against a health care provider for a claimed departure from accepted standards of safety which proximately resulted in injury to a claimant." See Texas Health Resources v. CABF, 552 S.W.3d 335 2018 (Tex. Ct. App. 2018).

The World Health Organization (WHO) panel decided that experimentation with unproven treatments is ethical "in the particular circumstances . . . provided certain conditions are met." See Annette Reid & Ezekiel J. Emmanuel, Ethical Considerations of Experimental Interventions in the Ebola Outbreak, 384 Lancet 1896 (2014). The conditions that they take into consideration to conduct trials for experimental treatments are: collaborative partnership (involve local communities to plan, conduct, and oversee trials); social value (share the knowledge learned); scientific validity (adequate means and use of known data); fair selection of study population (transparency); favorable risk-benefit ratio (minimize risks); independent review (ensure public accountability); informed consent (allow participants to freely participate without coercion); and respect for recruited participants and study communities (protect patients in various aspects). Id.

Additionally, a working group at the NYU Langone Medical Center has released findings from its studies on the research ethics of compassionate use. The following are the major findings:

> 1. Biotechnology companies have no legal or regulatory obligation to provide access to unapproved treatments on the grounds of compassionate use.
>
> 2. The U.S. Food and Drug Administration (FDA) is not an obstacle to those seeking compassionate use. . . . The FDA almost always defers to the company that is developing the unapproved treatment to decide whether to grant compassionate use acces [sic].
>
> 3. Increasing access to unapproved therapies may prove detrimental in the long run to longstanding and effective research and clinical trial systems through which interventions are proven effective and safe, and given regulatory approval.

Petrie-Flom Center, NYULMC: Compassionate Use Could Impact Long-Term Medical Benefits, Sept. 18, 2014, at http://blogs.law.harvard.edu/billofhealth/2014/09/18/nyulmc-compassionate-use-could-impact-long-term-medical-benefits/.

After the anthrax attacks around the time of September 11, 2001, the government mandated anthrax vaccination of military personnel even though the Anthrax Vaccine Adsorbed (AVA) was an investigational

drug that had not been approved for that use by the FDA. Do you agree that in these circumstances giving the vaccine was more important than worrying about its status in the FDA? Should the military enjoy all the rights to informed consent identified in this chapter, or can the government treat them differently because of its concerns about national defense? See Doe v. Rumsfeld, 294 F.Supp.2d 119 (D.D.C. 2003) (vaccine program violated statute prohibiting administration of investigational drugs to service members without informed consent).

> **Practice Exercise:** Would you approve this experiment and rule that it should be exempt from federal informed consent rules?

When there are emergency outbreaks and an unproven treatment exists, who should get the drug? The person closest to death? The person with the best chance of recovery? The person who is least sick? The youngest victim? The oldest victim? The health care workers who fight the disease? The military? Those more recently infected? Those who can be closely monitored? No one until the drug's use is successfully tested in a randomized clinical trial subject to the Common Rule and IRB review? How would you get informed consent from a patient in these circumstances?

Doctors at the University of Pittsburgh know that trauma patients with cardiac arrest have less than a ten percent chance of survival. They wanted to induce hypothermia in those patients to give them a better chance of recovery. As a first step, they must test whether their Emergency Preservation and Resuscitation for Cardiac Arrest from Trauma procedure (EPR-CAT) is safe and effective. In this procedure, emergency room personnel drain the blood of trauma patients suffering gun or knife wounds and replace it with freezing saltwater. The patients are then clinically dead because they lack heartbeat and brain activity. At that point doctors work to save the patients' lives and later resuscitate them, returning blood to their bodies. See Kate Murphy, Killing a Patient to Save His Life, N.Y. Times, Jun. 9, 2014, at D1; Acute Care Research, Emergency Preservation and Resuscitation for Cardiac Arrest from Trauma Procedure (EPR-CAT), at http://www.acutecareresearch.org/studies/current/emergency-preservation-and-resuscitation-cardiac-arrest-trauma-epr-cat.

The unconscious patients cannot consent to the procedure. Are you surprised that this project was sponsored by the U.S. Department of Defense? Or that the hospital provided yellow bracelets to residents of Pittsburgh so they could demonstrate if they wanted to opt out of this experiment? The project (University of Pittsburgh, Emergency Preservation and Resuscitation (EPR) for Cardiac Arrest from Trauma (EPR-CAT)) is described here: http://clinicaltrials.gov/ct2/show/NCT01042015?term=emergency+preservation+and+resuscitation&rank=1. Would you wear the yellow bracelet?

5. A NEW PUBLIC HEALTH EMERGENCY: COVID-19

The COVID-19 pandemic has reignited the discussion of Right to Try laws and whether such laws may help in the development of COVID treatments and vaccinations. In Spring 2020, as the pandemic was declared, the FDA used its "compassionate use" pathway to allow some patients to access proposed COVID treatments, including the Gilead drug remdesivir and the malaria drug chloroquine. Jacquie Lee, FDA Experimental Virus Drug Policy Highlights Right to Try Issue, Bloomberg Law, Mar. 19, 2020, https://news.bloomberglaw.com/pharma-and-life-sciences/fda-experimental-virus-drug-policy-highlights-right-to-try-issue. The Goldwater Institute has pushed to expand Right to Try even further amid the pandemic, allowing broader access to unapproved medications without the FDA's permission. Goldwater Institute, Right to Try Opens Door for Innovation in Coronavirus Crisis, https://goldwater institute.org/article/right-to-try-innovation-and-the-coronavirus-crisis/ (posted Mar. 19, 2020). While such efforts might have a positive impact, there is still potential danger in allowing experimental treatments to be given to COVID patients without knowledge of appropriate dosing, side effects, or possible long-term impacts.

Perhaps the best example of expanding the use of drugs during the pandemic was the use of the anti-malarial drug hydroxychloroquine, which President Trump supported as a treatment for COVID. On February 4, 2020, the Secretary of HHS determined there was a public health emergency; on March 28, FDA issued an Emergency Use Authorization (EUA) for emergency use of oral formulations of chloroquine phosphate and hydroxychloroquine sulfate for the treatment of COVID-19. On June 15, 2020, however, based on the FDA's continuing review of the scientific evidence, the agency determined that the drugs were unlikely to be effective and could cause serious cardiac and other adverse events, and revoked the EUA. See Food & Drug Administration, Authorizations and Revocation of Emergency Use of Drugs During the COVID-19 Pandemic; Availability, 85 Fed. Reg. 56231 (Sept. 11, 2020).

The global COVID-19 pandemic also spurred efforts to develop and produce a vaccine as quickly as possible. While the vaccine development process typically takes years to complete, both the government and private entities sought to expedite the process to develop and test COVID vaccine candidates. This push was highlighted by President Trump's announcement of "Operation Warp Speed," a public-private partnership aiming to have a vaccine available by January 2021. See United States Government Accountability Office, Operation Warp Speed: Accelerated COVID19 Vaccine Development Status and Efforts to Address Manufacturing Challenges (Feb. 2021), https://www.gao.gov/assets/gao-21-319.pdf. The program provided government assistance to support the development, manufacturing, and distribution of COVID-19 vaccines. Similarly, the World Health Organization, along with other global health actors such as the Wellcome Trust, announced the creation in April 2020

of the Access to COVID-19 Tools (ACT) Accelerator, designed to accelerate global development, production, and access to COVID-related health technologies. World Health Organization, Access to COVID-19 Tools (ACT) Accelerator: A Global Collaboration to Accelerate the Development, Production and Equitable Access to New COVID-19 Diagnostics, Therapeutics and Vaccines (Apr. 24, 2020), https://www.who.int/publications/m/item/access-to-covid-19-tools-(act)-accelerator. The FDA authorized a vaccine made by Pfizer for emergency use on December 11, 2020, followed a week later by authorization of one made by Moderna. Denise Grady, Abby Goodnough & Noah Weiland, F.D.A. Authorizes Moderna Vaccine, Adding Millions of Doses to U.S. Supply, N.Y. Times, Dec. 18, 2020, https://www.nytimes.com/2020/12/18/health/covid-vaccine-fda-moderna.html.

By May 3, 2021, more than 246 million vaccine doses had taken place in the United States. 40% of adults are estimated to have received two doses, while 56% have received one. President Biden hopes that by July 4, 2021, 70% of American adults would have received one dose, and thinks 160 million American adults will be fully vaccinated by then. Alana Wise, Biden Sets New Goal: At Least 70% of Adults Given 1 Vaccine Dose by July 4, NPR, May 4, 2021, https://www.npr.org/2021/05/04/993537622/biden-sets-new-goal-for-at-least-70-of-adults-to-be-vaccinated-by-july-4. Were you vaccinated? How did you get your vaccine? What would you recommend as the best way to distribute the vaccine across the United States? Across the world?

With the expedited start of Phase III trials for COVID vaccines, there was a prominent discussion regarding the ethics of testing a vaccine for a disease that does not have a cure. Much of the debate centered on "challenge trials," in which participants who receive a vaccine candidate are injected with a small amount of the virus and then monitored to see whether they become sick. The hope is that the amount of virus injected will be enough to spur the subjects to develop antibodies to the virus, but not enough for them to actually contract the disease. However, given the speed with which these trials have been proposed and the lack of knowledge about the virus itself, there are no clear guidelines regarding a safe dose. The ethical debate arises because there is (as of this writing) no known cure or treatment for COVID, which means that there is no clear way to treat any research subjects who do get sick. Whether the value of quickly developing a vaccine that could end the global pandemic can justify deliberately exposing healthy people to potential COVID infection is an ethical debate with no clear answer. Hannah Devlin, WHO Conditionally Backs Covid-19 Vaccine Trials That Infect People, The Guardian, May 8, 2020, https://www.theguardian.com/science/2020/may/08/who-conditionally-backs-covid-19-vaccine-trials-that-infect-people?CMP=share_btn_tw.

In Chapter 3, we explore the effects of new technology on traditional concepts of reproduction and parenthood, especially how technology affects the right to privacy.

CHAPTER 3

REPRODUCTIVE PRIVACY AND PARENTHOOD

Introduction. In Chapter 2, we learned about the importance of an individual's right to privacy and autonomy, particularly in the medical context. For example, regarding the criteria for an Institutional Review Board to approve research, there must be "adequate provisions to protect the privacy of subjects and to maintain the confidentiality of data." 45 C.F.R. § 690.111.

In this chapter, we learn more details about privacy and bodily autonomy, particularly in the context of reproduction, abortion, and surrogacy. We build on our knowledge of an individual's right to privacy and how that right can be limited in certain circumstances. At the beginning of the chapter, in Section A, we consider a woman's right to privacy in the abortion context and how that right has been limited regarding partial birth abortions and medication abortions. From there, in Section B we move to bioethical issues regarding reproduction and parenthood, focusing on surrogate motherhood and adoption.

Throughout the chapter, we focus on how legislators regulate bioethical issues through legislation. In the abortion context, state and federal legislators have consistently used legislation to try to restrict the right to abortion identified in *Roe v. Wade.* Meanwhile, in the reproductive technology setting, legislators have tried to keep pace with technology that now allows a child to have up to six parents. As you read this chapter, consider how you would go about passing legislation regulating reproductive privacy and whether the Constitution sets limits on what legislation can accomplish.

A. ABORTION LEGISLATION FROM PARTIAL BIRTH TO FETAL PAIN

The Supreme Court first identified a constitutional right to privacy in Griswold v. Connecticut, 381 U.S. 479 (1965). Connecticut law penalized the use of contraception or any assistance in its use with a fine of no less than fifty dollars and imprisonment of not less than sixty days or more than one year. The Supreme Court ruled that the Connecticut law was unconstitutional. Justice William Douglas wrote the opinion of the Court, which held that the law violated the constitutional right to privacy. Justice Douglas located that right in the "penumbras" of the Bill of Rights. Id. at 484. Just as the First Amendment protected an associational right of privacy, the Third Amendment a privacy right not to have soldiers quartered in the home, the Fourth Amendment a privacy

right against search and seizure, and the Fifth Amendment a privacy right against self-incrimination, so too was contraceptive privacy protected by the "penumbras" and "emanations" arising from the constitutional guarantees of the Bill of Rights. In a concurrence, Justice Arthur Goldberg argued that the Ninth Amendment was the constitutional provision that best protected the right to privacy.

Griswold emphasized marital privacy. Post-*Griswold*, the Court ruled in an equal protection case that single individuals enjoy a constitutional right to contraceptive use. Eisenstadt v. Baird, 405 U.S. 438 (1972).

A year later, the Court relied on the contraceptive line of cases to hold in Roe v. Wade, 410 U.S. 113 (1973), that the right to privacy protects the woman's decision to abort a fetus. The Court summarized its holding about abortion in the following manner:

> 1. A state criminal abortion statute of the current Texas type, that excepts from criminality only a life-saving procedure on behalf of the mother, without regard to pregnancy stage and without recognition of the other interests involved, is violative of the Due Process Clause of the Fourteenth Amendment.
>
> (a) For the stage prior to approximately the end of the first trimester, the abortion decision and its effectuation must be left to the medical judgment of the pregnant woman's attending physician.
>
> (b) For the stage subsequent to approximately the end of the first trimester, the State, in promoting its interest in the health of the mother, may, if it chooses, regulate the abortion procedure in ways that are reasonably related to maternal health.
>
> (c) For the stage subsequent to viability, the State in promoting its interest in the potentiality of human life may, if it chooses, regulate, and even proscribe, abortion except where it is necessary, in appropriate medical judgment, for the preservation of the life or health of the mother.

Id. at 164–65.

Although *Roe* was decided by a 7–2 vote of the Justices, the decision was controversial. In the legal realm, it provoked many state legislatures, and eventually Congress, to pass legislation to limit *Roe* and the abortion right. As the composition of the Supreme Court changed, the Justices became more willing to accept legislative restrictions on the abortion right. By 1992, many observers thought the Court would overrule *Roe*.

Instead, in 1992, the Court redefined *Roe* in Planned Parenthood of Southeastern Pennsylvania v. Casey, 505 U.S. 833 (1992). Led by a plurality of Justices Sandra Day O'Connor, Anthony Kennedy and David Souter, the Court concluded "the essential holding of *Roe v. Wade* should

be retained and once again reaffirmed." Id. at 846. According to the Court:

> *Roe's* essential holding, the holding we reaffirm, has three parts. First is a recognition of the right of the woman to choose to have an abortion before viability and to obtain it without undue interference from the State. Before viability, the State's interests are not strong enough to support a prohibition of abortion or the imposition of a substantial obstacle to the woman's effective right to elect the procedure. Second is a confirmation of the State's power to restrict abortions after fetal viability, if the law contains exceptions for pregnancies which endanger the woman's life or health. And third is the principle that the State has legitimate interests from the outset of the pregnancy in protecting the health of the woman and the life of the fetus that may become a child. These principles do not contradict one another; and we adhere to each.

Id. at 846. Following these principles, the plurality rejected *Roe's* trimester framework and adopted the "undue burden" standard: "An undue burden exists, and therefore a provision of law is invalid, if its purpose or effect is to place substantial obstacles in the path of a woman seeking an abortion before the fetus attains viability." Id.

Using the undue burden standard, the Court invalidated a spousal notification provision of the Pennsylvania abortion law. The Court upheld an informed consent requirement with a 24-hour waiting period and the requirement of informed consent by the parent of a minor, as long as a judicial bypass to parental consent was available. Given what you learned about informed consent in Chapter 2, how do you assess the following informed consent provision upheld by the Court in *Casey*?

> **(a) General rule.**—No abortion shall be performed or induced except with the voluntary and informed consent of the woman upon whom the abortion is to be performed or induced. Except in the case of a medical emergency, consent to an abortion is voluntary and informed if and only if:
>
> (1) At least 24 hours prior to the abortion, the physician who is to perform the abortion or the referring physician has orally informed the woman of:
>
> > (i) The nature of the proposed procedure or treatment and of those risks and alternatives to the procedure or treatment that a reasonable patient would consider material to the decision of whether or not to undergo the abortion.
> >
> > (ii) The probable gestational age of the unborn child at the time the abortion is to be performed.
> >
> > (iii) The medical risks associated with carrying her child to term.

(2) At least 24 hours prior to the abortion, the physician who is to perform the abortion or the referring physician, or a qualified physician assistant, health care practitioner, technician or social worker to whom the responsibility has been delegated by either physician, has informed the pregnant woman that:

(i) The department publishes printed materials which describe the unborn child and list agencies which offer alternatives to abortion and that she has a right to review the printed materials and that a copy will be provided to her free of charge if she chooses to review it.

(ii) Medical assistance benefits may be available for prenatal care, childbirth and neonatal care, and that more detailed information on the availability of such assistance is contained in the printed materials published by the department.

(iii) The father of the unborn child is liable to assist in the support of her child, even in instances where he has offered to pay for the abortion. In the case of rape, this information may be omitted.

(3) A copy of the printed materials has been provided to the pregnant woman if she chooses to view these materials.

(4) The pregnant woman certifies in writing, prior to the abortion, that the information required to be provided under paragraphs (1), (2) and (3) has been provided.

18 Pa. Cons. Stat. Ann. § 3205 (West).

Casey led to renewed state efforts to restrict abortion. The following case involves a Nebraska statute regulating "partial-birth abortion." As you read the following opinion, first ask yourself if you know what a partial-birth abortion is. Does the opinion do a good job of explaining what a partial birth abortion is? Then determine how the Court's analysis fits into the *Roe* and *Casey* frameworks described above.

1. PARTIAL BIRTH ABORTION

Stenberg v. Carhart

Supreme Court of the United States, 2000.
530 U.S. 914, 120 S.Ct. 2597.

■ JUSTICE BREYER delivered the opinion of the Court, in which STEVENS, O'CONNOR, SOUTER and GINSBURG, JJ., joined. STEVENS, J. filed concurring opinion in which GINSBURG, J., joined. O'CONNOR, J., filed a concurring opinion. GINSBURG, J., filed a concurring opinion in which STEVENS, J., joined. REHNQUIST, C.J., and SCALIA, J., filed dissenting opinions. KENNEDY, J., filed a dissenting opinion, in which REHNQUIST,

C.J., joined. THOMAS, J., filed a dissenting opinion, in which REHNQUIST, C.J., and SCALIA, J., joined.

. . . Three established principles determine the issue before us. We shall set them forth in the language of the joint opinion in *Casey*. First, before "viability . . . the woman has a right to choose to terminate her pregnancy."

Second, "a law designed to further the State's interest in fetal life which imposes an undue burden on the woman's decision before fetal viability" is unconstitutional. An "undue burden is . . . shorthand for the conclusion that a state regulation has the purpose or effect of placing a substantial obstacle in the path of a woman seeking an abortion of a nonviable fetus."

Third, "subsequent to viability, the State in promoting its interest in the potentiality of human life may, if it chooses, regulate, and even proscribe, abortion except where it is necessary, in appropriate medical judgment, for the preservation of the life or health of the mother."

We apply these principles to a Nebraska law banning "partial birth abortion." The statute reads as follows:

> "No partial birth abortion shall be performed in this state, unless such procedure is necessary to save the life of the mother whose life is endangered by a physical disorder, physical illness, or physical injury, including a life-endangering physical condition caused by or arising from the pregnancy itself."

The statute defines "partial birth abortion" as:

> "an abortion procedure in which the person performing the abortion partially delivers vaginally a living unborn child before killing the unborn child and completing the delivery."

It further defines "partially delivers vaginally a living unborn child before killing the unborn child" to mean

> "deliberately and intentionally delivering into the vagina a living unborn child, or a substantial portion thereof, for the purpose of performing a procedure that the person performing such procedure knows will kill the unborn child and does kill the unborn child." *Ibid.*

The law classifies violation of the statute as a "Class III felony" carrying a prison term of up to 20 years, and a fine of up to $25,000. It also provides for the automatic revocation of a doctor's license to practice medicine in Nebraska.

We hold that this statute violates the Constitution.

I

B

Because Nebraska law seeks to ban one method of aborting a pregnancy, we must describe and then discuss several different abortion procedures. . . .

3. D & E "refers generically to transcervical procedures performed at 13 weeks gestation or later." American Medical Association, Report of Board of Trustees on Late-Term Abortion, App. 490 (hereinafter AMA Report). The AMA Report, adopted by the District Court, describes the process as follows.

> Between 13 and 15 weeks of gestation:
>
> "D & E is similar to vacuum aspiration except that the cervix must be dilated more widely because surgical instruments are used to remove larger pieces of tissue. Osmotic dilators are usually used. Intravenous fluids and an analgesic or sedative may be administered. A local anesthetic such as a paracervical block may be administered, dilating agents, if used, are removed and instruments are inserted through the cervix into the uterus to removal fetal and placental tissue. Because fetal tissue is friable and easily broken, the fetus may not be removed intact. The walls of the uterus are scraped with a curette to ensure that no tissue remains."
>
> After 15 weeks:
>
> "Because the fetus is larger at this stage of gestation (particularly the head), and because bones are more rigid, dismemberment or other destructive procedures are more likely to be required than at earlier gestational ages to remove fetal and placental tissue."
>
> After 20 weeks:
>
> "Some physicians use intrafetal potassium chloride or digoxin to induce fetal demise prior to a late D & E (after 20 weeks), to facilitate evacuation."

There are variations in D & E operative strategy; compare *ibid.* with W. Hern, Abortion Practice 146–156 (1984), and Medical and Surgical Abortion 133–135. However, the common points are that D & E involves (1) dilation of the cervix; (2) removal of at least some fetal tissue using nonvacuum instruments; and (3) (after the 15th week) the potential need for instrumental disarticulation or dismemberment of the fetus or the collapse of fetal parts to facilitate evacuation from the uterus.

4. When instrumental disarticulation incident to D & E is necessary, it typically occurs as the doctor pulls a portion of the fetus through the cervix into the birth canal. Dr. Carhart testified at trial as follows:

"Dr. Carhart: . . . 'The dismemberment occurs between the traction of . . . my instrument and the counter-traction of the internal os of the cervix. . . .

"Counsel: 'So the dismemberment occurs after you pulled a part of the fetus through the cervix, is that correct?

"Dr. Carhart: 'Exactly. Because you're using—The cervix has two strictures or two rings, the internal os and the external os . . . that's what's actually doing the dismembering. . . .

"Counsel: 'When we talked before or talked before about a D & E, that is not—where there is not intention to do it intact, do you, in that situation, dismember the fetus in utero first, then remove portions?

"Dr. Carhart: 'I don't think so. . . . I don't know of any way that one could go in and intentionally dismember the fetus in the uterus. . . . It takes something that restricts the motion of the fetus against what you're doing before you're going to get dismemberment.' "

Dr. Carhart's specification of the location of fetal disarticulation is consistent with other sources.

5. The D & E procedure carries certain risks. The use of instruments within the uterus creates a danger of accidental perforation and damage to neighboring organs. Sharp fetal bone fragments create similar dangers. And fetal tissue accidentally left behind can cause infection and various other complications. See 11 F.Supp.2d, at 1110; Gynecologic, Obstetric, and Related Surgery 1045 (D. Nichols & D. Clarke-Pearson eds.2d ed.2000); F. Cunningham et al., Williams Obstetrics 598 (20th ed.1997). Nonetheless studies show that the risks of mortality and complication that accompany the D & E procedure between the 12th and 20th weeks of gestation are significantly lower than those accompanying induced labor procedures (the next safest midsecond trimester procedures). See Gynecologic, Obstetric, and Related Surgery, *supra,* at 1046; AMA Report, App. 495, 496; Medical and Surgical Abortion 139, 142; Lawson, 171 Am. J. Obstet. Gynecol., at 1368.

6. At trial, Dr. Carhart and Dr. Stubblefield described a variation of the D & E procedure, which they referred to as an "intact D & E." Like other versions of the D & E technique, it begins with induced dilation of the cervix. The procedure then involves removing the fetus from the uterus through the cervix "intact," *i.e.,* in one pass, rather than in several passes. It is used after 16 weeks at the earliest, as vacuum aspiration becomes ineffective and the fetal skull becomes too large to pass through the cervix. The intact D & E proceeds in one of two ways, depending on the presentation of the fetus. If the fetus presents head first (a vertex presentation), the doctor collapses the skull; and the doctor then extracts the entire fetus through the cervix. If the fetus presents feet first (a breech presentation), the doctor pulls the fetal body through the cervix,

collapses the skull, and extracts the fetus through the cervix. The breech extraction version of the intact D & E is also known commonly as "dilation and extraction," or D & X. In the late second trimester, vertex, breech, and traverse/compound (sideways) presentations occur in roughly similar proportions.

7. The intact D & E procedure can also be found described in certain obstetric and abortion clinical textbooks, where two variations are recognized. The first, as just described, calls for the physician to adapt his method for extracting the intact fetus depending on fetal presentation. See Gynecologic, Obstetric, and Related Surgery, *supra,* at 1043; Medical and Surgical Abortion 136–137. This is the method used by Dr. Carhart. A slightly different version of the intact D & E procedure, associated with Dr. Martin Haskell, calls for conversion to a breech presentation in all cases. See Gynecologic, Obstetric, and Related Surgery, *supra,* at 1043 (citing M. Haskell, Dilation and Extraction for Late Second Trimester Abortion (1992), in 139 Cong. Rec. 8605 (1993)).

8. The American College of Obstetricians and Gynecologists describes the D & X procedure in a manner corresponding to a breech-conversion intact D & E, including the following steps:

> 1. deliberate dilatation of the cervix, usually over a sequence of days;
>
> 2. instrumental conversion of the fetus to a footling breech;
>
> 3. breech extraction of the body excepting the head; and
>
> 4. partial evacuation of the intracranial contents of a living fetus to effect vaginal delivery of a dead but otherwise intact fetus." American College of Obstetricians and Gynecologists Executive Board, Statement on Intact Dilation and Extraction (Jan. 12, 1997) (hereinafter ACOG Statement), App. 599–560.

Despite the technical differences we have just described, intact D & E and D & X are sufficiently similar for us to use the terms interchangeably.

9. Dr. Carhart testified he attempts to use the intact D & E procedure during weeks 16 to 20 because (1) it reduces the dangers from sharp bone fragments passing through the cervix, (2) minimizes the number of instrument passes needed for extraction and lessens the likelihood of uterine perforations caused by those instruments, (3) reduces the likelihood of leaving infection-causing fetal and placental tissue in the uterus, and (4) could help to prevent potentially fatal absorption of fetal tissue into the maternal circulation. The District Court made no findings about the D & X procedure's overall safety. The District Court concluded, however, that "the evidence is both clear and convincing that Carhart's D & X procedure is superior to, and safer than, the . . . other abortion procedures used during the relevant gestational period in the 10 to 20 cases a year that present to Dr. Carhart."

10. The materials presented at trial referred to the potential benefits of the D & X procedure in circumstances involving nonviable fetuses, such as fetuses with abnormal fluid accumulation in the brain (hydrocephaly). See 11 F.Supp.2d, at 1107 (quoting AMA Report, App. 492 (" 'Intact D & X may be preferred by some physicians, particularly when the fetus has been diagnosed with hydrocephaly or other anomalies incompatible with life outside the womb' ")); see also Grimes, The Continuing Need for Late Abortions, 280 JAMA 747, 748 (Aug. 26, 1998) (D & X "may be especially useful in the presence of fetal anomalies, such as hydrocephalus," because its reduction of the cranium allows "a smaller diameter to pass through the cervix, thus reducing risk of cervical injury"). Others have emphasized its potential for women with prior uterine scars, or for women for whom induction of labor would be particularly dangerous.

11. There are no reliable data on the number of D & X abortions performed annually. Estimates have ranged between 640 and 5,000 per year.

II

A

. . . In sum, Nebraska has not convinced us that a health exception is "never necessary to preserve the health of women." Rather, a statute that altogether forbids D & X creates a significant health risk. The statute consequently must contain a health exception. This is not to say, as Justice THOMAS and Justice KENNEDY claim, that a State is prohibited from proscribing an abortion procedure whenever a particular physician deems the procedure preferable. By no means must a State grant physicians "unfettered discretion" in their selection of abortion methods. But where substantial medical authority supports the proposition that banning a particular abortion procedure could endanger women's health, *Casey* requires the statute to include a health exception when the procedure is " 'necessary, in appropriate medical judgment, for the preservation of the life or health of the mother.' " Requiring such an exception in this case is no departure from *Casey,* but simply a straightforward application of its holding.

B

The Eighth Circuit found the Nebraska statute unconstitutional because, in *Casey's* words, it has the "effect of placing a substantial obstacle in the path of a woman seeking an abortion of a nonviable fetus." It thereby places an "undue burden" upon a woman's right to terminate her pregnancy before viability. Nebraska does not deny that the statute imposes an "undue burden" *if* it applies to the more commonly used D & E procedure as well as to D & X. And we agree with the Eighth Circuit that it does so apply.

Our earlier discussion of the D & E procedure shows that it falls within the statutory prohibition. The statute forbids "deliberately and

intentionally delivering into the vagina a living unborn child, or a substantial portion thereof, for the purpose of performing a procedure that the person performing such procedure knows will kill the unborn child." We do not understand how one could distinguish, using this language, between D & E (where a foot or arm is drawn through the cervix) and D & X (where the body up to the head is drawn through the cervix). Evidence before the trial court makes clear that D & E will often involve a physician pulling a "substantial portion" of a still living fetus, say, an arm or leg, into the vagina prior to the death of the fetus. Indeed D & E involves dismemberment that commonly occurs only when the fetus meets resistance that restricts the motion of the fetus: "The dismemberment occurs between the traction of . . . [the] instrument and the counter-traction of the internal os of the cervix." And these events often do not occur until after a portion of a living fetus has been pulled into the vagina.

Even if the statute's basic aim is to ban D & X, its language makes clear that it also covers a much broader category of procedures. The language does not track the medical differences between D & E and D & X—though it would have been a simple matter, for example, to provide an exception for the performance of D & E and other abortion procedures. Nor does the statute anywhere suggest that its application turns on whether a portion of the fetus' body is drawn into the vagina as part of a process to extract an intact fetus after collapsing the head as opposed to a process that would dismember the fetus. Thus, the dissenters' argument that the law was generally intended to bar D & X can be both correct and irrelevant. The relevant question is *not* whether the legislature wanted to ban D & X; it is whether the law was intended to apply *only* to D & X. The plain language covers both procedures. A rereading of this opinion, as well as Justice THOMAS' dissent, will make clear why we can find no difference, in terms of *this* statute, between the D & X procedure as described and the D & E procedure as it might be performed. Both procedures can involve the introduction of a "substantial portion" of a still living fetus, through the cervix, into the vagina—the very feature of an abortion that leads Justice THOMAS to characterize such a procedure as involving "partial birth."

The Nebraska State Attorney General argues that the statute does differentiate between the two procedures. He says that the statutory words "substantial portion" mean "the child up to the head." He consequently denies the statute's application where the physician introduces into the birth canal a fetal arm or leg or anything less than the entire fetal body. He argues further that we must defer to his views about the meaning of the state statute.

We cannot accept the Attorney General's narrowing interpretation of the Nebraska statute. This Court's case law makes clear that we are not to give the Attorney General's interpretative views controlling weight.

The judgment of the Court of Appeals is

Affirmed.

■ JUSTICE O'CONNOR, concurring.

. . . I write separately to emphasize the following points.

First, the Nebraska statute is inconsistent with *Casey* because it lacks an exception for those instances when the banned procedure is necessary to preserve the health of the mother. Importantly, Nebraska's own statutory scheme underscores this constitutional infirmity. . . . Nebraska has recognized this constitutional limitation in its separate statute generally proscribing postviability abortions. That statute provides that "[n]o abortion shall be performed after the time at which, in the sound medical judgment of the attending physician, the unborn child clearly appears to have reached viability, *except when necessary to preserve the life or health of the mother.*" Because even a postviability proscription of abortion would be invalid absent a health exception, Nebraska's ban on previability partial birth abortions, under the circumstances presented here, must include a health exception as well, since the State's interest in regulating abortions before viability is "considerably weaker" than after viability. The statute at issue here, however, only excepts those procedures "necessary to save the life of the mother whose life is endangered by a physical disorder, physical illness, or physical injury." This lack of a health exception necessarily renders the statute unconstitutional.

Second, Nebraska's statute is unconstitutional on the alternative and independent ground that it imposes an undue burden on a woman's right to choose to terminate her pregnancy before viability. Nebraska's ban covers not just the dilation and extraction (D & X) procedure, but also the dilation and evacuation (D & E) procedure, "the most commonly used method for performing previability second trimester abortions."

It is important to note that, unlike Nebraska, some other States have enacted statutes more narrowly tailored to proscribing the D & X procedure alone. Some of those statutes have done so by specifically excluding from their coverage the most common methods of abortion, such as the D & E and vacuum aspiration procedures. For example, the Kansas statute states that its ban does not apply to the "(A) [s]uction curettage abortion procedure; (B) suction aspiration abortion procedure; or (C) dilation and evacuation abortion procedure involving dismemberment of the fetus prior to removal from the body of the pregnant woman." The Utah statute similarly provides that its prohibition "does not include the dilation and evacuation procedure involving dismemberment prior to removal, the suction curettage procedure, or the suction aspiration procedure for abortion." Likewise, the Montana statute defines the banned procedure as one in which "(A) the living fetus is removed intact from the uterus until only the head remains in the uterus; (B) all or a part of the intracranial contents of the

fetus are evacuated; (C) the head of the fetus is compressed; and (D) following fetal demise, the fetus is removed from the birth canal." By restricting their prohibitions to the D & X procedure exclusively, the Kansas, Utah, and Montana statutes avoid a principal defect of the Nebraska law.

If Nebraska's statute limited its application to the D & X procedure and included an exception for the life and health of the mother, the question presented would be quite different from the one we face today. . . . If there were adequate alternative methods for a woman safely to obtain an abortion before viability, it is unlikely that prohibiting the D & X procedure alone would "amount in practical terms to a substantial obstacle to a woman seeking an abortion." Thus, a ban on partial birth abortion that only proscribed the D & X method of abortion and that included an exception to preserve the life and health of the mother would be constitutional in my view.

■ JUSTICE KENNEDY, with whom THE CHIEF JUSTICE joins, dissenting.

II

. . . Substantial evidence supports Nebraska's conclusion that its law denies no woman a safe abortion. The most to be said for the D & X is it may present an unquantified lower risk of complication for a particular patient but that other proven safe procedures remain available even for this patient. Under these circumstances, the Court is wrong to limit its inquiry to the relative physical safety of the two procedures, with the slightest potential difference requiring the invalidation of the law. . . . Where the difference in physical safety is, at best, marginal, the State may take into account the grave moral issues presented by a new abortion method. . . . It is also important to recognize that the D & X is effective only when the fetus is close to viable or, in fact, viable; thus the State is regulating the process at the point where its interest in life is nearing its peak.

Courts are ill-equipped to evaluate the relative worth of particular surgical procedures. The legislatures of the several States have superior factfinding capabilities in this regard. Nebraska's judgment here must stand.

■ JUSTICE THOMAS, with whom THE CHIEF JUSTICE and JUSTICE SCALIA join, dissenting.

A

Starting with the statutory definition of "partial birth abortion," I think it highly doubtful that the statute could be applied to ordinary D & E. First, the Nebraska statute applies only if the physician "partially *delivers* vaginally a living unborn child," which phrase is defined to mean "deliberately and intentionally *delivering* into the vagina a living unborn child, or a substantial portion thereof." When read in context, the term "partially delivers" cannot be fairly interpreted to include removing pieces of an unborn child from the uterus one at a time.

The word "deliver," particularly delivery of an "unborn child," refers to the process of "assist[ing] in giving birth," which suggests removing an intact unborn child from the womb, rather than pieces of a child. Without question, one does not "deliver" a child when one removes the child from the uterus piece by piece, as in a D & E. Rather, in the words of respondent and his experts, one "remove[s]" or "dismember[s]" the child in a D & E. . . . No one, including the majority, understands the act of pulling off a part of a fetus to be a "delivery."

To make the statute's meaning even more clear, the statute applies only if the physician "partially delivers vaginally a living unborn child *before* killing the unborn child and completing the delivery." The statute defines this phrase to mean that the physician must complete the delivery "*for the purpose of* performing a procedure" that will kill the unborn child. It is clear from these phrases that the procedure that kills the fetus must be subsequent to, and therefore separate from, the "partia[l] deliver[y]" or the "deliver[y] into the vagina" of "a living unborn child or substantial portion thereof." In other words, even if one assumes, *arguendo,* that dismemberment—the act of grasping a fetal arm or leg and pulling until it comes off, leaving the remaining part of the fetal body still in the uterus—is a kind of "delivery," it does not take place "before" the death-causing procedure or "for the purpose of performing" the death-causing procedure; it *is* the death-causing procedure. Under the majority's view, D & E is covered by the statute because when the doctor pulls on a fetal foot until it tears off he has "delivered" a substantial portion of the unborn child and has performed a procedure known to cause death. But, significantly, the physician has not "delivered" the child *before* performing the death-causing procedure or "for the purpose of" performing the death-causing procedure; the dismemberment "delivery" is itself the act that causes the fetus' death.

Moreover, even if removal of a fetal foot or arm from the uterus incidental to severing it from the rest of the fetal body could amount to delivery *before,* or *for the purpose of,* performing a death-causing procedure, the delivery would not be of an "unborn child, or a substantial portion thereof." And even supposing that a fetal foot or arm could conceivably be a "substantial portion" of an unborn child, both the common understanding of "partial birth abortion" and the principle that statutes will be interpreted to avoid constitutional difficulties would require one to read "substantial" otherwise.

I respectfully dissent.

NOTES AND QUESTIONS

1. *Carhart I*. In this case (*Carhart I*), the Court found that the partial-birth abortion ban was unconstitutional because it was too vague and did not include a maternal health exception. What were the strongest arguments of each party? What were the weakest arguments of each party? Do you agree with the Court's decision?

a. *Justice Breyer*. In Justice Breyer's majority opinion, the Court concluded that the Nebraska ban on D & X procedures placed "an undue burden upon a woman's right to make an abortion decision" because "[a]ll those who perform abortion procedures using [the D & X] method must fear prosecution, conviction, and imprisonment." Justice Breyer gave very detailed descriptions of two procedures—D & E and D & X. Did you understand the difference between the two procedures? Why do you think he went into so much detail? Do you think his detailed description of each procedure was effective? Or do you think it made the abortion procedure sound too grotesque (e.g., dismembering the fetus or removing it and then crushing its skull)?

> **Go to** the website and read the WebMD resources on abortion, including information about D&E abortions. How does the medical description differ from the Nebraska statute and the Court's description of the procedures?

Justice Breyer emphasized the vagueness of the prohibition: "We do not understand how one could distinguish, using this language, between D & E (where a foot or arm is drawn through the cervix) and D & X (where the body up to the head is drawn through the cervix)." Why was that vagueness about whether the statute governed D & E or D & X essential to the Court's holding that the statute was unconstitutional?

b. *Justice O'Connor*. Justice O'Connor's concurrence focused on how the Nebraska statute comports with precedent. She emphasized that even statutes restricting post-viability abortions are required to have a maternal life and health exception. The Nebraska statute, however, pertained to pre-viability abortions, and did not include a maternal health exception. Why is the case stronger that a pre-viability abortion statute must have a maternal life and health exception?

> **Practice Exercise:** Go back and look at Justice O'Connor's description of those state laws. Now draft a new partial birth abortion statute for Nebraska that can survive constitutional scrutiny.

Justice O'Connor examined different state statutes to show that Nebraska could have been more specific with its ban.

c. *Justice Kennedy*. Justice Kennedy's dissent stressed the judicial incompetence argument—meaning that the Court is ill-equipped to decide matters best suited for the legislature. Further, Justice Kennedy questioned whether doctors, such as Doctor Carhart, actually perform D & X procedures because it is safer for the woman. Instead, Justice Kennedy stated that doctors are not

looking at the medical necessities of women, but choose abortion procedures based on their own preference. Also, Justice Kennedy stressed that there are other available procedures that are not as morally questionable as the D & X procedure that women can obtain to have an abortion. Do you think this argument is persuasive? Do you think there is a moral difference between dismembering the fetus and removing it piece-by-piece versus removing the fetus intact, then crushing its skull?

d. *Justice Thomas.* Justice Thomas' dissent stated that the Nebraska statute was not vague because the wording of the statute precluded its applicability to D & E abortions—abortions where the fetus is pulled out piece-by-piece. Justice Thomas emphasized that the term "delivery" and its etymology required a finding that the statute applies only to intact partial-birth abortions, such as D & X abortions. Do you agree with Justice Thomas' argument about the meaning of the words used in the statute? Or, do you think that the statute should be clear enough for the average person to understand it without consulting a dictionary?

2. *New Legislation.* In response to *Carhart I,* Congress passed 18 U.S.C. § 1531. Read the statute and ask whether you think the new statute passes the test that the Court required in *Carhart I.* If you were a legislator, would you vote to approve this statute? Would you draft the bill differently? If so, how?

18 U.S.C. § 1531

Partial Birth Abortion.

(a) Any physician who, in or affecting interstate or foreign commerce, knowingly performs a partial-birth abortion and thereby kills a human fetus shall be fined under this title or imprisoned not more than 2 years, or both. This subsection does not apply to a partial-birth abortion that is necessary to save the life of a mother whose life is endangered by a physical disorder, physical illness, or physical injury, including a life-endangering physical condition caused by or arising from the pregnancy itself. This subsection takes effect 1 day after the enactment.

(b) As used in this section—

(1) the term "partial-birth abortion" means an abortion in which the person performing the abortion—

(A) deliberately and intentionally vaginally delivers a living fetus until, in the case of a head-first presentation, the entire fetal head is outside the body of the mother, or, in the case of breech presentation, any part of the fetal trunk past the navel is outside the body of the mother, for the purpose of performing an overt act that the person knows will kill the partially delivered living fetus; and

(B) performs the overt act, other than completion of delivery, that kills the partially delivered living fetus; and

(2) the term "physician" means a doctor of medicine or osteopathy legally authorized to practice medicine and surgery by the State in which the doctor performs such activity, or any other individual legally authorized by the State to perform abortions: *Provided, however*, That any individual who is not a physician or not otherwise legally authorized by the State to perform abortions, but who nevertheless directly performs a partial-birth abortion, shall be subject to the provisions of this section.

(c)(1) The father, if married to the mother at the time she receives a partial-birth abortion procedure, and if the mother has not attained the age of 18 years at the time of the abortion, the maternal grandparents of the fetus, may in a civil action obtain appropriate relief, unless the pregnancy resulted from the plaintiff's criminal conduct or the plaintiff consented to the abortion.

(2) Such relief shall include—

(A) money damages for all injuries, psychological and physical, occasioned by the violation of this section; and

(B) statutory damages equal to three times the cost of the partial-birth abortion.

(d)(1) A defendant accused of an offense under this section may seek a hearing before the State Medical Board on whether the physician's conduct was necessary to save the life of the mother whose life was endangered by a physical disorder, physical illness, or physical injury, including a life-endangering physical condition caused by or arising from the pregnancy itself.

(2) The findings on that issue are admissible on that issue at the trial of the defendant. Upon a motion of the defendant, the court shall delay the beginning of the trial for not more than 30 days to permit such a hearing to take place.

(e) A woman upon whom a partial-birth abortion is performed may not be prosecuted under this section, for a conspiracy to violate this section, or for an offense under section 2, 3, or 4 of this title based on a violation of this section.

NOTES AND QUESTIONS

1. *Constitutionality*. Recall the two defects that the Court identified with the Nebraska statute in *Carhart I*. Did Congress address those defects in this legislation? For instance, is it vague? Does it include a maternal health exception? Does it pertain to pre-viability or post-viability abortions? Are there other safe alternatives if this type of abortion is banned?

Do you think this legislation was passed to follow the Court's guidance in *Carhart I*, or to push to ban more abortions?

2. *Carhart II*. In the following case, Gonzales v. Carhart (*Carhart II*), four physicians filed a facial challenge to the constitutionality of the Partial-Birth Abortion Ban Act of 2003. In a separate lawsuit, pro-choice advocates also facially challenged the Act's constitutionality. What are their best arguments?

In both district court cases, the courts held that the Act was unconstitutional and granted a permanent injunction against its enforcement. Both the Eighth Circuit and the Ninth Circuit approved the lower court decisions. The United States Supreme Court granted certiorari and consolidated the cases into *Carhart II*.

Practice Exercise: Write out the best arguments for each side in *Carhart II*. Then, go to the website to listen to the oral argument in the case. Compare your arguments with the arguments presented at the Supreme Court.

3. *Oral Argument*. After hearing the oral argument in this case, can you predict how the Justices will vote based on their questions to counsel?

Gonzales v. Carhart

Supreme Court of the United States, 2007.
550 U.S. 124, 127 S.Ct. 1610.

■ JUSTICE KENNEDY delivered the opinion of the Court, in which ROBERTS, C. J., and SCALIA, THOMAS, and ALITO, JJ., joined. THOMAS, J., filed a concurring opinion, in which SCALIA, J., joined. GINSBURG, J., filed a dissenting opinion, in which STEVENS, SOUTER, and BREYER, JJ., joined.

. . . Compared to the state statute at issue in *Stenberg,* the Act is more specific concerning the instances to which it applies and in this respect more precise in its coverage. We conclude the Act should be sustained against the objections lodged by the broad, facial attack brought against it.

III

We conclude that the Act is not void for vagueness, does not impose an undue burden from any overbreadth, and is not invalid on its face.

A

The Act punishes "knowingly perform[ing]" a "partial-birth abortion." § 1531(a). It defines the unlawful abortion in explicit terms. § 1531(b)(1).

First, the person performing the abortion must "vaginally delive[r] a living fetus." § 1531(b)(1)(A). The Act does not restrict an abortion procedure involving the delivery of an expired fetus. The Act, furthermore, is inapplicable to abortions that do not involve vaginal delivery (for instance, hysterotomy or hysterectomy). The Act does apply both previability and postviability because, by common understanding

and scientific terminology, a fetus is a living organism while within the womb, whether or not it is viable outside the womb.

Second, the Act's definition of partial-birth abortion requires the fetus to be delivered "until, in the case of a head-first presentation, the entire fetal head is outside the body of the mother, or, in the case of breech presentation, any part of the fetal trunk past the navel is outside the body of the mother." § 1531(b)(1)(A). The Attorney General concedes, and we agree, that if an abortion procedure does not involve the delivery of a living fetus to one of these "anatomical 'landmarks' "—where, depending on the presentation, either the fetal head or the fetal trunk past the navel is outside the body of the mother—the prohibitions of the Act do not apply.

Third, to fall within the Act, a doctor must perform an "overt act, other than completion of delivery, that kills the partially delivered living fetus." § 1531(b)(1)(B). For purposes of criminal liability, the overt act causing the fetus' death must be separate from delivery. And the overt act must occur after the delivery to an anatomical landmark. This is because the Act proscribes killing "the partially delivered" fetus, which, when read in context, refers to a fetus that has been delivered to an anatomical landmark.

Fourth, the Act contains scienter requirements concerning all the actions involved in the prohibited abortion. To begin with, the physician must have "deliberately and intentionally" delivered the fetus to one of the Act's anatomical landmarks. § 1531(b)(1)(A). If a living fetus is delivered past the critical point by accident or inadvertence, the Act is inapplicable. In addition, the fetus must have been delivered "for the purpose of performing an overt act that the [doctor] knows will kill [it]." *Ibid.* If either intent is absent, no crime has occurred. This follows from the general principle that where scienter is required no crime is committed absent the requisite state of mind.

C

We next determine whether the Act imposes an undue burden, as a facial matter, because its restrictions on second-trimester abortions are too broad. A review of the statutory text discloses the limits of its reach. The Act prohibits intact D & E; and, notwithstanding respondents' arguments, it does not prohibit the D & E procedure in which the fetus is removed in parts.

1

A comparison of the Act with the Nebraska statute struck down in *Stenberg* confirms this point. The statute in *Stenberg* prohibited " 'deliberately and intentionally delivering into the vagina a living unborn child, or a substantial portion thereof, for the purpose of performing a procedure that the person performing such procedure knows will kill the unborn child and does kill the unborn child.' " The Court concluded that this statute encompassed D & E because "D & E

will often involve a physician pulling a 'substantial portion' of a still living fetus, say, an arm or leg, into the vagina prior to the death of the fetus." The Court also rejected the limiting interpretation urged by Nebraska's Attorney General that the statute's reference to a "procedure" that " 'kill[s] the unborn child' " was to a distinct procedure, not to the abortion procedure as a whole.

Congress, it is apparent, responded to these concerns because the Act departs in material ways from the statute in *Stenberg*. It adopts the phrase "delivers a living fetus," § 1531(b)(1)(A), instead of " 'delivering . . . a living unborn child, or a substantial portion thereof[.]' " The Act's language, unlike the statute in *Stenberg*, expresses the usual meaning of "deliver" when used in connection with "fetus," namely, extraction of an entire fetus rather than removal of fetal pieces. The Act thus displaces the interpretation of "delivering" dictated by the Nebraska statute's reference to a "substantial portion" of the fetus. In interpreting statutory texts courts use the ordinary meaning of terms unless context requires a different result. Here, unlike in *Stenberg*, the language does not require a departure from the ordinary meaning. D & E does not involve the delivery of a fetus because it requires the removal of fetal parts that are ripped from the fetus as they are pulled through the cervix.

The identification of specific anatomical landmarks to which the fetus must be partially delivered also differentiates the Act from the statute at issue in *Stenberg*. § 1531(b)(1)(A). The Court in *Stenberg* interpreted " 'substantial portion' " of the fetus to include an arm or a leg. The Act's anatomical landmarks, by contrast, clarify that the removal of a small portion of the fetus is not prohibited. The landmarks also require the fetus to be delivered so that it is partially "outside the body of the mother." § 1531(b)(1)(A). To come within the ambit of the Nebraska statute, on the other hand, a substantial portion of the fetus only had to be delivered into the vagina; no part of the fetus had to be outside the body of the mother before a doctor could face criminal sanctions.

By adding an overt-act requirement Congress sought further to meet the Court's objections to the state statute considered in *Stenberg*. The Act makes the distinction the Nebraska statute failed to draw (but the Nebraska Attorney General advanced) by differentiating between the overall partial-birth abortion and the distinct overt act that kills the fetus. The fatal overt act must occur after delivery to an anatomical landmark, and it must be something "other than [the] completion of delivery." § 1531(b)(1)(B). This distinction matters because, unlike intact D & E, standard D & E does not involve a delivery followed by a fatal act. . . .

The Act's ban on abortions that involve partial delivery of a living fetus furthers the Government's objectives. No one would dispute that, for many, D & E is a procedure itself laden with the power to devalue human life. Congress could nonetheless conclude that the type of abortion proscribed by the Act requires specific regulation because it

implicates additional ethical and moral concerns that justify a special prohibition. Congress determined that the abortion methods it proscribed had a "disturbing similarity to the killing of a newborn infant," and thus it was concerned with "draw[ing] a bright line that clearly distinguishes abortion and infanticide." The Court has in the past confirmed the validity of drawing boundaries to prevent certain practices that extinguish life and are close to actions that are condemned. *Glucksberg* found reasonable the State's "fear that permitting assisted suicide will start it down the path to voluntary and perhaps even involuntary euthanasia."

Respect for human life finds an ultimate expression in the bond of love the mother has for her child. The Act recognizes this reality as well. Whether to have an abortion requires a difficult and painful moral decision. While we find no reliable data to measure the phenomenon, it seems unexceptionable to conclude some women come to regret their choice to abort the infant life they once created and sustained. Severe depression and loss of esteem can follow.

In a decision so fraught with emotional consequence some doctors may prefer not to disclose precise details of the means that will be used, confining themselves to the required statement of risks the procedure entails. From one standpoint this ought not to be surprising. Any number of patients facing imminent surgical procedures would prefer not to hear all details, lest the usual anxiety preceding invasive medical procedures become the more intense. This is likely the case with the abortion procedures here in issue.

It is, however, precisely this lack of information concerning the way in which the fetus will be killed that is of legitimate concern to the State. The State has an interest in ensuring so grave a choice is well informed. It is self-evident that a mother who comes to regret her choice to abort must struggle with grief more anguished and sorrow more profound when she learns, only after the event, what she once did not know: that she allowed a doctor to pierce the skull and vacuum the fast-developing brain of her unborn child, a child assuming the human form. . . .

There is documented medical disagreement whether the Act's prohibition would ever impose significant health risks on women. The three District Courts that considered the Act's constitutionality appeared to be in some disagreement on this central factual question. The District Court for the District of Nebraska concluded "the banned procedure is, sometimes, the safest abortion procedure to preserve the health of women." The District Court for the Northern District of California reached a similar conclusion. The District Court for the Southern District of New York was more skeptical of the purported health benefits of intact D & E. It found the Attorney General's "expert witnesses reasonably and effectively refuted [the plaintiffs'] proffered bases for the opinion that [intact D & E] has safety advantages over other second-trimester abortion procedures." In addition it did "not believe that many of [the

plaintiffs'] purported reasons for why [intact D & E] is medically necessary [were] credible; rather [it found them to be] theoretical or false." The court nonetheless invalidated the Act because it determined "a significant body of medical opinion . . . holds that D & E has safety advantages over induction and that [intact D & E] has some safety advantages (however hypothetical and unsubstantiated by scientific evidence) over D & E for some women in some circumstances."

The question becomes whether the Act can stand when this medical uncertainty persists. The Court's precedents instruct that the Act can survive this facial attack. The Court has given state and federal legislatures wide discretion to pass legislation in areas where there is medical and scientific uncertainty.

The Act is open to a proper as-applied challenge in a discrete case. No as-applied challenge need be brought if the prohibition in the Act threatens a woman's life because the Act already contains a life exception. 18 U.S.C. § 1531(a).

* * *

Respondents have not demonstrated that the Act, as a facial matter, is void for vagueness, or that it imposes an undue burden on a woman's right to abortion based on its overbreadth or lack of a health exception. For these reasons the judgments of the Courts of Appeals for the Eighth and Ninth Circuits are reversed.

It is so ordered.

■ JUSTICE THOMAS, with whom JUSTICE SCALIA joins, concurring.

I join the Court's opinion because it accurately applies current jurisprudence, including *Casey*. I write separately to reiterate my view that the Court's abortion jurisprudence, including *Casey* and *Roe* has no basis in the Constitution. I also note that whether the Partial-Birth Abortion Ban Act of 2013 constitutes a permissible exercise of Congress' power under the Commerce Clause is not before the Court. The parties did not raise or brief that issue; it is outside the question presented; and the lower courts did not address it.

■ JUSTICE GINSBURG, with whom JUSTICE STEVENS, JUSTICE SOUTER, and JUSTICE BREYER join, dissenting.

Today's decision is alarming. It refuses to take *Casey* and *Stenberg* seriously. It tolerates, indeed applauds, federal intervention to ban nationwide a procedure found necessary and proper in certain cases by the American College of Obstetricians and Gynecologists (ACOG). It blurs the line, firmly drawn in *Casey,* between previability and postviability abortions. And, for the first time since *Roe,* the Court blesses a prohibition with no exception safeguarding a woman's health.

I dissent from the Court's disposition. Retreating from prior rulings that abortion restrictions cannot be imposed absent an exception safeguarding a woman's health, the Court upholds an Act that surely

would not survive under the close scrutiny that previously attended state-decreed limitations on a woman's reproductive choices.

I

A

. . . In *Stenberg*, we expressly held that a statute banning intact D & E was unconstitutional in part because it lacked a health exception.

C

In contrast to Congress, the District Courts made findings after full trials at which all parties had the opportunity to present their best evidence. . . .

During the District Court trials, "numerous" "extraordinarily accomplished" and "very experienced" medical experts explained that, in certain circumstances and for certain women, intact D & E is safer than alternative procedures and necessary to protect women's health. . . .

Based on thoroughgoing review of the trial evidence and the congressional record, each of the District Courts to consider the issue rejected Congress' findings as unreasonable and not supported by the evidence. The trial courts concluded, in contrast to Congress' findings, that "significant medical authority supports the proposition that in some circumstances, [intact D & E] is the safest procedure."

The District Courts' findings merit this Court's respect. Today's opinion supplies no reason to reject those findings. Nevertheless, despite the District Courts' appraisal of the weight of the evidence, and in undisguised conflict with *Stenberg,* the Court asserts that the Partial-Birth Abortion Ban Act can survive "when . . . medical uncertainty persists." This assertion is bewildering. Not only does it defy the Court's longstanding precedent affirming the necessity of a health exception, with no carve-out for circumstances of medical uncertainty; it gives short shrift to the records before us, carefully canvassed by the District Courts. Those records indicate that "the majority of highly-qualified experts on the subject believe intact D & E to be the safest, most appropriate procedure under certain circumstances." . . .

Revealing in this regard, the Court invokes an antiabortion shibboleth for which it concededly has no reliable evidence: Women who have abortions come to regret their choices, and consequently suffer from "[s]evere depression and loss of esteem." Because of women's fragile emotional state and because of the "bond of love the mother has for her child," the Court worries, doctors may withhold information about the nature of the intact D & E procedure. The solution the Court approves, then, is *not* to require doctors to inform women, accurately and adequately, of the different procedures and their attendant risks. Instead, the Court deprives women of the right to make an autonomous choice, even at the expense of their safety.

This way of thinking reflects ancient notions about women's place in the family and under the Constitution—ideas that have long since been discredited. . . . Though today's majority may regard women's feelings on the matter as "self-evident," this Court has repeatedly confirmed that "[t]he destiny of the woman must be shaped . . . on her own conception of her spiritual imperatives and her place in society," *Casey*.

B

In cases on a "woman's liberty to determine whether to [continue] her pregnancy," this Court has identified viability as a critical consideration. . . . Today, the Court blurs that line, maintaining that "[t]he Act [legitimately] appl[ies] both previability and postviability because . . . a fetus is a living organism while within the womb, whether or not it is viable outside the womb." Instead of drawing the line at viability, the Court refers to Congress' purpose to differentiate "abortion and infanticide" based not on whether a fetus can survive outside the womb, but on where a fetus is anatomically located when a particular medical procedure is performed.

One wonders how long a line that saves no fetus from destruction will hold in face of the Court's "moral concerns." The Court's hostility to the right *Roe* and *Casey* secured is not concealed. Throughout, the opinion refers to obstetrician-gynecologists and surgeons who perform abortions not by the titles of their medical specialties, but by the pejorative label "abortion doctor." A fetus is described as an "unborn child," and as a "baby,"; second-trimester, previability abortions are referred to as "late-term"; and the reasoned medical judgments of highly trained doctors are dismissed as "preferences" motivated by "mere convenience." Instead of the heightened scrutiny we have previously applied, the Court determines that a "rational" ground is enough to uphold the Act. And, most troubling, *Casey's* principles, confirming the continuing vitality of "the essential holding of *Roe*" are merely "assume[d]" for the moment, rather than "retained" or "reaffirmed."

* * *

For the reasons stated, I dissent from the Court's disposition and would affirm the judgments before us for review.

NOTES AND QUESTIONS

1. *Comparison with Carhart I.* Justice Kennedy wrote the opinion finding that the Partial-Birth Abortion Ban that outlawed intact D & E is constitutional because it does not unduly burden a woman's right to abortion, even without a maternal health exception. How does he distinguish the federal law from the Nebraska law upheld in *Carhart I*? What was it about the way that Congress drafted the statute that allowed Justice Kennedy to conclude that the federal law was not vague? Do you agree that the description of the prohibited partial birth abortion was much clearer in

Carhart II than in *Carhart I*? Was it easier for you to read than the Nebraska statute?

How does Justice Kennedy handle the maternal health exception required by *Carhart I*? Do you agree with his conclusion that in a situation of disagreement in the medical community, Congress has the authority to decide that a certain procedure is never medically necessary? Is Justice Kennedy's analysis of congressional authority and medical uncertainty consistent with bioethical principles? Does it respect patient autonomy?

Do you agree with Justice Ginsburg that Justice Kennedy does not take *Casey* and *Carhart I* seriously? Why would Justice Ginsburg have deferred to the district courts' findings that intact D & E may be a safer procedure necessary to protect women's health? How does that affect her judgment that the statute should have contained a maternal health exception?

2. *Congressional Authority.* Did Congress have the authority to pass the Partial Birth Abortion Act? What congressional power allows Congress to regulate the subject of abortion? Is abortion a health matter that should be left to the states?

Justice Thomas raises the question whether Congress had the power under the Commerce Clause to pass the PBA legislation. What should the Court have concluded about Congress's power over abortion? How might this service affect interstate commerce? In Chapter 4, we learn that four Justices—Scalia, Kennedy, Thomas and Alito—concluded that Congress lacked power under the Commerce Clause to pass the Affordable Care Act. Is this a reason why the Court should have reached the congressional powers question? Why didn't the opponents of PBA legislation raise the Commerce Clause question?

3. *Women's Regret.* According to Justice Kennedy, "While we find no reliable data to measure the phenomenon, it seems unexceptionable to conclude some women come to regret their choice to abort the infant life they once created and sustained." Do you think Justice Kennedy's approach is too paternalistic? Or, do you think the State does have a legitimate interest in protecting women from regretting their decisions? If so, does the State have an interest in protecting women from regretting their decision to *have* the child? Do you agree or disagree with Justice Ginsburg's response that "[t]his way of thinking reflects ancient notions about women's place in the family and under the Constitution—ideas that have long since been discredited."? Is Justice Ginsburg faithful to bioethical principles when she writes that the majority "deprives women of the right to make an autonomous choice, even at the expense of their safety"?

4. *Shifting the Lens.* Partial birth abortion opponents were successful in proposing legislation because they described gruesome procedures that many legislators were reluctant to allow. Abortion opponents have more recently shifted the lens on the abortion controversy to "appeal to pain—a transcendent signifier, a universal proxy for empathy, and a subject that evokes visceral and moral horror." Amanda C. Pustilnik, Pain as Fact and Heuristic: How Pain Neuroimaging Illuminates Moral Dimensions of Law,

97 Cornell L. Rev. 801, 837 (2012). If legislators believe the fetus feels pain, do you think they will be more likely to outlaw abortion? Pustilnik argues:

> [F]ocusing on fetal pain allows the debate to shift away from the endless and irresoluble controversy over personhood. Instead, it permits anti-abortion advocates to propose, along with Bentham, that "[t]he question is not Can they reason?, nor, Can they talk?, but Can they suffer?" In addition to Bentham's moral question, the disgust factor related to thinking about fetal pain also plays a role, a factor that may be more viscerally effective than the philosophical and rhetorical strategies related to personhood.

Id. at 842. Do you think that shifting the lens to focus on fetal pain is a more effective argument than arguing about whether the fetus is a person? If you were a legislator or judge, would you give more or less weight to the pain of a fetus compared to the woman's right to choose? Is fetal pain a reason to ban abortion?

5. *Public Opinion.* Public opinion polls studying Americans' view on abortion consistently find that public support for abortion drops significantly after the first trimester. See Erik Eckholm, Theory on Pain Is Driving Rules for Abortions, N.Y. Times, Aug. 2, 2013, at A1 (finding that 61% of Americans support abortion in the first trimester, while only 27% support abortion in the second semester, and 14% in the final trimester).

Do you think this decline in support for abortion as the fetus grows parallels the public's conception of when a fetus becomes "human"? For example, pro-life advocates try to humanize the fetus by referring to it as a "baby," while pro-choice advocates prefer to use the term "fetus" because it is more dehumanizing. However, the use of the fetal pain argument humanizes the fetus, moving the public to empathize with the fetus as it would with a baby. Do you find this argument effective?

6. *Fetal Pain Science.* One of the arguments of pro-life advocates is that abortion causes pain to the fetus as early as twenty weeks into gestation, which becomes a reason for a state to pass a law prohibiting abortion whenever the fetus feels pain. However, studies published between 2005 and 2010 demonstrate that "fetal pain is unlikely to take place as early as 20 weeks after conception." Debra Cassens Weiss, Does Science Support Fetal-Pain Bills? Doc Wasn't Aware His Research Was Being Cited, ABA Journal, Sep. 18, 2013, at http://www.abajournal.com/news/article/does_science_support_fetal-pain_bills_doc_wasnt_aware_his_research_was/.

Some scientists who study fetal pain conclude that fetal pain is felt in the cortex or thalamus, which are not developed until after twenty weeks. Id. Moreover, expert committees in the United States and Great Britain agree that the fetus is not capable of feeling pain until twenty-six weeks. John A. Robertson, Fetal Pain Laws: Scientific and Constitutional Controversy, Harvard, June 26, 2013, at http://blogs.law.harvard.edu/billofhealth/2013/06/26/fetal-pain-laws-scientific-and-constitutional-controversy/. Further, the American Medical Association found that:

> Pain is an emotional and psychological experience that requires conscious recognition of a noxious stimulus. Consequently, the

> capacity for conscious perception of pain can arise only after thalamocortical pathways begin to function, which may occur in the third trimester around 29 to 30 weeks' gestational age, based on the limited data available. Small-scale histological studies of human fetuses have found that thalamocortical fibers begin to form between 23 to 30 weeks' gestational age, but these studies did not specifically examine thalamocortical pathways active in pain perception.

Susan J. Lee et al., Fetal Pain: A Systematic Multidisciplinary Review of the Evidence, 294 Am. Med. Ass'n, 947 (2005). Does this scientific evidence support restricting abortion to 20 weeks, or should a court conclude that a state relying on this evidence has no valid reason to ban abortion?

In Idaho, a fetal pain law failed after a federal judge struck down a law that banned abortions after twenty weeks. Idaho First State to Have Fetal Pain Law Rejected, USA Today, Mar. 7, 2013, https://www.usatoday.com/story/news/nation/2013/03/07/idaho-fetal-pain-law/1971527/. One supporter of the law said, "I'm very disappointed in the court in its decision to overturn the right to . . . protect a life from the pain of abortion." Id. Opponents of the law said banning pre-viability abortions is always unconstitutional. Id.

> **Practice Exercise:** Imagine that you are an attorney hired by the State of Arizona to draft a bill that would survive Supreme Court scrutiny and comply with Supreme Court decisions. Arizona would like a bill that restricts abortions that would cause the fetus pain. Before reading Arizona's Fetal Pain Bill, draft your own. Then, compare your bill, with the Arizona Fetal Pain Bill—what was different?

What do you think about fetal pain? If you were a woman seeking an abortion and a doctor told you that the abortion would be painful to the fetus, do you think that would deter you from getting an abortion? If so, do you think it is enough of a deterrent to constitute a substantial obstacle in the path of a woman seeking an abortion? Or, do you think the knowledge of potential pain to the fetus is necessary to have informed consent? For now, take a look at the Arizona Fetal Pain bill. In light of the U.S. Supreme Court precedent, do you think the Arizona legislature drafted this statute well?

2. FETAL PAIN

Ariz. Rev. Stat. § 36–2159 (2012)

Arizona Fetal Pain Bill.

A. Except in a medical emergency, a person shall not perform, induce or attempt to perform or induce an abortion unless the physician or the referring physician has first made a determination of the probable gestational age of the unborn child. In making that determination, the physician or referring physician shall make any inquiries of the pregnant

woman and perform or cause to be performed all medical examinations, imaging studies and tests as a reasonably prudent physician in the community, knowledgeable about the medical facts and conditions of both the woman and the unborn child involved, would consider necessary to perform and consider in making an accurate diagnosis with respect to gestational age.

B. Except in a medical emergency, a person shall not knowingly perform, induce or attempt to perform or induce an abortion on a pregnant woman if the probable gestational age of her unborn child has been determined to be at least twenty weeks.

C. A person who knowingly violates this section commits a class 1 misdemeanor.

D. A physician who knowingly violates this section commits an act of unprofessional conduct and is subject to license suspension or revocation pursuant to title 32, chapter 13 or 17.

E. In addition to other remedies available under the common or statutory law of this state, any of the following individuals may file a civil action to obtain appropriate relief for a violation of this section:

1. A woman on whom an abortion has been performed in violation of this section.
2. The father of the unborn child if the father is married to the mother at the time she received the abortion, unless the pregnancy resulted from the father's criminal conduct.
3. The maternal grandparents of the unborn child if the mother was not at least eighteen years of age at the time of the abortion, unless the pregnancy resulted from either of the maternal grandparent's criminal conduct.

F. A civil action filed pursuant to subsection E of this section shall be brought in the superior court in the county in which the woman on whom the abortion was performed resides. Relief pursuant to this subsection includes the following:

1. Money damages for all psychological, emotional and physical injuries resulting from the violation of this section.
2. Statutory damages in an amount equal to five thousand dollars or three times the cost of the abortion, whichever is greater.
3. Reasonable attorney fees and costs.

G. A civil action brought pursuant to this section must be initiated within six years after the violation occurred.

H. A woman on whom an abortion is performed or induced in violation of this section may not be prosecuted under this section or for conspiracy to commit a violation of this section.

NOTES AND QUESTIONS

1. *Ideal Plaintiffs.* If you wanted to challenge this law—the Arizona Fetal Pain Bill—who would be the ideal plaintiffs for your case? Would you pick a woman seeking an abortion? Would you want a doctor who performs abortions? Would you want a clinic that performs abortions?

2. Isaacson. In the following case, *Isaacson v. Horne*, the plaintiffs were three doctors who perform abortions. The doctors challenged the law claiming that banning abortion after twenty weeks based on alleged fetal pain is unconstitutional because it limits a woman's access to an abortion before viability. Only if a woman had a medical emergency could a woman have an abortion after twenty weeks. The Ninth Circuit held that the Arizona Fetal Pain Bill was unconstitutional. Was the Ninth Circuit's ruling consistent with Supreme Court precedent?

Isaacson v. Horne

United States Court of Appeals, Ninth Circuit, 2013.
716 F.3d 1213.

■ BERZON, CIRCUIT JUDGE:

Our question is whether the Constitution permits the Arizona legislature to prohibit abortion beginning at twenty weeks gestation, before the fetus is viable. We hold that it does not.

Arizona House Bill 2036 ("H.B.2036" or "the Act"), enacted in April 2012, forbids, except in a medical emergency, abortion of a fetus determined to be of a gestational age of at least twenty weeks. Arizona law separately prohibits abortions after fetal viability unless necessary to preserve the pregnant woman's life or health. *See* Ariz.Rev.Stat. § 36–2301.01(A)(1). The challenged provision in Section 7 of H.B.2036 ("Section 7" or "the twenty-week law") extends the abortion ban earlier in pregnancy, to the period between twenty weeks gestation and fetal viability. Because Section 7 deprives the women to whom it applies of the ultimate decision to terminate their pregnancies prior to fetal viability, it is unconstitutional under a long line of invariant Supreme Court precedents.

Since *Roe v. Wade*, the Supreme Court case law concerning the constitutional protection accorded women with respect to the decision whether to undergo an abortion has been unalterably clear regarding one basic point, although it has varied in other respects: a woman has a constitutional right to choose to terminate her pregnancy before the fetus is viable. A prohibition on the exercise of that right is *per se* unconstitutional. While the state may *regulate* the mode and manner of abortion prior to fetal viability, it may not *proscribe* a woman from electing abortion, nor may it impose an undue burden on her choice through regulation.

The challenged Arizona statute's medical emergency exception does not transform the law from a prohibition on abortion into a regulation of

abortion procedure. Allowing a *physician* to decide if abortion is medically necessary is not the same as allowing a *woman* to decide whether to carry her own pregnancy to term. Moreover, regulations involve limitations as to the mode and manner of abortion, not preclusion of the choice to terminate a pregnancy altogether. Arizona's twenty-week law is a preclusion prior to fetal viability and is thus invalid under binding Supreme Court precedent.

Background

I.

. . . The challenged portion of Section 7, codified at Arizona Revised Statutes § 36–2159, reads:

> A. Except in a medical emergency, a person shall not perform, induce or attempt to perform or induce an abortion unless the physician or the referring physician has first made a determination of the probable gestational age of the unborn child. In making that determination, the physician or referring physician shall make any inquiries of the pregnant woman and perform or cause to be performed all medical examinations, imaging studies and tests as a reasonably prudent physician in the community, knowledgeable about the medical facts and conditions of both the woman and the unborn child involved, would consider necessary to perform and consider in making an accurate diagnosis with respect to gestational age.
>
> B. Except in a medical emergency, a person shall not knowingly perform, induce or attempt to perform or induce an abortion on a pregnant woman if the probable gestational age of her unborn child has been determined to be at least twenty weeks.

Ariz.Rev.Stat. § 36–2159. Arizona law defines "medical emergency" as:

> a condition that, on the basis of the physician's good faith clinical judgment, so complicates the medical condition of a pregnant woman as to necessitate the immediate abortion of her pregnancy to avert her death or for which a delay will create serious risk of substantial and irreversible impairment of a major bodily function.

Ariz.Rev.Stat. § 36–2151(6). The stated purpose of the Act is to "[p]rohibit abortions at or after twenty weeks of gestation, except in cases of a medical emergency, based on the documented risks to women's health and the strong medical evidence that unborn children feel pain during an abortion at that gestational age." H.B.2036, sec. 9(B)(1). The Act lists a number of legislative findings in support of the assertions in the purpose provision, with citations to medical research articles. *See* H.B.2036, sec. 9(A)(1)–(7).

II.

The plaintiffs in this action are three board-certified obstetrician-gynecologists who practice in Arizona ("the Physicians"). In July 2012, they filed suit in the United States District Court for the District of Arizona, seeking declaratory and injunctive relief against enforcement of Section 7 on behalf of themselves and of their patients wishing to terminate pre-viability pregnancies at or after twenty weeks. Their complaint named three state defendants and two county defendants: the Attorney General of Arizona, Tom Horne; the Arizona Medical Board; and the Executive Director of the Arizona Medical Board, Lisa Wynn (collectively "State Defendants"); the County Attorney for Pima County, Barbara LaWall; and the County Attorney for Maricopa County, William Montgomery. . . .

Discussion

II.

A.

A woman has a constitutional right to choose to terminate her pregnancy before the fetus is viable without undue interference by the state. At bottom, the right recognized by *Roe* and reaffirmed by *Casey* is "the woman's right to make the *ultimate decision.*" . . .

Casey jettisoned this trimester framework and the strict scrutiny standard applied in *Roe*. But *Casey* reaffirmed—and *Gonzales v. Carhart* has since reiterated—*Roe's* central holding: "Before viability, the State's interests are not strong enough to support a prohibition of abortion or the imposition of a substantial obstacle to the woman's effective right to elect the procedure." That principle is binding upon us and decides this case.

B.

Defendants contend otherwise, characterizing the viability line first drawn in *Roe,* reaffirmed in *Casey,* and recognized again in *Gonzales,* as dicta rather than controlling Supreme Court precedent. That characterization is most certainly incorrect.

Roe identified fetal viability as the earliest point in pregnancy when the state's interest becomes sufficiently compelling to justify not just *regulation* of the abortion procedure, but *proscription* of abortion unless necessary to preserve the life or health of the mother. . . . Although the plurality opinion in *Casey* abandoned *Roe's* trimester framework, the Court yet again affirmed "*Roe's* central holding, that *viability* marks the earliest point at which the State's interest in fetal life is constitutionally adequate to justify a legislative ban on nontherapeutic abortions." The plurality opinion explained that the Court was again drawing the line at viability "so that before that time the woman has a right to choose to terminate her pregnancy," emphasizing that "there is no line other than viability which is more workable."

Echoing the joint opinion in *Casey*, *Stenberg* took as the starting point of its analysis the "established principle[ ]" that, "before 'viability . . . the woman has a right to choose to terminate her pregnancy.' "

Finally, the Supreme Court's most recent abortion decision, *Gonzales*, preserved the viability line as the limit on prohibitions of abortion, applying *Casey* rather than overturning it. *Gonzales* left in place the earlier rulings that,

> *[b]efore viability*, a State 'may not prohibit any woman from making the ultimate decision to terminate her pregnancy.' It also may not impose upon this right an undue burden, which exists if a regulation's 'purpose or effect is to place a substantial obstacle in the path of a woman seeking an abortion before the fetus attains viability.'

As *Roe* and its many progeny make clear, viability, although not a fixed point, is the critical point. The Supreme Court has recognized that viability varies among pregnancies and that improvements in medical technology will both push later in pregnancy the point at which abortion is safer than childbirth and advance earlier in gestation the point of fetal viability. Indeed, such trends led Justice O'Connor to remark, prior to *Casey*, that "the *Roe* framework . . . is on a collision course with itself." But while "time has overtaken some of *Roe*'s factual assumptions," prompting the abandonment of the trimester framework, "no changes of fact have rendered viability more or less appropriate as the point at which the balance of interests tips." Evolving medical realities have not eroded *Roe*'s central legal holding—that "viability marks the earliest point at which the State's interest in fetal life is constitutionally adequate to justify a legislative ban on nontherapeutic abortions." . . .

While viability is a "flexible" point, it is medically determinable. Precisely because viability varies from pregnancy to pregnancy, the Supreme Court has held repeatedly that "the determination of whether a particular fetus is viable is, and must be, a matter for the judgment of the responsible attending physician." That is why a state may not fix viability at a specific point in pregnancy.

The parties here agree that no fetus is viable at twenty weeks gestational age. The district court so recognized, declaring it undisputed that viability usually occurs between twenty-three and twenty-four weeks gestation. Accordingly, Arizona's ban on abortion from twenty weeks necessarily prohibits pre-viability abortions. Section 7 is therefore, without more, invalid.

NOTES AND QUESTIONS

1. *Necessity*. The purpose of the Arizona Fetal Pain Law was "based on the documented risks to women's health and the strong medical evidence that unborn children feel pain during an abortion at that gestational age." Isaacson v. Horne, 716 F.3d 1213 (9th Cir. 2013). However, studies have

documented that only about 1% of all abortions in the United States take place after the twentieth week of gestation. Amanda C. Pustilnik, Pain as Fact and Heuristic: How Pain Neuroimaging Illuminates Moral Dimensions of Law, 97 Cornell L. Rev. 801, 843 (2012). Knowing these statistics, do you think it would affect a court's view on how compelling the state interest is in limiting abortions to twenty weeks?

2. *Viability*. The Ninth Circuit emphasized that the Arizona Fetal Pain Law prohibited abortions prior to viability. Do you know when viability occurs? Did the Court establish the number of weeks at which a fetus is viable? Does a state have the power to define when a fetus is viable?

In another abortion case, attorneys for North Dakota argued that in vitro fertilization—which we will study later in this chapter—proves that a fertilized egg can survive outside the womb and therefore shows that viability occurs at conception. See Jessica Mason Pieklo, Attorneys Urge Federal Appeals Court to Take First Step in Overturning "Roe", RH Reality Check, Jan. 14, 2015, at http://rhrealitycheck.org/article/2015/01/14/attorneys-urge-federal-appeals-court-take-first-step-overturning-roe/. Has medical technology pushed viability back to conception? If so, do women retain any right to end a pregnancy?

3. *How Many Weeks?* Why did the Arizona legislators choose twenty weeks as the stopping point for non-emergency abortions? Twenty weeks has been a popular time frame in recent abortion statutes. Twelve states have passed bans on abortion after twenty weeks. In May 2015, the House of Representatives passed legislation banning abortion after twenty weeks. Is there any reason other than fetal pain to justify such legislation?

Arkansas legislators passed the Human Heartbeat Protection Act, Ark. Code Ann. §§ 20–16–1301 to 1307 (2013), which prohibits abortion after *twelve* weeks once a fetal heartbeat is detected. Does the detection of a heartbeat give the legislature reason to ban abortions? In litigation about the statute, Arkansas did not contest plaintiffs' medical testimony that a twelve-week fetus "cannot in any circumstance survive outside the uterus" and is therefore not viable. Is the Arkansas law unconstitutional? See Edwards v. Beck, 786 F.3d 1113 (8th Cir. 2015) (act is unconstitutional for banning pre-viability abortions). Despite ruling for the plaintiffs, the Eighth Circuit observed that viability is changing with medical technology, and described the survival of a twenty-one-weeks and six-days old fetus. The court urged the state to "develop[ ] the record in a meaningful way so as to present a real opportunity for the court to examine viability, case by case, as viability steadily moves back towards conception." Id. at 1119.

Practice Exercise: If you were in the Arkansas legislature, what evidence about viability would you include in your next statute? Is in vitro fertilization relevant?

4. *Informed Consent*. Another controversy surrounding abortion stems from doctors being required to give "informed consent" to women seeking an abortion. Post-*Casey*, many states have added detailed informed consent requirements to their abortion laws. In *Carhart II*, Justice Ginsburg

complained that the Court's rules were not serving patient autonomy, which is the usual goal of informed consent:

> Because of women's fragile emotional state and because of the "bond of love the mother has for her child," the Court worries, doctors may withhold information about the nature of the intact D & E procedure. The solution the Court approves, then, is *not* to require doctors to inform women, accurately and adequately, of the different procedures and their attendant risks. Cf. *Casey* (plurality opinion) ("States are free to enact laws to provide a reasonable framework for a woman to make a decision that has such profound and lasting meaning."). Instead, the Court deprives women of the right to make an autonomous choice, even at the expense of their safety.

Is informed consent different in the abortion context than in the research and general treatment settings we studied in Chapter 2? Should informed consent forms for abortion include the scientific evidence about fetal pain discussed above?

3. INFORMED CONSENT

Recently, states have enacted consent laws that require the woman to receive detailed information about the fetus through ultrasounds or sonograms. Unlike the informed consent discussed in Chapter 2, the informed consent at issue is whether doctors can be required to explain to the woman that the fetus has a heartbeat, have the woman listen to it, and show the woman the sonogram, before she can obtain an abortion.

> **Go to** the website to listen to and read about the two sides of the sonogram debate in Texas as represented by Senator Dan Patrick, the sponsor of the legislation, and Carolyn Jones, who had an abortion under the statute.

Now study the Texas Sonogram Abortion Bill, reprinted below. When reading this Bill, think about how you would draft a bill differently if you wanted to obtain informed consent to the abortion. Also, consider whether Texas' use of informed consent requirements are efforts to discourage a woman from seeking an abortion or authentic medical techniques necessary to protect patient autonomy. Does it matter whether the law permits women to close their eyes when the sonogram image is displayed? Whether the doctor believes the mandated information is scientifically accurate?

> **Go to** the website to see the actual informed consent form Texas requires. Then go through the Michigan process of informed consent. Go through as much of the process as you can.

Tex. Health & Safety Code Ann. § 171.012 (West 2003)

Texas Sonogram Abortion Bill.

(a) Consent to an abortion is voluntary and informed only if:

(1) the physician who is to perform the abortion informs the pregnant woman on whom the abortion is to be performed of:

(A) the physician's name;

(B) the particular medical risks associated with the particular abortion procedure to be employed, including, when medically accurate:

(i) the risks of infection and hemorrhage;

(ii) the potential danger to a subsequent pregnancy and of infertility; and

(iii) the possibility of increased risk of breast cancer following an induced abortion and the natural protective effect of a completed pregnancy in avoiding breast cancer;

(C) the probable gestational age of the unborn child at the time the abortion is to be performed; and

(D) the medical risks associated with carrying the child to term;

(2) the physician who is to perform the abortion or the physician's agent informs the pregnant woman that:

(A) medical assistance benefits may be available for prenatal care, childbirth, and neonatal care;

(B) the father is liable for assistance in the support of the child without regard to whether the father has offered to pay for the abortion; and

(C) public and private agencies provide pregnancy prevention counseling and medical referrals for obtaining pregnancy prevention medications or devices, including emergency contraception for victims of rape or incest;

(3) the physician who is to perform the abortion or the physician's agent:

(A) provides the pregnant woman with the printed materials described by Section 171.014; and

(B) informs the pregnant woman that those materials:

(i) have been provided by the Department of State Health Services;

(ii) are accessible on an Internet website sponsored by the department;

(iii) describe the unborn child and list agencies that offer alternatives to abortion; and

(iv) include a list of agencies that offer sonogram services at no cost to the pregnant woman;

(4) before any sedative or anesthesia is administered to the pregnant woman and at least 24 hours before the abortion or at least two hours before the abortion if the pregnant woman waives this requirement by certifying that she currently lives 100 miles or more from the nearest abortion provider that is a facility licensed under Chapter 245 or a facility that performs more than 50 abortions in any 12-month period:

(A) the physician who is to perform the abortion or an agent of the physician who is also a sonographer certified by a national registry of medical sonographers performs a sonogram on the pregnant woman on whom the abortion is to be performed;

(B) the physician who is to perform the abortion displays the sonogram images in a quality consistent with current medical practice in a manner that the pregnant woman may view them;

(C) the physician who is to perform the abortion provides, in a manner understandable to a layperson, a verbal explanation of the results of the sonogram images, including a medical description of the dimensions of the embryo or fetus, the presence of cardiac activity, and the presence of external members and internal organs; and

(D) the physician who is to perform the abortion or an agent of the physician who is also a sonographer certified by a national registry of medical sonographers makes audible the heart auscultation for the pregnant woman to hear, if present, in a quality consistent with current medical practice and provides, in a manner understandable to a layperson, a simultaneous verbal explanation of the heart auscultation;

(5) before receiving a sonogram under Subdivision (4)(A) and before the abortion is performed and before any sedative or anesthesia is administered, the pregnant woman completes and certifies with her signature an election form that states as follows: . . .

NOTES AND QUESTIONS

1. *The Debate in Texas.* The Fifth Circuit Court of Appeals upheld the Texas sonogram law against First Amendment and due process challenges in Texas Med. Providers Performing Abortion Servs. v. Lakey, 667 F.3d 570, 573 (5th Cir. 2012). Do you think doctors' speech about abortion to their patients deserves First Amendment protection?

The First Amendment argument was that the law compelled physicians to speak (about the sonogram) and women to become a compelled audience.

The court summarized the Supreme Court's abortion consent jurisprudence as follows:

> The import of these cases is clear. First, informed consent laws that do not impose an undue burden on the woman's right to have an abortion are permissible if they require truthful, nonmisleading, and relevant disclosures. Second, such laws are part of the state's reasonable regulation of medical practice and do not fall under the rubric of compelling "ideological" speech that triggers First Amendment strict scrutiny. Third, "relevant" informed consent may entail not only the physical and psychological risks to the expectant mother facing this "difficult moral decision," but also the state's legitimate interests in "protecting the potential life within her." Finally, the possibility that such information "might cause the woman to choose childbirth over abortion" does not render the provisions unconstitutional.

Id. at 575. Following these principles, the court concluded that it was "obvious" that the Texas law was constitutional because the sonogram, fetal heartbeat and other requirements were "the epitome of truthful non-misleading information." Id. Do you agree with the Fifth Circuit's statement? Or, is this information that, although truthful, may be misleading in a way because it appeals to emotion?

There is a circuit split on this issue. The Fourth Circuit disagreed with the Fifth Circuit, stating that requiring the sonogram violated the physicians' free speech rights because the requirement did not satisfy intermediate scrutiny. Stuart v. Camnitz, 774 F.3d 238, 245–46 (4th Cir. 2014). The Fourth Circuit described North Carolina's similar legislation as "quintessential compelled speech" that "explicitly promotes a pro-life message by demanding the provision of facts that all fall on one side of the abortion debate." Id. at 246. The Fourth Circuit found that the statute deviated from the traditions of informed consent. Do you agree? A circuit split often means that the Supreme Court decides to resolve the conflict. Are you surprised that the Court denied certiorari in the Fourth Circuit's case? Stuart v. Camnitz, 774 F.3d 238 (4th Cir. 2014) cert. denied sub nom. Walker-McGill v. Stuart, 576 U.S. 1028 (2015). Does this mean that the Court agreed with the Fourth Circuit? Justice Scalia dissented from the denial of cert. without explaining his reasons. Id. Why do you think Justice Scalia wanted the Court to hear the case?

2. *Anti-Ultrasound Lobbying*. Texas is not the only state that passed ultrasound requirements before a woman can have an abortion. In Virginia, legislators attempted to pass an "informed consent" bill that required a vaginal ultrasound, instead of the "jelly on the belly" type of ultrasound before a woman can obtain an abortion. Erik Eckholm, Ultrasound: A Pawn in the Abortion Wars, N.Y. Times, Feb. 26, 2012, at SR4. Pro-choice advocates called the vaginal ultrasound "forced vaginal penetration" that asks "doctors to commit a sex crime" that is "akin to rape." Id. The Virginia legislation eventually included an abdominal, but not a vaginal, scan. The Sixth Circuit upheld Kentucky's ultrasound law in 2019. EMW Women's Surg. Ctr. v. Beshear, 920 F.3d 421 (6th Cir. 2019). Is there a difference

between how vaginal and abdominal probes serve the goal of informed consent?

If you were a legislator, how would you draft a bill that requires informed consent for women seeking an abortion? Would you include a sonogram requirement? Would you make women read papers and then sign a consent form? Or, would you require the doctor to explain each issue to them? If so, would you require a mandatory waiting period after the doctor explains the procedure so the woman has a chance to think through the decision? How would abortion informed consent vary from the procedures you studied in Chapter 2?

Go to the website to look at the Virginia Ultrasound file. Assess whether the statute is constitutional or not. Be sure to consider the arguments on both sides. How does it compare to other state ultrasound laws?

4. THE SUPREME COURT'S LATEST CASES

Many (perhaps most) of the doctors who work at a hospital are not considered employees. Susan M. Brazas, The Doctor is In: How Doctors Work with Hospitals, Lawyers.com, http://medical-malpractice.lawyers.com/the-doctor-is-in-how-doctors-work-with-hospitals.html. Instead, they are independent contractors who have privileges at the hospital in accord with the hospital's Medical Staff Bylaws. Id. Consider how hospitals grant admitting privileges to doctors:

> Each hospital has its own set of rules, regulations and policies defining how doctors can admit patients, and how they're allowed to treat patients. Usually the rules require doctors to submit a written application for their privileges. The application contains extensive information about the doctor's education, license and experience.
>
> Different categories of privileges exist. These include:
>
> - **Admitting privileges**—allow a doctor to admit a patient to the hospital.
> - **Courtesy privileges**—allow a doctor to occasionally admit or to visit and treat patients in the hospital.
> - **Surgical privileges**—to perform surgery in the hospital's operating room or outpatient surgery area.
>
> Often the decision of whether to grant privileges to a doctor is a group decision made by a hospital's credentialing committee. The committee thoroughly reviews the doctor's application and conducts an in-person interview, then votes on whether to accept the doctor.

Id. What happens when the admitting privilege requirements conflict with the practice of abortion? Consider the Children's Hospital of San Antonio, a member-hospital of the Christus Santa Rosa Health System—

a Catholic organization. One of the "Obligations of Appointment and Reappointment" in the hospital's Medical Staff Bylaws includes that the "Physician and practitioner exercising temporary privileges under these Medical Staff Bylaws shall: abide by . . . the Ethical and Religious Directives for Catholic Health Care Services as approved by the Ordinary of the Archdiocese of San Antonio." If the Catholic Directives prohibit abortion, how do you think that will affect whether a doctor who performs abortion can be admitted to that hospital? What if this hospital were located in a jurisdiction that required abortion physicians to have admitting privileges? What if this hospital were the only hospital in a rural area? How do you feel about admitting privileges? Should each hospital have its own qualifications? Or, should there be uniformity among hospitals regarding admitting privileges?

The Supreme Court decided two cases about admitting privileges and abortion, *Whole Woman's Health* and *June Medical Services*. What insights do the cases give you about *women's health*? What are the bioethical issues involved in the cases? Are you surprised that the Justices disagree as much as they do? What do you think the next Supreme Court case will hold?

Whole Woman's Health v. Hellerstedt

Supreme Court of the United States, 2016.
579 U.S. ___, 136 S.Ct. 2292.

■ BREYER, J., delivered the opinion of the Court, in which KENNEDY, GINSBURG, SOTOMAYOR, and KAGAN, JJ., joined. GINSBURG, J., filed a concurring opinion. THOMAS, J., filed a dissenting opinion. ALITO, J., filed a dissenting opinion, in which ROBERTS, C. J., and THOMAS, J., joined.

■ JUSTICE BREYER.

We must here decide whether two provisions of Texas' House Bill 2 violate the Federal Constitution as interpreted in *Casey*. The first provision, which we shall call the *"admitting-privileges requirement,"* says that

> "[a] physician performing or inducing an abortion . . . must, on the date the abortion is performed or induced, have active admitting privileges at a hospital that . . . is located not further than 30 miles from the location at which the abortion is performed or induced." Tex. Health & Safety Code Ann. § 171.0031(a) (West Cum. Supp. 2015).

This provision amended Texas law that had previously required an abortion facility to maintain a written protocol "for managing medical emergencies and the transfer of patients requiring further emergency care to a hospital." 38 Tex. Reg. 6546 (2013).

The second provision, which we shall call the *"surgical-center requirement,"* says that

"the minimum standards for an abortion facility must be equivalent to the minimum standards adopted under [the Texas Health and Safety Code section] for ambulatory surgical centers." Tex. Health & Safety Code Ann. § 245.010(a).

We conclude that neither of these provisions confers medical benefits sufficient to justify the burdens upon access that each imposes. Each places a substantial obstacle in the path of women seeking a previability abortion, each constitutes an undue burden on abortion access, *Casey, supra,* at 878 (plurality opinion), and each violates the Federal Constitution. Amdt. 14, § 1.

II B

In sum, in our view, none of petitioners' claims are barred by res judicata. For all of the reasons described above, we conclude that the Court of Appeals' procedural ruling was incorrect. Cf. Brief for Professors Michael Dorf et al. as *Amici Curiae* 22 (professors in civil procedure from Cornell Law School, New York University School of Law, Columbia Law School, University of Chicago Law School, and Duke University Law School) (maintaining that "the panel's procedural ruling" was "clearly incorrect"). We consequently proceed to consider the merits of petitioners' claims.

III

The Court of Appeals wrote that a state law is "constitutional if: (1) it does not have the purpose or effect of placing a substantial obstacle in the path of a woman seeking an abortion of a nonviable fetus; and (2) it is reasonably related to (or designed to further) a legitimate state interest." 790 F. 3d, at 572. The Court of Appeals went on to hold that "the district court erred by substituting its own judgment for that of the legislature" when it conducted its "undue burden inquiry," in part because "medical uncertainty underlying a statute is for resolution by legislatures, not the courts." *Id.,* at 587 (citing *Gonzales* v. *Car-hart,* 550 U.S. 124, 163 (2007)).

The Court of Appeals' articulation of the relevant standard is incorrect. The first part of the Court of Appeals' test may be read to imply that a district court should not consider the existence or nonexistence of medical benefits when considering whether a regulation of abortion constitutes an undue burden. The rule announced in *Casey,* however, requires that courts consider the burdens a law imposes on abortion access together with the benefits those laws confer. See 505 U. S., at 887–898 (opinion of the Court) (performing this balancing with respect to a spousal notification provision); *id.,* at 899–901 (joint opinion of O'Connor, KENNEDY, and Souter, JJ.) (same balancing with respect to a parental notification provision). And the second part of the test is wrong to equate the judicial review applicable to the regulation of a constitutionally protected personal liberty with the less strict review applicable where, for example, economic legislation is at issue. See, *e.g., Williamson* v. *Lee*

Optical of Okla., Inc., 348 U.S. 483, 491 (1955). The Court of Appeals' approach simply does not match the standard that this Court laid out in *Casey*, which asks courts to consider whether any burden imposed on abortion access is "undue."

IV

The purpose of the admitting-privileges requirement is to help ensure that women have easy access to a hospital should complications arise during an abortion procedure. Brief for Respondents 32–37. But the District Court found that it brought about no such health-related benefit. The court found that "[t]he great weight of evidence demonstrates that, before the act's passage, abortion in Texas was extremely safe with particularly low rates of serious complications and virtually no deaths occurring on account of the procedure." 46 F. Supp. 3d, at 684. Thus, there was no significant health-related problem that the new law helped to cure.

We have found nothing in Texas' record evidence that shows that, compared to prior law (which required a "working arrangement" with a doctor with admitting privileges), the new law advanced Texas' legitimate interest in protecting women's health.

At the same time, the record evidence indicates that the admitting-privileges requirement places a "substantial obstacle in the path of a woman's choice." Eight abortion clinics closed in the months leading up to the requirement's effective date. Eleven more closed on the day the admitting-privileges requirement took effect.

In our view, the record contains sufficient evidence that the admitting-privileges requirement led to the closure of half of Texas' clinics, or thereabouts. Those closures meant fewer doctors, longer waiting times, and increased crowding. Record evidence also supports the finding that after the admitting-privileges provision went into effect, the "number of women of reproductive age living in a county . . . more than 150 miles from a provider increased from approximately 86,000 to 400,000 . . . and the number of women living in a county more than 200 miles from a provider from approximately 10,000 to 290,000." 46 F. Supp. 3d, at 681. We recognize that increased driving distances do not always constitute an "undue burden." See *Casey*, 505 U.S., at 885–887 (joint opinion of O'Connor, KENNEDY, and Souter, JJ.). But here, those increases are but one additional burden, which, when taken together with others that the closings brought about, and when viewed in light of the virtual absence of any health benefit, lead us to conclude that the record adequately supports the District Court's "undue burden" conclusion.

[T]he dissent suggests that one benefit of H. B. 2's requirements would be that they might "force unsafe facilities to shut down." To support that assertion, the dissent points to the Kermit Gosnell scandal.

Gosnell's behavior was terribly wrong. But there is no reason to believe that an extra layer of regulation would have affected that behavior.

V

The upshot is that this record evidence, along with the absence of any evidence to the contrary, provides ample support for the District Court's conclusion that "[m]any of the building standards mandated by the act and its implementing rules have such a tangential relationship to patient safety in the context of abortion as to be nearly arbitrary." 46 F. Supp. 3d, at 684. That conclusion, along with the supporting evidence, provides sufficient support for the more general conclusion that the surgical-center requirement "will not [provide] better care or . . . more frequent positive outcomes." *Ibid.* The record evidence thus supports the ultimate legal conclusion that the surgical-center requirement is not necessary.

At the same time, the record provides adequate evidentiary support for the District Court's conclusion that the surgical-center requirement places a substantial obstacle in the path of women seeking an abortion. The parties stipulated that the requirement would further reduce the number of abortion facilities available to seven or eight facilities, located in Houston, Austin, San Antonio, and Dallas/Fort Worth.

We agree with the District Court that the surgical-center requirement, like the admitting-privileges requirement, provides few, if any, health benefits for women, poses a substantial obstacle to women seeking abortions, and constitutes an "undue burden" on their constitutional right to do so.

* * *

For these reasons the judgment of the Court of Appeals is reversed, and the case is remanded for further proceedings consistent with this opinion.

■ JUSTICE GINSBURG, concurring.

So long as this Court adheres to *Roe* v. *Wade*, 410 U.S. 113 (1973), and *Planned Parenthood of Southeastern Pa.* v. *Casey*, 505 U.S. 833 (1992), Targeted Regulation of Abortion Providers laws like H. B. 2 that "do little or nothing for health, but rather strew impediments to abortion," *Planned Parenthood of Wis.*, 806 F. 3d, at 921, cannot survive judicial inspection.

■ JUSTICE THOMAS, dissenting.

I

This suit is possible only because the Court has allowed abortion clinics and physicians to invoke a putative constitutional right that does not belong to them—a woman's right to abortion. The Court's third-party standing jurisprudence is no model of clarity. See *Kowalski* v. *Tesmer*, 543 U.S. 125, 135 (2004) (THOMAS, J., concurring). Driving this doctrinal confusion, the Court has shown a particular willingness to undercut

restrictions on third-party standing when the right to abortion is at stake. And this case reveals a deeper flaw in straying from our normal rules: when the wrong party litigates a case, we end up resolving disputes that make for bad law.

II

I remain fundamentally opposed to the Court's abortion jurisprudence. *E.g., id.*, at 168–169 (THOMAS, J., concurring); *Stenberg,* 530 U. S., at 980, 982 (THOMAS, J., dissenting). Even taking *Casey* as the baseline, however, the majority radically rewrites the undue-burden test in three ways. First, today's decision requires courts to "consider the burdens a law imposes on abortion access together with the benefits those laws confer." *Ante,* at 19. Second, today's opinion tells the courts that, when the law's justifications are medically uncertain, they need not defer to the legislature, and must instead assess medical justifications for abortion restrictions by scrutinizing the record themselves. *Ibid.* Finally, even if a law imposes no "substantial obstacle" to women's access to abortions, the law now must have more than a "reasonabl[e] relat[ion] to . . . a legitimate state interest." *Ibid.* (internal quotation marks omitted). These precepts are nowhere to be found in *Casey* or its successors, and transform the undue-burden test to something much more akin to strict scrutiny.

* * *

Today's decision will prompt some to claim victory, just as it will stiffen opponents' will to object. But the entire Nation has lost something essential. The majority's embrace of a jurisprudence of rights-specific exceptions and balancing tests is "a regrettable concession of defeat—an acknowledgement that we have passed the point where 'law,' properly speaking, has any further application." Scalia, The Rule of Law as a Law of Rules, 56 U. Chi. L. Rev. 1175, 1182 (1989). I respectfully dissent.

■ JUSTICE ALITO, with whom THE CHIEF JUSTICE and JUSTICE THOMAS join, dissenting.

I D

For these reasons, what the Court has done here is to create an entirely new exception to the rule that a losing plaintiff cannot relitigate a claim just because it now has new and better evidence. As best I can tell, the Court's new rule must be something like this: If a plaintiff initially loses because it failed to provide adequate proof that a challenged law will have an unconstitutional effect and if subsequent developments tend to show that the law will in fact have those effects, the plaintiff may relitigate the same claim. Such a rule would be unprecedented, and I am unsure of its wisdom, but I am certain of this: There is no possible justification for such a rule unless the plaintiff, at the time of the first case, could not have reasonably shown what the effects of the law would be. And that is not the situation in this case.

* * *

In sum, the Court's holding that petitioners' second facial challenge to the admitting privileges requirement is not barred by claim preclusion is not supported by any of our cases or any body of lower court precedent; is contrary to the bedrock rule that a party cannot relitigate a claim simply because the party has obtained new and better evidence; is contrary to the first Restatement of Judgments and the actual rules of the second Restatement of Judgment; and is purportedly based largely on a single comment in the second Restatement, but does not even represent a sensible reading of that comment. In a regular case, an attempt by petitioners to relitigate their previously unsuccessful facial challenge to the admitting privileges requirement would have been rejected out of hand—indeed, might have resulted in the imposition of sanctions under Federal Rule of Civil Procedure 11. No court would even think of reviving such a claim on its own. But in this abortion case, ordinary rules of law—and fairness—are suspended.

III A

I do not dispute the fact that H. B. 2 caused the closure of some clinics. Indeed, it seems clear that H. B. 2 was intended to force unsafe facilities to shut down. The law was one of many enacted by States in the wake of the Kermit Gosnell scandal, in which a physician who ran an abortion clinic in Philadelphia was convicted for the first-degree murder of three infants who were born alive and for the manslaughter of a patient. Gosnell had not been actively supervised by state or local authorities or by his peers, and the Philadelphia grand jury that investigated the case recommended that the Commonwealth adopt a law requiring abortion clinics to comply with the same regulations as ASCs. If Pennsylvania had had such a requirement in force, the Gosnell facility may have been shut down before his crimes. And if there were any similarly unsafe facilities in Texas, H. B. 2 was clearly intended to put them out of business.

IV

Even if the Court were right to hold that res judicata does not bar this suit and that H. B. 2 imposes an undue burden on abortion access—it is, in fact, wrong on both counts—it is still wrong to conclude that the admitting privileges and surgical center provisions must be enjoined in their entirety. H. B. 2 has an extraordinarily broad severability clause that must be considered before enjoining any portion or application of the law. Both challenged provisions should survive in substantial part if the Court faithfully applies that clause. Regrettably, it enjoins both in full, heedless of the (controlling) intent of the state legislature. Cf. *Leavitt* v. *Jane L.*, 518 U. S. 137, 139 (1996) (*per curiam*) ("Severability is of course a matter of state law").

V

When we decide cases on particularly controversial issues, we should take special care to apply settled procedural rules in a neutral manner. The Court has not done that here.

I therefore respectfully dissent.

As the following case explains, post-*Whole Woman's Health,* Louisiana passed laws that were very similar to those ruled unconstitutional in Texas. The district court ruled that the laws were unconstitutional. The Fifth Circuit, however, upheld them. Why were such similar laws as the Texas and Louisiana laws heard in cases by the Supreme Court? Are you surprised by the results in these cases? Are you surprised that Chief Justice Roberts joined the majority in *June Medical*? How do you think the next abortion case at the Court will be argued, given that Justice Ruth Bader Ginsburg has been replaced by Justice Amy Coney Barrett?

June Medical Services, L.L.C. v. Russo

Supreme Court of the United States, 2020.
591 U.S. ___, 140 S.Ct. 2103.

■ BREYER, J., announced the judgment of the Court and delivered an opinion, in which GINSBURG, SOTOMAYOR, and KAGAN, JJ., joined. ROBERTS, C. J., filed an opinion concurring in the judgment. THOMAS, J., filed a dissenting opinion. ALITO, J., filed a dissenting opinion, in which GORSUCH, J., joined, in which THOMAS, J., joined except as to Parts III-C and IV-F, and in which KAVANAUGH, J., joined as to Parts I, II, and III. GORSUCH, J., and KAVANAUGH, J., filed dissenting opinions.

■ JUSTICE BREYER.

In this case, we consider the constitutionality of a Louisiana statute, Act 620, that is almost word-for-word identical to Texas' admitting-privileges law. We have examined the extensive record carefully and conclude that it supports the District Court's findings of fact. Those findings mirror those made in *Whole Woman's Health* in every relevant respect and require the same result. We consequently hold that the Louisiana statute is unconstitutional.

* * *

Taken together, we think that these findings and the evidence that underlies them are sufficient to support the District Court's conclusion that Act 620 would place substantial obstacles in the path of women seeking an abortion in Louisiana.

V

Benefits

We turn finally to the law's asserted benefits. The District Court found that there was " 'no significant health-related problem that the new law helped to cure.' " 250 F. Supp. 3d, at 86 (quoting *Whole Woman's*

Health, 579 U.S., at ___ (slip op., at 22)). It found that the admitting-privileges requirement "[d]oes [n]ot [p]rotect [w]omen's [h]ealth," provides "no significant health benefits," and makes no improvement to women's health "compared to prior law." 250 F. Supp. 3d, at 86 (boldface deleted). Our examination of the record convinces us that these findings are not "clearly erroneous."

VI

Conclusion

We conclude, in light of the record, that the District Court's significant factual findings—both as to burdens and as to benefits—have ample evidentiary support. None is "clearly erroneous." Given the facts found, we must also uphold the District Court's related factual and legal determinations. These include its determination that Louisiana's law poses a "substantial obstacle" to women seeking an abortion; its determination that the law offers no significant health-related benefits; and its determination that the law consequently imposes an "undue burden" on a woman's constitutional right to choose to have an abortion. We also agree with its ultimate legal conclusion that, in light of these findings and our precedents, Act 620 violates the Constitution.

VII

As a postscript, we explain why we have found unconvincing several further arguments that the State has made. First, the State suggests that the record supports the Court of Appeals' conclusion that Act 620 poses no substantial obstacle to the abortion decision. See Brief for Respondent 73, 80. This argument misconceives the question before us. "The question we must answer" is "not whether the [Fifth] Circuit's interpretation of the facts was clearly erroneous, but whether the *District Court's* finding[s were] clearly erroneous." *Anderson*, 470 U.S., at 577 (emphasis added). As we have explained, we think the District Court's factual findings here are plausible in light of the record as a whole. Nothing in the State's briefing furnishes a basis to disturb that conclusion.

Second, the State says that the record does not show that Act 620 will burden *every* woman in Louisiana who seeks an abortion. Brief for Respondent 69–70 (citing *United States* v. *Salerno*, 481 U.S. 739, 745 (1987)). True, but beside the point. As we stated in *Casey*, a State's abortion-related law is unconstitutional on its face if "it will operate as a substantial obstacle to a woman's choice to undergo an abortion" in "a large fraction of the cases in which [it] is relevant." 505 U.S., at 895 (majority opinion). In *Whole Woman's Health*, we reaffirmed that standard. We made clear that the phrase refers to a large fraction of "those women for whom the provision is an actual rather than an irrelevant restriction." 579 U.S., at ___ (slip op., at 39) (quoting *Casey*, 505 U.S., at 895; brackets omitted). That standard, not an "every woman" standard, is the standard that must govern in this case.

Third, the State argues that Act 620 would not make it "nearly impossible" for a woman to obtain an abortion. Brief for Respondent 71–72. But, again, the words "nearly impossible" do not describe the legal standard that governs here. Since *Casey*, we have repeatedly reiterated that the plaintiff's burden in a challenge to an abortion regulation is to show that the regulation's "purpose or effect" is to "plac[e] a substantial obstacle in the path of a woman seeking an abortion of a nonviable fetus." 505 U.S., at 877 (plurality opinion); see *Whole Woman's Health*, 579 U.S., at ___ (slip op., at 8); *Gonzales*, 550 U.S., at 156; *Stenberg*, 530 U.S., at 921; *Mazurek*, 520 U. S., at 971.

Finally, the State makes several arguments about the standard of review that it would have us apply in cases where a regulation is found *not* to impose a substantial obstacle to a woman's choice. Brief for Respondent 60–66. That, however, is not this case. The record here establishes that Act 620's admitting-privileges requirement places a substantial obstacle in the path of a large fraction of those women seeking an abortion for whom it is a relevant restriction.

* * *

This case is similar to, nearly identical with, *Whole Woman's Health*. And the law must consequently reach a similar conclusion. Act 620 is unconstitutional. The Court of Appeals' judgment is erroneous. It is *Reversed*.

■ CHIEF JUSTICE ROBERTS, concurring in the judgment.

I joined the dissent in *Whole Woman's Health* and continue to believe that the case was wrongly decided. The question today however is not whether *Whole Woman's Health* was right or wrong, but whether to adhere to it in deciding the present case. See *Moore* v. *Texas*, 586 U.S. ___, ___ (2019) (ROBERTS, C. J., concurring) (slip op., at 1).

Today's case is a challenge from several abortion clinics and providers to a Louisiana law nearly identical to the Texas law struck down four years ago in *Whole Woman's Health*. Just like the Texas law, the Louisiana law requires physicians performing abortions to have "active admitting privileges at a hospital . . . located not further than thirty miles from the location at which the abortion is performed." La. Rev. Stat. Ann. § 40:1061.10(A)(2)(a) (West Cum. Supp. 2020). Following a six-day bench trial, the District Court found that Louisiana's law would "result in a drastic reduction in the number and geographic distribution of abortion providers." *June Medical Services LLC* v. *Kliebert*, 250 F. Supp. 3d 27, 87 (MD La. 2017). The law would reduce the number of clinics from three to "one, or at most two," and the number of physicians providing abortions from five to "one, or at most two," and "therefore cripple women's ability to have an abortion in Louisiana." *Id.*, at 87–88.

The legal doctrine of *stare decisis* requires us, absent special circumstances, to treat like cases alike. The Louisiana law imposes a burden on access to abortion just as severe as that imposed by the Texas

law, for the same reasons. Therefore Louisiana's law cannot stand under our precedents.

II A

After faithfully reciting this [Casey] standard, the Court in *Whole Woman's Health* added the following observation: "The rule announced in *Casey* . . . requires that courts consider the burdens a law imposes on abortion access together with the benefits those laws confer." 579 U.S., at ___–___ (slip op., at 19–20). The plurality repeats today that the undue burden standard requires courts "to weigh the law's asserted benefits against the burdens it imposes on abortion access." *Ante,* at 2 (internal quotation marks omitted).

Read in isolation from *Casey*, such an inquiry could invite a grand "balancing test in which unweighted factors mysteriously are weighed." *Marrs* v. *Motorola, Inc.*, 577 F. 3d 783, 788 (CA7 2009). Under such tests, "equality of treatment is . . . impossible to achieve; predictability is destroyed; judicial arbitrariness is facilitated; judicial courage is impaired." Scalia, The Rule of Law as a Law of Rules, 56 U. Chi. L. Rev. 1175, 1182 (1989).

In this context, courts applying a balancing test would be asked in essence to weigh the State's interests in "protecting the potentiality of human life" and the health of the woman, on the one hand, against the woman's liberty interest in defining her "own concept of existence, of meaning, of the universe, and of the mystery of human life" on the other. *Casey*, 505 U. S., at 851 (opinion of the Court); *id.,* at 871 (plurality opinion) (internal quotation marks omitted). There is no plausible sense in which anyone, let alone this Court, could objectively assign weight to such imponderable values and no meaningful way to compare them if there were. Attempting to do so would be like "judging whether a particular line is longer than a particular rock is heavy," *Bendix Autolite Corp.* v. *Midwesco Enterprises, Inc.*, 486 U.S. 888, 897 (1988) (Scalia, J., concurring in judgment). Pretending that we could pull that off would require us to act as legislators, not judges, and would result in nothing other than an "unanalyzed exercise of judicial will" in the guise of a "neutral utilitarian calculus." *New Jersey* v. *T.L.O.*, 469 U.S. 325, 369 (1985) (Brennan, J., concurring in part and dissenting in part).

Nothing about *Casey* suggested that a weighing of costs and benefits of an abortion regulation was a job for the courts. On the contrary, we have explained that the "traditional rule" that "state and federal legislatures [have] wide discretion to pass legislation in areas where there is medical and scientific uncertainty" is "consistent with *Casey*." *Gonzales* v. *Carhart*, 550 U.S. 124, 163 (2007). *Casey* instead focuses on the existence of a substantial obstacle, the sort of inquiry familiar to judges across a variety of contexts.

The upshot of *Casey* is clear: The several restrictions that did not impose a substantial obstacle were constitutional, while the restriction that did impose a substantial obstacle was unconstitutional.

We accordingly will not disturb the factual conclusions of the trial court unless we are "left with the definite and firm conviction that a mistake has been committed." *United States* v. *United States Gypsum Co.*, 333 U.S. 364, 395 (1948). In my view, the District Court's work reveals no such clear error, for the reasons the plurality explains. *Ante*, at 19–35. The District Court findings therefore bind us in this case.

* * *

Stare decisis instructs us to treat like cases alike. The result in this case is controlled by our decision four years ago invalidating a nearly identical Texas law. The Louisiana law burdens women seeking previability abortions to the same extent as the Texas law, according to factual findings that are not clearly erroneous. For that reason, I concur in the judgment of the Court that the Louisiana law is unconstitutional.

■ JUSTICE THOMAS, dissenting.

Under a proper understanding of Article III, these plaintiffs lack standing to invoke our jurisdiction.

Despite the fact that we granted Louisiana's petition specifically to address whether "abortion providers [can] be presumed to have third-party standing to challenge health and safety regulations on behalf of their patients," Conditional Cross-Pet. in No. 18–1460, p. i, a majority of the Court all but ignores the question. The plurality and THE CHIEF JUSTICE ultimately cast aside this jurisdictional barrier to conclude that Louisiana's law is unconstitutional under our precedents. But those decisions created the right to abortion out of whole cloth, without a shred of support from the Constitution's text. Our abortion precedents are grievously wrong and should be overruled. Because we have neither jurisdiction nor constitutional authority to declare Louisiana's duly enacted law unconstitutional, I respectfully dissent.

■ JUSTICE ALITO, with whom JUSTICE GORSUCH joins, with whom JUSTICE THOMAS joins except as to Parts III-C and IV-F, and with whom JUSTICE KAVANAUGH joins as to Parts I, II, and III, dissenting.

The majority bills today's decision as a facsimile of *Whole Woman's Health* v. *Hellerstedt*, 579 U. S. ___, ___ (2016), and it's true they have something in common. In both, the abortion right recognized in this Court's decisions is used like a bulldozer to flatten legal rules that stand in the way.

In *Whole Woman's Health*, res judicata and our standard approach to severability were laid low. Even *Planned Parenthood of Southeastern Pa.* v. *Casey*, 505 U.S. 833 (1992), was altered.

Today's decision claims new victims. The divided majority cannot agree on what the abortion right requires, but it nevertheless strikes

down a Louisiana law, Act 620, that the legislature enacted for the asserted purpose of protecting women's health. To achieve this end, the majority misuses the doctrine of *stare decisis*, invokes an inapplicable standard of appellate review, and distorts the record.

The plurality eschews the constitutional test set out in *Casey* and instead employs the balancing test adopted in *Whole Woman's Health*. The plurality concludes that the Louisiana law does nothing to protect the health of women, but that is disproved by substantial evidence in the record. And the plurality upholds the District Court's finding that the Louisiana law would cause a drastic reduction in the number of abortion providers in the State even though this finding was based on an erroneous legal standard and a thoroughly inadequate factual inquiry.

THE CHIEF JUSTICE stresses the importance of *stare decisis* and thinks that precedent, namely *Whole Woman's Health,* dooms the Louisiana law. But at the same time, he votes to overrule *Whole Woman*'s *Health* insofar as it changed the *Casey* test.

Both the plurality and THE CHIEF JUSTICE hold that abortion providers can invoke a woman's abortion right when they attack state laws that are enacted to protect a woman's health. Neither waiver nor *stare decisis* can justify this holding, which clashes with our general rule on third-party standing. And the idea that a regulated party can invoke the right of a third party for the purpose of attacking legislation enacted to protect the third party is stunning. Given the apparent conflict of interest, that concept would be rejected out of hand in a case not involving abortion.

For these reasons, I cannot join the decision of the Court. I would remand the case to the District Court and instruct that court, before proceeding any further, to require the joinder of a plaintiff with standing. If a proper plaintiff is added, the District Court should conduct a new trial and determine, based on proper evidence, whether enforcement of Act 620 would diminish the number of abortion providers in the State to such a degree that women's access to abortions would be substantially impaired. In making that determination, the court should jettison the nebulous "good faith" test that it used in judging whether the physicians who currently lack admitting privileges would be able to obtain privileges and thus continue to perform abortions if Act 620 were permitted to take effect. Because the doctors in question (many of whom are or were plaintiffs in this case) stand to lose, not gain, by obtaining privileges, the court should require the plaintiffs to show that these doctors sought admitting privileges with the degree of effort that they would expend if their personal interests were at stake.

* * *

The decision in this case, like that in *Whole Woman's Health*, twists the law, and I therefore respectfully dissent.

■ JUSTICE GORSUCH, dissenting.

To arrive at today's result, rules must be brushed aside and shortcuts taken. While the concurrence parts ways with the plurality at the last turn, the road both travel leads us to a strangely open space, unconstrained by many of the neutral principles that normally govern the judicial process. The temptation to proceed this direction, closer with each step toward an unobstructed exercise of will, may be always with us, a danger inherent in judicial review. But it is an impulse this Court normally strives mightily to resist. Today, in a highly politicized and contentious arena, we prove unwilling, or perhaps unable, to resist that temptation. Either way, respectfully, it is a sign we have lost our way.

■ JUSTICE KAVANAUGH, dissenting.

Today, five Members of the Court reject the *Whole Woman's Health* cost-benefit standard. *Ante*, at 4–11 (ROBERTS, C.J., concurring in judgment); *ante*, at 14–20 (THOMAS, J., dissenting); *ante*, at 4 (ALITO, J., joined by THOMAS, GORSUCH, and KAVANAUGH, JJ., dissenting); *ante*, at 15–18 (GORSUCH, J., dissenting). A different five Members of the Court conclude that Louisiana's admitting-privileges law is unconstitutional because it "would restrict women's access to abortion to the same degree as" the Texas law in *Whole Woman's Health*. *Ante*, at 12 (opinion of ROBERTS, C.J.); see also *ante*, at 16–40 (opinion of BREYER, J., joined by GINSBURG, SOTOMAYOR, and KAGAN, JJ.).

I agree with the first of those two conclusions. But I respectfully dissent from the second because, in my view, additional factfinding is necessary to properly evaluate Louisiana's law. As JUSTICE ALITO thoroughly and carefully explains, the factual record at this stage of plaintiffs' facial, pre-enforcement challenge does not adequately demonstrate that the three relevant doctors (Does 2, 5, and 6) cannot obtain admitting privileges or, therefore, that any of the three Louisiana abortion clinics would close as a result of the admitting-privileges law. I expressed the same concern about the incomplete factual record more than a year ago during the stay proceedings, and the factual record has not changed since then. See *June Medical Services, L.L.C.* v. *Gee*, 586 U.S. ___ (2019) (opinion dissenting from grant of application for stay). In short, I agree with JUSTICE ALITO that the Court should remand the case for a new trial and additional factfinding under the appropriate legal standards.

NOTES AND QUESTIONS

1. In *Whole Woman's Health*, what test does Justice Breyer employ to decide if the regulations are constitutional? Does he employ the same test in *June Medical*? What test does Chief Justice Roberts recommend in *June*? What does he say about Breyer's test? Are they both following *Casey*?

2. Why is standing so important to this case? What is third party standing? Why is it so difficult for individual pregnant women to challenge the restrictions during their (nine-month) pregnancies? What are the different Justices saying about standing? Do women who want to have an

abortion have standing to bring a lawsuit about abortion regulations? Do you think doctors should have standing, or that they do not have standing because they are not having an abortion?

3. Why are the Justices arguing about the facts of the case?

4. What do you think the Texas and Louisiana abortion laws say about women's health? About bioethics? What is the best way for women's health and bioethics to be protected in abortion law?

Practice Exercise: Imagine that you represent one of the parties in a new abortion case. Pick a side and list the main reasons why the Supreme Court should grant certiorari (e.g., important constitutional question, circuit split, etc.). Draft the petition for certiorari.

5. *Medication Abortions.* In an effort to avoid surgical abortions, other abortion advocates are turning to the concept of medication abortions. As early as the year 2000, the United States Food and Drug Administration ("FDA") approved the use of a drug called mifepristone for early nonsurgical abortions. See Guttmacher Institute, Medication Abortions, Jan. 1, 2021, available at https://www.guttmacher.org/state-policy/explore/medication-abortion. However, some states have enacted legislation that limits the availability of medication abortions. For example, instead of allowing physician assistants and advanced practice nurses to prescribe mifepristone, thirty-two states "require clinicians who administer medication abortion to be a physician." Id. Also, in nineteen states, the clinician must be physically present when the medication is administered. Id.

Go to the website to learn more about Medication Abortions.

As we learned in Chapter 2, "[d]rugs approved by the FDA are approved only for specific uses based on extensive test data." 3 Attorneys Medical Deskbook 4th § 38:17. The FDA approved the use of mifepristone. See ACLU, Mifepristone (RU-486): Myths and Facts, available at https://www.aclu.org/other/mifepristone-ru-486-myths-and-facts.

Physicians regularly recommend "off-label" uses of FDA-approved drugs. The physicians have the authority to do so under 21 U.S.C. § 396, which states "[n]othing in this chapter shall be construed to limit or interfere with the authority of a health care practitioner to prescribe or administer any legally marketed device to a patient for any condition or disease within a legitimate health care practitioner-patient relationship." Therefore, physicians may give drugs to children or pregnant women, for example, even when the FDA has not approved that specific use. Id. Methotrexate, a drug approved for cancer and rheumatoid arthritis treatment, was used by physicians to treat psoriasis and later approved by the FDA for that purpose. Off-label use of drugs is especially common in cancer treatment. See American Cancer Society, Off-label Drug Use, at http://www.cancer.org/

treatment/treatmentsandsideeffects/treatmenttypes/chemotherapy/off-label-drug-use.

It is important to note that off-label marketing and promotion by drug manufacturers are different from off-label prescriptions because the off-label promotion means the drug may be "misbranded" by being introduced into interstate commerce for an unapproved use. See 21 U.S.C. § 352 (states what makes a drug or device misbranded). Therefore, manufacturers can't *promote* the drug for an off-label use, but a doctor is free to *prescribe* the drug for such a use. Given that physicians regularly prescribe off-label drugs, what do you think of state efforts to tightly restrict mifepristone to the current FDA protocol? What about requirements for in-person administration, which prevent providers from using telemedicine for medication abortion? Or efforts to require providers to share with patients the medically unsupported claim that medication abortion can be reversed? Is there any reason to apply ASC and admitting privileges requirements to medication abortions? Are these valid health regulations or an attempt to restrict abortion? See, e.g., Guttmacher Institute, Medication Abortion, (Feb. 2021), https://www.guttmacher.org/evidence-you-can-use/medication-abortion.

At the beginning of the COVID-19 pandemic many hospitals—some by order of state government, some on their own—stopped performing elective surgeries. Several states took the opportunity to designate abortions as elective procedures, thereby prohibiting the procedure except in extreme circumstances involving a serious threat to the mother's life or health. These decisions sparked outrage, especially on behalf of women whose pregnancies would have progressed too far to obtain an abortion once elective procedures were allowed to resume. While the claimed goal of the restrictions was to preserve hospital beds for a surge of potential COVID patients, critics argued that the clear ulterior motive was to reduce the number of abortions (if not to ban the procedure entirely). Several bans were challenged, leading to initial district court decisions overturning the state decisions—only for federal appeals courts to quickly overrule them. Jessica Glenza, States Use Coronavirus to Ban Abortions, Leaving Women Desperate: "You Can't Pause a Pregnancy," The Guardian, Apr. 20, 2020, https://www.theguardian.com/world/2020/apr/30/us-states-ban-abortions-coronavirus-leave-women-desperate.

The confusion and changing rules also led to an increase in the number of women seeking the prescription of abortion pills online; however, many states do not permit telehealth for this type of care, creating yet another obstacle to abortion access. Sarah McCammon, More Patients Seek Abortion Pills Online during Pandemic, But Face Restrictions, NPR, May 28, 2020, https://www.npr.org/2020/05/28/863512837/more-patients-seek-abortion-pills-online-during-pandemic-but-face-restrictions. At the federal level, the American College of Obstetricians and Gynecologists (ACOG) went to court, arguing that a requirement for patients to visit their doctors in order to get access to the drug during a pandemic placed a substantial obstacle in their path of a woman seeking an abortion. A district court judge agreed, and ordered the FDA not to enforce the in-person requirement until the pandemic was over. The Fourth Circuit affirmed that ruling. After a first challenge to

the Supreme Court, the district court reaffirmed its ruling against the FDA. The FDA then argued to the Supreme Court that the in-person ruling did not place a substantial burden on women because they could still receive a surgical abortion. In contrast, ACOG argued that the pandemic had worsened and that no one had been hurt by not having to pick up the drug in person. Amy Howe, Justices Grant FDA Request to Block Mail Delivery of Abortion Pills, Jan. 12, 2021, at https://www.scotusblog.com/2021/01/justices-grant-fda-request-to-block-mail-delivery-of-abortion-pills/#more-298537.

The Supreme Court granted the FDA's request to overturn the district court's injunction. Justice Breyer would have denied the application. Chief Justice Roberts explained that the legal question was not about the right to abortion, but about the district judge's capacity, as opposed to the FDA's, to make a public health ruling. Justice Sotomayor, joined by Justice Kagan, dissented, arguing that the abortion drugs were treated differently from all the other FDA drugs. In her view, the rule on abortion drugs put a substantial obstacle in the way of a woman's right to an abortion. Food and Drug Administration v. American College of Obstetricians and Gynecologists, 592 U.S. ___, 141 S.Ct. 578 (2021). What do you think of the Justices' arguments? In April 2021, under the Biden administration, the FDA reversed course and allowed patients to receive the pills via telemedicine and through the mail during the pandemic. Alice Miranda Ollstein & Darius Tahir, FDA lifts curbs on dispensing abortion pills during pandemic, Politico, Apr. 12, 2021, https://www.politico.com/news/2021/04/12/abortion-pills-481092.

6. *Still Questioning the Time of Viability.* States continue to pass different regulations banning abortions after a certain number of weeks. Mississippi, for example, the prohibits most abortions after 15 weeks gestational age. In ruling that law unconstitutional, Judge Patrick E. Higginbotham wrote: "This case concerns a Mississippi law that prohibits abortions, with limited exceptions, after 15 weeks' gestational age. The central question before us is whether this law is an unconstitutional ban on pre-viability abortions. In an unbroken line dating to *Roe v. Wade,* the Supreme Court's abortion cases have established (and affirmed, and re-affirmed) a woman's right to choose an abortion before viability. States may *regulate* abortion procedures prior to viability so long as they do not impose an undue burden on the woman's right, but they may not ban abortions. The law at issue is a ban. Thus, we affirm the district court's invalidation of the law, as well as its discovery rulings and its award of permanent injunctive relief." Jackson Women's Health Organization v. Dobbs, 945 F.3d 265, 268–69 (5th Cir. 2019). Do you think the courts should continue or change their reasoning about *Roe* and time of viability?

Professor Ziegler has argued that the debate about abortion has been about more than choice and life. "The abortion struggle offered a window into disagreements about poverty, personal responsibility, welfare reform, maturity, parenthood, marriage, the health care system, and the trustworthiness of the media and the government." Mary Ziegler, Abortion and the Law in America: Roe v. Wade to the Present (2020). How do those

issues affect your perspective on the legality or illegality of abortion? What do you think would happen to national debates about abortion if *Roe* is overturned?

In the next section, we will look at the topics of reproduction and parenthood. Specifically, we address issues such as new reproduction technology, surrogacy, and adoption, where new medical technology completely upended traditional ideas of what it means to be a parent.

B. REPRODUCTION AND PARENTHOOD

In later chapters, we will focus on many uses of reproductive technology and the bioethical questions associated with them. In this section, we focus on the issue of parenting and how changes in technology affect the definition of a parent. As you read the following materials, consider who, in these cases, should qualify as the child's parent. Then ask which parent(s) should have custody of the children.

1. SURROGATE MOTHERHOOD

Many technologies have helped people become parents. For example, men and women suffering from infertility have used artificial insemination ("AI"), where sperm is inserted directly into a woman's fallopian tubes, cervix, or uterus, to enhance the possibilities of conception. AI may help infertile men (who, e.g., have a low sperm count), infertile women (who have endometriosis or problems with their reproductive organs), as well as couples with infertility of no known cause.

Technology changed parenthood significantly after scientists perfected the technology of *in vitro* fertilization ("IVF"). Louise Brown, the first baby conceived through IVF, was born in 1978. Since then, IVF has helped couples conceive more than five million healthy babies. Helen Massy-Beresford, What's Next for the World's 5 Million IVF Babies?, The Observer, Nov. 23, 2014, at http://www.theguardian.com/society/2014/nov/23/whats-next-for-worlds-5-million-ivf-babies.

The IVF process starts when a woman is given hormones for several weeks until eggs or oocytes are produced in her body. Doctors then remove the eggs from her ovaries. Next, the eggs are mixed with sperm in the laboratory. The resulting fertilized eggs go through the first stages of cell division, or meiosis, in the laboratory, until the resulting pre-embryos are transferred into a woman's uterus. Once the pre-embryos are in the woman's uterus, cell division continues and the pregnancy develops until birth.

> **Go to** the website to read the materials and watch the videos describing IVF.

One implication of the IVF process is that it increases the number of persons who have claims to be a child's parent. Possible biological parents

include the sperm donor, the egg donor, and the woman who bears the child. There are also "intended" parent(s) who set the IVF process in motion so that they may have a child. Today, intended parents include not only a prospective father and/or mother, but also two gay fathers or two lesbian mothers. The permutations of possible parenthood have resulted in many of the cases discussed below as the law struggled to catch up with technology.

A woman who bears a child for someone else is usually referred to as a surrogate mother. A traditional surrogate mother is biologically related to the child. A gestational surrogate mother is not biologically related to the child, but instead gestates the child to birth. In the next case, *Baby M.*, the New Jersey Supreme Court addressed the issue whether a surrogacy contract is enforceable. Instead of looking at the surrogacy contract solely in contractual terms, the court addressed issues of parenthood and how pregnancy can create a maternal bond with the baby. Do you agree with the court's decision about who Baby M.'s parents are? *Baby M.* was decided in 1988. Is the court's reasoning now outdated?

In the Matter of Baby M.

Supreme Court of New Jersey, 1988.
537 A.2d 1227, 109 N.J. 396.

■ WILENTZ, C.J., delivered the opinion of the Court.

In this matter the Court is asked to determine the validity of a contract that purports to provide a new way of bringing children into a family. For a fee of $10,000, a woman agrees to be artificially inseminated with the semen of another woman's husband; she is to conceive a child, carry it to term, and after its birth surrender it to the natural father and his wife. The intent of the contract is that the child's natural mother will thereafter be forever separated from her child. The wife is to adopt the child, and she and the natural father are to be regarded as its parents for all purposes. The contract providing for this is called a "surrogacy contract," the natural mother inappropriately called the "surrogate mother."

We invalidate the surrogacy contract because it conflicts with the law and public policy of this State. While we recognize the depth of the yearning of infertile couples to have their own children, we find the payment of money to a "surrogate" mother illegal, perhaps criminal, and potentially degrading to women. Although in this case we grant custody to the natural father, the evidence having clearly proved such custody to be in the best interests of the infant, we void both the termination of the surrogate mother's parental rights and the adoption of the child by the wife/stepparent. We thus restore the "surrogate" as the mother of the child. We remand the issue of the natural mother's visitation rights to the trial court, since that issue was not reached below and the record before us is not sufficient to permit us to decide it *de novo*.

We find no offense to our present laws where a woman voluntarily and without payment agrees to act as a "surrogate" mother, provided that she is not subject to a binding agreement to surrender her child. Moreover, our holding today does not preclude the Legislature from altering the current statutory scheme, within constitutional limits, so as to permit surrogacy contracts. Under current law, however, the surrogacy agreement before us is illegal and invalid.

I.

FACTS

In February 1985, William Stern and Mary Beth Whitehead entered into a surrogacy contract. It recited that Stern's wife, Elizabeth, was infertile, that they wanted a child, and that Mrs. Whitehead was willing to provide that child as the mother with Mr. Stern as the father.

The contract provided that through artificial insemination using Mr. Stern's sperm, Mrs. Whitehead would become pregnant, carry the child to term, bear it, deliver it to the Sterns, and thereafter do whatever was necessary to terminate her maternal rights so that Mrs. Stern could thereafter adopt the child. Mrs. Whitehead's husband, Richard, was also a party to the contract; Mrs. Stern was not. Mr. Whitehead promised to do all acts necessary to rebut the presumption of paternity under the Parentage Act. Although Mrs. Stern was not a party to the surrogacy agreement, the contract gave her sole custody of the child in the event of Mr. Stern's death. Mrs. Stern's status as a nonparty to the surrogate parenting agreement presumably was to avoid the application of the baby-selling statute to this arrangement.

Mr. Stern, on his part, agreed to attempt the artificial insemination and to pay Mrs. Whitehead $10,000 after the child's birth, on its delivery to him. In a separate contract, Mr. Stern agreed to pay $7,500 to the Infertility Center of New York ("ICNY"). The Center's advertising campaigns solicit surrogate mothers and encourage infertile couples to consider surrogacy. ICNY arranged for the surrogacy contract by bringing the parties together, explaining the process to them, furnishing the contractual form, and providing legal counsel.

The history of the parties' involvement in this arrangement suggests their good faith. William and Elizabeth Stern were married in July 1974, having met at the University of Michigan, where both were Ph.D. candidates. Due to financial considerations and Mrs. Stern's pursuit of a medical degree and residency, they decided to defer starting a family until 1981. Before then, however, Mrs. Stern learned that she might have multiple sclerosis and that the disease in some cases renders pregnancy a serious health risk. Her anxiety appears to have exceeded the actual risk, which current medical authorities assess as minimal. Nonetheless that anxiety was evidently quite real, Mrs. Stern fearing that pregnancy might precipitate blindness, paraplegia, or other forms of debilitation. Based on the perceived risk, the Sterns decided to forego having their

own children. The decision had special significance for Mr. Stern. Most of his family had been destroyed in the Holocaust. As the family's only survivor, he very much wanted to continue his bloodline.

Initially the Sterns considered adoption, but were discouraged by the substantial delay apparently involved and by the potential problem they saw arising from their age and their differing religious backgrounds. They were most eager for some other means to start a family.

The paths of Mrs. Whitehead and the Sterns to surrogacy were similar. Both responded to advertising by ICNY. The Sterns' response, following their inquiries into adoption, was the result of their long-standing decision to have a child. Mrs. Whitehead's response apparently resulted from her sympathy with family members and others who could have no children (she stated that she wanted to give another couple the "gift of life"); she also wanted the $10,000 to help her family.

Both parties, undoubtedly because of their own self-interest, were less sensitive to the implications of the transaction than they might otherwise have been. Mrs. Whitehead, for instance, appears not to have been concerned about whether the Sterns would make good parents for her child; the Sterns, on their part, while conscious of the obvious possibility that surrendering the child might cause grief to Mrs. Whitehead, overcame their qualms because of their desire for a child. At any rate, both the Sterns and Mrs. Whitehead were committed to the arrangement; both thought it right and constructive.

Mrs. Whitehead had reached her decision concerning surrogacy before the Sterns, and had actually been involved as a potential surrogate mother with another couple. After numerous unsuccessful artificial inseminations, that effort was abandoned. Thereafter, the Sterns learned of the Infertility Center, the possibilities of surrogacy, and of Mary Beth Whitehead. The two couples met to discuss the surrogacy arrangement and decided to go forward. On February 6, 1985, Mr. Stern and Mr. and Mrs. Whitehead executed the surrogate parenting agreement. After several artificial inseminations over a period of months, Mrs. Whitehead became pregnant. The pregnancy was uneventful and on March 27, 1986, Baby M was born.

Not wishing anyone at the hospital to be aware of the surrogacy arrangement, Mr. and Mrs. Whitehead appeared to all as the proud parents of a healthy female child. Her birth certificate indicated her name to be Sara Elizabeth Whitehead and her father to be Richard Whitehead. In accordance with Mrs. Whitehead's request, the Sterns visited the hospital unobtrusively to see the newborn child.

Mrs. Whitehead realized, almost from the moment of birth, that she could not part with this child. She had felt a bond with it even during pregnancy. Some indication of the attachment was conveyed to the Sterns at the hospital when they told Mrs. Whitehead what they were going to name the baby. She apparently broke into tears and indicated

that she did not know if she could give up the child. She talked about how the baby looked like her other daughter, and made it clear that she was experiencing great difficulty with the decision.

Nonetheless, Mrs. Whitehead was, for the moment, true to her word. Despite powerful inclinations to the contrary, she turned her child over to the Sterns on March 30 at the Whiteheads' home.

The Sterns were thrilled with their new child. They had planned extensively for its arrival, far beyond the practical furnishing of a room for her. It was a time of joyful celebration—not just for them but for their friends as well. The Sterns looked forward to raising their daughter, whom they named Melissa. While aware by then that Mrs. Whitehead was undergoing an emotional crisis, they were as yet not cognizant of the depth of that crisis and its implications for their newly-enlarged family.

[After Mrs. Whitehead expressed her anxiety and depression to the Sterns, they agreed to her suggestion that the baby live with her for a week. When Mr. Stern took measures to get Melissa back, Whitehead fled to Florida with the baby.]

The Whiteheads immediately fled to Florida with Baby M. They stayed initially with Mrs. Whitehead's parents, where one of Mrs. Whitehead's children had been living. For the next three months, the Whiteheads and Melissa lived at roughly twenty different hotels, motels, and homes in order to avoid apprehension. From time to time Mrs. Whitehead would call Mr. Stern to discuss the matter; the conversations, recorded by Mr. Stern on advice of counsel, show an escalating dispute about rights, morality, and power, accompanied by threats of Mrs. Whitehead to kill herself, to kill the child, and falsely to accuse Mr. Stern of sexually molesting Mrs. Whitehead's other daughter.

Eventually the Sterns discovered where the Whiteheads were staying, commenced supplementary proceedings in Florida, and obtained an order requiring the Whiteheads to turn over the child. Police in Florida enforced the order, forcibly removing the child from her grandparents' home. She was soon thereafter brought to New Jersey and turned over to the Sterns. The prior order of the court, issued *ex parte,* awarding custody of the child to the Sterns *pendente lite,* was reaffirmed by the trial court after consideration of the certified representations of the parties (both represented by counsel) concerning the unusual sequence of events that had unfolded. Pending final judgment, Mrs. Whitehead was awarded limited visitation with Baby M.

The Sterns' complaint, in addition to seeking possession and ultimately custody of the child, sought enforcement of the surrogacy contract. Pursuant to the contract, it asked that the child be permanently placed in their custody, that Mrs. Whitehead's parental rights be terminated, and that Mrs. Stern be allowed to adopt the child, *i.e.,* that, for all purposes, Melissa become the Sterns' child.

The trial [court] . . . held that the surrogacy contract was valid; ordered that Mrs. Whitehead's parental rights be terminated and that sole custody of the child be granted to Mr. Stern; and, after hearing brief testimony from Mrs. Stern, immediately entered an order allowing the adoption of Melissa by Mrs. Stern, all in accordance with the surrogacy contract. . . . Although clearly expressing its view that the surrogacy contract was valid, the trial court devoted the major portion of its opinion to the question of the baby's best interests. The inconsistency is apparent. The surrogacy contract calls for the surrender of the child to the Sterns, permanent and sole custody in the Sterns, and termination of Mrs. Whitehead's parental rights, all without qualification, all regardless of any evaluation of the best interests of the child. As a matter of fact the contract recites (even before the child was conceived) that it is in the best interests of the child to be placed with Mr. Stern. In effect, the trial court awarded custody to Mr. Stern, the natural father, based on the same kind of evidence and analysis as might be expected had no surrogacy contract existed. Its rationalization, however, was that while the surrogacy contract was valid, specific performance would not be granted unless that remedy was in the best interests of the child. . . .

On the question of best interests—and we agree, but for different reasons, that custody was the critical issue—the court's analysis of the testimony was perceptive, demonstrating both its understanding of the case and its considerable experience in these matters. We agree substantially with both its analysis and conclusions on the matter of custody.

The court's review and analysis of the surrogacy contract, however, is not at all in accord with ours. . . .

II.

INVALIDITY AND UNENFORCEABILITY OF SURROGACY CONTRACT

We have concluded that this surrogacy contract is invalid. Our conclusion has two bases: direct conflict with existing statutes and conflict with the public policies of this State, as expressed in its statutory and decisional law. . . .

A. Conflict with Statutory Provisions

The surrogacy contract conflicts with: (1) laws prohibiting the use of money in connection with adoptions; (2) laws requiring proof of parental unfitness or abandonment before termination of parental rights is ordered or an adoption is granted; and (3) laws that make surrender of custody and consent to adoption revocable in private placement adoptions.

Considerable care was taken in this case to structure the surrogacy arrangement so as not to violate this prohibition. The arrangement was structured as follows: the adopting parent, Mrs. Stern, was not a party to the surrogacy contract; the money paid to Mrs. Whitehead was stated

to be for her services—not for the adoption; the sole purpose of the contract was stated as being that "of giving a child to William Stern, its natural and biological father"; the money was purported to be "compensation for services and expenses and in no way . . . a fee for termination of parental rights or a payment in exchange for consent to surrender a child for adoption"; the fee to the Infertility Center ($7,500) was stated to be for legal representation, advice, administrative work, and other "services." Nevertheless, it seems clear that the money was paid and accepted in connection with an adoption.

. . . The evils inherent in baby-bartering are loathsome for a myriad of reasons. The child is sold without regard for whether the purchasers will be suitable parents. The natural mother does not receive the benefit of counseling and guidance to assist her in making a decision that may affect her for a lifetime. In fact, the monetary incentive to sell her child may, depending on her financial circumstances, make her decision less voluntary. Furthermore, the adoptive parents may not be fully informed of the natural parents' medical history.

. . . Baby-selling potentially results in the exploitation of all parties involved. Conversely, adoption statutes seek to further humanitarian goals, foremost among them the best interests of the child. The negative consequences of baby-buying are potentially present in the surrogacy context, especially the potential for placing and adopting a child without regard to the interest of the child or the natural mother.

B. Public Policy Considerations

The surrogacy contract's invalidity, resulting from its direct conflict with the above statutory provisions, is further underlined when its goals and means are measured against New Jersey's public policy. The contract's basic premise, that the natural parents can decide in advance of birth which one is to have custody of the child, bears no relationship to the settled law that the child's best interests shall determine custody.

The surrogacy contract guarantees permanent separation of the child from one of its natural parents. Our policy, however, has long been that to the extent possible, children should remain with and be brought up by both of their natural parents. . . . This is not simply some theoretical ideal that in practice has no meaning. The impact of failure to follow that policy is nowhere better shown than in the results of this surrogacy contract. A child, instead of starting off its life with as much peace and security as possible, finds itself immediately in a tug-of-war between contending mother and father.

The surrogacy contract violates the policy of this State that the rights of natural parents are equal concerning their child, the father's right no greater than the mother's. "The parent and child relationship extends equally to every child and to every parent, regardless of the marital status of the parents." . . . The whole purpose and effect of the

surrogacy contract was to give the father the exclusive right to the child by destroying the rights of the mother.

The policies expressed in our comprehensive laws governing consent to the surrender of a child, stand in stark contrast to the surrogacy contract and what it implies. Here there is no counseling, independent or otherwise, of the natural mother, no evaluation, no warning.

The only legal advice Mary Beth Whitehead received regarding the surrogacy contract was provided in connection with the contract that she previously entered into with another couple. Mrs. Whitehead's lawyer was referred to her by the Infertility Center, with which he had an agreement to act as counsel for surrogate candidates. His services consisted of spending one hour going through the contract with the Whiteheads, section by section, and answering their questions. Mrs. Whitehead received no further legal advice prior to signing the contract with the Sterns. . . .

Under the contract, the natural mother is irrevocably committed before she knows the strength of her bond with her child. She never makes a totally voluntary, informed decision, for quite clearly any decision prior to the baby's birth is, in the most important sense, uninformed, and any decision after that, compelled by a pre-existing contractual commitment, the threat of a lawsuit, and the inducement of a $10,000 payment, is less than totally voluntary. Her interests are of little concern to those who controlled this transaction . . .

Worst of all, however, is the contract's total disregard of the best interests of the child. There is not the slightest suggestion that any inquiry will be made at any time to determine the fitness of the Sterns as custodial parents, of Mrs. Stern as an adoptive parent, their superiority to Mrs. Whitehead, or the effect on the child of not living with her natural mother.

This is the sale of a child, or, at the very least, the sale of a mother's right to her child, the only mitigating factor being that one of the purchasers is the father. Almost every evil that prompted the prohibition on the payment of money in connection with adoptions exists here.

The differences between an adoption and a surrogacy contract should be noted, since it is asserted that the use of money in connection with surrogacy does not pose the risks found where money buys an adoption.

First, and perhaps most important, all parties concede that it is unlikely that surrogacy will survive without money. Despite the alleged selfless motivation of surrogate mothers, if there is no payment, there will be no surrogates, or very few. That conclusion contrasts with adoption; for obvious reasons, there remains a steady supply, albeit insufficient, despite the prohibitions against payment. The adoption itself, relieving the natural mother of the financial burden of supporting an infant, is in some sense the equivalent of payment.

Second, the use of money in adoptions does not *produce* the problem—conception occurs, and usually the birth itself, before illicit funds are offered. With surrogacy, the "problem," if one views it as such, consisting of the purchase of a woman's procreative capacity, at the risk of her life, is caused by and originates with the offer of money.

Third, with the law prohibiting the use of money in connection with adoptions, the built-in financial pressure of the unwanted pregnancy and the consequent support obligation do not lead the mother to the highest paying, ill-suited, adoptive parents. She is just as well-off surrendering the child to an approved agency. In surrogacy, the highest bidders will presumably become the adoptive parents regardless of suitability, so long as payment of money is permitted.

Fourth, the mother's consent to surrender her child in adoptions is revocable, even after surrender of the child, unless it be to an approved agency, where by regulation there are protections against an ill-advised surrender. In surrogacy, consent occurs so early that no amount of advice would satisfy the potential mother's need, yet the consent is irrevocable.

The main difference, that the unwanted pregnancy is unintended while the situation of the surrogate mother is voluntary and intended, is really not significant. Initially, it produces stronger reactions of sympathy for the mother whose pregnancy was unwanted than for the surrogate mother, who "went into this with her eyes wide open." On reflection, however, it appears that the essential evil is the same, taking advantage of a woman's circumstances (the unwanted pregnancy or the need for money) in order to take away her child, the difference being one of degree.

In the scheme contemplated by the surrogacy contract in this case, a middle man, propelled by profit, promotes the sale. Whatever idealism may have motivated any of the participants, the profit motive predominates, permeates, and ultimately governs the transaction. The demand for children is great and the supply small. The availability of contraception, abortion, and the greater willingness of single mothers to bring up their children has led to a shortage of babies offered for adoption. The situation is ripe for the entry of the middleman who will bring some equilibrium into the market by increasing the supply through the use of money.

Intimated, but disputed, is the assertion that surrogacy will be used for the benefit of the rich at the expense of the poor. In response it is noted that the Sterns are not rich and the Whiteheads not poor. Nevertheless, it is clear to us that it is unlikely that surrogate mothers will be as proportionately numerous among those women in the top twenty percent income bracket as among those in the bottom twenty percent. Put differently, we doubt that infertile couples in the low-income bracket will find upper income surrogates. . . .

Beyond that is the potential degradation of some women that may result from this arrangement. In many cases, of course, surrogacy may bring satisfaction, not only to the infertile couple, but to the surrogate mother herself. The fact, however, that many women may not perceive surrogacy negatively but rather see it as an opportunity does not diminish its potential for devastation to other women.

In sum, the harmful consequences of this surrogacy arrangement appear to us all too palpable. In New Jersey the surrogate mother's agreement to sell her child is void. Its irrevocability infects the entire contract, as does the money that purports to buy it.

III.

TERMINATION

. . . Nothing in this record justifies a finding that would allow a court to terminate Mary Beth Whitehead's parental rights under the statutory standard. It is not simply that obviously there was no "intentional abandonment or very substantial neglect of parental duties without a reasonable expectation of reversal of that conduct in the future," *N.J.S.A.* 9:3–48c(1), quite the contrary, but furthermore that the trial court never found Mrs. Whitehead an unfit mother and indeed affirmatively stated that Mary Beth Whitehead had been a good mother to her other children. There is simply no basis, . . . to warrant termination of Mrs. Whitehead's parental rights. We therefore conclude that the natural mother is entitled to retain her rights as a mother.

IV.

CONSTITUTIONAL ISSUES

. . . The right asserted by the Sterns is the right of procreation; that asserted by Mary Beth Whitehead is the right to the companionship of her child. We find that the right of procreation does not extend as far as claimed by the Sterns. As for the right asserted by Mrs. Whitehead, since we uphold it on other grounds (*i.e.,* we have restored her as mother and recognized her right, limited by the child's best interests, to her companionship), we need not decide that constitutional issue, and for reasons set forth below, we should not.

. . . There is no constitutional basis whatsoever requiring that Mr. Stern's claim to the custody of Baby M be sustained. Our conclusion may thus be understood as illustrating that a person's rights of privacy and self-determination are qualified by the effect on innocent third persons of the exercise of those rights. . . . A sperm donor simply cannot be equated with a surrogate mother. The State has more than a sufficient basis to distinguish the two situations—even if the only difference is between the time it takes to provide sperm for artificial insemination and the time invested in a nine-month pregnancy—so as to justify automatically divesting the sperm donor of his parental rights without automatically divesting a surrogate mother. . . .

Mrs. Whitehead, on the other hand, asserts a claim that falls within the scope of a recognized fundamental interest protected by the Constitution. As a mother, she claims the right to the companionship of her child. This is a fundamental interest, constitutionally protected. Furthermore, it was taken away from her by the action of the court below. Whether that action under these circumstances would constitute a constitutional deprivation, however, we need not and do not decide. By virtue of our decision Mrs. Whitehead's constitutional complaint—that her parental rights have been unconstitutionally terminated—is moot. We have decided that both the statutes and public policy of this state require that that termination be voided and that her parental rights be restored.

V.

CUSTODY

. . . With the surrogacy contract disposed of, the legal framework becomes a dispute between two couples over the custody of a child produced by the artificial insemination of one couple's wife by the other's husband. Under the Parentage Act the claims of the natural father and the natural mother are entitled to equal weight, *i.e.,* one is not preferred over the other solely because he or she is the father or the mother. The applicable rule given these circumstances is clear: the child's best interests determine custody. . . . The issue here is which life would be *better* for Baby M, one with primary custody in the Whiteheads or one with primary custody in the Sterns.

. . . There were eleven experts who testified concerning the child's best interests, either directly or in connection with matters related to that issue. Our reading of the record persuades us that the trial court's decision awarding custody to the Sterns (technically to Mr. Stern) should be affirmed since "its findings . . . could reasonably have been reached on sufficient credible evidence present in the record." . . .

Our custody conclusion is based on strongly persuasive testimony contrasting both the family life of the Whiteheads and the Sterns and the personalities and characters of the individuals. The stability of the Whitehead family life was doubtful at the time of trial. Their finances were in serious trouble (foreclosure by Mrs. Whitehead's sister on a second mortgage was in process). Mr. Whitehead's employment, though relatively steady, was always at risk because of his alcoholism, a condition that he seems not to have been able to confront effectively. Mrs. Whitehead had not worked for quite some time, her last two employments having been part-time. One of the Whiteheads' positive attributes was their ability to bring up two children, and apparently well, even in so vulnerable a household. Yet substantial question was raised even about that aspect of their home life. The expert testimony contained criticism of Mrs. Whitehead's handling of her son's educational difficulties. Certain of the experts noted that Mrs. Whitehead perceived herself as omnipotent and omniscient concerning her children. She knew

what they were thinking, what they wanted, and she spoke for them. As to Melissa, Mrs. Whitehead expressed the view that she alone knew what that child's cries and sounds meant. Her inconsistent stories about various things engendered grave doubts about her ability to explain honestly and sensitively to Baby M—and at the right time—the nature of her origin. Although faith in professional counseling is not a *sine qua non* of parenting, several experts believed that Mrs. Whitehead's contempt for professional help, especially professional psychological help, coincided with her feelings of omnipotence in a way that could be devastating to a child who most likely will need such help. In short, while love and affection there would be, Baby M's life with the Whiteheads promised to be too closely controlled by Mrs. Whitehead. The prospects for wholesome, independent psychological growth and development would be at serious risk.

The Sterns have no other children, but all indications are that their household and their personalities promise a much more likely foundation for Melissa to grow and thrive. There *is* a track record of sorts—during the one-and-a-half years of custody Baby M has done very well, and the relationship between both Mr. and Mrs. Stern and the baby has become very strong. The household is stable, and likely to remain so. Their finances are more than adequate, their circle of friends supportive, and their marriage happy. Most important, they are loving, giving, nurturing, and open-minded people. They have demonstrated the wish and ability to nurture and protect Melissa, yet at the same time to encourage her independence. Their lack of experience is more than made up for by a willingness to learn and to listen, a willingness that is enhanced by their professional training, especially Mrs. Stern's experience as a pediatrician. They are honest; they can recognize error, deal with it, and learn from it. They will try to determine rationally the best way to cope with problems in their relationship with Melissa. When the time comes to tell her about her origins, they will probably have found a means of doing so that accords with the best interests of Baby M. All in all, Melissa's future appears solid, happy, and promising with them.

Based on all of this we have concluded, independent of the trial court's identical conclusion, that Melissa's best interests call for custody in the Sterns. . . . Although there is no substitute for reading the entire record, including the review of every word of each experts' testimony and reports, a summary of their conclusions is revealing. Six experts testified for Mrs. Whitehead: one favored joint custody, clearly unwarranted in this case; one simply rebutted an opposing expert's claim that Mary Beth Whitehead had a recognized personality disorder; one testified to the adverse impact of separation on *Mrs. Whitehead;* one testified about the evils of adoption and, to him, the probable analogous evils of surrogacy; one spoke only on the question of whether Mrs. Whitehead's consent in the surrogacy agreement was "informed consent"; and one spelled out the strong bond between mother and child. None of them unequivocally

stated, or even necessarily implied, an opinion that custody in the Whiteheads was in the best interests of Melissa—the ultimate issue. The Sterns' experts, both well qualified—as were the Whiteheads'—concluded that the best interests of Melissa required custody in Mr. Stern. Most convincingly, the three experts chosen by the court-appointed guardian *ad litem* of Baby M, each clearly free of all bias and interest, unanimously and persuasively recommended custody in the Sterns.

VI.

VISITATION

It is apparent to us that this factually sensitive issue, which was never addressed below, should not be determined *de novo* by this Court. We therefore remand the visitation issue to the trial court for an abbreviated hearing and determination. . . . the trial court should recall the touchstones of visitation: that it is desirable for the child to have contact with both parents; that besides the child's interests, the parents' interests also must be considered; but that when all is said and done, the best interests of the child are paramount.

We have decided that Mrs. Whitehead is entitled to visitation at some point, and that question is not open to the trial court on this remand. The trial court will determine what kind of visitation shall be granted to her, with or without conditions, and when and under what circumstances it should commence. It also should be noted that the guardian's recommendation of a five-year delay is most unusual—one might argue that it begins to border on termination. Nevertheless, if the circumstances as further developed by appropriate proofs or as reconsidered on remand clearly call for that suspension under applicable legal principles of visitation, it should be so ordered.

NOTES AND QUESTIONS

1. *Contract Law.* Why did the court rule that the surrogacy contract was unenforceable? Do you agree with the court's ruling as a matter of contract law? Do you think courts and legislatures today should look more favorably upon surrogate contracts? Would you place any limits on surrogacy contracts?

Practice Exercise: Imagine you were hired by a couple to draft a surrogacy contract. How would you draft the contract in light of the *Baby M* decision?

2. *Parents.* What did the court conclude about who Baby M's parents are? Was Mr. Stern her father? Was Mrs. Stern her mother? Was Mary Beth Whitehead her mother? Do you think all three were fit parents for Baby M?

3. *Adoption.* Do you think the Sterns should have adopted a child instead of using surrogate motherhood? Why do you think they rejected the adoption option? How does the court

describe the differences between an adoption contract and a surrogate contract? Do you agree that adoption and surrogacy offer different financial incentives for bearing children?

4. *Mothers.* Is your assessment of Mary Beth Whitehead's ability as a mother affected by the fact that she had other children? By the fact that she took Baby M to Florida without telling the Sterns? Does Baby M have two mothers, Whitehead and Stern?

Recall that in Section A, we discussed whether Justice Kennedy was overly paternalistic toward women in *Gonzales v. Carhart* when he suggested that the state had reason to control how much information women learned about partial birth abortion. How do you think the New Jersey court treated women in this case? Did it treat Stern and Whitehead equally? In a part of the opinion not included in the excerpt above, the court wrote:

> It seems to us that given her predicament, Mrs. Whitehead was rather harshly judged—both by the trial court and by some of the experts. She was guilty of a breach of contract, and indeed, she did break a very important promise, but we think it is expecting something well beyond normal human capabilities to suggest that this mother should have parted with her newly born infant without a struggle. Other than survival, what stronger force is there? We do not know of, and cannot conceive of, any other case where a perfectly fit mother was expected to surrender her newly born infant, perhaps forever, and was then told she was a bad mother because she did not. We know of no authority suggesting that the moral quality of her act in those circumstances should be judged by referring to a contract made before she became pregnant. We do not countenance, and would never countenance, violating a court order as Mrs. Whitehead did, even a court order that is wrong; but her resistance to an order that she surrender her infant, possibly forever, merits a measure of understanding. We do not find it so clear that her efforts to keep her infant, when measured against the Sterns' efforts to take her away, make one, rather than the other, the wrongdoer. The Sterns suffered, but so did she. And if we go beyond suffering to an evaluation of the human stakes involved in the struggle, how much weight should be given to her nine months of pregnancy, the labor of childbirth, the risk to her life, compared to the payment of money, the anticipation of a child and the donation of sperm?

Do you agree with the court? How did you react when you read the facts of the case that mentioned Whitehead had violated court orders and fled with Melissa to Florida? Did that affect your judgment of her as a mother?

5. *Money.* What should the role of money be in an adoption case? In a surrogate motherhood case? Should financial payments ever be allowed to surrogate mothers? Do you see an important distinction between reimbursing a surrogate mother for medical expenses and paying her money as a fee for the surrogacy? Was the court's decision about custody influenced

by the Sterns' wealth compared to the Whiteheads' financial situation? Do you think paid surrogacy always takes advantage of poor women?

6. *Melissa.* After the decision, Melissa lived with the Sterns while Whitehead enjoyed broad visitation rights. Does it surprise you to learn that when Melissa turned 18, she started the adoption process allowing Elizabeth Stern to adopt her and terminated Whitehead's rights? See Allison Pries, Whatever Happened to Baby M?, The Record (Bergen County, NJ), Jan. 5, 2010, at A02.

7. *Gestational Surrogacy.* Five years after *Baby M*, the California Supreme Court upheld a gestational surrogacy contract in Johnson v. Calvert, 851 P.2d 776 (Cal. 1993); see also Lisa C. Ikemoto, Johnson v. Calvert: Technology, Family, and Commerce, in Health Law & Bioethics: Cases in Context, 79–95 (S.H. Johnson et al., eds. 2009). Mark and Crispina Calvert wanted to have a child, but Crispina was unable to bear a child due to a hysterectomy. She could, however, produce eggs. Therefore, the Calverts entered into a surrogacy contract with Anna Johnson, where Mark provided the sperm, Crispina the eggs, and Anna the gestation. Over time, the Calverts and Johnson disagreed about the pregnancy. Johnson was angry about the Calverts' efforts to find health insurance and about their neglect of her during a medical crisis. The Calverts were angry when they learned that Johnson had never informed them of past miscarriages and stillbirths.

Eventually the dispute went to the California Supreme Court to determine parentage. Under California law, the child had two possible mothers—Anna, because she bore the child, and Crispina, because she contributed the ova. The Supreme Court rejected the opportunity to declare that a child could have two mothers, and recognized Crispina as the child's mother because she was the intended parent according to the surrogacy contract:

> We conclude that although the Act recognizes both genetic consanguinity and giving birth as means of establishing a mother and child relationship, when the two means do not coincide in one woman, she who intended to procreate the child—that is, she who intended to bring about the birth of a child that she intended to raise as her own—is the natural mother under California law.

In dissent, Justice Kennard argued that because the child had two mothers under California law, parenthood should be decided according to a "best interests of the child" standard instead of according to the surrogacy contract. Do you agree? What outcome would have been in the best interests of the child? Should California have vacated the surrogacy contract as New Jersey did? Or is gestational surrogacy a different matter? How does the California majority's reasoning in the quotation above differ from the reasoning in *Baby M*?

8. *Surrogacy in the United States.* Surrogates still cannot collect a fee in New Jersey. Post-*Johnson*, however, "fertility tourists" traveled to California, which became "Surrogacy Central" in the United States. Judith Daar, Litowitz v. Litowitz: Feuding over Frozen Embryos and Forecasting

the Future of Reproductive Medicine, in Health Law & Bioethics: Cases in Context, 99 (S.H. Johnson et al., eds. 2009).

Post *Baby M*, states developed different laws regarding surrogacy contracts. Some states require a surrogate to have already had a child before agreeing to a surrogacy arrangement. See Jennifer Ludden, Surrogacy Experts Help Navigate Murky Legal Waters, NPR, Apr. 13, 2012, available at http://www.npr.org/2012/04/13/150498711/surrogacy-aides-spring-from-murky-legal-waters. Others require that the surrogate be financially stable so as to not seek surrogacy as a way to generate an income. Id.

Go back to the website to get an overview of the different laws regulating surrogacy across the United States. Then, draft a law that you think should govern surrogacy in your home state. What would you include as necessary requirements for a surrogacy contract to be legal?

Jordan and Tammy Myers had twins, a boy named Eames and a girl named Ellison, with a surrogate mother. Michigan will not recognize them as the twins' parents until they adopt the twins. State law recognizes the surrogate and her husband as the twins' parents, even though a fertility doctor said that the Myerses are the twins' biological parents. The surrogate and her husband also filled out an affidavit acknowledging that Jordan and Tammy are the parents of the twins. To become the adoptive parents, the Myerses have to go through a review to prove they are fit to adopt the children. They need to give reference letters to the state, and had to get the surrogate's permission to bring the twins home. Paying a woman to be a surrogate is illegal in Michigan, and surrogate contracts are void, meaning that parents must go through the adoption process. The Michigan surrogate volunteered to carry the babies for the Myerses. Should Michigan change its laws, or keep them as they are? See Maria Cramer, Couple Forced to Adopt Their Own Children After a Surrogate Pregnancy, N.Y. Times, Jan. 31, 2021.

Go back to the website and spend time visiting two websites that offer surrogate services, SelectSurrogate and ConceiveAbilities. Does seeing how the process works online persuade you to change your draft law in any way?

9. *Taxable Income.* Nichelle Perez, an egg donor who went through the painful procedures associated with egg donation—repeated injections and operations—signed a contract stating she would receive $20,000 in "consideration for all of her pain, suffering, time, inconvenience, and efforts" connected with the procedure. In tax law, compensation for services is taxed as income, but "a taxpayer who suffers physical pain or injury while performing a contract for personal services may exclude the amounts paid under that service contract as 'damages received on account of personal physical injuries or physical sickness.' " Should the $20,000 count as income subject to tax? See Perez v. Commissioner, 144 T.C. No. 4 (Jan. 22, 2015).

The Tax Court clarified at the outset of its opinion that the contract was not for the sale of eggs. It then ruled that the money was taxable income because "the injury here, as painful as it was . . . was exactly within the scope of the medical procedures to which she contractually consented." Do you agree with the Tax Court that compensation for egg donation should not count as damages? The court gave the following reasoning in support of its decision:

> We see no limit on the mischief that ruling in Perez's favor might cause: A professional boxer could argue that some part of the payments he received for his latest fight is excludable because they are payments for his bruises, cuts, and nosebleeds. A hockey player could argue that a portion of his million-dollar salary is allocable to the chipped teeth he invariably suffers during his career. And the same would go for the brain injuries suffered by football players and the less-noticed bodily damage daily endured by working men and women on farms and ranches, in mines, or on fishing boats. We don't doubt that some portion of the compensation paid all these people reflects the risk that they will feel pain and suffering, but it's a risk of pain and suffering that they agree to before they begin their work. And that makes it taxable compensation and not excludable damages.

Id. Do you think egg donation should be analogized to boxing, hockey and football?

A California district court certified a class action against the American Society for Reproductive Medicine and the Society for Assisted Reproductive Technology. Plaintiffs alleged that the societies' guidelines capping compensation for egg donors at $5,000 or $10,000 constituted a horizontal price fixing agreement that violated the Sherman Antitrust Act. The result is that egg donors are undercompensated. Kamakahi v. American Society for Reproductive Medicine, No. 11–cv–01781–JCS, N.D. Cal., Feb. 3, 2015, at http://blurblawg.typepad.com/files/kamakahi-classcert.pdf. The case ultimately settled, with ASRM agreeing to remove the cap on payments and paying $1.5 million in attorneys' fees and costs. See Egg Donors Get Pay Limits Axed With Antitrust Settlement, Law360, Feb. 1, 2016, https://www.law360.com/competition/articles/753389?nl_pk=ad0ed999-c219-40d1-a23f-addcaed2be7c&utm_source=newsletter&utm_medium=email&utm_campaign=competition. What do you think the compensation for an egg donor should be? Should there be any recommended caps?

10. *Effect of COVID-19.* For a discussion of how COVID-19 has affected access to reproductive health services, see David Dodge, How Coronavirus Is Affecting Surrogacy Foster Care and Adoption, N.Y. Times, April 1, 2020, https://www.nytimes.com/2020/04/01/parenting/coronavirus-adoption-surrogacy-foster-care.html. What do you think will be the long-term effects of COVID-19 on reproductive care?

11. *Gay and Lesbian Parents.* As you read the next case, consider what laws should govern gay and lesbian parentage, including their adoption of children and their use of surrogate motherhood.

Sha'Kayla St. Mary v. Veronica Lynn Damon

Supreme Court of Nevada, 2013.
309 P.3d 1027, 129 Nev. Adv. Op. 68.

■ By the Court, SAITTA, J.

This appeal concerns the establishment of custodial rights over a minor child born to former female partners, appellant Sha'Kayla St. Mary and respondent Veronica Lynn Damon. The couple became romantically involved and decided to have a child. They drafted a co-parenting agreement, and eventually, St. Mary gave birth to a child through in vitro fertilization, using Damon's egg and an anonymous donor's sperm. Thereafter, their relationship ended, leading to the underlying dispute concerning the parties' custodial rights over the child.

The district court, apparently relying on a previous order that recognized Damon as the child's legal mother and granted her the right to be added as a mother to the child's birth certificate, concluded that St. Mary was a mere surrogate. The district court refused to uphold the parties' co-parenting agreement or consider whether St. Mary was a parent entitled to any custodial rights. St. Mary appealed, challenging the district court's conclusion that she was a surrogate and its refusal to uphold the co-parenting agreement.

We first conclude that the district court erred in determining, without holding an evidentiary hearing on the issue, that St. Mary was a surrogate lacking any legal rights to parent the child. The version of NRS 126.041(1) that existed at the time of the district court's determinations, as well as the version that exists now, provides that a mother-child relationship may be established by "proof of [the mother] having given birth." Here, the parties agree that St. Mary gave birth to the child but disagree about whether they intended for St. Mary to be a mother to the child or a mere surrogate. Nothing in either Nevada law or in this case's record, including the birth certificate order, conclusively demonstrates that NRS 126.041(1) does not apply to St. Mary's relationship with the child. Accordingly, a factual issue exists regarding whether St. Mary was a legal mother to the child or was a surrogate or gestational carrier without legal rights to the child, and we remand this matter for an evidentiary hearing on that issue.

Second, we conclude that St. Mary and Damon's co-parenting agreement is not void as unlawful or against public policy. When two parents, presumptively acting in the child's best interest, reach an agreement concerning post-separation custody, that agreement must not be deemed unenforceable on the basis of the parents being of the same sex. In this matter, the parties' co-parenting agreement stated that if their relationship ended, they would continue to share in the responsibilities and privileges of being the child's parent. Thus, if the district court determines on remand that both St. Mary and Damon are

the child's legal parents, the district court should consider the co-parenting agreement and its enforceability in determining custody.

FACTS AND PROCEDURAL HISTORY

Approximately one year after entering into a romantic relationship with each other, St. Mary and Damon moved in together. They planned to have a child, deciding that Damon would have her egg fertilized by a sperm donor, and St. Mary would carry the fertilized egg and give birth to the child. In October 2007, Damon's eggs were implanted into St. Mary. Around the same time, Damon drafted a co-parenting agreement, which she and St. Mary signed. The agreement indicated that Damon and St. Mary sought to "jointly and equally share parental responsibility, with both of [them] providing support and guidance." In it, they stated that they would "make every effort to jointly share the responsibilities of raising [their] child," including paying for expenses and making major child-related decisions. The agreement provided that if their relationship ended, they would each work to ensure that the other maintained a close relationship with the child, share the duties of raising the child, and make a "good-faith effort to jointly make all major decisions affecting" the child.

St. Mary gave birth to a child in June 2008. The hospital birth confirmation report and certificate of live birth listed only St. Mary as the child's mother. The child was given both parties' last names, however, in the hyphenated form of St. Mary-Damon.

For several months, St. Mary primarily stayed home caring for the child during the day while Damon worked. But, nearly one year after the child's birth, their romantic relationship ended, St. Mary moved out of the home, and St. Mary and Damon disagreed about how to share their time with the child. St. Mary signed an affidavit declaring that Damon was the biological mother of the child, and in 2009, Damon filed an ex parte petition with the district court to establish maternity, seeking to have the child's birth certificate amended to add Damon as a mother. The district court issued an order stating that St. Mary gave birth to the child and that Damon "is the biological and legal mother of said child." The 2009 order also directed that the birth certificate be amended to add Damon's name as a mother.

Thereafter, St. Mary instituted the underlying case by filing a complaint and motion, in a separate district court case, to establish custody, visitation, and child support. In response, Damon contended that, due to her biological connection, she was entitled to sole custody of the child. Damon attached the 2009 order to her opposition.

[The district court concluded that St. Mary had already been designated a surrogate, not the child's mother, and focused only on the question whether St. Mary should have visitation rights.] St. Mary and Damon gave conflicting testimonies regarding their relationship, the co-parenting agreement's purpose, and their intentions in using in vitro

fertilization to produce the child. St. Mary testified that she and Damon intended to create the child together, wanted the child to be their child, and fertilized and implanted Damon's eggs into St. Mary so that both women would be "related" to the child. But Damon testified that she and St. Mary orally agreed that St. Mary would be a mere surrogate. St. Mary further testified that she and Damon created the co-parenting agreement together, believing that it would be required by the fertility clinic as a prerequisite for the performance of the reproductive procedure. St. Mary indicated that despite the fertility clinic not asking for the agreement before the procedure, she and Damon completed the agreement after the procedure. Damon asserted that she and St. Mary did not intend to create an enforceable co-parenting agreement but created the agreement to satisfy the fertility clinic's requirements and to seek insurance coverage for the pregnancy.

Following the hearing, in March 2011, the district court issued an order providing that St. Mary was entitled to third-party visitation but not custody. . . .

DISCUSSION

St. Mary argues that the district court erred in determining that, legally, she was a surrogate and not the child's legal mother and in deeming the co-parenting agreement unenforceable as a matter of law. As a result of our de novo review of these legal questions, we agree.

St. Mary may be the child's legal mother

To determine parentage in Nevada, courts must look to the Nevada Parentage Act, which is modeled after the Uniform Parentage Act (UPA). The Nevada Parentage Act is "applied to determine legal parentage." Absent an ambiguity, we focus on the statutory language and "give effect to the plain and ordinary meaning of the words." Our ultimate goal in interpreting the Nevada Parentage Act "is to give effect to the legislature's intent."

As the Legislature's adoption of the UPA recognizes, the relationship between a parent and a child is of fundamental societal and constitutional dimension. In Nevada, all of the "rights, privileges, duties and obligations" accompanying parenthood are conferred on those persons who are deemed to have a parent-child relationship with the child, regardless of the parents' marital status. Surrogates who bear a child conceived through assisted conception for another, on the other hand, are often not entitled to claim parental rights. Accordingly, whether St. Mary is treated as someone other than a legal mother, such as a surrogate, is of the upmost significance.

The multiple ways to prove maternity

Given the medical advances and changing family dynamics of the age, determining a child's parents today can be more complicated than it was in the past. To this end, although perhaps not encompassing every possibility, the Nevada Parentage Act provides several ways to

determine a child's legal mother: a mother with a parent-child relationship with the child "incident to which the law confers or imposes rights, privileges, duties, and obligations." NRS 126.021 (3). Under the pre-2013 and current versions of NRS 126.041(1), a woman's status as a legal mother can be established by "proof of her having given birth to the child." *See* NRS 126.041 (2009); 2013 Nev. Stat., ch. 213, § 34, at 812. In maternity actions under NRS Chapter 126, the statutes under which paternity may be determined apply "[i]nsofar as practicable." NRS 126.231. Paternity may be established in a variety of ways, including through presumptions based on marriage and cohabitation, NRS 126.051(1)(a)–(c), presumptions based on receiving the child into the home and openly holding oneself out as a parent, NRS 126.051(1)(d), genetic testing, NRS 126.051(2), and voluntary acknowledgment, NRS 126.053. Hence, a determination of parentage rests upon a wide array of considerations rather than genetics alone.

This case presents a situation where two women proffered evidence that could establish or generate a conclusive presumption of maternity to either woman. St. Mary testified that she gave birth to the child, thereby offering proof to establish that she is the child's legal mother. Damon showed that her egg was used to produce the child, demonstrating a genetic relationship to the child that may be a basis for concluding that she is the child's legal mother. By dividing the reproductive roles of conceiving a child, St. Mary and Damon each assumed functions traditionally used to evidence a legal maternal relationship. Hence, this matter raises the issue of whether the Nevada Parentage Act and its policies preclude a child from having two legal mothers where two women split the genetic and physical functions of creating a child.

The law does not preclude a child from having two legal mothers

. . . contrary to [the district court's] premise, the Nevada Parentage Act and its policies do not preclude such a child from having two legal mothers.

Although NRS 126.051(3) contains procedures for rebutting paternity presumptions by clear and convincing evidence or "a court decree establishing *paternity* . . . by another *man*," (emphases added), and while NRS 126.051(3) arguably applies in maternity cases, we decline to read this provision of the statute as conveying clear legislative intent to deprive a child conceived by artificial insemination of the emotional, financial, and physical support of an intended mother who "actively assisted in the decision and process of bringing [the child] into this world." In Nevada, as in other states, the best interest of the child is the paramount concern in determining the custody and care of children. Both the Legislature and this court have acknowledged that, generally, a child's best interest is served by maintaining two actively involved parents. To that end, the Legislature has recognized that the children of same-sex domestic partners bear no lesser rights to the enjoyment and

support of two parents than children born to married heterosexual parents. *See* NRS 122A.300(1) (indicating that NRS Chapter 125 applies to registered domestic partners terminating their relationship); NRS 122A.300(3)(b) (recognizing former domestic partners' custody agreements). Certainly, the Legislature has not instructed that children born to unregistered domestic partners bear any less rights to the best-interest considerations set forth in these statutes than children born to registered domestic partners, married persons, and unmarried persons. Ultimately, "the preservation and strengthening of family life is a part of the public policy of this State."

Of the jurisdictions that have addressed the issue of maternity between two women who created a child through assisted reproduction, California is highly instructive. California, like Nevada, enacted statutes modeled after the UPA. The California Supreme Court has determined that its laws do not preclude two women from being the legal mothers of a child. *See Elisa B. v. Superior Court,* 37 Cal.4th 108, 33 Cal.Rptr.3d 46, 117 P.3d 660, 666 (2005) (providing that, under the California UPA, there is "no reason why both parents of a child cannot be women"); *see also K.M.,* 33 Cal.Rptr.3d 61, 117 P.3d at 675. In *K.M.,* the California Supreme Court dealt with a maternity case that presented facts analogous to the instant case. There, K.M.'s eggs were implanted in E.G., her lesbian partner who gave birth to twins. Thereafter, K.M. and E.G.'s relationship ended, and K.M. sought custody and visitation of the twins, but the trial court denied her request, determining that she had relinquished her parental rights. On appeal, the California Supreme Court agreed with K.M.'s contention that she was the twins' legal mother because her eggs were used for the twins' birth. It concluded that because "K.M.'s genetic relationship with the twins constitutes evidence of a mother and child relationship under the UPA," and "[t]he circumstance that E.G. gave birth to the twins also constitutes evidence of a mother and child relationship[,] . . . both K.M. and E.G. are mothers of the twins under the UPA." The court held that when a woman provides her eggs to her lesbian partner so that the partner can bear children by in vitro fertilization, both women are the child's legal mothers.

California's precedent is highly persuasive because it pertains to a statutory scheme that is substantially similar to Nevada's and advances the policies that underlie the Nevada Parentage Act—preventing children from "becom[ing] wards of the state," As other jurisdictions have acknowledged, recognizing two legal parents, such as two legal mothers, supports these policies. *See, e.g., Elisa B.,* 33 Cal.Rptr.3d 46, 117 P.3d at 669 (concluding that a woman was a legal mother with an obligation to pay child support to her former lesbian partner; although the woman was not a genetic or gestational mother, she held the children out as her own, and concluding otherwise "would leave [the children] with only one parent and would deprive them of the support of their second parent"); *Chatterjee v. King,* 280 P.3d 283, 292 (N.M.2012) (explaining that a child

can have two legal mothers under the New Mexico UPA because "the state has a strong interest in ensuring that a child will be cared for, financially and otherwise, by two parents"); *Miller-Jenkins v. Miller-Jenkins,* 180 Vt. 441, 912 A.2d 951, 970 (2006) (determining that two women were both legal mothers of a child where, among other things, concluding otherwise "would leave [the child] with only one parent").

Hence, there is no legal or policy-based barrier to the establishment under NRS Chapter 126, as it existed at the time of the district court's determinations and as it exists now, of a legal parent and child relationship with both St. Mary and Damon. Rather, the Nevada Parentage Act and its policies permit a child created by artificial insemination, where one woman had her egg fertilized by a sperm donor and implanted into her female partner, to have two legal mothers.

[The court concluded that the district court had mistakenly decided that St. Mary was not the child's biological mother.]

St. Mary asserts that she is a legal mother of the child in addition to Damon, not instead of Damon. This claim must be given consideration under the Nevada Parentage Act, which does not preclude the child from having two legal mothers. Because the district court erroneously concluded that St. Mary was a mere surrogate and limited the scope of the evidentiary hearing to third-party visitation issues, the district court did not consider the parentage statutes with respect to St. Mary's and Damon's testimonies regarding their intent in creating the child and the nature of their relationship to one another and the child. Although St. Mary's parentage can be established by virtue of her having given birth to the child, the parties dispute whether they intended for St. Mary to be the child's parent or simply a surrogate or gestational carrier who lacked a legal parent-child relationship to the child. Therefore, upon remand, the district court must hold an evidentiary hearing to determine whether St. Mary is the child's legal mother or if she is someone without a legal relationship to the child, during which the court may consider any relevant evidence for establishing maternity under the Nevada Parentage Act.

The co-parenting agreement was not a surrogacy agreement and was consistent with Nevada's public policy

St. Mary asserts that the co-parenting agreement demonstrates the parties' intent regarding parentage and custody of the child and that the district court erred in determining that the co-parenting agreement was an unenforceable surrogacy agreement under NRS 126.045. Damon responds that, because the agreement was between an unmarried intended parent and a surrogate and purported to resolve issues of parentage and child custody, the district court correctly deemed that the co-parenting agreement was prohibited by NRS 126.051(3) (2009).

At the time of the district court's determinations, NRS 126.051(3) (2009) governed contracts between two married persons and a

gestational carrier, or surrogate, for assisted reproduction. It required such contracts to specify the parties' rights, including the "[p]arentage of the child," the "[c]ustody of the child in the event of a change of circumstances," and the "respective responsibilities and liabilities of the contracting parties." NRS 126.045(1)(a)–(c) (2009). Additionally, the statute defined a "[s]urrogate" as "an adult woman who enters into an agreement to bear a child conceived through assisted conception for the intended parents," and "[i]ntended parents" were defined as "a man and woman, married to each other," who agree to "be the parents of a child born to a surrogate through assisted conception." NRS 126.045(4)(b), (c) (2009). Here, St. Mary and Damon's co-parenting agreement was not within the scope of NRS 126.045. The agreement lacked any language intimating that St. Mary acted as a surrogate, such as language indicating that she surrendered custody of the child or relinquished her rights as a mother to the child. Rather, the agreement expressed that St. Mary would share the parental duties of raising the child and would jointly make major parenting decisions with Damon.[3]

Nevertheless, Damon insists that, because the agreement covered issues of parentage and child custody, it necessarily addressed issues contemplated by NRS 126.045 and, as a result, is void for failing to meet the statute's other terms. In other words, Damon argues that outside of NRS 126.045, agreements (at least those with a non-parent) concerning parentage, custody, and responsibilities over a child are void. But, as explained above, parentage is governed by NRS Chapter 126. In the event that both parties are determined to be the child's parents, nothing in Nevada law prevents two parents from entering into agreements that demonstrate their intent concerning child custody.

"Parties are free to contract, and the courts will enforce their contracts if they are not unconscionable, illegal, or in violation of public policy." It is presumed that fit parents act in the best interest of their children. Thus, public policy favors fit parents entering agreements to resolve issues pertaining to their minor child's "custody, care, and visitation."

When a child has the opportunity to be supported by two loving and fit parents pursuant to a co-parenting agreement, this opportunity is to be given due consideration and must not be foreclosed on account of the parents being of the same sex. To bar the enforceability of a co-parenting agreement on the basis of the parents' genders conflicts with the Nevada Parentage Act's policies of promoting the child's best interest with the support of two parents.

---

[3] In 2013, the Legislature repealed NRS 126.045, substituted the term "surrogate" with "gestational carrier," and defined "[g]estational carrier" as one "who is not an intended parent and who enters into a gestational agreement" under which she "[s]urrender[s] legal and physical custody" of the child to the intended parent or parents and may "relinquish all rights and duties as the parent[ ] of a child." The language of St. Mary and Damon's co-parenting agreement does not appear to be within the scope of this new statute.

St. Mary and Damon's co-parenting agreement was aligned with Nevada's policy of allowing parents to agree on how to best provide for their child. Within their co-parenting agreement, St. Mary and Damon sought to provide for their child's best interest by agreeing to share the responsibilities of raising the child, even if the relationship between St. Mary and Damon ended. The agreement's language provides the indicia of an effort by St. Mary and Damon to make the child's best interest their priority. Thus, in the event that St. Mary is found to be a legal mother, the district court must consider the parties' co-parenting agreement in making its child custody determination.

CONCLUSION

The district court, in issuing its 2011 order, erred in determining that St. Mary lacked "legal rights" to the child because it misinterpreted the 2009 order, which recognized Damon's relationship to the child without affecting the same of St. Mary. The Nevada Parentage Act does not preclude St. Mary and Damon from both being legal mothers of the child. Hence, the district court abused its discretion in limiting the evidentiary hearing to the issue of third-party visitation. The district court also erred in deeming the co-parenting agreement unenforceable under NRS 126.045. The agreement's plain language indicated that it was not a surrogacy arrangement within the scope of that statute. Moreover, the parties' co-parenting agreement aligns with Nevada's policy of encouraging parents to enter into parenting agreements that resolve matters pertaining to their child's best interest.

As a result, we reverse the 2011 order. We remand this matter to the district court for further proceedings to determine the child's parentage, custody, and visitation.

■ We concur: PICKERING, C.J., and GIBBONS, HARDESTY, PARRAGUIRRE, DOUGLAS, and CHERRY, JJ.

NOTES AND QUESTIONS

1. *Mothers.* What is the best argument that St. Mary is the child's mother? What is the best argument that Damon is the child's mother? What do you think of a law that states that a child may have only one mother? What do you think of a law that states that a child may have two mothers? Is it possible for a child to have three mothers? How?

2. *Frozen Embryos.* What should happen to frozen embryos in the event of a divorce? In a leading case on this subject, David and Becky Litowitz decided to use IVF to bear a child. Because Becky could not produce eggs, the Litowitzes paid an egg donor and had those eggs inseminated with David's sperm. Another woman served as the gestational surrogate and gave birth to a healthy baby girl.

As frequently occurs with IVF, the remaining embryos were put into cryopreservation. When the couple divorced, they argued over the embryos. Becky wanted to retain custody of them in case she wanted to bear children, while David did not want Becky to bear his child. Who should get custody? See Litowitz v. Litowitz, 48 P.3d 261 (Wash. 2002); Judith Daar, Litowitz v. Litowitz: Feuding over Frozen Embryos and Forecasting the Future of Reproductive Medicine, in Health Law & Bioethics: Cases in Context (S.H. Johnson et al., eds. 2009). The court relied on the IVF contract, which stated that the embryos could be thawed after five years. Thus neither party gained custody over them. A settlement allowed the embryos to be given anonymously to another party instead of being thawed. Id. To whom would you have awarded the embryos? Are you influenced by the knowledge that only David was genetically related to them? Are you influenced by finding out that the egg donor wanted Becky to take custody of the eggs?

> **Go to** the website and read the new Nevada law to see the law referenced in the opinion. The text is edited so that you can see how the legislature amended the statute. What do you think of the amendments? Would you change this new law in any way? Do the surrogate websites developed in Nevada describe the new law accurately?

The courts have split over custody of frozen embryos. Daar, *supra*, at 113–14; see also In re Marriage of Dahl and Angle, 194 P.2d 834 (Or.App. 2008) (Court upheld contract designating wife as person whose interest controls in case of disagreement; wife is allowed to choose destruction of the embryos); Roman v. Roman, 193 S.W.3d 40 (Tex.App.-Houston (1st Dist.) 2006) (allowing enforcement of prior agreement to award frozen embryos to wife). Recently, appeals courts in Pennsylvania and Illinois allowed women who were infertile from chemotherapy (and thus unable to create new embryos) to use their frozen embryos despite their partners' opposition. The Pennsylvania court identified three options for embryo custody: enforcing the contract, requiring the consent and agreement of both parties, and balancing the interests of the parties. Because the wife did not have an agreement with her ex-husband about the embryos, the court applied the balancing test and weighed the woman's interests in procreation above the man's interest in avoiding unwanted procreation. Reber v. Reiss, 42 A.3d 1131, 1135 (Pa. Super. 2012). In Illinois, because the parties had an oral contract that the woman could use the embryos without her partner's consent, the court awarded her the embryos. Szafranski v. Dunston, 2015 IL

> **Practice Exercise:** How would you decide who should gain custody? Draft a contract that addresses this concern. Would you consider the best-fit parent, the best interest of the child, or the parties' original intent? What about the inconvenience, pain and suffering, and compensation of the donor? Should each state have a law that determines who gets custody instead of leaving it to contract? Draft that law.

App (1st) 122975. Both courts left the question of child support open, although the Pennsylvania wife had agreed not to seek child support. How do you think questions of future child support should be resolved in these circumstances? See David Orentlicher, Frozen Embryo Disputes and Unwanted Parenthood, HealthLawProfBlog, Jun. 15, 2015 at http://lawprofessors.typepad.com/healthlawprof_blog/2015/06/frozen-embryo-disputes-and-unwanted-parenthood.html. Do you agree that it is problematic to "bind people to advance agreements about procreation"? Id.

3. *International Surrogacy.* The United States is one of the few countries that allow paid surrogacy. See Tamar Lewin, Coming to U.S. for Baby, and Womb to Carry It, N.Y. Times, July 6, 2014, at A1. Even though surrogacy is a recent development, foreigners often choose the United States because "many states have sophisticated fertility clinics, experienced lawyers, a large pool of egg donors and surrogates, and, especially, established legal precedent." Id. However, fertility lawyers have encountered ethical issues when dealing with foreigners. For example, some foreigners have asked to implant six embryos simultaneously in the surrogate mother so that they can pick two of the babies and put the rest up for adoption. Id. One fertility lawyer told the foreigners that they could not have "the pick of the litter" and that he would not work with them. Id. Other ethical issues arise when a couple asks the surrogate to abort the fetus. One surrogate mother was asked to abort the twenty-one-week-old fetus after the intended parents discovered the fetus had a cleft in his brain. Id. How should US law handle this type of issue? For a discussion of these issues, see Noelia Igareda González, Legal and Ethical Issues in Cross-Border Gestational Surrogacy, 113 Fertility and Sterility 916 (2020), https://www.sciencedirect.com/science/article/abs/pii/S001502822030248X.

> **Go to** the website and review India's treatment of surrogacy law. What do you think of India as a destination for surrogacy?

Thailand is considered a cheaper alternative to America in terms of surrogacy and is one of the only two countries in Asia to allow surrogacy. As a result, the government is concerned with wealthier Asians taking advantage of the Thai people and their surrogacy laws. Thomas Fuller, Thailand's Business in Paid Surrogate May Be Foundering in a Moral Quagmire, N.Y. Times, Aug. 26, 2014, at A12. Due to the poverty in Thailand, the need for money makes it easy for women to become surrogates. Id. For instance, a Japanese man fathered around twelve babies with surrogates, some only weeks or months apart. Id. Additionally, an Australian couple hired a surrogate and when the woman gave birth to twins, the Australian couple took only one of them because the other had Down syndrome. Id. Thailand is now being referred to as the "womb of Asia" due to the number of people who travel there for surrogates. Although the Thai government is concerned with the surrogacy laws, many Thai people see it as an opportunity to make money and help a couple in need. Id.

The judges in the surrogacy cases frequently compared surrogacy to adoption. How are surrogacy and adoption similar? How are they different? Can the same laws that govern adoption govern surrogacy?

Whose rights should have been protected in the following case? Do you view the case differently from *Baby M* or *St. Mary* because it involves a father's parental claims instead of a mother's?

2. ADOPTIVE PARENTS AND FORGOTTEN FATHERS

Adoptive Couple v. Baby Girl

Supreme Court of the United States, 2013.
570 U.S. 637, 133 S.Ct. 2552.

■ JUSTICE ALITO delivered the opinion of the Court.

This case is about a little girl (Baby Girl) who is classified as an Indian because she is 1.2% (3/256) Cherokee. Because Baby Girl is classified in this way, the South Carolina Supreme Court held that certain provisions of the federal Indian Child Welfare Act of 1978 required her to be taken, at the age of 27 months, from the only parents she had ever known and handed over to her biological father, who had attempted to relinquish his parental rights and who had no prior contact with the child. The provisions of the federal statute at issue here do not demand this result.

Contrary to the State Supreme Court's ruling, we hold that 25 U.S.C. § 1912(f)—which bars involuntary termination of a parent's rights in the absence of a heightened showing that serious harm to the Indian child is likely to result from the parent's "continued custody" of the child—does not apply when, as here, the relevant parent never had custody of the child. We further hold that § 1912(d)—which conditions involuntary termination of parental rights with respect to an Indian child on a showing that remedial efforts have been made to prevent the "breakup of the Indian family"—is inapplicable when, as here, the parent abandoned the Indian child before birth and never had custody of the child. Finally, we clarify that § 1915(a), which provides placement preferences for the adoption of Indian children, does not bar a non-Indian family like Adoptive Couple from adopting an Indian child when no other eligible candidates have sought to adopt the child. We accordingly reverse the South Carolina Supreme Court's judgment and remand for further proceedings.

I

"The Indian Child Welfare Act of 1978 (ICWA) was the product of rising concern in the mid-1970's over the consequences to Indian children, Indian families, and Indian tribes of abusive child welfare practices that resulted in the separation of large numbers of Indian children from their families and tribes through adoption or foster care placement, usually in non-Indian homes." Congress found that "an

alarmingly high percentage of Indian families [were being] broken up by the removal, often unwarranted, of their children from them by nontribal public and private agencies." This "wholesale removal of Indian children from their homes" prompted Congress to enact the ICWA, which establishes federal standards that govern state-court child custody proceedings involving Indian children.

Three provisions of the ICWA are especially relevant to this case. *First,* "[a]ny party seeking" an involuntary termination of parental rights to an Indian child under state law must demonstrate that "active efforts have been made to provide remedial services and rehabilitative programs designed to prevent the breakup of the Indian family and that these efforts have proved unsuccessful." § 1912(d). *Second,* a state court may not involuntarily terminate parental rights to an Indian child "in the absence of a determination, supported by evidence beyond a reasonable doubt, including testimony of qualified expert witnesses, that the continued custody of the child by the parent or Indian custodian is likely to result in serious emotional or physical damage to the child." § 1912(f). *Third,* with respect to adoptive placements for an Indian child under state law, "a preference shall be given, in the absence of good cause to the contrary, to a placement with (1) a member of the child's extended family; (2) other members of the Indian child's tribe; or (3) other Indian families." § 1915(a).

II

In this case, Birth Mother (who is predominantly Hispanic) and Biological Father (who is a member of the Cherokee Nation) became engaged in December 2008. One month later, Birth Mother informed Biological Father, who lived about four hours away, that she was pregnant. After learning of the pregnancy, Biological Father asked Birth Mother to move up the date of the wedding. He also refused to provide any financial support until after the two had married. The couple's relationship deteriorated, and Birth Mother broke off the engagement in May 2009. In June, Birth Mother sent Biological Father a text message asking if he would rather pay child support or relinquish his parental rights. Biological Father responded via text message that he relinquished his rights.

Birth Mother then decided to put Baby Girl up for adoption. Because Birth Mother believed that Biological Father had Cherokee Indian heritage, her attorney contacted the Cherokee Nation to determine whether Biological Father was formally enrolled. The inquiry letter misspelled Biological Father's first name and incorrectly stated his birthday, and the Cherokee Nation responded that, based on the information provided, it could not verify Biological Father's membership in the tribal records.

Working through a private adoption agency, Birth Mother selected Adoptive Couple, non-Indians living in South Carolina, to adopt Baby Girl. Adoptive Couple supported Birth Mother both emotionally and

financially throughout her pregnancy. Adoptive Couple was present at Baby Girl's birth in Oklahoma on September 15, 2009, and Adoptive Father even cut the umbilical cord. The next morning, Birth Mother signed forms relinquishing her parental rights and consenting to the adoption. Adoptive Couple initiated adoption proceedings in South Carolina a few days later, and returned there with Baby Girl. After returning to South Carolina, Adoptive Couple allowed Birth Mother to visit and communicate with Baby Girl.

It is undisputed that, for the duration of the pregnancy and the first four months after Baby Girl's birth, Biological Father provided no financial assistance to Birth Mother or Baby Girl, even though he had the ability to do so. Indeed, Biological Father "made no meaningful attempts to assume his responsibility of parenthood" during this period.

Approximately four months after Baby Girl's birth, Adoptive Couple served Biological Father with notice of the pending adoption. (This was the first notification that they had provided to Biological Father regarding the adoption proceeding.) Biological Father signed papers stating that he accepted service and that he was "not contesting the adoption." But Biological Father later testified that, at the time he signed the papers, he thought that he was relinquishing his rights to Birth Mother, not to Adoptive Couple.

Biological Father contacted a lawyer the day after signing the papers, and subsequently requested a stay of the adoption proceedings.[2] In the adoption proceedings, Biological Father sought custody and stated that he did not consent to Baby Girl's adoption. Moreover, Biological Father took a paternity test, which verified that he was Baby Girl's biological father.

[The South Carolina Supreme Court affirmed a family court order giving Father custody.]

III

. . . assuming for the sake of argument that he is a "parent," we hold that neither § 1912(f) nor § 1912(d) bars the termination of his parental rights.

A

Section 1912(f) addresses the involuntary termination of parental rights with respect to an Indian child. Specifically, § 1912(f) provides that "[n]o termination of parental rights may be ordered in such proceeding in the absence of a determination, supported by evidence beyond a reasonable doubt, . . . that the *continued custody* of the child by the parent or Indian custodian is likely to result in serious emotional or physical damage to the child." (Emphasis added.)

---

[2] Around the same time, the Cherokee Nation identified Biological Father as a registered member and concluded that Baby Girl was an "Indian child" as defined in the ICWA. The Cherokee Nation intervened in the litigation approximately three months later.

. . . Our reading of § 1912(f) comports with the statutory text demonstrating that the primary mischief the ICWA was designed to counteract was the unwarranted *removal* of Indian children from Indian families due to the cultural insensitivity and biases of social workers and state courts. The statutory text expressly highlights the primary problem that the statute was intended to solve: "an alarmingly high percentage of Indian families [were being] broken up by the *removal,* often unwarranted, of their children from them by nontribal public and private agencies." And if the legislative history of the ICWA is thought to be relevant, it further underscores that the Act was primarily intended to stem the unwarranted removal of Indian children from intact Indian families. . . . In sum, when, as here, the adoption of an Indian child is voluntarily and lawfully initiated by a non-Indian parent with sole custodial rights, the ICWA's primary goal of preventing the unwarranted removal of Indian children and the dissolution of Indian families is not implicated.

Under our reading of § 1912(f), Biological Father should not have been able to invoke § 1912(f) in this case, because he had never had legal or physical custody of Baby Girl as of the time of the adoption proceedings. . . .

B

Section 1912(d) provides that "[a]ny party" seeking to terminate parental rights to an Indian child under state law "shall satisfy the court that active efforts have been made to provide remedial services and rehabilitative programs designed *to prevent the breakup of the Indian family* and that these efforts have proved unsuccessful." (Emphasis added.) . . . Consistent with the statutory text, we hold that § 1912(d) applies only in cases where an Indian family's "breakup" would be precipitated by the termination of the parent's rights. . . . [W]hen an Indian parent abandons an Indian child prior to birth and that child has never been in the Indian parent's legal or physical custody, there is no "relationship" that would be "discontinu[ed]"—and no "effective entity" that would be "end[ed]"—by the termination of the Indian parent's rights. In such a situation, the "breakup of the Indian family" has long since occurred, and § 1912(d) is inapplicable.

In sum, the South Carolina Supreme Court erred in finding that § 1912(d) barred termination of Biological Father's parental rights.

IV

In the decision below, the South Carolina Supreme Court suggested that if it had terminated Biological Father's rights, then § 1915(a)'s preferences for the adoptive placement of an Indian child would have been applicable. In so doing, however, the court failed to recognize a critical limitation on the scope of § 1915(a).

Section 1915(a) provides that "[i]n any adoptive placement of an Indian child under State law, a preference shall be given, in the absence

of good cause to the contrary, to a placement with (1) a member of the child's extended family; (2) other members of the Indian child's tribe; or (3) other Indian families." Contrary to the South Carolina Supreme Court's suggestion, § 1915(a)'s preferences are inapplicable in cases where no alternative party has formally sought to adopt the child. This is because there simply is no "preference" to apply if no alternative party that is eligible to be preferred under § 1915(a) has come forward.

In this case, Adoptive Couple was the only party that sought to adopt Baby Girl in the Family Court or the South Carolina Supreme Court. Biological Father is not covered by § 1915(a) because he did not seek to *adopt* Baby Girl; instead, he argued that his parental rights should not be terminated in the first place. Moreover, Baby Girl's paternal grandparents never sought custody of Baby Girl.

* * *

The Indian Child Welfare Act was enacted to help preserve the cultural identity and heritage of Indian tribes, but under the State Supreme Court's reading, the Act would put certain vulnerable children at a great disadvantage solely because an ancestor—even a remote one—was an Indian. As the State Supreme Court read §§ 1912(d) and (f), a biological Indian father could abandon his child *in utero* and refuse any support for the birth mother—perhaps contributing to the mother's decision to put the child up for adoption—and then could play his ICWA trump card at the eleventh hour to override the mother's decision and the child's best interests. If this were possible, many prospective adoptive parents would surely pause before adopting any child who might possibly qualify as an Indian under the ICWA. Such an interpretation would raise equal protection concerns, but the plain text of §§ 1912(f) and (d) makes clear that neither provision applies in the present context. Nor do § 1915(a)'s rebuttable adoption preferences apply when no alternative party has formally sought to adopt the child. We therefore reverse the judgment of the South Carolina Supreme Court and remand the case for further proceedings not inconsistent with this opinion.

It is so ordered.

■ JUSTICE SCALIA, dissenting.

. . . While I am at it, I will add one thought. The Court's opinion, it seems to me, needlessly demeans the rights of parenthood. It has been the constant practice of the common law to respect the entitlement of those who bring a child into the world to raise that child. We do not inquire whether leaving a child with his parents is "in the best interest of the child." It sometimes is not; he would be better off raised by someone else. But parents have their rights, no less than children do. This father wants to raise his daughter, and the statute amply protects his right to do so. There is no reason in law or policy to dilute that protection.

■ JUSTICE SOTOMAYOR, with whom JUSTICE GINSBURG and JUSTICE KAGAN join, and with whom JUSTICE SCALIA joins in part, dissenting.

II

B

On a more general level, the majority intimates that ICWA grants Birth Father an undeserved windfall: in the majority's words, an "ICWA trump card" he can "play . . . at the eleventh hour to override the mother's decision and the child's best interests." The implicit argument is that Congress could not possibly have intended to recognize a parent-child relationship between Birth Father and Baby Girl that would have to be legally terminated (either by valid consent or involuntary termination) before the adoption could proceed.

But this supposed anomaly is illusory. In fact, the law of at least 15 States did precisely that at the time ICWA was passed. And the law of a number of States still does so.

Without doubt, laws protecting biological fathers' parental rights can lead—even outside the context of ICWA—to outcomes that are painful and distressing for both would-be adoptive families, who lose a much wanted child, and children who must make a difficult transition. On the other hand, these rules recognize that biological fathers have a valid interest in a relationship with their child. And children have a reciprocal interest in knowing their biological parents. These rules also reflect the understanding that the biological bond between a parent and a child is a strong foundation on which a stable and caring relationship may be built. Many jurisdictions apply a custodial preference for a fit natural parent over a party lacking this biological link. This preference is founded in the "presumption that fit parents act in the best interests of their children."

Balancing the legitimate interests of unwed biological fathers against the need for stability in a child's family situation is difficult, to be sure, and States have, over the years, taken different approaches to the problem. Some States, like South Carolina, have opted to hew to the constitutional baseline established by this Court's precedents and do not require a biological father's consent to adoption unless he has provided financial support during pregnancy. Other States, however, have decided to give the rights of biological fathers more robust protection and to afford them consent rights on the basis of their biological link to the child. At the time that ICWA was passed, as noted, over one-fourth of States did so.

ICWA, on a straightforward reading of the statute, is consistent with the law of those States that protected, and protect, birth fathers' rights more vigorously. This reading can hardly be said to generate an anomaly. ICWA, as all acknowledge, was "the product of rising concern . . . [about] abusive child welfare practices that resulted in the separation of large numbers of Indian children from their families." It stands to reason that the Act would not render the legal status of an Indian father's relationship with his biological child fragile, but would instead grant it a

degree of protection commensurate with the more robust state-law standards.

III

Because I would affirm the South Carolina Supreme Court on the ground that § 1912 bars the termination of Birth Father's parental rights, I would not reach the question of the applicability of the adoptive placement preferences of § 1915. I note, however, that the majority does not and cannot foreclose the possibility that on remand, Baby Girl's paternal grandparents or other members of the Cherokee Nation may formally petition for adoption of Baby Girl. If these parties do so, and if on remand Birth Father's parental rights are terminated so that an adoption becomes possible, they will then be entitled to consideration under the order of preference established in § 1915. The majority cannot rule prospectively that § 1915 would not apply to an adoption petition that has not yet been filed. Indeed, the statute applies "[i]n *any* adoptive placement of an Indian child under State law," 25 U.S.C. § 1915(a) (emphasis added), and contains no temporal qualifications. It would indeed be an odd result for this Court, in the name of the child's best interests, to purport to exclude from the proceedings possible custodians for Baby Girl, such as her paternal grandparents, who may have well-established relationships with her.

* * *

The majority opinion turns § 1912 upside down, reading it from bottom to top in order to reach a conclusion that is manifestly contrary to Congress' express purpose in enacting ICWA: preserving the familial bonds between Indian parents and their children and, more broadly, Indian tribes' relationships with the future citizens who are "vital to [their] continued existence and integrity."

The majority casts Birth Father as responsible for the painful circumstances in this case, suggesting that he intervened "at the eleventh hour to override the mother's decision and the child's best interests." I have no wish to minimize the trauma of removing a 27-month-old child from her adoptive family. It bears remembering, however, that Birth Father took action to assert his parental rights when Baby Girl was four months old, as soon as he learned of the impending adoption. As the South Carolina Supreme Court recognized, " '[h]ad the mandate of . . . ICWA been followed [in 2010], . . . much potential anguish might have been avoided[;] and in any case the law cannot be applied so as automatically to "reward those who obtain custody, whether lawfully or otherwise, and maintain it during any ensuing (and protracted) litigation." ' "

The majority's hollow literalism distorts the statute and ignores Congress' purpose in order to rectify a perceived wrong that, while heartbreaking at the time, was a correct application of federal law and that in any case cannot be undone. Baby Girl has now resided with her

father for 18 months. However difficult it must have been for her to leave Adoptive Couple's home when she was just over 2 years old, it will be equally devastating now if, at the age of 3 1/2, she is again removed from her home and sent to live halfway across the country. Such a fate is not foreordained, of course. But it can be said with certainty that the anguish this case has caused will only be compounded by today's decision.

I believe that the South Carolina Supreme Court's judgment was correct, and I would affirm it. I respectfully dissent.

NOTES AND QUESTIONS

1. *Justice Alito's Opinion*. Why did Congress pass ICWA? Justice Alito addressed three provisions of the statute to conclude that ICWA did not bar Adoptive Couple from custody of Baby Girl:

> 25 U.S.C. § 1912(f)—which bars involuntary termination of a parent's rights in the absence of a heightened showing that serious harm to the Indian child is likely to result from the parent's "continued custody" of the child—does not apply when, as here, the relevant parent never had custody of the child.
>
> We further hold that § 1912(d)—which conditions involuntary termination of parental rights with respect to an Indian child on a showing that remedial efforts have been made to prevent the "breakup of the Indian family"—is inapplicable when, as here, the parent abandoned the Indian child before birth and never had custody of the child.
>
> Finally, we clarify that § 1915(a), which provides placement preferences for the adoption of Indian children, does not bar a non-Indian family like Adoptive Couple from adopting an Indian child when no other eligible candidates have sought to adopt the child.

How do you assess his conclusion about each of these three sections of the statute?

2. *Justice Sotomayor's Dissent*. What does Justice Sotomayor conclude about how these three sections of the statute should be interpreted?

3. *Justice Scalia's Dissent*. Justice Scalia stated "We do not inquire whether leaving a child with his parents is 'in the best interest of the child.' It sometimes is not; he would be better off raised by someone else." Do you think courts should make this inquiry? Do you think that a parent's right should trump a child's best interest? How would you assess a child's best interest?

4. *Fathers*. Do you think the Court paid too little attention to the biological father's right to custody of a child? What do you think of the discussion among the Justices about the father's "abandonment" of Baby Girl? Did the father's conduct influence your assessment of whether he should have custody of Baby Girl or not?

5. *Parents*. Does this case make you rethink the importance of biology to parenthood? In the surrogate motherhood context, we saw that courts

frequently defer to "intended" parents over parents with biological connections to the child. Are there intended parents in this case? Should adoptive parents be viewed as intended parents, similar to those who use surrogacy, or are adoptive parents morally and legally different from couples who use surrogacy to bear a child?

6. *Indian Commerce Clause.* In a separate concurrence, Justice Thomas argued that adoptions are usually regulated by state law and that Congress lacks the authority to regulate Indian adoptions. He rejected the argument that the Indian Commerce Clause of Article I, Section 8 gives Congress authority over this area. Recall that Justice Thomas made a similar Commerce Clause argument about the partial-birth abortion statute in Section A. Should all the laws about reproduction, parenthood and abortion be left to state legislatures without interference from the federal government?

7. *Post-Adoptive Couple v. Baby Girl.* ICWA was enacted in 1978 to "discourage adoptions outside tribes." Robert Barnes, Despite Justices' Ruling, Baby Veronica's Case is Far From Over, Wash. Post, Sept. 16, 2013, at A15. Although the Supreme Court held that ICWA does not apply when "the parent abandoned the Indian child before birth and never had custody of the child," the adoptive couple in the case above struggled to regain custody of Baby Veronica—"Baby Girl"—due to the number of courts involved, including various South Carolina and Oklahoma courts. See id.

On remand, the Supreme Court of South Carolina terminated the parental rights of the Indian father and granted custody to the adoptive couple. Id. However, the Cherokee Nation Court awarded temporary custody to the Indian father and the Oklahoma Supreme Court prohibited the adoptive couple from taking custody of Veronica pending the Indian father's appeal. Id. Finally, the Oklahoma Supreme Court decided it did not have jurisdiction over the child, so it removed the stay and ordered that Veronica be returned to the adoptive couple. See "Baby Veronica" Handed over to Adoptive Parents, Cherokee Nation Confirms, CBSNews, Sept. 24, 2013, at http://www.cbsnews.com/news/baby-veronica-handed-over-to-adoptive-parents-cherokee-nation-confirms/. It took an exhaustion of all legal remedies before the adoptive couple could regain custody of Baby Veronica. Barnes, *infra*. After the Indian father ceased litigation, he and Veronica's adoptive parents attempted to form a relationship where he could still play some role in Veronica's life. "Baby Veronica" Handed over to Adoptive Parents, Cherokee Nation Confirms, *infra*.

Should the state courts have deferred to the Cherokee Nation Court and awarded custody to the father?

Does the Uniform Parentage Act, excerpted below, help you to answer the questions about parenthood identified in this section? Does it give you answers to the new problems identified in Section C?

Uniform Parentage Act (2017)

NATIONAL CONFERENCE OF COMMISSIONERS ON UNIFORM STATE LAWS.

PREFATORY NOTE

UPA (2017) makes five major changes to the UPA. First, UPA (2017) seeks to ensure the equal treatment of children born to same-sex couples. UPA (2002) was written in gendered terms, and its provisions presumed that couples consist of one man and one woman.

... UPA (2017) helps state legislatures address this potential constitutional infirmity by amending provisions throughout the act so that they address and apply equally to same-sex couples. These changes include broadening the presumption, acknowledgment, genetic testing, and assisted reproduction articles to make them gender-neutral.

UPA (2017) updates the act to address this potential constitutional infirmity by amending provisions throughout the act so that they address and apply equally to same-sex couples. These changes include broadening the presumption, acknowledgment, genetic testing, and assisted reproduction articles to make them gender-neutral.

Second, UPA (2017) includes a provision for the establishment of a de facto parent as a legal parent of a child. Most states recognize and extend at least some parental rights to people who have functioned as parents to children but who are unconnected to those children through either biology or marriage. These states span the country; ranging from Massachusetts, to West Virginia, to North and South Carolina, to Texas. Some states recognize such people under a variety of equitable doctrines—sometimes called de facto parentage, or in loco parentis, or the psychological parent doctrine. Other states extend rights to such people through broad third party standing statutes. And, more recently, states have begun to treat such people as legal parents under their parentage provisions. Two states—Delaware and Maine—achieve this result by including "de facto parents" in their definition of parent in their state versions of the Uniform Parentage Act. Other states, including California, Colorado, Kansas, New Hampshire, and New Mexico, reached this conclusion by applying their existing parentage provisions to such persons. New Section 609 provides a process for the establishment of parentage by those who claim to be de facto parents.

Third, UPA (2017) includes a provision that precludes establishment of a parent-child relationship by the perpetrator of a sexual assault that resulted in the conception of the child. The United States Congress adopted the Rape Survivor Child Custody Act in 2015, which provides incentives for states to enact "a law that allows the mother of any child that was conceived by rape to seek court-ordered termination of the parental rights of her rapist with regard to that child, which the court shall grant upon clear and convincing evidence of rape." In 2017, at least 17 state legislatures were considering bills to enact such statutes. New Section 614 provides language to implement the federal law.

Fourth, UPA (2017) updates the surrogacy provisions to reflect developments in that area. States have been particularly slow to enact Article 8 of UPA (2002). Eleven states adopted versions of UPA (2002). Of these 11 states, only two—Texas and Utah—enacted the surrogacy provisions based on Article 8 of UPA (2002). At least five of the 11 states that enacted UPA (2002) enacted surrogacy provisions that are *not* premised on the 2002 UPA. These states include: Delaware (permitting) (enacted 2013); Illinois (permitting) (enacted 2004); Maine (permitting) (enacted 2015); North Dakota (banning) (enacted 2005); and Washington (banning compensated) (enacted 1989).

The fact that very few states enacted Article 8 is likely the result of a confluence of factors. One likely factor is the controversial nature of surrogacy itself. But the fact that four of the states that enacted UPA (2002) have provisions permitting surrogacy that are not modeled on Article 8 of UPA (2002) suggests that the small number of enactments is also affected by the substance of Article 8. Accordingly, UPA (2017) updates the surrogacy provisions to make them more consistent with current surrogacy practice.

Finally, UPA (2017) includes a new article—Article 9—that addresses the right of children born through assisted reproductive technology to access medical and identifying information regarding any gamete providers. Based on data from 2015, the CDC reports that "approximately 1.6% of all infants born in the United States every year are conceived using ART." Data suggest that this percentage continues to increase. Gaia Bernstein, *Unintended Consequences: Prohibitions on Gamete Donor Anonymity and the Fragile Practice of Surrogacy*, 10 Ind. Health L. Rev. 291, 298 (2013) (noting that "from 2004 to 2008 the number of IVF cycles used for gestational surrogacy grew by 60%, the number of births by gestational surrogates grew by 53% and the number of babies born to gestational surrogates grew by 89%"). Accordingly, it is increasingly important for states to address the right of children to access information about their gamete donor. Article 9 does not require disclosure of the identity of a gamete donor, but it does require gamete banks and fertility clinics to ask donors if they want to have their identifying information disclosed when the resulting child attains 18 years of age. It does require disclosure of non-identifying medical history of the gamete donor.

UNIFORM PARENTAGE ACT

ARTICLE 2

PARENT-CHILD RELATIONSHIP

SECTION 201. ESTABLISHMENT OF PARENT-CHILD RELATIONSHIP. A parent-child relationship is established between an individual and a child if:

(1) the individual gives birth to the child[, except as otherwise provided in [Article] 8];

(2) there is a presumption under Section 204 of the individual's parentage of the child, unless the presumption is overcome in a judicial proceeding or a valid denial of parentage is made under [Article] 3;

(3) the individual is adjudicated a parent of the child under [Article] 6;

(4) the individual adopts the child;

(5) the individual acknowledges parentage of the child under [Article] 3, unless the acknowledgment is rescinded under Section 308 or successfully challenged under [Article] 3 or 6; [or]

(6) the individual's parentage of the child is established under [Article] 7[; or

(7) the individual's parentage of the child is established under [Article] 8].

ARTICLE 7

ASSISTED REPRODUCTION

SECTION 701. SCOPE OF [ARTICLE]. This [article] does not apply to the birth of a child conceived by sexual intercourse [or assisted reproduction under a surrogacy agreement under [Article] 8].

SECTION 702. PARENTAL STATUS OF DONOR. A donor is not a parent of a child conceived by means of assisted reproduction.

SECTION 703. PARENTAGE OF CHILD OF ASSISTED REPRODUCTION.

An individual who consents under Section 704 to assisted reproduction by a woman with the intent to be a parent of a child conceived by the assisted reproduction is a parent of the child.

SECTION 704. CONSENT TO ASSISTED REPRODUCTION.

(a) Except as otherwise provided in subsection (b), the consent described in Section 703 must be in a record signed by a woman giving birth to a child conceived by assisted reproduction and an individual who intends to be a parent of the child.

(b) Failure to consent in a record as required by subsection (a), before, on, or after birth of the child, does not preclude the court from finding consent to parentage if:

(1) the woman or the individual proves by clear-and-convincing evidence the existence of an express agreement entered into before conception that the individual and the woman intended they both would be parents of the child; or

(2) the woman and the individual for the first two years of the child's life, including any period of temporary absence, resided together in the same household with the child and both openly held out the child as the individual's child, unless the individual dies or

becomes incapacitated before the child attains two years of age or the child dies before the child attains two years of age, in which case the court may find consent under this subsection to parentage if a party proves by clear-and-convincing evidence that the woman and the individual intended to reside together in the same household with the child and both intended the individual would openly hold out the child as the individual's child, but the individual was prevented from carrying out that intent by death or incapacity.

SECTION 705. LIMITATION ON SPOUSE'S DISPUTE OF PARENTAGE.

(a) Except as otherwise provided in subsection (b), an individual who, at the time of a child's birth, is the spouse of the woman who gave birth to the child by assisted reproduction may not challenge the individual's parentage of the child unless:

(1) not later than two years after the birth of the child, the individual commences a proceeding to adjudicate the individual's parentage of the child; and

(2) the court finds the individual did not consent to the assisted reproduction, before, on, or after birth of the child, or withdrew consent under Section 707.

(b) A proceeding to adjudicate a spouse's parentage of a child born by assisted reproduction may be commenced at any time if the court determines:

(1) the spouse neither provided a gamete for, nor consented to, the assisted reproduction;

(2) the spouse and the woman who gave birth to the child have not cohabited since the probable time of assisted reproduction; and

(3) the spouse never openly held out the child as the spouse's child.

(c) This section applies to a spouse's dispute of parentage even if the spouse's marriage is declared invalid after assisted reproduction occurs.

ARTICLE 8

SURROGACY AGREEMENT

Sections 801 through 807 establish the rules that apply to both types of surrogacy agreements. Sections 808 through 812 include rules that apply only to gestational surrogacy agreements. Sections 813 through 818 include rules that apply only to genetic surrogacy agreements.

SECTION 804. REQUIREMENTS OF GESTATIONAL OR GENETIC SURROGACY AGREEMENT: CONTENT.

(a) A surrogacy agreement must comply with the following requirements:

(1) A surrogate agrees to attempt to become pregnant by means of assisted reproduction.

(2) Except as otherwise provided in Sections 811, 814, and 815, the surrogate and the surrogate's spouse or former spouse, if any, have no claim to parentage of a child conceived by assisted reproduction under the agreement.

(3) The surrogate's spouse, if any, must acknowledge and agree to comply with the obligations imposed on the surrogate by the agreement.

(4) Except as otherwise provided in Sections 811, 814, and 815, the intended parent or, if there are two intended parents, each one jointly and severally, immediately on birth will be the exclusive parent or parents of the child, regardless of number of children born or gender or mental or physical condition of each child.

(5) Except as otherwise provided in Sections 811, 814, and 815, the intended parent or, if there are two intended parents, each parent jointly and severally, immediately on birth will assume responsibility for the financial support of the child, regardless of number of children born or gender or mental or physical condition of each child.

(6) The agreement must include information disclosing how each intended parent will cover the surrogacy-related expenses of the surrogate and the medical expenses of the child. If health-care coverage is used to cover the medical expenses, the disclosure must include a summary of the health-care policy provisions related to coverage for surrogate pregnancy, including any possible liability of the surrogate, third-party-liability liens, other insurance coverage, and any notice requirement that could affect coverage or liability of the surrogate. Unless the agreement expressly provides otherwise, the review and disclosure do not constitute legal advice. If the extent of coverage is uncertain, a statement of that fact is sufficient to comply with this paragraph.

(7) The agreement must permit the surrogate to make all health and welfare decisions regarding herself and her pregnancy. This [act] does not enlarge or diminish the surrogate's right to terminate her pregnancy.

(8) The agreement must include information about each party's right under this [article] to terminate the surrogacy agreement.

(b) A surrogacy agreement may provide for:

(1) payment of consideration and reasonable expenses; and

(2) reimbursement of specific expenses if the agreement is terminated under this [article].

(c) A right created under a surrogacy agreement is not assignable and there is no third-party beneficiary of the agreement other than the child.

SECTION 805. SURROGACY AGREEMENT: EFFECT OF SUBSEQUENT CHANGE OF MARITAL STATUS.

(a) Unless a surrogacy agreement expressly provides otherwise:

(1) the marriage of a surrogate after the agreement is signed by all parties does not affect the validity of the agreement, her spouse's consent to the agreement is not required, and her spouse is not a presumed parent of a child conceived by assisted reproduction under the agreement; and

(2) the [divorce, dissolution, annulment, declaration of invalidity, legal separation, or separate maintenance] of the surrogate after the agreement is signed by all parties does not affect the validity of the agreement.

(b) Unless a surrogacy agreement expressly provides otherwise:

(1) the marriage of an intended parent after the agreement is signed by all parties does not affect the validity of a surrogacy agreement, the consent of the spouse of the intended parent is not required, and the spouse of the intended parent is not, based on the agreement, a parent of a child conceived by assisted reproduction under the agreement; and

(2) the [divorce, dissolution, annulment, declaration of invalidity, legal separation, or separate maintenance] of an intended parent after the agreement is signed by all parties does not affect the validity of the agreement and, except as otherwise provided in Section 814, the intended parents are the parents of the child.

SECTION 808. TERMINATION OF GESTATIONAL SURROGACY AGREEMENT.

(a) A party to a gestational surrogacy agreement may terminate the agreement, at any time before an embryo transfer, by giving notice of termination in a record to all other parties. If an embryo transfer does not result in a pregnancy, a party may terminate the agreement at any time before a subsequent embryo transfer.

(b) Unless a gestational surrogacy agreement provides otherwise, on termination of the agreement under subsection (a), the parties are released from the agreement, except that each intended parent remains responsible for expenses that are reimbursable under the agreement and incurred by the gestational surrogate through the date of termination.

(c) Except in a case involving fraud, neither a gestational surrogate nor the surrogate's spouse or former spouse, if any, is liable to the intended parent or parents for a penalty or liquidated damages, for terminating a gestational surrogacy agreement under this section.

SECTION 809. PARENTAGE UNDER GESTATIONAL SURROGACY AGREEMENT.

(a) Except as otherwise provided in subsection (c) or Section 810(b) or 812, on birth of a child conceived by assisted reproduction under a gestational surrogacy agreement, each intended parent is, by operation of law, a parent of the child.

(b) Except as otherwise provided in subsection (c) or Section 812, neither a gestational surrogate nor the surrogate's spouse or former spouse, if any, is a parent of the child.

(c) If a child is alleged to be a genetic child of the woman who agreed to be a gestational surrogate, the court shall order genetic testing of the child. If the child is a genetic child of the woman who agreed to be a gestational surrogate, parentage must be determined based on [Articles] 1 through 6.

(d) Except as otherwise provided in subsection (c) or Section 810(b) or 812, if, due to a clinical or laboratory error, a child conceived by assisted reproduction under a gestational surrogacy agreement is not genetically related to an intended parent or a donor who donated to the intended parent or parents, each intended parent, and not the gestational surrogate and the surrogate's spouse or former spouse, if any, is a parent of the child, subject to any other claim of parentage.

SPECIAL RULES FOR GENETIC SURROGACY AGREEMENT

SECTION 813. REQUIREMENTS TO VALIDATE GENETIC SURROGACY AGREEMENT.

(a) Except as otherwise provided in Section 816, to be enforceable, a genetic surrogacy agreement must be validated by the [designate court]. A proceeding to validate the agreement must be commenced before assisted reproduction related to the surrogacy agreement.

(b) The court shall issue an order validating a genetic surrogacy agreement if the court finds that:

(1) Sections 802, 803, and 804 are satisfied; and

(2) all parties entered into the agreement voluntarily and understand its terms. (c) An individual who terminates under Section 814 a genetic surrogacy agreement shall file notice of the termination with the court. On receipt of the notice, the court shall vacate any order issued under subsection (b). An individual who does not notify the court of the termination of the agreement is subject to sanctions.

SECTION 814. TERMINATION OF GENETIC SURROGACY AGREEMENT.

(a) A party to a genetic surrogacy agreement may terminate the agreement as follows:

(1) An intended parent who is a party to the agreement may terminate the agreement at any time before a gamete or embryo transfer by giving notice of termination in a record to all other parties. If a gamete or embryo transfer does not result in a pregnancy, a party may terminate the agreement at any time before a subsequent gamete or embryo transfer. The notice of termination must be attested by a notarial officer or witnessed.

(2) A genetic surrogate who is a party to the agreement may withdraw consent to the agreement any time before 72 hours after the birth of a child conceived by assisted reproduction under the agreement. To withdraw consent, the genetic surrogate must execute a notice of termination in a record stating the surrogate's intent to terminate the agreement. The notice of termination must be attested by a notarial officer or witnessed and be delivered to each intended parent any time before 72 hours after the birth of the child.

(b) On termination of the genetic surrogacy agreement under subsection (a), the parties are released from all obligations under the agreement except that each intended parent remains responsible for all expenses incurred by the surrogate through the date of termination which are reimbursable under the agreement. Unless the agreement provides otherwise, the surrogate is not entitled to any non-expense related compensation paid for serving as a surrogate.

(c) Except in a case involving fraud, neither a genetic surrogate nor the surrogate's spouse or former spouse, if any, is liable to the intended parent or parents for a penalty or liquidated damages, for terminating a genetic surrogacy agreement under this section.

ARTICLE 9

INFORMATION ABOUT DONOR

SECTION 904. DECLARATION REGARDING IDENTITY DISCLOSURE.

(a) A gamete bank or fertility clinic licensed in this state which collects gametes from a donor shall:

(1) provide the donor with information in a record about the donor's choice regarding identity disclosure; and

(2) obtain a declaration from the donor regarding identity disclosure.

(b) A gamete bank or fertility clinic licensed in this state shall give a donor the choice to sign a declaration, attested by a notarial officer or witnessed, that either:

(1) states that the donor agrees to disclose the donor's identity to a child conceived by assisted reproduction with the donor's gametes on request once the child attains 18 years of age; or

(2) states that the donor does not agree presently to disclose the donor's identity to the child.

(c) A gamete bank or fertility clinic licensed in this state shall permit a donor who has signed a declaration under subsection (b)(2) to withdraw the declaration at any time by signing a declaration under subsection (b)(1).

SECTION 905. DISCLOSURE OF IDENTIFYING INFORMATION AND MEDICAL HISTORY.

(a) On request of a child conceived by assisted reproduction who attains 18 years of age, a gamete bank or fertility clinic licensed in this state which collected, stored, or released for use the gametes used in the assisted reproduction shall make a good-faith effort to provide the child with identifying information of the donor who provided the gametes, unless the donor signed and did not withdraw a declaration under Section 904(b)(2). If the donor signed and did not withdraw the declaration, the gamete bank or fertility clinic shall make a good-faith effort to notify the donor, who may elect under Section 904(c) to withdraw the donor's declaration.

(b) Regardless whether a donor signed a declaration under Section 904(b)(2), on request by a child conceived by assisted reproduction who attains 18 years of age, or, if the child is a minor, by a parent or guardian of the child, a gamete bank or fertility clinic licensed in this state shall make a good-faith effort to provide the child or, if the child is a minor, the parent or guardian of the child, access to nonidentifying medical history of the donor.

C. LOOKING AHEAD: DESIGNER PARENTHOOD

1. THREE-WAY PARENTHOOD—HOW MANY PARENTS?

Even with IVF and egg freezing, a mother can give birth to a child with deleterious mutations in his or her mitochondrial DNA (mtDNA), which can lead to, among other problems, heart conditions, liver failure, and blindness. Ian Sample, "Three-Parent" Babies Explained, The Guardian, Feb. 3, 2015, at S1. Approximately 1,000 to 4,000 children born in the United States will have an mtDNA mutation with symptoms ranging from mild to severe. Marcy Darnovsky, Genetically Modified Babies, N.Y. Times, Feb. 23, 2014, at A25. These mutations in the mtDNA are passed along only by the mother, not the father. Gene Editing Technique Could Prevent Inherited Diseases, Nursing Times, May 2, 2015, at http://www.nursingtimes.net/nursing-practice/specialisms/genetics/gene-editing-technique-could-prevent-inherited-diseases/5084281.article. Studies suggest that women begin to become infertile after the age of thirty due to changes in their mtDNA. Maurice Bernstein, Tampering With Evolution? "Three Parent Embryos", Bioethics.net, Mar.

4, 2014, available at http://www.bioethics.net/2014/03/tampering-with-evolution-three-parent-embryos/.

To prevent the mutations, scientists have developed a process that creates an embryo from the eggs of two women and the sperm obtained from one man. Sample, *supra*. The DNA from the egg of the woman that carries the mutation can be transferred into the donor egg that does not have the mutation. For a review of the technology, see Hana Carolina et al., Three-Parent Babies: Mitochondrial Replacement Therapies, 27 JBRA Assist Reprod. 189 (2020), https://www.ncbi.nlm.nih.gov/pmc/articles/PMC7169912/.

Go to the website to see an illustration of this process.

The result is a woman with mutated mtDNA carrying an embryo that contains genetic material from the three donors, but does not carry the mutation. Id. The child would end up having inherited eye and hair color, e.g., but not the mutation. Sample, *supra*. This process carries many questions. Consider: Is this process ethical? Who would be considered the actual parents of the child? What if the donation is not used; who owns it? Do the benefits of this process outweigh the potential ethical risks? What risks may arise from mixing mtDNA?

The House of Commons of the United Kingdom has approved mitochondrial DNA replacement. According to Professor Caplan, the usual three arguments against the transplants are "safety; creating babies with three parents; and the danger of opening the doors to more genetic engineering." Do you think any of these concerns provides sufficient reason to ban the procedure? See Arthur Caplan, Is It Ethical To Create Babies from Three DNA Sources? Absolutely, Wired, Feb. 3, 2015, at http://www.wired.com/2015/02/ethical-create-babies-three-dna-sources-absolutely/ (concluding the science from studies of monkeys and human embryos now demonstrates the process is safe; babies have had three parents before; genetic engineering concerns are overstated).

If scientists can manipulate DNA to eliminate certain defects, consider what could come next. What would happen if this new process of eliminating certain defects led to genetic engineering? Some state that the mtDNA process does not involve changing existing genes, just eliminating certain harmful ones. Matt, Smith, FDA Considering 3-Parent Embryos, CNN, Feb. 27, 2014, available at http://www.cnn.com/2014/02/26/health/ivf-mitochondria/. Others, however, believe that moving in this direction is moving one step closer to consumer eugenics, by making the "perfect baby" that is taller, smarter, or faster than it otherwise would have been. Id. Do you think these are legitimate concerns? How could legislation remedy these concerns? What regulations would need to be in place? What problems could arise from piecing together a future child? What are the ethical concerns? Where would the genetic engineering stop? What benefits could come from genetic engineering? Would you want to "design" your own child?

2. FORCED PARENTHOOD?

What if a parent voluntarily agreed to create embryos for the future, and then withdrew his or her consent before the embryo was implanted in the woman's uterus because the individual no longer intended to parent the child? For example, a thirty-eight year old female doctor, who has never been married or has never had children, finds out that she has cancer. She needs to start chemotherapy to get rid of the cancer, but the chemotherapy will render her infertile. So, she asks her boyfriend of five months to artificially inseminate embryos so that she can have a biological child. The boyfriend agrees. However, a few months later, the boyfriend changes his mind and decides he does not want to become a parent. Should the boyfriend be forced into parenthood? If so, should he be legally responsible for the child (i.e. legal custody, physical custody, or child support)? Should the woman not be able to use the embryos even though she relied on his consent before she started chemotherapy? See Roy Strom, Frozen Embryos: Who Do They Belong to?, Chicago Lawyer, Sept. 1, 2014, at http://chicagolawyermagazine.com/Articles/2014/09/Frozen–Embryos–Legal–Rights.aspx.

What should happen if frozen embryos are unclaimed? See John Robertson, Two Year Old Boy to Inherit 11 Frozen Embryos, Harvard Law, Feb. 23, 2014, available at https://blogs.law.harvard.edu/billofhealth/2014/02/23/ (discussing whether embryos should be considered property). Should anyone be allowed to adopt them? What happens if a donor wishes to become the parent of the child after the donation? Consider California Senate Bill 115, proposed legislation that discusses how a sperm donor can establish paternity. See Naomi Cahn & June Carbone, When Does a Father Become One?, L.A. Times, Aug. 12, 2013, at A13.

> **Go to** the website to see the proposed legislation. Would you vote for it?

3. DELAYED PARENTHOOD?

Egg freezing, along with sperm donation, are other options women may utilize to help increase and prolong fertility. Seema Mohapatra, Using Egg Freezing to Extend the Biological Clock: Fertility Insurance or False Hope?, 8 Harv. L. & Pol'y Rev. 381 (2014); Molly Elizalde, How Egg Freezing Went Mainstream, N.Y. Times, Apr. 17, 2020, https://www.nytimes.com/2020/04/17/parenting/fertility/egg-freezing.html. Silicon Valley companies Apple and Facebook attracted a lot of attention after they announced they would pay for egg freezing for women employees. The process can cost up to $20,000. Tech companies traditionally haven't had many women employees, and this was seen as a means of hiring more women workers. See David Orentlicher, Egg Freezing and Women's Decision Making, Bill of Health, Oct. 17, 2014, at http://blogs.law.harvard.edu/billofhealth/2014/10/17/egg-freezing-and-womens-decision-

making/; Linda Wertheimer, Silicon Valley Companies Add New Benefit for Women: Egg-Freezing, NPR, Oct. 17, 2014, at http://www.npr.org/blogs/alltechconsidered/2014/10/17/356765423/silicon-valley-companies-add-new-benefit-for-women-egg-freezing.

Is this a good advancement for women's equality? "After all, if a woman can delay procreation and put in long hours at the office, why shouldn't she do so?" Wertheimer, *supra*. Should the companies provide more child support for workers at the office rather than more opportunities to freeze eggs? See id. ("I could teach this idea round or teach it flat. I mean, this could be a generous offer to working women who are trying to make sensible career decisions. Or it could be a nasty warning that pregnancies and babies and advancement in high tech don't really go together.").

Go to the website to watch the videos about egg freezing. Would you participate in a clinical trial about egg freezing?

However positive these options are, opponents still find problems with them due to the lack of consumer protections, the cost, and doctors treating the options solely like a business. See Karen Brown, Can Fertility Clinics Deliver on Promises?, WBUR, Aug. 12, 2013, available at https://wbur.org/2013/08/12/fertility-industry-deliver; Mohapatra, 8 Harv. L. Pol'y Rev. 381–90. How much consumer protection did you write into your sample surrogacy law?

4. SAVIOR SIBLINGS?

Parents can now use pre-implantation genetic diagnosis (PGD) to figure out whether an embryo is healthy and to decide whether to bear a child. The combination of PGD with IVF also leads to the possibility that parents of an unhealthy child could create a "savior sibling" whose bone marrow, blood, or other biological material could be used to help the unhealthy child. Should there be regulations on the savior sibling practice, or is this a matter of parental autonomy? Do you think parents can be good parents to their savior sibling children? What about using IVF and PGD to create an heir, continue a legacy, serve as a playmate, strengthen a relationship or even save a marriage? See Zachary Shapiro, Savior Siblings in the United States, Bill of Health, Oct. 23, 2014, at http://blogs.law.harvard.edu/billofhealth/2014/10/23/savior-siblings-in-the-united-states/.

Go to the website and learn about PGD.

Has technology really changed anything about the issue of savior siblings? Twenty years ago, Mary and Abe Ayala decided to have a baby who could serve as a bone marrow donor for their daughter, Anissa. Doctors said Anissa, then 16, would die unless she received a bone marrow transplant. The Ayalas conceived their daughter Marissa after they were unable to find a matching donor for Anissa. Against long odds,

Marissa was a match and became a bone marrow donor when she was fourteen months old. Marissa graduated from college in 2013. Anissa's leukemia has been in remission for many years. See Original 'Savior Sibling' Marissa Ayala Who Sparked Ethics Storm 20 Years Ago When She Was Born Just to Save Life of Leukaemia-Stricken Sister Graduates from College, Daily Mail, May 23, 2013, at http://www.dailymail.co.uk/news/article–2329429/Marissa–Ayala-graduates-college-decades-saving-life-leukemia-stricken-sister.html. Would it make a moral or legal difference if parents used IVF and PGD to do the same thing? Why?

5. MATERNAL IMPRISONMENT AND INFANTICIDE?

According to Indiana law, a "person who knowingly or intentionally terminates a human pregnancy with an intention other than to produce a live birth or to remove a dead fetus commits feticide, a Level 3 felony." Ind. Code 35–42–1–6.

Which of the following women should be prosecuted for feticide after suffering a miscarriage?

- Bei Shuai, who became depressed and attempted suicide while pregnant; she survived, but the fetus did not. Sally Kolm, Indiana "Feticide" Charge is the Latest Fallout from States' Strict Anti-Abortion Laws, U.S. News, Aug. 27, 2014.
- Christine Taylor, who became anxious during the second trimester of her pregnancy that her husband might leave her. During the anxiety, she tripped and fell in her house. She told the hospital nurse that she didn't feel sure about having the baby. Michele Goodwin, Fetal Protection Laws: Moral Panic and the New Constitutional Battlefront, 102 Cal. L. Rev. 781, 806 (2014).

Professor Goodwin has explained that the criminalization of mothers does terrible things for maternal and fetal health; "children of incarcerated mothers are one of the most at-risk groups in American society." Michele Goodwin, Policing the Womb: Invisible Women and the Criminalization of Motherhood 202 (2020). The medical relationship with patients is also undermined by the growing requests the law puts on nurses and doctors to become informants about what women are doing with their prenatal health. Fetal protection laws, which were supposed to protect women from domestic violence, are instead used to intervene in and sanction women's pregnancies. Id.

What do you think of Goodwin's argument that

> medical professionals are ten times more likely to report African American pregnant women to state disciplinary authorities if they test positive for illicit substances . . . Researchers found that only 1.1 percent of pregnant white women testing positive

> for illicit drug ingestion are reported, compared to 10.7 percent of Black women?

Id. at 201.

In Chapter 4, we examine the role of the bioethical principle of justice in health care by considering how health care and organs should be distributed.

CHAPTER 4

JUSTICE: HOW SHOULD HEALTH CARE AND ORGANS BE DISTRIBUTED?

Introduction. In Chapter 3, we built on our knowledge of privacy in the context of bodily autonomy and how it relates to reproduction, abortion, and surrogacy. We learned about the Supreme Court's different views regarding partial birth abortion statutes in *Carhart I* and *II*. We learned that States may have an interest in protecting women from the regret of obtaining a partial birth abortion. For example, Justice Kennedy wrote in his opinion that:

> The State has an interest in ensuring so grave a choice is well informed. It is self-evident that a mother who comes to regret her choice to abort must struggle with grief more anguished and sorrow more profound when she learns, . . . that she allowed a doctor to pierce the skull and vacuum the fast-developing brain of her unborn child, a child assuming the human form.

Gonzales v. Carhart, 550 U.S. 124, 159–60 (2007). After *Carhart I* and *II*, we looked at different state statutes that attempted to regulate abortions, such as the Arizona Fetal Pain Bill and the Texas Sonogram Bill. We focused on how these regulations and their judicial decision-counterparts comport with the concept of privacy and bodily autonomy. Finally, we shifted the lens to look at adoption, surrogacy, and other technological advances in the field of reproduction.

In this chapter, we examine another principle that guides bioethics—the principle of justice. In philosophy, the concept of justice requires that every person receive his or her due, and usually examines what persons are entitled to as a matter of human rights. Questions of justice focus on the fair and equitable distribution of society's resources.

In the American health care system, two types of questions about the just distribution of resources have received constant attention over the last forty years. The first involves the question of health care itself. Do individuals have a right to health care? Is health care something that is due to them as human persons? If so, how can the law ensure that this right is protected? The second question involves the distribution of scarce resources to people in need, especially to people who need organ transplants. In the United States, as of September 2020, there were more than 109,000 men, women and children candidates waiting for transplant on the U.S. national waiting list. 39,718 transplants took place in 2019. 17 people die each day waiting for a transplant. Although

90% of adults support organ donation, only 60% are signed up to be donors. Dep't of Health & Human Services, Organ Donation Statistics, at http://www.organdonor.gov/about/graphdescription.html. More than half the people on the transplant list are from a racial or ethnic minority because some end-stage organ diseases are more common in them than in the rest of the population. For example, African Americans, Native Hawaiians, Asians and Pacific Islanders are three times more likely to suffer end stage kidney disease than Whites, and Native Americans four times more likely to have diabetes. Id. at https://www.organdonor.gov/about/facts-terms/donation-faqs.html.

Practice Exercise: Go to the website or to https://www.organdonor.gov/register.html and see how you can register to be an organ donor in your state.

How should these organs be distributed in a just and fair manner? In a 1974 article, Professor Gene Outka identified five standard accounts of social justice and applied them to health care. The five relevant theories of justice are:

I. To each according to his merit or desert.

II. To each according to his societal contribution.

III. To each according to his contribution in satisfying whatever is freely desired by others in the open marketplace of supply and demand.

IV. To each according to his needs.

V. Similar treatment for similar cases.

Gene Outka, Social Justice and Equal Access to Health Care, 2 J. Religious Ethics 11 (1974). Keep these five theories of justice in mind as you read this chapter.

In the United States, health care is accessed through the purchase of insurance. Indeed, there is "no other product that is purchased with insurance benefits. . . . [I]ndividuals seek health insurance to buy the initial 'product'—healthcare—before seeking that care." Wendy K. Mariner, Health Insurance is Dead; Long Live Health Insurance, 40 Am. J. Law & Med. 195, 197 (2014). For that reason, Section A focuses on what it means to have a just health care system by examining the *Sebelius* decision regarding the Affordable Care Act ("ACA"), which changed the health insurance system in the United States. Nat'l Fed'n of Indep. Bus. v. Sebelius, 567 U.S. 519 (2012). Section B concentrates on the just distribution of organs.

Practice Exercise: Write down which theories you think should apply to health care and to organ distribution. Then, reconsider your choices after reading this Chapter.

A. RIGHT TO HEALTH CARE

Before considering the just distribution of health care resources, it is helpful to understand how people in the United States pay for their health care. While it once was the norm, it is now rare to pay the full cost of care out-of-pocket; instead, most people try to obtain health insurance to finance their care. Health insurance developed in response to the Great Depression, which made it difficult for many patients to pay for medical care—and thus difficult for physicians and hospitals to remain solvent. In the United States, the majority of people have private health insurance; others are covered through government-sponsored programs, or lack insurance entirely. For a thorough history of the origins of health insurance in this country, see Paul Starr, The Social Transformation of American Medicine 235–334 (1982); Jeff Griffin, The History of Medicine and Organized Health Care in America, Mar. 27, 2020, https://www.griffinbenefits.com/blog/history-of-healthcare.

In contrast, other countries have universal health care systems, in which all residents are guaranteed access to health care. Some systems are government-funded, while others require all citizens to purchase private health insurance. Currently, many countries in Latin America, the Caribbean, Africa, and Asia-Pacific regions have some form of universal health care system, including China, which has the world's largest universal health care system. World Health Report 2010, Health Systems Financing: the Path to Universal Coverage, https://www.who.int/whr/2010/en/.

According to the U.S. Census Bureau, in 2013, before the major changes in the ACA went into effect, 86.6% of the United States population had health insurance for all or part of the year. See Jessica C. Smith & Carla Medalia, United States Census Bureau, Health Insurance Coverage in the United States: 2013, Sept. 2014, https://www.census.gov/library/publications/2014/demo/p60-250.html. The majority—64.2%—of those with coverage had private health insurance, with 53.9% having employment-based insurance and 11% purchasing insurance directly from an insurance company. Id. Government health insurance covered 34.3% of the population, with 17.3% covered by Medicaid and 15.6% covered by Medicare. Id. Approximately 42 million people—13.4% of the population—were without health insurance coverage for the entire year. Id.

Medicare and Medicaid. Medicare was created in 1965 in response to concerns that the elderly had limited financial resources and were unable to purchase health insurance due to their underlying medical conditions, which made them poor insurance risks. Medicare primarily was designed to serve people over 65, who are eligible if they—or a spouse—are eligible for Social Security benefits and have made payroll tax contributions for at least ten years. Over the years, the program has been expanded to also cover nonelderly disabled individuals who receive

Social Security Disability Insurance—after a two-year waiting period—as well as individuals diagnosed with end-stage renal disease and amyotrophic lateral sclerosis ("Lou Gehrig's Disease").

Medicare coverage consists of four parts. Part A covers hospital stays, care in a skilled nursing facility, hospice care, and some home health care. Part B covers outpatient doctors' services and other outpatient care, some home health care, medical supplies and preventative services. Part C, also known as "Medicare Advantage" ("MA"), consists of plans that provide all of Part A and Part B coverage, as well as other services such as outpatient prescription drugs. MA plans are offered by private companies approved by Medicare and function similar to private managed care plans such as health maintenance organizations ("HMOs") or preferred provider organizations ("PPOs"). MA plans may also offer extra coverage for vision, hearing, dental, and/or health and wellness services. Part D consists of optional Medicare-approved plans that cover prescription drugs, including freestanding Medicare drug plans as well as MA plans. Congressional Research Service, Medicare Overview, May 21, 2020, https://fas.org/sgp/crs/misc/IF10885.pdf.

People who qualify for Medicare are automatically enrolled in premium-free Part A coverage when they turn 65. They can pay extra—starting at $144.60 a month in 2020—to get Part B coverage, with premiums rising with income level. Unless enrolled in MA plans that already cover prescription drugs, enrollees usually pay monthly premiums for Part D coverage.

In 2019, Medicare served roughly 60 million beneficiaries. KFF, An Overview of Medicare, Feb. 13, 2019, https://www.kff.org/medicare/issue-brief/an-overview-of-medicare/. Medicare is funded by a combination of payroll taxes, beneficiary premiums, copayments and deductibles, and Federal appropriations from the U.S. Treasury. Congressional Research Service, Medicare Overview, May 21, 2020, https://fas.org/sgp/crs/misc/IF10885.pdf. In 2020, total Medicare spending was about $836 billion—almost 15% of total federal spending and 3.1% of GDP. Id.

While Medicare was created as an entitlement program for the elderly population, Medicaid was designed as a welfare program, serving individuals based on economic need. Traditionally, eligibility for Medicaid has been quite restrictive: federal funding has been limited to low-income individuals such as children, pregnant women, parents of dependent children, individuals with disabilities, and the elderly. States are required to cover the "categorically needy" in these groups with incomes below federal thresholds, and have the option to expand coverage to additional categories of similar populations with slightly higher income levels. As you will read below, the ACA sought to expand Medicaid to reach additional low-income individuals beyond these limited populations. Medicaid covers a broad range of services, including a large percentage of long-term nursing home care. Almost 72 million

people are enrolled in Medicaid, which is the largest insurer in the United States. While the federal government pays for Medicare, the federal and state governments jointly fund Medicaid. Each state runs its own Medicaid program, subject to federal requirements. The federal contribution varies depending on each state's per capita income, ranging from 50 to 76%; the state must fund the rest. The Commonwealth Fund, What Is Medicaid's Value?, Dec. 13, 2019, https://www.commonwealthfund.org/publications/explainer/2019/dec/medicaids-value. We will see in the case below that the ACA expanded Medicaid, with varying results from the states.

Private Insurance. The large percentage of individuals who receive health insurance through their employer—or the employer of a family member—is something of an historical accident that can be traced back to World War II.

> [T]o control inflation in the overheated wartime economy, the federal government in 1942 limited employers' freedom to raise wages and thus to compete on the basis of pay for scarce workers. However, the federal government allowed employers to expand benefits for workers, such as health insurance, which resulted in a rapid increase in employer sponsored insurance. Several additional federal rulings followed that increased the attractiveness of the provision of employer-sponsored insurance to workers and their unions. . . . Finally, in 1954, the Internal Revenue Service decided that the contributions that employers made to the purchase of health insurance for their employees were not taxable as income to workers.

David Blumenthal, Employer-Sponsored Health Insurance in the United States—Origins and Implications, 355 New Engl. J. Med. 82 (2006).

Receiving group health insurance from an employer has numerous advantages, particularly for people who suffer from—or are at risk for—underlying medical conditions: because the employer negotiates with insurers on behalf of a large group of employees, it is likely to be able to negotiate lower prices than an at-risk individual would be able to do. Employers usually pay a substantial contribution towards the cost of coverage for their employees. Employers typically pay about 85% of the premium amount for their employees, and about 75% of the premium amount for the employees' dependents. The employees cover the rest of the premium. KFF, 2019 Employer Health Benefits Survey, Sep. 25, 2019, https://www.kff.org/health-costs/report/2019-employer-health-benefits-survey/. Amid growing concerns that employer-sponsored health insurance contributed to "job lock"—where employees would be unable to switch jobs due in part to concerns that they would lose their health insurance—Congress passed the Health Insurance Portability and Accountability Act of 1996 ("HIPAA"). Pub. L. No. 104–191, 110 Stat. 1936 (1996). Among other things, HIPAA included provisions designed to make insurance more "portable" by requiring that new employees be

permitted to join the employer's group insurance plan, prohibiting group plans from discriminating in coverage or price based on health status, and limiting the period in which the new insurer could refuse to cover preexisting conditions.

Prior to the ACA, individuals who were not able to obtain employer-sponsored insurance, and who were not eligible for government health programs, could purchase insurance directly from insurers on the open market. However, such purchases were subject to strict insurance underwriting practices. Individuals or families with pre-existing medical conditions, or at risk for such conditions, could be denied coverage entirely or offered coverage only at rates that were unaffordable. While HIPAA contained a few provisions designed to increase access to individual insurance, generally for those who had maintained insurance previously, the law imposed no limits on the rates that could be charged, nor did it prevent common underwriting techniques that unfairly disadvantaged certain populations—including women, who tend to incur higher health costs.

As you will see in the next case, the ACA was designed to remedy many of these problems, notably by setting up a system of insurance "exchanges" in which people could shop for standardized insurance policies, with many individuals eligible for income-based premium subsidies. The ACA required insurance companies to offer comprehensive packages to all applicants, regardless of pre-existing health conditions or mental health needs, at premiums that were affordable and did not fluctuate depending on health care needs or status. In return, the law required that virtually all U.S. citizens obtain some form of health insurance—the so-called "individual mandate." The goal of the mandate was to get younger and healthier people to obtain health insurance and pay premiums so that they could help share the cost of insuring more high-risk participants.

The major ACA coverage provisions went into effect as of January 1, 2014. Six months later, the percentage of uninsured adults was estimated to have fallen by 22.3%. See Sharon K. Long et al., Urban Institute, Taking Stock at Mid-Year: Health Insurance Coverage under the ACA as of June 2014, July 29, 2014, http://hrms.urban.org/briefs/taking-stock-at-mid-year.html. Coverage rates rose significantly after implementation of the ACA, only to fall again amid ongoing affordability concerns. "The number of uninsured nonelderly individuals dropped from more than 46.5 million in 2010 to fewer than 26.7 million in 2016 before climbing to 28.9 million individuals in 2019." Jennifer Tolbert & Kendal Orgera, Key Facts about the Uninsured Population, Kaiser Family Foundation, Nov. 6, 2020, https://www.kff.org/uninsured/issue-brief/key-facts-about-the-uninsured-population/. Yet, "[i]n spite of the recent increases, the number of uninsured individuals remains well below levels prior to enactment of the ACA." Id.

The central constitutional question about the ACA was whether Congress exceeded its limited constitutional powers in passing the legislation. Many commentators expected the Court's opinion to focus on Congress's Commerce Clause power, and some believe that there were originally five votes—Justices Roberts, Scalia, Kennedy, Thomas, and Alito—to invalidate the Act. In a close and surprising 5–4 decision, however, Chief Justice John Roberts joined Justices Ginsburg, Breyer, Sotomayor and Kagan to rule that Congress had acted within its constitutional taxing power when it passed the individual mandate provision of the ACA. Then, with only Justices Ginsburg and Sotomayor dissenting, seven Justices ruled that Congress had exceeded its authority under the Spending Clause by passing the mandatory Medicaid expansion provision of the ACA, which had expanded Medicaid to cover all individuals under the age of 65 with incomes below 133% of the federal poverty line. However, the majority ruled that the Medicaid expansion could be severed, rather than necessitating that the entire statute be struck down.

As you read the opinion, consider whether the constitutional discussion of Congress's authority bears any relationship to the policy issues of access to health care. Could the Obama administration have passed health care legislation that was more just than the ACA? Do you think the ACA addresses the fundamental issues in the health care industry? Do you think the Justices understood how health care works? Do you think the people who wrote the ACA understood how health care works?

National Federation of Independent Business v. Sebelius

Supreme Court of the United States, 2012.
567 U.S. 519, 132 S.Ct. 2566.

■ ROBERTS, C.J., announced the judgment of the Court and delivered the opinion of the Court with respect to Parts I, II, and III-C, in which GINSBURG, BREYER, SOTOMAYOR, and KAGAN, JJ., joined; an opinion with respect to Part IV, in which BREYER and KAGAN, JJ., joined; and an opinion with respect to Parts III-A, III-B, and III-D. GINSBURG, J., filed an opinion concurring in part, concurring in the judgment in part, and dissenting in part, in which SOTOMAYOR, J., joined, and in which BREYER and KAGAN, JJ., joined as to Parts I, II, III, and IV. SCALIA, KENNEDY, THOMAS, and ALITO, JJ., filed a dissenting opinion. THOMAS, J., filed a dissenting opinion.

Today we resolve constitutional challenges to two provisions of the Patient Protection and Affordable Care Act of 2010: the individual mandate, which requires individuals to purchase a health insurance policy providing a minimum level of coverage; and the Medicaid expansion, which gives funds to the States on the condition that they

provide specified health care to all citizens whose income falls below a certain threshold. We do not consider whether the Act embodies sound policies. That judgment is entrusted to the Nation's elected leaders. We ask only whether Congress has the power under the Constitution to enact the challenged provisions.

I

In 2010, Congress enacted the Patient Protection and Affordable Care Act, 124 Stat. 119. The Act aims to increase the number of Americans covered by health insurance and decrease the cost of health care. The Act's 10 titles stretch over 900 pages and contain hundreds of provisions. This case concerns constitutional challenges to two key provisions, commonly referred to as the individual mandate and the Medicaid expansion.

The individual mandate requires most Americans to maintain "minimum essential" health insurance coverage. 26 U.S.C. § 5000A. The mandate does not apply to some individuals, such as prisoners and undocumented aliens. § 5000A(d). Many individuals will receive the required coverage through their employer, or from a government program such as Medicaid or Medicare. See § 5000A(f). But for individuals who are not exempt and do not receive health insurance through a third party, the means of satisfying the requirement is to purchase insurance from a private company.

Beginning in 2014, those who do not comply with the mandate must make a "[s]hared responsibility payment" to the Federal Government. § 5000A(b)(1). That payment, which the Act describes as a "penalty," is calculated as a percentage of household income, subject to a floor based on a specified dollar amount and a ceiling based on the average annual premium the individual would have to pay for qualifying private health insurance. § 5000A(c). In 2016, for example, the penalty will be 2.5 percent of an individual's household income, but no less than $695 and no more than the average yearly premium for insurance that covers 60 percent of the cost of 10 specified services (*e.g.*, prescription drugs and hospitalization). *Ibid.*; 42 U.S.C. § 18022. The Act provides that the penalty will be paid to the Internal Revenue Service with an individual's taxes, and "shall be assessed and collected in the same manner" as tax penalties, such as the penalty for claiming too large an income tax refund. 26 U.S.C. § 5000A(g)(1). The Act, however, bars the IRS from using several of its normal enforcement tools, such as criminal prosecutions and levies. § 5000A(g)(2). And some individuals who are subject to the mandate are nonetheless exempt from the penalty—for example, those with income below a certain threshold and members of Indian tribes. § 5000A(e).

... The second provision of the Affordable Care Act directly challenged here is the Medicaid expansion. Enacted in 1965, Medicaid offers federal funding to States to assist pregnant women, children, needy families, the blind, the elderly, and the disabled in obtaining

medical care. See 42 U.S.C. § 1396a(a)(10). In order to receive that funding, States must comply with federal criteria governing matters such as who receives care and what services are provided at what cost. By 1982 every State had chosen to participate in Medicaid. Federal funds received through the Medicaid program have become a substantial part of state budgets, now constituting over 10 percent of most States' total revenue.

The Affordable Care Act expands the scope of the Medicaid program and increases the number of individuals the States must cover. For example, the Act requires state programs to provide Medicaid coverage to adults with incomes up to 133 percent of the federal poverty level, whereas many States now cover adults with children only if their income is considerably lower, and do not cover childless adults at all. See § 1396a(a)(10)(A)(i)(VIII). The Act increases federal funding to cover the States' costs in expanding Medicaid coverage, although States will bear a portion of the costs on their own. § 1396d(y)(1). If a State does not comply with the Act's new coverage requirements, it may lose not only the federal funding for those requirements, but all of its federal Medicaid funds. See § 1396c.

III

The Government advances two theories for the proposition that Congress had constitutional authority to enact the individual mandate. First, the Government argues that Congress had the power to enact the mandate under the Commerce Clause. Under that theory, Congress may order individuals to buy health insurance because the failure to do so affects interstate commerce, and could undercut the Affordable Care Act's other reforms. Second, the Government argues that if the commerce power does not support the mandate, we should nonetheless uphold it as an exercise of Congress's power to tax. According to the Government, even if Congress lacks the power to direct individuals to buy insurance, the only effect of the individual mandate is to raise taxes on those who do not do so, and thus the law may be upheld as a tax.

A

The Government's first argument is that the individual mandate is a valid exercise of Congress's power under the Commerce Clause and the Necessary and Proper Clause. According to the Government, the health care market is characterized by a significant cost-shifting problem. Everyone will eventually need health care at a time and to an extent they cannot predict, but if they do not have insurance, they often will not be able to pay for it. Because state and federal laws nonetheless require hospitals to provide a certain degree of care to individuals without regard to their ability to pay, hospitals end up receiving compensation for only a portion of the services they provide. To recoup the losses, hospitals pass on the cost to insurers through higher rates, and insurers, in turn, pass on the cost to policy holders in the form of higher premiums. Congress estimated that the cost of uncompensated care raises family health insurance premiums, on average, by over $1,000 per year.

In the Affordable Care Act, Congress addressed the problem of those who cannot obtain insurance coverage because of preexisting conditions or other health issues. It did so through the Act's "guaranteed-issue" and "community-rating" provisions. These provisions together prohibit insurance companies from denying coverage to those with such conditions or charging unhealthy individuals higher premiums than healthy individuals.

The guaranteed-issue and community-rating reforms do not, however, address the issue of healthy individuals who choose not to purchase insurance to cover potential health care needs. In fact, the reforms sharply exacerbate that problem, by providing an incentive for individuals to delay purchasing health insurance until they become sick, relying on the promise of guaranteed and affordable coverage. The reforms also threaten to impose massive new costs on insurers, who are required to accept unhealthy individuals but prohibited from charging them rates necessary to pay for their coverage. This will lead insurers to significantly increase premiums on everyone.

The individual mandate was Congress's solution to these problems. By requiring that individuals purchase health insurance, the mandate prevents cost-shifting by those who would otherwise go without it. In addition, the mandate forces into the insurance risk pool more healthy individuals, whose premiums on average will be higher than their health care expenses. This allows insurers to subsidize the costs of covering the unhealthy individuals the reforms require them to accept. The Government claims that Congress has power under the Commerce and Necessary and Proper Clauses to enact this solution.

1

The Government contends that the individual mandate is within Congress's power because the failure to purchase insurance "has a substantial and deleterious effect on interstate commerce" by creating the cost-shifting problem. . . . Given its expansive scope, it is no surprise that Congress has employed the commerce power in a wide variety of ways to address the pressing needs of the time. But Congress has never attempted to rely on that power to compel individuals not engaged in commerce to purchase an unwanted product. Legislative novelty is not necessarily fatal; there is a first time for everything. But sometimes "the most telling indication of [a] severe constitutional problem . . . is the lack of historical precedent" for Congress's action. . . .

The Constitution grants Congress the power to "*regulate* Commerce." The power to *regulate* commerce presupposes the existence of commercial activity to be regulated. If the power to "regulate" something included the power to create it, many of the provisions in the Constitution would be superfluous. . . . As expansive as our cases construing the scope of the commerce power have been, they all have one thing in common: They uniformly describe the power as reaching "activity." . . .

The individual mandate, however, does not regulate existing commercial activity. It instead compels individuals to *become* active in commerce by purchasing a product, on the ground that their failure to do so affects interstate commerce. Construing the Commerce Clause to permit Congress to regulate individuals precisely *because* they are doing nothing would open a new and potentially vast domain to congressional authority. Every day individuals do not do an infinite number of things. In some cases they decide not to do something; in others they simply fail to do it. Allowing Congress to justify federal regulation by pointing to the effect of inaction on commerce would bring countless decisions an individual could *potentially* make within the scope of federal regulation, and—under the Government's theory—empower Congress to make those decisions for him.

. . . Indeed, the Government's logic would justify a mandatory purchase to solve almost any problem. . . . To consider a different example in the health care market, many Americans do not eat a balanced diet. That group makes up a larger percentage of the total population than those without health insurance. The failure of that group to have a healthy diet increases health care costs, to a greater extent than the failure of the uninsured to purchase insurance. Those increased costs are borne in part by other Americans who must pay more, just as the uninsured shift costs to the insured. Congress addressed the insurance problem by ordering everyone to buy insurance. Under the Government's theory, Congress could address the diet problem by ordering everyone to buy vegetables. See Dietary Guidelines ("Improved nutrition, appropriate eating behaviors, and increased physical activity have tremendous potential to . . . reduce health care costs").

People, for reasons of their own, often fail to do things that would be good for them or good for society. Those failures—joined with the similar failures of others—can readily have a substantial effect on interstate commerce. Under the Government's logic, that authorizes Congress to use its commerce power to compel citizens to act as the Government would have them act.

That is not the country the Framers of our Constitution envisioned. James Madison explained that the Commerce Clause was "an addition which few oppose and from which no apprehensions are entertained." While Congress's authority under the Commerce Clause has of course expanded with the growth of the national economy, our cases have "always recognized that the power to regulate commerce, though broad indeed, has limits." The Government's theory would erode those limits, permitting Congress to reach beyond the natural extent of its authority, "everywhere extending the sphere of its activity and drawing all power into its impetuous vortex." Congress already enjoys vast power to regulate much of what we do. Accepting the Government's theory would give Congress the same license to regulate what we do not do,

fundamentally changing the relation between the citizen and the Federal Government.

To an economist, perhaps, there is no difference between activity and inactivity; both have measurable economic effects on commerce. But the distinction between doing something and doing nothing would not have been lost on the Framers, who were "practical statesmen," not metaphysical philosophers. As we have explained, "the framers of the Constitution were not mere visionaries, toying with speculations or theories, but practical men, dealing with the facts of political life as they understood them, putting into form the government they were creating, and prescribing in language clear and intelligible the powers that government was to take." The Framers gave Congress the power to *regulate* commerce, not to *compel* it, and for over 200 years both our decisions and Congress's actions have reflected this understanding. There is no reason to depart from that understanding now.

The Government sees things differently. It argues that because sickness and injury are unpredictable but unavoidable, "the uninsured as a class are active in the market for health care, which they regularly seek and obtain." The individual mandate "merely regulates how individuals finance and pay for that active participation—requiring that they do so through insurance, rather than through attempted self-insurance with the back-stop of shifting costs to others." . . . The phrase "active in the market" cannot obscure the fact that most of those regulated by the individual mandate are not currently engaged in any commercial activity involving health care, and that fact is fatal to the Government's effort to "regulate the uninsured as a class."

The individual mandate's regulation of the uninsured as a class is, in fact, particularly divorced from any link to existing commercial activity. The mandate primarily affects healthy, often young adults who are less likely to need significant health care and have other priorities for spending their money. It is precisely because these individuals, as an actuarial class, incur relatively low health care costs that the mandate helps counter the effect of forcing insurance companies to cover others who impose greater costs than their premiums are allowed to reflect. If the individual mandate is targeted at a class, it is a class whose commercial inactivity rather than activity is its defining feature. . . .

Everyone will likely participate in the markets for food, clothing, transportation, shelter, or energy; that does not authorize Congress to direct them to purchase particular products in those or other markets today. The Commerce Clause is not a general license to regulate an individual from cradle to grave, simply because he will predictably engage in particular transactions.

The Government argues that the individual mandate can be sustained as a sort of exception to this rule, because health insurance is a unique product. According to the Government, upholding the individual mandate would not justify mandatory purchases of items such as cars or

broccoli because, as the Government puts it, "[h]ealth insurance is not purchased for its own sake like a car or broccoli; it is a means of financing health-care consumption and covering universal risks." But cars and broccoli are no more purchased for their "own sake" than health insurance. They are purchased to cover the need for transportation and food.

B

That is not the end of the matter. Because the Commerce Clause does not support the individual mandate, it is necessary to turn to the Government's second argument: that the mandate may be upheld as within Congress's enumerated power to "lay and collect Taxes." Art. I, § 8, cl. 1. . . . the Government asks us to read the mandate not as ordering individuals to buy insurance, but rather as imposing a tax on those who do not buy that product. . . .

Under the mandate, if an individual does not maintain health insurance, the only consequence is that he must make an additional payment to the IRS when he pays his taxes. That, according to the Government, means the mandate can be regarded as establishing a condition—not owning health insurance—that triggers a tax—the required payment to the IRS. Under that theory, the mandate is not a legal command to buy insurance. Rather, it makes going without insurance just another thing the Government taxes, like buying gasoline or earning income. And if the mandate is in effect just a tax hike on certain taxpayers who do not have health insurance, it may be within Congress's constitutional power to tax.

C

The exaction the Affordable Care Act imposes on those without health insurance looks like a tax in many respects. The "[s]hared responsibility payment," as the statute entitles it, is paid into the Treasury by "taxpayer[s]" when they file their tax returns. It does not apply to individuals who do not pay federal income taxes because their household income is less than the filing threshold in the Internal Revenue Code. For taxpayers who do owe the payment, its amount is determined by such familiar factors as taxable income, number of dependents, and joint filing status. The requirement to pay is found in the Internal Revenue Code and enforced by the IRS, which—as we previously explained—must assess and collect it "in the same manner as taxes." This process yields the essential feature of any tax: it produces at least some revenue for the Government. Indeed, the payment is expected to raise about $4 billion per year by 2017.

[Although the ACA labeled the mandate as a penalty and not a tax, the Court concluded that labeling a tax as a penalty did not alter its fundamental character. Under the *Drexel* analysis, the Court determined that the individual mandate is valid as a tax because it invokes no other legal consequences, along with the following three reasons: (1) the

amount due will be less than the price of insurance; (2) the individual mandate does not contain a scienter (intent) element—intentional crimes are more punitive; and (3) the payment is collected through the IRS—the normal means of taxation.]

. . . The Affordable Care Act's requirement that certain individuals pay a financial penalty for not obtaining health insurance may reasonably be characterized as a tax. Because the Constitution permits such a tax, it is not our role to forbid it, or to pass upon its wisdom or fairness.

IV

A

The States also contend that the Medicaid expansion exceeds Congress's authority under the Spending Clause. They claim that Congress is coercing the States to adopt the changes it wants by threatening to withhold all of a State's Medicaid grants, unless the State accepts the new expanded funding and complies with the conditions that come with it. This, they argue, violates the basic principle that the "Federal Government may not compel the States to enact or administer a federal regulatory program."

There is no doubt that the Act dramatically increases state obligations under Medicaid. The current Medicaid program requires States to cover only certain discrete categories of needy individuals—pregnant women, children, needy families, the blind, the elderly, and the disabled. There is no mandatory coverage for most childless adults, and the States typically do not offer any such coverage. The States also enjoy considerable flexibility with respect to the coverage levels for parents of needy families. On average States cover only those unemployed parents who make less than 37 percent of the federal poverty level, and only those employed parents who make less than 63 percent of the poverty line.

The Medicaid provisions of the Affordable Care Act, in contrast, require States to expand their Medicaid programs by 2014 to cover *all* individuals under the age of 65 with incomes below 133 percent of the federal poverty line. The Act also establishes a new "[e]ssential health benefits" package, which States must provide to all new Medicaid recipients—a level sufficient to satisfy a recipient's obligations under the individual mandate. The Affordable Care Act provides that the Federal Government will pay 100 percent of the costs of covering these newly eligible individuals through 2016. In the following years, the federal payment level gradually decreases, to a minimum of 90 percent. In light of the expansion in coverage mandated by the Act, the Federal Government estimates that its Medicaid spending will increase by approximately $100 billion per year, nearly 40 percent above current levels.

. . . Permitting the Federal Government to force the States to implement a federal program would threaten the political accountability

key to our federal system. "[W]here the Federal Government directs the States to regulate, it may be state officials who will bear the brunt of public disapproval, while the federal officials who devised the regulatory program may remain insulated from the electoral ramifications of their decision." Spending Clause programs do not pose this danger when a State has a legitimate choice whether to accept the federal conditions in exchange for federal funds. In such a situation, state officials can fairly be held politically accountable for choosing to accept or refuse the federal offer. But when the State has no choice, the Federal Government can achieve its objectives without accountability, just as in *New York* and *Printz*. Indeed, this danger is heightened when Congress acts under the Spending Clause, because Congress can use that power to implement federal policy it could not impose directly under its enumerated powers.

. . . In this case, the financial "inducement" Congress has chosen is much more than "relatively mild encouragement"—it is a gun to the head. Section 1396c of the Medicaid Act provides that if a State's Medicaid plan does not comply with the Act's requirements, the Secretary of Health and Human Services may declare that "further payments will not be made to the State." A State that opts out of the Affordable Care Act's expansion in health care coverage thus stands to lose not merely "a relatively small percentage" of its existing Medicaid funding, but *all* of it. Medicaid spending accounts for over 20 percent of the average State's total budget, with federal funds covering 50 to 83 percent of those costs. The Federal Government estimates that it will pay out approximately $3.3 trillion between 2010 and 2019 in order to cover the costs of *pre*-expansion Medicaid. Brief for United States 10, n. 6. In addition, the States have developed intricate statutory and administrative regimes over the course of many decades to implement their objectives under existing Medicaid. It is easy to see how the *Dole* Court could conclude that the threatened loss of less than half of one percent of South Dakota's budget left that State with a "prerogative" to reject Congress's desired policy, "not merely in theory but in fact." The threatened loss of over 10 percent of a State's overall budget, in contrast, is economic dragooning that leaves the States with no real option but to acquiesce in the Medicaid expansion.

B

Nothing in our opinion precludes Congress from offering funds under the Affordable Care Act to expand the availability of health care, and requiring that States accepting such funds comply with the conditions on their use. What Congress is not free to do is to penalize States that choose not to participate in that new program by taking away their existing Medicaid funding. Section 1396c gives the Secretary of Health and Human Services the authority to do just that. It allows her to withhold *all* "further [Medicaid] payments . . . to the State" if she determines that the State is out of compliance with any Medicaid requirement, including those contained in the expansion. In light of the Court's holding, the

Secretary cannot apply § 1396c to withdraw existing Medicaid funds for failure to comply with the requirements set out in the expansion.

* * *

The Affordable Care Act is constitutional in part and unconstitutional in part. The individual mandate cannot be upheld as an exercise of Congress's power under the Commerce Clause. That Clause authorizes Congress to regulate interstate commerce, not to order individuals to engage in it. In this case, however, it is reasonable to construe what Congress has done as increasing taxes on those who have a certain amount of income, but choose to go without health insurance. Such legislation is within Congress's power to tax.

As for the Medicaid expansion, that portion of the Affordable Care Act violates the Constitution by threatening existing Medicaid funding. Congress has no authority to order the States to regulate according to its instructions. Congress may offer the States grants and require the States to comply with accompanying conditions, but the States must have a genuine choice whether to accept the offer. The States are given no such choice in this case: They must either accept a basic change in the nature of Medicaid, or risk losing all Medicaid funding. The remedy for that constitutional violation is to preclude the Federal Government from imposing such a sanction. That remedy does not require striking down other portions of the Affordable Care Act.

The Framers created a Federal Government of limited powers, and assigned to this Court the duty of enforcing those limits. The Court does so today. But the Court does not express any opinion on the wisdom of the Affordable Care Act. Under the Constitution, that judgment is reserved to the people.

The judgment of the Court of Appeals for the Eleventh Circuit is affirmed in part and reversed in part.

It is so ordered.

■ JUSTICE GINSBURG, with whom JUSTICE SOTOMAYOR joins, and with whom JUSTICE BREYER and JUSTICE KAGAN join as to Parts I, II, III, and IV, concurring in part, concurring in the judgment in part, and dissenting in part.

I agree with THE CHIEF JUSTICE . . . that the minimum coverage provision is a proper exercise of Congress' taxing power. I therefore join Parts I, II, and III-C of THE CHIEF JUSTICE's opinion. Unlike THE CHIEF JUSTICE, however, I would hold, alternatively, that the Commerce Clause authorizes Congress to enact the minimum coverage provision. I would also hold that the Spending Clause permits the Medicaid expansion exactly as Congress enacted it.

I

. . . Not all U.S. residents, however, have health insurance. In 2009, approximately 50 million people were uninsured, either by choice or,

more likely, because they could not afford private insurance and did not qualify for government aid. As a group, uninsured individuals annually consume more than $100 billion in healthcare services, nearly 5% of the Nation's total Over 60% of those without insurance visit a doctor's office or emergency room in a given year.

B

The large number of individuals without health insurance, Congress found, heavily burdens the national health-care market. As just noted, the cost of emergency care or treatment for a serious illness generally exceeds what an individual can afford to pay on her own. Unlike markets for most products, however, the inability to pay for care does not mean that an uninsured individual will receive no care. Federal and state law, as well as professional obligations and embedded social norms, require hospitals and physicians to provide care when it is most needed, regardless of the patient's ability to pay.

As a consequence, medical-care providers deliver significant amounts of care to the uninsured for which the providers receive no payment. In 2008, for example, hospitals, physicians, and other health-care professionals received no compensation for $43 billion worth of the $116 billion in care they administered to those without insurance.

Health-care providers do not absorb these bad debts. Instead, they raise their prices, passing along the cost of uncompensated care to those who do pay reliably: the government and private insurance companies. In response, private insurers increase their premiums, shifting the cost of the elevated bills from providers onto those who carry insurance. The net result: Those with health insurance subsidize the medical care of those without it. As economists would describe what happens, the uninsured "free ride" on those who pay for health insurance.

The size of this subsidy is considerable. Congress found that the cost-shifting just described "increases family [insurance] premiums by on average over $1,000 a year." Higher premiums, in turn, render health insurance less affordable, forcing more people to go without insurance and leading to further cost-shifting.

And it is hardly just the currently sick or injured among the uninsured who prompt elevation of the price of health care and health insurance. Insurance companies and health-care providers know that some percentage of healthy, uninsured people will suffer sickness or injury each year and will receive medical care despite their inability to pay. In anticipation of this uncompensated care, health-care companies raise their prices, and insurers their premiums. In other words, because any uninsured person may need medical care at any moment and because health-care companies must account for that risk, every uninsured person impacts the market price of medical care and medical insurance.

The failure of individuals to acquire insurance has other deleterious effects on the health-care market. Because those without insurance

generally lack access to preventative care, they do not receive treatment for conditions—like hypertension and diabetes—that can be successfully and affordably treated if diagnosed early on. See Institute of Medicine, National Academies, Insuring America's Health: Principles and Recommendations 43 (2004). When sickness finally drives the uninsured to seek care, once treatable conditions have escalated into grave health problems, requiring more costly and extensive intervention. *Id.*, at 43–44. The extra time and resources providers spend serving the uninsured lessens the providers' ability to care for those who do have insurance.

C

States cannot resolve the problem of the uninsured on their own. Like Social Security benefits, a universal health-care system, if adopted by an individual State, would be "bait to the needy and dependent elsewhere, encouraging them to migrate and seek a haven of repose." An influx of unhealthy individuals into a State with universal health care would result in increased spending on medical services. To cover the increased costs, a State would have to raise taxes, and private health-insurance companies would have to increase premiums. Higher taxes and increased insurance costs would, in turn, encourage businesses and healthy individuals to leave the State.

D

Aware that a national solution was required, Congress could have taken over the health-insurance market by establishing a tax-and-spend federal program like Social Security. Such a program, commonly referred to as a single-payer system (where the sole payer is the Federal Government), would have left little, if any, room for private enterprise or the States. Instead of going this route, Congress enacted the ACA, a solution that retains a robust role for private insurers and state governments. To make its chosen approach work, however, Congress had to use some new tools, including a requirement that most individuals obtain private health insurance coverage. As explained below, by employing these tools, Congress was able to achieve a practical, altogether reasonable, solution.

A central aim of the ACA is to reduce the number of uninsured U.S. residents. The minimum coverage provision advances this objective by giving potential recipients of health care a financial incentive to acquire insurance. Per the minimum coverage provision, an individual must either obtain insurance or pay a toll constructed as a tax penalty.

The minimum coverage provision serves a further purpose vital to Congress' plan to reduce the number of uninsured. Congress knew that encouraging individuals to purchase insurance would not suffice to solve the problem, because most of the uninsured are not uninsured by choice. Of particular concern to Congress were people who, though desperately in need of insurance, often cannot acquire it: persons who suffer from preexisting medical conditions.

Before the ACA's enactment, private insurance companies took an applicant's medical history into account when setting insurance rates or deciding whether to insure an individual. Because individuals with preexisting medical conditions cost insurance companies significantly more than those without such conditions, insurers routinely refused to insure these individuals, charged them substantially higher premiums, or offered only limited coverage that did not include the preexisting illness.

To ensure that individuals with medical histories have access to affordable insurance, Congress devised a three-part solution. First, Congress imposed a "guaranteed issue" requirement, which bars insurers from denying coverage to any person on account of that person's medical condition or history. Second, Congress required insurers to use "community rating" to price their insurance policies. Community rating, in effect, bars insurance companies from charging higher premiums to those with preexisting conditions.

But these two provisions, Congress comprehended, could not work effectively unless individuals were given a powerful incentive to obtain insurance.

. . . In sum, Congress passed the minimum coverage provision as a key component of the ACA to address an economic and social problem that has plagued the Nation for decades: the large number of U.S. residents who are unable or unwilling to obtain health insurance. Whatever one thinks of the policy decision Congress made, it was Congress' prerogative to make it. Reviewed with appropriate deference, the minimum coverage provision, allied to the guaranteed-issue and community-rating prescriptions, should survive measurement under the Commerce and Necessary and Proper Clauses.

II

1

a

. . . Everyone will, at some point, consume health-care products and services. Thus, if THE CHIEF JUSTICE is correct that an insurance-purchase requirement can be applied only to those who "actively" consume health care, the minimum coverage provision fits the bill.

. . . Maintaining that the uninsured are not active in the health-care market, THE CHIEF JUSTICE draws an analogy to the car market. An individual "is not 'active in the car market,' " THE CHIEF JUSTICE observes, simply because he or she may someday buy a car. The analogy is inapt. The inevitable yet unpredictable need for medical care and the guarantee that emergency care will be provided when required are conditions nonexistent in other markets. That is so of the market for cars, and of the market for broccoli as well. Although an individual *might* buy a car or a crown of broccoli one day, there is no certainty she will ever do so. And if she eventually wants a car or has a craving for broccoli, she

will be obliged to pay at the counter before receiving the vehicle or nourishment. She will get no free ride or food, at the expense of another consumer forced to pay an inflated price. Upholding the minimum coverage provision on the ground that all are participants or will be participants in the health-care market would therefore carry no implication that Congress may justify under the Commerce Clause a mandate to buy other products and services.

... THE CHIEF JUSTICE also calls the minimum coverage provision an illegitimate effort to make young, healthy individuals subsidize insurance premiums paid by the less hale and hardy. This complaint, too, is spurious. Under the current health-care system, healthy persons who lack insurance receive a benefit for which they do not pay: They are assured that, if they need it, emergency medical care will be available, although they cannot afford it. Those who have insurance bear the cost of this guarantee. By requiring the healthy uninsured to obtain insurance or pay a penalty structured as a tax, the minimum coverage provision ends the free ride these individuals currently enjoy.

... As an example of the type of regulation he fears, THE CHIEF JUSTICE cites a Government mandate to purchase green vegetables. One could call this concern "the broccoli horrible." Congress, THE CHIEF JUSTICE posits, might adopt such a mandate, reasoning that an individual's failure to eat a healthy diet, like the failure to purchase health insurance, imposes costs on others.

Consider the chain of inferences the Court would have to accept to conclude that a vegetable-purchase mandate was likely to have a substantial effect on the health-care costs borne by lithe Americans. The Court would have to believe that individuals forced to buy vegetables would then eat them (instead of throwing or giving them away), would prepare the vegetables in a healthy way (steamed or raw, not deep-fried), would cut back on unhealthy foods, and would not allow other factors (such as lack of exercise or little sleep) to trump the improved diet.[9]

V

A

Expansion has been characteristic of the Medicaid program. Akin to the ACA in 2010, the Medicaid Act as passed in 1965 augmented existing federal grant programs jointly administered with the States. . . .

Since 1965, Congress has amended the Medicaid program on more than 50 occasions, sometimes quite sizably. Most relevant here, between

9 The failure to purchase vegetables in THE CHIEF JUSTICE's hypothetical, then, is *not* what leads to higher health-care costs for others; rather, it is the failure of individuals to maintain a healthy diet, and the resulting obesity, that creates the cost-shifting problem. Requiring individuals to purchase vegetables is thus several steps removed from solving the problem. The failure to obtain health insurance, by contrast, is the *immediate cause* of the cost-shifting Congress sought to address through the ACA. Requiring individuals to obtain insurance attacks the source of the problem directly, in a single step.

1988 and 1990, Congress required participating States to include among their beneficiaries pregnant women with family incomes up to 133% of the federal poverty level, children up to age 6 at the same income levels, and children ages 6 to 18 with family incomes up to 100% of the poverty level.

. . . Compared to past alterations, the ACA is notable for the extent to which the Federal Government will pick up the tab. Medicaid's 2010 expansion is financed largely by federal outlays. In 2014, federal funds will cover 100% of the costs for newly eligible beneficiaries; that rate will gradually decrease before settling at 90% in 2020. By comparison, federal contributions toward the care of beneficiaries eligible pre-ACA range from 50% to 83%, and averaged 57% between 2005 and 2008.

Nor will the expansion exorbitantly increase state Medicaid spending. The Congressional Budget Office (CBO) projects that States will spend 0.8% more than they would have, absent the ACA. Whatever the increase in state obligations after the ACA, it will pale in comparison to the increase in federal funding

B

. . . This case does not present the concerns that led the Court in *Dole* even to consider the prospect of coercion. In *Dole,* the condition—set 21 as the minimum drinking age—did not tell the States how to use funds Congress provided for highway construction. Further, in view of the Twenty-First Amendment, it was an open question whether Congress could directly impose a national minimum drinking age.

The ACA, in contrast, relates solely to the federally funded Medicaid program; if States choose not to comply, Congress has not threatened to withhold funds earmarked for any other program. Nor does the ACA use Medicaid funding to induce States to take action Congress itself could not undertake. The Federal Government undoubtedly could operate its own health-care program for poor persons, just as it operates Medicare for seniors' health care. See *supra,* at 2632.

That is what makes this such a simple case, and the Court's decision so unsettling. Congress, aiming to assist the needy, has appropriated federal money to subsidize state health-insurance programs that meet federal standards. The principal standard the ACA sets is that the state program cover adults earning no more than 133% of the federal poverty line. Enforcing that prescription ensures that federal funds will be spent on health care for the poor in furtherance of Congress' present perception of the general welfare.

C

THE CHIEF JUSTICE asserts that the Medicaid expansion creates a "new health care program." Moreover, States could "hardly anticipate" that Congress would "transform [the program] so dramatically." Therefore, THE CHIEF JUSTICE maintains, Congress' threat to withhold "old" Medicaid funds based on a State's refusal to participate in

the "new" program is a "threa[t] to terminate [an]other . . . independent gran[t]." And because the threat to withhold a large amount of funds from one program "leaves the States with no real option but to acquiesce [in a newly created program]," THE CHIEF JUSTICE concludes, the Medicaid expansion is unconstitutionally coercive.

1

The starting premise on which THE CHIEF JUSTICE's coercion analysis rests is that the ACA did not really "extend" Medicaid; instead, Congress created an entirely new program to co-exist with the old. THE CHIEF JUSTICE calls the ACA new, but in truth, it simply reaches more of America's poor than Congress originally covered.

■ JUSTICE SCALIA, JUSTICE KENNEDY, JUSTICE THOMAS, and JUSTICE ALITO, dissenting.

. . . The Act before us here exceeds federal power both in mandating the purchase of health insurance and in denying nonconsenting States all Medicaid funding. These parts of the Act are central to its design and operation, and all the Act's other provisions would not have been enacted without them. In our view it must follow that the entire statute is inoperative.

I

The Individual Mandate

. . . The Government was invited, at oral argument, to suggest what federal controls over private conduct (other than those explicitly prohibited by the Bill of Rights or other constitutional controls) could *not* be justified as necessary and proper for the carrying out of a general regulatory scheme. It was unable to name any. As we said at the outset, whereas the precise scope of the Commerce Clause and the Necessary and Proper Clause is uncertain, the proposition that the Federal Government cannot do everything is a fundamental precept. Section 5000A is defeated by that proposition.

II

The Taxing Power

. . . The Government contends, however, as expressed in the caption to Part II of its brief, that "THE MINIMUM COVERAGE PROVISION IS INDEPENDENTLY AUTHORIZED BY CONGRESS'S TAXING POWER." The phrase "independently authorized" suggests the existence of a creature never hitherto seen in the United States Reports: A penalty for constitutional purposes that is *also* a tax for constitutional purposes. In all our cases the two are mutually exclusive. The provision challenged under the Constitution is either a penalty or else a tax. Of course in many cases what was a regulatory mandate enforced by a penalty *could have been* imposed as a tax upon permissible action; or what was imposed as a tax upon permissible action *could have been* a regulatory mandate enforced by a penalty. But we know of no case, and the Government cites none, in which the imposition was, for constitutional purposes, both. The

two are mutually exclusive. Thus, what the Government's caption should have read was "ALTERNATIVELY, THE MINIMUM COVERAGE PROVISION IS NOT A MANDATE-WITH-PENALTY BUT A TAX." It is important to bear this in mind in evaluating the tax argument of the Government and of those who support it: The issue is not whether Congress had the *power* to frame the minimum-coverage provision as a tax, but whether it *did* so.

So the question is, quite simply, whether the exaction here is imposed for violation of the law. It unquestionably is. The minimum-coverage provision is found in 26 U.S.C. § 5000A, entitled "*Requirement* to maintain minimum essential coverage." (Emphasis added). It commands that every "applicable individual *shall* . . . ensure that the individual . . . is covered under minimum essential coverage." And the immediately following provision states that, "[i]f . . . an applicable individual . . . fails to meet the *requirement* of subsection (a) . . . there is hereby imposed . . . a *penalty*." And several of Congress' legislative "findings" with regard to § 5000A confirm that it sets forth a legal requirement and constitutes the assertion of regulatory power, not mere taxing power. See 42 U.S.C. § 18091(2)(A) ("The requirement regulates activity . . ."); § 18091(2)(C) ("The requirement . . . will add millions of new consumers to the health insurance market . . ."); § 18091(2)(D) ("The requirement achieves near-universal coverage"); § 18091(2)(H) ("The requirement is an essential part of this larger regulation of economic activity, and the absence of the requirement would undercut Federal regulation of the health insurance market"); § 18091(3) ("[T]he Supreme Court of the United States ruled that insurance is interstate commerce subject to Federal regulation").

IV
The Medicaid Expansion

Once it is recognized that spending-power legislation cannot coerce state participation, two questions remain: (1) What is the meaning of coercion in this context? (2) Is the ACA's expanded Medicaid coverage coercive? We now turn to those questions.

E

Whether federal spending legislation crosses the line from enticement to coercion is often difficult to determine, and courts should not conclude that legislation is unconstitutional on this ground unless the coercive nature of an offer is unmistakably clear. In this case, however, there can be no doubt. In structuring the ACA, Congress unambiguously signaled its belief that every State would have no real choice but to go along with the Medicaid Expansion. If the anticoercion rule does not apply in this case, then there is no such rule.

1

. . . For these reasons, the offer that the ACA makes to the States—go along with a dramatic expansion of Medicaid or potentially lose all

federal Medicaid funding—is quite unlike anything that we have seen in a prior spending-power case. In *South Dakota v. Dole,* the total amount that the States would have lost if every single State had refused to comply with the 21-year-old drinking age was approximately $614.7 million—or about 0.19% of all state expenditures combined. South Dakota stood to lose, at most, funding that amounted to less than 1% of its annual state expenditures. See *ibid.* Under the ACA, by contrast, the Federal Government has threatened to withhold 42.3% of all federal outlays to the states, or approximately $233 billion. Withholding $614.7 million, equaling only 0.19% of all state expenditures combined, is aptly characterized as "relatively mild encouragement," but threatening to withhold $233 billion, equaling 21.86% of all state expenditures combined, is a different matter.

2

What the statistics suggest is confirmed by the goal and structure of the ACA. In crafting the ACA, Congress clearly expressed its informed view that no State could possibly refuse the offer that the ACA extends. . . .

F

Seven Members of the Court agree that the Medicaid Expansion, as enacted by Congress, is unconstitutional. See Part IV-A to IV-E, *supra*; Part IV-A, *ante* (opinion of ROBERTS, C.J., joined by BREYER and KAGAN, JJ.).

1

The Act's Major Provisions

Major provisions of the Affordable Care Act—*i.e.,* the insurance regulations and taxes, the reductions in federal reimbursements to hospitals and other Medicare spending reductions, the exchanges and their federal subsidies, and the employer responsibility assessment—cannot remain once the Individual Mandate and Medicaid Expansion are invalid. That result follows from the undoubted inability of the other major provisions to operate as Congress intended without the Individual Mandate and Medicaid Expansion. Absent the invalid portions, the other major provisions could impose enormous risks of unexpected burdens on patients, the health-care community, and the federal budget. That consequence would be in absolute conflict with the ACA's design of "shared responsibility," and would pose a threat to the Nation that Congress did not intend.

2

The Act's Minor Provisions

The next question is whether the invalidation of the ACA's major provisions requires the Court to invalidate the ACA's other provisions. It does.

The ACA is over 900 pages long. Its regulations include requirements ranging from a break time and secluded place at work for nursing mothers, see 29 U.S.C. § 207(r)(1) (2006 ed., Supp. IV), to displays of nutritional content at chain restaurants, see 21 U.S.C. § 343(q)(5)(H). The Act raises billions of dollars in taxes and fees, including exactions imposed on high-income taxpayers, see ACA §§ 9015, 10906; HCERA § 1402, medical devices, see 26 U.S.C. § 4191 (2006 ed., Supp. IV), and tanning booths, see § 5000B. It spends government money on, among other things, the study of how to spend less government money. 42 U.S.C. § 1315a. And it includes a number of provisions that provide benefits to the State of a particular legislator. For example, § 10323, 124 Stat. 954, extends Medicare coverage to individuals exposed to asbestos from a mine in Libby, Montana. Another provision, § 2006, *id.*, at 284, increases Medicaid payments only in Louisiana.

* * *

The Court today decides to save a statute Congress did not write. It rules that what the statute declares to be a requirement with a penalty is instead an option subject to a tax. And it changes the intentionally coercive sanction of a total cut-off of Medicaid funds to a supposedly noncoercive cut-off of only the incremental funds that the Act makes available.

The Court regards its strained statutory interpretation as judicial modesty. It is not. It amounts instead to a vast judicial overreaching. It creates a debilitated, inoperable version of health-care regulation that Congress did not enact and the public does not expect. It makes enactment of sensible health-care regulation more difficult, since Congress cannot start afresh but must take as its point of departure a jumble of now senseless provisions, provisions that certain interests favored under the Court's new design will struggle to retain. And it leaves the public and the States to expend vast sums of money on requirements that may or may not survive the necessary congressional revision.

The Court's disposition, invented and atextual as it is, does not even have the merit of avoiding constitutional difficulties. It creates them. The holding that the Individual Mandate is a tax raises a difficult constitutional question (what is a direct tax?) that the Court resolves with inadequate deliberation. And the judgment on the Medicaid Expansion issue ushers in new federalism concerns and places an unaccustomed strain upon the Union. Those States that decline the Medicaid Expansion must subsidize, by the federal tax dollars taken from their citizens, vast grants to the States that accept the Medicaid Expansion. If that destabilizing political dynamic, so antagonistic to a harmonious Union, is to be introduced at all, it should be by Congress, not by the Judiciary.

The values that should have determined our course today are caution, minimalism, and the understanding that the Federal

Government is one of limited powers. But the Court's ruling undermines those values at every turn. In the name of restraint, it overreaches. In the name of constitutional avoidance, it creates new constitutional questions. In the name of cooperative federalism, it undermines state sovereignty.

The Constitution, though it dates from the founding of the Republic, has powerful meaning and vital relevance to our own times. The constitutional protections that this case involves are protections of structure. Structural protections—notably, the restraints imposed by federalism and separation of powers—are less romantic and have less obvious a connection to personal freedom than the provisions of the Bill of Rights or the Civil War Amendments. Hence they tend to be undervalued or even forgotten by our citizens. It should be the responsibility of the Court to teach otherwise, to remind our people that the Framers considered structural protections of freedom the most important ones, for which reason they alone were embodied in the original Constitution and not left to later amendment. The fragmentation of power produced by the structure of our Government is central to liberty, and when we destroy it, we place liberty at peril. Today's decision should have vindicated, should have taught, this truth; instead, our judgment today has disregarded it.

> **Practice Exercise:** Summarize the Court's holdings about Congress's Commerce Clause, Taxing and Spending powers. Which Justices believe that Congress had commerce power to pass the ACA? Taxing power? Spending power?

For the reasons here stated, we would find the Act invalid in its entirety. We respectfully dissent.

NOTES AND QUESTIONS

1. *Constitutional Arguments.* Do you believe this lawsuit was about "saving the country from Obamacare and saving the Constitution for the country"? Randy Barnett, No Small Feat: Who Won the Health Care Case (And Why Did So Many Law Professors Miss the Boat)?, 65 Fla. L. Rev. 1331 (2013).

How do you assess the following arguments that are central to the opinion?

a. Citizens who do not desire to purchase health insurance or use the health care system are inactive. Congress may not regulate inactivity in the marketplace under its commerce powers.

b. Because medical institutions are required to provide health care even to the uninsured, everyone participates in the health care market even when they are not using health care.

c. Even though Congress identified the shared responsibility payment as a *penalty* for not complying with the

ACA, the Court ruled the ACA falls within the Congress's taxing powers. Why do you think Congress did not call the penalty a tax?

d. The Act's Medicaid provisions coerced the states by threatening to take away their existing Medicaid funding.

2. *The Health Care Market and the Commerce Clause.* Do you think the Justices understand the health care market? The market for health *insurance*? The difference between the two? Assess the government's argument that the health care market is different from other markets because everyone participates in it at some time or another. Assess the government's argument that the health care market is different from other markets because hospitals are required to provide emergency care to individuals whether they have insurance or not. How much is the discussion affected by EMTALA, *infra*?

Given the structure of the health care insurance market, do you agree with the government that the mandate was necessary? Do you agree with the Chief Justice that allowing the mandate would expand Congress's powers beyond anything previously available or imaginable?

3. *The Importance of Insurance.* After reading the *Sebelius* decision and learning how much a major role health insurance plays in our society, it is important to understand the different conceptions of insurance. To understand the value of insurance, we must understand its formation. Professor Kenneth S. Abraham identified four different conceptions of insurance:

> It is worthwhile at the outset to briefly summarize the four conceptions [of insurance]. The contract conception understands insurance as a voluntary agreement between an individual policyholder and an insurer, subject to the constraints and rules of construction that are ordinarily placed on such agreements by the law of contracts. This conception supplies the "literal" view of insurance to which the other conceptions, understood as metaphors or analogies, contrast themselves. Under the public utility/regulated industry conception, contract is a mere tool for bringing the regulated relationship into existence. On this view, insurance is a cartelized industry selling a good sufficiently essential that it requires government regulation in the public interest. The product conception sees insurance more as a tangible good than a promise to perform financial services, and therefore appropriately subject to rules analogous to those that govern defectively designed products. Tort, rather than contract, is the core paradigm in this conception. Finally, the governance conception views insurance as a surrogate for government in controlling behavior and protecting against misfortune, as well as an organizational arrangement among policyholders. These governance relationships create the risk of abuse by the insurer for its own ends, and for the ends of the majority of policyholders at the expense of the minority. Insurance law rules, analogous to those that protect the populace against government and the

> minority of the populace against overreaching by the majority, are therefore desirable.

Kenneth S. Abraham, Four Conceptions of Insurance, 161 U. Pa. L. Rev. 653, 657 (2013). Which of these conceptions of insurance did the ACA adopt?

4. *Alternatives.* Can you think of any way that the government could have abolished preexisting conditions limitations on insurance without requiring everyone to become part of the health care system?

Should the government have pursued a single payer system, in which the government runs the health care system, instead of leaving health insurance coverage to private insurance companies?

> Single payer health care is a universal health care system where a "single payer" (fund), rather than private insurers, pays for health care costs. Much like our current Medicare system, in a single payer system everyone pays into a single fund, then that fund pays for all medical services, typically with delivery of care remaining private. The single fund is controlled by an agency, typically organized and overseen by the government. Single payer describes funding and not delivery, allowing for public health insurance while maintaining a private or quasi-private health care system.

ObamaCare Facts, What is a Single Payer System?, at http://obamacarefacts.com/single-payer/. Why do you think the Obama administration did not opt for a single-payer system? What are the benefits you can see with a single-payer system? The drawbacks?

5. *Health Care Market Analogies: Buying Cars and Broccoli.* The Chief Justice rejected the government's interpretation of the individual mandate by talking about cars and broccoli:

> According to the Government, upholding the individual mandate would not justify mandatory purchases of items such as cars or broccoli because, as the Government puts it, "[h]ealth insurance is not purchased for its own sake like a car or broccoli; it is a means of financing health-care consumption and covering universal risks." But cars and broccoli are no more purchased for their "own sake" than health insurance. They are purchased to cover the need for transportation and food.

Is buying health insurance like buying a car, as the Chief Justice suggested? If the mandate were constitutional under the Commerce Clause, could the government force people to buy broccoli for their health?

Professor Mariner provided a detailed explanation why the health care market is unique, and not at all like buying a car:

> One might argue that repairs to one's house or car are often paid directly by homeowners or car insurance. However, that analogy ignores an important distinction. Individuals do not seek repairs in a vacuum. First, they must buy a house or a car with money from their own assets or a loan. Then they may buy insurance to pay for any repairs needed in the future. Later, if damage occurs, they may call upon insurance to pay for repairs, but

they do not use car insurance proceeds to buy the car in the first place.

In contrast, individuals seek health insurance to buy the initial "product"—healthcare—before seeking that care. One might claim that health insurance is like a car loan obtained to buy the car in the first place, except that the "loan" does not have to be repaid. Health insurance is not analogous to car insurance, unless we consider the human body to be the original product and health insurance as the source of payment for repairs to the body. Of course, the human body is not a product; the Thirteenth Amendment has prohibited treating a human being as a commodity since 1865.

In his opinion on the ACA's individual mandate in *National Federation of Independent Business v. Sebelius,* Chief Justice John Roberts rejected the idea that health insurance differs from car insurance. Very few things are purchased for their own sake, he asserted: a car is purchased for transportation to go places. If health insurance is similarly purchased for an ultimate purpose, as the Chief Justice implied, that purpose can only be to buy healthcare, which, under his reasoning, is itself purchased for the further purpose of getting well. This theory makes analogies—a mainstay of legal reasoning—unmanageable. At issue is the source of payment for products or services like cars and health care. Intangible states of being, like going places and getting well, are not products that can be bought. Buying health insurance is at least one step too far removed from buying a car to satisfy the Chief Justice's attempt at analogy.

Wendy K. Mariner, Health Insurance is Dead; Long Live Health Insurance, 40 Am. J. Law & Med. 195, 197–98 (2014). Whose reasoning is more persuasive, the Chief Justice's or Professor Mariner's?

Justice Scalia introduced the broccoli analogy during oral argument about Obamacare:

Justice SCALIA: Could you define the market—everybody has to buy food sooner or later. So, you define the market as food; therefore, everybody's in the market; therefore, you can make people buy broccoli.

General VERRILLI: No, that is quite different. It is quite different. The food market, while it shares that trait that everybody's in it, it is not a market in which your participation is often unpredictable and often involuntary. It is not a market in which you often don't know before you go in what you need, and it is not a market in which, if you go in and—and seek to obtain a product or service, you will get it even if you can't pay for it.

Department of Health & Human Services v. Florida, 2012 WL 1017220 (U.S.), 13 (U.S. Oral Arg. 2012).

Do you think the broccoli argument is persuasive? Do you agree with Justice Scalia that the broccoli argument parallels the health care

argument? Or, do you find the two things distinguishable? If so, how? Do you agree that a Commerce Clause ruling for the government would have allowed the government to force us all to buy broccoli? Or do you think Justice Ginsburg gets the better of the broccoli and cars argument:

> . . . Maintaining that the uninsured are not active in the health-care market, THE CHIEF JUSTICE draws an analogy to the car market. An individual "is not 'active in the car market,'" THE CHIEF JUSTICE observes, simply because he or she may someday buy a car. The analogy is inapt. The inevitable yet unpredictable need for medical care and the guarantee that emergency care will be provided when required are conditions nonexistent in other markets. That is so of the market for cars, and of the market for broccoli as well. Although an individual *might* buy a car or a crown of broccoli one day, there is no certainty she will ever do so. And if she eventually wants a car or has a craving for broccoli, she will be obliged to pay at the counter before receiving the vehicle or nourishment. She will get no free ride or food, at the expense of another consumer forced to pay an inflated price. Upholding the minimum coverage provision on the ground that all are participants or will be participants in the health-care market would therefore carry no implication that Congress may justify under the Commerce Clause a mandate to buy other products and services.

6. *EMTALA—a Free Ride.* The Emergency Medical Treatment and Active Labor Act ("EMTALA"), originally passed in 1986 and signed by President Ronald Reagan, requires that hospitals that accept Medicare and operate an emergency department provide an "appropriate medical screening" to anyone who "comes to" the emergency department, regardless of their ability to pay, their citizenship, or legal status. The act was created to ensure public access to emergency services, specifically by prohibiting patient "dumping"—turning patients away because they could not pay. Because almost all hospitals participate in Medicare, the Act applies to most hospitals and to anyone needing treatment, not just someone with Medicare. If a hospital seeks to transfer a patient with an emergency medical condition that has not been stabilized, the hospital must obtain written, informed consent from the patient or patient's representative. If the patient or their representative is not available, EMTALA requires a physician's signed certification that the medical benefits of the transfer are expected to outweigh the risks. EMTALA is codified at 42 U.S.C. § 1395dd and requires the following:

> (a) Medical screening requirement
>
> In the case of a hospital that has a hospital emergency department, if any individual (whether or not eligible for benefits under this subchapter) comes to the emergency department and a request is made on the individual's behalf for examination or treatment for a medical condition, the hospital must provide for an appropriate medical screening examination within the capability of the hospital's emergency department, including ancillary services routinely available to the emergency department, to determine

> whether or not an emergency medical condition (within the meaning of subsection (e)(1) of this section) exists.
>
> (b) Necessary stabilizing treatment for emergency medical conditions and labor
>
> (1) In general
>
> If any individual (whether or not eligible for benefits under this subchapter) comes to a hospital and the hospital determines that the individual has an emergency medical condition, the hospital must provide either—
>
> (A) within the staff and facilities available at the hospital, for such further medical examination and such treatment as may be required to stabilize the medical condition, or
>
> (B) for transfer of the individual to another medical facility in accordance with subsection (c) of this section.

42 U.S.C. § 1395dd(a)–(b) (2012). Failure to comply with this Act may result in a penalty of not more than $50,000.00 for a negligent hospital or physician. In addition, there is a private right of action available against hospitals by an individual who suffers personal harm or by another medical facility that suffers a financial loss due to the hospital's violation of the statute. Id. § 1395dd(d).

Was Congress correct to take account of EMTALA in the ACA by enforcing the mandate? Or should Congress abolish EMTALA and let people get health care only if they pay for it? Do you agree with the following comment from a *Washington Post* reader regarding the link from EMTALA to the ACA?

> If we are going to mandate that hospitals treat and stabilize patients with emergency medical conditions, we should mandate that individuals purchase insurance to pay for that care. If we don't, then we truly have a health care system where the few pay for the many. . . . The government has been mandating health care coverage for more than 25 years—only now President Obama wants those who utilize the system to pay for it.

Ezra Klein, Repeal EMTALA!, Wash. Post, Jan. 27, 2011. As Justice Scalia suggested at oral argument in *Sebelius*, does it make sense to repeal EMTALA? Would repealing EMTALA take care of the problem by keeping free riders out of the health care system?

7. *State Exchanges and the Implementation of the ACA*. The ACA required the states to establish American Health Benefit Exchanges (Exchanges) to make it easier for consumers to buy qualified health plans. 42 U.S.C.A. § 18031. An Exchange is "a governmental agency or nonprofit entity that is established by a State," 42 U.S.C.A. § 18031, in order to "make available qualified health plans to qualified individuals and qualified employers." 42 U.S.C.A. § 18031. According to the ACA, if states decide not to create an Exchange, the federal government will establish an Exchange that state residents can use. See 42 U.S.C.A. § 18041 ("the Secretary shall

(directly or through agreement with a not-for-profit entity) establish and operate such Exchange within the State and the Secretary shall take such actions as are necessary to implement such other requirements.").

The federal Exchange is available at www.HealthCare.gov. In states that have not established Exchanges, individuals who don't have coverage through an employer, Medicare, Medicaid, or the Children's Health Insurance Program (CHIP), may use HealthCare.gov to purchase health insurance. The website is designed to act as a single portal that will connect individuals with the most appropriate coverage source, including Medicaid or CHIP as well as ACA plans. See https://www.healthcare.gov/.

Go to the website and figure out how to work your way through the Health Insurance Marketplace.

As of February 2021, fourteen states (CA, CO, CT, ID, MA, MD, MN, NV, NJ, NY, PA, RI, VT, WA) and the District of Columbia operate their own exchanges. Pennsylvania and New Jersey began operating their own exchanges effective November 1, 2020. In 2015, Hawaii and Kentucky originally operated their own exchanges, but have since adopted the federal exchange. Health Insurance Marketplaces by State, https://www.health insurance.org/state-health-insurance-exchanges/. The other states have federal-run, federally-supported, or state-federal partnerships.

The ACA provides a premium tax credit to low- and middle-income Exchange users to offset the cost of their insurance. 26 U.S.C. § 36B. IRS regulations give the credit to purchasers who use either the federal or the state-run Exchanges. 26 C.F.R. § 1.36B–1(k); Health Insurance Premium Tax 7 Credit, 77 Fed.Reg. 30,377, 30,378 (May 23, 2012). During the 2020 open enrollment period, more than 7.2 million (87%) of the 8.3 million individuals enrolled through HealthCare.gov qualified for tax credits. Katie Keith, Final Marketplace Enrollment Data For 2020, HealthAffairs Blog, April 2, 2020, https://www-healthaffairs-org.libproxy.lib.unc.edu/do/10.1377/hblog20200402.109653/full/.

After the Exchanges were underway, challengers in Virginia and other states without Exchanges who did not want to purchase comprehensive health insurance filed lawsuits challenging the tax credit's applicability to HealthCare.gov. King v. Burwell, 759 F.3d 358, 364 (4th Cir. 2014) cert. granted,; Halbig v. Burwell, 758 F.3d 390, 399 (D.C. Cir. 2014) reh'g en banc granted, judgment vacated, No. 14–5018, 2014 WL 4627181 (D.C. Cir. Sept. 4, 2014). They argued that the specific wording of the statute allowed tax credits for the state Exchanges only, i.e., in practice only for the thirteen states and the District of Columbia who ran their own Exchanges.

According to Section 1311 of the ACA, "Each State shall, not later than January 1, 2014, establish an American Health Benefit Exchange (referred to in this title as an "Exchange")." 42 U.S.C. § 18031. If a state "elects" not to establish an Exchange, Section 1321 then clarifies that "the Secretary [of HHS] shall (directly or through agreement with a not-for-profit entity) establish and operate such Exchange within the State." 42 U.S.C. § 18041.

According to the tax credit section of the statute, tax credits apply to individuals who "were enrolled in through an Exchange established by the State under [Section] 1311 of the Patient Protection and Affordable Care Act." 26 U.S.C. § 36B(b)(2)(A). "The plaintiffs argued that in defining the terms 'coverage months' and 'premium assistance amount' by reference to Exchanges that are 'established by the State under [§] 1311,' Congress limited the availability of tax credits to individuals purchasing insurance on state Exchanges. Under the plaintiffs' construction, the premium credit amount for individuals purchasing insurance through a federal Exchange would always be zero." King v. Burwell, 759 F.3d 358, 368 (4th Cir.) cert. granted, 574 U.S. 988.

The Fourth Circuit ruled for the government; however, the D.C. Circuit ruled for the challengers because "a federal Exchange is not an 'Exchange established by the State,' and section 36B does not authorize the IRS to provide tax credits for insurance purchased on federal Exchanges." Halbig v. Burwell, 758 F.3d 390, 399 (D.C. Cir. 2014) reh'g en banc granted, judgment vacated, No. 14–5018, 2014 WL 4627181 (D.C. Cir. Sept. 4, 2014). The Supreme Court granted cert. in King v. Burwell.

In June 2015, in a 6–3 decision written again by Chief Justice Roberts, the Court affirmed the Fourth Circuit and upheld the availability of tax credits to health insurance purchased through both types of exchanges. King v. Burwell, 576 U.S. 473 (2015). While acknowledging that the Petitioners' arguments regarding the plain meaning of the phrase were strong, the majority nonetheless sided with the Government in holding that the context and structure of the overall statute led to the conclusion that the statute permitted tax credits for insurance purchased on "any Exchange created under the Act" (id. at 2496).

> **Go to** the website and listen to the oral argument in *King v. Burwell*.

8. *Medicaid*. Part of the ACA included an expansion of Medicaid increasing the eligibility levels to include individuals under age 65 with incomes up to133% of the federal poverty level. In *Sebelius*, the Supreme Court overturned the requirement under the ACA that states are required to expand Medicaid. Before the decision, states that did not comply with the expanded Medicaid requirement would lose all their federal funding for traditional Medicaid as well. However, the Supreme Court held that states could opt out of the Medicaid expansion without losing federal funding. That left states the option of deciding whether they would participate in the expansion or not. As of November 2020, 12 states (TX, WY, SD, KS, WI, TN, MS, AL, GA, FL, SC, and NC) have not adopted the Medicaid expansion. Two states, (MO and OK) have adopted the expansion, but have not implemented it. KFF, Status of State Action on the Medicaid Expansion Decision, Nov. 2, 2020, https://www.kff.org/medicaid/issue-brief/status-of-state-medicaid-expansion-decisions-

> **Go to** the website and decide if you would adopt the Medicaid Expansion.

interactive-map/. Initially, the federal government paid 100% of the cost for new Medicaid recipients. The matching rate slowly declined each year until 2020 when the match reached 90%. According to the federal government, the 90% match is where it will remain indefinitely. See State and Federal spending under the ACA, MACPAC, https://www.macpac.gov/subtopic/state-and-federal-spending-under-the-aca/.

What do you think about the Medicaid expansion? If you were a state governor, would you choose to participate in it? What are the benefits of participation? What are the drawbacks?

9. *The Next Phase of the ACA.* In 2017, Congress enacted the Tax Cuts and Jobs Act of 2017, Pub. L. No. 115–97, 131 Stat. 2054, which set the cost of the individual mandate at $0. Thus, patients had no dollar amount to pay for violating the individual mandate. However, Congress left the rest of the ACA in place. A group of 20 states, led by Texas, challenged the amended ACA in 2018, saying that the minimum coverage provision was now unconstitutional because the tax had been reduced to zero. When the Trump Administration chose not to defend the constitutionality of the ACA, 17 states, led by California, were allowed to intervene to defend the law. The district court agreed with the plaintiffs and invalidated the entire ACA because the mandate was "interwoven" with the rest of the act. The Fifth Circuit agreed, ruling that the mandate was now an unconstitutional command to purchase health insurance, and remanded the case for the district court to consider in more detail the severability of the mandate from the rest of the act. Texas v. U.S., 945 F.3d 355 (5th Cir. 2019). The Supreme Court granted cert. to hear the appeal of the Fifth Circuit's decision.

Go to the website and listen to the oral argument in *California v. Texas.* What are the best arguments? What are the worst? Which side do you think will win? Which side did win?

States on one side (CA, CO, CT, DE, HI, IL, IA, MA, MI, MN, NV, NJ, NY, NC, OR, RI, VT, VA, WA, the Governor of KY, and D.C.) challenged the Fifth Circuit's decision and supported the ACA, while other states (TX, AL, AZ, AR, FL, GA, IN, KS, LA, MS, MO, NE, ND, SC, SD, TE, UT, WV) asked for the district court's opinion to be affirmed. One argument was that the critics of the act did not have standing because they had not suffered any injury by incurring a $0 penalty. How do you think the Supreme Court will rule?

The briefing and oral argument in this case took place during the Trump administration. In February 2021, the new Biden administration notified the Court that it should uphold the entire law. It told the Court that it no longer adhered to the view espoused in the prior administration's brief. It said the mandate was still a constitutional mandate, and if the Court ruled it was not, the rest of the ACA was still severable. Amy Howe, Biden administration notifies court of new position on Affordable Care *Act*, SCOTUS blog (Feb. 10, 2021, 5:30 PM), https://www.scotusblog.com/2021/02/biden-administration-

notifies-court-of-new-position-on-affordable-care-act/. Should this notification change anything at the Court?

10. *Historical Background to Quest for Social Justice.* Now consider whether the ACA effectuates social justice by making health care available to all Americans. Consider the following extended debate about a right to health care that took place during the past forty years before giving your verdict on the ACA.

a. *The Seventies.* As you learned at the beginning of this chapter, in a 1974 article, Professor Gene Outka identified five standard accounts of social justice and applied them to health care. Gene Outka, Social Justice and Equal Access to Health Care, 2 J. Religious Ethics 11 (1974). Outka examined different principles to determine which would be the most applicable to a national health care system. Outka understood the difficulty of having a national health care system because of the American concept of health care as a "good or service." Id. at 20. Americans do not believe that goods and services are given as gifts by nature; rather, they are earned through the effort of the individual. Id. With this American societal view in mind, Outka examines all five standards. See Outka, *supra*, at 13. Which of Outka's standards do you think is the most relevant principle of justice for the health care system? Outka rejected the first theory—*"To each according to his merit or desert"*—because he believed that health issues are non-meritarian, meaning that it is not based upon who deserves health care based on their merits, because health issues "occur for reasons beyond our control or power to predict. They frequently fall without discrimination on the (according-to-merit) just and unjust, i.e., the virtuous and the wicked, the industrious and the slothful alike." Id. at 15. Further, Outka argued that unlike virtues and vices, health crises depend upon natural contingencies. "It makes sense therefore to say that we are equal in being randomly susceptible to these crises." Id. For example, Outka reasoned, "it would be odd to maintain that a newborn child deserves his hemophilia or the tumor afflicting her spine." Do you agree with Outka that it would be odd for someone to say that a newborn deserves a health issue? What if it was an adult?

> **Practice Exercise:** Consider the following reasons why individuals may visit an emergency room and ask yourself if you think some are more deserving of care than others:

In contrast, is there a merit-based argument for deaths? Outka discusses that not all deaths are beyond our control, such as automobile accidents, drugs, tobacco, obesity, etc. Id. at 16.

> (1) a person with a heart attack who is seriously overweight; (2) a football hero who has suffered a concussion; (3) a man with lung cancer who has smoked

> cigarettes for forty years; (4) a 60 year old man who has always taken excellent care of himself and is suddenly stricken with leukemia; (5) a three year old girl who has swallowed poison left out carelessly by her parents; (6) a 14 year old boy who has been beaten without provocation by a gang and suffers brain damage and recurrent attacks of uncontrollable terror; (7) a college student who has slashed his wrists (and not for the first time) from a psychological need for attention; (8) a woman raised in the ghetto who is found unconscious due to an overdose of heroin.

Id. Did you think that some of these health issues were brought upon by the individual's own faults or assumption of risk? If you had limited health resources, whom would you help first? Would you help those in need of care? Or, would you look at who was considered the biggest victim compared to someone who brought the health issue upon him or her?

Outka also rejected the second theory—*"To each according to his social contribution."* Id. at 17. He recounted the example of a Swedish Hospital in Seattle in the early 1960s. The Hospital had a dilemma; it was short on resources. The Hospital only had a limited amount of kidney machines, with a larger amount of patients suffering chronic renal failure. Id. at 18. The Hospital used the following criteria to determine who received dialysis: "age, sex, marital status, number of dependents, income, net worth, educational background, occupation, past performance and future potential." Id. Under these circumstances, Outka posed the question of whether "someone with six children [should] always have priority over an artist or composer?"

Outka also rejected the third principle for justice—*"To each according to his contribution in satisfying whatever is freely desired by others in the open marketplace of supply and demand."* Id. at 19. Outka stated that this idea would typically fail because of the argument about a consumer's free choice. Id. The reason, Outka argued, that a national health care system will be so heavily debated is because opponents will appeal to the liberty of Americans to express their preferences and choose from different goods and services, not a mandated national system. Id.

The fourth principle—*"To each according to his needs"*—Outka argued is the most applicable principle in the health care marketplace. Id. at 21. Unlike the first principle, which dealt with merits and deserts (rewards), this principle deals with essential needs. Outka explained, "essential needs are likewise distinguishable from deserts. Where needs are unequal, one thinks of them fortuitously distributed, as part, perhaps, of a kind of 'natural lottery.'" Id. at 22. For example, Outka distinguishes between hunger and cancer. Hunger is a constant threat, which allows humans to use the power of prediction to store up on food to

combat hunger in the winter. Id. Cancer, on the other hand, is a "contingent disaster" and is "particularly random and uncontrollable." Id. Consequently, a responsible person—who always stores food as a way of safeguarding their health—cannot predict or control if they will be diagnosed with cancer. In summary, Outka stated, "[J]ustice has properly to do with pleas of 'But I could not help it.' It seeks to distinguish such cases from those acknowledged to be praiseworthy or blameworthy. The formula 'to each according to his needs' is one cogent way of identifying the moral relevance of these pleas." Id. at 23.

The final theory is *"Similar treatment for similar cases."* Outka concluded it is "necessary but not sufficient" because it could wind up with everyone without treatment. Outka argued:

> Illness is the proper ground for the *receipt* of medical care. However, the *distribution* of medical care in less-than-optimal circumstances requires us to face the collisions. I would argue that in such circumstances the formula of similar treatment for similar cases may be construed so as to guide actual choices in the way most compatible with the goal of equal justice.

Id. at 24. To address what is the most appropriate way to conduct a national health care system, Outka proposed his plan. Outka propositioned:

> Each citizen is (in effect) issued a card by the government. Whenever "legitimate" medical expenses (however determined for a given society) exceed, say 10 per cent of his or her annual taxable income, the card may be presented so that additional costs incurred will be paid for out of the general tax revenues.

Id. at 26. What do you think about Outka's plan? How would a government decide what type of medical expenses are "legitimate"? Do you think it would open up the floodgates of litigation if Americans had to litigate every issue to have the courts determine if a certain procedure was considered "legitimate," i.e. abortion, vasectomy, braces, plastic surgery, etc.? Further, what type of federal resources would it take to keep track of all citizens' annual taxable income when individuals apply for insurance? Do you think it would require the IRS to be stricter on taxes to ensure that Americans are not underreporting to save on health care? Do you agree with Outka's plan? Why or why not? If so, how would you change it?

Are you surprised that in 1974, Outka expected that Americans would get comprehensive health care? Outka stated in the beginning of his article that the goal is "the assurance of comprehensive health services for every person irrespective of income or geographic location." Id. at 11. Do you think the ACA adopted any of Outka's principles? If so, which ones?

b. *The Eighties and Nineties.* The 1980s brought EMTALA, which required health care treatment for the uninsured as described above, to the American health care system. In the 1980s and 1990s, attention turned increasingly to the health insurance market. Professor Deborah Stone observed two principles by which insurance could be regulated—the solidarity principle and the principle of actuarial fairness. Deborah A. Stone, The Struggle for the Soul of Health Insurance, 18 J. Health Pol. Pol'y & L. 287 (1993). Stone argued that the concept of actuarial fairness—where each person pays for his own risk—fragments communities "by fostering in people a sense of their differences, rather than their commonalities, and their responsibilities for themselves only, rather than their interdependence," and leads to the destruction of mutual aid. Id. at 290. On the other hand, "[s]ocial insurance operates by the logic of solidarity. Its purpose is to guarantee that certain agreed-upon individual needs will be paid for by a community or group." Id. at 290–91. Stone observed the issues of actuarial fairness:

> If medical care were financed like most market goods, by charging people for exactly the goods and services they consume, the ultimate distribution of medical care would be only partially according to need. Those who are sick and need care would come forward to purchase it, but among the sick, only those who could afford it would actually receive care. In addition, some who are not sick but who have resources might try to purchase care as well. People who could not afford to buy care would not receive any, regardless of their need for it or ability to benefit from it.

Id. at 291. Further, under the theory of actuarial fairness, premium rates are different per person based on the quality of risk—meaning the likely value of a person's medical needs. Id. at 293. Similar to life insurance, where insurance companies use factors to assess life expectancy, medical insurance companies try to use factors to determine a person's use of medical care. These factors "include one's occupation, hobbies (since some are very dangerous), family medical history, personal medical history, and any medical information that is prognostic of disease, even if disease hasn't yet occurred." Id. What do you think about actuarial fairness versus the concept of the solidarity principle—where individuals receive care and the community will help cover the costs? Which of these principles was most prevalent in the ACA?

c. *The Aughts.* After considering health care in America, scholars in the new millennium focused on global justice and providing medical treatment and health care systems to everyone, not just in America or other industrialized nations. See Sabina Alkire & Lincoln Chen, Global Health and Moral Values, 364 Lancet 1069 (2004). To justify global health initiatives, scholars

formed four different schools of thought: humanitarianism, utilitarianism, equity, and rights. Id. at 1070. Alkire and Chen define humanitarianism as "acting virtuously towards those in need." Id. The authors argued that humanitarianism is the most common school of moral values for global health action, as evidenced by the voluntary actions of non-governmental organizations and public donations. Id. Utilitarianism is defined as maximizing aggregate subjective happiness. Id. Utilitarians focus on the public utility that good health provides to the economy and in society. Alkire and Chen observed:

> Many contemporary health policies are based on a form of utilitarianism in which good health is valued as instrumental to maximizing aggregate utility. For example, the WHO Commission on Macroeconomics and Health calculated the costs and benefits of burdens of disease and argued that investing in health would generate economic growth, thereby enhancing incomes and aggregate utility.

Id. Equity is based on the goal of achieving a fairer distribution of health capabilities. Id. at 1071. Alkire and Chen posed the question of "equity of what?" Id. Does Global Justice require that everyone in the world have equal health care? Should a family in a third world country that cannot afford to pay for health care receive the same health care treatment as a middle-class family in the United States that can afford treatment? What does equity really mean? Does it mean emergency treatment for the sick? Does it mean flu shots? Does it mean teeth cleanings? The authors stated, "equity in health should be assessed in terms of health capabilities and achievements rather than healthcare activities." Id. The authors recognized "health care is a human activity; what people actually value is the capability to attain good health." Id. So, does equity mean that everyone has equal access to health care, even if they cannot afford to receive it? If equity requires that everyone receive equal treatment, how would that endeavor be financed and enforced? What do you think is the difference between health capabilities and health care activities? Does it sound like another way of saying that those that can afford treatment should have access to it?

The last school of moral thought is "rights." Rights are defined as "fulfilling our obligations so others are dignified." Principally, the authors evaluated what human rights mean: "things which are owed to man because of the very fact that he is man." Id. However, with a right comes an obligation "on the part of the state, firms, groups, and individuals." Id. In summary, "[a] human rights approach often assumes some health minimum that all people should be able to realize for human dignity." Id.

Which of these schools of moral thought is the most persuasive to support global health initiatives? Do you think there is a God-given right to health care? Do you think that someone in a third world country deserves lifesaving drugs because they are in need, even if it requires other countries, individuals, or organizations to support the cost? Do you think that eradicating disease will provide the most utility to our global economy and

society? Or, do you think that helping others attain good health care is just the right thing to do, even without all of the other benefits?

Global health initiatives have been very successful on many different levels. For example, the World Health Organization and the World Bank "help governments improve the public administration needed to deliver quality health care to all," whether it is on the "macro level (e.g., standardizing diagnostic categories) or the micro level (e.g., providing antiretroviral medicines for AIDS patients)." Jennifer Prah Ruger, Health and Social Justice, 364 Lancet 1075, 1079 (2004). Regardless of whether individuals donated or volunteered to help achieve these goals based on humanitarian, utilitarian, equity, or rights schools of moral thought, the impact has been very successful. Do you think global health initiatives are important? How so?

11. *COVID and the ACA.* Under the Affordable Care Act, enrollment in ACA plans occurs during a set time each year, called "open enrollment." However, a life-changing event, such as loss of coverage due to job loss, may qualify a person for a special enrollment period ("SEP"). The Center for Medicare and Medicaid Services ("CMS") may authorize a broad SEP during crises, a move that has been supported by many during the COVID-19 pandemic. However, under the Trump Administration, CMS did not do so. A June 25, 2020, CMS report showed that HealthCare.gov enrollment through *existing* SEPs skyrocketed during the pandemic, leading to a 27% increase in enrollment over the same period in 2019. Special enrollment due to loss-of-coverage from job loss peaked in April 2020 and represented a 46% increase relative to the same period in 2019.

Enrollment through state-based marketplaces was even higher during the pandemic. For example, in California, Covered California enrollment because of SEP was 2.5 times higher than during the same period in 2019. Even though elevated SEP enrollment was expected because of the COVID-19 pandemic and widespread economic disruption and job loss, the CMS data could have shown an even higher enrollment due to the number of job losses suffered by Americans during the pandemic months. This suggests that enrollment through SEP would have been even higher if CMS had advertised and reached out more to the public about the availability of SEPs. Soon after assuming office in January 2021, President Biden announced a plan to reopen exchange enrollment in the states that use Healthcare.gov. Margot Sanger-Katz, Biden Plans to Reopen Obamacare Exchanges in Many States, N.Y. Times, Jan. 27, 2021, https://www.nytimes.com/2021/01/27/us/biden-obamacare-aca.html. The exchanges opened on Feb. 15, 2021. Megan Leonhardt, Biden Sign Order to Open Obamacare in 2 Weeks, Feb. 1. 2021, https://www.cnbc.com/2021/02/01/biden-to-reopen-obamacare-in-2-weeks what-you-need-to-know.html.

B. ORGAN TRANSPLANTS

39,035 transplants were performed in 2020. In the United States, there are around 109,000 Americans on a waiting list for organ transplants. 17 people die each day waiting for a transplant. See Department of Health and Human Services, Organ Donation Statistics, at organdonor.gov/statistics-stories/statistics.html; Data, at https://optn.transplant.hrsa.gov/data/. The shortage is due to a lack of registered donors as well as to difficulties in obtaining organs. Some people may not register for religious reasons or because they fear they will not get good health care if they agree to be a donor. Only 3 of 1,000 people die in a way that allows organ transplantation. Advances in medical treatments are good for patients, but they reduce the number of organs available for transplantation. Life Center, The Organ Shortage and the Need for Donors, https://lifepassiton.org/the-organ-shortage-the-need-for-donors/. Once a donation is secured, a threshold question in organ transplantation is which recipient should receive the organ.

> **Practice Exercise:** Based on what type of need you see, coupled with the type of donor pool available, consider how you would create an ideal system for organ donation.

With this information in mind, ask yourself: how would your system distribute the organs? Is it first come, first served? Is it based on who can afford to pay? Is it based on need (medical or otherwise)? Is age a factor—what if you had a seventy-year-old man who was in more need than a ten-year-old boy, but the man had lived a long life, while the boy has his whole life ahead of him? Does a person's contribution to society matter—what if you had to choose between a convicted felon in prison or a law-abiding citizen? Between your spouse and the President of the United States? What about an individual's location—should the patient closer to the organ be favored over a person across the country? Should the length of time a patient has been on the waiting list affect her chances? Will your decision be influenced by the different theories of justice developed in Section A of this Chapter? If so, which principle most affects your decision of distribution?

In the United States, organ transplants are governed by the National Organ Transplant Act ("NOTA"). Passed in October 1984 and amended in 1988, 1990, and 2007, the National Organ Transplant Act also outlawed the sale of human organs. The 2007 amendment added, among other things, the paired donation language considered below. See https://www.govtrack.us/congress/bills/110/hr710. The possibility of organ sale was prohibited because lawmakers feared commercializing organ transplantation would force the poor and disenfranchised into being manipulated into donating their organs. They feared such an outcome would create intolerable dehumanization. Gwen Mayes, Buying

and Selling Organs for Transplantation in the United States. Medscape Education 4, no. 3 (2003): 1–4.

On the specific question of organ distribution, NOTA "provided for the establishment and operation of an Organ Procurement and Transplantation Network ("OPTN"), a private nonprofit entity with expertise in organ procurement and transplantation composed of representatives of organ procurement organizations ("OPOs"), transplant centers, voluntary health associations, and the general public." Noel Barnard, Throw Me a Bone Marrow Transplant: Peripheral Blood Stem Cells and the National Organ Transplant Act, 13 N.C. J.L. & Tech. 387, 396–98 (2012). The United Network for Organ Sharing ("UNOS") "manages the nation's organ transplant system under contract with the federal government." See About Us, UNOS, https://unos.org/about/. UNOS manages the national transplant waiting list and maintains a database of every organ transplant that occurs in the United States. Id. Did your ideal system include such an agency? According to regulations implementing NOTA,

> (b) Allocation performance goals. Allocation policies shall be designed to achieve equitable allocation of organs among patients . . . through the following performance goals:
>
> (1) Standardizing the criteria for determining suitable transplant candidates through the use of minimum criteria (expressed, to the extent possible, through objective and measurable medical criteria) for adding individuals to, and removing candidates from, organ transplant waiting lists;
>
> (2) Setting priority rankings expressed, to the extent possible, through objective and measurable medical criteria, for patients or categories of patients who are medically suitable candidates for transplantation to receive transplants. These rankings shall be ordered from most to least medically urgent (taking into account, in accordance with paragraph (a) of this section, and in particular in accordance with sound medical judgment, that life sustaining technology allows alternative approaches to setting priority ranking for patients). There shall be a sufficient number of categories (if categories are used) to avoid grouping together patients with substantially different medical urgency;
>
> (3) Distributing organs over as broad a geographic area as feasible under paragraphs (a)(1)–(5) of this section, and in order of decreasing medical urgency; and
>
> (4) Applying appropriate performance indicators to assess transplant program performance under paragraphs (c)(2)(i) and (c)(2)(ii) of this section and reducing the inter-transplant program variance to as small as can reasonably be achieved in any performance indicator under paragraph (c)(2)(iii) of this section as the Board determines appropriate, and under

> paragraph (c)(2)(iv) of this section. If the performance indicator "waiting time in status" is used for allocation purposes, the OPTN shall seek to reduce the inter-transplant program variance in this indicator, as well as in other selected performance indicators, to as small as can reasonably be achieved, unless to do so would result in transplanting less medically urgent patients or less medically urgent patients within a category of patients.

42 C.F.R. 121.8. Do these standards help you to design your ideal system?

On July 10, 2019, President Trump issued an executive order titled, "Advancing American Kidney Health." See Exec. Order 13879, 84 Fed. Reg. 33817 (2019). Among other things, the order directed the Secretary of HHS to: create an initiative to increase awareness of kidney-related diseases; create new payment models to identify and treat at-risk individuals and increase home dialysis and kidney transplants; encourage the development of an artificial kidney; develop regulations to enhance procurement and utilization of organs from deceased donations by revising evaluation metrics for Organ Procurement Organizations (OPOs); streamline kidney matching and delivery in order to reduce the rate of discarded organs; and develop a regulation to reduce financial barriers to living organ donations. Id. The rule revising OPO conditions was finalized in December 2020, to take effect in February 2021. Centers for Medicare and Medicaid Services, Medicare and Medicaid Programs; Organ Procurement Organizations Conditions for Coverage: Revisions to the Outcome Measure Requirements for Organ Procurement Organizations, 85 Fed. Reg. 77898 (Dec. 2020) (to be codified in 42 C.F.R. Part 486).

To be placed on the OPTN National Transplant Waiting List, patients need to be referred by a physician. See U.S. Dep't Health & Human Servs., Organ Transplantation: The Process, OrganDonor.gov, http://www.organdonor.gov/about/transplantationprocess.html. Once a donor—typically deceased—is ready to donate, the local OPO contacts the OPTN "to begin the search for matching recipients." Id. From there, a donor and recipient are matched as follows:

> A computer program matches donor organs with recipients based on certain characteristics. These include blood type, tissue type, height, and weight. The length of time the patient has been waiting, the severity of the patient's illness, and the distance between the donor's and the recipient's hospitals also figure into who is the best match for a specific organ. The list does not reference race, gender, income or social status. The OPTN computer system stores the matching information for all waiting patients and the [Organ Procurement Organization] representative enters the same information for the donor.
>
> A list of patients (by organ type) who match the donor is generated. Each organ is offered to the first patient on the

> computer match list. The transplant surgeon may determine that the organ is medically suitable for that patient or may refuse the organ for a number of reasons, such as the patient is too sick to be transplanted or the patient cannot be reached in time. Most organs (75%) go to local patients. The others are shared with patients in other regions of the country.

Id. Although these factors demonstrate what the OPTN searches for, there are some organizations that exclude certain individuals. For example, the Hastings Center—a nonpartisan bioethics research institution—found that many times, the following individuals are excluded from consideration:

- Many transplant centers will not accept people without insurance.
- Transplant teams rarely consider anyone over 75 years of age.
- Some centers exclude patients with moderate mental retardation, HIV, a history of addiction, or a long criminal record.
- Though American transplant centers can list foreigners, they can make up no more than 5% of any center's list. Most of non-U.S. citizens listed have substantial financial resources and pay in cash.
- Some transplant programs will admit illegal aliens, but most are children. Some transplant centers have caused controversy by refusing to retransplant illegal aliens whose initial organs, received at the same hospital during childhood, have failed.

Arthur Caplan, Organ Transplantation, Hastings Center, http://www.thehastingscenter.org/Publications/BriefingBook/Detail.aspx?id=2198.

In addition to these considerations, some commentators question whether patients who are ill because of their own risky personal conduct, such as alcoholism or drug abuse, are less deserving of transplants. See Daniel Brudney, Are Alcoholics Less Deserving of Liver Transplants?, Hastings Center (2007). For example, David Crosby, a founding member of the singing groups The Byrds and Crosby, Stills, Nash, and Young, spent time in jail on drug charges and fought drug addiction throughout his career. Crosby admitted he had been frequently stoned while writing and performing his music. Nonetheless, Crosby received a liver transplant in 1994 after he suffered liver failure. David Crosby Gets Liver Transplant, L.A. Times, Nov. 21, 1994, at A19.

Does this argument sound familiar? Recall Outka's argument about merit in Section A of this Chapter. After reading how the system works in the United States, how would you change the OPTN? Would your

decision be influenced by the theories of justice in Section A of this Chapter?

Although questions about fair organ distribution are recurring, most of the current debate about organ transplants in the United States focuses on the shortage of organs. Jason Millman has argued that the discrepancy between the increase of patients versus the number of donors is based on not asking the public to donate enough. Jason Millman, One Way to Boost Organ Donations: Just Keep Asking, Wash. Post, Aug. 18, 2014. Typically, the American public is asked whether or not they want to donate their organs one time—usually when they check the box at the DMV. Id. However, studies have shown that persistently asking the American public to donate may be better. First, it will increase awareness about the issue. Second, it will influence Americans to think this is a pressing and important issue. Third, it will give individuals another opportunity to decide whether they want to donate. Id.

Some states have increased efforts to raise awareness and recruit more people to organ donation causes. For example, in 2017, New York Governor Andrew Cuomo signed an executive order that made increasing the number of registered organ donors a priority. The order directed the State Health Department to work with other state agencies and Donate Life NYS to provide the public with more opportunities to register as organ donors. As a result, hundreds of thousands of people signed up to become donors as they purchased or renewed health insurance through the marketplace. 2.5 Million New Enrollees Since New Initiatives Began in 2015; Nearly 10,000 New Yorkers Await a Life-Saving Transplant, https://www.governor.ny.gov/news/organ-donor-enrollment-day-governor-cuomo-urges-new-yorkers-register-organ-donors.

Many advocates of organ transplants argue that donation simply cannot meet the need for organs, and recommend instead that organ distribution be market-based. NOTA, however, bans compensation for organs, as the following section explains. As one commentator notes, "the U.S. organ transplant system, particularly as it relates to kidneys, has been constrained by an ethos built around altruistic donations." Simon Haeder, Thinking the Unthinkable: Buying and Selling Human Organs, Milken Institute Review, July 30, 2020, https://www.milkenreview.org/articles/thinking-the-unthinkable.

1. THE BAN ON COMPENSATION

Throw Me a Bone Marrow Transplant: Peripheral Blood Stem Cells and the National Organ Transplant Act

Noel Barnard.
13 N.C. J.L. & Tech. 387, 396–98 (2012).

III. History of Organ Transplant Legislation

The history of organ transplant legislation in the United States is relatively brief since the technology only became a medical reality within the last fifty years. Joseph E. Murray performed the first successful organ transplant in 1954. However, it took many years before medical advances like HLA-typing [also called tissue typing] and anti-rejection drugs made transplantation available to a widespread population. [HLA, human leukocyte antigen, is a protein found on the body's cells. It helps the body to identify what belongs to it and what does not, and therefore affects the body's ability to accept or reject a transplant.]

As transplants became more prevalent, individual states began passing laws regulating the practice. Initially, these laws tended to be vague and varied greatly in scope and content. By 1968, six states still had no laws regarding organ transplants and four states had statutes providing for eye donation only. The remaining forty states had donation statutes providing for the donation of some or all organs. However, these statutes varied greatly in their provisions regarding next of kin authority to donate, donor cards, revocation authority, and conflict of laws. Many legal professionals saw a need to standardize organ donor practices across the country.

The first significant attempt to harmonize organ transplantation law came, not from Congress, but the National Conference of Commissioners on Uniform State Laws (also known as the Uniform Law Commission, "ULC"). The ULC is an organization designed to provide "states with non-partisan, well-conceived and well-drafted legislation that brings clarity and stability to critical areas of state statutory law." Established in 1892, the ULC is composed of practicing lawyers, judges, legislators, and law professors "who have been appointed by state governments . . . to research, draft and promote enactment of uniform state laws in areas of state law where uniformity is desirable and practical."

Recognizing the need to address issues associated with organ transplants, the ULC approved the Uniform Anatomical Gift Act ("UAGA") in 1968. The core of the UAGA grants any individual over eighteen years old the authority to donate all or part of his body upon death. The UAGA also provides several mechanisms for donation, including will, written instrument or donor card. The law also limits the ability to accept donations to "persons or institutions licensed or authorized to practice medicine and to engage in tissue banking or

related matters." The UAGA's provisions make organs more akin to other property interests. By 1972, all states had adopted some version of the UAGA.

In 1987 and again in 2006, the UAGA was updated to reflect changes in transplant technology. These updates aimed to increase the supply of donor organs to meet the heightened demand associated with more prevalent transplantation procedures.

The second piece of legislation to deal with the subject of organ transplantation was NOTA, passed in 1984. The main feature of NOTA is a blanket prohibition on organ purchases. The law states, "[i]t shall be unlawful for any person to knowingly acquire, receive, or otherwise transfer any human organ for valuable consideration for use in human transplantation. . . ." NOTA defines a human organ to include the kidney, liver, heart, lung, pancreas, bone marrow, cornea, eye, bone, skin, and any other organ designated by the Secretary of Health and Human Services ("HHS"). While outright organ purchase is illegal, NOTA does allow the donor to be paid reasonable expenses associated with the transplant, such as travel and lost wages.

One provision of President Trump's July 2019 executive order directed the Secretary of HHS to remove financial barriers to living organ donations by expanding the definition of reimbursable costs, raising the limit on the donor income, permitting reimbursement for lost wages, and providing reimbursement for child- and elder-care expenses. Exec., Order 13879, 84 Fed. Reg. at 33818. A Final Rule was published on September 22, 2020. Dept. of Health & Human Servs., Removing Financial Disincentives to Living Organ Donation, 85 Fed. Reg. 59438 (2020) (codified at 42 C.F.R. Part 121).

Following is the statutory text of NOTA that bans compensation for organs.

42 U.S.C. § 274e

Prohibition of Organ Purchases

(a) Prohibition

It shall be unlawful for any person to knowingly acquire, receive, or otherwise transfer any human organ for valuable consideration for use in human transplantation if the transfer affects interstate commerce. The preceding sentence does not apply with respect to human organ paired donation.

(b) Penalties

Any person who violates subsection (a) of this section shall be fined not more than $50,000 or imprisoned not more than five years, or both.

(c) Definitions

For purposes of subsection (a) of this section:

(1) The term "human organ" means the human (including fetal) kidney, liver, heart, lung, pancreas, bone marrow, cornea, eye, bone, and skin or any subpart thereof and any other human organ (or any subpart thereof, including that derived from a fetus) specified by the Secretary of Health and Human Services by regulation.

(2) The term "valuable consideration" does not include the reasonable payments associated with the removal, transportation, implantation, processing, preservation, quality control, and storage of a human organ or the expenses of travel, housing, and lost wages incurred by the donor of a human organ in connection with the donation of the organ.

(3) The term "interstate commerce" has the meaning prescribed for it by section 321 (b) of title 21.

(4) The term "human organ paired donation" means the donation and receipt of human organs under the following circumstances:

(A) An individual (referred to in this paragraph as the "first donor") desires to make a living donation of a human organ specifically to a particular patient (referred to in this paragraph as the "first patient"), but such donor is biologically incompatible as a donor for such patient.

(B) A second individual (referred to in this paragraph as the "second donor") desires to make a living donation of a human organ specifically to a second particular patient (referred to in this paragraph as the "second patient"), but such donor is biologically incompatible as a donor for such patient.

(C) Subject to subparagraph (D), the first donor is biologically compatible as a donor of a human organ for the second patient, and the second donor is biologically compatible as a donor of a human organ for the first patient.

(D) If there is any additional donor-patient pair as described in subparagraph (A) or (B), each donor in the group of donor-patient pairs is biologically compatible as a donor of a human organ for a patient in such group.

(E) All donors and patients in the group of donor-patient pairs (whether 2 pairs or more than 2 pairs) enter into a single agreement to donate and receive such human organs, respectively, according to such biological compatibility in the group.

(F) Other than as described in subparagraph (E), no valuable consideration is knowingly acquired, received, or otherwise transferred with respect to the human organs referred to in such subparagraph.

NOTA was put to the test in a 2012 case involving technological advances in the donation of bone marrow cells. Several plaintiffs challenged the constitutionality of NOTA's compensation ban under the Equal Protection Clause by arguing "there was no rational basis for allowing compensation for donations of renewable human products such as blood, eggs, and sperm, but not for donations of similarly renewable bone marrow stem cells." Jay S. Reidler & Joshua Berkowitz, Compensation for Organ Donations: A Landmark Ruling on Hematopoietic Stem Cell Transplantation Refuels the Debate, 40 J.L. Med. & Ethics 409, 410 (2012). Do you agree with the Ninth Circuit's resolution of the issue on statutory, but not equal protection, grounds in the following case?

Flynn v. Holder

United States Court of Appeals, Ninth Circuit, 2012.
684 F.3d 852.

■ KLEINFELD, SENIOR CIRCUIT JUDGE:

This is a challenge to a criminal statute prohibiting compensation for "bone marrow" donations.

I. Facts.

The district court dismissed the complaint for failure to state a claim upon which relief could be granted. We take the facts from the allegations in the complaint to determine whether, if proved, they would state an actionable claim.

The complaint challenges the constitutionality of the ban on compensation for human organs in the National Organ Transplant Act, as applied to bone marrow transplants. Plaintiffs seek declaratory and injunctive relief to allow harvesting of "hematopoietic stem cells." The complaint is not crystal clear on whether plaintiffs claim that compensation for all bone marrow transplantation is constitutionally protected, but the focus of the arguments is on cells extracted by "peripheral blood stem cell apheresis." This is a relatively new method of bone marrow transplant that avoids the need to invade the bone for marrow.

Some plaintiffs are parents of sick children who have diseases such as leukemia and a rare type of anemia, which can be fatal without bone marrow transplants. Another plaintiff is a physician and medical school professor, and an expert in bone marrow transplantation. He says that at least one out of five of his patients dies because no matching bone marrow donor can be found, and many others have complications when scarcity of matching donors compels him to use imperfectly matched donors. One plaintiff is a parent of mixed race children, for whom sufficiently matched donors are especially scarce, because mixed race

persons typically have the rarest marrow cell types. One plaintiff is an African-American man suffering from leukemia who received a bone marrow transplant from his sister. She was an imperfect match and, though the transplant saved his life, he continues to suffer from life-threatening and disabling complications on account of the slight genetic mismatch.

Another plaintiff is a California nonprofit corporation that seeks to operate a program incentivizing bone marrow donations. The corporation proposes to offer $3,000 awards in the form of scholarships, housing allowances, or gifts to charities selected by donors, initially to minority and mixed race donors of bone marrow cells, who are likely to have the rarest marrow cell type. The corporation, MoreMarrowDonors.org, alleges that it cannot launch this program because the National Organ Transplant Act criminalizes payment of compensation for organs, and classifies bone marrow as an organ.

We generally use the word "marrow" to refer to the soft, fatty material in the central cavities of big bones, what some people suck out of beef bones. Bone marrow is the body's blood manufacturing factory. Bone marrow transplants enable sick patients, whose own blood cells need to be killed to save their lives, to produce new blood cells. For example, patients with leukemia, which is cancer of the blood or bone marrow, may need chemotherapy or radiation to kill the cancer cells in their blood. The treatments kill the white blood cells essential to their immune systems. The patients will die if the killed cells are not quickly replaced with healthy cells. And they cannot be replaced without the stem cells, which we describe below, that can mature into white blood cells. These stem cells can only be obtained through bone marrow transplants.

Until about twenty years ago, bone marrow was extracted from donors' bones by "aspiration." Long needles, thick enough to suck out the soft, fatty marrow, were inserted into the cavities of the anesthetized donor's hip bones. These are large bones with big central cavities full of marrow. Aspiration is a painful, unpleasant procedure for the donor. It requires hospitalization and general or local anesthesia, and involves commensurate risks.

The complaint explains that a new technology has superseded this technique during the last twenty years, after enactment of the National Organ Transplant Act. With this new technique, now used for at least two-thirds of bone marrow transplants, none of the soft, fatty marrow is actually donated. Patients who need bone marrow transplants do not need everything that the soft, fatty substance from bone cavities contains, just some of the marrow's "hematopoietic stem cells." These stem cells are seeds from which white blood cells, red blood cells, and platelets grow.

These are not the embryonic stem cells often the subject of controversy. Those stem cells, taken from human embryos, are

"pluripotent," that is, they can turn into any kind of cell—brain, blood, retina, toenail, whatever. The stem cells at issue in this case are "hematopoietic stem cells." "Hema" refers to blood, and "poietic" means "pertaining to production." Hematopoietic stem cells turn into blood cells and nothing else. Humans and other large mammals produce these blood stem cells constantly in vast numbers, because our blood cells die within a few months and need continual replacement. The dead blood cells are flushed out in the spleen, the body's garbage disposal for used-up blood cells, and new ones are made in the bone marrow, as long as we live.

Most blood stem cells stay in the bone marrow cavity and grow into mature blood cells there, before passing into the blood vessels. But some blood stem cells flow into and circulate in the bloodstream before they mature. These are called "peripheral" blood stem cells, "peripheral" meaning outside the central area of the body. The new bone marrow donation technique, developed during the past twenty years, is called "peripheral blood stem cell apheresis." "Apheresis" means the removal or separation of something. This procedure begins with five days of injections of a medication called a "granulocyte colony-stimulating factor" into the donor's blood. The medication accelerates blood stem cell production in the marrow, so that more stem cells go into the bloodstream. Then, with no need for sedatives or anesthesia, a needle is inserted into the donor's vein. Blood is withdrawn from the vein and filtered through an apheresis machine to extract the blood stem cells. The remaining components of the blood are returned to the donor's vein. The blood stem cells extracted in the apheresis method are replaced by the donor's bone marrow in three to six weeks. Complications for the donor are exceedingly rare.

The main difference between an ordinary blood donation and apheresis is that instead of just filling up a plastic bag with whole blood, the donor sits for some hours in a recliner while the blood passes through the apheresis machine. This same apheresis technique is sometimes used for purposes other than bone marrow donations, such as when the machine is set up to collect plasma or platelets, rather than stem cells, from a donor's blood. When it is used for these other purposes, the identical technique is called a "blood donation" or "blood plasma donation." When used to separate out and collect hematopoietic stem cells from the donor's bloodstream, apheresis is called "peripheral blood stem cell apheresis" or a "bone marrow donation."

Though the new process makes bone marrow donations much like ordinary blood donations, the matching problem remains. Deep genetic compatibility is critical in bone marrow transplants, because our bodies are xenophobic: white blood cells produced from a donor's imperfectly matched blood stem cells treat the recipient patient's body as foreign, attacking it. This is graft-versus-host disease, which can be fatal or can result in lifelong medical problems for the transplant recipient. All donations from another person, except for one's identical twin, produce

at least some graft-versus-host disease in the recipient, but the closer the genetic match, the less disease. Matching is easy in ordinary blood transfusions, because there are only four basic blood types. But there are millions of marrow cell types, so good matches are hard to find. The more diverse the patient's genetic heritage, the rarer the match. For example, African-Americans have especially great difficulty finding a compatible unrelated donor, as they tend to have a mix of African, Caucasian, and Native-American genes, and fewer potential donors are registered in the national civilian registry.

The establishment of this registry, the National Marrow Donor Program, which is funded by the federal government to assist in finding matches, was an important aspect of the statute at issue here. But even with this registry, good matches often cannot be found. And even when a good match is found in the registry, tracking down the potential donor from what may be an outdated address may be impossible to accomplish in time to save the patient's life—assuming the potential donor is willing to go through with the process when found.

The plaintiff nonprofit proposes to mitigate this matching problem by using a financial incentive. The idea is that the financial incentive will induce more potential donors to sign up, stay in touch so that they can be located when necessary, and go through with the donations. The nonprofit plans to focus its attention initially on minority and mixed race donors, because their marrow cell types are rarer. The financial incentives would be $3,000 in scholarships, housing allowances, or gifts to charities of the donor's choice, which the nonprofit acknowledges would be "valuable consideration" under the statutory prohibition.

Plaintiffs argue that the National Organ Transplant Act, as applied to MoreMarrowDonors.org's planned pilot program, violates the Equal Protection Clause. They claim that blood stem cell harvesting is not materially different from blood, sperm, and egg harvesting, which are not included under the statutory or regulatory definitions of "human organ." Like donors of blood and sperm, a bone marrow donor undergoing apheresis suffers no permanent harm, experiences no significant risk, and quickly regenerates what is donated. Plaintiffs also argue that any rational basis that Congress had when it passed the statute no longer exists with respect to the pilot program, because of the subsequent development of the apheresis method. Plaintiffs seek declaratory and injunctive relief so that MoreMarrowDonors.org can proceed with the initiative.

II. Analysis.

A. The arguments.

The core of plaintiffs' argument is that there is no rational basis for allowing compensation for blood, sperm, and egg donations, while disallowing compensation for bone marrow donations, because bone marrow donations can now be accomplished through apheresis without

removing marrow, and the donor's body quickly regenerates the donated stem cells. Since the distinction, they argue, is without a rational basis, it violates the Equal Protection Clause, despite highly deferential "rational basis" review.

The Attorney General responds that the statute plainly classifies "bone marrow" as an organ for which compensation is prohibited, and that the congressional determination is indeed rational. The statute makes it a felony "to knowingly acquire, receive, or otherwise transfer any human organ for valuable consideration for use in human transplantation." And it defines the term "human organ" to include "bone marrow." Ergo, the statute expressly prohibits compensating bone marrow donors. According to the government's brief, Congress took the view that "human body parts should not be viewed as commodities," and had several policy reasons for disallowing compensation to donors, which suffice to serve as a rational basis for the prohibition.

As for plaintiffs' argument that there is no rational basis for a distinction between peripheral blood stem cell apheresis and blood donations, the government argues that because it is much harder to find a match for patients who need bone marrow transplants than for patients who need blood transfusions, exploitative market forces could be triggered if bone marrow could be bought. The government also asserts that peripheral blood stem cell apheresis poses greater health risks for the donor than blood donations do, because of the side effects of the medicine used to increase stem cell secretion. The government bases this factual assertion on information taken not from the complaint, which says that there is no significant risk, but from a patient handout called "Now That You Are a Match," published by the National Marrow Donor Program. Since the case was dismissed on a 12(b)(6) motion, the complaint controls. If material allegations of fact are mistaken, summary judgment or trial can so establish. We do not imply that patient risk is material to what the statute means and whether the distinctions it draws are constitutionally permissible. There are significant risks from egg donations, but the government concedes that the statute allows them. The statute does not prohibit trials of new medicines, which often involve risks and create discomfort or worse for participants. Other provisions of law and medical ethics may address these concerns, but the statute before us does not.

B. Bone marrow transplants by aspiration.

Plaintiffs address their arguments largely to the peripheral blood stem cell apheresis method of extracting hematopoietic stem cells, but their complaint appears to challenge the prohibition on bone marrow transplants regardless of method. They do not, in their complaint or their brief, confine their challenge to transplants by means of apheresis. They apparently propose to give compensated donors the choice between aspiration and apheresis. To the extent that plaintiffs challenge the constitutionality of the compensation ban on bone marrow donation by

the old aspiration method—where a long needle is inserted into the cavity of the hip bone to extract the soft, fatty marrow—the challenge must fail.

The statute says that the term "human organ" includes "bone marrow." The soft, fatty stuff that the needle extracts is bone marrow. It is irrelevant that the legislative history indicates that Congress viewed certain types of regenerable tissue, such as blood, as falling outside the statutory definition of "human organ." It may be that senators themselves, their staffs, or lobbyists for blood banks argued for an exception for body substances that can regenerate, and persuaded committee staffers to put that reason in the legislative history. But the statute does not say that compensation is permitted for organs or body parts that regenerate and prohibited for those that do not. Nor is the statute consistent with such a construction. The statute defines the liver "or any subpart thereof" as an organ for which compensation is prohibited. The drafters doubtless knew that a partial resection of a liver can yield a donation that will save the recipient's life, and that the donor's liver will grow back. So the statute does expressly prohibit compensation for at least one explicitly denoted "human organ" that will regenerate.

As for whether the distinction between the organs or other body substances for which compensation is permitted and those for which it is prohibited has a rational basis, there are two classes of rational basis here: policy concerns and philosophical concerns. The policy concerns are obvious. Some are mentioned in the legislative history, though they need not be. Congress may have been concerned that if donors could be paid, rich patients or the medical industry might induce poor people to sell their organs, even when the transplant would create excessive medical risk, pain, or disability for the donor. Or, looking from the other end, Congress might have been concerned that every last cent could be extracted from sick patients needful of transplants, by well-matched potential donors making "your money or your life" offers. The existing commerce in organs extracted by force or fraud by organ thieves might be stimulated by paying for donations. Compensation to donors might also degrade the quality of the organ supply, by inducing potential donors to lie about their medical histories in order to make their organs marketable. Plaintiffs argue that a $3,000 housing subsidy, scholarship, or charitable donation is too small an amount to create a risk of any of these evils, but for a lot of people that could amount to three to six months' rent.

Congress may have had philosophical as well as policy reasons for prohibiting compensation. People tend to have an instinctive revulsion at denial of bodily integrity, particularly removal of flesh from a human being for use by another, and most particularly "commodification" of such conduct, that is, the sale of one's bodily tissue. While there is reportedly a large international market for the buying and selling of human organs, in the United States, such a market is criminal and the commerce is generally seen as revolting. Leon Kass examines the philosophical issue

of commodification with his observation that nonprofit hospitals, donor registries, and physicians are permitted to make a lot of money from organ transplants, and the only people who get nothing are those whose organs are donated:

> [A]lthough we allow no commerce in organs, transplant surgeons and hospitals are making handsome profits from the organ-trading business, and even the not-for-profit transplant registries and procurement agencies glean for their employees a middleman's livelihood. Why . . . should everyone be making money from this business except the person whose organ makes it possible? Could it be that [the] real uneasiness [lies] with organ donation or with transplantation itself, for if not, what would be objectionable about its turning a profit?

Kass suggests that the revulsion for commodification of human flesh is reflected in our language: we call donors who are paid for their organs "donors" rather than "sellers" or "vendors." To account for why most of us are revolted by the notion of a poor person selling a kidney to feed his family, Kass cites the taboos we have against cannibalism, defilement of corpses, and necrophilia. Kass points to the idea of "psychophysical unity, a position that regards a human being as largely, if not wholly, self-identical with his enlivened body," so that, as Kant put it, to " 'dispose of oneself as a mere means to some end of one's own liking is to degrade the humanity in one's person.' " In this view, "organ transplantation . . . is—once we strip away the trappings of the sterile operating rooms and their astonishing technologies—simply a noble form of cannibalism."

These reasons are in some respects vague, in some speculative, and in some arguably misplaced. There are strong arguments for contrary views. But these policy and philosophical choices are for Congress to make, not us. The distinctions made by Congress must have a rational basis, but do not need to fit perfectly with that rational basis, and the basis need merely be rational, not persuasive to all. Here, Congress made a distinction between body material that is compensable and body material that is not. The distinction has a rational basis, so the prohibition on compensation for bone marrow donations by the aspiration method does not violate the Equal Protection Clause.

C. Bone marrow transplants by apheresis.

The focus, though, of plaintiffs' arguments is compensation for "bone marrow donations" by the peripheral blood stem cell apheresis method. For this, we need not answer any constitutional question, because the statute contains no prohibition. Such donations of cells drawn from blood flowing through the veins may sometimes anachronistically be called "bone marrow donations," but none of the soft, fatty marrow is donated, just cells found outside the marrow, outside the bones, flowing through the veins.

Congress could not have had an intent to address the apheresis method when it passed the statute, because the method did not exist at that time. We must construe the words of the statute to see what they imply about extraction of hematopoietic stem cells by this method. This issue has not been addressed by any of our sister circuits.

Since payment for blood donations has long been common, the silence in the National Organ Transplant Act on compensating blood donors is loud. "Blood" is omitted from the list of examples of "human organs" in the statute and the regulation. The statute says "human organ" is defined as a human "kidney, liver, heart, lung, pancreas, bone marrow, cornea, eye, bone, and skin or any subpart thereof and any other human organ . . . specified by the Secretary of Health and Human Services by regulation." The regulation adds intestines and the rest of the gastrointestinal tract to the list: "kidney, liver, heart, lung, pancreas, bone marrow, cornea, eye, bone, skin, and intestine, including the esophagus, stomach, small and/or large intestine, or any portion of the gastrointestinal tract." Neither the statute nor the regulation defines "human organ" to include "blood." The government concedes that the common practice of compensating blood donors is not prohibited by the statute.

The government argues that hematopoietic stem cells in the veins should be treated as "bone marrow" because "bone marrow" is a statutory organ, and the statute prohibits compensation not only for donation of an organ, but also "any subpart thereof." Hematopoietic stem cells are formed in the bone marrow, and most are found there because they generally mature into blood cells and platelets in the marrow. Therefore, the government argues, they should be viewed as "subparts" of the bone marrow, even when these stem cells are obtained through apheresis, which is to say, from blood flowing through veins.

We reject this argument, because it proves too much, and because it construes words to mean something different from ordinary usage. If the government's argument that what comes from the marrow is a subpart of the marrow were correct, then the statute would prohibit compensating blood donors. The red and white blood cells that flow through the veins come from the bone marrow, just like hematopoietic stem cells. But the government implicitly concedes that these red and white blood cells are not "subparts" of bone marrow under the statute, because it explicitly concedes that the statute does not prohibit compensation for blood donations.

As for ordinary usage, the bloodstream consists of plasma containing red cells, white cells, platelets, stem cells that will mature into one of these, and other material. We call this liquid as a whole "blood." No one calls it "bone marrow," even though these cells come from the marrow. There is no reason to think that Congress intended "bone marrow" to mean something so different from ordinary usage. Also, the blood contains not only blood cells and stem cells, but also other substances

that come from elsewhere in the body. For example, the blood contains vitamin B12, which enters the bloodstream after binding with intrinsic factor and being absorbed from the small intestine. The government's argument would treat vitamin B12 as a "subpart" of the intestines, and the regulation prohibits paying donors for their intestines or subparts thereof. But every blood draw contains some vitamin B12, and we still call the red liquid "blood," not "guts."

Likewise, every blood draw includes some hematopoietic stem cells. All that differentiates the blood drawn in peripheral blood stem cell apheresis from the blood drawn from a compensated blood donor, other than the filtration process, is the medicine given to donors in the days before the blood draw to increase hematopoietic stem cell secretion. Once the stem cells are in the bloodstream, they are a "subpart" of the blood, not the bone marrow. The word "subpart" refers to the organ from which the material is taken, not the organ in which it was created. Taking part of the liver for a liver donation would violate the statute because of the "subpart thereof" language. But taking something from the blood that is created in the marrow takes only a subpart of the blood.

In its petition for rehearing, the government makes a new argument, not made in its initial brief, for the proposition that Congress did indeed intend "bone marrow" to mean something different from ordinary usage. We have amended our opinion to address that argument. The argument is that because Congress defined "bone marrow" in another statute to include cells found in peripheral blood, "bone marrow" should be so understood in the National Organ Transplant Act. This argument is mistaken, for two reasons. First, in the statute the government cites, the definition of "bone marrow" is limited to provisions "[i]n this part." Title 42 of the United States Code is divided into chapters, subchapters, parts, subparts, and sections. The prohibition on organ purchases is in a different "part" of the title, not "this" part. Had Congress meant to say "title," "chapter," or "subchapter," no doubt that is what it would have said.

Second, the "part" prohibiting organ purchases addresses one subject, the part defining bone marrow to include the cells found in peripheral blood quite another. The first provides for organ donations, prohibits purchases of human organs, and defines these organs to exclude blood. The second provides for acquisition of information on as broad a basis as possible to facilitate research on "neonatal blood remaining in the placenta and umbilical cord after separation from . . . newborn bab[ies]." The National Organ Transplant Act, promulgated in 1984, establishes a regulatory scheme for organ transplants. The 2005 statute addresses the hope some people had for medical advances from embryonic stem cells, and the concern other people had with the possible breeding and killing of embryos for their stem cells. Congress and the President responded to these concerns with the Stem Cell Therapeutic and Research Act of 2005, "[t]o provide for the collection and maintenance

of human cord blood stem cells for the treatment of patients and research." The Stem Cell Act is directed partly at the same problem plaintiffs seek to address with MoreMarrowDonors.org's pilot program: "increasing the representation of racial and ethnic minority groups" by obtaining more data to assist in matching donors to patients. But the Stem Cell Act carefully avoids extending its definition of "bone marrow" to the prohibition on organ purchases by limiting application of the definition to "this part." And it defines bone marrow broadly, to include blood cells in the veins, serving its explicit purpose of facilitating stem cell research and a broadly inclusive donor registry.

This new argument by the government, like its old arguments, cannot be reconciled with the government's concession that the National Organ Transplant Act does not prohibit buying blood. After all, the Stem Cell Act defines "bone marrow" to include "the" cells, not just stem cells, "found in . . . peripheral blood." This definition includes all blood cells found in veins: red, white, and stem. Had Congress said "in this subchapter" instead of "in this part," when it defined all the cells in the bloodstream as "bone marrow," compensation for blood donations would be prohibited.

We construe "bone marrow" to mean the soft, fatty substance in bone cavities, as opposed to blood, which means the red liquid that flows through the blood vessels. The statute does not prohibit compensation for donations of blood and the substances in it, which include peripheral blood stem cells. The Secretary of Health and Human Services has not exercised regulatory authority to define blood or peripheral blood stem cells as organs. We therefore need not decide whether prohibiting compensation for such donations would be unconstitutional.

III. Conclusion.

It may be that "bone marrow transplant" is an anachronism that will soon fade away, as peripheral blood stem cell apheresis replaces aspiration as the transplant technique, much as "dial the phone" is fading away now that telephones do not have dials. Or it may live on, as "brief" does, even though "briefs" are now lengthy arguments rather than, as they used to be, brief summaries of authorities. Either way, when the "peripheral blood stem cell apheresis" method of "bone marrow transplantation" is used, it is not a transfer of a "human organ" or a "subpart thereof" as defined by the statute and regulation, so the statute does not criminalize compensating the donor.

REVERSED. The judgment is VACATED and the case REMANDED for such additional proceedings as may be appropriate. Costs on appeal awarded to Plaintiffs-Appellants.

NOTES AND QUESTIONS

1. *Apheresis and Aspiration*. Do you understand the distinction between apheresis and aspiration? See Jay S. Reidler & Joshua Berkowitz,

Compensation for Organ Donation: A Landmark Ruling on Hematopoietic Stem Cell Transplantation Refuels the Debate, 40 J.L. Med. & Ethics 409 (2012). Aspiration "harvests stem cells in their fatty milieu inside the bone." Id. Apheresis, on the other hand, "harvests stem cells when they are separated from the fat and bone." Id. Does the difference in harvesting have a bearing on whether donors would be likely to extort money from those in dire need?

2. *Equal Protection.* Does the Equal Protection argument resonate with you? Plaintiffs argued that the Equal Protection Clause required a finding of unconstitutionality of the NOTA compensation ban because there was no rational basis for allowing compensation for blood, eggs, and sperm, but not for bone marrow. Was there a rational basis to distinguish hematopoietic stem cells from blood, sperm, and egg cells? See id. Blood, eggs, and sperm can be regenerated and do not compromise the health of the donor, just like bone marrow; does the distinction of when the bone marrow is harvested matter? Id.

3. *Statutory Outcome.* What was the purpose of the National Organ Transplant Act? If the concerns regarding organ donation stemmed from the possibility of poor patients using organ donation as a way to get money even in unsafe conditions or donors extorting large amounts of money from desperate patients, would the difference between apheresis and aspiration matter? Id. Do you think the way the stem cells are harvested has an impact on the statute's ultimate goal? What incentives does the court have to rule the way that it did?

4. *Compensation for Bone Marrow.* Should people be compensated for donating an organ? See id. Society tends to compensate those engaged in highly dangerous activities (bomb disposal units, stunt persons, professional boxers, among many others). Should organ donation fall under a "dangerous activity"? Would allowing compensation make the procedure safer? Should the cost of organs be a fixed price or should competitive bidding be allowed? Does your opinion on the questions above change knowing that 3,000 Americans die per year awaiting marrow transplants and 80,000 patients are in need of kidneys? Id

5. *Leon Kass Argument.* The court referred to the work of physician and philosopher Leon Kass, who identified the revulsion that some people feel toward organ donation: "People tend to have an instinctive revulsion at denial of bodily integrity, particularly removal of flesh from a human being for use by another, and most particularly 'commodification' of such conduct, that is, the sale of one's bodily tissue." Do you feel any revulsion toward organ donation? Toward compensation for organ donation? If every person involved in the donation except the donor benefits from the procedure, should the donors be able to sell and receive monetary compensation for their organs? Do you think that allowing people to sell their organs dehumanizes them? Which parts of Kass's argument do you find most persuasive? Do you find the argument that organ donation is basically cannibalism without the medical techniques and sterile operating rooms compelling?

6. *Post-Flynn Blog Debate*. Some of the nation's leading bioethicists participated in an extensive debate about the merits of the *Flynn* decision. The blogs help you to understand the important issues easily without needing to unpack every sentence. Additionally, they help you form your own educated opinion with regards to the above case.

Go to the website and read the list of Flynn-related blogs, starting with Cohen-Flynn and ending with WSJ marrow.

7. *Proposed New Rule*. In response to *Flynn*, the Department of Health and Human Services proposed a new rule to govern bone marrow transplants. The new rule would have amended the term "human organ" to include hematopoietic stem cells in peripheral blood as part of the definition of "bone marrow." Human Organ, 78 Fed. Reg. 60812 (proposed Oct. 2, 2013). This rule would have eliminated the distinction in bone marrow collection method, meaning that compensation for all types of bone marrow transplantation would be illegal under the Act. Id. The amendment would, in effect, have reversed the Ninth Circuit's *Flynn v. Holder* decision. In proposing the change, the Department argued that compensation for donation by apheresis might 1) lead to exploitation of those in medical need, 2) discourage charitable donations, and 3) increase the likelihood of transmission of disease through the collection and use of infected biological products. These are all arguments we have seen before. What do you think of the proposed amendment and its rationale? See Hank Greely, My Comments on the HHS Notice of Proposed Rulemaking to Overturn Flynn v. Holder, https://law.stanford.edu/2013/12/02/lawandbiosciences-2013-12-02-my-comments-on-the-hhs-notice-of-proposed-rulemaking-to-overturn-flynn-v-holder/. Would this change have followed the statute's original purpose? Can you think of any other rules or changes that might work better? The Department withdrew the proposed rule on Nov. 27, 2018, saying, "Given the number of substantive comments, at this time HHS has decided to consider the issue further and may issue an NPRM in the future." Change to the Definition of "Human Organ" under Section 301 of the National Organ Transplant Act of 1984; Withdrawal, 83 FR 60804.

8. *Paid Organ Donations*. *Flynn* demonstrates that whether organ donors should be paid is a controversial issue with constitutional implications. In the following reading, Professor John Robertson discusses this matter and questions whether NOTA's ban is constitutional. As you read the article, ask yourself if you think there is a way to pay organ donors and maintain the principles of NOTA. Did Professor Robinson do a better job of identifying the constitutional arguments against the ban on organ compensation than the plaintiffs did in *Flynn*?

Paid Organ Donations and the Constitutionality of NOTA

John Robertson.
40 Hastings Const. L.Q. 221 (2013).

A recurring issue in talk of ways to increase organ supply has been the use of financial incentives. Since money works so well in allocating goods and services in markets, why not allow a market system for organ donations? . . . Despite the clamor of more voices in favor of payment, no major change in NOTA may occur for years to come, even for experimental programs.

Might a constitutional attack on NOTA advance the process? The idea is rooted in the notion of self-defense as a basic right. An organ transplant is critically important to a person with end-stage organ disease who is fighting for her life against the depredations of trauma, illness, and disease. Some argue that the Supreme Court's interpretation of the Second Amendment as protecting an individual right to possess a handgun in the home for self-defense should extend to medical self-defense as well. Others rely more directly on substantive due process for a negative right to safe and effective medical care to protect life and liberty.

Whatever the theory, it will be a hard slog—but not an impossible one—to get courts to recognize such a right.

IV. The Case for Strict Scrutiny

[The article first analyzed *Flynn v. Holder*, *supra*.] Having seen how heightened scrutiny would require the government to show a much stronger justification to ban paid apheresis or aspiration than it needs under rational basis review, I now address the case for heightened scrutiny. That case rests on whether there is a (negative) constitutional right to medical care from a willing doctor to a willing patient of a safe and effective medical treatment such as organ transplant.

The case for strict scrutiny hinges on the preservation and importance of life and health and whether restrictions on pursuing that interest, such as a ban on paid donations, are unconstitutional without a strong showing of governmental need to limit them. I will focus on the right to have an organ transplant, which would include the right to pay a doctor and donor for the services needed to obtain it, but this same issue would arise with access to cancer drugs, tissue cloned from embryonic stem cells, and many other situations. Access to these treatments are, of course, only a small part of the health services that people need and pale beside the challenges of providing affordable health care to everyone. But they are crucial for those in need of organ transplants or other medical treatments for which they can pay but which the law denies them the access to do so. Why should they not have a right to get them from a willing donor or provider when these treatments are essential to preserve their lives?

Eugene Volokh has elegantly presented this case, terming it a right of medical self-defense. His article draws on the common law tradition of lethal self-defense, which applies even if the attacker is innocent or the defender mistaken that there is a viable threat. He sees a constitutional basis for the standard case of self-defense and would extend it to medical needs as well. Indeed, the Supreme Court, in holding that the Second Amendment protected the right to have a handgun in the home drew upon the natural right of self-preservation as the source of its reading of the Second Amendment. Volokh also argues that the right to abort a viable fetus to protect a woman's life or health is further recognition of such a right, as is the right to have burdensome medical treatment withheld, even at the cost of one's life. He argues that this right includes the right to take on risks, such as the use of experimental drugs under Phase II FDA approval for clinical research. Medical self-defense, in one sense, is an apt and resonant term for the right to safe and effective medical care.

To protect one's body from the effects of trauma, virus, cancer, infection, etc., is to defend one's self in that sense. Yet trauma, illness, and disease are not agents or individuals directly attacking one, the usual terrain of self-defense. As Volokh points out, however, self-defense applies against animals and persons who due to infancy or mental illness are not responsible agents. A virus, bacteria, or a cancer cell gone awry is also an intruder or occupant of sorts who is acting outside of ordinary bounds, though strictly speaking, not outside the law. The concept of self-defense should thus apply to the situation caused by a smaller, biologic attacker, especially when it masses in such multitudes as to overwhelm the body. Self-defense in this instance would be understood as a right to use safe and effective medical treatments to ward off those attacks.

In another way, however, pushing the right of access to safe and effective medical treatment into the category of self-defense is not apt. The cost of self-defense is the life of an innocent attacker (not relevant to disease) or an innocent bystander due to the defensive actions of the person who reasonably thinks she is being attacked. Invalidating a ban on a safe and effective medical procedure that is independent of other persons would not have those costs. However, invalidating a ban on paid organ donations would mean that paid donors would bear the cost of the loss of the organ sold or the morbidity that occurs in the process of obtaining it. If the donor is fully informed and makes an intelligent and knowing choice to donate for money, these costs are lessened though they still exist. Such costs may be worth the preservation of the life of the recipient, just as a paid bodyguard knowingly takes on the risk of death or injury as an aspect of the right to self-defense. To be acceptable, however, there must be a further balancing of the donor's interests versus the recipient's interests. The question under strict scrutiny would be whether the interests at stake in barring a system of paid donation are sufficiently greater than allowing the current system of unpaid

donation, which denies needy recipients the opportunity to extend their lives through a system that increases organ supply through financial rewards.

With this qualification in mind, medical self-defense thus may be articulated as a right against unjustified governmental interference with access to safe and effective medical treatment. By prohibiting payment for the life-saving medical means to attack disease or organ failure, the Legislature denies patients, and the doctors supporting them, the right to self-preservation, a right so basic it should be treated by the Court as fundamental—or at least subject to a greater scrutiny than the standard rational basis analysis of *Carolene Products* and *Lee Optical*.

In short, the ban on paid organ donation deprives patients in need of such transplants the "life" and "liberty" specified in the Fifth and Fourteenth Amendments' clauses. Being alive is a necessary precondition to the exercise of other rights. Rights to free exercise of religion, to free speech, to assembly, to association, to vote, to raise children, to sexual and reproductive autonomy, or to pursue any right or interest depends on possessing life itself. Because life is a primary good on which realizing all other goods depends, it should have at least the same protection when "life" and "liberty" are specified in the constitutional text. State deprivation or interference with life, therefore, should require at least as strong a justification as is needed for depriving a person of other fundamental liberties, or at least a scrutiny stricter than rational basis. A full exposition of the right to use safe and effective medical treatments would extend beyond lifesaving treatments such as organ transplants. One cannot pursue liberty interests if one is unable to participate in ordinary life activities due to severe disability or pain. Thus, the right to use safe and effective medical treatments could also be grounded in liberty rights to be free of pain or disability. I leave the scope of that right to future analysis.

The Second Amendment cases give support here, but they are distinguishable by the Second Amendment's more explicit language. Yes, *District of Columbia v. Heller* and *McDonald v. City of Chicago* draw on a natural right to life, which includes repelling one's attacker and having the means to do so. But because of the Second Amendment text and the presence of a physical assailant, the cases are not directly apposite. Still, the notion of self-defense does lend support to the notion of a (negative) right to established health care from a willing doctor to ward off viral, bacterial, or cellular attacks. An organ transplant occurs at the point of attack when—by analogy—there is a need to wield the gun. Banning payment for organ donations is the equivalent of banning payment to buy a handgun or the ammunition necessary to repel an expected invader. However, buying the handgun per se does not threaten the life or health of third-party individuals in the same way that paying for removal of an organ does.

Adding rights via substantive due process, even one as narrowly specified as a negative right to safe and effective medical treatment to protect life, is always problematic for the Supreme Court. It is poor consolation that the Court has previously done so with rights of family, marriage, child rearing, sexuality, reproduction, and the like, because each step forward is controversial and bitterly fought over. Indeed, the Second Amendment cases, *Heller* and *McDonald*, take an originalist approach but rest on a traditional acceptance of a deeper right of self-preservation or self-defense against attackers. But why should that deeper right of self-preservation or defense be predicated upon a human or mammal attacker, rather than a virus, bacteria, or an immune system gone awry? If people may buy and use handguns to protect themselves from human attackers, even if innocent lives are lost in taking reasonable defensive action, why shouldn't individuals be able to buy organs for transplant or some other medical service when necessary to defeat an even more imminent viral or bacterial attack, and when the donor, whether paid or unpaid, has intelligently, competently, and knowingly assumed the risks involved?

In principle, that right should also apply, and if burdened by anti-payment legislation, should be recognized by the courts. To make that leap requires an even greater jump across a gap that the Court is now extremely cautious about taking and appeared to reject in *Washington v. Glucksberg* with regard to physician-assisted suicide. While the Supreme Court is far from admitting the right to safe and effective medical treatment into the due process pantheon, lower courts might occasionally do so. At the very least, such action might prod Congress and state legislatures to look more kindly on legislative proposals to use financial incentives to spur more organ donation. Before turning to medical self-defense challenges to NOTA's ban on paying bone marrow and organ donors, I examine the barriers to recognition of a substantive due process right to medical care presented by *Washington v. Glucksberg* and *Abigail Alliance v. Eschenbach*. A different outcome in *Glucksberg* or *Abigail Alliance* would not necessarily give a person the right to pay donors for organ or tissue donations, but it would shift the burden on government to show there is a more compelling need to justify NOTA's near total ban on paying donors.

* * *

VII. Burdens and Standing in Litigating the Right to Paid Donation

Recognition of a constitutional right to access organ transplants presents reasons why Congress should rethink NOTA's sweeping ban on paid donations. If there is a right to use such treatments, then a law prohibiting or greatly burdening their use would have to withstand a higher level of scrutiny than rational basis. I will assume that stricter scrutiny in such a case will entail the fundamental right, compelling state interest, and no less restrictive means requirements that have

become standard in substantive due process analysis, despite some hesitation by the Court in using such language.

The argument might not immediately spur legislative action, but it could lead to a judicial challenge that would have that effect. A facial attack on the ban would not work because there are situations of paid donation that should be subject to prohibition. An as-applied attack, however, is another matter. One strategy would be for an individual in need of an organ donation, e.g., a kidney, to come forward with a live donor who is willing to donate only if paid and challenge the Act on an as-applied individual basis. His case would be stronger if he could show that the would-be donor was fully aware of the risks of donation, had been carefully screened, was in good health, was not especially poor, felt strongly that there should be some reward for what he is doing, etc. Another approach would be to have a private organization create a system to recruit paid live kidney or cadaveric donors, screen and protect them, and pay rewards with price caps—along the lines of MMD.org approach—for patients in need of organ transplants. Those healthy informed donors would also join the suit under the premise that they will only donate if they are paid.

The ban on payment may substantially burden patients in particular situations unless there are paid donors, thus satisfying the standing requirements of injury in fact, causation, and redressability. Banning payment to an identified living donor of marrow or a kidney who is the best match for a plaintiff presents the clearest case of standing. In the case of kidney transplant, dialysis is more onerous and has serious health effects, which a transplant will alleviate. Banning payment to a scheme that encourages persons to register as potential donors and then follow through to receive the reward is less directly harmful to a specific patient and could have presented standing problems in Flynn v. Holder. But there is no question that it will affect some persons on organ waitlists even if they are not identifiable at the time of the suit, so that current plaintiffs, who are less immediately threatened, may raise their interests. Their interest is close enough that the plaintiffs should withstand objections to standing based on causation or redressability, if in fact paid donation would materially increase their chance of a transplant.

NOTES AND QUESTIONS

1. *Distinguish Abigail Alliance*. One of the issues Robertson discussed in his article is the case of *Abigail Alliance*, which you read in Chapter 2. In order for supporters of paid organ donations to legalize their cause, they must distinguish paid organ donations from *Abigail Alliance*. Robertson summarized the case as follows:

> Abigail Alliance grew out of a young woman's losing battle with late-stage esophageal cancer. She had failed several chemotherapy regimens and wanted to receive a new drug called Iressa, which the

> FDA had approved only for a Phase II study of efficacy. She was denied access to that drug, and died a few months later. Iressa was eventually approved for lung and colon cancers. Oncologists now use it off-label for other cancers. Iressa, of course, is not a magic bullet. It was approved based on evidence that it delayed tumor growth for esophageal cancer, not that it extended life significantly. It may or may not even have had that effect for the young woman that sought it.
>
> As a result of this experience the patient's father, the families of cancer patients, and others who thought that the FDA had been too restrictive about approving new cancer drugs formed an organization that sought expanded access to experimental drugs for the terminally ill. Finding that that access was often barred by the investigational new drug and clinical testing program required by the FDA, the Alliance submitted its own proposals and then a "citizen petition" to the FDA, arguing that there is a "different risk-benefit tradeoff facing patients who are terminally ill and who have no other treatment options," and that a lower evidentiary standard for safety and efficacy should be applied in those cases. The FDA never responded to the Alliance's citizen petition. The Alliance then sued, arguing that the United States Constitution provided terminally ill patients without other treatment options a right of access to experimental drugs that had passed Phase I clinical testing unless strict scrutiny of the need to deny that access could be shown. The district court rejected its claim, but the circuit court upheld it in a 2–1 decision. The circuit court en banc then reversed the panel decision.

Id. In summary, Abigail Alliance argued that the FDA was interfering with the right of terminally ill patients to rescue themselves by not allowing those patients to take experimental drugs. The United States Court of Appeals for the District of Columbia found—when rehearing the case en banc—that there is a tradition in United States history of preventing unsafe drugs from public use. Id. Even though Abigail Alliance argued that the standard should be different for terminally ill patients, the court rejected that argument and held that there is no constitutional right to unapproved drugs for terminally ill patients. Id.

Robertson distinguished the Abigail Alliance case from paid organ donations:

> Abigail Alliance's holding that experimental or unproven therapies are not within a due process or medical self-defense right of a terminally ill patient should not prevent a scrutiny stricter than rational basis to apply to bans on payment for safe and effective therapies such as organ and tissue transplants. Although there is always the question of whether a transplant will be successful for a given patient, organ and tissue transplants are not experimental or unproven for blood disorders and end stage organ disease.

> As a result, the en banc court's rejection in Abigail Alliance of self-defense and tortious interference with a rescue as precedents for the right claimed in that case would not be applicable to a ban on safe and effective organ transplants or any other established therapy. Established treatments such as organ transplant are appropriate for a rescue since we know they work. They also are a form of self-defense, in that they are as effective against a "medical intruder"—a virus, bacteria, or cellular system gone awry—as a handgun against an attacker. Indeed, someone who stole or destroyed the container with the organ that has been donated to another, causing the death or increased suffering of the intended recipient would be liable criminally for homicide and civilly liable for tortious interference with a rescue. A law that barred transplantation or substantially burdened access to it should thus be subject to a scrutiny stricter than rational basis. The established nature of organ transplantation sidesteps Abigail Alliance's reasoning about access to unproven treatments, but it still leaves open the question of whether there is a due process negative right to safe and effective medical treatments. As we have seen, that issue will turn on whether Glucksberg's requirements of being "deeply rooted in this nation's history" and "essential to ordered liberty" are met when a person's life is at stake and he seeks an established medical treatment to defend it.

Id. What do you think about Robertson's distinction between paid organ donations and *Abigail Alliance*? What arguments would you make if you support paid organ donations? What arguments would you make if you oppose paid organ donations? How are the two things—compensation for organ donation and access to unproven drugs—different?

2. *Distinguish Glucksberg*. In another section of the article, Robertson argued that in order to win, his plaintiffs would have to distinguish their lawsuit from the physician-assisted suicide case, *Washington v. Glucksberg*, which you read in Chapter 1. In *Glucksberg*, the Court refused to recognize a new substantive due process right due to our nation's history and tradition of banning physician-assisted suicide. According to Robertson, "[s]upporters of a right to medical treatment will argue that a right to use safe and effective medical treatments to extend life or reduce pain and disability is also 'deeply rooted in this Nation's history and tradition.' " Do you agree? Do you think the Supreme Court would recognize a constitutional right to safe and effective medical treatment broad enough to include a right to an organ?

> **Practice Exercise:** As you read the different types of payment programs below, ask yourself which of these you think is the most appropriate and why.

3. *Different Payment Programs*. In another section of the article, Robertson proposed three different types of payment programs and discussed the constitutionality of each program under NOTA. Id.

a. *Free Market Libertarianism*. Robertson discussed the idea of a free market for paid organ donations—no government interference at all. However, Robertson acknowledged that this concept is unlikely to provide a successful constitutional challenge to NOTA, for good reason. Id. Robertson gave the example of an organ broker in New York who posted ads in Israel. Poor Israelis agreed to come to the United States to donate an organ. Even though the recipient paid over $150,000.00 for the donation, the donor received only $10,000.00. Eventually, the FBI caught the broker. Although families of the recipients looked at the broker as a saint, it was not always the same for the donors. Although the donors may have received $10,000.00, the fees did not cover all their future medical expenses and problems post-donation. Also, the chances of fraud and coercion are so high in such a market, that Robertson concluded that free market libertarianism is not the best method because some regulation is needed. Id.

b. *Paid Live Kidney Donations*. Next, Robertson suggested a regulated system in which individuals can be paid for live kidney donations. Id. He gave an example of a system that would cap payment around $20,000.00, which is relatively proportionate considering egg donors can receive around $10,000.00. Further, there are many structures and processes in place to ensure that needy individuals are not exploited, such as the requirement for U.S. citizenship. Robertson argued that this type of method would likely pass strict scrutiny if a court finds that terminally ill patients have a fundamental right to receive life-sustaining kidney transplants. If a court does so find, it will be difficult for NOTA to overcome that finding of strict scrutiny by arguing fraud or coercion. Id.

c. *Paid Cadaveric Donations*. Third, Robertson focused on the constitutionality under NOTA of paid cadaveric donations. Id. Robertson addressed the issues that opponents may raise, such as the influence of financial incentives on family members and the concept of commodifying death—profiting on death. Id. However, Robertson rejected these arguments. Just because there is a financial incentive, does not make it coercive. Robertson projected that paid cadaveric donations will likely pose a successful constitutional challenge to NOTA. Id.

> **Practice Exercise:** Compare Professor Robertson's arguments to the constitutional arguments presented in *Richards v. Holder*.

4. *Richards v. Holder*. Next, *Richards* involved a constitutional challenge to the federal statute prohibiting the sale of human organs. Could you have improved upon Richards's constitutional arguments? Are you surprised that the district court dismissed his case? Are you surprised that the court relied on *Glucksberg* and *Abigail Alliance* in its ruling?

Richards v. Holder

United States District Court for the District of Massachusetts, 2014.
No. 13–13195–LTS, 2014 WL 2805280.

■ SOROKIN, DISTRICT JUDGE.

Plaintiff James Richards has sued Defendant Eric Holder in his official capacity as United States Attorney General, alleging that the federal statute prohibiting the sale of human organs for transplantation, 42 U.S.C. § 274e, violates his due process rights and exacts a taking without just compensation. . . . Defendant has moved to dismiss the counts alleging due process violations and a taking, arguing that those counts fail to state a claim. For the reasons that follow, Defendant's motion to dismiss is ALLOWED, . . .

I. *BACKGROUND*

The following facts, drawn from Richards's complaint, are taken as true for the purposes of resolving this motion. The Court draws all reasonable inferences from these factual allegations in Richards's favor.

Richards currently suffers from end stage renal disease, which is a product of kidney damage that was caused by previously prescribed medication. The only treatment for the disease at this stage is dialysis or a kidney transplant. Richards is currently receiving dialysis treatment, which requires lengthy treatment sessions several times per week. The sessions range from uncomfortable to painful and can have significant negative side effects. Richards avers that his life expectancy would be meaningfully longer if he received a kidney transplant rather than continuing dialysis. He further states that the longer he is on dialysis, the less likely it is that any eventual transplant will be successful and the less likely a significant increase in life expectancy will result from that transplant.

Richards has asked family members to donate a kidney for transplant, but they are not willing or able to do so. He is eligible for a "perfect match" kidney donation, but, thus far, none has been found. Without a "perfect match," Richards will likely wait four to five years in order to receive a kidney for transplant. In order to minimize the time waiting for a kidney, Richards's family is willing to pay a donor at least $50,000 for the donation of a kidney. His intention to offer payment to incentivize the donation of a kidney is thwarted, however, by 42 U.S.C. § 274e, which makes it a federal crime "for any person to knowingly acquire, receive, or otherwise transfer any human organ for valuable consideration for use in human transplantation." § 274e(a). Violations of the statute are punishable by fines of up to $50,000 and imprisonment of not more than five years. § 274e(a)(b).

Richards argues that if he were able to pay a donor to donate a kidney, he would likely be able to procure a kidney with less delay, with the attendant benefit of increased life expectancy, than if he were forced to wait to receive a kidney off the waiting list. As such, Richards argues

that, as applied to him, § 274e deprives him of both life and liberty without due process of the law, in violation of the Fifth Amendment to the United States Constitution.

Richards also states his preference to have his own organs harvested and sold upon his death, such that the proceeds of those sales may be included in his estate and passed to his heirs. He argues that because § 274e prevents him from selling his organs and because the United States will not provide just compensation for those organs, the statute effects an unconstitutional taking in violation of the Fifth Amendment of the Constitution. . . .

III. *SUBSTANTIVE DUE PROCESS CLAIM*

The Due Process Clause of the Fifth Amendment provides that "[n]o person shall . . . be deprived of life, liberty, or property, without due process of law." Noting that the Clause "guarantees more than fair process," the Supreme Court in *Washington v. Glucksberg* set forth the analysis to evaluate substantive due process claims. The Court noted that the inquiry has "two primary features":

> First, we have regularly observed that the Due Process Clause specially protects those fundamental rights and liberties which are, objectively, deeply rooted in this Nation's history and tradition, and implicit in the concept of ordered liberty, such that neither liberty nor justice would exist if they were sacrificed. Second, we have required in substantive-due-process cases a careful description of the asserted fundamental liberty interest.

In applying this analysis, courts carefully describe the asserted right and then address whether that right falls within the category of fundamental rights and liberty interests described above. If the asserted right is considered fundamental, any infringement of that right will be subject to strict scrutiny and will be deemed unconstitutional "unless the infringement is narrowly tailored to serve a compelling state interest." The Supreme Court, however, has warned that courts should be reluctant to add to the list of fundamental rights, noting that "[b]y extending constitutional protection to an asserted right or liberty interest, [the Court], to a great extent, place[s] the matter outside the arena of public debate and legislative action." Alternatively, for those rights and liberty interests which are not deemed fundamental, infringement is subject only to rational basis review and will be upheld "so long as the law is rationally related to a legitimate governmental interest."

Richards first contends that 42 U.S.C. § 274e constitutes a deprivation of life and liberty without due process of law. The Supreme Court has gone to lengths to caution lower courts to carefully define rights asserted in the substantive due process context. Richards cannot claim that Congress has prohibited outright the form of treatment he seeks—an organ transplant—as the statute does no such thing. Rather,

the statute of which § 274e is a part creates a system to permit and to encourage transplants. Further, the statute does not block the only treatment available to him, as he currently receives another form of medical treatment, dialysis, for his condition.

Richards's complaint, in fact, is that Congress has banned a particular means of encouraging transplants—monetary payments—which he asserts would speed the availability of an organ for him. He does not argue that Congress cannot regulate the transfer of organs at all, as he concedes in his complaint that some regulation by Congress of the exchange of money for an organ would be appropriate, and by implication, constitutional. Carefully read then, Richards claims a due process right to procure a kidney by buying one.

Richards's substantive due process claim fails for three reasons. First, the Ninth Circuit considered and rejected a challenge to the constitutionality of § 274e. In *Flynn v. Holder*, the court upheld the ban on the sale of body parts for transplant against an equal protection challenge brought by a collection of plaintiffs who sought to incentivize bone marrow transplants by providing valuable consideration to persons who provided bone marrow for donation. The court upheld the law without applying heightened scrutiny to the statute, which would be required if the ban implicated a fundamental right, and found the statute constitutional after rational basis review. This decision is persuasive authority for the proposition that Richards does not have a fundamental constitutional right to buy a kidney.

Second, the District of Columbia Circuit rejected a substantive due process challenge that raised a similarly asserted right, notwithstanding the fact that the plaintiffs in that case presented an even more compelling case than Richards in law and fact. *Alliance for Better Access to Developmental Drugs v. von Eschenbach,* 495 F.3d 695, 701 (D.C. Cir. 2007) (en banc). In *Abigail,* the law (in the form of federal regulations) barred access to certain experimental drugs sought by the plaintiffs, who, factually, were terminally ill and without *any* treatment options other than the experimental drugs they sought. In this case, by contrast, the law (in the form of the larger act of which § 274e is a part) facilitates, albeit not without limitation, Richards's access to kidney transplants, and, factually, he is currently availing himself of an alternative treatment for his condition. Yet, notwithstanding stronger factual and legal arguments, the *Abigail* court determined that terminally ill individuals do not have "a fundamental right to experimental drugs that have passed [initial phase] clinical testing" and rejected the plaintiffs' constitutional claim. In so doing, the court emphasized both the high hurdle that must be cleared to establish a right as fundamental and the deference due to legislatures in crafting a balance between the risks and benefits of medical technology where no fundamental right is implicated. The persuasive reasoning of the *Abigail* court applies with even more force to Richards's challenge.

Finally, Richards's due process claim fails because he has not articulated how the asserted right is "deeply rooted in this Nation's history and tradition" or "implicit in the concept of ordered liberty, such that neither liberty nor justice would exist if [it] were sacrificed." He has not made any showing of a historical basis for the right to encourage donation of organs by offering cash payments. Nor does the complaint set forth sufficient detail to bring into sharp relief a deprivation, both immediate and springing directly from the statute, of such a magnitude as to implicate rights implicit in the concept of ordered liberty. Instead, Richards generally objects to the balance Congress has struck between incentivizing the donation of organs for transplant and limiting the individual and societal risks attendant to the sale of human organs. Such an argument is not sufficient to invoke heightened scrutiny of the statute nor to establish that the statute lacks a rational relationship to a legitimate government interest.

For these reasons, the Court finds the right to offer cash for the donation of an organ for transplant not to be fundamental. As such, the statute is subject only to rational basis review, which it easily satisfies. Accordingly, Defendant's motion to dismiss Richards's count alleging a due process deprivation is ALLOWED.

IV. *TAKING CLAIM*

The Takings Clause of the Fifth Amendment instructs that "private property [shall not] be taken for public use, without just compensation." "To make a cognizable claim of a taking in violation of the Fifth Amendment, the plaintiff[ ] must first show that [he] possess[es] a recognized property interest which may be protected by the Fifth Amendment."

Richards contends that the statute, by prohibiting him from selling his organs upon his death, has exacted a taking without just compensation. His claim of a taking fails, however, because he can make no showing that any independent source, such as state law or traditional common law principles, supports a constitutionally protected property interest in the sale of one's organs after death.

Looking first to state law, Massachusetts has made clear that it does not recognize such a property right by adopting the Uniform Anatomical Gifts Act, which provides criminal penalties for the purchase or sale of organs intended for transfer after death. Looking more broadly at Massachusetts common law, there appears to be no current or historical recognition of a right to transfer one's organs for valuable consideration. Further, there appears to be no support for such a property right under traditional common law principles.

Because Richards does not and can not show that he possesses a constitutionally protected property interest in the sale of his organs upon his death, he cannot state a claim for an unconstitutional taking.

Accordingly, Defendant's motion to dismiss the taking count is ALLOWED.

SO ORDERED.

NOTES AND QUESTIONS

1. *Paid Organ Donation.* After reading Richards's argument, are you persuaded that individuals should be able to pay donors in order to increase their chance of receiving a needed organ, or at least expedite the process? Do you think there is a due process right to pay for organs?

2. *Level of Scrutiny.* The court awarded the right to purchase organs only rational basis review after determining that it was not a fundamental right. If you were on the court, what level of scrutiny would you have awarded the right to purchase organs?

3. *Glucksberg and Abigail Alliance.* As predicted in Professor Robertson's article, Plaintiff Richards needed to distinguish his claim from the decisions in *Glucksberg* and *Abigail.* Are there arguments in Robertson's article that the district court should have considered? Did the district court misinterpret those cases?

4. *Property.* Are organs property? Should the court have allowed Richards to dispose of his body's property as he liked by selling his organs after death?

5. *Kidneys.* Note that Richards suffered from end stage renal disease. Kidneys have prompted particular interest in the organ transplant debate because, unlike many other organs, they can be taken from living donors. Nonetheless, severe shortages of kidneys plague the transplant system. In the next section, we consider whether the history of kidney transplants justifies a market in organs and the overcoming of NOTA's compensation ban.

> **Go to** the website and decide if you would go through the process of being a kidney donor.

2. THE SPECIAL CASE OF KIDNEYS: REASON TO START A MARKET FOR ORGANS?

The shortage of kidneys available for transplantation is particularly acute. See, e.g., Henri Astier, Should Organ Donors be Paid? The Heavy Toll of US Kidney Shortage, BBC New, Feb. 18, 2020, https://www.bbc.com/news/world-us-canada-51266959. The American Kidney Fund called on President Biden to "prioritize our country's kidney disease epidemic by focusing on policies that address health disparities, and protect and expand access to affordable, high-quality health coverage." AP, American Kidney Fund Calls on President-elect Biden, Jan. 8, 2021, https://apnews.com/press-release/accesswire/joe-biden-business-pandemics-public-health-race-and-ethnicity-9b1c6db191ebacb8f0495c8fee0af8e0.

"Kidney disease and kidney failure, also known as end-stage renal disease (ESRD), have a disproportionate impact on racial and ethnic minorities. Compared to white Americans, Black Americans are 3.4 times more likely to develop kidney failure, Native Americans are 1.9 times more likely and Asian Americans are 1.3 times more likely. Additionally, people of Hispanic ethnicity are 1.5 times more likely to develop kidney failure than non-Hispanics." *Id.* What can the new administration do about this?

Recall that NOTA prohibits any compensation for organs, including kidneys. In response to kidney shortages, the nonsimultaneous, extended, altruistic donor ("NEAD") chain idea described in the article below developed. Then NOTA was amended to allow this type of NEAD kidney exchange. What do you think of NEAD exchanges as a solution to the shortage of organs?

a. ALTRUISTIC NEAD CHAINS

Custom, Contract, and Kidney Exchange

Kieran Healy & Kimberly D. Krawiec.
62 Duke L.J. 645 (2012).

Introduction

... In a nonsimultaneous, extended, altruistic donor (NEAD) chain, an altruistic donor freely gives a kidney to a patient, initiating a chain of transplants among a series of donor-patient pairs. Each donor has a kidney that is incompatible with "her" patient, so instead each donates her kidney to the compatible patient of another donor-patient pair, forming the next link in the chain. NEAD chains are a relatively recent innovation in the transplant system, and they seem set to become more common in the future.

What sort of exchange is this? In some ways, a NEAD chain resembles a form of generalized exchange, an ancient and widespread instance of the norm of reciprocity that can be thought of simply as the obligation to "pay it forward" rather than the obligation to reciprocate directly with the giver. Generalized exchange has long been seen as an extremely effective customary means of generating commitment and solidarity in social groups, because everyone participates in the exchange of values, rather than in a system of directly reciprocated dyadic transfers. This imagery of solidarity and collective commitment generated through a chain of gifts has been important to the success of NEAD chains. The most notable similarity between NEAD chains and true generalized exchange is the presence of a gap in time between exchanges, which introduces some standard elements of gift giving, especially the social obligation to reciprocate (pay forward) and the problem of trust that arises along with it. But these chains are an odd kind of generalized exchange. They do not cycle back on themselves as

classical generalized exchange systems do; they occur between sets of pairs rather than between individuals; and, most importantly, they are to a large degree organizationally manufactured rather than locally emergent.

Looked at from a different point of view, though, a NEAD chain is not like gift exchange at all. Instead, it resembles a string of promises and commitments to deliver something in exchange for some valuable consideration—in short, a series of contracts. After the first free donation, each donor-patient dyad in the chain in effect promises to pay the donor's incompatible kidney forward upon receipt of a compatible kidney for the patient. But again, the fit is not perfect. These chains are an odd kind of contract. For one thing, of course, contracting for the sale of human organs is illegal, and NEAD-chain professionals explicitly disavow any role of formal contract. At the same time, it does seem as though each NEAD-chain pair offers something of value (a healthy, but incompatible, kidney) explicitly in exchange for something else of value (a healthy, compatible kidney) by mutual agreement at each point in the chain. Isn't this the essence of contract?

I. NEAD Chains

The demand for kidneys for transplantation far outstrips supply. As of October 5, 2012, the Organ Procurement and Transplantation Network reported 94,005 candidates on the kidney transplant waiting list, many of whom will die due to lack of available donors. In 2008 alone, 4,573 kidney patients died while waiting for an organ transplant. In an attempt to close this gap between supply and demand in the face of restrictions on compensation for organ donation, which limit the number of transplants from unrelated donors, the medical community has developed innovative exchange mechanisms that seek to overcome barriers to related-party exchange stemming from immune-system or blood-type incompatibility.

Consider two patients in need of kidney transplants, each of whom has found a living donor (a spouse, perhaps, or another relative, or a friend). Within each patient-donor dyad, the donor's kidney is incompatible with the patient's immune system—yet it is suitable for the patient in the other pair. There are thus two donor-patient pairs, each incompatible internally but compatible with their counterparts. The obvious solution is a straightforward, simultaneous swap of kidneys between the two dyads. With the right combination of compatibilities across dyads, simultaneous swaps of three or four or even more pairs are possible in principle. In swaps of this sort, parties to the exchange cannot back out in the middle of things—either everything happens at once, or nothing does. Although multi-way pairings are possible in principle, they are rare in practice because the logistical demands of organizing simultaneous swaps grow rapidly as the number of pairs increases. Each individual in the swap requires her own surgical theater and team, either to remove the donor kidney or to transplant it into a recipient. Doing all

of this at once is very difficult. As a result, simultaneous kidney exchanges typically involve only a limited number of swaps.

A NEAD chain converts the simultaneous, cyclical exchange of kidneys amongst two or more donor pairs into a chain of donations and transplants. The process begins with a kidney from an altruistic donor, who gives a kidney without having a particular recipient in mind. With this "extra" kidney in the system, the transplants do not need to take place all at once. Instead, a patient can have her donor pay it forward later—say, when another suitable patient-donor pair is found. In the meantime, the donor in the last dyad affirms her commitment to give, and awaits her turn to donate.

Figure 1.

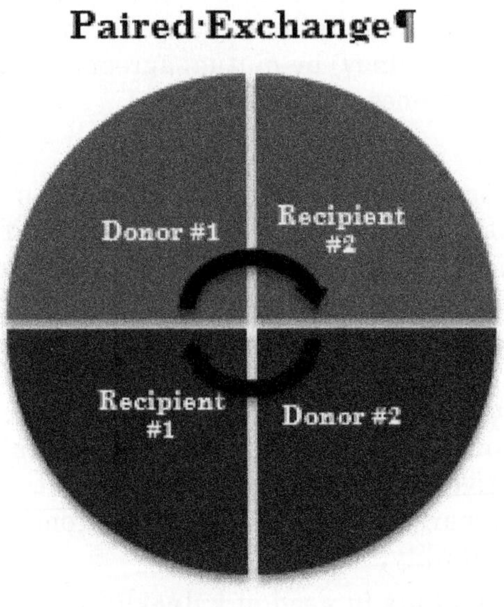

Figure 2.

NEAD·Chain·¶

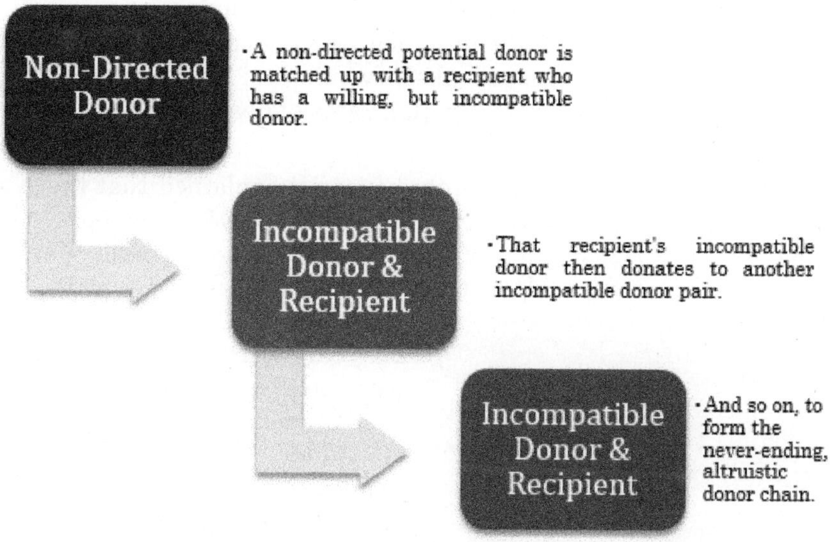

Now that you've learned about NEAD chains, do you think that they should be the main source of kidneys, or do you think markets would more effectively handle the problem? We consider the market for kidneys in the next section.

b. LET THE MARKET DECIDE

According to some bioethics scholars, kidneys offer a special case of organ donation. See Philip J. Cook & Kimberly D. Krawiec, A Primer on Kidney Transplantation: Anatomy of the Shortage, 77 Law & Contemp. Probs. 1 (2014). First, living donation is possible because people have two kidneys, but need only one, while the health risks associated with kidney removal and transplant are lower than for other organs. Second, patients who need kidneys can wait for a longer period of time for organ transplant because of the availability of dialysis and Medicare coverage for End Stage Renal Disease treatment. Third, the need for kidneys is desperate; in February 2021, 91,311 people were on the waiting list for kidney transplants; the next highest number is 11,913 waiting for liver transplants. Organ Procurement and Transportation Network, Data, Feb. 11, 2021, https://optn.transplant.hrsa.gov/data/.

> **Practice Exercise:** How would you persuade people to donate kidneys? Identify all the options.

With this background, the authors argue that there is no likely increase in available organs under the existing systems, including NEAD. There is no reason to think deceased donor numbers will increase.

> For all these reasons, we believe the time is ripe to reconsider inducement to kidney donation, and financial inducements in particular. Needless to say, a system that provided cash rewards for living donors could produce unsavory consequences, and would have to be carefully designed and managed. But without such a system, the most likely version of the future is a continuation of unnecessarily high rates of death and disability from kidney failure.

In 2014, a Nobel-prize winning economist explained that there was an average wait of 4.5 years for a kidney, with 95,000 people on the waiting list in 2012. See Gary S. Becker & Julio J. Elias, Cash for Kidneys: The Case for a Market for Organs, Wall St. J., Jan. 18, 2014. Ten years earlier, there had been a 2.9-year wait and 54,000 people were on the waiting list. A kidney patient on dialysis can live 8 years; a kidney patient with kidney transplant can expect to live 23 years (for persons between ages 45–49). Dialysis costs $80,000.00 per year, while a transplant costs $150,000.00. The authors report that kidney exchanges—"in which pairs of living would-be donors and recipients who prove incompatible look for another pair or pairs of donors and recipients who would be compatible for transplants, cutting their wait time—have become more popular, but still only account for 9% of live donations and 3% of after-death donations." Id.

Practice Exercise: Stop here and consider how you would develop a market for kidneys. How much would a kidney cost?

Do these statistics persuade you that we need a market for kidneys? The authors recommend a price of $15,000.00 per kidney. Does that sound like the right amount? Would you take that amount for your kidney? Iran, which allows the sale of kidneys at a market price of about $4,000.00, has largely eliminated the waiting list for kidneys. Does that influence your analysis of markets for organs? Do you agree with the authors that living donors should be able to negotiate now for the sale of organs after death, like lungs and hearts?

The authors argued that a market for body parts is no different from the ethics of a volunteer military and surrogate motherhood. Do you agree? Is it more immoral to sell organs or to allow people to die without transplants?

An alternative to a pure market solution to kidney problems is to have government programs, either tax credits or pure cash payments. Professors Bilgel and Galle argue that tax incentive legislation increased unrelated kidney donation rates by about 52% in New York. See Firat Bilgel & Brian Galle, Paying for Altruism: The Case of Organ Donation Revisited, Sept. 23, 2014, at http://papers.ssrn.com/sol3/papers.cfm?abstract_id=2499686.

Or, do you agree with those who find the idea of the sale of organs morally repugnant? See Alvin E. Roth, Repugnance as a Constraint on Markets, J. Econ. Perspectives, vol. 21, no. 3, at 37 (Summer 2007). Roth argued that there are three main arguments why the American public would find the selling of kidneys morally repugnant.

> Concerns about the monetization of transactions fall into three principal classes. One concern is objectification: that is, the fear that putting a price on certain things and buying or selling them might move them into a class of impersonal objects to which they should not belong. The sociology literature has shown a longstanding interest in how the introduction of money changes many kinds of social relationships and their meanings. A second concern is that offering substantial monetary payments might be coercive, in the sense that it might leave some people, particularly the poor, open to exploitation from which they deserve protection. A third concern, sometimes less clearly articulated, is that monetizing certain transactions that might not themselves be objectionable may cause society to slide down a slippery slope to genuinely repugnant transactions.

Id. at 44–45. Now, review the arguments for and against a free market in organs in an article written by Professor I. Glenn Cohen. According to Professor Cohen, "[t]hree arguments are commonly deployed against organ sale generally":

> **Corruption:** allowing the sale of organs to go forward will do violence or denigrate our views of how goods (organs, personhood) are properly valued, in that it may "dehumanize society by viewing human beings and their parts as mere commodities."
>
> **Crowding Out:** allowing the sale of organs will cause individuals who would have donated organs to instead sell them, thus reducing the number of *donated* organs, or it will cause individuals to refuse to donate at all, leading to an *overall* reduction in procured organs. This claim has its roots in behavioral economic work on motivational crowding out, suggesting that contrary to the classical economic model allowing payment for goods may change its social meaning in a way that discourages altruistic giving and ultimately decreases supply.
>
> **Coercion:** Poor sellers are coerced into selling their organs by brokers or recipients who have no right to propose this, because they have no reasonable economic alternative.

I. Glenn Cohen, Transplant Tourism: The Ethics and Regulation of International Markets for Organs, 41 J.L. Med. & Ethics 269, 273 (2013) (footnotes omitted). Do you think that these reasons are persuasive?

Instead of having a market for organs, should we find a way to encourage more people to donate organs?

c. ENCOURAGING DONATION

Would presumed consent to organ donation increase the number of available kidneys? In some states, in order to register to be an organ donor, you must affirmatively check a box at the DMV that you want to donate your organs. However, Florida took a different approach. See Kelly Ann Keller, The Bed of Life: A Discussion of Organ Donation, Its Legal and Scientific History, and A Recommended "Opt-Out" Solution to Organ Scarcity, 32 Stetson L. Rev. 855, 888–90 (2003). Instead of affirmatively deciding to become an organ donor, Florida presumes that everyone consents to be an organ donor unless a decedent carries a non-organ donor card or the decedent's family objects. Read the following statute and determine if you think it is positive because it increases harvestable organs or negative because it may violate people's wishes.

Presumed Consent to Organ Donation for Transplantation

(1) In any case in which a patient needs an organ for transplantation and it is possible to remove the organ within the useful life of the organ, the organ of a decedent may be harvested if all of the following conditions have been met:

(a) a decedent who may provide a suitable organ for donation has been certified dead by a physician using either cardiac or whole brain death standards;

(b) no objection to organ donation by the decedent or the decedent's family is known or suspected;

(c) the surgeon, physician, or technician who harvests the organ is not the same individual who certifies the death of the decedent;

(d) all reasonable efforts are made to restore cosmetically the decedent's appearance after the organ is harvested;

(e) the removal is in accordance with accepted medical standards;

(f) the organ removal does not interfere with the subsequent course of an investigation or autopsy; and

(g) no individual or organization involved in the organ procurement process may be held liable in any civil or criminal action for failure to obtain the consent of the donor's family.

(2) If an individual does not wish to become an organ donor, he or she may carry a non-organ donor card.

(a) The Florida Department of Motor Vehicles shall present to every individual receiving a driver's license or other

identification card the option to have placed on such identification card the designation of non-organ donor.

(b) In the absence of a non-organ donor card or an objection by the decedent or decedent's family, individuals and organizations involved in the organ-procurement process may assume that all decedents are organ donors.

In addition to the proposed statutory language above, the "definitions" section of the Florida Statute should be amended to include the following definition of "organ": any part or subpart of the human body including but not limited to the kidneys, heart, lungs, liver, pancreas, intestine, stomach, eyes, tissue, bone, and skin.

Id. Do you agree with Florida's presumed consent for organ donation? Or, do you think states that require individuals to affirmatively state they are organ donors protect individuals from being violated against their wishes, religion, etc.? For more information on the history of presumed consent laws, see David Orentlicher, Presumed Consent to Organ Donation: Its Rise and Fall in the United States, 61 Rutgers L. Rev. 295 (2009). For a good discussion on the topic of presumed consent and routine removal on organ donation, please see Institute of Medicine, Organ Donation: Opportunities for Action (2006).

After 32-year-old Todd Krampitz discovered he had liver cancer, he had trouble finding a donor. He posted two billboards, like the one pictured below, along highways in Houston, Texas. A donor who read the billboard donated a relative's organ specifically for Todd. See AP, Man gets liver after using Billboards, Net, NBCNews, Aug. 13, 2004, at http://www.nbcnews.com/id/5685485/ns/health-cancer/t/man-gets-liver-after-using-billboards-net/#.VPTt2LPF–Xx. What do you think of this system of encouraging kidney donation? Do you agree with the United Network for Organ Sharing (UNOS), which "believe[s] public pleas for directed donations, like what Todd Krampitz did, run the risk of bypassing the established allocation system and can create an uneven playing field for all individuals on the national waiting list for organs"? Id. Would you respond to a billboard seeking an organ donor?

If the organ transplant system is donor-based, what rights should the donor and donee have over the organs? What if someone was gifted organs? Does he have a property right in those organs? Read the *Colavito* case below and ask yourself whether gifting organs creates different rights for the recipient than the rights of an individual to purchase organs.

Colavito v. New York Organ Donor Network

New York Court of Appeals, 2006.
8 N.Y.3d 43, 860 N.E.2d 713.

■ ROSENBLATT, J.

The case before us involves the purported gift of a kidney to plaintiff. He asserts that as the specified donee of the organ, he acquired a property right in it, giving rise to claims against defendants for delivering it to someone else. Plaintiff brought suit in federal court, and the United States Court of Appeals for the Second Circuit has certified questions to us relating to whether he has rights that would support his common-law conversion action or a statutory claim under Public Health Law articles 43 and 43–A.

I

In August 2002 Peter Lucia died at defendant Good Samaritan Hospital on Long Island, from massive intracranial bleeding. His widow, Debra Lucia, sought to donate his kidney (or kidneys) to plaintiff, Peter's longtime friend who had been suffering from end stage renal disease. Debra proceeded by going through defendant New York Organ Donor Network (NYODN). NYODN transplant coordinator defendant Spencer Hertzel concluded that Peter's kidneys were "not a perfect match, but they [were] good enough." Peter's left kidney was airlifted to Jackson

Memorial Hospital in Miami, Florida, where plaintiff was awaiting its transplantation; Peter's other kidney remained in New York.

While preparing for the transplant during the early afternoon of August 23, 2002, Dr. George W. Burke, a surgeon at Jackson Memorial, inspected the donated kidney and discovered an aneurysm of the renal artery, making the kidney unsuitable for transplantation. He immediately contacted NYODN, asking for Peter's other kidney, and was informed that it had been allocated to someone else. The parties agree that NYODN had allocated the other kidney to another patient at about 11:25 A.M. that day.

Plaintiff brought suit against NYODN and others in the United States District Court for the Eastern District of New York, alleging fraud, conversion and violations of New York Public Health Law articles 43 and 43–A. Defendants moved for summary judgment and in support presented the deposition of Dr. Burke, in which he recounted the relevant events of August 23, 2002. He testified that when he found the first kidney unacceptable (owing to the aneurysm) the tissue-typing lab was performing other tests, reconfirming the blood group, retesting plaintiff's tissue and running cross-matching. About 12 hours after discovering the aneurysm, Dr. Burke learned of the positive cross-match which, he said, would have prevented the successful transplant of either kidney.

. . . Dr. Robert S. Gaston, Medical Director of the Kidney and Pancreas Transplantation programs at the University of Alabama . . . concluded that plaintiff was an inappropriate donee for either of Peter's kidneys and that any attempt at transplant would result in "hyperacute rejection" by plaintiff, whose antibodies would attack either of Peter's kidneys and cause damage immediately after transplantation. Defendants argued that for these and other reasons plaintiff had no viable common-law or statutory claim against them.

Plaintiff cross-moved for summary judgment, maintaining, as he does before us, that incompatibility is irrelevant to his claim that defendants misappropriated or diverted Peter's second kidney. He characterized the incompatibility determination as belated and suspect.

The District Court . . . determined that plaintiff failed to state a cause of action for fraud, not having shown how he was harmed by any justifiable reliance on defendants' alleged misrepresentation.

In rejecting the conversion claim, the District Court held, in essence, that contract law ill-suits organ donations and that it would be "inappropriate to expand the limited right that courts recognize in a deceased's body, which only belongs to the next of kin to ensure proper burial." Lastly, the court concluded that in the absence of a clear legislative expression, neither Public Health Law article 43 nor article 43–A gives donees standing to bring a lawsuit.

The Second Circuit agreed that he did not state a cause of action for fraud, but determined that the legal issues necessary to address the two

remaining causes of action raised novel and important questions of New York law. The Second Circuit certified to us, and we accepted, the following questions:

> (1) Do the applicable provisions of the New York Public Health Law vest the intended recipient of a directed organ donation with rights that can be vindicated in a private party's lawsuit sounding in the common law tort of conversion or through a private right of action inferred from the New York Public Health Law? . . .

II
Conversion

To answer the first question we begin by addressing the tort of conversion. A conversion takes place when someone, intentionally and without authority, assumes or exercises control over personal property belonging to someone else, interfering with that person's right of possession. Two key elements of conversion are (1) plaintiff's possessory right or interest in the property and (2) defendant's dominion over the property or interference with it, in derogation of plaintiff's rights.

The first element is pivotal to our inquiry insofar as plaintiff's conversion cause of action necessarily rests on his claimed property right in the second kidney. We must examine the relevant common law to see whether he has such a right.

The Common Law Relative to Property Rights in the Body of a Deceased Person

We begin with an observation. The common law on this subject extends back for centuries while organ donation and transplantation are measured by mere decades. When discussing body parts of deceased persons, it is unlikely that our forbears had in mind that human organs might be transplanted to extend life or improve health. . . .

Considering, however, that the "no property right" jurisprudence was developed long before the age of transplants and other medical advances, we need not identify or forecast the circumstances in which someone may conceivably have actionable rights in the body or organ of a deceased person. For purposes of this case it is enough to say, in answer to the first part of the first certified question, that plaintiff, as a specified donee of an incompatible kidney, has no common-law right to the organ. For that reason, his cause of action for conversion must fail, as it is necessarily based on his claimed right to possess the kidney in question.

We therefore turn to the second half of the first question: does plaintiff, a specified donee of an incompatible kidney, have a viable right of action under New York's Public Health Law?

III
Public Health Law Articles 43 and 43-A: New York's Version of the Uniform Anatomical Gift Act and Its Implementation

Article 43

Given the lack of uniformity among state laws regulating organ donation, the National Conference of Commissioners on Uniform State Laws introduced the Uniform Anatomical Gift Act (UAGA) of 1968. The UAGA was designed to provide a nationwide law to "encourage the making of anatomical gifts" and "serve the needs of the several conflicting interests in a manner consistent with prevailing customs and desires in this country respecting dignified disposition of dead bodies." The UAGA identified the principal competing interests as:

> (1) the wishes of the deceased during his lifetime concerning the disposition of his body; (2) the desires of the surviving spouse or next of kin; (3) the interest of the state in determining by autopsy, the cause of death in cases involving crime or violence; (4) the need of autopsy to determine the cause of death when private legal rights are dependent upon such cause; and (5) the need of society for bodies, tissues and organs for medical education, research, therapy and transplantation" (*id.*).

The UAGA gave any individual, of sound mind and 18 years or more of age, the right to donate all or any part of his or her body for any purpose specified in the act, with the gift to take effect upon death. If an individual does not express such a desire, family members may donate a deceased's organs posthumously, but are prohibited from making an anatomical gift if they know it contravenes the deceased's wishes. Every state, and the District of Columbia, has adopted some variation of the UAGA.

With minor variation, New York codified the UAGA in 1970 as Public Health Law article 43 (L. 1970, ch. 466), describing who may be a donor or donee of an anatomical gift, and how a gift may be executed or revoked. The law expressly prohibits the exchange of valuable consideration for body parts for human transplantation. Section 4301(5) recognizes that the "rights of the donee created by the gift are paramount to the rights of others." The statute, however, is silent as to what rights a donee has in a donated organ.

Article 43 contains a good faith immunity provision: section 4306(3) states, "A person who acts in good faith in accord with the terms of this article or with the anatomical gift laws of another state is not liable for damages in any civil action or subject to prosecution in any criminal proceeding for his act." The immunization was intended to help increase the organ supply by encouraging medical professionals to participate in the organ procurement process.

Article 43–A

To enhance organ procurement and increase the supply of organs, the Legislature passed Public Health Law article 43–A in 1985, entitled "Request for Consent to an Anatomical Gift" (L. 1985, ch. 801, § 1). Section 4351, as originally enacted, obligated hospital administrators to follow certain procedures when seeking consent from a decedent's family members for an anatomical gift. In 1997 the Legislature repealed the 1985 law and replaced it with the current version of section 4351 (L. 1997, ch. 668, § 1). The statute now prescribes the duties of hospital administrators, organ procurement organizations, eye banks and tissue banks. Article 43–A also sets forth procedures for anatomical gift requests, and designates who may qualify as a "requestor" to "ensure[ ] that the request for [the] gift will be both effective with regard to organ procurement and sensitive to the needs of the family during a very difficult time."

Section 4351(4) obligates hospitals to ask a deceased's family member (in a prescribed order of priority) to consent to the gift of all or part of the deceased's body, unless there is reason to believe that the deceased would have objected. In keeping with concerns of tact and sensitivity, the statute goes so far as to provide that the person asking for consent be a trained "designated requestor."

The most vexing provision in article 43–A is section 4351(7), to which the parties have dedicated an appreciable part of their arguments. It provides that "any person or organization acting pursuant to this section, involving the duties of hospitals *shall be legally responsible for any negligent or intentional act or omission committed by such entity or its employees or agents*" (emphasis added). The import of these words is altered, however, by the phrase preceding them, notably that the good faith immunity provision of article 43's section 4306(3) applies. Thus, section 4351(7) incorporates section 4306's good faith immunity provision and states that violators will be held responsible only "[t]o the extent permissible under such subdivision."

Plaintiff argues that the language—"legally responsible for any negligent or intentional act or omission"—implies a statutory cause of action for anyone harmed by defendants, and that he qualifies. He further asserts that the incorporated language of Public Health Law § 4306(3) creates not a qualified immunity, requiring dismissal unless plaintiff can prove bad faith, but merely an affirmative defense, as to which defendants have the burden of proof—a burden he says they have not met.

Defendants maintain that the "legally responsible for any negligent or intentional act or omission" phrase in section 4351(7) has nothing to do with rights of donors or donees, and that the words "legally responsible" contemplate responsibility as opposed to liability. Section 4351(7), defendants argue, comes into play if, for example, a hospital fails to notify a federally designated organ procurement organization of a

potential donor, enabling the commission to hold the hospital "responsible." Defendants thus maintain that, absent bad faith, they are immune from liability by virtue of section 4306(3)'s imported "good faith" language.

The Second Circuit called section 4351(7) "odd," in that when combined with the superimposed language of section 4306, it states that negligent persons "will be held legally responsible to the extent permissible under a provision which shields negligent persons from liability" (438 F.3d at 231 n.16). The court went on to speculate that good faith might be meant to include some but not all acts of negligence, or that section 4351(7) makes negligent parties responsible for injunctive relief but section 4306(3) shields them from personal liability.

The Attorney General offers yet another explanation of 4351(7)'s perplexing language, suggesting that it refers only to article 43–A wrongdoing, involving procurement of anatomical gifts. He asserts it has no bearing on article 43, which deals with donors and donees and the type of allegations made here—the asserted misdelivery of an organ—which is covered by the good faith immunity of section 4306(3). While we agree that the language of section 4351(7) is unclear, it does not control our decision. We rest our answer to the second half of the first question on section 4302(4), which provides that a qualified donor may make a gift to any specified donee "for therapy or transplantation *needed by him*" (emphasis added). In other words, a donee is defined as someone who needs the donated organ.

As we have seen, plaintiff did not need the kidney in question. While he was in need of a functioning kidney, both of Peter's kidneys were of no use to plaintiff. Under the statutory scheme, gifts of a deceased donor are conditioned upon medical benefit to the intended recipient. Indeed, medical compatibility tests are specifically authorized "to *assure* medical acceptability of [the] gift" for transplant. Although plaintiff was the specified donee, that does not alter his status as someone who could not benefit from either kidney. In answer to the second part of the first question we conclude that because the kidneys were medically incompatible with plaintiff, he has no private right of action against defendants under the New York Public Health Law.

Accordingly, under the circumstances of this case, certified question No. 1 should be answered in the negative.

NOTES AND QUESTIONS

1. *Donee's Rights.* Do you agree with the Court of Appeals' resolution of the question of the donee's rights? The court held that there was no right at common law. Why not? On the statutory question, do you think the court dodged the question whether donees have property rights in a certain organ? What would the result of the case have been if one of Peter's kidneys could have been of use to Colavito?

2. *UAGA.* The Court explains the Uniform Anatomical Gift Act (UAGA), which was established to encourage a uniform system of organ donation. Do you think these procedures encourage donation? Do you agree that family members should be allowed to donate a relative's organs after that relative dies?

3. *Back to the Market.* Now that you understand more about a donor-based system for organs, do you find the idea of a market for organs more appealing? How do you assess the following guidelines for a market-based system?

> **a.** A publicly funded and controlled monopsony will procure all organs, and will be the sole agent legally allowed to compensate donors and to distribute organs for transplant. This organization will not be permitted to solicit kidneys, beyond the provision of the sort of factual information that transplant centers now make available for potential living donors.
>
> **b.** Organs obtained will be distributed according to existing algorithms.
>
> **c.** The default position of all persons is that of being a nondonor: Multiple affirmative steps must be taken to facilitate moving to living donor status, and opt in (or forced choice) will remain in place for the deceased-donor system.
>
> **d.** Cadaveric donors (or their families), living directed donors, and living undirected donors will all receive compensation packages, although they will differ substantially, in part for reasons of donor substitution. The underlying attitude governing the system will be that "donors are heroes," and the compensation will reflect this status.
>
> **e.** Compensation to donors will consist of a package of benefits and recognition, of which financial payments, some of them delayed, are but a part.
>
> **f.** Criteria that must be met for qualification as a donor will be public, and undirected living donors, in particular, will continue to undergo a rigorous vetting process to ensure medical and psychological suitability.

T. Randolph Beard & Jim Leitzel, Designing A Compensated-Kidney Donation System, 77 Law & Contemp. Probs. 253, 278–79 (2014). How would you fill in the details of this system? What do you think of their suggestion that living undirected donations receive $50,000 while living directed donations receive $10,000? Id. at 283. For discussion of other models, see, e.g., Iris Jacobs, Selling Kidneys: an Ethical and Economical Approach, Penn Bioethics J., vol. XV, no. 1, at 14, http://bioethicsjournal.com/wp-content/uploads/2019/11/PBJ-Volume-XV-Issue-i.pdf.

4. *Remembering Bioethical Principles.* We started the chapter by reflecting on the bioethical principle of justice. What insight does the principle of justice give about a market for kidneys? According to Professor Capron, the

argument for allowing payments for organs rests on the principle of utility (that the greatest good consists in saving or, in the case of kidney transplants, extending and improving, human life) and the principle of liberty (that freedom of contract must be protected). Yet these principles provide no grounds for erecting impediments to patients, physicians, or indeed health systems seeking potential organ sellers anywhere in the world. As philosopher Janet Radcliffe Richards argues, "If it is presumptively bad to prevent sales altogether, because lives will be lost and adults deprived of an option some would choose if they could, it is for the same reason presumptively bad *to restrict* the selling of organs." Thus, if restrictions are to be placed on markets, principles other than utility and liberty must justify them. Such justification can be found in the three basic principles of medical ethics: justice, beneficence, and autonomy.

Practice Exercise: Write out the implications of these three principles for kidney organ markets.

Alexander M. Capron, Six Decades of Organ Donation and the Challenges That Shifting the United States to A Market System Would Create Around the World, Law & Contemp. Probs., 2014, at 25, 51. What insight do those three principles provide in these circumstances?

In Chapter 2, we asked whether drugs that hadn't been tested in humans in a clinical trial should be made available in emergency circumstances. During the Ebola outbreak in Western Africa, e.g., a local doctor did not receive a dose of ZMapp, one of the products that is hoped to treat the disease, while two American missionaries did. Has this chapter given you a better sense of how all scarce medical resources, not only organs, should be distributed?

d. RETHINKING WHO SHOULD RECEIVE KIDNEYS

At the beginning of this section you decided how you would distribute organs in conditions of scarcity. Do you have any changes to your system now that you know more about organ donation?

In 2014, UNOS released new guidelines for kidney transplants in the United States. Following are their announced goals and policies:

Key goals of the new system include:

- Extending the length of time kidney recipients may have a functioning transplant
- Making better use of available kidneys through increasing organ usage and reducing the need for repeat transplants
- Improving the likelihood of receiving a transplant for candidates who are difficult to match with most donors

To achieve these goals, a number of new and revised policies will be implemented. Key features of the new system include:

Practice Exercise: After understanding these new guidelines, how would you distribute organs in a regulated market in which donors could be compensated? If a donor in Los Angeles signed up on a database to sell her kidneys, who would likely receive her kidneys—a recipient in Los Angeles, a needier recipient in New York, an equally needy recipient in Montana?

What about limited supply of medication? Who should be the first to receive treatment/medicine? Should geography outweigh need? Should age outweigh geography? Should money be a factor?

- Individual calculations of the likely length of function of a donor kidney and of the expected length of time an adult candidate may need a kidney transplant
- Priority matching of kidneys likely to function the longest with candidates likely to need a kidney for the longest amount of time
- Revisions to blood type matching to provide more opportunities to candidates with more rare types
- Increased priority for candidates whose immune system is not compatible with most donor kidneys
- Calculation of transplant waiting time (a key factor in allocation priority) from the date a patient begins dialysis, even if he or she started dialysis before being accepted for listing at a transplant center
- Elimination of kidney payback offers and local logistical exceptions to the national system

UNOS, Revised National Kidney Transplant Allocation System is Now in Place, Dec. 4, 2014, at http://optn.transplant.hrsa.gov/news/revised-national-kidney-transplant-allocation-system-is-now-in-place/. Can you cut through the jargon to figure out what these policies mean? According to the rules, recipients will go on the waiting list when they start dialysis, not when they formally join the list; the best kidneys will be matched with the healthiest and youngest patients; lower-functioning kidneys will be offered in a wider geographical area, so if someone high on the waiting list is far away, the kidney can be used locally; and patients who have less common blood types or immune sensitivity may be moved to the top of the waiting list. See Steven Reinberg, New Rules Aim to Make Kidney Transplants More Fair, CBSNews, Dec. 4, 2014, at http://www.

Go to the website and watch the video describing the revised system. HHS is providing monthly reports about how the system works. Read the most recent report and find out how the new rules have affected kidney transplants.

cbsnews.com/news/new-rules-aim-to-make-kidney-transplants-more-fair/; Victoria Colliver, New Rules for Kidney Allocations, SFGate, Jan. 21, 2014, at http://www.sfgate.com/health/article/New-rules-for-kidney-allocations–5164066.php. What do you think of these changes?

In December 2019, UNOS announced a new policy for kidney and pancreas transplants, which will become effective in February 2021. The new rules should make the distribution system "more fair and equitable," and increase access for "children, women, ethnic minorities and those who are hard to match due to high immune sensitivity."

The new policies remove donation service area (DSA) and OPTN region from kidney and pancreas allocation. Instead of using these inconsistent boundaries as units of distribution, kidneys and pancreata will now be allocated using a 250 nautical mile (NM) circle around the donor's hospital. This will help ensure that the system is based appropriately on the medical needs of patients rather than artificial dictates of geography.

In this distance-based allocation system, up to two proximity points will be awarded to candidates inside the circle to offer organs efficiently to candidates listed closer to or farther from the donor location. If no candidates inside the circle accept the offer, then up to four proximity points will be awarded to candidates outside the circle. Additional policies will address how organs from Alaska are allocated and how medically urgent kidney candidates are prioritized in the new system.

UNOS noted that they have had "seven consecutive years of increases in the number of transplants performed." UNOS, Kidney-pancreas policy, https://unos.org/policy/kidney-pancreas/. Why is this rule an improvement over the past? What do you think of the human values in systems that "first elicit from human subjects a list of patient attributes they consider acceptable for the purpose of prioritizing patients (e.g., medical characteristics, lifestyle choices, and so on). Then, we ask subjects comparison queries between patient profiles and estimate weights in a principled way from their responses. We show how to use these weights in kidney exchange market clearing algorithms. We then evaluate the impact of the weights in simulations and find that the precise numerical values of the weights we computed matter little, other than the ordering of profiles that they imply. However, compared to not prioritizing patients at all, there is a significant effect, with certain classes of patients being (de)prioritized based on the human-elicited value judgments." Rachel Freedman et al., Adapting a Kidney Exchange Algorithm to Align with Human Values, 283 Artificial Intelligence 103261 (2020), https://arxiv.org/abs/2005.09755. Is that a system that aligns with human values?

Although organ donation after cardiac death is popular, it is still "highly controversial and practically inefficient." An alternative is imminent death organ donation, where patients work to make sure that their organs are not wasted, as they can be after cardiac death. What

would you need to know about imminent death organ donation to convince you it is a good idea? See Jordan Potter, Imminent Death Donation: Ethical and Practical Policy Considerations, 46 J. of Law, Medicine and Ethics 524 (2018).

New technologies raise the possibility that organs could be created, rather than harvested, including using three-dimensional "bioprinting" or using genetically modified pigs to "grow" human organs. Anna MacDonald, Bioprinting Organs—A Future Alternative to Organ Donation?, Technology Networks, Sept. 2, 2019, https://www.technologynetworks.com/cell-science/articles/bioprinting-organs-a-future-alternative-to-organ-donation-323422; Karen Weintraub, Meet the pigs that could solve the human organ transplant crisis, MIT Tech. Rev., Nov. 1, 2019, https://www.technologyreview.com/2019/11/01/132110/meet-the-pigs-that-could-solve-the-human-organ-transplant-crises/. What ethical issues might be raised by these new efforts?

C. LOOKING AHEAD: MORE MARKETS FOR MORE BODY PARTS

1. OVARIES AND UTERUSES

"I Love Being a Mom, So I Donated My Uterus to Help Someone Else Become One." Would you do that? 31-year-old Heather Bankos tells her story donating her uterus in Time Magazine, Jun. 3, 2019, https://time.com/5598232/heather-bankos-uterus-donation/. She has three children, and wanted to help others have children. She was thinking of being a surrogate mother until she read a story about a uterus transplant. Her surgery took about 11 hours, and the transplant recipient is doing well. "I'd do it again in a heartbeat," even though there was some pain attached to the surgery, she concludes.

There have been many breakthroughs in the battle against infertility. In 2008 Susanne Butscher was the first to receive a whole ovary transplant. Valarie K. Blake, Ovaries, Testicles, and Uteruses, Oh My! Regulating Reproductive Tissue Transplants, 19 Wm. & Mary J. Women & L. 353, 353–56 (2013). Susanne received her sister's ovary and within three months of the transplant, she began ovulating naturally and then after a short time became pregnant. Id. A few months prior, a woman in Denmark gave birth to her second child after the transplantation of her own ovarian tissue. Id. After these successes, the Gotheburg University of Sweden gained permission to pursue uterus transplants at the end of 2012. Id. Doctors in the United Kingdom have also started to experiment with uterus transplants. Id.

Reproductive tissue transplants are starting to take on a host of new ethical and legal challenges. Id. Reproductive tissue transplants are still in the research phase, which means that they still must adhere to the Institutional Review Board's approved research protocols, including the

ethical and legal requirements therein. Id. This means that the doctors will still need to consider how to regulate the new procedures, how to obtain informed consent, who gets first access to the resources, whether donors can be paid, and whether donors would have parental rights to resulting offspring. Id.

Practice Exercise: Consider these concerns that doctors face and develop solutions to each.

Further, consider the repercussions that allowing uterus transplants would cause. Generally, patients who have new organs must take medicine to prevent their immune systems from rejecting the organ. David Orentlicher, Uterus Transplants?, PrawfsBlog, Oct. 9, 2014, http://prawfsblawg.blogs.com/prawfsblawg/2014/10/uterus-transplants.html. This means that people who receive uterus transplants will need long-term immunosuppression to keep their body from rejecting the transplant. Id. Additionally, there are risks like low birth weight to the unborn child from the mother taking the immunosuppressive drugs. Id. However, the children exposed to the drugs during pregnancy do not appear to be at an elevated risk of physical malformations or other serious side effects. Id. While most organ transplants have been used for patients to live longer, they are now being used to promote a higher quality of living instead of longevity (consider hands/face transplants). Id. Do you think this matters? What ethical concerns does this raise? It is important to note, however, that the donated uteruses can be removed after use. Id. See also Bethany Bruno & Kavita Shah Arora, Uterus Transplantation: The Ethics of Using Deceased vs. Living Donors, 18 Am. J. Bioeth. 6 (2018), https://www.ncbi.nlm.nih.gov/pmc/articles/PMC6296249/.

2. THE FOREIGN MARKET FOR ORGANS

Organ trafficking is a serious problem that has been occurring for decades. Jacqueline Bowden, Feeling Empty? Organ Trafficking & Trade: The Black Market for Human Organs, 8 Intercultural Hum. Rts. L. Rev. 451, 452–53 (2013). People in foreign countries are grabbed off the street, forced into a vehicle, and put through excruciating pain by having a surgeon remove their kidney without any pain reliever. Id. Furthermore, no medication is given after the procedure to prevent infection and if there is a complication because of the surgery, there are no forms of emergency assistance available. Id. How would you solve this problem? Would you approach the government? What if the government was involved in the activity?

Although many people believe organ trafficking is a myth, there are many reports that suggest otherwise. Id. Fortunately, many countries have enacted laws to prevent and prohibit organ trafficking. Id. Organ trafficking is increasingly global. Id. at 456. The countries most involved are China, Mexico, Kosovo, South Africa, Mozambique, India, and the

United States. Id. The problem with the United States is that it is one of the major destinations for the trafficked organs. (Israel is also a top destination for trafficked organs.) Id. Below is a list of countries and their problems associated with organ trafficking. Determine what options you would consider when combating these major issues.

China: China is one of the few countries that permit the taking of organs from death row prisoners. Id. at 458. Since ninety-nine percent of the transplanted organs come from prisoners, China has an incentive to sentence more prisoners to death. Id. The more people on death row, the more money China can generate. Id. There are many problems with this, but one of the major ones is that there are reports that prisoners are coerced into consenting for the threat of being killed prior to their execution date. Id. at 460.

Mexico: In Mexico, some authorities deny that organs are trafficked; yet multiple bodies of young women have been found in the desert with their organs removed. Id. at 461.

Kosovo: Organ trafficking has been present in Kosovo for many years. Id. at 462. Some reported accounts reveal that the Kosovo Liberation Army would take Serbian and Albanian captives for organ removal. Id. at 463. However, after U.N. officials investigated the place where the transplants were alleged to have taken place and found evidence of the alleged misconduct, government officials still claimed that the allegations were unsubstantiated. Id. at 464.

South Africa: A major hospital in Durban, South Africa was charged with organ trafficking in 2010. Id. at 465. The belief is that over 100 illegal kidney transplants took place at that hospital. Id. People from countries like Brazil and Romania are enticed to go to South Africa to surrender their kidneys for compensation. Id. Even though the government prosecutes these illegal transplants, they still occur. Id.

Mozambique: Although Mozambique passed the Human Tissue Act of 1983, which "permits the removal of organs from cadavers after attempts to contact the family of the deceased have failed," organ trafficking is still a huge problem. Id. The problem is still a large one because enforcers of the Act are suspected of colluding with the organ traffickers. Id.

India: India is unique because, unlike many other at-risk countries, the people in India willingly give up their organs because they are in desperate need of money. Id. at 467. Most of the time, the impoverished individuals who donate their kidneys for compensation rarely are compensated the amount promised. Id. Furthermore, many of the surgeries are performed at the individual's home by people posing as surgeons, not by

actual surgeons. Id. Although India has the Transplantation of Human Organs Act, the government does not enforce it due to police and doctor corruption. Id. at 468.

3. REVERSE TRANSPLANT TOURISM

On the other hand, the existence of an international organ system may promote more transplantation. Professors Krawiec and Rees recommend "reverse transplant tourism" (RTT), also known as "cross-border kidney-paired donation," as a means to enhance transplants. Kimberly D. Krawiec & Michael A. Rees, Reverse Transplant Tourism, 77 Law & Contemp. Probs. 145 (2014). RTT is a more complicated version of NEAD chains, which

> takes this approach a step further by redefining incompatibility to include not only immunological barriers, but also a more prevalent incompatibility when transplantation is considered worldwide: the barrier of poverty. In the United States, there are many patients with kidney failure (known as end-stage renal disease (ESRD)) who have insurance to pay for a transplant, but whose donors have the wrong blood type or human leukocyte antigens (HLAs) and thus are not immunologically compatible. In contrast, there are many poor patients outside of the United States with willing compatible living donors, who are not able to afford the immunosuppression necessary to sustain a renal transplant. In both these cases, the patients face barriers that prevent the transplant from moving forward.

Id. at 145–46. To illustrate RTT, Krawiec and Rees describe the situation of Amanda, Bob, Carlos and Diana, which is also illustrated in the diagram. In the United States, Amanda and Bob are biologically incompatible.

> Carlos and Diana, rather than facing biological incompatibility, face a different problem: They are poor and live in a country where poverty is a barrier to transplantation—let's assume Mexico, which does not pay for all of the necessary costs of transplantation. . . . RTT can help both Bob and Diana, allowing each to receive a kidney that they otherwise could not—in Bob's case because of his biological incompatibility with Amanda, and in Diana's case because of her poverty and lack of adequate health care coverage.

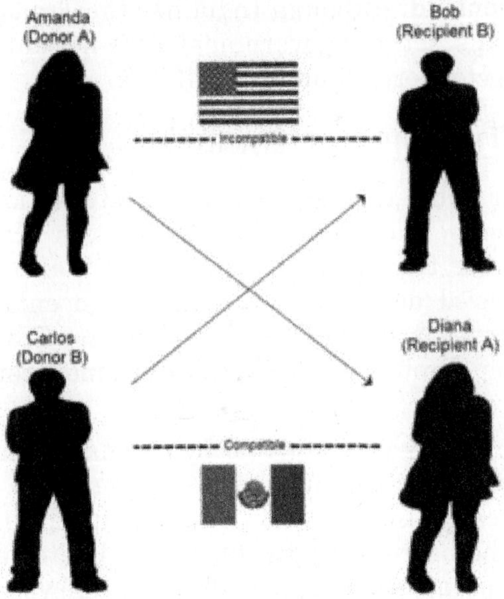

Id. at 152–53.

Dr. Rees was able to participate in an actual RTT. A husband from the Philippines needed a kidney and his wife was willing to donate one. They could not afford the transplant. Dr. Rees raised $150,000 from private sources. The couple came to the United States, where the husband received a kidney removed from a donor in Georgia and the wife's kidney was sent to a recipient in Minnesota. Marlene Harris-Taylor, Reverse-Transplant-Tourism: Kidney doctor pairs foreign, U.S. recipients, Toledo Blade, Feb. 8, 2015, at http://www.toledoblade.com/Medical/2015/02/08/Kidney-doctor-pairs-foreign-U–S-recipients.html. Doctor raised $150,000 from private donors to bring the Filipinos to Toledo, Ohio. Would you recommend or participate in this type of system?

4. MIND OVER MATTER: ORGAN DONATION BY THE MENTALLY INCOMPETENT

Should a mentally incompetent person be allowed to donate organs? Consider a case in Kentucky where a court authorized doctors to remove a kidney from an incompetent man to give to the man's brother. Strunk v. Strunk, 445 S.W.2d 145 (Ky. 1969). The court rationalized its decision by stating that the incompetent man's well-being depended on his brother being alive. Id. at 146.

Consider another case in Wisconsin where the court did not allow a mentally incompetent brother to give his kidney to his sibling with whom he did not have a close relationship because there was no indication that the mentally incompetent brother had agreed to the transplant, nor that he would otherwise benefit. In re Guardianship of Pescinski, 226 N.W.2d 180 (Wis. 1975). Do you think allowing a mentally incompetent

individual to donate a kidney is ethical? Would you allow it? What safeguards would you put in place if it were allowed?

5. ORGAN DONATION IN U.S. PRISONS

Prisons and states typically do not allow inmates to donate organs as living donors to anyone but immediate family members and other close relatives. Technically, there is no law against prisoner organ donation; however, the transplant community and lawmakers have discouraged use of prisoners' organs since the early 1990s due to concern over prisons' high-risk environment for infectious diseases. In addition, physicians and ethicists also criticize the idea because a prisoner is not able to consent to the procedure in a free and non-coercive environment, especially if given inducements and incentives to participate.

The problem of death row inmates becoming organ donors is even more acute. Some considerations for organ donation from those on death row reflect those of general prison population, although more pronounced. Indirect and direct coercion and undue stress and force can possibly frustrate the ability of a death row inmate to make a fully informed decision. As of 2013, all requests by state death row inmates to donate their organs have been denied.

As organ recipients, prisoners also face problems. Because donor organs are in short supply, there are more people waiting for a transplant than there are available organs. When a prisoner receives an organ, that means someone else in the general population may die while waiting for the next available organ. Some people insist that felons and criminals who have a history of violent crime and have violated others' basic rights in society, have lost the right to receive priority for an organ transplant, and that it would be fundamentally unfair to allow the criminal to receive an organ while a law-abiding citizen must die waiting. Prisoner organ donation proposal worrisome, American Medical News. 2007-04-09; David L. Perry, Should Violent Felons Receive Organ Transplants? Markkula Center for Applied Ethics, Jan. 31, 2002, https://www.scu.edu/ethics/focus-areas/bioethics/resources/should-violent-felons-receive-organ-transplants/.

In Chapter 5, we examine the role of conscience in health care by identifying when reasons of conscience give individuals and institutions authorization to opt out of certain forms of medical care.

CHAPTER 5

CONSCIENCE: AN EXERCISE OF PATERNALISM OR AUTONOMY?

Introduction. In Chapter 4, we focused on how to achieve justice in the health care system. We evaluated different schools of moral thought regarding how an ideal health system would operate. We studied the Supreme Court's decision on the Affordable Care Act and discussed whether the Act achieves the principles that scholars advocate to ensure a just health care system. Then we applied those same principles of justice to the organ distribution system. We tried to develop a response to the vexing question of the best way to distribute organs when the supply never matches the demand.

One moral issue that Chapter 4 did not address is whether it violates the rights of hospitals or physicians to force them to perform certain medical procedures. In this chapter, we learn about conscience protection for medical institutions and individuals. First, in Section A, we look at conscientious objection in medicine, such as a Catholic hospital or doctor refusing to perform abortions because it is against the Catholic faith. In response to Roe v. Wade, 410 U.S. 113 (1973), numerous federal and state governments drafted "conscience clauses" or "refusal clauses" that allowed religious individuals and institutions to refuse medical treatments that they find morally objectionable. Since then, increasing numbers of medical practitioners have been given conscience protection to deny an increasing range of services to patients. In Chapter 1, we identified patient autonomy as a central principle of bioethics. Are conscience clauses consistent with patient autonomy? Or do they favor paternalism by letting doctors and other medical personnel decide what services they will provide?

Conscience has also influenced the development of stem cell research, the topic of Section B. As exemplified by President George W. Bush, many Americans believed that stem cell research was immoral because it destroyed human embryos and therefore should be outlawed. Others thought that the potential medical benefits of stem cell research to cure numerous diseases outweighed the harm to the embryo. Both sides argued over the proper basis of stem cell laws. Should conscientious lawmakers prohibit the research or promote it?

Thus, in this chapter, we study the proper balance between caregivers' consciences and patients' needs in Section A, and between politicians' consciences and scientific research in Section B.

A. WHOSE CONSCIENCE COUNTS?

Is it appropriate to refuse certain treatments to patients if the health care provider has voluntarily entered the medical profession? For a review of the ethics of conscientious objection in medicine, see Julian Savulescu, Conscientious Objection in Medicine, 332 Brit. Med. J. 294 (2006). In the United States, the primary discussions about conscientious objection and medical personnel have involved reproductive health, especially sterilization, contraception, abortion and assisted reproductive technologies. Medical participation in the death and dying process, including euthanasia, assisted suicide and withdrawal of feeding, has also become a subject of moral concern. Do you think there should be a constitutional right to conscience for medical personnel?

In all these areas, the usual legal solution has been for state and federal governments to draft legislation containing conscience clauses, which protect employees who refuse to perform abortion, euthanasia and other contested procedures from firing or demotion. Many conscience clauses shield individuals from sanction for adhering to their religious beliefs; others protect religious hospitals and health care institutions from any obligation to perform the contested services.

Such conscience clauses are controversial. They may protect the conscience of the medical provider, but not the needs of the patient who conscientiously desires—and may desperately need—a certain form or level of treatment. Furthermore, religious institutions that enjoy the protections of conscience may receive government funding for some of their programs, raising difficult questions of Establishment and Free Exercise under the First Amendment. On one side are religious health care providers who have moral reasons not to perform a medical service; on the other are citizens who, following their own consciences, desire that medical treatment.

As you read the following materials, consider how the courts and the legislatures should strike the proper balance between those two groups. Keep in mind four recurring themes. First, is the protection of conscience a constitutional right or a statutory privilege that can be given or taken away by the state? Second, should both individuals and institutions enjoy rights of conscience? Third, what jobs warrant conscience protection—doctors, nurses, pharmacists, administrators, janitors? Fourth, what procedures warrant conscience protection—abortion, sterilization, provision of contraceptive insurance, sale of pharmaceuticals, euthanasia? Or all medical procedures?

Means v. United States Conference of Catholic Bishops

Sixth Circuit Court of Appeals, 2016.
836 F.3d 643.

■ ALICE M. BATCHELDER, CIRCUIT JUDGE.

Plaintiff Tamesha Means miscarried at eighteen weeks' gestation. She sought treatment at a Catholic hospital in western Michigan, which allegedly failed to provide her accurate information or diagnose and treat a serious bacterial infection. Three years later, Means sued, not the hospital or any of its physicians, but the United States Conference of Catholic Bishops (USCCB) and three individuals who have served as chair of the unincorporated organization Catholic Health Ministries (CHM). Means has alleged that USCCB and the CHM defendants are liable in ordinary negligence for promulgating and enforcing a publication of mandatory ethical guidelines dictated by Catholic doctrine (the "Directives"), which she claims dictated the poor treatment she received. The district court dismissed Means's complaint for lack of personal jurisdiction over USCCB and failure to state a claim against the CHM defendants. We AFFIRM.

I. FACTS AND PROCEDURAL HISTORY

Means was eighteen weeks pregnant when she went into labor on December 1, 2010. She went to Mercy Health Partners, the only hospital within thirty minutes of her residence. Doctors at Mercy Health diagnosed Means with preterm premature rupture of membrane. This condition usually results in a stillbirth or the baby's death soon after birth. At this time, however, the unborn baby still had a heartbeat.

Despite the gravity of Means's condition, which created serious risks to herself and her baby, Mercy Health sent her home with some pain medication and told her to return the following week for her regularly scheduled appointment. Although Means was told that her baby was not yet viable, no one told her that the baby would likely not survive or that continuing her pregnancy could endanger her own health. Mercy Health did not give Means the option of artificially completing the miscarriage or terminating the pregnancy.

The next morning, Means returned to the hospital with a fever, excruciating pain, and bleeding. Mercy Health did not give her additional treatment or treatment options, even though Means's treating physician suspected she had a serious bacterial infection that can cause infertility and even death. Instead, once Means's fever went down, the hospital sent her home. Means was told to return if her fever came back or if her contractions worsened.

Means returned to Mercy Health that night with regular, extremely painful contractions. While the hospital was preparing to discharge her for the third time, shortly after midnight, Means delivered her baby breech. The baby died within three hours. The placental pathology report

confirmed that Means did in fact have two acute bacterial infections at the time she gave birth.

Two years later, a public health educator working on a federally funded public health surveillance project on infant and fetal mortality discovered and inquired into Means's case. Mercy Health's Vice President of Mission Services Joseph O'Meara explained the hospital's inaction by stating that the Directives prohibited the hospital from inducing labor or taking similar action in Means's situation. Since the statute of limitations had run out on any medical malpractice claim Means may have had, she sued the Catholic entities responsible for the Directives on a theory of ordinary negligence, alleging that the Directives caused Mercy Health's harmful inaction.

USCCB is a national public policy agency established by the Roman Catholic Bishops of the United States. It is a not-for-profit entity incorporated in the District of Columbia. USCCB published the Fifth Edition of *Ethical and Religious Directives for Catholic Health Care Services* in December 2009.

The other three defendants—Stanley Urban, Robert Ladenburger, and Mary Mollison ("the CHM defendants")—are current and former chairs of an unincorporated entity known as Catholic Health Ministries. CHM is the Catholic sponsor of Trinity Health, the healthcare system that operates Mercy Health and other hospitals. CHM's "Canonical Bylaws state that CHM 'will adhere to [the Directives] promulgated by [USCCB].' " In turn, Trinity Health's Amended Articles of Incorporation provide that its "activities . . . shall be carried out in a manner consistent with," among other sources, "directives promulgated from time to time by [CHM] and the values and principles inherent in the medical-moral teachings of the Church (such as the [Directives]) as promulgated from time to time by [USCCB]." The most recent versions of CHM's Canonical Bylaws and Trinity Health's Articles of Incorporation were adopted in 2009, when Mollison was chair of CHM. Ladenburger was chair in 2010, when Means's alleged injury occurred. Urban is CHM's current chair. Urban, Ladenburger, and Mollison are residents of Pennsylvania, Colorado, and Wisconsin, respectively. Means has alleged that CHM's decision to adopt the Directives took place within the Eastern District of Michigan.

II. PERSONAL JURISDICTION AND VENUE

. . . Turning to the substance of USCCB's defense, we agree with the district court that it lacked personal jurisdiction over USCCB.

In order to demonstrate personal jurisdiction over USCCB, Means must satisfy the requirements of constitutional due process as set forth in the three-prong test of *Southern Machine Co. v. Mohasco Industries, Inc.*:

> First, the defendant must purposefully avail himself of the privilege of acting in the forum state or causing a consequence

> in the forum state. Second, the cause of action must arise from the defendant's activities there. Finally, the acts of the defendant or consequences caused by the defendant must have a substantial enough connection with the forum state to make the exercise of jurisdiction over the defendant reasonable.

401 F.2d 374, 381 (6th Cir. 1968). Where, as here, the district court decides the personal jurisdiction issue on the basis of written submissions without an evidentiary hearing, the plaintiff must make only a prima facie showing that personal jurisdiction exists. *Schneider v. Hardesty*, 669 F.3d 693, 697 (6th Cir. 2012).

Southern Machine's first prong, "purposeful availment," is " 'essential' to a finding of personal jurisdiction." *Intera Corp. v. Henderson*, 428 F.3d 605, 616 (6th Cir. 2005). " 'Purposeful availment' . . . is present where the defendant's contacts with the forum state 'proximately result from actions by the defendant *himself* that create a "substantial connection" with the forum state . . . .' " *Neogen Corp. v. Neo Gen Screening, Inc.*, 282 F.3d 883, 889 (6th Cir. 2002) (quoting *Burger King Corp. v. Rudzewicz*, 471 U.S. 462, 475 (1985)). "[T]he defendant's conduct and connection with the forum" must be "such that he 'should reasonably anticipate being haled into court there.' " *Id.* (quoting *Burger King Corp.*, 471 U.S. at 474). "Due process requires that a defendant be haled into court in a forum State based on his own affiliation with the State, not based on the 'random, fortuitous, or attenuated' contacts he makes by interacting with other persons affiliated with the State." *Walden v. Fiore*, 134 S. Ct. 1115, 1123 (2014) (quoting *Burger King Corp.*, 471 U.S. at 475).

USCCB's action of publishing the Directives does not "create a substantial connection" between USCCB and Michigan. Michigan—like every state—does have Catholic hospitals, and USCCB does intend the Directives to be implemented by all Catholic healthcare institutions. USCCB may even have known that Trinity Health is a Catholic hospital network operating in Michigan. But this is not a "substantial connection" such that USCCB would reasonably expect to be haled into court in the state of Michigan. *Cf. Calder v. Jones*, 465 U.S. 783, 788–89 (1984) (holding that a libelous article published in Florida established personal jurisdiction in California because it was about a California resident and was drawn from California sources).

Rather, USCCB is connected to Michigan through exactly the sort of "attenuated contacts" that do *not* permit the exercise of personal jurisdiction. The actions that connect USCCB to Michigan are the actions of CHM (in adopting the Directives in the state of Michigan), of Trinity Health (in operating Catholic hospitals in the state of Michigan), and of Mercy Health (in being a Catholic hospital in the state of Michigan). USCCB has not required Trinity Health or Mercy Health to affiliate with the Catholic Church. Nor did USCCB impose the Directives on Mercy Health. USCCB has simply set forth the ethical standards necessary for

an institution to call itself "Catholic." Accordingly, USCCB's connection to Michigan is too attenuated to create personal jurisdiction in a Michigan court.

. . . Means has not alleged any other connection between USCCB and Michigan, and she has failed to make a prima facie case of personal jurisdiction. We affirm the district court's dismissal of Means's claim against USCCB for lack of personal jurisdiction.

III. FAILURE TO STATE A CLAIM OF ORDINARY NEGLIGENCE

. . . Means's complaint brought a single cause of action for ordinary negligence against the CHM defendants. "[I]n order to state a negligence claim on which relief may be granted, [a] plaintiff[ ] must prove (1) that defendant[s] owed [her] a duty of care, (2) that defendant[s] breached that duty, (3) that [the] plaintiff[ ] w[as] injured, and (4) that defendant[s'] breach caused [the] plaintiff['s] injuries." *Henry v. Dow Chem. Co.*, 701 N.W.2d 684, 688 (Mich. 2005). The district court held that Means's complaint did not state a claim for ordinary negligence because Michigan law does not create a cause of action against healthcare policy makers for "independent negligence" that is distinct from malpractice or vicarious liability.

Means asks us to recognize a duty under Michigan law on the part of a religious organization to a specific patient to adopt ethical directives that do not contradict the medical standard of care. Whether such a duty exists is far from certain, especially if the standard of care violates the organization's religious beliefs. Nevertheless, even if the CHM defendants had such a duty, Means's factual allegations do not create the plausible inference that any breach of that duty proximately caused any injury to Means within the strictures of Michigan negligence law.

In Michigan, "[i]n order to be a proximate cause, the negligent conduct must have been a cause of the plaintiff's injury and the plaintiff's injury must have been a natural and probable result of the negligent conduct." *O'Neal v. St. John Hosp. & Med. Ctr.*, 791 N.W.2d 853, 858 (Mich. 2010). The first of these prongs "generally requires showing that 'but for' the defendant's actions, the plaintiff's injury would not have occurred." *Id.* (quoting *Skinner v. Square D Co.*, 516 N.W.2d 475, 479 (Mich. 1994)). The second prong "relates to the foreseeability of the consequences." *Id.*

Here, the defendants' actions were the adoption of the USCCB Directives, so we will look to any action the Directives may have caused. To understand what action the Directives may have caused, it is necessary to examine the offending portions. Under Directive 45, [a]bortion (that is, the directly intended termination of pregnancy before viability or the directly intended destruction of a viable fetus) is never permitted. Every procedure whose sole immediate effect is the termination of pregnancy before viability is an abortion . . . .

Counterbalancing this prohibition, Directive 47 permits "[o]perations, treatments, and medications that have as their direct purpose the cure of a proportionately serious pathological condition of a pregnant woman" and that "cannot be safely postponed until the unborn child is viable, even if they will result in the death of the unborn child." Finally, as relevant here, Directive 27 requires that the patient receive all reasonable information about the essential nature of the proposed treatment and its benefits; its risks, side-effects, consequences, and cost; and any reasonable and morally legitimate alternatives, including no treatment at all.

As noted above, the Directives themselves require adoption of the Directives "as policy" in Catholic healthcare institutions.

Means alleges that these Directives dictated Mercy Health's inaction in her situation. In her view, Mercy Health should have: (1) informed Means of the option to terminate her pregnancy before discharging her; (2) informed her of the health risks of continuing her pregnancy; (3) informed her that her baby would likely not survive; and (4) "provide[d] appropriate medical care to" Means. Means alleges that Mercy Health did not do these things because it was following the Directives.

It is not clear that the Directives restricted Mercy Health from giving Means all the information she alleges it withheld. But we will not attempt to interpret the Directives, because even if we were to accept Means's allegations that the Directives dictated Mercy Health's inaction and restriction of information, her complaint suffers from another deficiency.

Means alleges—and we do not doubt—that she suffered physical and mental pain, emotional injuries, a riskier delivery, shock and emotional trauma from making funeral arrangements for her dead child, and other "discomforts and pain." But these allegations are not sufficient to state an injury under Michigan negligence law. In Michigan, "present physical injury" is necessary to state a claim for negligence. *Henry v. Dow Chem. Co.*, 701 N.W.2d 684, 691 (Mich. 2005). Pain alone is not "physical injury." *See People v. DeKorte*, 593 N.W.2d 203, 206 (Mich. Ct. App. 1999) (discussing the ordinary meaning of the term "physical injury" by looking to negligence law). Means's allegation of emotional trauma does not cure the problem, because a claim of negligent infliction of emotional distress requires "physical manifestations of that distress." *Henry*, 701 N.W.2d at 692 (emphasis omitted). And although a defendant who causes a miscarriage can be liable for the resulting mental anguish, even when there is no physical injury to the mother, *McClain v. Univ. of Mich. Bd. of Regents*, 665 N.W.2d 484, 496 (Mich. Ct. App. 2003), *superseded by statute on unrelated grounds as noted in Simpson v. Alex Pickens, Jr. & Assocs., MD, PC*, 874 N.W.2d 359, 365 & n.6 (Mich. Ct. App. 2015), here the defendants—by reason of the Directives—neither caused nor are alleged to have caused the miscarriage. Means was in labor when she first arrived at the hospital, and while her delivery may have been

riskier, she has not alleged any physical consequences. Nor has she alleged any long-term effects of her bacterial infections. The complaint does not suggest that Means incurred more medical expenses as a result of Mercy Health's inaction, although even that would be insufficient to state a claim for negligence in Michigan. *See Henry*, 701 N.W.2d at 690 ("[A] plaintiff must demonstrate a present physical injury to person or property in addition to economic losses that result from that injury in order to recover under a negligence theory.").

Because Means has not alleged that the defendants, by adopting the Directives, caused her any cognizable injury, she has not stated a claim of negligence. We accordingly AFFIRM the district court's decision dismissing Means's complaint.

What do you think of the reasoning of the Sixth Circuit in the *Means* case? Do you think it protects the rights of conscience? Does it protect the rights of the patient? Is there another way you would have written it? What do you think of Professor Sawicki's analysis of the *Means* case at the beginning of the following article? What do you learn from her article about conscience?

The Conscience Defense to Malpractice

Nadia N. Sawicki.
108 Calif. L. Rev. 1255 (2020).

According to Tamesha Means' complaint in federal court, at no point did any of the health care providers at Mercy tell her that there was no chance her fetus would survive the amniotic rupture, or that terminating the pregnancy and extracting the fetus would reduce the risk of serious health complications. Rather than offering her the option of termination, the providers at Mercy discharged her from the hospital without informing her of the risks she faced in continuing the miscarriage without active medical management.

In doing so, it is very likely that the physicians, nurses, and other individual health care providers at Mercy committed medical malpractice, and that Mercy as an institution breached legal duties owed to her.

However, even if Tamesha Means could prove that the hospital or its doctors deviated from the medical standard of care, she would be barred from bringing a malpractice suit to recover damages for her injuries. This is because Michigan law, like many states' health care conscience laws, creates a "conscience defense" to malpractice—that is, it immunizes health care providers from civil liability, even when their conscience-driven refusal to provide information or treatment violates the standard of care. In Tamesha Means' case, Mercy was protected from suit because it was a Catholic hospital and had a religious justification for turning her

away without treatment: Mercy was obligated to follow the U.S. Conference of Catholic Bishops' Ethical and Religious Directives for Catholic Health Care Services, which prohibit intentional termination of pregnancy in all circumstances.

For nearly a half century, scholars of law, medicine, medical ethics, and philosophy have debated the role that conscience and religion should play in the delivery of health care. Much of the literature in this area has focused on the laws that codify the rights of refusing health care providers—specifically, who should be protected by these laws, what conduct should be protected, and whether and when there should be any limitations on a provider's right to act in accordance with his conscientious beliefs. But in these debates, a fundamental issue has been overlooked—the procedural question of how, exactly, law protects health care providers who exercise their conscience in the course of their professional practice. That is, when a provider refuses on grounds of conscience to participate in a health care service, what consequences is he protected from?

While the precise procedural protections established by health care conscience laws vary widely from state to state, they often include protections from civil liability, criminal prosecution, discipline by state licensing boards or other administrative agencies, adverse action by employers, discrimination in educational opportunities, and loss of funding, among others. However, there is scant scholarship critically evaluating, or even acknowledging, the breadth of these legal protections. Perhaps even more surprisingly, given the significant attention that has been paid to tracking legislative developments related to U.S. conscience law, there exists no empirical data on how frequently these various types of procedural protections arise. In the absence of such data as a starting point for academic analysis, contemporary debates about health care conscience laws are necessarily incomplete.

. . . The Article focuses exclusively on conscience laws that apply in the context of abortion and other reproductive health services, with a particular emphasis on the laws' protections from civil liability in cases of conscientious objection to abortion. It demonstrates that immunity from civil liability is by far the most common type of procedural protection explicitly established. Further, the majority of conscience laws are absolute in their protections—they permit providers to refuse to participate in reproductive health services and shield them from civil liability for their refusals, even when their conduct violates the medical profession's standard of care and causes patient harm. Effectively, many reproductive health care conscience laws create an absolute and unchallengeable "conscience defense" to medical malpractice. . . .

II. OVERVIEW OF U.S. HEALTH CARE CONSCIENCE LAWS

Public debates about conscientious objection in health care began in earnest around the time that abortion bans faced their first challenges in

court. These debates reached a tipping point after the Supreme Court's 1973 decision in Roe v. Wade established that a woman has a constitutional right to choose to terminate a pregnancy in consultation with her physician, and effectively legalized abortion nationwide. Individual and institutional health care providers expressed concern that as a result of the Court's decision, they might be forced to participate in a procedure they found morally objectionable. The first federal and state conscience laws were enacted shortly thereafter in response to these concerns, but the passage of these laws by no means settled the issue.

Today, the scope of conscientious objection in health care has extended beyond physicians' objections to participation in abortion. Other licensed health care professionals—like nurses, pharmacists, emergency medical technicians, and physician assistants—also claim rights to decline to participate in medical services they find objectionable. Individuals who work in the health or public health industries but who are not licensed by the state—like public health officials, medical students, and researchers—claim these rights as well. Finally, institutional health care providers—like hospitals and skilled nursing facilities—also regularly claim religious and conscientious objections to certain medical services. In the 45 years since Roe, conscience laws at both the state and federal level have extended to protect this broader scope of providers.

Conscientious refusals arise most commonly in the context of reproductive health services, like abortion, sterilization, emergency contraception, and contraception. However, refusals arise in other contexts as well. The treatments available to patients at the end of life—for example, aid in dying, terminal sedation, artificial nutrition and hydration, and other life-sustaining medical treatments—are often impacted by health care providers' conscientious beliefs. Medical services that have a connection with embryos or human stem cells—such as vaccines derived from research on fetal stem cells—are also a point of contention for some providers. Others rely on conscience to justify their refusal to treat LGBTQ individuals. As a result, health care conscience laws in many states have expanded to encompass a broad variety of medical services that some providers deem objectionable. Indeed, a few states offer protections to health care providers who object on grounds of conscience to any medical service. Given their historical grounding in the abortion debate, conscience laws have often been viewed as redounding only to the benefit of religious conservatives. However, providers with beliefs falling on the liberal side of the political spectrum also have the opportunity to benefit from their protections, especially as these laws have expanded to encompass a broader variety of medical services.

Finally, conscience laws have extended to protect not only providers who are unwilling to directly perform medical services they deem objectionable, but also those whose involvement is more tangential. Health care providers have raised objections to various types of

participation in medical services that they view as morally complicit—such as providing referrals for an objectionable service, informing patients about the availability of the service, transferring prescriptions and medical records, providing transportation, and providing translation services. Depending on how broadly a state's conscience law is worded, many of these indirect forms of involvement may be protected as well . . .

IV. RESEARCH FINDINGS

. . . D. Summary of Civil Liability Protections

Taken together, the findings above paint a troubling picture for patients who have suffered injuries as a result of conscience-based deviations from the medical standard of care. Where an individual or institutional health care provider's refusal to terminate a pregnancy (or inform a patient that termination would be medically appropriate) violates the standard of care—as may be the case for patients experiencing inevitable miscarriages, ectopic pregnancies, or other pregnancies that threaten the woman's life or health—patients in most states are denied the opportunity for legal recovery.

Out of 50 states and the District of Columbia, 46 states have abortion-specific conscience laws. The remaining five jurisdictions do not have legislation explicitly protecting health care providers who decline to participate in abortion for reasons of conscience. That said, one of those jurisdictions—Mississippi—has a general conscience law that grants individual and institutional providers the right to refuse to participate in any health care service (without specifically delineating abortion) and explicitly establishes civil immunity in such cases. The District of Columbia also has a general conscience law, but it is limited in scope to employees of public benefit corporations, protecting them from employment discrimination for their conscientious refusal to participate in "certain aspects of direct patient care that are in conflict with their religious, or ethical beliefs." Although the law does not specifically reference immunity from civil liability, for the reasons described in Part IV-A, supra, a judge might nevertheless interpret it as implicitly establishing civil immunity. That said, the District of Columbia law, unlike Mississippi's, establishes exceptions in cases where the patient's "safety is in jeopardy," and requires that managers "assess and ensure appropriate staffing so that patient care needs are met." Colorado has laws protecting providers' rights of conscience in the context of sterilization, contraception, and emergency contraception, but not abortion. The remaining two jurisdictions—New Hampshire and Vermont—appear to have no health care conscience laws. Thus, in only four of the five jurisdictions with no abortion-specific conscience law is it possible that an injured patient could, in some situations, bring a tort action if a health care provider's refusal to participate in abortion violated the standard of care.

Of the remaining 46 states, 37 states explicitly immunize providers from civil liability for their conscience-based refusals, and the remaining

nine have conscience laws that would likely be interpreted as creating civil immunity despite the absence of explicit language to this effect. Thirteen of the 46 states with abortion conscience laws limit providers' right to refuse treatment and/or permit patients to bring civil suit in life-threatening or emergency situations—but only against some providers and in some circumstances. No state withdraws providers' rights to immunity from civil liability when they have committed general malpractice in non-emergent situations.

Considering all these data together, in only 17 U.S. states might a patient who is injured by a provider's conscience-driven refusal to participate in abortion be able to recover damages under the common law of malpractice—and even then, only in life-threatening or emergency situations (rather than in all contexts where the provider's conscientious refusal violates the standard of care), and only against some providers.

VI. CONCLUSIONS AND DIRECTIONS FOR FUTURE RESEARCH

. . . These new insights into the details of conscience protections relating to reproductive health services offer scholars and policymakers an opportunity to revisit, in a more nuanced fashion, the debates surrounding law's role in protecting health care providers' rights of conscience. Recognition of the fact that individual and institutional providers in most states are granted absolute (or near-absolute) immunity from civil suit should prompt discussion of whether such broad protections are justified as a policy matter. Likewise, recognition of the wide variety of procedural protections states might choose from—including immunity in the context of criminal prosecution, adverse employment action, loss of funding, disciplinary action by licensing authorities, and beyond—should inspire policymakers to critically evaluate which of these protections best balance providers' conscience rights against state interests in protecting patient health and safety.

NOTES AND QUESTIONS

1. How do you analyze the Sixth Circuit's decision that it had no personal jurisdiction over the Catholic bishops? How do you assess its decision that Means had no tort injuries? Were you persuaded by both arguments? The opinion protects the consciences of doctors who would not want to provide an abortion or information surrounding it. Would the court protect doctors who wanted to provide abortion at a Catholic hospital as a matter of conscience? Do you agree that all lawsuits like Means's should be barred by a conscience defense, which protects health care providers' rights to follow their consciences not to provide services?

2. *The Church Amendment.* In October 1972, James and Gloria Taylor went to St. Vincent's Hospital in Billings, Montana, to deliver their second child. Earlier that year St. Vincent's, a Roman Catholic hospital run by the Sisters of Charity, had combined its maternity department with that of the only other hospital in town, the Billings Deaconess Hospital. During the

merger negotiations, St. Vincent's had told Deaconess that it would not provide surgical sterilizations, which violate the "Ethical and Religious Directives for Catholic Hospitals." Instead, the two hospitals had an agreement that St. Vincent's would send patients desiring sterilization to Deaconess. The Taylors wanted to have a sterilization operation during Mrs. Taylor's cesarean section, but St. Vincent's refused their request.

The Taylors sued St. Vincent's for violation of their constitutional rights under 42 U.S.C. § 1983. Usually plaintiffs may sue only the government for violations of their constitutional rights. The Taylors, however, argued that St. Vincent's was a state actor, to be held to the government's standards, because it received tax benefits from the State of Montana and federal funding under the Hill-Burton Act, 42 U.S.C. § 291, which had paid for some of the hospital's construction. The district court of Montana agreed, and took jurisdiction over the case on October 27, 1972, because of the government funding. Taylor v. St. Vincent's Hospital, 369 F. Supp. 948, 950 (D. Mont. 1973).

Subsequently, however, in June 1973, Congress passed the Church Amendment to the Health Programs Extension Act of 1973 (see current version at 42 U.S.C. § 300a–7). The Church Amendment provided that a hospital that receives federal funding is not a state actor. Specifically, under that amendment courts could not order an entity that received federal funding to "make its facilities available for the performance of any sterilization procedure or abortion if the performance of such procedure or abortion in such facilities is prohibited by the entity on the basis of religious beliefs or moral convictions." Accordingly, the district court then refused jurisdiction over the still-pending Taylors' case because St. Vincent's was not a state actor. See Taylor v. St. Vincent's Hospital, 369 F. Supp. 948, 951 (D. Mont. 1973), aff'd by 523 F.2d 75 (9th Cir. 1975). The court concluded that Congress did not intend different treatment of hospitals that received funding before and after the Church Amendment passed. Id. The courts did not reach the Taylors' argument that the Church Amendments violated the Establishment Clause. St. Vincent's was not forced to perform a sterilization that contradicted Catholic principles and modern conscience clauses were born.

The Church Amendment was prompted by the Supreme Court's January 1973 decision, Roe v. Wade, 410 U.S. 113 (1973), which held that the decision whether to abort or bear a pregnancy is protected by the constitutional right to privacy. Several religious groups, including Catholics, Mormons, Seventh-Day Adventists, Baptists and Muslims, have moral objections to abortion and have insisted on the necessity of conscience clauses as a matter of free exercise. See Abortion: A Reader (Lloyd H. Steffan ed., 1996) for denominational statements and attitudes toward abortions; see also Ronald M. Green, Religions' "Bioethical Sensibility:" A Research Agenda, in Notes from a Narrow Ridge: Religion and Bioethics 165–81 (Dena S. Davis & Laurie Zoloth eds., 1999).

3. *Conscience Clauses.* The Guttmacher Institute summarizes state reproductive conscience clauses in the following manner:

> "46 states allow some health care providers to refuse to provide abortion services.
>
> All of these states permit individual health care providers to refuse to provide abortion services.
>
> 44 states allow health care institutions to refuse to provide abortion services; 13 limit the exemption to private health care institutions and 1 state allows only religious health care entities to refuse to provide such care.
>
> 12 states allow some health care providers to refuse to provide services related to contraception.
>
> 9 states allow individual health care providers to refuse to provide services related to contraception.
>
> 6 states explicitly permit pharmacists to refuse to dispense contraceptives. (6 additional states have broad refusal clauses that do not specifically include pharmacists, but may apply to them.)
>
> 8 states allow health care institutions to refuse to provide services related to contraception; 5 states limit the exemption to private entities.
>
> 18 states allow some health care providers to refuse to provide sterilization services.
>
> 17 states allow individual health care providers to refuse to provide sterilization services.
>
> 16 states allow health care institutions to refuse to provide sterilization services; 4 limit the exemption to private entities."

Refusing to Provide Health Services, Jan.1, 2021. What are the strengths and weaknesses of these provisions?

Although the early conscience clauses involved abortion or (occasionally) sterilization, since 1973 conscience clause protection has grown to include numerous additional medical procedures and providers. In 1974, for example, the Church Amendment was expanded to include protection for religious or moral objection to *any* health service in which funds were received from the Secretary of Health, Education and Welfare; in 1997 it was broadened to include Medicare- and Medicaid-managed care plans. See Kathleen M. Boozang, Deciding the Fate of Religious Hospitals in the Emerging Health Care Market, 31 Hous. L. Rev. 1429, 1481 (1995). State conscience clause legislation has been piecemeal, providing different coverage from state to state. Most state conscience clauses cover a few procedures instead of providing a blanket exemption for any objectionable health service. Although the early conscience clauses developed immediately post-*Roe*, since the 1990s conscience clauses have expanded considerably. See Thaddeus Mason Pope, Legal Briefing: Conscience Clauses and Conscientious Refusal, 21 J. Clinical Ethics 163 (2010); Lynn D. Wardle, Protecting the Rights of Conscience of Health Care Providers, 14 J. Legal

Med. 177 (1993); Katherine A. White, Crisis of Conscience: Reconciling Religious Health Care Providers' Beliefs and Patients' Rights, 51 Stan. L. Rev. 1703, 1708 (1999).

In 1996, an amendment to the Public Health Act extended conscience protection to medical education and training programs. In 2004, President George W. Bush signed legislation including the Weldon Amendment, which blocks funding to any federal or state agency or program that discriminates against entities that do not provide abortion. The coverage was broad, extending not only to hospitals and individual doctors, but also to insurance companies and any health care facility. As the Bush administration ended, the Department of Health and Human Services (HHS) issued a new rule about conscience protection that became effective on the last day of Bush's presidency. Dep't of Health and Human Servs., "Ensuring that Department of Health and Human Services Funds Do Not Support Coercive or Discriminatory Policies or Practices in Violation of Federal Law," 45 C.F.R. Pt. 88, 73 Fed. Reg. 78071 (Dec. 19, 2008). Although HHS acknowledged that the Church Amendments, the Public Health Service Act, and the Weldon Amendment already protected conscience and that no federal statute mandated the passage of the new administrative rule, it cited concerns about the intolerance of the health care field toward religion to justify adding new certification requirements for recipients of HHS funds, who must certify in writing that they comply with the federal legislation. See Jane W. Walker, Comment, The Bush Administration's Midnight Provider Refusal Rule: Upsetting the Emerging Balance in State Pharmacist Refusal Laws, 46 Hous. L. Rev. 939 (2009). Do you agree that health care is hostile toward religion?

Attentive to the complaints of some critics who argued that the new rule would keep patients from accessing needed services, the Obama administration promised a reconsideration of the Bush rule. Dep't of Health and Human Services, Rescission of the Regulation Entitled "Ensuring that Department of Health and Human Services Funds Do Not Support Coercive or Discriminatory Policies or Practices in Violation of Federal Law," 45 C.F.R. Pt. 88, 74 Fed. Reg. 10207, 10209 (Mar. 10, 2009). Yet President Obama supported conscience clause legislation and pledged support for "reasonable" conscience clauses. Transcript: Obama's Notre Dame Speech, L.A. Times, May 17, 2009. Consider that, in addition to the forty-six states that allow some refusal of abortion services, eighteen states allow some refusal of sterilization services and thirteen states allow some refusal of contraceptive services. See State Policies in Brief, *supra*. Is that reasonable?

The Obama administration eventually issued a new rule governing conscience clauses that rescinded parts of the 2008 Bush rule. In particular, the revised regulations did not include the written certification requirement, which was viewed as too burdensome, and replaced that requirement with a provision that grant documents make clear that health employers would be held to the conscience protection laws. The Obama regulations include strong language about the importance of conscience protection and authorize vigorous enforcement of conscience legislation by the Office of Civil Rights. The Obama rules left "intact only long-standing 'conscience' protections for

doctors and nurses who do not want to perform abortions or sterilizations." Interpreters of the Bush regulations feared that *every* employee of a health care institution could refuse to participate in *all* medical services. See Rob Stein, Obama Administration Replaces Controversial "Conscience" Regulation for Health Care Workers, Wash. Post, Feb. 18, 2011. Did Obama go too far in cutting back on Bush's rules?

On the other hand, the Affordable Care Act prohibits qualified health plans from discriminating against health care providers due to their "unwillingness to provide, pay for, provide coverage of, or refer for abortions." 42 U.S.C. § 18023(b)(4). Does that statute give too much protection to providers who refuse abortion care? Why should referral be included on the list?

A Trump administration rule, Protecting Statutory Rights in Health Care, was released in 2019. This rule was based on Trump's announced commitment to protect religious freedom. "In order to ensure that recipients of Federal financial assistance and other Department funds comply with their legal obligations, this final rule requires certain recipients to maintain records; cooperate with OCR's [the Office of Civil Rights] investigations, reviews, or other proceedings; and submit written assurances and certifications of compliance to the Department. The final rule also encourages the recipients of HHS funds to provide notice to individuals and entities about their right to be free from coercion or discrimination on account of religious beliefs or moral convictions." Protecting Statutory Conscience Rights in Health Care, 84 FR 23170. Federal fund recipients would lose their funding if they violated the consciences of their providers.

What did Trump add to his predecessors' protections of conscience? The rule was challenged in different lawsuits around the country. What would be the basis for upholding the law? For saying it is illegal?

The Trump administration also made access to health care more difficult for transgender people by removing them from the protections of the health antidiscrimination laws and by allowing health care personnel to refuse treatment based on their moral commitments against transgender rights. Do you think conscience clauses should be used to limit transgender rights to health? Kathy L. Cerminara, Today's Crusades: A Therapeutic Jurisprudential Critique of Faith-Based Civil Rights in Health Care, 13 Alb. Gov't L. Rev. 1 (2020).

Soon after taking office, President Biden issued an executive order prohibiting gender identity or sexual orientation discrimination, and assuring medical care for transgender people in the military. Transgender Students and Title IX: Biden Administration Signals Shift, XI:45 Nat'l Law Review, Jan. 29, 2021, https://www.natlawreview.com/article/transgender-students-and-title-ix-biden-administration-signals-shift; Jim Garamone, Biden Administration Overturns Transgender Exclusion Policy, Defense News, Jan. 25, 2021, https://www.defense.gov/Explore/News/Article/Article/2482048/biden-administration-overturns-transgender-exclusion-policy/. Why do you think he changed the Trump policies? Which is the better rule?

4. *Sara Hellwege.* Sara Hellwege, a nurse who applied for a job as a nurse-midwife at the Tampa Family Health Centers ("TFHC"), does not believe in prescribing some "hormonal" birth control drugs, which she would have to do as part of her job at the health center. Hellwege "believes that 'birth control can cause the death of a human embryo.' " Katie McDonough, Nurse Won't Prescribe Birth Control, Sues Because She Didn't Get a Job that Requires Prescribing Birth Control, Salon, Jul. 21, 2014, at http://www.salon.com/2014/07/21/nurse_wont_prescribe_birth_control_sues_because_she_didnt_get_a_job_that_requires_prescribing_birth_control/. Hellwege wrote in her application to TFHC that she had no religious objections to counseling women about contraception. After Hellwege did not get an interview for the job, she filed a lawsuit alleging religious discrimination against TFHC, in particular discrimination because she is pro-life. The lawsuit lists violations of a federal public health law and two Florida statutes. Id.

Title X of the Public Health Service Act, 42 U.S.C. § 300, provides federal funding for family planning services. TFHC is a Title X organization, which receives federal funding to provide family planning services to clients. Hellwege's lawsuit relied on one Title X provision, stating that an individual cannot be required to "perform or assist in the performance of any sterilization procedure or abortion if his performance or assistance in the performance of such part of such program or activity would be contrary to his religious beliefs or moral convictions." 42 U.S.C. § 300a–7(a)(1). Florida has similar laws preventing retaliation against employees for refusal to participate in family planning or abortion services. See Complaint, Hellwege v. Tampa Family Health Ctrs., Case No. 8:14–cv–01576–VMC–AEP (M.D. Fla. Jun. 27, 2014), https://docplayer.net/8712630-Case-8-14-cv-01576-vmc-aep-document-1-filed-06-27-14-page-1-of-13-pageid-1.html.

The complaint asked for $400,000 and attorneys' fees in damages and asked the court to divest Tampa Family Health Centers of its federal funding, which could possibly involve millions of dollars. Id. What do you think the result of the lawsuit should be?

The federal district court held that Title X did not create a private right of action. In addition, the court declined to exercise supplemental jurisdiction over novel questions posed by the Florida statutes, on which the plaintiff had based some of her complaints. As a result, Tampa Family Health Center's motion to dismiss the case was granted. Hellwege v. Tampa Family Health Ctrs., 103 F.Supp. 3d 1303 (M.D. Fla. 2015).

The Trump administration also adopted a Title X regulation ensuring that institutions that provide abortion coverage do not receive federal funding. Was this a good idea? HHS, Trump Administration Actions to Protect Life and Conscience, Jan. 24, 2020, https://www.hhs.gov/about/news/2020/01/23/trump-admin-actions-to-protect-life-and-conscience-factsheet-released-01-23-20.html. President Biden reversed the ban on abortion funding going to international aid groups and ordered the health department to remove Title X restrictions on domestic family planning. See Biden Allows US Aid for Abortion Providers and Expands Obamacare, BBC News, Jan. 28, 2021, https://www.bbc.com/news/world-us-canada-55844717. The Biden

administration thought public health was not served by the Trump rules. Why not? HHS, Ensuring Access to Equitable, Affordable, Client-Centered, Quality Family Planning Services, Apr. 15 2021, https://public-inspection.federalregister.gov/2021-07762.pdf. Why did Biden reverse Trump's actions?

The Supreme Court granted cert. on three cases about Trump's rule prohibiting Title X funds to anyone who refers patients for abortion. Jessie Hellman, Supreme Court to hear challenge on family planning program, The Hill, Feb. 22, 2021. About one-quarter of Title X providers had left the program in response to the Trump rule. Id. What do you think the Court will say about the Title X rule?

5. *Jehovah's Witnesses.* Jehovah's Witnesses refuse blood transfusions because they believe transfusions are forbidden by scriptural passages, including Genesis 9:4, Leviticus 17:12, Deuteronomy 12:23–25 and Acts 15:28–29. Receiving a transfusion jeopardizes their everlasting life with God. Should Jehovah's Witnesses be allowed to refuse medical treatment that will save their lives? See generally Heather Payne & Norman Doe, Public Health and the Limits of Religious Freedom, 19 Emory Int'l L. Rev. 539 (2005) (explaining that adult refusal is usually accepted because of informed consent requirements). What should happen if medical personnel wish to give transfusions to a Jehovah's Witness because they want to save their patient's life? Should the conscience of the provider overcome the conscience of the adult in any circumstances? Compare Application of President and Directors of Georgetown College, Inc., 331 F.2d 1000 (D.C. Cir. 1964) (allowing transfusion over the objection of the patient and her husband because she was the mother of a seven-month-old child) with In the Matter of Fosmire v. Nicoleau, 551 N.E.2d 77 (N.Y. 1990) (holding that competent adult's right to decline blood transfusion was not outweighed by state's interest in preserving her life for the benefit of her child).

Should doctors try to persuade their Jehovah's Witnesses patients that their religion may allow some transfusions? See Raanan Gillon, Refusal of Potentially Life-Saving Blood Transfusions by Jehovah's Witnesses: Should Doctors Explain That Not All JWs Think It's Religiously Required?, 26 J. Med. Ethics 299, 299–301 (2000).

What should happen if parents refuse transfusions for their ill children? See, e.g., In re Elisha McCauley, 409 Mass. 134, 565 N.E.2d 411 (1991) (ordering transfusions for an eight-year-old girl with leukemia over her parents' objections). "Courts are nearly unanimous in authorizing state intervention, over the religion-based objections of parents, to give blood transfusions to children who require them." Karen L. Diaz, Refusal of Medical Treatment Based on Religious Beliefs: Jehovah's Witness Parents, 16 J. Contemp. Legal Issues 85, 86 (2007). While adult Jehovah's Witnesses enjoy some right of refusal over their own health care, the right does not extend to children. Do Jehovah's Witnesses parents have a good argument that giving their children transfusions violates parents' rights of conscience? Is the parent or the state best qualified to speak for the best interests of the child in these circumstances?

6. *Pharmacists.* As explained above, the original conscience clauses usually covered sterilization and abortion, and applied to medical personnel like doctors and nurses. The development of emergency contraceptives expanded the conscience debate. In addition to their regular contraceptive prescriptions, women could go to a pharmacy to receive emergency contraception.

Plan B was the best known of the emergency contraceptives. The moral and scientific debate about Plan B revolves around ovulation, fertilization and implantation. According to NPR,

> For years, scientists knew the pills, particularly Plan B, were highly effective in preventing pregnancy after unprotected sex but weren't exactly sure how they managed that. "It wasn't really clear whether it worked before ovulation or after ovulation," . . . Scientists did know the drug worked primarily by preventing ovulation. It stops an egg from being released from a woman's ovary and thus prevents any chance of fertilization and pregnancy. But they also thought the drug might make it more difficult for a fertilized egg to implant in a woman's uterus.

Julie Rovner, Morning-After Pills Don't Cause Abortion, Study Says, NPR, Feb. 21, 2013, at http://www.npr.org/blogs/health/2013/02/22/172595689/morning-after-pills-dont-cause-abortion-studies-say. Scientifically, blocking implantation of a fertilized egg is not an abortion. Id.

Nonetheless, some religious pharmacists believe as a matter of faith that emergency contraceptives cause abortion by blocking fertilization or implantation. Scientists disagree that such contraceptives are abortifacient. Other pharmacists believe that all artificial contraception is morally wrong. Do you think such pharmacists are entitled to conscience clause protection? Should drugstores be required to inform customers of their refusal to sell contraceptives? Or are customers responsible for finding a drugstore to meet their needs?

What do you think of the argument that pharmacists need discretion in dispensing drugs, and that taking away their freedom could be dangerous to patients? See Susan Paynter, Prescription for Calm Amid the Morning After Pill Fever, Seattle Post-Intelligencer, Sept. 2, 2005, at E1 ("Pharmacists are not robots unquestioningly filling physicians' orders without a second look. Sometimes that second look saves lives when a prescription is a mistake. So how can you ask pharmacists to exercise ethics on one end of the process and not on the other?") What do you think would be the result if the pharmacist conscientiously objected to filling another prescription other than contraceptives, for example, drugs that have harmful side effects or drugs such as methadone, used to wean people from illegal drugs? What about drugs to be used in physician-assisted suicide? Drugs used to treat AIDS?

> **Practice Exercise:** Draft your own pharmacist conscience clause based on what you think is necessary to balance the protections of the public and an individual's religious beliefs.

Should pharmacists who refuse to fill prescriptions be required to make referrals to other pharmacists? What if they believe that even referring someone for contraception is a sin? Republican Representative Chris Shays of Connecticut "told reporters he was shocked to learn of instances in which some pharmacists would not even return prescriptions to contraceptive-seeking customers." What do you think of that practice, or of the pharmacist at K-Mart, who said "she simply lied to the patient and told her the drug was not in stock to avoid a public confrontation or embarrassment"? Ryan Holeywell, Mandatory Contraceptive Prescriptions Eyed, UPI, June 10, 2005. Should the courts uphold laws that require pharmacists to refuse and refer? Or should they require pharmacists to fill the prescription? Should the law require all pharmacies to stock emergency contraception? If one pharmacy employs a C.O. pharmacist, should another pharmacist always be required to be in attendance to fill prescriptions? California law, for example, allows a pharmacist to decline to dispense a drug or device on ethical, moral, or religious grounds only if the pharmacist "has previously notified his or her employer, in writing, of the drug or class of drugs to which he or she objects, and the [ ] employer can, without creating undue hardship, provide a reasonable accommodation of the [ ] objection. The [ ] employer shall establish protocols that ensure that the patient has timely access to the prescribed drug or device despite the [ ] refusal to dispense the prescription or order." Cal. Bus. & Prof. Code § 733(b)(3). Does this provision strike an acceptable balance among the interests of the patient, pharmacist, and employer?

7. *Different Standards for Rape Victims.* Should a rape survivor be allowed to sue a religious hospital for failing to advise her about emergency contraception? See Brownfield v. Daniel Freeman Marina Hosp., 208 Cal.App.3d 405, 256 Cal.Rptr. 240 (1989) (finding that a rape survivor could state a cause of action by showing that: (1) a skilled practitioner of good standing would have provided her with information about emergency contraception under similar circumstances; (2) she would have elected such treatment if it had been available; and (3) she suffered damages as a result of the hospital's failure to provide her with information about this treatment option). What about suing a pharmacist for failure to provide post-rape contraception?

8. *Sterilization.* The Ethical and Religious Directives do not allow sterilizations in Catholic institutions. According to Eleanor Barczak, "Conscientious objection to postpartum tubal ligations violates medical best practices, regardless of whether the objector is an individual or an organization. However, the individual provider makes this objection by applying expert knowledge, morals and religious values in real situations involving actual, rather than hypothetical, patients. The institution may reach the same conclusion, but it does so by adhering to bright line rules without conscientious deliberation. Because of this, the Conscience Clause is misapplied to the institution as a whole and creates an incurable barrier to women's health care, impermissibly violates medical best practices, and systemically suppresses the conscientious practice of physicians within Catholic institutions." Ethical Implications of the Conscience Clause on

Access to Postpartum Tubal Ligations, 70 Hastings L.J. 1613, 1637 (2019); Esther Ju, Unclear Conscience: How Catholic Hospitals and Doctors are Claiming Conscientious Objections to Deny Healthcare to Transgender Patients, 2020 U.Ill. L. Rev. 1289 (2020) Do you agree? Does this give a reason for individual doctors to decide not to follow Catholic rules when they work in Catholic hospitals? Is there any way that this problem can be solved so that best practices are met?

As you read the next article, ask yourself whether doctors who want to *provide* contraception, sterilization or abortion should have claims of conscience to do so, as the following article suggests. Do you agree with the article's distinction between individuals and institutions?

Taking Conscience Seriously

Elizabeth Sepper.
98 Va. L. Rev. 1501 (2012).

Introduction

At a Catholic hospital in a large Eastern city, Dr. S admits a patient nineteen weeks pregnant and miscarrying. He recommends, and the patient agrees to, the medically indicated treatment—ending the pregnancy. But the hospital ethics committee denies his request because of the institution's moral objection to abortion: although the fetus has no chance of survival, an ultrasound still detects a fetal heartbeat. The woman becomes septic, with a 106-degree fever and profuse bleeding. Watching the patient "dying before our eyes," the doctor makes a decision: he performs the abortion. The patient spends another ten days in intensive care and suffers permanent injuries. Horrified, Dr. S quits, saying "I just can't do this. . . . This is not worth it to me."

This story is not unique. . . . Yet claims to conscience of medical providers like Dr. S are virtually absent from scholarly and legislative debates over conscience in medicine. Lawmakers and scholars focus instead on the archetypal doctor who refuses to participate in contested treatments that his or her institution provides. . . .

II. Problematizing Legislation's Inconsistent Defense of Conscience

Consider two hypothetical physicians. The first, Dr. Abbott, refuses to administer contraception, but works at a hospital committed to delivering all necessary care to patients. By contrast, the second, Dr. Baker, feels a moral imperative to ensure his patients have autonomy over their reproductive lives, but his employer has moral policies against contraceptives. Under the approach taken by most legislation, Dr. Abbott can refuse to prescribe emergency contraception to a rape victim in violation of her institution's policy—without consequence. Dr. Baker, however, can be fired for prescribing emergency contraception to a rape victim—even if he acts in good conscience—because he has violated the institutional policy of refusal.

This Part argues that these asymmetries render current legislation fundamentally and conceptually incoherent. It takes seriously the claim of medical providers to act on conscience. It uses relevant philosophical literature theorizing conscience to outline a basic understanding of what we mean by conscience, and why as a society we care about protecting it. Based on this literature, it introduces two interconnected arguments. First, willing providers equally may claim to act on conscience. The strongest arguments about the nature of conscience cannot justify their disparate treatment under current legislation. Second, no theory of institutional conscience arrives at describing a concept akin to human conscience. Instead, institutional conscience might be said to reflect the value of moral association. Under any conception of institutional conscience, however, the disparate treatment of refusing and willing institutions cannot be justified. . . .

Two objections—one practical, one theoretical—might be made to recognizing the conscience of the willing provider. The first is that a doctor or nurse who wants to provide prohibited services should simply work elsewhere. This argument, however, is equally valid (or invalid) for refusing providers, who could equally seek out a refusing employer. Moreover, there are a number of reasons why doctors and nurses may be unable to change employment or affiliation. First, they may be under multi-year contracts at the time the conflict arises. With regard to residencies, in particular, if the institution later imposes restrictions, the resident will be required to stay on for the remainder of the contract. Second, in many areas of the country, a limited number of hospitals exist. By necessity, a provider practicing in the area may be affiliated with a particular hospital. Third, consolidation of healthcare means fewer choices for providers. Many managed care organizations enter into exclusive contracts with hospitals or require doctors to secure admitting privileges at a particular hospital (irrespective of moral limitations). Omitting Catholic healthcare alone, to say nothing of all other refusing institutions, would mean giving up association with four of the ten largest health systems.

The second objection claims that a moral distinction exists between being compelled to perform and being compelled to refrain from an action. As the argument goes, legislators should be most concerned that doctors not be forced to perform procedures that violate their deepest convictions. Compelling doctors to refrain from treatments they are called to do by conscience, by contrast, may be tolerated.

However, the distinction between acts and omissions is insufficient to explain moral responsibility in the medical field, even if the theory were generally to hold. A doctor who omits to perform CPR at a patient's request has committed no wrong. A doctor, however, who unilaterally omits to deliver CPR to a patient will be considered morally (and legally) responsible. Moreover, whether medical treatments involve acts or omissions is often difficult to discern. An oft-cited example involves

stopping a respirator at a patient's request: "Does the physician omit continuing the treatment or act to disconnect it?" Withholding or removing artificial nutrition similarly may be described as either omitting feeding or actively starving a patient. . . .

Even if we were to set aside the flaws in the act-omission theory, it still fails to explain the law's asymmetrical treatment of the willing and refusing provider. Existing legislation does not draw any such fundamental distinction between acts and omissions, as end-of-life care makes plain. Consider a terminally ill patient who has indicated he wishes not to receive life support. In this situation, a supposedly refusing provider would seek to "act," to impose life-sustaining treatment. The willing provider, by contrast, believes honoring the patient's decision is morally required and seeks to "omit" life support. In this case, the usual roles are reversed. The refusing provider would be required by institutional policy to refrain from delivering treatment she believes is required; and the willing provider would be compelled to perform a procedure she believes is prohibited. . . .

As we have seen, legislative frameworks do not acknowledge willing providers' consciences. Instead, they exacerbate conflicts by recognizing institutional conscience for refusing health facilities. The next Section examines whether permitting institutional policies to trump individual conscience only in refusing institutions is theoretically defensible.

C. The Curious Case of Institutional Conscience Understanding

How individual conscience works is relatively straightforward; we can identify the bearers of conscience, the manner in which it is expressed, and (generally speaking) its bases. Institutional conscience poses greater difficulties for legal and moral argumentation. Corporations are creatures of law without the capacity to feel, reason, or act without mediating agents. Although healthcare businesses are typically designed for "moral ends . . . such as rendering charitable service, relieving suffering, . . . curing the sick, or saving life," most focus primarily on generating revenue in order to survive (or profit). They lack distinctly human characteristics—such as the capacities to discern right from wrong, to be conscious of specific circumstances in making moral judgments, and to comport one's acts to context—that seem to be required to exercise conscience. Indeed, various secular and theological traditions share the position that conscience is intimately connected to human nature. . . .

3. No Theoretical Support for Favoring Refusing Institutions

Even if we were to accept the theoretical justifications for protecting institutional conscience, the distinction that legislation draws between refusing and willing institutions cannot be supported. To the extent existing legislation seeks to promote either mission adherence or moral collectives, it misses the mark. No principle explains why a refusing employer may impose its moral norms on staff, but a willing institution

must accommodate individual providers' refusing consciences with which it disagrees. . . .

* * *

Ignoring the willing provider and privileging the refusing institution are opposite sides of the same coin. Each alone generates asymmetries in the treatment of willing and refusing individuals and of willing and refusing institutions. Each lacks a strong theoretical foundation to justify the disparate treatment of refusing and willing providers.

The next Part introduces a new way to balance the inherent tension between legislative protection of institutional conscience and societal respect for individual conscience.

III. A Better Balance Between Individual Conscience and Institutional Norms

A. Evaluating the Absolutist Alternatives

Three alternatives have been proposed to address the problem of morality in medicine. The first prioritizes institutional conscience, stripping away protection for individual doctors and nurses. The second takes the opposite approach and favors individual conscience over institutional policies. The third refrains from enacting conscience legislation at all and, instead, requires institutions and individuals to exercise their consciences within the boundaries of medical ethics, generally applicable law, and competent medical practice. Unfortunately, as this Section shows, each falls short—indicating the need for a new approach. . . .

B. A Framework for Identifying Moral Associations and Protecting Patients

In contrast to absolutist positions, this Section proposes a more nuanced approach to determining whether institutional interest or individual conscience wins out. First, it sets forth a framework that considers the size of the institution, how cohesive it is, and whether it is focused around expressing a message on the relevant issue to decide whether an institution embodies an interest in moral association that supersedes the interest in individual conscience. Although this framework has some limitations, it provides a theoretically coherent rule that treats willing and refusing providers and their institutions alike. Second, this Section recommends that conscience legislation be limited to nondiscrimination, resolving the individual-institution conflict while leaving in place legal and ethical standards that protect patients. Together, these reforms would improve the balance between conscience, moral association, and patient care.

1. Cohesion, Size, and Message Central to Moral Associations

To identify whether a particular healthcare institution reflects the value of moral association, the proposed framework looks to three connected factors: cohesion, size, and message. . . .

Distinguishing between institutions based on their cohesion, size, and messaging has the advantage of a strong theoretical foundation. It equally protects the ability of a reproductive rights clinic to exclude employees who refuse to deliver contraceptives and of a natural family planning clinic to reject employees who disagree with its methods. It acknowledges that demanding accommodation of countervailing employee conscience is especially likely to impinge on associational interests of these smaller, cohesive, and dedicated groups. In the most extreme case, such as the solo abortion provider who hires a nurse who then refuses to participate in abortions, accommodation disallows any possibility of moral association. . . .

In sum, under this framework, small, cohesive institutions with clear messages would receive protection of the interest in moral association. At the other extreme, large business entities like hospitals, which are pluralistic by their nature, would be excluded from legislative protection. For other types of institutions—such as nursing homes, hospices, clinics, or ambulatory surgery centers—decisions about including or excluding them would turn on whether they are sufficiently cohesive and devoted to a message so as to supersede the interest in individual conscience. . . .

Ultimately, a legislative framework based on institutional category, distinguished by cohesion, size, and message, would promote pluralism in medicine. Smaller facilities with cohesive staff and clear moral positions could represent an array of moral or religious approaches to medicine. Large, pluralistic institutions, though providing the same baseline level of care, could distinguish themselves in other ways as well. A hospital might have the kindest nursing staff, adopt a team-based approach to patient care, or remunerate its employees especially well. . . .

Conclusion

Correcting the asymmetry that characterizes conscience clauses matters, most immediately, for willing doctors, nurses, and institutions. Nonetheless, it has potentially broad implications. Invoking conscience in order to refuse to perform employment obligations is rapidly spreading beyond medicine—to pharmacists, ambulance drivers, supermarket cashiers, and lawyers. Even further afield, some suggest exemptions from anti-discrimination norms for business owners who object to same-sex marriage. Conscience legislation—modeled on medical conscience clauses, which this analysis has shown to be deeply flawed—has been proposed and sometimes passed in these ever-wider areas.

Future legislative efforts and scholarly thinking should strive to take conscience seriously. No longer should employees or staff within a refusing institution be presumed to share its moral positions. Instead, potential conflicts between institutional interests and individual conscience should be explored and justified. Similarly, courts should consider the equality of individual conscience in interpreting current statutes, especially those broad medical conscience clauses that plausibly

can be read to allow willing providers to exercise conscience in face of countervailing policies.

NOTES AND QUESTIONS

1. *Dr. S.* How do you assess the conscience of Professor Sepper's Dr. S, who wants to perform abortions, to the consciences of those who do not want to do so? Are their consciences equal in stature? Should they both be protected by the law?

2. *Dr. Abbott and Dr. Baker.* How does Professor Sepper treat the situations of Dr. Abbott, who refuses to administer contraception at a hospital committed to delivering all necessary care to patients, and Dr. Baker, who wants to provide forms of birth control in an institution opposed to contraception? How do current laws treat them? How would Dr. Sepper's proposal for institutions treat them? What would you have to know about Dr. Abbott's and Dr. Baker's employers before you could decide how Sepper's proposal applies to them?

3. *Four Alternatives.* What are the three alternatives that have been suggested to resolve the questions of morality in medicine? What is the fourth alternative suggested by Professor Sepper? Which alternative do you prefer?

4. *Pharmacies.* Does Professor Sepper's analysis suggest that every pharmacy should be free to decide whether it wants to provide emergency contraception? Does the analysis apply only to contraception or to other prescriptions? Is there a difference under her theory between one locally-owned drug store and a chain like Walgreens or CVS? Under her theory, would every Walgreens have to follow the same rule because they share a common institutional name?

5. *Hospital Mergers.* Since the 1990s, changes in health care and the economic climate have led to increasing numbers of hospital mergers. The Affordable Care Act (ACA) also encouraged consolidation of medical institutions as a way to reduce costs:

> The ACA encourages consolidation in two respects. One is the unintended byproduct of shaking up the healthcare landscape; the other is an intentional effort to reduce costs. In the first respect, the ACA has spurred consolidation by empowering commercial payors to negotiate prices with healthcare providers, including hospitals, which had been criticized for exorbitant costs. Concerned about their leverage in negotiations, some hospital systems are responding to the ACA by seeking to expand and thereby improve their bargaining position. In this respect, hospital consolidation is an unintended, though foreseeable, byproduct of the ACA.
>
> In another respect, healthcare consolidation is explicitly part of the ACA's blueprint for reform. Some ACA programs are aimed at wringing excess costs out of the healthcare system. One such mechanism is clinical integration, which involves coordinating patient care across a "continuum" of services and platforms, both

> inpatient and outpatient. The ACA encouraged clinical integration by providing financial incentives and support for various forms of partnership between medical providers. To benefit from the ACA's perks, healthcare entities must demonstrate increased efficiency and reduced cost to patients by showing that their proposed consolidation will meaningfully integrate the two healthcare entities. An example of such integration might be reducing the number of empty hospital beds and eliminating redundant, expensive technology. Demonstrating such integration frequently allows consolidating hospitals to avoid antitrust scrutiny. That is, because the ACA incentivizes a particular form of merger—one that leads to clinical integration and produces cost savings—hospitals may be permitted to consolidate in ways that otherwise would raise red flags for the federal antitrust agencies. Hospitals therefore have increasing incentives and legal power to consolidate.

Elizabeth B. Deutsch, Expanding Conscience, Shrinking Care: The Crisis in Access to Reproductive Care and the Affordable Care Act's Nondiscrimination Mandate, 124 Yale L.J. 2470, 2484–86 (2015).

"Comprised of more than 600 hospitals and 1,600 long-term care and other health facilities in all 50 states, the Catholic health ministry is the largest group of nonprofit health care providers in the nation. Every day, more than one in seven patients in the U.S. is cared for in a Catholic hospital." Catholic Health Association of the United States, Catholic Health Care in the United States, Jan. 2020, https://www.chausa.org/about/about/facts-statistics. As discussed in *Means*, Catholic hospitals are run according to the Ethical and Religious Directives for Catholic Health Care Services (ERDs), which prohibit abortion and sterilization. Thomas Olmstead, the Catholic bishop of Phoenix, Arizona, removed St. Joseph's Hospital's Catholic status after an abortion occurred there. St. Joseph's was part of Catholic Healthcare West, which has 41 hospitals in Arizona, California and Nevada. Id. The hospital's administrator (Sister Margaret McBride) and its Ethics Committee approved an abortion for a twenty-seven-year old mother of four who was eleven weeks pregnant and had pulmonary hypertension, which had a greater than 50% chance of ending her life. Dan Harris, Bishop Strips Hospital of Catholic Status After Abortion, ABC News, Dec. 22, 2010, at http://abcnews.go.com/Health/abortion-debate-hospital-stripped-catholic-status/story?id=12455295. In contrast to the bishop, Sr. Carol Keehan, President and CEO of the Catholic Health Association, argued that the hospital had acted in accord with the ERDs by saving the life of the mother. Jerry Filteau, Catholic Health Association Backs Phoenix Hospital, National Catholic Reporter, Dec. 22, 2010, at http://ncronline.org/news/catholic-health-association-backs-phoenix-hospital.

What should happen when a community hospital merges with a Catholic hospital, usually in order to save money and offer health care more efficiently? Must the hospital be run according to the ERDs? What is the best way to protect conscience in merger situations? Do Professor Sepper's options help you to identify the best outcome in merger talks?

In Troy, New York, the secular Samaritan Hospital merged with Catholic St. Mary's. The two sides negotiated a deal that the Burdette Care Center, a secular, separately-incorporated hospital within a hospital, would be created to offer reproductive care prohibited by church teaching. Nina Martin, Catholic Bishops Vote to Revise Rules for Health Care Partnerships, ProPublica, Nov. 11, 2014, at http://www.propublica.org/article/catholic-bishops-weigh-tightening-rules-for-health-care-partnerships. After that merger, however, the Catholic bishops voted to approve stricter rules to ensure Catholic institutions wouldn't cooperate with immoral practices. Id.

Go to the website and complete the Merger Exercise.

What laws should regulate hospital mergers?

6. *Corporate Conscience.* The federal Religious Freedom Restoration Act (RFRA) arose in response to the Supreme Court's decision in Employment Div., Department of Human Resources of Oregon v. Smith, 494 U.S. 872 (1990). No citizen shall "become a law unto himself," wrote Justice Antonin Scalia in *Smith,* when he denied Native Americans an exemption from the criminal and unemployment compensation statutes for their peyote use; the law applies to all. Id. at 885. *Smith* held that "the right of free exercise does not relieve an individual of the obligation to comply with a 'valid and neutral law of general applicability' on the ground that the law proscribes (or prescribes) conduct that his religion prescribes (or proscribes)." Id. at 880. According to *Smith's* author, that standard was consistent with the Court's earlier Free Exercise decisions, including Reynolds v. United States, an 1879 case that upheld the application of the monogamous marriage laws to a Mormon polygamist. Under *Smith,* Congress, but not the Court, may exempt citizens from the law. Thus, exemptions may be statutorily required, but are not compelled by the Free Exercise Clause of the First Amendment.

In response, Congress, with the support of a broad array of religious groups, in 1993 passed the Religious Freedom Restoration Act (RFRA), to require the use of the "compelling state interest" test whenever religion was substantially burdened by a state or federal government. The original RFRA prohibited both state and federal governments from substantially burdening a person's exercise of religion, even if the burden resulted from a rule of general applicability, unless the government could demonstrate that the burden "(1) is in furtherance of a compelling governmental interest; and (2) is the least restrictive means of furthering that compelling governmental interest." 42 U.S.C. § 2000bb–1(a)(b). In City of Boerne v. Flores, 521 U.S. 507 (1997), the Court ruled that RFRA could not be applied to the states because Congress lacked the power to pass the Act under Section 5 of the Fourteenth Amendment. RFRA, however, continues to apply to the federal government. Moreover, at the same time that the federal RFRA developed, many states enacted state RFRAs to hold state governments to the compelling state interest test. Hence, the federal and state governments may be held to the *Smith* standard in Free Exercise cases and to the compelling state interest/least restrictive means test for statutory claims.

RFRA provided a means for opponents to challenge some of the requirements of the Affordable Care Act (ACA), especially those requiring reproductive health care for women. Although Congress discussed passing women's contraceptive equality legislation during the 1990s, it did not do so. Many years later, however, President Barack Obama's health care reform bill, the Patient Protection and Affordable Care Act (ACA), Public Law 111–148, addressed problems in the national insurance market for health care. The ACA required the Secretary of Health and Human Services (HHS) to identify the details of preventive care for women. See 42 U.S.C. § 300gg–13(a)(4). Among the implementing regulations was a requirement that employers provide all Food and Drug Administration-approved contraceptive methods and sterilization procedures without charge or cost-sharing to employees. The regulations exempted purely religious employers like houses of worship and their ministerial employees from coverage, but otherwise applied the contraceptive regulations to religious employers. See Group Health Plans and Health Insurance Issuers Relating to Coverage of Preventive Services Under the Patient Protection and Affordable Care Act, 76 Fed. Reg. 46621 (Aug. 3, 2011).

Constitutional and statutory challenges to the regulations by religious organizations immediately began across the country. See Becket Fund for Religious Liberty, HHS Mandate Information Central, at http://www.becketfund.org/hhsinformationcentral/. In response to the lawsuits by religious organizations that did not qualify for the initial exemption as houses of worship complaining that the administration opposed religious liberty, in February 2013, the Obama administration released a new regulation governing religious institutions and contraceptive insurance. Under the new regulations, an objecting religious employer would inform its insurance company that it opposed contraceptive coverage. The insurance company would then contact the employees and provide coverage to them without any cost to the employer. See Coverage of Certain Preventive Services under the Affordable Care Act, 78 Fed. Reg. 8456 (proposed February 6, 2013) (to be codified at 45 C.F.R. § 147–48, 156).

The new, 2013 regulation generally applied to religious nonprofit employers. Then *for-profit* corporations also went to court arguing that the contraceptive mandate violated *their* religious freedom. The for-profit challenges were addressed in Burwell v. Hobby Lobby Stores, 573 U.S. 682 (2014). In a 5–4 decision, the Court ruled that under RFRA, employers who were closely held corporations and opposed contraception were exempt from the requirement to provide insurance coverage. Thus women had to figure out how to access contraceptive insurance without their employer providing it. Obama's plan allowed the employer's insurance policy to continue to provide some coverage without the employer's active participation. Justice Ginsburg disagreed that for-profit corporations could exercise religion, noting, "The Court, I fear, has ventured into a minefield, by its immoderate reading of RFRA. I would confine religious exemptions . . . to organizations formed "for a religious purpose," [and] "engage[d] primarily in carrying out that religious purpose. . . ."

However, some employers argued that even signing the form notifying the third party insurer of their decision not to cover contraception violated their consciences because it "triggered" contraception, of which they disapproved. The Sixth, Seventh, and D.C. Circuits ruled that the religions were not substantially burdened by the signature because the law, not the signature, triggered the coverage. See Mich. Catholic Conference & Catholic Family Servs. v. Burwell, 755 F.3d 372 (6th. Cir. 2014); Univ. of Notre Dame v. Sebelius, 743 F.3d 547 (7th Cir. 2014); Priests For Life v. U.S. Dep't of Health & Human Servs., 772 F.3d 229 (D.C. Cir. 2014). The Court remanded those opinions to be considered in light of *Hobby Lobby*.

Right after the Court issued *Hobby Lobby*, one of those non-profits, Wheaton College, a Christian school in Illinois, applied for an injunction against the mandate. The Court issued an injunction that the mandate could not be applied to Wheaton if it told the *Secretary of Health and Human Services* that it objected to contraception; Wheaton College need not use the government form or send copies to health insurers and third-party administrators. Wheaton Coll. v. Burwell, 573 U.S. 958 (2014). On appeal, the eight-member Court did not issue an opinion on this split, but remanded the case for the parties to work out a compromise. Zubik v. Burwell, 136 S.Ct. 1557 (2016).

The Trump administration then expanded the availability of the exemption to more employers by extending it to include anyone who had a religious or moral objection to women's access to birth control. Newspapers suggested some 126,000 women would lose their contraceptive insurance under the new rule. See Little Sisters of the Poor Saints Peter and Paul Home v. Pennsylvania, 591 U.S. ___, 140 S.Ct. 2367 (2020) (upholding the Trump expansion).

What bioethical issues are involved in these decisions about contraception? Does anything you learned from Prof. Sawicki's article suggest better ways that the law could handle the conflict between religious beliefs and contraception?

7. *What Comes Next?* What kind of RFRA cases would you expect corporations to file now? What should happen to lawsuits by employers refusing to provide health insurance coverage for same-sex partners and spouses? See Ira Lupu and Robert Tuttle, *Hobby Lobby* in the Long Run, Cornerstone, Jul. 1, 2014, at http://berkleycenter.georgetown.edu/rfp/blog/hobby-lobby-in-the-long-run.

Does RFRA give medical personnel a right to opt out of health care treatment for gays and lesbians? Should conscience clauses also be interpreted to allow medical personnel to opt out of treating LGBTs if they believe homosexuality is immoral? See Rob Stein, Proposals Pit Religious Values Against Patient Rights, Houston Chron., Feb. 5, 2006, at A20. How much discretion should pharmacists enjoy?

"[A]fter one patient with HIV disclosed to a hospital that he had sex with other men, the hospital staff refused to provide his HIV medication. In another case, a transgender teenager who was admitted to a hospital for suicidal ideation and self-inflicted injuries was repeatedly misgendered and

then discharged early by hospital staff. He later committed suicide. Discrimination affects LGBTQ parents as well: In Michigan, an infant was turned away from a pediatrician's office because she had same-sex parents." Shabab Ahmed Mirza & Caitlin Rooney, Discrimination Prevents LGBTQ People from Accessing Health Care, Center for American Progress, Jan. 18, 2018, https://www.americanprogress.org/issues/lgbtq-rights/news/2018/01/18/445130/discrimination-prevents-lgbtq-people-accessing-health-care/. Should RFRA allow all this discrimination?

Do these decisions persuade you that American health care should not be employer-based?

In this section, we saw how religious and moral beliefs about the beginnings of human life led to claims of conscience by pharmacists and employers who believe that some forms of contraception cause abortion. Opposition to abortion also led to significant restrictions on stem cell research, as we learn in the next section. Recall that in Chapter 2 we learned how important stem cells are to medical research, as in the cases of Henrietta Lacks and John Moore. Those cases, however, involved cells taken from adults, and asked if the adults had given proper consent to the use of their body parts. The complication in the following cases is whether stem cells should be taken from human embryos, which die in the process of removing the cells.

B. STEM CELL RESEARCH

In this section, we examine whether stem cell research should be banned or limited for moral reasons or pursued energetically for its possible scientific benefits. Stem cell research, of course, may be linked to embryonic stem cells, and therefore due special protection, as the embryo frequently is.

The Flaws of Stem Cell Legislation: Sherley, Brüstle, and Future Policy Challenges Posed by Induced Pluripotent Stem Cells

Nicholas J. Diamond.
14 Minn. J.L. Sci. & Tech. 259, 265–67 (2013).

II. A BRIEF INTERLUDE: THE SCIENCE OF STEM CELLS

At present, the scope of stem cell research includes three different types of stem cells: adult stem cells (ASCs), hESCs [human embryonic stem cells], and iPSCs [induced pluripotent stem cells]. Research on ASCs is the oldest of the three, dating to the 1950s. ASCs are undifferentiated cells found in adult tissues and organs in the body amongst already differentiated cells. ASCs are multipotent, which means that they can be specialized into but a few different cell types. As such, the utility of ASCs for research and therapeutic purposes is greatly limited. For researchers using ASCs, the area of the body from which the

ASCs were harvested limits the utility of the cell. For instance, neural stem cells in the brain can replace neurons in the nervous system, but neural stem cells are unable to become heart, liver, or lung cells, to mention just a few. In contrast to hESCs, ASCs are considered uncontroversial because harvesting them does not require the use and subsequent destruction of human embryos.

hESCs are found in the embryonic layer of week-old human embryos. Unlike ASCs, which have limited utility, hESCs are pluripotent, which means that they can divide into nearly any type of cell in the human body, but do not have the capacity to develop into an independent, fully functional organism, e.g., a human being. In contrast to ASCs, which are harvested with the informed consent of adult donors, hESCs are harvested from human embryos—in most cases, surplus preimplantation embryos from in vitro fertilization (IVF) procedures—which have been donated for research purposes with the informed consent of both parents. The process of harvesting hESCs from a donated embryo necessitates the destruction of the embryo. Opinion as to the moral status of the human embryo differs widely. Because human embryos are necessarily destroyed during the harvesting of hESCs, such research is considered morally and politically controversial. While the full therapeutic potential of hESCs has not yet been fully realized, promising research results exist in animal studies of Parkinson's disease, spinal injury, type 1 diabetes, and cardiovascular disease.

iPSCs are the result of genetically reprogramming ASCs to behave like hESCs, which is to say that they have the utility of pluripotency. Being that ASCs are more abundant than hESCs, iPSCs stand to make pluripotency theoretically limitless. Notwithstanding this potential spike in the availability of pluripotency, current research suggests that iPSCs and hESCs will complement one another, rather than having iPSCs negate the need for hESCs, which had been hypothesized in early iPSC research publications. At minimum, the ability to alter the fate of ASCs through reprogramming has changed researchers' views on the stability of cellular identity, thereby spurring new directions in research possibilities. iPSC technology, however, has not yet been perfected. Ultimately, researchers hope that encouraging advancements made in recent years augur well the chance that iPSCs will eventually offer the therapeutic benefits that hESCs have been slow to provide.

In 2001, President George W. Bush announced an executive order limiting stem cell research to certain pre-existing lines. Eight years later, President Barack Obama revoked Bush's order so that more stem cell research could be funded. Which president's remarks do you find more persuasive on the topic—George W. Bush or Barack Obama? In 2019, President Trump then added a prohibition on research with human fetal tissue from elective abortions. Is his position consistent with President

Bush's? President Biden then reversed Trump's position on fetal tissue. Which position is most persuasive?

Remarks by President George W. Bush on Stem Cell Research

August 9, 2001.
The Bush Ranch, Crawford, Texas.

Good evening. I appreciate you giving me a few minutes of your time tonight so I can discuss with you a complex and difficult issue, an issue that is one of the most profound of our time.

The issue of research involving stem cells derived from human embryos is increasingly the subject of a national debate and dinner table discussions. The issue is confronted every day in laboratories as scientists ponder the ethical ramifications of their work. It is agonized over by parents and many couples as they try to have children or to save children already born.

The issue is debated within the church, with people of different faiths, even many of the same faith, coming to different conclusions. Many people are finding that the more they know about stem cell research, the less certain they are about the right ethical and moral conclusions.

My administration must decide whether to allow federal funds, your tax dollars, to be used for scientific research on stem cells derived from human embryos. A large number of these embryos already exist. They are the product of a process called in vitro fertilization which helps so many couples conceive children. When doctors match sperm and egg to create life outside the womb, they usually produce more embryos than are implanted in the mother. Once a couple successfully has children or if they are unsuccessful, the additional embryos remain frozen in laboratories.

Some will not survive during long storage, others are destroyed. A number have been donated to science and used to create privately funded stem cell lines. And a few have been implanted in an adoptive mother and born and are today healthy children.

Based on preliminary work that has been privately funded, scientists believe further research using stem cells offers great promise that could help improve the lives of those who suffer from many terrible diseases, from juvenile diabetes to Alzheimer's, from Parkinson's to spinal cord injuries. And while scientists admit they are not yet certain, they believe stem cells derived from embryos have unique potential.

You should also know that stem cells can be derived from sources other than embryos: from adult cells, from umbilical cords that are discarded after babies are born, from human placentas. And many scientists feel research on these types of stem cells is also promising.

Many patients suffering from a range of diseases are already being helped with treatments developed from adult stem cells.

However, most scientists, at least today, believe that research on embryonic stem cells offers the most promise because these cells have the potential to develop in all of the tissues in the body . . .

As I thought through this issue I kept returning to two fundamental questions. First, are these frozen embryos human life and therefore something precious to be protected? And second, if they're going to be destroyed anyway, shouldn't they be used for a greater good, for research that has the potential to save and improve other lives?

I've asked those questions and others of scientists, scholars, bioethicists, religious leaders, doctors, researchers, members of Congress, my Cabinet and my friends. I have read heartfelt letters from many Americans. I have given this issue a great deal of thought, prayer, and considerable reflection, and I have found widespread disagreement.

On the first issue, are these embryos human life—well, one researcher told me he believes this five-day-old cluster of cells is not an embryo, not yet an individual but a pre-embryo. He argued that it has the potential for life, but it is not a life because it cannot develop on its own.

An ethicist dismissed that as a callous attempt at rationalization. "Make no mistake," he told me, "that cluster of cells is the same way you and I, and all the rest of us, started our lives. One goes with a heavy heart if we use these," he said, "because we are dealing with the seeds of the next generation."

And to the other crucial question—If these are going to be destroyed anyway, why not use them for good purpose?—I also found different answers.

Many argue these embryos are byproducts of a process that helps create life and we should allow couples to donate them to science so they can be used for good purpose instead of wasting their potential. Others will argue there is no such thing as excess life and the fact that a living being is going to die does not justify experimenting on it or exploiting it as a natural resource. . . .

My position on these issues is shaped by deeply held beliefs. I'm a strong supporter of science and technology, and believe they have the potential for incredible good—to improve lives, to save life, to conquer disease. Research offers hope that millions of our loved ones may be cured of a disease and rid of their suffering. I have friends whose children suffer from juvenile diabetes. Nancy Reagan has written me about President Reagan's struggle with Alzheimer's. My own family has confronted the tragedy of childhood leukemia. And like all Americans, I have great hope for cures.

I also believe human life is a sacred gift from our creator. I worry about a culture that devalues life, and believe as your president I have an important obligation to foster and encourage respect for life in America and throughout the world. And while we're all hopeful about the potential of this research, no one can be certain that the science will live up to the hope it has generated. . . .

As a result of private research, more than 60 genetically diverse stem cell lines already exist. They were created from embryos that have already been destroyed, and they have the ability to regenerate themselves indefinitely, creating ongoing opportunities for research. I have concluded that we should allow federal funds to be used for research on these existing stem cell lines, where the life-and-death decision has already been made. . . .

I have made this decision with great care, and I pray it is the right one.

Thank you for listening. Good night, and God bless America.

Executive Order: Removing Barriers to Responsible Scientific Research Involving Human Stem Cells

Exec. Order No.13505, 74 Fed. Reg. 10667 (Mar. 11, 2009).
The White House Office of the Press Secretary.

By the authority vested in me as President by the Constitution and the laws of the United States of America, it is hereby ordered as follows:

Section 1. Policy. Research involving human embryonic stem cells and human non-embryonic stem cells has the potential to lead to better understanding and treatment of many disabling diseases and conditions. Advances over the past decade in this promising scientific field have been encouraging, leading to broad agreement in the scientific community that the research should be supported by Federal funds.

For the past 8 years, the authority of the Department of Health and Human Services, including the National Institutes of Health (NIH), to fund and conduct human embryonic stem cell research has been limited by Presidential actions. The purpose of this order is to remove these limitations on scientific inquiry, to expand NIH support for the exploration of human stem cell research, and in so doing to enhance the contribution of America's scientists to important new discoveries and new therapies for the benefit of humankind. . . .

Sec. 5. Revocations. (a) The Presidential statement of August 9, 2001, limiting Federal funding for research involving human embryonic stem cells, shall have no further effect as a statement of governmental policy.

(b) Executive Order 13435 of June 20, 2007, which supplements the August 9, 2001, statement on human embryonic stem cell research, is revoked.

Remarks by President Barack Obama: Signing of Stem Cell Executive Order and Scientific Integrity Presidential Memorandum

March 9, 2009.
The White House, Washington, D.C.

But in recent years, when it comes to stem cell research, rather than furthering discovery, our government has forced what I believe is a false choice between sound science and moral values. In this case, I believe the two are not inconsistent. As a person of faith, I believe we are called to care for each other and work to ease human suffering. I believe we have been given the capacity and will to pursue this research—and the humanity and conscience to do so responsibly.

It is a difficult and delicate balance. Many thoughtful and decent people are conflicted about, or strongly oppose, this research. I understand their concerns, and we must respect their point of view.

But after much discussion, debate and reflection, the proper course has become clear. The majority of Americans—from across the political spectrum, and of all backgrounds and beliefs—have come to a consensus that we should pursue this research. That the potential it offers is great, and with proper guidelines and strict oversight, the perils can be avoided. . . .

I can also promise that we will never undertake this research lightly. We will support it only when it is both scientifically worthy and responsibly conducted. We will develop strict guidelines, which we will rigorously enforce, because we cannot ever tolerate misuse or abuse. And we will ensure that our government never opens the door to the use of cloning for human reproduction. It is dangerous, profoundly wrong, and has no place in our society, or any society. . . .

Thank you, God bless you, and may God bless America.

Statement from the Department of Health and Human Services of President Donald Trump

June 5, 2019.
HHS Press Office.

In September 2018, the Department of Health and Human Services (HHS) terminated a contract between Advanced Bioscience Resources, Inc. and the Food and Drug Administration that provided human fetal tissue from elective abortions to develop testing protocols. The Department was not sufficiently assured that contract included the appropriate protections applicable to fetal tissue research or met all other

procurement requirements. As a result, HHS also initiated a comprehensive review of all HHS research involving human fetal tissue from elective abortions to ensure consistency with statutes and regulations governing such research, and to ensure the adequacy of procedures and oversight of this research in light of the serious regulatory, moral, and ethical considerations involved.

When the audit and review began, HHS had an existing contract with the University of California, San Francisco (UCSF) regarding research involving human fetal tissue from elective abortions. HHS has been extending the UCSF contract by means of 90-day extensions while conducting its audit and review. The current extension expires on June 5, 2019, and there will be no further extensions.

Promoting the dignity of human life from conception to natural death is one of the very top priorities of President Trump's administration. The audit and review helped inform the policy process that led to the administration's decision to let the contract with UCSF expire and to discontinue intramural research—research conducted within the National Institutes of Health (NIH)—involving the use of human fetal tissue from elective abortion. Intramural research that requires new acquisition of fetal tissue from elective abortions will not be conducted.

No current extramural research projects (research conducted outside NIH, e.g., at universities, that are funded by NIH grants) will be affected during their currently approved project period. For new extramural research grant applications or current research projects in the competitive renewal process (generally every five years) that propose to use fetal tissue from elective abortions and that are recommended for potential funding through NIH's two-level external scientific review process, an ethics advisory board will be convened to review the research proposal and recommend whether, in light of the ethical considerations, NIH should fund the research project—pursuant to a law passed by Congress.

HHS will also undertake changes to its regulations and NIH grants policy to adopt or strengthen safeguards and program integrity requirements applicable to extramural research involving human fetal tissue.

Finally, HHS is continuing to review whether adequate alternatives exist to the use of human fetal tissue from elective abortions in HHS-funded research and will ensure that efforts to develop such alternatives are funded and accelerated. In December 2018, NIH announced a $20 million funding opportunity for research to develop, demonstrate, and validate experimental models that do not rely on human fetal tissue from elective abortions. HHS is committed to providing additional funding to support the development and validation of alternative models.

Update on Changes to NIH Requirements Regarding Proposed Human Fetal Tissue Research

April 16, 2021.
Office of the Director, National Institutes of Health.

This notice informs the extramural research community that HHS is reversing its 2019 decision that all research applications for NIH grants and contracts proposing the use of human fetal tissue from elective abortions will be reviewed by an Ethics Advisory Board. Accordingly, HHS/NIH will not convene another NIH Human Fetal Tissue Research Ethics Advisory Board.

NIH reminds the community of expectations to obtain informed consent from the donor for any NIH-funded research using human fetal tissue, and of continued obligations to conduct such research only in accord with any applicable federal, state, or local laws and regulations, including prohibitions on the payment of valuable consideration for such tissue.

NOTES AND QUESTIONS

1. *President Bush.* What do you think about President Bush's statement? President Bush allowed federal funding for pre-existing stem cell lines, but would not fund the creation of new embryonic stem cell lines. Do you think President Bush's order was based on science or religion? Or a pragmatic compromise?

2. *President Obama's Executive Order.* In 2009, President Obama revoked President Bush's statement and corresponding Executive Order. Consequently, federal funding could be used for embryonic stem cell research beyond the limitations President Bush gave. How do you feel about Executive Orders? Do you think it would be better if Congress passed a law that allowed embryonic stem cell research so the advancement of the science is not dependent on who is president? Does it bother you that one president can revoke the executive order of another president?

3. *President Trump's HHS and President Biden's response.* Trump's statement says "[p]romoting the dignity of human life from conception to natural death is one of the very top priorities of President Trump's administration." How does his policy meet those goals? What would be the alternatives to fetal tissue research that the administration should consider? If you were on one of the ethics advisory boards, how would you decide which projects to fund?

Democratic members of the House of Representatives later called on Trump to dismiss these restrictions in order to promote research for COVID-19. "Because of your restrictions, NIH is unable to utilize human fetal tissue to develop animal models of COVID-19 that can test potential vaccines and treatments to decelerate or even end this global health crisis. This inaction may ultimately put Americans further at risk of disease or death from COVID-19," some of them wrote. Some scientists reported that the rule would limit their research on confronting the virus. In their research,

sometimes they put parts of human fetal tissue into animals and then test how drugs perform there. See House Democrats call on Trump administration to lift restrictions on fetal tissue for coronavirus research, 2020 WL 1676642. Stem cells also made news related to COVID vaccines, when abortion opponents objected to the fact that vaccine candidates were manufactured using the human cell lines originally derived from elective abortions. See Meredith Wadman, Abortion Opponents Protest COVID-19 Vaccines' Use of Fetal Cells, Science, Jun. 5, 2020, https://www.sciencemag.org/news/2020/06/abortion-opponents-protest-covid-19-vaccines-use-fetal-cells.

Trump's ethics board had rejected 13 of 14 scientific projects submitted to it. In contrast, Biden followed the advice of medical groups who wanted to continue scientific research, including research on Parkinson's, HIV and COVID-19. New HHS Secretary Xavier Becerra said "We believe that we have to do the research it takes to make sure that we are incorporating innovation and getting all of those types of treatments and therapies out there to the American people." Alice Miranda Ollstein, Biden administration reverses Trump restrictions on fetal tissue research, Politico, Apr. 16, 2021, https://www.politico.com/news/2021/04/16/biden-reverses-fetal-tissue-research-restrictions-482503. What health advances do you expect from these new standards? Are you surprised that anti-abortion groups oppose the changes?

4. *Dickey-Wicker Amendment*. In 1996, prior to the stem cell debate, Congress passed the Dickey-Wicker Amendment, which provides that federal funds shall not be used for "research in which a human embryo or embryos are destroyed, discarded, or knowingly subjected to risk of injury or death greater than that allowed for research on fetuses in utero. . . ." Pub. L. No. 111–117, § 509(a)(2), 123 Stat. 3032, 3280–81. Do you think Congress's intent *about stem cell research* is clear from passing the Dickey-Wicker Amendment? Or, do you think it is ambiguous? Do you think the Dickey-Wicker Amendment would invalidate or trump President Obama's order allowing federal funding for embryonic stem cell research?

5. *Sherley v. Sebelius*. In response to President Obama's Executive Order allowing federal funding for human embryonic stem cells ("hESCs") research, adult stem cell (ASC) researchers who opposed embryonic stem cell research filed suit against the Secretary of Health and Human Services (HHS) and the National Institutes of Health (NIH) claiming that President Obama's hESCs research funding policy violated the Dickey-Wicker Amendment. The federal district court issued a preliminary injunction against the NIH after deciding that there was sufficient evidence to warrant the freezing of funds for embryo-destructive research while the case was pending. In the case that follows, the Court of Appeals lifted the injunction against NIH after holding that the Dickey-Wicker Amendment was ambiguous, and that a reasonable interpretation of the Amendment did allow stem cell research because stem cell research does not involve the direct destruction of embryos.

What more do you need to understand about human stem cell research before deciding whether you agree with the Court of Appeals' reasoning about Dickey-Wicker?

Sherley v. Sebelius

United States Court of Appeals, District of Columbia Circuit, 2012.
689 F.3d 776, 402 U.S. App. D.C. 178, cert. denied, 568 U.S. 1087 (2013).

■ SENTELLE, CHIEF JUDGE:

. . . At the time of the adoption of the first Dickey-Wicker rider, scientists had not yet isolated embryonic stem cells (ESC), and the original enactment was apparently directed at another type of research performed on human embryos in the field of in vitro fertilization. By 1998, researchers had generated a stable line of ESCs available for further research. Although more mature stem cells were and remain available, many researchers consider the ESCs far more valuable because they are pluripotent—that is, they can be developed into any of nearly 200 different types of human cells for use in a broad range of medical research.

Isolating ESCs for research requires that the cells be removed from a human embryo, cultured, and stabilized into a "stem cell line." This process of "derivation" destroys the embryo. The cells from this line may then be used for years by researchers, who differentiate the cells into whatever kinds of cells they need for a particular research project. Thus, the initial derivation process requires the destruction of a human embryo. The particular research projects using the earlier derived stem cells, however, does not involve the destruction of any further embryos.

It is this distinction between funding research projects directly involving the destruction of a human embryo and projects using embryonic stem cells derived from an earlier destruction that underlies the controversy giving rise to the present litigation. In 2001, President George W. Bush, for ethical reasons, declared that federal funds would be used in research on embryonic stem cells only if such cells were drawn from one of the sixty or so stem cell lines already existing at the time of President Bush's declaration.

So matters stood until 2009, when President Obama issued an Executive Order revoking Executive Order No. 13,435. The Order stated that NIH "may support and conduct responsible, scientifically worthy human stem cell research, including human embryonic stem cell research, to the extent permitted by law."

As required by the Executive Order and after notice and comment, NIH issued new "Guidelines for Human Stem Cell Research." The Guidelines "recognize the distinction, accepted by Congress, between the derivation of stem cells from an embryo that results in the embryo's destruction, for which Federal funding is prohibited, and research involving [ESCs] that does not involve an embryo nor result in an

embryo's destruction, for which Federal funding is permitted." Under the Guidelines, an ESC research project may receive NIH funding as long as it utilizes cells from lines (1) created by in vitro fertilization for reproductive purposes, (2) no longer needed for that purpose, and (3) voluntarily donated by the individuals who owned them—even if that line was derived after 2001.

III. Analysis

. . . 1. Dickey-Wicker

Appellants . . . asserted then and assert now that the Dickey-Wicker ban "unambiguously" extends to any research project that uses ESCs. Their argument, now and before, is that if a funded research project involves the use of an ESC, then an embryo necessarily has been destroyed, and the ban of Dickey-Wicker has been violated. Briefly put, appellants contend that all ESC research is "research" in which a human embryo or embryos are destroyed and, therefore, NIH's guidelines violate Dickey-Wicker by authorizing federal funding of such research. This is precisely the same argument we rejected in our review of the preliminary injunction order.

[There] we held that NIH had reasonably interpreted Dickey-Wicker's ban on funding "research in which . . . embryos are destroyed" to allow federal funding of ESC research. We explained that "research" as used in Dickey-Wicker was a "flexible" (i.e., ambiguous) term. It could be understood as the plaintiffs construed the term—an "extended process" that would include the initial derivation of stem cells. Or "research" could take on NIH's narrow interpretation as a "discrete project" separate from derivation. Id. Given that ambiguity, we deferred . . . to NIH's permissible construction of Dickey-Wicker: "research" as used in Dickey-Wicker may reasonably be understood to mean a "discrete endeavor" that excludes the initial derivation of ESCs. Under that interpretation, Dickey-Wicker permits federal funding of research projects that utilize already-derived ESCs—which are not themselves embryos—because no "human embryo or embryos are destroyed" in such projects.

. . . 2. Subjected to Risk

Appellants make a second argument that is intertwined with their first. They note that Dickey-Wicker also bans "research in which a human embryo or embryos are . . . knowingly subjected to risk of injury or death." . . . They theorize that conducting a federally funded ESC research project increases the demand for more ESC lines, which in turn incentivizes the destruction of more embryos to create those lines, thus subjecting those embryos to risk. NIH responds that no embryos are subjected to risk of injury or death in any ESC research project using already derived ESCs and not otherwise involving the use of embryos.

. . . Under [NIH's] definition of "research," the destruction of embryos that occurs in the ESC derivation process is not a part of

individual ESC research projects using already derived ESCs. Therefore, ESC research is no more "research in which . . . embryos are . . . subjected to risk" than it was "research in which . . . embryos are . . . destroyed." Appellants' theory shifts focus from the embryo destroyed in the past to embryos for which an ESC research project "incentivizes" future destruction. But none of those embryos are "destroyed" or "subjected to risk" in an ESC research project. The language of Dickey-Wicker does not ban funding for, e.g., "research which provides an incentive to harm, destroy, or place at risk human embryos." As we have held before, the NIH interpretation of the statute's actual language is reasonable.

Conclusion

For the above reasons, we affirm the district court's grant of summary judgment in favor of the government.

So ordered.

■ KAREN LECRAFT HENDERSON, CIRCUIT JUDGE, concurring:

The Amendment prohibits federal funding of "research in which a human embryo or embryos are destroyed." Contrary to the holding in *Sherley I*, this ban plainly prohibits federal funding that the Guidelines expressly permit—namely, the funding of human embryonic stem cell (hESC) research that is conducted after the destruction of the embryo. This conclusion is compelled by the dictionary definition of "research" as a "systematic inquiry or investigation," which necessarily includes not only "the first sequence of hESC research [involving] the derivation of stem cells from the human embryo" but also "the succeeding sequences of hESC research."

■ BROWN, CIRCUIT JUDGE, concurring:

Even Dr. James Thompson, the researcher credited with being the first to successfully derive human embryonic stem cells, has admitted: "If human embryonic stem cell research does not make you at least a bit uncomfortable, you have not thought about it enough." Gina Kolata, Man Who Helped Start Stem Cell War May End It, N.Y. Times, Nov. 22, 2007.

Congressional efforts to grapple with the ethical challenges arising from the extraordinary advances in biomedicine and biotechnology date back at least to the passage of the National Research Act in 1974. Since then, there has been no shortage of committees, boards, and panels all dedicated to the study and consideration of the moral, legal, and ethical dimensions of using human subjects, or human cellular or genetic materials, in scientific experiments. More recently, Congress passed the NIH Revitalization Act of 1993, under which NIH established the Human Embryo Research Panel ("HERP"). While the bill's focus was human reproductive biology, HERP concluded that "[r]esearch involving the development of embryonic stem cells [done] with embryos resulting from IVF treatment for infertility or clinical research that have been donated" was "acceptable" and could receive federal funding.

Congress passed the Dickey-Wicker Amendment in 1996 partially in response to some of HERP's bolder recommendations, perhaps agreeing with the Washington Post that the Panel had gone "a step too far." The Amendment was not directed at the precise research at issue here, but whatever the Amendment's original purpose, President Clinton's decision in 1999 to announce a policy of federal funding for embryonic stem cell research—and Congress's decision to pass the Amendment unchanged the following year—altered the interpretive calculus. In the same vein, Congress's decision to pass the Amendment unchanged for all eight years of the Bush Administration seems to confirm its acquiescence to some federal funding of research involving human embryonic stem cells. Indeed, Congress supplemented this implicit approval of funding for embryonic stem cell research with contemporaneous Senate and House reports explicitly stating that the amendment "should not be construed to limit federal support for research involving human embryonic stem cells listed on an NIH registry and carried out in accordance with the policy outlined by the President."

The challenging—and constantly evolving—issues presented by bioethics are critical and complex. Striking the right balance is not easy and not, in the first instance, a task for judges. What must be defended is "the integrity of science, the legitimacy of government, and the continuing vitality" of concepts like human dignity. Given the weighty interests at stake in this encounter between science and ethics, relying on an increasingly Delphic, decade-old single paragraph rider on an appropriations bill hardly seems adequate.

NOTES AND QUESTIONS

1. *Statutory Reasoning.* The court distinguished the destruction of a human embryo during the stem cell derivation process from later research involving derived stem cells. Do you agree with the court and NIH that this two-step process means that embryos are not destroyed during stem cell research? Do you agree with the reasoning of the majority about the destruction of embryos in research or with the concurrence by Judge Henderson?

The plaintiffs argued that ongoing stem cell research encourages the destruction of more embryos for future research. Do you agree? Do you believe this is reason to stop stem cell research? What did the court conclude about this argument?

Practice Exercise: Redraft the Dickey-Wicker amendment to either allow or prohibit stem cell research.

2. *Stem Cell Controversy Creator and Ender.* Dr. James Thomson's laboratory was one of the first two laboratories to retrieve stem cells from human embryos. See Gina Kolata, Man Who Helped Start Stem Cell War May End It, N.Y. Times, Nov. 22, 2007, at A1. Little did Dr. Thomson know

this practice would start a political controversy that "took on an almost iconic quality the same way Roe v. Wade has." Id. The idea of using human embryos created an ethical struggle for Dr. Thomson. However, his research has found a way around the need for human embryos. Id. Dr. Thomson discovered a "way to turn ordinary human skin cells into what appear to be embryonic stem cells without ever using a human embryo" by adding four genes to the skin cells. Id. The skin cells, after being turned into stem cells, have the power to morph into any of the body's 220 different cells. Id. So, the doctor who helped create the controversy of human embryonic stem cell research has taken steps to avoid the controversial embryos, while still advancing the medical science.

Dr. Thomson's work, although esteemed in the field of stem cell research, is not as well received in the overall scientific community. See Jacob Sherkow, Of Stem Cell: Prizes and Controversy, Stanford Law School: Center for Law and the Biosciences, Blog, Oct. 11, 2012. Sherkow discussed that many scientific breakthroughs in stem cell research, including those of Dr. Thomson, have been absent from the Nobel Prize community, which, Sherkow speculated, could be because of the Nobel Prize's moral barriers to stem cell research. Id.

3. *Stem Cell Fraud.* What once appeared to be a breakthrough in stem cell research, soon turned out to be a fabrication of scientific findings. See Martin Fackler, Japan Questions Stem Cell Breakthrough, N.Y. Times, Apr. 2, 2014, at B14. At Japan's leading research institute, the Riken Institute, a thirty-year-old female scientist claimed to have discovered a way to turn mouse cells into stem cells by immersing them in an acidic bath. Id. However, after a thorough investigation and skepticism from the scientific community, the scientist's procedures were flawed and partially fabricated. Id. The investigation did not reveal whether or not the stem cells could be created, but only concluded that more research was needed. Id.

This is not the first time that scientists and physicians have taken advantage of the modern day medical miracle science. In a 60 Minutes investigation, reporters found many different online scams that offered stem cell therapy—a treatment that is illegal in the United States and many other places in the world, due to the lack of scientific findings. Sadly, many terminally ill patients are taken advantage of by the false hope created from these con artists claiming to have cured or improved many incurable diseases and illnesses. A Missouri state legislator was removed from her position after being accused of stem cell fraud. The legislator, Patricia Ashton Derges, "claimed her Regenerative Biologics stem cells would treat patients suffering from 'tissue damage, kidney disease, chronic obstructive pulmonary disease. . ., Lyme Disease, erectile dysfunction, and urinary incontinence.' " But her product did not contain any stem cells. Jaclyn Peiser, A Missouri lawmaker sold a 'potential cure' for coronavirus. It was a fake stem cell treatment, feds say," Wash. Post, Feb. 3, 2021, at https://www.washingtonpost.com/nation/2021/02/03/missouri-lawmaker-stemcell-covid-indicted/. See also Andy Marso, Peddling

Go to the website to watch the 60 Minutes investigation video.

Unproven Treatments, Stem Cell Industry 'Fleeces,' Sometimes Harms Patients, Kansas City Star, Aug. 18, 2019, https://www.kansascity.com/news/business/health-care/article233635472.html. While not necessarily fraud, other companies are trying to benefit financially from the stem cell movement. Companies are starting to emerge that encourage individuals to bank their stem cells for the possibility that modern medicine will advance enough to provide a cure later on in life, if need be. See Dan Morgan, Banking Stem Cells in the Hope of a Lifesaving Cure, CNBC, July 28, 2013. A French Company, known as Cellectic, created a stem-cell bank called Scéil. Id. The French Company is banking on the fact that the rate of medical research and development will allow individuals to have "a personal deposit of your cell[s]" as a backup in case of a medical need. Id. For a one-time payment of $60,000.00, individuals can store their stem cells for life. Id. The new motto is "Forget about cash. Start banking your body." Id.

4. *Treatment with ASCs.* The availability of adult stem cells makes it possible for many physicians to offer patients treatments using their own cells. The physician can harvest cells from the patient, process them, and then apply them to the same patient's disease. Given the complexity of stem cell research, how much do you think the government should regulate ASC treatments?

> **Go to** the website and, as background to the following case, read the Chirba and Epstein blogs with contrasting views of how the FDA should regulate stem cells.

United States v. Regenerative Sciences, LLC

United States Court of Appeals, District of Columbia Circuit, 2014.
741 F.3d 1314.

■ GRIFFITH, CIRCUIT JUDGE:

In this civil enforcement action, we must decide whether the appellants—three individuals and a related corporate entity—violated federal laws regulating the manufacture and labeling of drugs and biological products by producing, as part of their medical practice, a substance consisting of a mixture of a patient's stem cells and the antibiotic doxycycline. Because we conclude that they did, we affirm the district court's judgment and the permanent injunction it entered against appellants.

I

A

This case involves two statutes under which the Food and Drug Administration (FDA) regulates the healthcare industry: the Federal Food, Drug & Cosmetic Act (FDCA), 21 U.S.C. § 301 *et seq.*, and the Public Health Service Act (PHSA), 42 U.S.C. § 201 *et seq.* Those statutes promote the safety of drugs and biological products, respectively, by setting forth detailed requirements for how such substances are to be manufactured and labeled. Drugs and biological products not satisfying

those requirements are deemed "adulterated" or "misbranded," and doing any act that causes a drug or biological product to be adulterated or misbranded is a violation of federal law. The FDA may seek an injunction to prohibit such violations.

B

The substance at issue in this case is produced by appellants Dr. Christopher Centeno, Dr. John Schultz, Michelle Cheever, and Regenerative Sciences, LLC, as part of a medical therapy that they market as the "Cultured Regenexx Procedure" (the Procedure). Drs. Centeno and Schultz, who practice medicine together at the Centeno-Schultz Clinic in Colorado, jointly developed the Procedure to treat patients' orthopedic conditions. They are the majority shareholders of Regenerative Sciences, which they founded and which, in turn, owns the Procedure and licenses it exclusively to the Centeno-Schultz Clinic. Michelle Cheever is the laboratory director for Regenerative Sciences.

The Procedure begins with the extraction of a sample of a patient's bone marrow or synovial fluid. From that sample, Regenerative Sciences isolates mesenchymal stem cells (MSCs), which are capable of differentiating into bone and cartilage cells. The MSCs are then placed in a solution to culture them—that is, to cause them to divide and proliferate. Other substances are sometimes added to the solution that affect the MSCs' differentiation. The culturing process determines the growth and biological characteristics of the resulting cell population. When the MSCs are sufficiently numerous for re-injection, they are combined with doxycycline, an antibiotic obtained in interstate commerce and used to prevent bacterial contamination of the MSCs. The resulting mixture (the Mixture) is injected into the patient from whom the stem cell sample was initially taken, at the site of the damaged tissue.

Appellants promote the Procedure as an alternative to surgery for various orthopedic conditions and diseases. In court filings, they have described the Procedure as a "treatment [for] orthopedic injuries and arthritis" and for "musculoskeletal and spinal injury." Their promotional materials recommend the Procedure for treatment of osteoarthritis, non-healing bone fractures, chronic bulging lumbar discs, and soft tissue injuries.

In August 2010, the government filed this action for a permanent injunction against appellants, alleging that the Mixture is both a drug and a biological product that is adulterated and misbranded in violation of § 331(k) of the FDCA and § 262(j) of the PHSA, which incorporates § 331(k) by reference. Appellants counterclaimed, asserting that the Mixture is not subject to federal regulation and that, even if it is, the FDA's effort to regulate the Mixture is defective under both the PHSA and the Administrative Procedure Act (APA), 5 U.S.C. § 706(2).

The district court granted the government's motion for summary judgment and dismissed appellants' counterclaims, holding that they had

violated the FDCA and the PHSA. *United States v. Regenerative Scis., LLC*, 878 F.Supp.2d 248, 263 (D.D.C.2012). Then, finding a "cognizable danger of a recurrent violation," the district court entered a permanent injunction prohibiting appellants from committing further violations of the FDCA's adulteration and misbranding restrictions. Appellants timely appealed both orders. . . .

II

Appellants' principal argument is that the Mixture is not subject to regulation under the FDCA or PHSA because it is neither a drug nor a biological product but is, rather, a medical procedure. The text of those statutes forecloses this argument.

The FDCA defines a "drug" as any "article[ ] intended for use in the diagnosis, cure, mitigation, treatment, or prevention of disease" or "intended to affect the structure or any function of the body." The PHSA defines "biological product" in similarly broad terms as any "virus, therapeutic serum, toxin, antitoxin, vaccine, blood, blood component or derivative . . . or analogous product . . . applicable to the prevention, treatment, or cure of a disease or condition of human beings." Both of these wide-ranging definitions clearly apply to the Mixture, an article derived mainly from human tissue and intended to treat orthopedic diseases and to affect musculoskeletal function. Indeed, appellants do not actually dispute that the plain language of the statutes compels this conclusion.

Rather, appellants urge us to construe the FDCA in light of purported federalism concerns. But appellants' concerns lack merit. They boil down to the following syllogism: the FDCA was not intended to infringe on states' traditional role in regulating the practice of medicine; the Procedure fits Colorado's statutory definition of the "practice of medicine"; therefore, the FDA's regulation of the Procedure exceeds the FDA's authority under the FDCA. This syllogism is flawed twice over.

First, it misapprehends what this case is about. Notwithstanding appellants' attempt to characterize this case as an effort by the FDA to "restrict[ ] the use of an autologous stem cell *procedure*," the focus of the FDA's regulation is the *Mixture*. That is, the FDA does not claim that the procedures used to administer the Mixture are unsafe; it claims that the Mixture itself is unsafe. Appellants' arguments about the practice-of-medicine exemption are therefore wide of the mark.

Second, appellants are wrong to suggest that the scope of the FDCA depends on state-by-state definitions of the "practice of medicine." The FDCA enacts a comprehensive, uniform regulatory scheme for the distribution of drugs. The scheme's breadth—and, more specifically, its applicability to doctors—is evident in the fact that the FDCA *carves out* certain exceptions from its requirements for doctors who manufacture and administer drugs in the course of their professional practice. Those exceptions would be unnecessary if the FDCA did not otherwise regulate

the distribution of drugs by licensed physicians. Appellants' construction of the FDCA, by contrast, would allow states to gut the FDCA's regulation of doctors, and thereby create an enormous gap in the FDCA's coverage, by classifying the distribution of drugs by doctors as the practice of medicine. Given Congress's intent that the FDCA's "coverage be as broad as its literal language indicates," such a construction is not tenable.

Equally untenable is appellants' contention that because the Procedure occurs entirely within the state of Colorado, the Mixture lacks a sufficient connection to interstate commerce to permit federal regulation under the Commerce Clause. It is simply impossible to square this argument with the last seventy years of Commerce Clause jurisprudence, which, in recognition of Congress's authority to regulate even "purely local activities that are part of an economic 'class of activities' that have a substantial effect on interstate commerce," has upheld federal laws prohibiting the possession of home-grown marijuana intended solely for personal use, and restricting the amount of wheat a farmer can grow purely for his farm's consumption. Here, not only does the Mixture undoubtedly have effects on interstate markets for orthopedic care, but it actually includes an article shipped in interstate commerce, namely, doxycycline. The Commerce Clause poses no obstacle to regulating the Mixture under the FDCA.

Nor can appellants prevail on their argument that even if the Mixture may be federally regulated in principle, it falls outside the scope of the statute appellants are charged with violating. That provision prohibits "the doing of any . . . act with respect to [ ] a . . . drug . . . if such act is done while such [drug] is held for sale . . . *after shipment in interstate commerce* and results in such [drug] being adulterated or misbranded." Appellants read § 331(k) to require that the entire Mixture have been shipped in interstate commerce. They contend that merely using an ingredient that travelled in interstate commerce—here, doxycycline—is insufficient to trigger the bar. We disagree. Not only does the FDCA define the term "drug" to include a drug's components, but to interpret § 331(k) as appellants suggest would severely narrow a statutory scheme designed to regulate the safety of drugs at every stage of their distribution. The two circuits to have considered this issue have reached the same conclusion. In *United States v. Dianovin Pharmaceuticals, Inc.*, which involved a pharmaceutical company that used raw vitamin K purchased in interstate commerce to manufacture injectable vitamin K, the First Circuit held that the company's "use of components shipped in interstate commerce . . . brought their activities within § 331(k)." Similarly, in *Baker v. United States*, the Ninth Circuit held that § 331(k)'s " 'shipment in interstate commerce' requirement is satisfied even when only an ingredient is transported interstate." We therefore hold that, by virtue of its use of doxycycline, the Mixture is

within the scope of drugs—and, by extension, biological products, *see* 42 U.S.C. § 262(j)—regulated by § 331(k).

III

Appellants next advance two arguments why the Mixture is exempt from the FDCA's manufacturing and labeling requirements even if it is otherwise subject to federal regulation. Each argument fails.

A

In addition to regulating biological products directly, the PHSA gives the FDA authority to issue regulations to prevent the interstate spread of communicable disease. Pursuant to that authority, in 2001 the FDA promulgated regulations to ensure the safety of human cells, tissues, and cellular or tissue-based products (HCT/Ps) used for therapeutic purposes. Those regulations, which appear at 21 C.F.R. part 1271, define HCT/Ps, in relevant part, as "articles containing or consisting of human cells or tissues that are intended for implantation, transplantation, infusion, or transfer into a human recipient." HCT/Ps may qualify as drugs or biological products, and when they do, the FDA generally regulates them accordingly under the FDCA, PHSA, and corresponding regulations. The Part 1271 Regulations, however, create a regulatory exemption from the manufacturing and labeling requirements that normally apply to drugs and biological products for any HCT/P that is no more than "minimally manipulated." "Minimal manipulation" of cells means "processing that does not alter the relevant biological characteristics." Appellants claim this exemption applies to the Mixture, but the government offers several reasons why appellants' culturing process alters the MSCs' relevant biological characteristics and is therefore more than minimal manipulation. As to some of those reasons, such as the government's claim that culturing MSCs alters the genes and proteins they express, appellants have created genuine issues of fact by submitting expert affidavits arguing that the government's views are based on scientific studies that are inapplicable to appellants' culturing process. But appellants give no response to other reasons offered by the government. For example, appellants admit that the culturing process is designed to "determine the growth and biological characteristics of the resulting cell population." It is also undisputed that, in at least some cases, appellants add substances to the cell culture that affect the differentiation of bone marrow cells.

These concessions are fatal to appellants' attempt to claim refuge under § 1271.10(a). Given that § 1271.10(a) is an exemption from the otherwise applicable provisions of the FDCA, appellants ultimately bear the burden of establishing that it applies to the Mixture. Because appellants concede that culturing MSCs affects their characteristics and offer no evidence that those effects constitute only minimal manipulation, they fail to carry that burden as a matter of law.

We emphasize that we reach this conclusion based on the evidence in the record, and not merely by deferring to the FDA's statement in the preamble to the Part 1271 Regulations that expansion of MSCs in culture automatically constitutes more than minimal manipulation. Appellants devote considerable energy to challenging that statement as an invalid legislative rule that the FDA now seeks to enforce against them. That is, they claim that the FDA seeks to give legal effect to a statement that was not promulgated through formal rule-making procedures, which the APA forbids. Our decision, however, is based on, and gives effect to, the Part 1271 Regulations, not the preamble. Appellants' procedural challenge to the preamble is therefore irrelevant.

Surprisingly, appellants also challenge the Part 1271 Regulations as *ultra vires* if applied to autologous stem cell procedures because, they argue, such procedures do not carry the risk of spreading communicable disease and thus are not subject to regulation under 42 U.S.C. § 264. It is unclear what appellants hope to achieve with this claim; to prevail would only mean invalidating the very exemption from the FDCA in which they hope to take refuge. In any case, the FDA's findings, which appellants do not challenge, undercut appellants' argument. In promulgating the Part 1271 Regulations, the FDA noted that any procedure involving HCT/Ps risks spreading disease through, for example, "[e]rrors in labeling, mixups of testing records, failure to adequately clean work areas, and faulty packaging." Indeed, Regenerative Sciences' own standard operating procedure takes a similar view, recognizing the risk of "[c]ontamination" as a "major problem in tissue culture" and stressing the need for "good tissue practices" to "prevent the introduction, transmission, or spread of communicable diseases." Appellants thus offer no basis to conclude that the Part 1271 Regulations exceed the FDA's authority to issue regulations "to prevent the introduction, transmission, or spread of communicable diseases" between states.

B

Alternatively, appellants contend that the Mixture is exempt from the FDCA's manufacturing and labeling requirements because it is a compounded drug. A compounded drug must be produced using certain types of "bulk drug substances," one of which is "bulk drug substances . . . that . . . are components of drugs approved by the [government]." Appellants assert that the Mixture meets this definition because cultured MSCs are a component of the FDA-approved drug Carticel. But even if that were the case—and the affidavits appellants cite only suggest that it might be—it would not be enough to bring the Mixture within § 353a. To qualify as a "bulk drug substance," an item must be "represented for use in a drug," and appellants point to no evidence in the record even suggesting that MSCs are held out for use in Carticel, or any other drug for that matter. Appellants therefore fail to establish that the Mixture is

exempt from the FDCA's manufacturing and labeling requirements, and we proceed to consider whether the Mixture violated them.

IV

A

The FDCA provides that a drug "*shall be deemed to be adulterated* . . . if . . . the methods used in, or the facilities or controls used for, its manufacture, processing, packing, or holding do not conform to or are not operated or administered in conformity with current good manufacturing practice." The FDA has established the specific elements of current good manufacturing practice at 21 C.F.R. parts 210–211. Here, it is undisputed that appellants' facilities, methods, and controls for processing the Mixture violated federal manufacturing standards in numerous respects. Therefore, the Mixture is *per se* adulterated, regardless of any other safety protocols appellants happen to use.

B

The FDCA also provides that a drug "shall be deemed to be misbranded" if its label omits certain information. As relevant here, the FDCA requires that a drug's label provide "adequate directions for use," and, in the case of prescription drugs, bear the symbol "Rx only." Appellants admit that the Mixture's labeling satisfies neither of these requirements.

Appellants nevertheless argue that it is inappropriate to hold them liable for not providing adequate directions because they produced the Mixture only for their own use. This argument, however, misunderstands how the FDCA's labeling scheme applies to prescription drugs. To satisfy § 352(f)'s requirement of providing "adequate directions for use," a drug's label must provide "directions under which the *layman* can use a drug safely and for the purposes for which it is intended." A prescription drug, however, is by definition "not safe for use except under the supervision of a *practitioner licensed by law to administer such drug.*" It is thus impossible to provide "adequate directions for use" for prescription drugs. As the Seventh Circuit has observed, this means that prescription drugs are "presumptively misbranded." A prescription drug can avoid being actually misbranded only by qualifying for either of two exemptions from § 352(f): the statutory exemption, which applies when licensed practitioners distribute drugs to patients via prescriptions, or the regulatory exemption, which applies to prescription drugs at any stage of distribution. A prescription drug's label must contain specific information in order for either exemption to apply. If the label does not contain every piece of required information, the prescription drug will remain subject to the impossible mandate of § 352(f) and will be misbranded.

Here, there is no doubt that the Mixture qualifies as a prescription drug. Before the Mixture can be injected into a patient, a physician must review the cultured MSCs to ensure that there are no visible signs of

bacterial contamination or genetic mutation. Then, if the MSCs are safe, appellants inject the Mixture using sophisticated imaging devices to ensure that it reaches the right spot on a patient's bone or tissue so that it has the intended therapeutic effect. Because the Mixture can be safely administered only under a physician's supervision, the question for us is whether the Mixture qualifies for either § 352(f) exemption. The answer is clear. Both exemptions require that the label bear the symbol "Rx only," and it is undisputed that the Mixture's label does not. Because its label fails to provide the minimum information necessary to qualify for either exemption from § 352(f), the Mixture is misbranded.

In reaching this conclusion, we reject appellants' broad reading of *United States v. Evers,* in which the Fifth Circuit held that a doctor was not liable for violating § 352(f)(1) by advertising his off-label use of a prescription drug without providing adequate directions for that use. Appellants read *Evers* for the proposition that doctors need not comply with the FDCA's labeling requirements when they prescribe drugs only within their own practices. But *Evers* cannot bear the weight of this interpretation, which is inconsistent with the fact that the FDCA does not exempt doctors in such a categorical manner. As the Fifth Circuit made clear, the "object of the government's case" in *Evers* was not the off-label "*prescription*" of the drug at issue, but rather the "*promotion and advertising*" of such off-label use. *Evers* thus differs from this case in two important ways: the drug at issue in *Evers* was FDA approved, and the FDA did not question Evers's right to prescribe that drug to his patients. Neither of those circumstances is present here. The FDA has not approved the Mixture as safe for any use and hence challenges appellants' right to prescribe the Mixture at all. We will not broaden *Evers* to vitiate the FDCA's labeling requirements in these circumstances. The strict exemption criteria presumably reflect the judgment of both Congress and the FDA about the minimum information necessary to safely distribute prescription drugs. Because appellants did not meet those criteria, they misbranded their drug. . . .

VI

For the foregoing reasons, we affirm the district court's orders granting summary judgment to the government, dismissing appellants' counterclaims, and permanently enjoining appellants from committing future violations of the FDCA's manufacturing and labeling provisions.

NOTES AND QUESTIONS

1. *The FDA, the Practice of Medicine, and Marketing Drugs.* In Chapter 3, in the context of medication abortions, we learned that physicians regularly and legally prescribe off-label uses of FDA-approved drugs under the authority of 21 U.S.C. § 396, which states "[n]othing in this chapter shall be construed to limit or interfere with the authority of a health care practitioner to prescribe or administer any legally marketed device to a patient for any condition or disease within a legitimate health care

practitioner-patient relationship." Should the same reasoning permit the doctors in this case to perform the stem cell treatment?

In contrast, we also learned that off-label promotions by drug manufacturers are different from off-label prescriptions because the off-label promotion may cause the drug to be "misbranded" by being introduced into interstate commerce for an unapproved use. See 21 U.S.C. § 352 (states what makes a drug or device misbranded). Therefore, manufacturers can't *promote* the drug for an off-label use, but a doctor is free to *prescribe* the drug for such a use. How does the court resolve the misbranding issue in *Regenerative Sciences*? In this case, are Drs. Centeno and Schultz manufacturers or physicians? Why did the court conclude the Mixture in this case was misbranded?

> **Practice Exercise:** A patient wants access to services that will help him use his own stem cells to fight his disease. As an attorney, how would you help him? What would you argue on his behalf?

2. *Commerce Clause.* Regenerative Sciences argued that the FDA lacked jurisdiction over its medical procedure because it was not part of interstate commerce. We learned in Chapter 3 (with the Partial Birth Abortion Act) and Chapter 4 (with the Affordable Care Act) that Congress usually relies on its Commerce Clause authority when it passes federal health legislation. Given that *five* Justices in Nat'l Fed'n of Indep. Bus. v. Sebelius, 567 U.S. 519 (2012) concluded that Congress lacked Commerce Clause power to pass the Affordable Care Act, do you agree with the court's conclusion here that the Mixture not only has "effects on interstate markets for orthopedic care, but it actually includes an article shipped in interstate commerce, namely, doxycycline"? If the therapy could not be regulated as a drug, do you think the Supreme Court would agree that the FDA can regulate the doctors' practice of medicine in Colorado in these circumstances?

3. *United States v. Regenerative Sciences, LLC*. The opinion held that the process by which stem cells are used for autologous purposes is considered a "drug" that may be regulated by the FDA. If the FDA defines a "drug" as anything used to diagnose, cure, mitigate, treat, or prevent disease or anything intended to affect the structure or function of the body, do you believe that definition is too far-reaching or not broad enough? What do you think was lacking in this opinion? How often was "patient" mentioned? Does this concern you? Should the patient have the ultimate decision regarding his or her own body? How does this relate to the abortion cases? How does this relate to the concerns of members of the Abigail Alliance, who, as we learned in Chapters 2 and 4, have repeatedly argued that terminally ill patients should have access to drugs not yet approved by the FDA? If the patients in this case were terminally ill, would the court have ruled differently? Should the court have ruled differently?

In 2017, the FDA released several guidance documents as "part of a comprehensive policy framework to address how the agency plans to support and expedite the development of regenerative medicine products" using a "risk-based, flexible regulatory framework [to] underscore the agency's

commitment to help bring new and innovative treatment options to patients." The most recent version of those guidance documents is available on the FDA website. See FDA, Framework for the Regulation of Regenerative Medicine Products, https://www.fda.gov/vaccines-blood-biologics/cellular-gene-therapy-products/framework-regulation-regenerative-medicine-products. For a detailed analysis of the FDA's approach, see Pew Charitable Trusts, FDA's Framework for Regulating Regenerative Medicine Will Improve Oversight, Oct. 17, 2019, https://www.pewtrusts.org/en/research-and-analysis/reports/2019/10/17/fdas-framework-for-regulating-regenerative-medicine-will-improve-oversight.

4. *Stem Cell Treatments Overtake Science.* With which side of this issue do you agree—do you believe that people should have the opportunity to try experimental treatments or do you agree with bioethicist Leigh Turner when she states that experimental treatments blur the boundaries between trials and treatments? If you needed stem cell therapy, would you pay to receive the treatment overseas or would you volunteer for a trial in the United States, with the possibility of receiving a placebo? What are your rationales? Doctors worry that if too many patients do not see positive results from experimental clinics, then funding for actual trials will cease. How do you think this problem could be addressed or remedied? How would you combat the conflict between focusing on getting a product to the market and publishing material regarding the trials in medical journals?

5. *FDA Regulations.* Do you believe that the Regenxx™ Procedure should be regulated? What are your arguments for and against it being regulated given the above listed criteria for regulation: 1) no more than minimally manipulated; 2) used for their same original or "homologous" purpose; and 3) autologous? Does the fact that the FDA regulations normally do not target the actual treatment of a patient matter to you when making your arguments? Why or why not?

A Florida stem cell clinic removed adipose (fat) tissue from individuals, isolated certain stem cells within it, and then injected it back into the same patients to treat a range of illnesses. The clinic would use a multi-step process to separate stromal and vascular stem cells, known as the stromal vascular fraction (SVF). The process would include taking out sections of the fat tissue, adding enzymes, and also a cell wash solution to the mix. The mixture is strained so that only SVF can pass through. The SVF are then injected into patient. Why do you think the district court deferred to the FDA's request for an injunction in these circumstances? United States v. US Stem Cell Clinic, LLC, 403 F.Supp.3d 1279 (S.D. Fla. 2019).

6. *FDA and Medical Devices.* A well-known website, 23andMe, that offers DNA testing and analysis has recently undergone scrutiny from the FDA. Robert C. Green & Nita A. Farahany, Regulation: The FDA is Overcautious on Consumer Genomics, 505 Nature 286–87 (Jan. 16, 2014). The FDA states that it can regulate companies that give consumers genetic interpretations that relate to health because supplying that information is considered medical advice, and may meet the definition of a "medical device." Id. This is concerning to many people because if that statement is true, then the FDA may be able to "regulate as medical devices information-based

products such as questionnaires that evaluate the risk of a heart attack or the plethora of fitness trackers that help people to follow their weight, body temperature, heart rate, sleep disorders, seizures, or heart attacks." Id. The FDA has stepped in because it fears that patients may misunderstand the information from such websites and the effects could be more harmful than beneficial. Id. The FDA prefers to be overly cautious in its regulations to prevent future harm. Id. Do you agree with the FDA's reasoning? Where should the line be drawn? Should the FDA be concerned about consumers misinterpreting information? Should clients in legal trouble be prohibited from reading case law because they could misinterpret it? Is that a valid analogy, why or why not? After 23andMe was able to show the FDA that its tests were reliable and accurate, it was allowed to continue its operations in October 2015. Andrew Pollack, 23andMe Will Resume Giving Users Health Data, Oct. 21, 2015, https://www.nytimes.com/2015/10/21/business/23andme-will-resume-giving-users-health-data.html. The business continued to be successful: in February 2021, the company announced that it planned to go public. Casey Ross et al., 23andMe to Go Public via Richard Branson's SPAC, STAT, Feb. 4, 2021.

> **Practice Exercise:** How would you advise a client who wants to travel to Tijuana for experimental treatment or who wants to give experimental treatment to patients in Tijuana? How would you advise a client who has found a clinic in the United States that is willing to offer experimental treatments? Would your advice change depending on whether the patient or the doctor was your client? Would your advice change depending on the severity of your client's need?

7. *Government Overreach*. Now that you have read the opinion, go back and reconsider the blogs by Chirba and Epstein. Have you changed your mind about which blog has the better argument?

C. LOOKING AHEAD: WILL NEW TECHNOLOGY RAISE NEW QUESTIONS OF CONSCIENCE?

1. A HEALTH CARE SYSTEM BASED ON HEALTH

Throughout this chapter we've seen the importance of conscience, as well as moral and religious arguments, to the history of American health care, medicine and research. What would the health care system look like if it always focused *first and primarily* on the patient's health? Go back and read through all the cases and legal developments in this chapter. How would they change if their primary goal was patient health?

2. STEM CELL BREAKTHROUGHS

Scientists have managed to convert skin cells into brain cells by exposing them to a particular combination of cell programming. Catherine Paddock, Scientists Convert Human Skin Cells Directly into

Brain Cells, Medical News Today, Oct. 2, 2014. This is unique because "unlike many cell conversion techniques, the cells did not return to a stem cell stage first—they converted directly into brain cells—thus avoiding the risk of producing many other types of cells." Id. Additionally, "the team managed to reprogram the skin cells to become a particular type of brain cell instead of a range of brain cells." Id. Adult human skin cells were used, which is important because this means that the therapies can use readily available cells and avoid immune rejection. Id.

Furthermore, scientists with the Harvard Stem Cell Institute have developed a new way to use stem cells in the fight against brain cancer. D. W. Stuckey et al., Scientists Engineer Toxin-Secreting Stem Cells to Treat Brain Tumors, Oct. 24, 2014, at http://hsci.harvard.edu/news/scientists-engineer-toxin-secreting-stem-cells-treat-brain-tumors. The scientists have devised a way to "genetically engineer stem cells so they can produce and secrete tumor-killing toxins." Id. This means that the stem cells can enter a tumor and excrete a toxin to kill the cancer cells without killing the healthy cells or the stem cell. Id. The toxin "disrupts the cell's ability to make proteins and, within days, the cell starts to die." Id. The trials have prolonged the survival rate in animal trials. Id. Right now the trials have only been conducted on mice, but the scientists are looking to introduce these "therapies into clinical trials within the next five years." Id. Do you have any moral concerns about these trials on brain cancer?

What other breakthroughs do you anticipate in stem cell research? What would be of most interest to you and your family? Does it worry you that "the U.S. Food and Drug Administration is concerned that some patients seeking cures and remedies are vulnerable to stem cell treatments that are illegal and potentially harmful. And the FDA is increasing its oversight and enforcement to protect people from dishonest and unscrupulous stem cell clinics, while continuing to encourage innovation so that the medical industry can properly harness the potential of stem cell products." See FDA Warns About Stem Cell Therapies, Sept. 3, 2019, https://www.fda.gov/consumers/consumer-updates/fda-warns-about-stem-cell-therapies.

3. UMBILICAL CORD BLOOD BANKING

Umbilical cord blood is an alternative source of hematopoietic stem cells. These cells are easier to collect than the bone marrow stem cells described in Chapter 4 in Flynn v. Holder, 684 F.3d 852 (2011), because the procedure involves clamping the umbilical cord at delivery instead of using aspiration or apheresis to remove cells from bone marrow. Parents now have the option to bank their newborns' umbilical cord blood as a source of stem cells for future use. For a fee, private banks store cells for future use by the individual who opens the account. Public banks take donations of cells for use by any medically appropriate recipient. The public banks are searchable but the private banks are not. See Merlin G.

Butler & Jay E. Menitove, Umbilical Cord Blood Banking: An Update, 28(8) J. Assist. Reprod. Genet. 669 (2011); Health Resources and Services Administration, Options for Umbilical Cord Blood Banking & Donation, https://bloodstemcell.hrsa.gov/donor-information/donate-cord-blood/options-umbilical-cord-blood-banking-donation.

Should every parent bank umbilical cord blood for future use? In a private or public bank? Does it influence your answer to learn that there is only an "estimated 0.04% to 0.005% chance that an individual will develop a disease treatable with their own stored cord blood by 21 years of age"? Id. Or to learn that children who have certain diseases can't use their own stem cells for treatment because those cells are already infected? Id. Does this scientific development cause you to think more favorably of the "savior siblings" we discussed in Chapter 3, because stem cells from a new baby could be used to heal an older sibling?

Go to the website and decide whether the cord blood banking informed consent form is adequate and how much banking should cost.

Recall that in *Flynn*, the Ninth Circuit ruled that donors could be compensated for donation of hematopoietic stem cells when obtained by peripheral blood stem cell apheresis. Based on that ruling, should donors be compensated for donating umbilical cord blood?

Do you think adults should bank their stem cells for future medical use? Should adults be encouraged to donate stem cells just as organ donors were encouraged to donate in Chapter 4? Aren't both umbilical cord stem cell donation and adult stem cell donation both so easy that everyone should donate them?

Practice Exercise: Imagine your client banked the umbilical cord blood of her child with a private bank. Her child now needs the umbilical cord blood but when your client contacts the private bank, she discovers it went out of business. How would you counsel your client in this situation?

4. THE PLACENTA

The placenta is an often-ignored part of the body of reproductive justice. Professor Mathilde Cohen argues that its role needs reconsideration. In her words,

> The inequities at stake in placenta regulation can be summed up in the following supply and demand chain. Pregnant people produce placental tissue through their reproductive labor. Generally constructed by the law as waste products, placentas may be simultaneously inaccessible to postpartum patients on the ground that they are infectious and available for use by third parties on the ground that they are discarded. In states seeking

> to ban or restrict abortions, however, patients may have more ready access to their placenta following an abortion or a miscarriage than after the delivery of a baby by reason of fetal remains being categorized as cadavers of born persons whose remains must be dignified and cannot be classified as waste. Finally, while some patients may be denied access to their own placentas, others may purchase poorly regulated placenta-based cosmetics and therapies.
>
> To curb this cycle, this Article proposes that pregnant patients' right to choose what to do with their placenta should be legally protected and that placenta-based cosmetics should be regulated more strictly. To develop a comprehensive legal regime pertaining to placentas, data must be collected on the ins and outs of current placental economies, as there is much we do not currently know about how placentas are collected, transformed, marketed, labeled, and more. This Article has broader implications for the law of the body in general, as it shows that placentas disrupt some of the assumptions underpinning the functioning and regulation of the bioeconomy. Placentas contradict the happy story according to which, after diagnostic or therapeutic procedures, patients do not think about what happens to their tissues, which can therefore be retained as waste and utilized without obtaining patient consent or providing compensation. The idea of protecting patients' autonomy over their placentas could thus serve as a blueprint for exploring whether and how similar protections should be extended to other body parts and biological materials.

Mathilde Cohen, The Law of Placenta, 31 Yale J.L. & Feminism 337, 408–409 (2020). How would patients' autonomy be protected in these circumstances? How does opposition to abortion affect the ethics of the treatment of the placenta? How could a woman give true informed consent on what happened to her placenta?

In Chapter 6, we consider the property aspects of technology, with special emphasis on whether patent law protects researchers as well as patients who need access to new medical technologies. We examine the role of gene editing in bioethics.

CHAPTER 6

PROPERTY: THE BALANCE BETWEEN RESEARCH, PROFITS, AND PATIENTS

Introduction. In Chapter 5, we focused on ethical considerations in the medical community from two different perspectives. First, we looked at conscience objections in medicine—ethical considerations from a physician or hospital's viewpoint that oppose certain types of medical procedures. Second, we examined many dissimilar viewpoints, whether political or professional, regarding stem cell research. We questioned whether stem cell research comported with the concepts of beneficence and non-maleficence. Specifically, we reviewed different types of stem cell research, the benefits of each type, and the controversy surrounding human embryonic stem cell research.

In this chapter, we focus on the commercialization of stem cell and genetic research. In Section A, we examine the process for obtaining patents, and whether that process does and should allow for genetic patents. The patent area demonstrates a tension between rewarding researchers for their efforts and making new technologies widely available to patients who need them. In Section B, we shift our focus to research profits by examining how much medical researchers should be allowed to profit from their research. We question whether profits can create flawed incentives in research and ask whether patients should enjoy more property rights in the products of research based on their body parts. In Section C, we look forward to new patent and property questions that arise from developing technology.

A. PATENTS

When drafting the U.S. Constitution, the Framers recognized the importance of patents and accordingly protected them in Article 1, Section 8, Clause 8—"To promote the progress of science and useful arts, by securing for limited times to authors and inventors the exclusive right to their respective writings and discoveries." The Framers realized the necessity of public disclosure of information and intellectual property and how it benefits society. See David L. Newman, Standing on the Shoulders of the Framers of the U.S. Constitution's Patent and Copyright Clause, 31 Westlaw J. 1 (2013). Consequently, the Framers incentivized potential investors by protecting their intellectual property "for a short period of time in

Go to the website in order to review the basics of patent law.

exchange for publicly disclosing their intellectual property." Id. Without the protection of patents, inventors would not necessarily front the costs of invention if any other company or individual could copy it. A temporary monopoly is necessary to make the invention worth the cost to inventors.

Federal statutes implement the constitutional protection. Holders of federal patents receive a twenty-year period of exclusivity, during which they may "forbid anyone else from making, using, selling or offering to sell their invention." Lori B. Andrews et al., Genetics: Ethics, Law & Policy 194 (2009). Pharmaceutical patents are particularly valuable to drug manufacturers, which explains why they undergo the detailed review process described in Chapter 2. Id.

In order to obtain a patent, the invention must be patentable under 35 U.S.C. § 101, which states: "Whoever invents or discovers any new and useful process, machine, manufacture, or composition of matter, or any new and useful improvement thereof, may obtain a patent therefor, subject to the conditions and requirements of this title." Note that under Section 101, the patented invention must be "useful." Section 102 requires inventions to be novel, id. § 102, and Section 103 requires patents to be non-obvious. Id. § 103. An invention is considered obvious "if the differences between the claimed invention and the prior art are such that the claimed invention as a whole would have been obvious before the effective filing date of the claimed invention to a person having ordinary skill in the art to which the claimed invention pertains." Id.

There are three types of patents: utility patents, design patents, and plant patents. Patents, U.S. Patent and Trademark Office, http://www.uspto.gov/patent. For a general overview of the patents and their functionality, see Introduction to Understanding Patents, MLibrary, Nov. 4, 2014, http://guides.lib.umich.edu/content.php?pid=35640 & sid=288824. Utility patents apply to new and useful processes (an invention that does something). Id. Utility patents can be split into three categories: mechanical, electrical, and chemical. Id. Design patents apply to new, original, and ornamental designs and plant patents apply to an asexually reproduced distinct or new variety of plant. Id.

U.S. patents protect only inventions within the United States. Protecting Your Inventions Abroad: Frequently Asked Questions About the Patent Cooperation Treaty, World Intellectual Prop. Org., Jul. 2014, http://www.wipo.int/pct/en/faqs/faqs.html. This means that a U.S. inventor can prohibit an inventor from another country from selling his or her invention in the United States or the U.S. inventor can prohibit an inventor from creating the invention in the United States and then selling it abroad. Id. However, a patent filed in the United States will not prohibit an inventor from developing the same invention in another country and selling it there. Id. Nonetheless, the Patent Cooperation Treaty allows U.S. citizens to file for an "international" patent. Id. This "international" patent protects the invention for thirty months, which

gives U.S. citizens thirty months to file for patents in each country where the inventor wants to protect his or her invention. Id.

Under the Supreme Court's patent jurisprudence, "laws of nature, natural phenomena, and abstract ideas are not patentable." Mayo Collaborative Servs. v. Prometheus Laboratories, Inc., 566 U.S. 66, 70 (2012). The Court has explained that "a new mineral discovered in the earth or a new plant found in the wild is not patentable subject matter. Likewise, Einstein could not patent his celebrated law that $E=mc^2$; nor could Newton have patented the law of gravity. Such discoveries are 'manifestations of . . . nature, free to all men and reserved exclusively to none.'" Id. at 71.

In *Prometheus*, the Court addressed the question of whether a medical process that "help[s] doctors who use thiopurine drugs to treat patients with autoimmune diseases" by determining "whether a given dosage level is too low or too high" was patentable. Id. at 72. In the Court's opinion—written by Justice Stephen Breyer—the medical process was not patentable because "the steps in the claimed process (apart from the natural laws themselves) involve well-understood, routine, conventional activity previously engaged in by researchers in the field." Id. at 73. The Court recognized that "a process is not unpatentable simply because it contains a law of nature or a mathematical algorithm." Id. at 71. Instead, if a law of nature or a mathematical formula is *applied* to a known structure or process, it may be patentable. Id. Nevertheless, the Court emphasized: "to transform an unpatentable law of nature into a patent-eligible *application* of such a law, one must do more than simply state the law of nature while adding the words 'apply it.'" Id. at 72.

In *Prometheus*, the Court concluded that the thiopurine drug process was not patentable because it did not incorporate inventive, or non-obvious, concepts in its application of the law of nature. The Court ruled that "a process that focuses upon the use of a natural law also [must] contain other elements or a combination of elements, sometimes referred to as an 'inventive concept,' sufficient to ensure that the patent in practice amounts to significantly more than a patent upon the natural law itself." Id. The Court refused to allow the drug process to be patentable based on the fear that it "would risk disproportionately tying up the use of the underlying natural laws, inhibiting their use in the making of further discoveries." Id. at 73.

Prometheus provided the background for the Court's treatment of laws of nature as the issue of gene patents reached the Court. Starting in 1982, the U.S. Patent and Trademark Office began issuing patents on genetic materials. See Michael Franco, How Gene Patents Work, How Stuff Works, October 3, 2011. There are approximately "3,000 to 5,000 patents on human genes in the United States alone with another 47,000 on inventions involving genetic material." Id. "[G]enes can count as altered products of nature only if they have been removed from the body and processed in some way. The patent applies to that processed end

product." Id. Gene patents usually cover "a purified and isolated gene, the protein for which the gene codes, the correlation between mutations of the gene and disease, cells or biological entities that have been engineered to express the gene, and [or] the use of the gene or protein to detect or treat a disease or condition." Andrews, *infra*, at 195. According to Michael Franco,

> Gene patents break down generally into four categories: diagnostics, functional use, process and compositions of matter. These patents might be on a single gene, but more often than not, they are on a process involving genetic material or on a small strand of linked genes, and they generally focus on the parts of genes involved in the production of proteins.
>
> When it comes to diagnostics, gene researchers are looking to patent methods that test for genetic differences or abnormalities. These types of patents are occasionally referred to as disease gene patents, because they are most often associated with spotting genetic markers involved in ailments such as cancer, Alzheimer's disease and cystic fibrosis. Things get complicated in this category of gene patents because one gene can have many different mutations, or one test can analyze different genes for the same disease—and all of the different combinations of engineered mutations and tests can be patented.
>
> Functional use patents stem from research that discovers the roles played by various genes in causing disease in the body or in regulating bodily functions. These patents are typically issued for drugs which affect the functioning of genes.
>
> Process patents are relatively self-explanatory and are used to protect a method by which genes are extracted or manipulated. In the furor surrounding gene patenting, these types of patents are relatively benign, as they patent a process rather than actual human genetic material.
>
> Composition of matter patents are filed to protect "inventions" that generally stem from combining different genetic material and are typically filed for drugs and vaccines such as insulin and human growth hormone (HGH).

Franco, *infra*.

In the following case, *Myriad*, the Supreme Court considered whether Myriad Genetics, Inc. could patent two types of biological material, BRCA1 and BRCA2, which helped identify mutations that are linked to an increased hereditary risk for breast cancer and ovarian cancer. See Bill Mears, Court: Human Genes Cannot Be Patented, CNN, June 13, 2013.

Scientists study genes in order to determine how diseases are caused. By means of DNA sequencing, Myriad identified two genes,

BRCA1 and BRCA2, that cause breast and ovarian cancer. Myriad then received patents for the genes.

Because Myriad owned the patent on BRCA1 and BRCA2, "it was the only company that could perform tests for abnormalities." Id. The Plaintiffs in the case below, a group of patients, doctors and patient advocacy groups, challenged Myriad's patent as denying them access to medical procedures due to the high cost of the BRCA testing. Id. Each test could cost as much as $3,000. Although the procedure was costly, Myriad argued that it spent hundreds of millions of dollars and several years to develop its research. Id. As you read the Court's opinion, focus on the reasoning about the nature of the patents, the policies behind patents, and the Court's weighing of those policies. Can you understand the Court's treatment of the science? Does the Court's decision about patents protect the property interests of all involved in the development of research on BRCA1 and BRCA2?

Go to the website to understand the science behind the case.

Practice Exercise: Practice genetic sequencing on the website.

DNA sequencing is a central part of genetic research and is part of the *Myriad* opinion. It identifies the order in which the four bases (adenine, guanine, cytosine, and thymine) appear in a strand of DNA. The opinion below also distinguishes DNA from synthetic or complementary DNA (cDNA).

Association for Molecular Pathology v. Myriad Genetics, Inc.

United States Supreme Court, 2013.
569 U.S. 576, 133 S.Ct. 2107.

■ JUSTICE THOMAS delivered the opinion of the Court.

Respondent Myriad Genetics, Inc. (Myriad), discovered the precise location and sequence of two human genes, mutations of which can substantially increase the risks of breast and ovarian cancer. Myriad obtained a number of patents based upon its discovery. This case involves claims from three of them and requires us to resolve whether a naturally occurring segment of deoxyribonucleic acid (DNA) is patent eligible under 35 U.S.C. § 101 by virtue of its isolation from the rest of the human genome. We also address the patent eligibility of synthetically created DNA known as complementary DNA (cDNA), which contains the same protein-coding information found in a segment of natural DNA but omits portions within the DNA segment that do not code for proteins. For the reasons that follow, we hold that a naturally occurring DNA segment is a product of nature and not patent eligible merely because it has been

isolated, but that cDNA is patent eligible because it is not naturally occurring. We, therefore, affirm in part and reverse in part the decision of the United States Court of Appeals for the Federal Circuit.

I

A

Genes form the basis for hereditary traits in living organisms. The human genome consists of approximately 22,000 genes packed into 23 pairs of chromosomes. Each gene is encoded as DNA, which takes the shape of the familiar "double helix" that Doctors James Watson and Francis Crick first described in 1953. Each "cross-bar" in the DNA helix consists of two chemically joined nucleotides. The possible nucleotides are adenine (A), thymine (T), cytosine (C), and guanine (G), each of which binds naturally with another nucleotide: A pairs with T; C pairs with G. The nucleotide cross-bars are chemically connected to a sugar-phosphate backbone that forms the outside framework of the DNA helix. Sequences of DNA nucleotides contain the information necessary to create strings of amino acids, which in turn are used in the body to build proteins. Only some DNA nucleotides, however, code for amino acids; these nucleotides are known as "exons." Nucleotides that do not code for amino acids, in contrast, are known as "introns."

Creation of proteins from DNA involves two principal steps, known as transcription and translation. In transcription, the bonds between DNA nucleotides separate, and the DNA helix unwinds into two single strands. A single strand is used as a template to create a complementary ribonucleic acid (RNA) strand. The nucleotides on the DNA strand pair naturally with their counterparts, with the exception that RNA uses the nucleotide base uracil (U) instead of thymine (T). Transcription results in a single strand RNA molecule, known as pre-RNA, whose nucleotides form an inverse image of the DNA strand from which it was created. Pre-RNA still contains nucleotides corresponding to both the exons and introns in the DNA molecule. The pre-RNA is then naturally "spliced" by the physical removal of the introns. The resulting product is a strand of RNA that contains nucleotides corresponding only to the exons from the original DNA strand. The exons-only strand is known as messenger RNA (mRNA), which creates amino acids through translation. In translation, cellular structures known as ribosomes read each set of three nucleotides, known as codons, in the mRNA. Each codon either tells the ribosomes which of the 20 possible amino acids to synthesize or provides a stop signal that ends amino acid production.

DNA's informational sequences and the processes that create mRNA, amino acids, and proteins occur naturally within cells. Scientists can, however, extract DNA from cells using well known laboratory methods. These methods allow scientists to isolate specific segments of DNA—for instance, a particular gene or part of a gene—which can then be further studied, manipulated, or used. It is also possible to create DNA synthetically through processes similarly well known in the field of

genetics. One such method begins with an mRNA molecule and uses the natural bonding properties of nucleotides to create a new, synthetic DNA molecule. The result is the inverse of the mRNA's inverse image of the original DNA, with one important distinction: Because the natural creation of mRNA involves splicing that removes introns, the synthetic DNA created from mRNA also contains only the exon sequences. This synthetic DNA created in the laboratory from mRNA is known as complementary DNA (cDNA).

Changes in the genetic sequence are called mutations. Mutations can be as small as the alteration of a single nucleotide—a change affecting only one letter in the genetic code. Such small-scale changes can produce an entirely different amino acid or can end protein production altogether. Large changes, involving the deletion, rearrangement, or duplication of hundreds or even millions of nucleotides, can result in the elimination, misplacement, or duplication of entire genes. Some mutations are harmless, but others can cause disease or increase the risk of disease. As a result, the study of genetics can lead to valuable medical breakthroughs.

B

This case involves patents filed by Myriad after it made one such medical breakthrough. Myriad discovered the precise location and sequence of what are now known as the BRCA1 and BRCA2 genes. Mutations in these genes can dramatically increase an individual's risk of developing breast and ovarian cancer. The average American woman has a 12- to 13-percent risk of developing breast cancer, but for women with certain genetic mutations, the risk can range between 50 and 80 percent for breast cancer and between 20 and 50 percent for ovarian cancer. Before Myriad's discovery of the BRCA1 and BRCA2 genes, scientists knew that heredity played a role in establishing a woman's risk of developing breast and ovarian cancer, but they did not know which genes were associated with those cancers.

Myriad identified the exact location of the BRCA1 and BRCA2 genes on chromosomes 17 and 13. Chromosome 17 has approximately 80 million nucleotides, and chromosome 13 has approximately 114 million. Within those chromosomes, the BRCA1 and BRCA2 genes are each about 80,000 nucleotides long. If just exons are counted, the BRCA1 gene is only about 5,500 nucleotides long; for the BRCA2 gene, that number is about 10,200. Knowledge of the location of the BRCA1 and BRCA2 genes allowed Myriad to determine their typical nucleotide sequence. That information, in turn, enabled Myriad to develop medical tests that are useful for detecting mutations in a patient's BRCA1 and BRCA2 genes and thereby assessing whether the patient has an increased risk of cancer.

Once it found the location and sequence of the BRCA1 and BRCA2 genes, Myriad sought and obtained a number of patents. Nine composition claims from three of those patents are at issue in this case.

Claims 1, 2, 5, and 6 from the '282 patent are representative. The first claim asserts a patent on "[a]n isolated DNA coding for a BRCA1 polypeptide," which has "the amino acid sequence set forth in SEQ ID NO:2." App. 822. SEQ ID NO:2 sets forth a list of 1,863 amino acids that the typical BRCA1 gene encodes. See *id.*, at 785–790. Put differently, claim 1 asserts a patent claim on the DNA code that tells a cell to produce the string of BRCA1 amino acids listed in SEQ ID NO:2.

Claim 2 of the '282 patent operates similarly. It claims "[t]he isolated DNA of claim 1, wherein said DNA has the nucleotide sequence set forth in SEQ ID NO:1." Like SEQ ID NO:2, SEQ ID NO:1 sets forth a long list of data, in this instance the sequence of cDNA that codes for the BRCA1 amino acids listed in claim 1. Importantly, SEQ ID NO:1 lists only the cDNA exons in the BRCA1 gene, rather than a full DNA sequence containing both exons and introns. See *id.*, at 779 (stating that SEQ ID NO:1's "MOLECULE TYPE:" is "cDNA"). As a result, the Federal Circuit recognized that claim 2 asserts a patent on the cDNA nucleotide sequence listed in SEQ ID NO:1, which codes for the typical BRCA1 gene.

Claim 5 of the '282 patent claims a subset of the data in claim 1. In particular, it claims "[a]n isolated DNA having at least 15 nucleotides of the DNA of claim 1." The practical effect of claim 5 is to assert a patent on any series of 15 nucleotides that exist in the typical BRCA1 gene. Because the BRCA1 gene is thousands of nucleotides long, even BRCA1 genes with substantial mutations are likely to contain at least one segment of 15 nucleotides that correspond to the typical BRCA1 gene. Similarly, claim 6 of the '282 patent claims "[a]n isolated DNA having at least 15 nucleotides of the DNA of claim 2." This claim operates similarly to claim 5, except that it references the cDNA-based claim 2. The remaining claims at issue are similar, though several list common mutations rather than typical BRCA1 and BRCA2 sequences.

C

Myriad's patents would, if valid, give it the exclusive right to isolate an individual's BRCA1 and BRCA2 genes (or any strand of 15 or more nucleotides within the genes) by breaking the covalent bonds that connect the DNA to the rest of the individual's genome. The patents would also give Myriad the exclusive right to synthetically create BRCA cDNA. In Myriad's view, manipulating BRCA DNA in either of these fashions triggers its "right to exclude others from making" its patented composition of matter under the Patent Act.

But isolation is necessary to conduct genetic testing, and Myriad was not the only entity to offer BRCA testing after it discovered the genes. The University of Pennsylvania's Genetic Diagnostic Laboratory (GDL) and others provided genetic testing services to women. Petitioner Dr. Harry Ostrer, then a researcher at New York University School of Medicine, routinely sent his patients' DNA samples to GDL for testing. After learning of GDL's testing and Ostrer's activities, Myriad sent letters to them asserting that the genetic testing infringed Myriad's

patents. In response, GDL agreed to stop testing and informed Ostrer that it would no longer accept patient samples. Myriad also filed patent infringement suits against other entities that performed BRCA testing, resulting in settlements in which the defendants agreed to cease all allegedly infringing activity. Myriad, thus, solidified its position as the only entity providing BRCA testing.

Some years later, petitioner Ostrer, along with medical patients, advocacy groups, and other doctors, filed this lawsuit seeking a declaration that Myriad's patents are invalid under 35 U.S.C. § 101. . . .

With respect to the merits, the court held that both isolated DNA and cDNA were patent eligible under § 101. The central dispute among the panel members was whether the act of *isolating* DNA—separating a specific gene or sequence of nucleotides from the rest of the chromosome—is an inventive act that entitles the individual who first isolates it to a patent. Each of the judges on the panel had a different view on that question. Judges Lourie and Moore agreed that Myriad's claims were patent eligible under § 101 but disagreed on the rationale. Judge Lourie relied on the fact that the entire DNA molecule is held together by chemical bonds and that the covalent bonds at both ends of the segment must be severed in order to isolate segments of DNA. This process technically creates new molecules with unique chemical compositions. Judge Lourie found this chemical alteration to be dispositive, because isolating a particular strand of DNA creates a nonnaturally occurring molecule, even though the chemical alteration does not change the information-transmitting quality of the DNA. Accordingly, he rejected petitioners' argument that isolated DNA was ineligible for patent protection as a product of nature.

Judge Moore concurred in part but did not rely exclusively on Judge Lourie's conclusion that chemically breaking covalent bonds was sufficient to render isolated DNA patent eligible. Instead, Judge Moore also relied on the United States Patent and Trademark Office's (PTO) practice of granting such patents and on the reliance interests of patent holders. However, she acknowledged that her vote might have come out differently if she "were deciding this case on a blank canvas."

Finally, Judge Bryson concurred in part and dissented in part, concluding that isolated DNA is not patent eligible. As an initial matter, he emphasized that the breaking of chemical bonds was not dispositive: "[T]here is no magic to a chemical bond that requires us to recognize a new product when a chemical bond is created or broken." Instead, he relied on the fact that "[t]he nucleotide sequences of the claimed molecules are the same as the nucleotide sequences found in naturally occurring human genes." Judge Bryson then concluded that genetic "structural similarity dwarfs the significance of the structural differences between isolated DNA and naturally occurring DNA, especially where the structural differences are merely ancillary to the breaking of covalent bonds, a process that is itself not inventive." Moreover, Judge Bryson

gave no weight to the PTO's position on patentability because of the Federal Circuit's position that "the PTO lacks substantive rulemaking authority as to issues such as patentability."

Although the judges expressed different views concerning the patentability of isolated DNA, all three agreed that patent claims relating to cDNA met the patent eligibility requirements of § 101.

II

A

Section 101 of the Patent Act provides:

> "Whoever invents or discovers any new and useful . . . composition of matter, or any new and useful improvement thereof, may obtain a patent therefor, subject to the conditions and requirements of this title." 35 U.S.C. § 101.

We have "long held that this provision contains an important implicit exception[:] Laws of nature, natural phenomena, and abstract ideas are not patentable." Rather, " 'they are the basic tools of scientific and technological work' " that lie beyond the domain of patent protection. As the Court has explained, without this exception, there would be considerable danger that the grant of patents would "tie up" the use of such tools and thereby "inhibit future innovation premised upon them." This would be at odds with the very point of patents, which exist to promote creation.

The rule against patents on naturally occurring things is not without limits, however, for "all inventions at some level embody, use, reflect, rest upon, or apply laws of nature, natural phenomena, or abstract ideas," and "too broad an interpretation of this exclusionary principle could eviscerate patent law." As we have recognized before, patent protection strikes a delicate balance between creating "incentives that lead to creation, invention, and discovery" and "imped[ing] the flow of information that might permit, indeed spur, invention." We must apply this well-established standard to determine whether Myriad's patents claim any "new and useful . . . composition of matter," § 101, or instead claim naturally occurring phenomena.

B

It is undisputed that Myriad did not create or alter any of the genetic information encoded in the BRCA1 and BRCA2 genes. The location and order of the nucleotides existed in nature before Myriad found them. Nor did Myriad create or alter the genetic structure of DNA. Instead, Myriad's principal contribution was uncovering the precise location and genetic sequence of the BRCA1 and BRCA2 genes within chromosomes 17 and 13. The question is whether this renders the genes patentable.

Myriad recognizes that our decision in *Chakrabarty* is central to this inquiry. In *Chakrabarty,* scientists added four plasmids to a bacterium, which enabled it to break down various components of crude oil. The

Court held that the modified bacterium was patentable. It explained that the patent claim was "not to a hitherto unknown natural phenomenon, but to a nonnaturally occurring manufacture or composition of matter—a product of human ingenuity 'having a distinctive name, character [and] use.'" The *Chakrabarty* bacterium was new "with markedly different characteristics from any found in nature," due to the additional plasmids and resultant "capacity for degrading oil." In this case, by contrast, Myriad did not create anything. To be sure, it found an important and useful gene, but separating that gene from its surrounding genetic material is not an act of invention.

Groundbreaking, innovative, or even brilliant discovery does not by itself satisfy the § 101 inquiry. In *Funk Brothers Seed Co. v. Kalo Inoculant Co.,* 333 U.S. 127, 68 S.Ct. 440, 92 L.Ed. 588 (1948), this Court considered a composition patent that claimed a mixture of naturally occurring strains of bacteria that helped leguminous plants take nitrogen from the air and fix it in the soil. The ability of the bacteria to fix nitrogen was well known, and farmers commonly "inoculated" their crops with them to improve soil nitrogen levels. But farmers could not use the same inoculant for all crops, both because plants use different bacteria and because certain bacteria inhibit each other. Upon learning that several nitrogen-fixing bacteria did not inhibit each other, however, the patent applicant combined them into a single inoculant and obtained a patent. The Court held that the composition was not patent eligible because the patent holder did not alter the bacteria in any way. His patent claim thus fell squarely within the law of nature exception. So do Myriad's. Myriad found the location of the BRCA1 and BRCA2 genes, but that discovery, by itself, does not render the BRCA genes "new . . . composition[s] of matter," § 101, that are patent eligible.

Indeed, Myriad's patent descriptions highlight the problem with its claims. For example, a section of the '282 patent's Detailed Description of the Invention indicates that Myriad found the location of a gene associated with increased risk of breast cancer and identified mutations of that gene that increase the risk. In subsequent language Myriad explains that the location of the gene was unknown until Myriad found it among the approximately eight million nucleotide pairs contained in a subpart of chromosome 17. The '473 and '492 patents contain similar language as well. Many of Myriad's patent descriptions simply detail the "iterative process" of discovery by which Myriad narrowed the possible locations for the gene sequences that it sought. Myriad seeks to import these extensive research efforts into the § 101 patent-eligibility inquiry. But extensive effort alone is insufficient to satisfy the demands of § 101.

Nor are Myriad's claims saved by the fact that isolating DNA from the human genome severs chemical bonds and thereby creates a nonnaturally occurring molecule. Myriad's claims are simply not expressed in terms of chemical composition, nor do they rely in any way on the chemical changes that result from the isolation of a particular

section of DNA. Instead, the claims understandably focus on the genetic information encoded in the BRCA1 and BRCA2 genes. If the patents depended upon the creation of a unique molecule, then a would-be infringer could arguably avoid at least Myriad's patent claims on entire genes (such as claims 1 and 2 of the '282 patent) by isolating a DNA sequence that included both the BRCA1 or BRCA2 gene and one additional nucleotide pair. Such a molecule would not be chemically identical to the molecule "invented" by Myriad. But Myriad obviously would resist that outcome because its claim is concerned primarily with the information contained in the genetic *sequence,* not with the specific chemical composition of a particular molecule.

Finally, Myriad argues that the PTO's past practice of awarding gene patents is entitled to deference. We disagree. *J.E.M.* held that new plant breeds were eligible for utility patents under § 101 notwithstanding separate statutes providing special protections for plants. After analyzing the text and structure of the relevant statutes, the Court mentioned that the Board of Patent Appeals and Interferences had determined that new plant breeds were patent eligible under § 101 and that Congress had recognized and endorsed that position in a subsequent Patent Act amendment. In this case, however, Congress has not endorsed the views of the PTO in subsequent legislation. While Myriad relies on Judge Moore's view that Congress endorsed the PTO's position in a single sentence in the Consolidated Appropriations Act of 2004, that Act does not even mention genes, much less isolated DNA.

Further undercutting the PTO's practice, the United States argued in the Federal Circuit and in this Court that isolated DNA was *not* patent eligible under § 101, and that the PTO's practice was not "a sufficient reason to hold that isolated DNA is patent-eligible." These concessions weigh against deferring to the PTO's determination.

C

cDNA does not present the same obstacles to patentability as naturally occurring, isolated DNA segments. As already explained, creation of a cDNA sequence from mRNA results in an exons-only molecule that is not naturally occurring. Petitioners concede that cDNA differs from natural DNA in that "the non-coding regions have been removed." They nevertheless argue that cDNA is not patent eligible because "[t]he nucleotide sequence of cDNA is dictated by nature, not by the lab technician." That may be so, but the lab technician unquestionably creates something new when cDNA is made. cDNA retains the naturally occurring exons of DNA, but it is distinct from the DNA from which it was derived. As a result, cDNA is not a "product of nature" and is patent eligible under § 101, except insofar as very short series of DNA may have no intervening introns to remove when creating cDNA. In that situation, a short strand of cDNA may be indistinguishable from natural DNA.

III

It is important to note what is *not* implicated by this decision. First, there are no method claims before this Court. Had Myriad created an innovative method of manipulating genes while searching for the BRCA1 and BRCA2 genes, it could possibly have sought a method patent. But the processes used by Myriad to isolate DNA were well understood by geneticists at the time of Myriad's patents "were well understood, widely used, and fairly uniform insofar as any scientist engaged in the search for a gene would likely have utilized a similar approach," and are not at issue in this case.

Similarly, this case does not involve patents on new *applications* of knowledge about the BRCA1 and BRCA2 genes. Judge Bryson aptly noted that, "[a]s the first party with knowledge of the [BRCA1 and BRCA2] sequences, Myriad was in an excellent position to claim applications of that knowledge. Many of its unchallenged claims are limited to such applications."

Nor do we consider the patentability of DNA in which the order of the naturally occurring nucleotides has been altered. Scientific alteration of the genetic code presents a different inquiry, and we express no opinion about the application of § 101 to such endeavors. We merely hold that genes and the information they encode are not patent eligible under § 101 simply because they have been isolated from the surrounding genetic material.

* * *

For the foregoing reasons, the judgment of the Federal Circuit is affirmed in part and reversed in part.

It is so ordered.

■ JUSTICE SCALIA, concurring in part and concurring in the judgment.

I join the judgment of the Court, and all of its opinion except Part I-A and some portions of the rest of the opinion going into fine details of molecular biology. I am unable to affirm those details on my own knowledge or even my own belief. It suffices for me to affirm, having studied the opinions below and the expert briefs presented here, that the portion of DNA isolated from its natural state sought to be patented is identical to that portion of the DNA in its natural state; and that complementary DNA (cDNA) is a synthetic creation not normally present in nature.

NOTES AND QUESTIONS

1. *Myriad Decision.* In Myriad, the Court held that the BRCA1 and BRCA2 genes are considered naturally occurring DNA sequences. Consequently, even when isolated from the body, they cannot be patented because they are products of nature. However, the Court allowed artificially

created DNA to be patent eligible because artificial DNA is not naturally occurring.

a. *Creation or Modification.* Justice Clarence Thomas, who wrote the majority opinion, noted the distinction between natural genes and natural genes that have been modified or genes that have been created. Justice Thomas wrote, when comparing *Myriad* to *Chakrabarty*: "In this case, by contrast, Myriad did not create anything. To be sure, it found an important and useful gene, but separating that gene from its surrounding genetic material is not an act of invention." Compare the facts of *Myriad* to those of *Chakrabarty* and *Funk Brothers*. Why were the *Chakrabarty* bacteria patentable while the *Funk Brothers* bacteria were not? Do you think the *Myriad* facts are more analogous to those of *Chakrabarty* or *Funk Brothers?* How does Justice Thomas answer that question?

b. *Method Patents.* Why didn't Myriad apply for a method patent in this case? Instead of trying to patent the gene, do you think Myriad should have tried to patent the process for finding the gene? What do you think the Court would have been more receptive to?

c. *Scalia's Concurrence.* In his concurrence, Justice Antonin Scalia refused to join the opinion discussing the detailed biology of the genes. However, he felt that the briefs presented and the opinions below gave him sufficient information to make a decision on the rest of the Court's holding. Do you think Part I-A would be too complex for you to join if you were a Justice of the United States Supreme Court? Would you feel comfortable relying only on the information provided by the lower courts and briefs?

Do you agree with Seventh Circuit Judge Richard Posner's criticism that Justice Scalia should "learn a little science"? According to Posner,

> Part I-A of the majority opinion attempts a brief explanation of the basics of genetic biology. It is dense with scientific jargon and would be largely unintelligible to a nonscientist unwilling to look up the terms and maybe consult an elementary textbook on genetics. One might expect a judge to be willing to make the rather modest investment in time and intellectual effort required to puzzle out the majority's description. Yet some commentators, rather than criticizing Scalia for being unwilling to do so, have commended him for candor in acknowledging his scientific ignorance.
>
> But if Justice Scalia was unwilling to make the necessary effort to understand the discussion of genetics in the majority opinion, how was he able to understand the discussion of genetics in the lower-court opinions or the friend-of-the-court briefs submitted by experts such as

> James Watson, the co-discoverer of the double helix, the foundation of modern genetic theory? I have dipped into what Scalia calls the "expert" briefs, and their discussions of genetics tend to be as technical as the most technical parts of the majority opinion. So if Scalia understood those discussions, why wouldn't that enable him to understand the discussion of genetics in the majority opinion? If he didn't understand the briefs, on what basis could he join the decision?
>
> Although Scalia may be the extreme case, the justices of the Supreme Court (Justice Breyer may be the only exception), and federal judges generally (state judges as well), tend to be uncomfortable with science and technology. Scalia's discomfort with biochemistry seems of a piece with his embrace of "familiar tools of textual interpretation"—familiar to judges because the tools do not require any scientific understanding. But neither can they replace a willingness to learn a bit of science, at least.

Richard A. Posner, Can't Justice Scalia Learn a Little Science?, Slate, June 24, 2013. Do you think Posner is right that there is a conflict between being able to understand the lower-courts and amicus briefs, but not the majority opinion? Do you think Justices should look only at the facts presented? Or, do you think Justices should do independent research, like Posner suggests? If so, how much independent research do you think the Supreme Court Justices must do in a case if they do not understand the issues presented?

How would Scalia's concurrence and Posner's commentary influence the way you litigate cases involving science?

What do you think of a proposed congressional revision to Section 101, which states, "The provisions of section 101 shall be construed in favor of eligibility. No implicit or other judicially created exceptions to subject matter eligibility, including 'abstract ideas,' 'laws of nature,' or 'natural phenomena,' shall be used to determine patent eligibility under section 101, and all cases establishing or interpreting those exceptions to eligibility are hereby abrogated"? Kelly Servick, Controversial U.S. Bill Would Lift Supreme Court Ban on Patenting Human Genes, Science Mag., Jun. 4, 2019, https://www.sciencemag.org/news/2019/06/controversial-us-bill-would-lift-supreme-court-ban-patenting-human-genes. Would such a change in the law be good or bad for patients? For researchers? For the health care industry?

2. *Public Awareness*. Genetic testing can provide many benefits. Take the story of actress and director Angelina Jolie, for example. Jolie's mother died of breast cancer at age 56. Angelina Jolie, My Medical Choice, N.Y. Times, May 14, 2013, at A25. After her mother's death, Jolie got tested through Myriad's patented procedure to see if she carried the defect in the gene, BRCA1, which is responsible for increasing the chances of developing breast and ovarian cancer (remember BRCA1 and BRCA2 are the same

genes that the Myriad decision discussed patenting). Id. Jolie did have the defect and doctors said that carrying that defect gave her a 50 percent chance of developing ovarian cancer and an 87 percent chance of developing breast cancer. Id. Women who have the mutation have about a 65 percent chance of getting breast cancer, where most women are at 12 percent. Denise Grady et al., Jolie's Disclosure of Preventative Mastectomy Highlights Dilemma, N.Y. Times, May 14, 2014, at A1. Due to her increased chances of developing cancer, Jolie decided to take preventive measures and attempt to minimize her chances by undergoing a double mastectomy. Angelina Jolie, My Medical Choice, N.Y. Times, May 14, 2013, at A25. The double mastectomy consisted of three separate procedures. Id. After the three procedures, Jolie was very satisfied with how they left her looking and, more importantly, the procedures decreased her risk of developing breast cancer from 87 percent to under 5 percent. Id.

According to the World Health Organization, breast cancer kills around 458,000 people every year. Id. Testing for the defects in genes can help minimize the risks for many women. Id. However, before the *Myriad* decision, the cost of testing for such defects was more than $3,000 in the United States. Id. This cost created an obstacle for women who generally cannot afford such testing. Id. Post-*Myriad*, testing costs are now as low as $300. Anna Farias-Eisner, Patenting Human Genes Violates Laws of Nature, Impedes Patient Care, Stifles Research, and Inhibits Long-Term Business Opportunities, 35 Nw. J. Int'l L. & Bus. Ambassador 1A, 20A (2014). Does this change in price convince you that *Myriad* was correctly decided?

Jolie's disclosure and open acknowledgment of cancer has empowered women to take their own preventative measures. Id. However, some doctors worry that public exposure to preventative mastectomies could start a trend among women to get mastectomies that are not medically necessary. Grady et al., *supra*. Jolie's case was unique and mutations of her kind are rare, but some women believe that their risk of new or recurring cancer is much higher than it really is. Id. Doctors do not want women to automatically jump to surgery because there are other procedures to diminish the risk of getting cancer. Id. This is especially true due to the high cost of the screening for the mutations. Id. What some doctors hope women took away from Jolie's article is that there are tremendous benefits in genetic counseling to ensure the mother is not passing the mutation to her children. Id. Additionally, there are options for in vitro fertilizations to have the embryos screened for the mutation prior to getting them implanted. Id.

Do you think you would remove a body part to combat a disease? Do you think genetic testing would help combat cancer? Do you think that genetic testing should be patented? Would that make getting screened more or less expensive? Would you consider genetic counseling?

Two years after writing about her mastectomies, Jolie wrote another op-ed describing the removal of her ovaries and fallopian tubes, surgeries that force menopause. Angelina Jolie Pitt, Diary of a Surgery, N.Y. Times, Mar. 24, 2015, at A23. Jolie explained that women have a number of nonsurgical options when faced with BRCA1 gene mutations. She opted for surgery

because three women in her family—her mother, her aunt and her grandmother—had died from similar cancers. Ovarian cancer is more difficult to detect than breast cancer. Many doctors think Jolie's choice was the smartest one for her health. Can you imagine having so many preventive surgeries?

3. *Genetic Testing.* As the experience of Angelina Jolie and the plaintiffs in *Myriad* demonstrates, individuals undergo genetic testing to determine if they have the genetic makeup that makes it more likely for them to have a disease such as breast cancer or Huntington's disease. Genetic testing examines the DNA of a person's cells, looking for changes or mutations in a person's genes as well as the number and placement of chromosomes that may cause medical problems. Who should have genetic testing? Should all women be genetically tested, or just those whose family history indicates a history of breast or ovarian cancer?

Go to the website and consider who should seek genetic testing. Does the HGP chart help you to understand what information genetic testing might provide? Is BCM's consent form to genetic testing adequate?

Pregnant women may also choose genetic testing for their fetus. Should all women arrange genetic testing before the child is born, or only those with a family history of genetic diseases? What about after the child is born? Imagine that Jane has tested positive for BRCA and that her sisters have had breast cancer. Jane takes her 6-month-old daughter Emily to the pediatrician and asks for BRCA testing for Emily. The pediatrician explains that predictive genetic testing for an adult-onset disease is not in Emily's best interests because Emily should be allowed to make the choice, as an adult, whether she wants the testing. Some adults prefer not to know their genetic status, and Emily might be harmed by learning that she is at risk of a disease. Jane is very anxious and prefers to know if Emily has BRCA. See Lainie Friedman Ross, Predictive Genetic Testing of Children and the Role of the Best Interest Standard, 41 J.L. Med. & Ethics 899, 903 (Winter 2013).

Should the pediatrician refuse to test Emily? Should the physician enjoy a right of conscience not to test Emily, as we discussed in Chapter 5? Does it depend on whether there are any steps that could be taken during Emily's childhood to address the condition, such as additional screenings or therapeutic interventions? Does this situation confirm that Jane should have tested Emily prenatally? Id. at 904. Does this situation demonstrate the importance of direct-to-consumer (DTC) testing, where Jane can choose to purchase a genetic test without going through the pediatrician? Or will Jane get the best information and treatment by following her pediatrician's advice? Id.

Widespread genetic testing became possible because of the success of the 13-year-long Human Genome Project (HGP), a federally funded project that was completed in 2003. HGP's goals were to "*identify* all the approximately 20,500 genes in human DNA, *determine* the sequences of the 3 billion chemical base pairs that make up human DNA, *store* this

information in databases, *improve* tools for data analysis, *transfer* related technologies to the private sector, and *address* the ethical, legal, and social issues (ELSI) that may arise from the project. Human Genome Project Information Archive 1990–2003, http://web.ornl.gov/sci/techresources/Human_Genome/index.shtml. There are now over 26,000 genetic tests available for 5,400 conditions, including colon, endometrial, and pancreatic cancer, as well as Alzheimer's and Parkinson's diseases. Elizabeth Cohen, Learning From Angelina Jolie's Genetic Testing for Our Own Health, CNN, Mar. 25, 2015, at http://www.cnn.com/2015/03/25/health/cohen-angelina-jolie-genetic-tests/.

The Genetic Information Nondiscrimination Act of 2008 (GINA), Pub. L. No. 110–233, 122 Stat. 881, prohibits genetic-information discrimination in health insurance and employment. Health insurers may not use genetic information to determine eligibility for insurance coverage and employers may not hire, fire or otherwise disadvantage employees on the basis of that information. See Jessica L. Roberts, Preempting Discrimination: Lessons from the Genetic Information Nondiscrimination Act, 63 Vand. L. Rev. 439, 451–52 (2010). Would the existence of GINA make you more comfortable in deciding to have genetic testing?

Go to the website and listen to the oral argument in *Myriad* starting at minute 32.

4. *Myriad Oral Argument*. How would you make the science clear to the Justices if you were arguing *Myriad*? What could you have done to help even Justice Scalia understand the science? Would you use videos and pictures like the ones with which we started this section? Could you argue by analogy?

5. *Follow-Up Litigation*. After the Supreme Court decided *Myriad,* several companies announced plans to make less expensive BRCA1 and BRCA2 testing available to consumers. Myriad went back to court arguing that companies providing BRCA testing were infringing other Myriad patents not covered by the Court's opinion. The district court ruled that, although Myriad was likely to suffer irreparable harm without an injunction, it was unlikely to succeed on the merits of its claim. The court therefore refused to enjoin the other companies from offering the less expensive tests. In re BRCA1-, BRCA2-Based Hereditary Cancer Test Patent Litig., 3 F. Supp. 3d 1213 (D. Utah Mar. 10, 2014); In re BRCA1- & BRCA2-Based Hereditary Cancer Test Patent Litig., 774 F.3d 755 (Fed. Cir. 2014).

Practice Exercise: As you're listening to the *Myriad* oral argument, write down each analogy as you hear it made by the advocates or Justices. Then, decide which analogies were most effective and least effective and why.

Myriad argued that it had Primer and Method Claims that prevented the defendants from testing for breast cancer. A primer is a short, isolated strand of DNA that starts DNA synthesis. Can you figure out why the district

court decided primers are patent ineligible products of nature? See In re BRCA–1, 3 F. Supp. 3d at 1264 ("Primers Claims are directed to compositions structurally similar to the DNA found in nature" and "are likewise similar in utility to naturally occurring DNA"); id. at 1266 ("Like the primers at issue here, the isolate DNA compositions Myriad claimed in *AMP* were 'nonnaturally occurring,' but were drawn to natural genes and their sequences—'the information they encode.' ").

The Method Claims involved Myriad's processes of comparing a patient's BRCA1 and BRCA2 genes to normal samples. The court ruled that there was nothing inventive in those processes and therefore the methods claims were patent ineligible. Id. at 1267. Can you see why the *Prometheus* decision, explained above, was relevant to this ruling? Is comparing genes inventive? Is comparing genes an abstract idea? The Federal Circuit affirmed the district court's ruling. In re BRCA1- & BRCA2-Based Hereditary Cancer Test Patent Litig., 774 F.3d 755 (Fed. Cir. 2014).

The Federal Circuit analyzed a patent claim about hepatocytes and multiple freeze-thaw cycles. Hepatocytes are liver cells that are useful for testing, diagnosis, and treatment. They help researchers understand how drugs are used by the liver or how toxic the drugs are. The supply of hepatocytes is limited and their life is short. Originally people thought the cells could be frozen only once. Then the '929 patent holders discovered the cells could be frozen several times. The district court found the patent invalid, but the appeals court reversed. The court asked "whether the claims here are 'directed to a patent-ineligible concept.' " Rapid Litigation Management v. CellzDirect, 827 F,3d 1042, 1047 (Fed. Cir. 2016). The district court said yes, they were, because they involved an "ineligible law of nature" showing that hepatocytes could survive several freezing cycles. Id. The circuit disagreed because the patent was "directed to a new and useful laboratory technique for preserving hepatocytes. This type of constructive process, carried out by an artisan to achieve 'a new and useful end,' is precisely the type of claim that is eligible for patenting." Id. at 1048. This case was distinguishable from *Myriad* because there was no innovative method in that case, but there was in the liver cells case. Do you understand the difference?

6. *Settlement.* After its losses in the Utah District Court and the Federal Circuit, Myriad settled its infringement cases. Both sides agreed to drop claims and counterclaims against each other, and Myriad will stop any lawsuits for patent infringement regarding BRCA testing. Andrew Pollack, Myriad Genetics Ending Patent Dispute on Breast Cancer Risk, N.Y. Times, Jan. 27, 2015, at http://www.nytimes.com/2015/01/28/business/myriad-genetics-ending-patent-dispute-on-breast-cancer-risk-testing.html. Was this a fair result for Myriad? For consumers?

7. *COVID-19 and Patents.* COVID reminds us that "[w]hen patents relate to medical technologies this has the *potential* for significant implications for human health." See Aisling McMahon, Covid-19, Patents & Healthcare: The Need for A (Bio)ethics Space within Patent Law, Journal of Medical Ethics, Apr. 16, 2020, https://blogs.bmj.com/medical-ethics/2020/04/16/covid-19-patents-healthcare-the-need-for-a-bioethics-space-within-

patent-law/. In one lawsuit, a company holding rights to two Theranos patents sued another company, arguing it was infringing its patents as it worked on COVID-19 tests. The suit was later withdrawn. Another patent holder challenged the use of a 3D printing ventilator for COVID treatment, although those claims were successfully denied by the patent holder. People are also asking whether robust patent protections could make future treatments or vaccines for COVID more expensive and therefore blocked for some users. The Open-Covid Pledge "encourages patent holders to make intellectual property (including patents) available free of charge for use in ending Covid-19, and the World Health Organisation has endorsed the development of a voluntary pool of patented technology related to Covid-19." Id. Initial opposition came primarily from the United States, United Kingdom, Russia, China, and France, countries that are home to some of the largest health care research and production entities and consequently rely heavily on health care industry revenue. As a political matter it is difficult to overcome the focus on profits, especially in countries where the pharmaceutical industry lobbies extensively and has significant government support. Sarah Boseley, US and UK "Lead Push against Global Patent Pool for Covid-19 Drugs," The Guardian, May 17, 2020, https://www.theguardian.com/world/2020/may/17/us-and-uk-lead-push-against-global-patent-pool-for-covid-19-drugs.

In May 2021, President Biden announced that he was willing to waive patent protection for COVID-19 drugs. The United States trade representative said, "The administration believes strongly in intellectual property protections, but in service of ending this pandemic, supports the waiver of those protections for COVID-19 vaccines." Thomas Kaplan and Sheryl Gay Stolberg, The Biden administration says it will support lifting patent protections to help produce more vaccinates globally, N.Y. Times, https://www.nytimes.com/live/2021/05/05/world/covid-vaccine-coronavirus-cases#covid-vaccine-patent-biden. Do you agree with the Biden administration's position on waiving patents? Does COVID change the way you think about patents?

8. Consumer Watchdog v. WARF. After the Supreme Court's holding in *Myriad*—striking down genetic patents on the ground that the patents claimed were mere "products of nature"—the Court had another opportunity to extend or clarify the *Myriad* rule. See Hank Greely, *Myriad* Decision Invoked in Appeal of Suit to Invalidate Embryonic Stem Cell Patent Claims, Stanford Law School: Center for Law & Biosciences, Blog, July 4, 2013, available at https://law.stanford.edu/2013/07/04/lawandbiosciences-2013-07-04-myriad-decision-invoked-in-appeal-of-suit-to-invalidate-embryonic-stem-cell-patent-claims/. In *Consumer Watchdog v. Wisconsin Alumni Research Foundation* ("*WARF*"), adult stem cell researchers challenged the patentability of WARF's human embryonic stem cells lines, claiming that the *Myriad* rationale renders the stem cells "products of nature" and therefore not patentable. Id.

Consumer Watchdog claimed that the human embryonic stem cell lines are considered obvious to researchers in that field. Id. The Patent and Trademark Office Board ruled that the stem cell lines were considered obvious, and, thus, unpatentable. Id. However, on appeal, the Examiner and the Board ruled that the stem cell lines were patentable—leading to the appeal before the United States Court of Appeals for the Federal Circuit. Id. In addition to the obviousness argument, Consumer Watchdog argued that the ruling in *Myriad* prohibits patents on products of nature, while WARF's patents involve characteristics that are present in all human embryonic stem cells. Id.

Go to the website and read the stem cell patent at issue to fully understand the issues presented in Consumer Watchdog. This is a good opportunity for you to see what a patent application looks like. Rely on what you learned about stem cells in Chapter 5 to try to understand the science. Focus on the brief summary of the invention at pages 55–56 of the patent application.

9. *Brief for Consumer Watchdog*. Now that you have an understanding of the background issues in the case, read the Appellant's Opening Brief. When reading the brief, ask yourself: What are the strongest arguments for Appellant? Does the argument correctly interpret *Myriad*? If you were on the Federal Circuit Court of Appeals, would you find the human embryonic stem cells patentable or not? How much difference would it make to consumers if the stem cells could not be patented?

Practice Exercise: After reading the stem cell patent at issue, make an argument that this patent involves a product of nature and an argument that it does not involve a product of nature. Who should win the lawsuit?

Consumer Watchdog v. Wisconsin Alumni Research Foundation

United States Court of Appeals for the Federal Circuit, 2013.
Appellant's Opening Brief, No. 2013–1377, July 2, 2013.

STATEMENT OF THE ISSUES

Whether an in vitro culture of human embryonic stem cells is patent eligible under 35 U.S.C. § 101.

Whether claims to an in vitro culture of human embryonic stem cells are anticipated or rendered obvious by prior art that discloses methods for deriving and maintaining mammalian embryonic stem cells that one of ordinary skill in the art would have expected would produce human embryonic stem cells if used with human embryos.

STATEMENT OF THE CASE

Appellant Consumer Watchdog ("CW") is a not-for-profit public charity dedicated to providing a voice for taxpayers and consumers in special interest-dominated public discourse, government and politics. Appellee Wisconsin Alumni Research Foundation ("WARF") is the assignee of U.S. Patent No. 7,029,913 issued April 18, 2006 ("the '913 patent"), entitled "Primate Embryonic Stem Cells." The '913 patent's three claims cover in vitro cultures of human embryonic stem ("hES") cells that are not markedly different from naturally occurring hES cells.

WARF's broad and aggressive assertion of the '913 patent has put a severe burden on taxpayer-funded research in the State of California where CW is located. Concerned that the '913 patent gives WARF the potential to completely preempt all uses of hES cells, including particularly for scientific and medical research, CW filed a request for *inter partes* reexamination of the '913 patent on July 17, 2006.

In its request, CW explained how prior art available at the time the '913 patent was filed provided step-by-step directions for the derivation and maintenance of mammalian embryonic stem cells. As such, the three claims of the '913 patent directed to hES cells were obvious in light of that prior art because one of ordinary skill in the art of ES cell derivation would expect that the same process for deriving other mammalian ES cells could also be used to derive hES cells. At minimum, it was obvious to try the known mammalian ES cell techniques with human embryos.

The PTO Board first agreed with CW that the claims were all invalid as anticipated by and obvious in light of the prior art. But it later flip-flopped and upheld the claims based, in part, on a biased and flawed declaration submitted by an expert retained by WARF that was not questioned by the Board or CW and several errors regarding secondary considerations of obviousness. The Board never considered whether the claims to hES cells are patent eligible subject matter. CW now appeals to this Court to rule that each of the '913 patent's claims is invalid.

STATEMENT OF FACTS

Embryonic stem ("ES") cells are cells from the cellular structure formed in the early gestation of vertebrates called a blastocyst. ES cells are "pluripotent" in that they retain the ability to differentiate into all of the various cell types that form a more mature (non-embryonic) organism. ES cells can be cultured and manipulated in vitro and then returned to the embryonic environment to contribute normally to the development of a mature organism. As such, ES cells have substantial potential for medical research and clinical purposes.

The '913 patent claims a replicating culture (i.e. cluster) of pluripotent hES cells and has an effective filing date of January 20, 1995. A164. At that time, much was already known about ES cells, as several publications had already taught how to create and maintain ES cells of various species.

For example, U.S. Patent No. 5,166,065, issued November 24, 1995 to Robert L. Williams et al. ("Williams") taught methods for isolating and maintaining mammalian ES cells in vitro. Williams first taught specific methods for isolating ES cells from embryos of humans, mice, birds, sheep, pigs, cattle, goats and fish. Williams specified that feeder cells may or may not be present in the culture medium in which isolation takes place. Second, Williams taught a process for maintaining the same animal ES cells in vitro while retaining their pluripotency, again in culture medium that may or may not contain feeder cells. Williams exemplified its methods with derivation of ES cells from murine (mouse) blastocysts using two different processes, one of which involved first letting the blastocyst attach to the culture dish and grow for a week and the other of which involved immunosurgery, or isolating the cells of the inner cell mass (ICM) of the embryo prior to culture. In both methods, the cells were then dissociated and cultured.

Other researchers also contributed significantly to the body of stem cell knowledge before 1995. Examples include two publications authored by Robertson, one by Piedrahita, and a patent naming Hogan as the inventor.

Hogan described human, pluripotent ES cells derived from germ cells. Piedrahita described protocols for isolating ES cells from murine, ovine (sheep) and porcine (pig) embryos. Robertson '83 described isolation of pluripotent cells from blastocysts of mice. Robertson '87 described the same two methods of producing ES cells described in Williams, one prescribing the transfer of intact blastocysts into culture for a limited period of continued growth and the other prescribing immunosurgery, both followed by dissociation and culture in conditioned medium. Robertson '87 stressed that "feeder layers are absolutely essential for both the isolation of stem cell lines from embryos and for the routine maintenance of established cell lines."

It is undisputed that interest in hES cells was high at the time the '913 patent was filed. However, much of the ES cell research prior to that time, including most of the examples above, attempted to advance hES cell research by using cells from other species. The reason for using non-human cells was two-fold. First, the use of human embryos in research was, and continues to be, controversial. Many countries even made such research illegal. Human embryos were therefore scarce and difficult to obtain for research. Second, funding to support hES cell research was also extremely scarce in the mid-to-late 1990s.

Dr. James A. Thomson at the University of Wisconsin was one of the lucky few stem cell researchers who managed to obtain both funding for hES cell research and human embryos with which to work. At a time when the federal government was not funding ES cell research, Geron Corporation funded Thomson's laboratory. Thomson obtained human embryos through an Israeli colleague, Itskovitz-Eldor, who in 1997 sent Thomson frozen embryos donated from Israeli couples in IVF clinics.

Thomson's unique access to human embryos provided him the rare opportunity to succeed in isolating hES cells, and four of the five hES cell lines Thomson's team first described in 1998 came from the Israeli embryos.

Thomson is listed as the sole inventor of the '913 patent, entitled "Primate Embryonic Stem Cells." Claim 1, the only independent claim, as amended reads:

> 1. (Amended) A replicating in vitro cell culture of pluripotent human embryonic stem cells derived from a pre-implantation embryo, wherein the stem cells (i) will proliferate in an in vitro culture for over one year in an undifferentiated state without the application of exogenous leukemia inhibitory factor, (ii) maintain a karyotype in which the chromosomes are euploid through prolonged culture, (iii) maintain the potential to differentiate to derivatives of endoderm, mesoderm, and ectoderm tissues throughout the culture, and (iv) are inhibited from differentiation when cultured on a fibroblast feeder layer.

Claims 2 and 3 are dependent on claim 1 and were not separately argued during the reexamination process, as they do not add limitations that affect the validity analysis. As is evident from the claim language, the '913 patent claims a culture of hES cells itself, not a method of producing such hES cells.

As noted above, Thomson was able to work with hES cells when most of his colleagues in the field could not. But when he filed the application in January 1995 that eventually resulted in the '913 patent, he had not yet received the human embryos from which he first isolated hES cell lines. Thus, the '913 specification, which described Thomson's process for isolating and maintaining hES cells of the type claimed in the '913 patent, was written years before Dr. Thomson actually isolated hES cells. The cell lines described in the patent are exemplified by the isolation of ES cell lines from two non-human primate species, the marmoset and the rhesus monkey. Thus, Thomson claimed hES cells even though he had not yet made them. Instead, he had made ES cells of other mammals and used that as a basis to claim he could make hES cells.

Thomson described the method by which he obtained the monkey cell lines as follows:

> The present invention is also a method of isolating a primate embryonic stem cell line. The method comprises the steps of isolating a primate blastocyst, isolating cells from the inner cellular mass (ICM) of the blastocyst, plating the ICM cells on a fibroblast layer (wherein ICM-derived cell masses are formed) removing an ICM-derived cell mass and dissociating the mass into dissociated cells, replating the dissociated cells on embryonic feeder cells and selecting colonies with compact morphology containing cells with a high nucleus/cytoplasm

ratio, and prominent nucleoli. The cells of the selected colony are then cultured.

In the '913 patent, Thomson acknowledged the body of ES cell knowledge that came before his research. For example, Thomson describes how the colony morphology of his monkey cell lines compares to that of mouse ES cells:

> The colony morphology of primate embryonic stem cell lines is similar to, but distinct from, mouse embryonic stem cells. Both mouse and primate ES cells have the characteristic features of undifferentiated stem cells, with high nuclear/cytoplasmic ratios, prominent nucleoli, and compact colony formation. The colonies of primate ES cells are flatter than mouse ES cell colonies and individual primate ES cells can be easily distinguished.

Thomson also wrote about ES cells that had been isolated in other species:

> Strong evidence of [the properties required of true ES cells] have been published only for rodents ES cells including mouse, hamster, and rat, and less conclusively for rabbit ES cells. However, only established ES cell lines from the rat and the mouse have been reported to participate in normal development in chimeras.

Multiple stem cell researchers succeeded in producing hES cells as claimed in the '913 patent following methods known in the art for mouse, rat, pig and sheep ES cells, such as methods taught in Robertson '83 and '87 and Piedrahita, before Thomson filed his patent. They did not depend on Thomson's publications for their success.

Believing that these facts rendered all three claims of the '913 patent invalid. CW requested *inter partes* reexamination of the '913 patent on July 17, 2006. After granting the request for reexamination, the Examiner found all of the pending claims allowable. CW appealed to the Board of Patent Appeals and Interferences (now known as the Patent Trial Appeal Board). The Board reversed the Examiner's decision on April 29, 2010 ("Reversal") and designated new grounds of rejection, entitling WARF to reopen prosecution. The Board's rejections were as follows:

1. Claims 1–3 under 35 U.S.C. § 102(b) as anticipated by, or in the alternative, under 35 U.S.C. § 103(a) as obvious based on, Williams;

2. Claims 1–3 under 35 U.S.C. § 103(a) as obvious based on Robertson '83, Robertson '87, Williams, and Hogan;

3. Claims 1–3 under 35 U.S.C. § 103(a) as obvious based on Piedrahita, Williams, and Hogan; and

4. Claims 1–3 under 35 U.S.C. § 103(a) as obvious based on Robertson '83, Robertson '87, Piedrahita, Williams, and Hogan.

WARF filed a Request to Reopen Prosecution along with an amendment and new evidence. In response, the Examiner determined that the claims were patentable over the rejections made by the Board. On January 22, 2013, the Board affirmed the Examiner. ("Affirmance"). CW now appeals.

SUMMARY OF ARGUMENT

As a threshold matter, the claims of the '913 patent are invalid under 35 U.S.C. § 101 for claiming subject matter that is not patent eligible. Specifically, the claimed hES cell culture falls within the "product of nature" exception to statutory subject matter. It is within the Court's discretion to address this issue despite the fact that the Board failed to address it below, and is especially appropriate in light of the recent Supreme Court ruling on Section 101 in *Ass'n. for Molecular Pathology v. Myriad Genetics, Inc.*, 2013 U.S. LEXIS 4540 (June 13, 2013).

The '913 patent's claims are also invalid because they were anticipated by Williams. The Board erred in finding that Williams did not teach the "cultured on a fibroblast feeder layer" claim limitation, as Williams expressly teaches using feeder cells during isolation. The Board's dependence on a biased and unchallenged declaration submitted by WARF late in these proceedings to interpret Williams in a manner inconsistent with its express teaching was legal error.

The '913 patent's claims are also invalid because they were obvious in light of the numerous prior art teachings of ways to derive and maintain ES cells of several mammalian species. Each of the four reasons cited by the Board to support non-obviousness conflicts with the facts and law.

First, invention was not required for Thomson to derive and identify the colonies that contained primate ES cells, because the three characteristics Thomson taught as bases for selection of primate ES cells are the exact same three characteristics Thomson identified as common to mouse ES cells.

Second, the Board erred in finding that 2008 evidence that rat ES cells were not isolated until that year made it non-obvious to attempt to make primate ES cells in 1995 using the methods that succeeded for mouse and other mammalian ES cells. The '913 specification itself concedes that others had made rat ES cells, and information learned more than a decade later, in 2008, can not change what would have been obvious to one skilled in the art in 1995. Regardless of whether Thomson thought rat cells had been isolated before 1995, the Board offers no reason one skilled in the art would not have applied the known successful methods of isolating other mammalian ES cells to primate and human embryos at that time.

Third, the Board erred in (i) finding that Dr. Melton's citation of Thomson's work with human ES cells in a scientific publication indicated that Melton somehow depended on Thomson's work and then (ii) using that finding as a reason to discount Melton's sworn statement that he

had produced hES cells using the methods taught in the prior art without recourse to Thomson's publications. It is customary for scientists to credit those making certain accomplishments previously even if they did not follow the teachings and methods of those accomplishments.

Fourth, the Board erred in relying on industry acclaim for Thomson's successful isolation of hES cells in 1997–8 to support the validity of his 1995 patent application for primate ES cells. Acclaim is no more indicative of invention than it is of logistical achievement, especially in a climate where human embryos and funding for research thereon were scarce. Thus, the public acclaim received by Thomson is not a factor that should weigh in support of non-obviousness.

For these reasons, all three claims of the '913 patent are invalid under 35 U.S.C. §§ 101, 102, and 103.

ARGUMENT

II. The Court Should Rule The Claims Invalid Under Section 101

A. The Claimed Cell Culture Is An Ineligible Product of Nature

The Supreme Court restated just last month that discovery and isolation of a product that occurs in nature does not render that product patent eligible under Section 101. *Ass'n. for Molecular Pathology v. Myriad Genetics, Inc*, 2013 U.S. LEXIS 4540, at 25 (June 13, 2013) ("*AMP*"). The claims in *AMP* that the Supreme Court held were not eligible for patenting covered "isolated DNA."

The '913 patent claims a "replicating in vitro cell culture of pluripotent human embryonic stem cells derived from a pre-implantation embryo" in which the cells have certain enumerated characteristics exhibited by all ES cells. As in *AMP*, the '913 patent's claims are drawn to neither a method of preparation nor a scientific application of the claimed composition. They place no restriction on the conditions in which the ES cells should be grown or the methods of derivation and maintenance. The enumerated factors in claim 1 merely identify properties that are inherent in all ES cells, including those that exist naturally. Indeed, if the claimed ES cells were not the same as natural ES cells, the claimed invention would offer very little benefit for medical research.

The '913 patent's requirement that the claimed culture of cells be in vitro is analogous to the claim limitation in *AMP* that the DNA be "isolated." But here there is not even a chemical change between ES cells in an in vivo embryo and ES cells in an vitro culture as there is between human DNA in vivo and isolated DNA in vitro.

The '913 patent does not in any way distinguish the claimed ES cells from those that exist in nature. Williams, the prior art patent, highlights the fact that the cells that scientists culture and those that exist in the natural embryo are intended to be identical: "Embryonic stem (ES) cells

. . . can be cultured and manipulated in vitro and then returned to the embryonic environment to contribute normally to all tissues including the germline."

WARF did not create or alter the properties inherent in stem cells any more than Myriad created or altered the genetic information encoded in the DNA it claimed. Because the '913 claims merely describe ES cells that are the same as ES cells inside a human embryo (*i.e.* they maintain the potential to differentiate, refrain from differentiation when cultured on a fibroblast feeder layer, etc.), the '913 patent gives WARF the right to preempt any and all making or using of any hES cells. Such broad claims to products of nature are not patent eligible under 101 and thus should be declared invalid. . . .

IV. The Board Erred In Reversing Its Findings of Obviousness

In the Affirmance, the Board cited four reasons for its decision to flip-flop and find the '913 patent's claims non-obvious. Not only is each reason unsupported by the facts and law, even if one assumes they are supported by substantial evidence and a correct application of the law, they still do not contradict the Board's original determination that the claimed invention was invalid for being obvious to try. In short, the prior art teaching of methods for deriving mammalian ES cells would have, and indeed did, motivate one of ordinary skill in the art to attempt to derive hES cells in the same way. All one needed was access to human embryos, which is something Thomson eventually had when many others did not.

A. Isolation of Human Embryonic Stem Cells Did Not Require Innovation

The Board concluded that Thomson's identification of hES cells required innovation. The Board's basis for this conclusion came from a declaration submitted by WARF's retained expert, Dr. Stewart, in which he said hES cell colonies are flatter and more compact than mouse ES cell colonies, that flat colonies of hES cells had not been described before Thomson's invention, and that there was a plethora of colonies to choose from.

However, Stewart's bald biased claim that Thomson's colony selection required insight is inconsistent with and insufficient to overcome all of the other evidence regarding colony morphology, including evidence cited by the Board itself. First, even the Board acknowledged that language from the '913 patent conceded colony morphology of primate ES cells is "similar to" that of mouse ES cells and that both "have the characteristic features of undifferentiated stem cells, with high nuclear/cytoplasmic ratios, prominent nucleoli, and compact colony formation." But these three similarities do not merely represent a partial overlap between hallmarks of mouse ES cells and hallmarks of hES cells. Instead, these three characteristics common to mouse ES cells are the very same three characteristics that Thomson revealed in his

"method of isolating a primate embryonic stem cell line" as the bases on which to choose colonies from those that form during the isolation process:

> The method comprises . . . replating the dissociated cells on embryonic feeder cells and selecting colonies with **compact morphology** containing cells with a **high nucleus/cytoplasm ratio**, and **prominent nucleoli**.

If Thomson recognized flatness of cells was a key to their identification, Thomson failed to include such recognition in the instructions in the patent. Thus, the disclosure contained in the '913 patent itself does not support Stewart's (and thus the Board's) conclusion on that point.

Second, in its previous decision rejecting the '913 patent's claims, the Board rebutted WARF's argument regarding ordinary skilled scientists not knowing which colony to select by saying, "common sense would have directed her or him to pick different colony types to determine which possessed ES properties." The Board's second decision to the contrary assumes either that it would not have been sensible to test different colony types for ES properties (which, by Thomson's description, were visually obvious in any event) or that an ordinary skilled scientist would not have had common sense. The evidence citing a distinction between hES colonies and mouse ES colonies supports neither of those propositions.

In any case, the significance of the distinction between mouse ES cell colonies and hES cell colonies is vastly overstated. Thomson was not required to pick a hES colony out of a sea of mouse ES colonies. He instead had to select it from a culture of human cells. Like a mouse ES colony, the hES colony has the three "characteristic features" that distinguish it from surrounding non-ES cells. Thomson himself characterized the colony morphology of the mouse and primate as "similar" and pronounced identical hallmarks.

If the characteristic features of hES colonies didn't immediately identify the colonies as such, common sense would have guided an ordinary skilled scientist to test different colony types for those features. It is thus not true that identifying the ES colonies in the human cell cultures required innovation or insight. The Board's finding that such identification was an inventive act rather than an application of known technology is legally erroneous.

B. Obviousness Was Not Negated By Failure to Make Rat ES Cells

The Board relied on evidence that WARF cited in its Request to Reopen Prosecution to conclude that all attempts to make rat ES cells before 2008 had failed, and thus the path to isolating hES cells was not obvious in light of the prior art that taught how to isolate mouse ES cells. A10. The new evidence submitted by WARF late in the reexamination was a December 2008 publication by Buehr that found the process for

reproducibly deriving ES cells from inbred mouse strains did not yield ES cells when applied to the rat. In its earlier decision rejecting the '913 patent's claims, the Board had relied in part on the inventor's own statements in the '913 patent that rat ES cells had been isolated prior to 1995. The earlier decision was the correct one.

There are several critical flaws in the Board's decision to rely on the Buehr publication instead of the '913 patent's own admissions about the prior art. First, the Board acknowledged in its earlier decision a difference of opinion within the field regarding the production of rat ES cells. It pointed out that, regardless of whether WARF could resolve the question of the extent to which stem cells had been obtained from embryos of other species, case law supported finding that it was obvious to try when evidence cut both ways and there were "predictable options taught in the prior art for making ES cells." Even if the Board found that WARF managed to resolve that question, nothing about the 2008 Buehr article changed the principle that options taught in the prior art were obvious to try.

Second and more importantly, regardless of whether Buehr conclusively established that all of the rat cells thought in 1995 to be ES cells were not ES cells, it does not change what a person skilled in the art thought in 1995. Section 103(a) forbids issuance of a patent when "the differences between the subject matter sought to be patented and the prior art are such that the subject matter as a whole would have been obvious *at the time the invention was made* to a person having ordinary skill in the art to which said subject matter pertains." Thomson himself explicitly stated in the '913 patent specification that "[s]trong evidence of these [properties required of true ES cells] have been published only for rodents [*sic*] ES cells including . . . rat," and "established cell lines from the rat . . . have been reported to participate in normal development in chimeras."

Thomson thus clearly believed in 1995 that rat ES cells had been produced. He at minimum did not question the assumption of ordinary skilled scientists that rat ES cells could be produced with the known and familiar techniques for deriving ES cells of other mammals. If after applying for and receiving the '913 patent Thomson came to believe that rat ES cells did not exist before 1995, that belief could not have changed his beliefs, or the beliefs of others, in 1995, which is the relevant time for an obviousness analysis. The Board's consideration of a publication from 2008 to determine what was obvious in 1995 was legal error.

C. The Evidence Does Not Support That Others Who Made Human Embryonic Stem Cells Depended On Thomson's Work

The Board held the '913 patent's claims non-obvious because, in part, it found that, "[t]hose (Melton) making human embryonic stem cells followed Thomson's work." The Board made this finding despite the fact that it had originally stated as one basis for finding the claims obvious that both Drs. Melton and Cowan, scientists with expertise in cell culture

who submitted declarations in the reexamination proceeding, stated that they had isolated hES cells by simply following methods taught for deriving mouse, rat, pig and sheep ES cells. The Board's flip-flop on this issue resulted from its decision to discount Dr. Melton's sworn statement because he had cited Dr. Thomson's work in his own published research on hES cells that appeared in the New England Journal of Medicine. In short, the Board stated, "despite Dr. Melton's statements to the contrary, in his own research in making human embryonic stem cells, Dr. Melton credited Dr. Thomson' published work."

Dr. Melton's sworn statement, however, was not "contrary" to his NEJM article. The fact that Dr. Melton did not depend on Thomson's work to do his own was not a good reason to omit Thomson from the list of scientists Melton credited with earlier isolation of hES cells. The "published protocols" Melton referenced in his article noted Thomson's work alongside the work of two other human ES cell researchers. This credit makes perfect sense given that the three cited publications describing ES cells derived from human blastocysts preceded Dr. Melton's publication. For Dr. Melton to not credit other scientists with earlier publication of hES cell derivation, or for him to credit only scientists who published research describing ES cell derivation from other species, such as Robertson and Piedrahita, would amount to a false representation that Dr. Melton himself was the only scientist at the time to have derived hES cells. His citation to other scientists, including Dr. Thomson, was a respectable and conventional way to recognize the accomplishments of those who did related work before him, regardless of whether he used their work to perform his own research.

Melton did, as the Board found, "follow" Thomson's work—but he did so only in a chronological sense. A13. The fact that Melton did his work "according to published protocols [that he modified]" does not mean he relied on the publications he cited. It means that if a scientist reading the Melton research wanted to repeat his experiments, (s)he could follow the steps in the cited publications to achieve the same results. Alternatively, and importantly, (s)he could follow the steps taught in Williams since, as established above, Williams teaches the same steps.

Melton's sworn statement that he derived hES cells "without recourse to Dr. Thomson's publications or patents" (A341) is consistent with the acknowledgments he made in his NEJM article: he did his hES cell research without depending on other hES cell research, and yet he credited other hES researchers for their earlier work with human embryos. His sworn statement should not have been discounted by the Board.

D. Acclaim By the Scientific Community Does Not In Itself Support a Finding of Non-Obviousness

The fourth basis for the Board's non-obviousness finding was noted acclaim in *Harvard Magazine* and other examples of recognition of Thomson by scientists. Such acclaim does not support a finding of non-

obviousness in this case because it did not result from Thomson's patent. Instead Thomson received acclaim for work with the human embryos that he managed to obtain years after he filed for the '913 patent.

Given the advanced state of the art and the scarcity of human embryos and funding to support hES cell research in 1995, the "breakthrough" needed for the isolation and maintenance of hES cells was of the logistical, not innovative, type. Thomson's manufacture of hES cells was acclaimed because hES cells are useful and their production had not been reported before, but that does not mean his feat required invention. Acclaim is warranted for many things other than inventiveness, and in this case it was warranted by Dr. Thomson's ability to procure human embryos to which he could apply the known techniques for deriving mammalian ES cells as taught by, e.g., Williams. Thomson was the first to derive hES cells not because he invented something new or non-obvious, but instead because he had special access to the necessary human embryos and funding.

The Examiner involved in the appeal proceeding below considered and erroneously rejected the argument that access to human embryos was relevant to the validity of the invention. His mistake resulted from his quotation of the language from 35 U.S.C. 103(a) which states that "patentability shall not be negatived by the manner in which the invention is made." But the Examiner misunderstood the argument, as Appellant does not argue that Thomson's receipt of embryos and funding "negative" his invention. Rather, it is the prior art that renders Thomson's work anticipated and obvious that "negatives" Thomson's claims. The fact that obtaining embryos and funding was difficult merely negates secondary considerations of non-obviousness. Any argument about other scientists' "failure" to produce hES cells or long-felt unmet need or critical acclaim does not indicate that the way to derive hES cells was not obvious. Instead, it evidences merely other scientists' lack of resources.

Indeed, neither the Board, nor the Examiner, nor WARF has cited any evidence of a scientist who had access to human embryos who failed to derive hES cells. Nor is there any reference in the record that would have taught ordinary skilled scientists to not use feeder cells to derive hES cells as claimed in the '913 patent. All the Board cites, and all WARF can cite, is the fact that others did not actually derive hES cells. But they fail to recognize that was due to a lack of access to human embryos and financial resources, not a lack of knowledge of how to do so.

CONCLUSION

Claims 1–3 of the '913 patent are each invalid because they cover ineligible subject matter and were anticipated and obvious. The Court should rule each claim of the '913 patent invalid.

NOTES AND QUESTIONS

1. *Dodging the Issues.* In his blog, Professor Hank Greely discussed the remaining questions that courts, practitioners, and inventors are grappling with post-*Myriad*. See Hank Greely, *Myriad* Decision Invoked in Appeal of Suit to Invalidate Embryonic Stem Cell Patent Claims, Stanford Law School: Center for Law & Biosciences, Blog, July 4, 2013, available at https://law.stanford.edu/2013/07/04/lawandbiosciences-2013-07-04-myriad-decision-invoked-in-appeal-of-suit-to-invalidate-embryonic-stem-cell-patent-claims/. Greely predicted that the Federal Circuit might not even address the issues in the case. Id. Instead, the Federal Circuit could have dismissed the case because the issue was not properly appealed. Id.

2. *Consumer Watchdog Decision.* Professor Greely was correct; the Federal Circuit did not address the issues, but, instead, dismissed the case for a lack of standing:

> Consumer Watchdog does not identify any alleged injury aside from the Board denying Consumer Watchdog the particular outcome it desired in the reexamination, i.e., canceling the claims of the '913 patent. Appellant's Br. in Response to United States 3. Consumer Watchdog does not allege that it is engaged in any activity involving human embryonic stem cells that could form the basis for an infringement claim. It does not allege that it intends to engage in such activity. Nor does it allege that it is an actual or prospective licensee, or that it has any other connection to the '913 patent or the claimed subject matter. Instead, Consumer Watchdog relies on the Board's denial of Consumer Watchdog's requested administrative action—namely, the Board's refusal to cancel claims 1–4 of the '913 patent. That denial, however, is insufficient to confer standing.

Consumer Watchdog v. Wis. Alumni Research Found., 753 F.3d 1258 (Fed. Cir. 2014). Although Consumer Watchdog attempted to meet the injury portion of the standing requirement by analogizing its injury to those suffered under the Freedom of Information Act, the court did not find that argument persuasive. Id. Instead, the court found that Consumer Watchdog had only shown a general grievance, and not a concrete injury. Id. Although the Patent and Trademark Office allows for third parties to request reexamination of a patent, that right does not extend to an appeal to the courts. Id. In sum, the court determined that Consumer Watchdog had not suffered an injury; thus, it had no standing for the court to address its appeal.

3. *Myriad and Consumer Watchdog.* If the Federal Circuit had addressed the issues that Consumer Watchdog appealed under the *Myriad* framework, do you think WARF's patents would have been revoked? Do you think human embryonic stem cells in a petri dish should be considered products of nature? Or, do you think that WARF modified them enough—WARF's stem cells could survive indefinitely in a petri dish, while normal stem cells could not?

Think back to all the analogies the parties used in arguing *Myriad*, e.g., that BRCA1 had been "snipped" out of the body, was like a baseball bat, was

like chocolate chip cookies, and so forth. What analogies could you use for stem cell research?

4. *European Stem Cell Patent Ban.* Although the United States is currently grappling with what types of stem cells can be patented—and has not yet drawn a clear line of demarcation between patentable and unpatentable stem cells—the European Union issued a ruling that bans all human embryonic stem cell patents. See Case C–34/10, Brüstle v. Greenpeace eV., 2011 Celex No. 610CC0034 (Mar. 10, 2011). In Brüstle, a German professor—Oliver Brüstle—filed a patent involving the creation of nerve cells derived from human embryonic stem cells. See Fergus Walsh, Stem Cell Patent Ban, BBC News, Oct. 18, 2011, available at http://www.bbc.com/news/health–15355991. This patent and medical procedure is a treatment that can help patients with Parkinson's disease. Id. The European Court of Justice struck down the patent and ruled—on ethical grounds—that patents for embryonic stem cell research are prohibited. Id. The holding discussed the ethical considerations of the "respect for human dignity." Id.

> **Go to** the website to read the press releases about the two European opinions, *Brüstle* and *ISCC*, as well as ISCC's existing patent in the United States.

The ruling stated that "no patents can be granted for inventions based on embryonic stem cells, even if the cell lines were established in the laboratory many years ago and the invention itself does not involve obtaining new embryonic stem cells." Emma Kemp, European Court Bans Stem Cell Patents, EuroStemCell, Oct. 18, 2011. The court's key legal test was whether the stem cells "are capable of commencing the process of development of a human being, and therefore, are included within the concept of 'human embryo.'" The ruling does permit patents on human embryos if the technique was useful "to correct a malformation and improve the chances of life" for the embryo itself. Walsh, *supra.*

Researchers in the European Union are not happy with the ban:

> This unfortunate decision by the Court leaves scientists in a ridiculous position. We are funded to do research for the public good, yet prevented from taking our discoveries to the market place where they could be developed into new medicines. One consequence is that the benefits of our research will be reaped in America and Asia.

Id. (quoting Professor Austin Smith of the Wellcome Trust Centre for Stem Cell Research at the University of Cambridge).

In a follow-up case to *Brüstle*, the California-based International Stem Cell Corporation successfully sought a patent in the UK on the "parthenogenetic activation of oocytes for the production of embryonic stem cells," during which the company uses chemical and electrical techniques to activate a human ovum. These activated oocytes (called "parthenotes") cannot develop past the blastocyst stage. The new opinion clarified the *Brüstle* analysis to ask whether the parthenote must have the "inherent

capacity of developing into a human being." See Case C–364/13, International Stem Cell Corporation v. Comptroller General of Patents, Designs and Trademarks (Dec. 18, 2014); Anna Dannreuther, The CJEU Clarifies When Stem Cells Can be Patented in Europe, EU Law Analysis, Dec. 19, 2014, at http://eulawanalysis.blogspot.com/2014/12/the-cjeu-clarifies-when-stem-cells-can.html ("The Court ruled that in order to constitute a 'human embryo' for the purposes of the Directive, the stimulated ovum must have the 'inherent capacity to develop into a human being'. This is in contrast to its previous ruling in *Brüstle* where it held that such an ovum would only constitute a 'human embryo' if it were 'capable of *commencing* the process of development of a human being'."); Aurora Plomer, International Stem Cell Corporation v. Comptroller General of Patents, Designs and Trade Marks, https://www.cambridge.org/core/journals/international-legal-materials/article/abs/international-stem-cell-corporation-v-comptroller-general-of-patents-designs-and-trade-marks-cjeu/DAA40A6D44B94FCE47DF08806B6F26D1 ("The Court held that the term 'human embryo' does not cover unfertilized human eggs produced by parthenogenesis (parthenotes).").

How does that standard differ from *Brüstle*? Do you think this new standard strikes the proper balance between protecting patents and protecting the dignity of the human embryo?

The opinion left open the possibility that member states could still prohibit patenting of parthenotes on the grounds of public order or morality. Dannreuter, *infra*. Do you think they should do so? Would this lead to "patent tourism" as researchers leaves jurisdictions unfriendly to patenting parthenotes? See id.

Does this European embryonic stem cell discussion remind you of the Dickey-Wicker Amendment (studied in the stem cell controversy in Chapter 5, which prohibited federal funding from going to the creation or destruction of human embryos)? Or, do you think the ban is even broader than the Dickey-Wicker Amendment? Can the parthenotes be patented in the U.S.? Are they a product of nature under *Myriad*?

5. *Funding Stem Cell Research.* Who should fund stem cell research? Who should profit from it? California voters passed Proposition 71 in 2004 to authorize the sale of bonds to support stem cell research, with priority given to hESC research. Andrew T. Serafini & Gene H. Yee, IP Provisions and ROI for State-Funded Stem-Cell-Based Products and Technologies in California, 24 No. 9 Intell. Prop. & Tech. L.J. 3 (2012). Under the stem cell law, the California Institute of Regenerative Medicine (CIRM) provides grants to researchers, who own the rights to their inventions and file and report their patent applications. Id. at 3. Grantees are required to share some of their revenues with the state. Grantees who produce drugs must provide a plan for drugs to be made available to uninsured Californians. Id. at 5. Does the law strike the right balance between taxpayers and researchers? Do you think the requirements to share revenues will dampen commercial interest in stem cell research in California?

Scientists used $3 billion in California funds for this research, but the fund has run out of money. The CIRM is no longer taking applications. Do you expect California to re-fund this research in a new bond initiative? See Jocelyn Kaiser, California's Stem Cell Research Fund Dries Up, Science Mag., Jul. 9, 2019, https://www.sciencemag.org/news/2019/07/california-s-stem-cell-research-fund-dries. Would you recommend that it continue the funding?

6. *Encouraging Technology Transfer.* For many years, confusion over the ownership of patents on government-funded research slowed the movement of research into the commercial sector. "In 1980, fewer than 5 percent of the 28,000 patents being held by federal agencies had been licensed, compared with 25 percent to 30 percent of the small number of federal patents for which the government had allowed companies to retain title to the invention." General Accounting Office, Technology Transfer: Administration of the Bayh-Dole Act by Research Universities, at 3, GAO/RCED-98-126, May 1998, https://www.gao.gov/assets/rced-98-126.pdf. To encourage the transfer of technology to private industries, Congress passed The Patent and Trademark Law Amendments Act (the Bayh-Dole Act), 35 U.S.C. §§ 200–211, which gave universities and nonprofits the right to retain title to inventions made or discovered with government funding. Federal Grant Practice § 51:16 (2015 ed.); see also Ashley J. Stevens, The Enactment of Bayh-Dole, 29 J. Technology Transfer 93 (2004). Bayh-Dole also established patent and licensing policies that promoted the commercialization of research by encouraging universities to collaborate with private industry so that inventions would be more widely used. Id. Do you think patients' interests would be affected if the government, a research university, or a private business held the patent to a medical technology? Would one type of patent owner serve patient interests better than another?

Should the government have the right—or obligation—to intercede if the taxpayer-funded invention is not being used in a way that benefits the public? "[T]he federal government retains a non-exclusive, non-transferable, royalty-free license to use the invention, a provision intended to permit further research by federal agencies. . . . . [M]uch more controversially, the federal agency that funded the research can 'march in' and compel the granting of a license (or grant one itself) to 'a responsible applicant or applicants' if the patent owner is not holding up its end of the agreement to use the invention for the benefit of the public [such as if the] . . . patentee and its licensees have not taken effective steps to achieve practical application of the invention and are not expected to do so within a reasonable time [or the] . . . march-in license 'is necessary to alleviate health or safety needs which are not [being] reasonably satisfied' by the rights-holders. . . ." John Conley, Government Refuses to March-In Under Bayh-Dole—Again, Genomics L. Rep., Jan. 18, 2011, available at http://www.genomicslawreport.com/index.php/2011/01/18/government-refuses-to-march-in-under-bayh-dole-again/. The government has been reluctant to exercise those rights, however, even when patients are adversely affected. Id. (describing NIH denial of 2010 petition asking the agency to exercise its right to grant a compulsory license for Fabrazyme, an enzyme replacement therapy for

Fabry disease that was developed with NIH support, after the existing manufacturer licensee experienced severe production problems that left patients without adequate access.)

The issues have come to the forefront during the COVID-19 pandemic, as researchers have tested a variety of new and existing drugs—some of which were developed with significant public funding—for possible efficacy against the virus. In August 2020, a group of state attorneys general asked the government to exercise its march-in rights and license the new Gilead drug remdesivir to third-party manufacturers. See Letter to Alex M. Azar, Secretary, U.S. Department of Health & Human Services, Dr. Francis S. Collins, Director, National Institutes of Health, and Stephen Hahn, Commissioner, U.S. Food & Drug Administration, Aug. 4, 2020, https://www.oag.ca.gov/system/files/attachments/press-docs/Remdesivir%20Letter%2020200804.pdf. For a discussion of the issues involved in exercising march-in rights for COVID-19 treatments, see Jordan Paradise, COVID-IP: Staring Down the Bayh-Dole Act with 2020 Vision, J. L. & Biosciences, vol. 7, no. 1, Jan.–June 2020, https://doi.org/10.1093/jlb/lsaa073.

7. *Pharmaceutical Patents.* We learned in Chapter 2 that drug manufacturers spend extensive time and money going through IRB requirements and the research process before they can bring their products to market. It is estimated that in 2013 each medicine approved by the FDA cost about $5 billion to bring to market, and that global sales of pharmaceuticals reached $980 billion in 2013 and $1 trillion in 2014. Gene Quinn & Steve Brachmann, The High Cost of Making Pharmaceuticals, IP Watchdog, Oct. 19, 2014, at http://www.ipwatchdog.com/2014/10/19/the-high-cost-of-making-pharmaceuticals/id=51737/; Emma Stoye, Pharma Sales "Will Reach $1 Trillion" in 2014, Chemistry World, Sept. 11, 2014. Patent law protects manufacturers' ability to profit from their work. Do you think patent law incentivizes pharmaceutical manufacturers? Are any public policy concerns important enough to limit patent protection?

In 1984, Congress passed the Drug Price Competition and Patent Term Restoration Act of 1984, Pub. L. No. 98–417, 98 Stat. 1585 (1984) (codified as amended 21 U.S.C. § 355), commonly known as the Hatch-Waxman Act, in order to encourage the production of generic drugs. Generic drugs are comparable to the brand-name, patented drugs, and can be sold once the brand name's patent expires. "The Act allows a generic manufacturer to file an abbreviated new drug application (ANDA) while the term of the patent for that pharmaceutical is still active. This filing is particularly advantageous to generic manufacturers because it often allows for a significant reduction in the amount of time it takes to place the generic on the market. Production time for the generic is also reduced as the actual manufacturing processes are typically easy to replicate once a patent has been disclosed. With a properly filed ANDA, generic versions of the patented pharmaceutical are frequently introduced into the market the moment the patent term expires." Katelyn J. Bernier, Obviating the Obvious? An Appraisal of Pharmaceutical Patents, 10 J. High Tech. L. 208 (2010).

Why would Congress have legislated such protection of generic drugs? Are there other ways that patent laws should be amended to help consumers

or patients? Are there other people like the *Myriad* plaintiffs who should be filing lawsuits challenging patents? Should legislators pass new legislation to balance patent profits with public policy?

You can see a database of all DNA-based patents and patent applications issued by the United States Patent and Trademark Office at https://bioethics.georgetown.edu/library-materials/bioethics-research-library-databases/dna-patent-database/.

In the next section, we study the flawed incentives that arise when doctors and researchers earn profits from their research.

B. PROFITS

In Chapter 2, we read about Henrietta Lacks and the commercial development of the HeLa cells from tumor material removed from Lacks's body. Lacks never consented to the use of her tissue by her doctors. Researchers later made large commercial profits from her cell lines. Should her doctors have given her a consent form, or were the researchers entitled to use her tumor waste without Lacks's consent?

In this section, we examine how lawyers and ethicists should think about the use of human biospecimens in research. Must consent always accompany this research, or are doctors entitled to use whatever products they take from the human body? Be sure to rely on the principles developed in Chapter 2 as you read the following materials. You read the informed consent parts of the *Moore* case in Chapter 2, and the facts of the case are available there. We now address the property issues that arise when doctors receive patents based on biospecimens acquired without informed consent. This excerpt focuses on the tort of conversion, a tort that protects against interference with possessory and ownership interests in personal property.

Moore v. Regents of the University of California

Supreme Court of California, 1990.
51 Cal.3d 120, 793 P.2d 479.

I. INTRODUCTION

■ PANELLI, JUSTICE.

We granted review in this case to determine whether plaintiff has stated a cause of action against his physician and other defendants for using his cells in potentially lucrative medical research without his permission. Plaintiff alleges that his physician failed to disclose preexisting research and economic interests in the cells before obtaining consent to the medical procedures by which they were extracted. The superior court sustained all defendants' demurrers to the third amended complaint, and the Court of Appeal reversed. We hold that the complaint states a cause of action for breach of the physician's disclosure obligations, but not for conversion.

. . . Sometime before August 1979, Golde established a cell line from Moore's T-lymphocytes. On January 30, 1981, the Regents applied for a patent on the cell line, listing Golde and Quan as inventors. "[B]y virtue of an established policy . . . [the] Regents, Golde, and Quan would share in any royalties or profits . . . arising out of [the] patent." The patent issued on March 20, 1984, naming Golde and Quan as the inventors of the cell line and the Regents as the assignee of the patent. (U.S. Patent No. 4,438,032 (Mar. 20, 1984)).

The Regent's patent also covers various methods for using the cell line to produce lymphokines. Moore admits in his complaint that "the true clinical potential of each of the lymphokines . . . [is] difficult to predict, [but] . . . competing commercial firms in these relevant fields have published reports in biotechnology industry periodicals predicting a potential market of approximately $3.01 Billion Dollars by the year 1990 for a whole range of [such lymphokines]. . . ."

With the Regents' assistance, Golde negotiated agreements for commercial development of the cell line and products to be derived from it. Under an agreement with Genetics Institute, Golde "became a paid consultant" and "acquired the rights to 75,000 shares of common stock." Genetics Institute also agreed to pay Golde and the Regents "at least $330,000 over three years, including a pro-rata share of [Golde's] salary and fringe benefits, in exchange for . . . exclusive access to the materials and research performed" on the cell line and products derived from it. On June 4, 1982, Sandoz "was added to the agreement," and compensation payable to Golde and the Regents was increased by $110,000. "[T]hroughout this period, . . . Quan spent as much as 70 [percent] of her time working for [the] Regents on research" related to the cell line.

* * *

B. Conversion

Moore also attempts to characterize the invasion of his rights as a conversion—a tort that protects against interference with possessory and ownership interests in personal property. He theorizes that he continued to own his cells following their removal from his body, at least for the purpose of directing their use, and that he never consented to their use in potentially lucrative medical research. Thus, to complete Moore's argument, defendants' unauthorized use of his cells constitutes a conversion. As a result of the alleged conversion, Moore claims a proprietary interest in each of the products that any of the defendants might ever create from his cells or the patented cell line.

No court, however, has ever in a reported decision imposed conversion liability for the use of human cells in medical research. While that fact does not end our inquiry, it raises a flag of caution. In effect, what Moore is asking us to do is to impose a tort duty on scientists to investigate the consensual pedigree of each human cell sample used in research. To impose such a duty, which would affect medical research of

importance to all of society, implicates policy concerns far removed from the traditional, two-party ownership disputes in which the law of conversion arose. Invoking a tort theory originally used to determine whether the loser or the finder of a horse had the better title, Moore claims ownership of the results of socially important medical research, including the genetic code for chemicals that regulate the functions of every human being's immune system. . . .

1. Moore's Claim Under Existing Law

"To establish a conversion, plaintiff must establish an actual interference with his *ownership* or *right of possession*. . . . Where plaintiff neither has title to the property alleged to have been converted, nor possession thereof, he cannot maintain an action for conversion."

Since Moore clearly did not expect to retain possession of his cells following their removal, to sue for their conversion he must have retained an ownership interest in them. But there are several reasons to doubt that he did retain any such interest. First, no reported judicial decision supports Moore's claim, either directly or by close analogy. Second, California statutory law drastically limits any continuing interest of a patient in excised cells. Third, the subject matters of the Regents' patent—the patented cell line and the products derived from it—cannot be Moore's property.

Neither the Court of Appeal's opinion, the parties' briefs, nor our research discloses a case holding that a person retains a sufficient interest in excised cells to support a cause of action for conversion. We do not find this surprising, since the laws governing such things as human tissues, transplantable organs, blood, fetuses, pituitary glands, corneal tissue, and dead bodies deal with human biological materials as objects sui generis, regulating their disposition to achieve policy goals rather than abandoning them to the general law of personal property. It is these specialized statutes, not the law of conversion, to which courts ordinarily should and do look for guidance on the disposition of human biological materials. . . .

Finally, the subject matter of the Regents' patent—the patented cell line and the products derived from it—cannot be Moore's property. This is because the patented cell line is both factually and legally distinct from the cells taken from Moore's body. Federal law permits the patenting of organisms that represent the product of "human ingenuity," but not naturally occurring organisms. *Chakrabarty*. Human cell lines are patentable because "[l]ong-term adaptation and growth of human tissues and cells in culture is difficult—often considered an art. . . ." and the probability of success is low. It is this *inventive effort* that patent law rewards, not the discovery of naturally occurring raw materials. Thus, Moore's allegations that he owns the cell line and the products derived from it are inconsistent with the patent, which constitutes an authoritative determination that the cell line is the product of invention.

Since such allegations are nothing more than arguments or conclusions of law, they of course do not bind us.

2. Should Conversion Liability Be Extended?

As we have discussed, Moore's novel claim to own the biological materials at issue in this case is problematic, at best. Accordingly, his attempt to apply the theory of conversion within this context must frankly be recognized as a request to extend that theory. While we do not purport to hold that excised cells can never be property for any purpose whatsoever, the novelty of Moore's claim demands express consideration of the policies to be served by extending liability rather than blind deference to a complaint alleging as a legal conclusion the existence of a cause of action.

There are three reasons why it is inappropriate to impose liability for conversion based upon the allegations of Moore's complaint. First, a fair balancing of the relevant policy considerations counsels against extending the tort. Second, problems in this area are better suited to legislative resolution. Third, the tort of conversion is not necessary to protect patients' rights. For these reasons, we conclude that the use of excised human cells in medical research does not amount to a conversion. . . . Liability based upon existing disclosure obligations, rather than an unprecedented extension of the conversion theory, protects patients' rights of privacy and autonomy without unnecessarily hindering research. . . .

The extension of conversion law into this area will hinder research by restricting access to the necessary raw materials. Thousands of human cell lines already exist in tissue repositories, such as the American Type Culture Collection and those operated by the National Institutes of Health and the American Cancer Society. These repositories respond to tens of thousands of requests for samples annually. Since the patent office requires the holders of patents on cell lines to make samples available to anyone, many patent holders place their cell lines in repositories to avoid the administrative burden of responding to requests. At present, human cell lines are routinely copied and distributed to other researchers for experimental purposes, usually free of charge. This exchange of scientific materials, which still is relatively free and efficient, will surely be compromised if each cell sample becomes the potential subject matter of a lawsuit.

. . . [T]he theory of liability that Moore urges us to endorse threatens to destroy the economic incentive to conduct important medical research. If the use of cells in research is a conversion, then with every cell sample a researcher purchases a ticket in a litigation lottery. Because liability for conversion is predicated on a continuing ownership interest, "companies are unlikely to invest heavily in developing, manufacturing, or marketing a product when uncertainty about clear title exists." In our view, "[i]t is not unreasonable to conclude in these circumstances that the imposition of a harsher test for liability would not further the public

interest in the development and availability of these important products."

For these reasons, we hold that the allegations of Moore's third amended complaint state a cause of action for breach of fiduciary duty or lack of informed consent, but not conversion.

■ LUCAS, C.J., and EAGLESON and KENNARD, JJ., concur.

■ BROUSSARD, JUSTICE, concurring and dissenting.

When it turns to the conversion cause of action, however, the majority opinion fails to maintain its focus on the specific allegations before us. Concerned that the imposition of liability for conversion will impede medical research by innocent scientists who use the resources of existing cell repositories—a factual setting not presented here—the majority opinion rests its holding, that a conversion action cannot be maintained, largely on the proposition that a patient generally possesses no right in a body part that has already been removed from his body. Here, however, plaintiff has alleged that defendants interfered with his legal rights before his body part was removed. Although a patient may not retain any legal interest in a body part after its removal when he has properly consented to its removal and use for scientific purposes, it is clear under California law that before a body part is removed it is the patient, rather than his doctor or hospital, who possesses the right to determine the use to which the body part will be put after removal. If, as alleged in this case, plaintiff's doctor improperly interfered with plaintiff's right to control the use of a body part by wrongfully withholding material information from him before its removal, under traditional common law principles plaintiff may maintain a conversion action to recover the economic value of the right to control the use of his body part. Accordingly, I dissent from the majority opinion insofar as it rejects plaintiff's conversion cause of action.

■ MOSK, JUSTICE, dissenting.

The majority's third and last reason for their conclusion that Moore has no cause of action for conversion under existing law is that "the subject matter of the Regents' patent—the patented cell line and the products derived from it—cannot be Moore's property." The majority then offer a dual explanation: "This is because the patented cell line is *factually* and *legally* distinct from the cells taken from Moore's body." Neither branch of the explanation withstands analysis.

First, in support of their statement that the Mo cell line is "factually distinct" from Moore's cells, the majority assert that "Cells change while being developed into a cell line and continue to change over time," and in particular may acquire an abnormal number of chromosomes. No one disputes these assertions, but they are nonetheless irrelevant. For present purposes no distinction can be drawn between Moore's cells and the Mo cell line. It appears that the principal reason for establishing a cell line is not to "improve" the quality of the parent cells but simply to

extend their life indefinitely, in order to permit long-term study and/or exploitation of the qualities already present in such cells. The complaint alleges that Moore's cells naturally produced certain valuable proteins in larger than normal quantities; indeed, that was why defendants were eager to culture them in the first place. Defendants do not claim that the cells of the Mo cell line are in any degree more productive of such proteins than were Moore's own cells. Even if the cells of the Mo cell line in fact have an abnormal number of chromosomes, at the present stage of this case we do not know if that fact has any bearing whatever on their capacity to produce proteins; yet it is in the commercial exploitation of that capacity—not simply in their number of chromosomes—that Moore seeks to assert an interest. For all that appears, therefore, the emphasized fact is a distinction without a difference.

Second, the majority assert in effect that Moore cannot have an ownership interest in the Mo cell line because defendants patented it. The majority's point wholly fails to meet Moore's claim that he is entitled to compensation for defendants' unauthorized use of his bodily tissues *before* defendants patented the Mo cell line: defendants undertook such use immediately after the splenectomy on October 20, 1976, and continued to extract and use Moore's cells and tissue at least until September 20, 1983; the patent, however, did not issue until March 20, 1984, more than seven years after the unauthorized use began. Whatever the legal consequences of that event, it did not operate retroactively to immunize defendants from accountability for conduct occurring long before the patent was granted.

Nor did the issuance of the patent in 1984 necessarily have the drastic effect that the majority contend. To be sure, the patent granted defendants the exclusive right to make, use, or sell the invention for a period of 17 years. But Moore does not assert any such right for himself. Rather, he seeks to show that he is entitled, in fairness and equity, to some share in the profits that defendants have made and will make from their commercial exploitation of the Mo cell line. I do not question that the cell line is primarily the product of defendants' inventive effort. Yet likewise no one can question Moore's crucial contribution to the invention—an invention named, ironically, after him: but for the cells of Moore's body taken by defendants, *there would have been no Mo cell line.* Thus the complaint alleges that Moore's "Blood and Bodily Substances were absolutely essential to defendants' research and commercial activities with regard to his cells, cell lines, [and] the Mo cell-line, . . . and that defendants could not have applied for and had issued to them the Mo cell-line patent and other patents described herein without obtaining and culturing specimens of plaintiff's Blood and Bodily Substances." Defendants admit this allegation by their demurrers, as well they should: for all their expertise, defendants do not claim they could have extracted the Mo cell line out of thin air.

Nevertheless the majority conclude that the patent somehow cut off all Moore's rights—past, present, and future—to share in the proceeds of defendants' commercial exploitation of the cell line derived from his own body tissue. The majority cite no authority for this unfair result, and I cannot believe it is compelled by the general law of patents: a patent is not a license to defraud. Perhaps the answer lies in an analogy to the concept of "joint inventor." I am aware that "patients and research subjects who contribute cells to research will not be considered inventors." Nor is such a person strictly speaking a "joint inventor" within the meaning of the term in federal law. But he does fall within the spirit of that law: "The joint invention provision guarantees that all who contribute in a substantial way to a product's development benefit from the reward that the product brings. Thus, the protection of joint inventors encourages scientists to cooperate with each other and ensures that each contributor is rewarded fairly.

. . . Concededly, the patent is not granted for the cell as it is found in nature, but for the modified biogenetic product. However, the uniqueness of the product that gives rise to its patentability stems from the uniqueness of the original cell. *A patient's claim to share in the profits flowing from a patent would be analogous to that of an inventor whose collaboration was essential to the success of a resulting product. The patient was not a coequal, but was a necessary contributor to the cell line.*"

Under this reasoning, which I find persuasive, the law of patents would not be a bar to Moore's assertion of an ownership interest in his cells and their products sufficient to warrant his sharing in the proceeds of their commercial exploitation.

NOTES AND QUESTIONS

1. *Doctors and Researchers.* How do you assess the court's holding that Moore could sue for breach of fiduciary duty or lack of informed consent, but not conversion? Do you agree with the majority that the first two torts are sufficient to protect Moore's interests? Or are the dissenting Justices correct that the conversion lawsuit should have been allowed? Are you surprised that the court, in rejecting the conversion claim, ruled that Moore had no property interest in his cells? Do you agree with the court that Moore's doctors should have informed him of their economic interests in his cells before surgery? Did the court strike the proper balance between protecting subjects and promoting research?

Does it make a difference to you that Moore travelled to UCLA from Seattle after his surgery numerous times for over seven years to remove blood, skin, bone marrow and semen because Dr. Golde told Moore that Moore should see only Dr. Golde? See Rebecca Skloot, Taking the Least of You: The Tissue-Industrial Complex, N.Y. Times Magazine, Apr. 16, 2006, at 38 (stating that Dr. Golde offered to pay for Moore's plane tickets and put him up in a "ritzy" hotel when Moore started to question why he could not see a doctor in Seattle). If Moore had known that Dr. Golde was profiting

from Moore's cells, do you think he would have questioned whether the extra visits were necessary for Moore's health compared to Dr. Golde's research? Do you think Moore should have received compensation for the Mo Cell Line that was valued at approximately $3 billion? See id. Did the court confuse Moore's status as a patient with his status as a research subject?

Compare Moore with Ted Slavin, a hemophiliac who was exposed to hepatitis B through blood transfusions. Slavin's doctor told him he had a high number of antibodies in his blood, and Slavin sold his antibodies for $10 a milliliter. He also tracked down the best hepatitis researcher and gave him antibodies for free so the cure would be discovered more quickly. Slavin's blood was then used to create the first hepatitis B vaccine. Id. Would you want money or other compensation for your tissue if you were in Moore's or Slavin's situation?

Do you agree with Skloot that the difference between Moore and Slavin was information, not property or privacy? Skloot argued that:

> The difference between Ted Slavin and John Moore wasn't that Slavin owned his tissues and Moore didn't. (No court ruled that Slavin had the right to control his excised tissues; he just did it.) The difference was information. Someone told Slavin that his tissues were special and that scientists might want them. So he was able to control his tissues by establishing his terms *before* anything left his body. In other words, he was informed, and he gave consent. In the end, the question isn't whether people have the ability to control their tissues; it is how much science should be obligated (ethically and legally) to put them in the position to do so.

Does Skloot's analysis confirm that the tort that occurred here was informed consent and not conversion?

2. *Patents.* Given what you learned about patent law in Section A, do you agree with the court that "the subject matter of the Regents' patent—the patented cell line and the products derived from it—cannot be Moore's property?" This is because the patented cell line is both "factually and legally distinct from the cells taken from Moore's body"? In *Moore*, the court wrote that

> Human cell lines are patentable because "[l]ong-term adaptation and growth of human tissues and cells in culture is difficult—often considered an art. . . ." and the probability of success is low. It is this *inventive effort* that patent law rewards, not the discovery of naturally occurring raw materials. Thus, Moore's allegations that he owns the cell line and the products derived from it are inconsistent with the patent, which constitutes an authoritative determination that the cell line is the product of invention. Since such allegations are nothing more than arguments or conclusions of law, they of course do not bind us.

How would you apply this reasoning to the WARF case about stem cell patents, which we studied at the end of Section A? Does this language from *Moore* support the conclusion that the stem cells cultured in the WARF case

were patentable because they were the product of ingenuity and inventive effort?

Do you think the dissent provides a better analysis of the patent than the majority? According to the dissent, the wrong to Moore was done long before the patent on the Mo cell line issued. Is Moore entitled to some type of joint inventor status and share in the profits? How can it be possible that Moore would not profit from the Mo cell line that bears his name?

3. Greenberg. Plaintiffs who were committed to finding a cure for Canavan disease contributed human tissue to a research doctor who later isolated the Canavan gene and developed a screening test for the disease. Unknown to plaintiffs, the researcher and his employer received a patent for their work. Although the plaintiffs wanted the research to be publicly accessible on an affordable basis, patent law allowed the research team to limit Canavan disease testing and to license the testing restrictively. Recall that plaintiffs in *Myriad*, in Section A, were similarly concerned that patients were unable to gain access to medical testing due to restrictive patent laws.

A Florida district court followed *Moore* and ruled that there was no conversion lawsuit because donor plaintiffs had no property interest in their donation. The court then distinguished *Moore* on the grounds that there was no fiduciary duty or duty of informed consent between a researcher and donors. Greenberg v. Miami Children's Research Inst., 264 F. Supp. 2d 1064, 1070 (S.D. Fla. 2003) ("Defendants here are solely medical researchers and there was no therapeutic relationship as in *Moore*."). On the other hand, plaintiffs were allowed to sue under a theory of unjust enrichment because plaintiffs invested "time and significant resources" to the research effort. Id. at 1072. Do you think the court made the right analysis of the applicability of the tort laws to the Canavan disease researchers?

What would it take for you to figure out whether the Canavan patent was consistent with *Myriad*? Could you make a WARF claim about the Canavan patent?

4. *Henrietta Lacks.* Recall from Chapter 2 that in 1951 Henrietta Lacks went to John Hopkins Hospital seeking medical care for cervical cancer. Doctors removed two "dime-sized" samples of her tumor. The samples were given to researcher George Gey, who produced the HeLa cell line that proliferated more than any other cells in prior research. Gey gave the cells away to fellow researchers around the world. Biotech companies and for-profit cell banks later earned enormous profits from medical discoveries based on research on the HeLa cell line. See generally Rebecca Skloot, The Immortal Life of Henrietta Lacks (2010). Lacks died from her cancer. Lacks' family was very poor and never received any money from the research. Under what tort theories, if any, should they have been allowed to sue defendants who profited from the use of the HeLa cells?

After European scientists published the genome of the HeLa cells and made it available for download (thus making public genetic information about Henrietta's relatives) the National Institutes of Health entered into an agreement with Lacks' family. The family received no financial

compensation, but the genome data are stored in NIH databases, where researchers can apply for access. Two members of the Lacks family will be members of the NIH committee that decides who gets access. See Carl Zimmer, Family Gets Role in Use of 'Immortal Life' Cells, N.Y. Times, Aug. 8, 2013, at A1. Is this a satisfactory resolution of Henrietta's case?

5. *Other Tissues.* What should happen to all the tissues that are currently collected in doctors' offices, hospitals and research centers around the country? Do you agree with Professor Javitt's analysis in the following article?

Take Another Little Piece of My Heart: Regulating the Research Use of Human Biospecimens

Gail H. Javitt.
41 J.L. Med. & Ethics 424 (2013).

II. Biobanking Background

A biobank, also known as a biorepository, is a place that "collects, stores, processes, and distributes biological materials and the data associated with those materials." These "biological materials" are typically human biospecimens, including tissue or blood, and the "data" are the clinical information pertaining to the donor of that biospecimen. Biobanks allow researchers to conduct a range of studies, including genome-wide association studies (GWAS), which are studies of entire genome of large numbers of people to identify genetic markers for disease. In recent years, biobanks have been increasingly used to study complex diseases that are believed to have both genetic and environmental causes. According to one estimate, in 1999 there were 178 million unique samples contained in biorepositories, and that number was expected to increase by more than 20 million samples per year.

Assuming that rate of growth is correct, there currently are, in 2013, 458 million samples. Unfortunately, the actual number of existing biobanks and the discrete specimens contained therein is not known because no mandated centralized registry of biobanks exists, either nationally or internationally.

Human Subjects Protection and Biospecimens

A. HISTORICAL ROOTS

. . . The Common Rule, when promulgated, did not contemplate research on tissue specimens, but today, the collection and use of stored tissue for research has become commonplace, from a newborn's first day of life forward. As discussed below, there are no generally applicable rules governing the research use of such tissues. Whether and to what extent federal rules apply depends on (1) whether the research at issue is federally funded, and (2) whether the tissue samples used in the research can be linked back to their source, in other words, whether they are "identifiable." Even where federal regulations do apply, they do not address many of the concerns and preferences of the contributors of such

tissue. For non-federally funded research, the applicable requirements vary based on individual state laws, and, as described below, different courts have invoked different legal theories to resolve disputes between researchers, participants, and institutions.

B. FEDERAL OVERSIGHT OF RESEARCH INVOLVING HUMAN TISSUE

. . . The Rule applies to "all research involving human subjects conducted, supported or otherwise subject to regulation by any federal department or agency which takes appropriate administrative action to make the policy applicable to such research." Although the federal regulations do not explicitly define research with human tissue specimens as human subjects research, if such research involves "identifiable private information," it is clearly encompassed within the definition. However, the regulations specifically exempt research that uses *existing* stored tissue specimens if "the information is recorded by the investigator in such a manner that *subjects cannot be identified*, directly or through identifiers linked to the subjects." In addition, guidance issued by the Office of Human Research Protections (OHRP), within the National Institutes of Health (NIH), states that research involving "coded," or non-identifiable, human specimens is not considered human subjects research.

In short, federally funded research involving identifiable human biological specimens generally is considered human subjects research for the purposes of the Common Rule, while federally funded research involving samples whose identity has been removed or has not been recorded generally is not considered human subject research according to the statutory definition. Even where the use of specimens is considered human subjects research, however, researchers are not required to address all of the issues that participants in such research might view as important. For example, the federal regulations do not require researchers to inform participants of every possible use of their tissue or to provide information to them about study results. Nor do the regulations require researchers to disclose whether and to what extent the research may have commercial application. Thus, even where they apply, the protections provided under the Common Rule may not be consonant with the expectations and preferences of those who contribute their tissue for research. Additionally, the regulations do not apply to research conducted by private entities that do not receive federal funds. . . .

III. Case Law

Although there have been only a few legal cases involving disputes between the parties to human tissue research, their resolutions starkly reveal the gaps in the current oversight framework, as well as a lack of shared perceptions by the different parties to the enterprise. Furthermore, the lack of consistency in the court decisions (including among judges reviewing the same case), demonstrates the wide

divergence of views on the issues and the need prospectively to establish and apply clear and consistent rules.

A. *Moore v. Regents of the University of California*

. . . In holding in favor of Moore's informed consent claim, but against his conversion claim, the court appears to have been balancing its desire to prevent blatant deception of patients while protecting the research enterprise. However, the court's reasoning with respect to informed consent is flawed. In particular, the court failed to distinguish between Moore as a patient and Moore as a research subject. Although there was evidence presented to the district court that Golde was aware of the potentially lucrative nature of Moore's cells before he removed his spleen, and therefore had a *potentially* conflicting interest, there was no evidence that this actually motivated his decision to perform the surgery or, moreover, that the surgery was not the appropriate treatment for Moore's underlying medical condition. Disclosing his financial interest might have led Moore to seek a different doctor, but presumably that doctor also would have concluded that the surgery was necessary to treat his leukemia. Thus, at least in this instance, there is no evidence that disclosure of Golde's financial interest in his cells would have made Moore-the-patient better off, and might have needlessly led him to reject a competent physician.

Moreover, even recognizing that there are circumstances where a patient's well-being may be compromised by his or her treating physician's conflict of interest, financial or otherwise, and that financial disclosure therefore may be an important element of informed consent to *treatment*, the court's reasoning nevertheless was insufficient in its failure to consider Moore the-research-subject separately from Moore-the-patient. When Golde took Moore's cells for a research purpose—as opposed to a purpose related to Moore's treatment—Moore became a research subject, even if he did not know it at the time. In failing to inform Moore that he planned to use the cells in research, Golde therefore committed a wrong to Moore the-research-subject independently of whatever duties he owed Moore as a patient. The court failed to acknowledge Moore's transition from patient to research subject, and therefore failed to consider the duties owed to Moore in that capacity. Had Golde not been his treating physician, or if he had had no inkling of the cells' potential research value at the time of the surgery, he would have been under no obligation, by the court's reasoning, to inform Moore of the value of his cells. Nor, by the court's reasoning, did Quan or UCLA have any duty to obtain Moore's consent to use his cells. The court's limited holding therefore does little to protect the interests of the vast majority of contributors of tissue samples. . . .

[B]. Post-Moore Decisions

Since *Moore*, courts facing analogous disputes have likewise failed to properly consider the status of the "third party to the biotechnology enterprise," and have instead relied on a variety of legal arguments to

rule in favor of the institutions at which the research took place. In *Greenberg v. Miami Children's Hospital*, family members with children suffering from Canavan disease, a rare genetic disorder, along with non-profit organizations with an interest in the disease, sought help from the defendant, Dr. Matalon, in identifying the genetic mutation causing the illness and in developing a test to detect the mutation. The plaintiffs provided support to Matalon by contributing tissue, developing a patient registry, and raising money. Matalon identified the gene and developed a test to detect the mutation, but his research institution, Miami Children's Hospital, patented the gene, listed him as an inventor, and sought to enforce the patent and collect royalties for the test's performance.

The plaintiffs, who were not told that the gene would be patented and had expected the test to be freely available, sued Matalon and Miami Children's Hospital, alleging lack of informed consent, breach of fiduciary duty, unjust enrichment, fraudulent concealment, conversion, and misappropriation of trade secrets. With the exception of unjust enrichment, the court dismissed all of the plaintiffs' claims. In particular, the *Greenberg* court held that Matalon did not have a duty of informed consent with respect to the plaintiffs because, unlike Dr. Golde in *Moore*, Matalon was not the plaintiffs' treating physician. The court then questioned whether the duty of informed consent was applicable, under state law, to medical research (while acknowledging that the duty did apply under federal law, which was not at issue in the case). Even if the duty did apply, moreover, the court held that it did not include a duty to disclose the researcher's financial interests in research, because the plaintiffs were tissue donors, and not "objects of human experimentation."

Like the majority in *Moore*, the *Greenberg* court appeared to give priority to the needs of medical research over the concerns of research participants. Also like the *Moore* decision, the *Greenberg* court's reasoning is flawed. Just as the *Moore* court conflated the contexts of medical treatment and human subjects research in a manner that discounted Moore's interest as a research subject, the *Greenberg* court confused the differing premises underlying informed consent and donation—again to the plaintiffs' disadvantage. The plaintiffs in *Greenberg* were required by the research institution to sign an informed consent document. The context of such signature was clearly a research context—the whole point of providing their tissue was to have research performed with their tissues. Thus, at the time the tissue was provided by the plaintiffs, they had been assigned the role of human subject by the institution, a role necessarily required the institution to act in a protective—if not strictly fiduciary—capacity. The scope of such duties of protection is delineated in the Common Rule, which includes the obligation to ensure that subjects are given all the information necessary to make an informed decision about participation.

The court's after-the-fact designation of the plaintiffs as "donors" thus seems to take advantage of the plaintiffs' trust. Nothing in the informed consent process would have alerted plaintiffs to the fact that they were engaging in a legal transaction with the defendants. Plaintiffs clearly were knowledgeable about how to mobilize research resources, but there is no evidence to suggest they understood that by signing a consent form they were simultaneously engaging in a legal transaction in which they were renouncing any potential rights over the uses of their specimens. They signed an informed consent document, which signaled only an investigator-subject relationship, not a donor-donee relationship. Had they appreciated that they were in the latter category, they might have made more effort to reach an independent assessment of their own best interests before agreeing to donate their tissues, for example, by requesting the inclusion of specific terms as a condition of their donation. As a consequence, the plaintiffs failed to receive the protective benefits of informed consent, since they were not provided sufficient information about the researcher and institution's financial interests to make an informed decision to participate, and also were not given the requisite access to information and ability to negotiate on equal terms that one would expect to accompany the status of donor.

This status conflation is echoed yet again in *Washington University v. Catalona, Catalona II*, 490 F.3d 667 (8th Cir. 2007), *aff'g* 437 F. Supp. 2d 985 (E.D. Mo. 2006) (*Catalona I*). In that case, the dispute was between a researcher, Dr. Catalona, and the institution that had employed him. Catalona had established a biorepository containing an extensive collection of tissue samples from patients with prostate cancer, many of whom he had treated personally. The biorepository was housed at Washington University and funded by the institution. Patients were invited to participate in genetic research by providing their tissue samples to the biorepository and were required to sign a consent form. The forms typically used the word "donation" to characterize the delivery of the sample, and the participants were informed that their samples might be used by different entities, that they had a right to withdraw from the research and have their samples destroyed, and that they did not have any claim to the donated tissues or materials or processes derived from them.

When Catalona left Washington University, he sought to take the collection with him to his new institution. To that end, he obtained release forms from the research participants indicating that they sought transfer of their samples to him. Washington University then sought a declaration that it owned the bio-repository and the tissue samples, while Dr. Catalona sought a declaration that participants could directly transfer their materials to him.

In this case, the legal status of the tissue samples' contributors was the determining factor in the court's ruling. The district court ruled that

Washington University owned the samples, a decision that was upheld on appeal.

IV. Public Attitudes toward Biobanking

. . . Studies to date appear to support the following with respect to American attitudes: (1) there is significant public support for the goals of biobank research; (2) a majority of the public would agree, at least under some conditions, to contribute tissue samples for research; (3) there is significant public concern about ensuring the privacy of information derived from tissue samples as well as any associated medical information included about individuals as part of research; and (4) receiving health-related information from research conducted with one's tissues, and having a choice regarding what information is received, are factors that would influence many people's decisions to participate in such research.

Analysis

One of the threshold questions raised by the regulatory oversight of and case law regarding research with human biospecimens is defining the legal status of those specimens once they have been removed from the human body. Are they waste? The subject's property? Something else? There are no easy answers; as one scholar has explained, "[T]he law of the body remains in a state of confusion and chaos."

Under the biospecimens-as-property theory, an individual's body—including his or her biospecimens—is viewed as his or her property. On this view, the uninvited removal or use of bodily tissue is theft or trespass. One concern with recognizing an individual's property right to his or her excised tissue, however, is that it could threaten investigators' and universities' access to use stored samples effectively, which is "essential to everything from advances in pharma-cogenomics and genetic epidemiology, to the development of new tests for clinically significant mutations, to the investigation of historical events and epidemics through the medical testing of cadavers."

There are other reasons to be leery of the "property" construction as well, including the effects such a construction could have on public health laws prohibiting the sale and governing the handling of transplantable human organs, as well as on laws governing the disposal of biological materials including human tissue, blood, fetuses, pituitary glands, corneal tissue, and dead bodies. As the court in *Moore* explained, the laws regarding biological materials primarily seek to ensure the safe handling of potentially hazardous biological waste materials, but

> one cannot escape the conclusion that the [laws'] practical effect is to limit, drastically, a patient's control over excised cells. By restricting how excised cells may be used and requiring their eventual destruction, the [laws] eliminate[ ] so many of the rights ordinarily attached to property that one cannot simply

> assume that what is left amounts to 'property' or 'ownership'. . . .

Accordingly, affording an individual a property right in his or her biospecimens, if a court were ever to recognize such interest, could potentially require modification of numerous existing public health measures.

An alternative to the biospecimens-as-property view is that biospecimens are entitled to protection under an individual's right to privacy. The privacy viewpoint generally accords with the findings from surveys of public attitudes regarding the use of human biospecimens, in which participants expressed significant concern about ensuring the privacy of the information derived from their tissue samples as well as any associated medical information that is included about them as a part of the research. A concern about the privacy framework is that it "bundles all interests in the body together within a single person. As a result, bodily privacy is generally inalienable and unassailable: it can neither be contracted away to private parties nor confiscated by the government." The privacy view also may not be applicable in the research context, where there is often a lack of intimacy and a relationship of trust between the individual and the researcher. Nor is there much legal support to be found in the case law for this position.

Regardless of whether biospecimens are viewed as property or as protected under an individual's right to privacy, it is clear that the public generally expects that some type of authorization from an individual should be required before his or her biospecimens are used in research. Indeed, public opinion research reveals that many people harbor strong possessive, or at least protective, feelings towards their tissue. Such feelings may find their source in religious views on the body. Alternatively, they may reside in notions of bodily integrity—for example, the conviction that, as a matter of autonomy, individuals should retain the power to control the use of their body parts by virtue of the fact that those parts originated in, and once were a part of, their body. Even individuals who do not care about the fate of their excised tissues may well care about whether the information derived from that tissue could help, or harm, them in the future. Thus, there are numerous non-property based reasons—rooted in religion, autonomy, or privacy (including individual, family, and group privacy)—why tissue contributors may care, and therefore should be consulted about, the use of their tissues in research.

Respect for these interests requires that researchers both ask would-be contributors if they are willing to have their tissue used for research, and offer a meaningful opportunity for the would-be contributors to decline. Failure to provide such respect, moreover, can result in negative consequences. For example, the Texas and Minnesota blood spot litigation led to the destruction of millions of valuable biospecimens that could have furthered research. The Havasupai case, in addition to

causing negative publicity for the researcher and institution, led to the termination of a research relationship that could have yielded important research findings that might also have benefited the participants.

... [T]he choice to contribute one's tissue should be provided regardless of whether the tissue is "deidentified." Although deidentification may alleviate privacy concerns, it does not change the fact that the tissue was derived from an individual and that such individual may desire or expect to be consulted as to its disposition. While some individuals may elect not to contribute their tissues, thereby reducing the number of samples available for research, providing such choice is a requirement of respectful engagement with the contributors. As a practical matter, it is likely that most people, when treated with such respect, will choose to contribute; but such choice should not be presumed. Also as a practical matter, in most cases it is unlikely that any one individual's tissue will be individually valuable enough to afford significant bargaining power, but if prospective contributors do possess such ability to bargain, either individually or collectively, then researchers will need to weigh the importance of the research against their willingness and ability to meet the terms.

NOTES AND QUESTIONS

1. *The Current Standard.* As the article explains, if tissue research involves "identifiable private information," it is human subjects research governed by the Common Rule. This case was decided under the older version of the Common Rule; the new rule is provided in Chapter 2. If the subjects cannot be identified in existing stored tissue, it is exempt. Research involving "coded," or non-identifiable, human specimens is not considered human subjects research and is also exempt from review.

> **Practice Exercise:** Draft your own standard governing research with human biospecimens.

Professor Javitt argues that *Moore*'s reasoning was "flawed" because it "failed to distinguish between Moore as a patient and Moore as a research subject." What standard can protect both patients and research subjects? Should researchers owe a fiduciary duty and a duty of informed consent to tissue donors? On what basis?

How much information do you think doctors and researchers should give patients about their tissue before it is removed? The Cancer Human Biobank is a biobank created by the National Cancer Institute to supply research scientists with tissue, blood, and other human material. A patient who has to have some human material removed at the request of her doctor can consent to have the unused portion of that material given to scientists for purposes of research.

> **Go to** the website and assess the adequacy of the Cancer Human Biobank's form.

The material will be linked to the patient, but will be anonymous to researchers. Should such research be conducted on an opt-in or opt-out basis?

2. Greenberg. Do you agree with the Florida court that Dr. Matalon did not owe the Canavan disease patients a duty of informed consent? Do you think it makes a difference that Dr. Matalon was not the treating physician? See Kevin L.J. Oberdorfer, Note, The Lessons of *Greenberg*: Informed Consent and the Protection of Tissue Sources' Research Interests, 93 Geo. L.J. 365, 367 (2004) (stating that the tissue obtained in *Greenberg* was obtained by a medical researcher "solely for research purposes from individuals who are not patients but who wish to contribute to biomedical research"). Why should an informed consent lawsuit fail and an unjust enrichment claim succeed on the facts of *Greenberg*?

3. Catalona. What does Professor Javitt mean when she concludes that the Missouri court confused informed consent with donation in *Catalona*?

4. *Exculpatory Language*. Why do IRB regulations prohibit researchers from including exculpatory language in their informed consent forms?

> **Practice Exercise:** Can you tell which of the following statements are acceptable for informed consent forms and which are unacceptable because they are exculpatory?

- I voluntarily and freely donate any and all blood, urine, and tissue samples to the [name of research institution] and hereby relinquish all property rights, title, and interest I may have in those samples.
- Tissue obtained from you in this research may be used to establish a cell line that could be patented and licensed. No financial compensation will be provided to you should this occur.
- I waive any possibility of compensation, including any right to sue, for injuries that I may receive as a result of participation in this research.
- In the event that you suffer a research-related injury, your medical expenses will be your responsibility or that of your third-party payer.
- In the event that you suffer a research-related injury, your medical expenses will be your responsibility or that of your third-party payer, although you are not precluded from seeking to collect compensation for injury related to malpractice, fault, or blame on the part of those involved in the research.
- Because of hospital policy, the hospital is not able to offer financial compensation should you be injured as a result of participating in this research. However, you are not precluded from seeking to collect compensation for injury related to

malpractice, fault, or blame on the part of those involved in the research, including the hospital.

- If you suffer a research-related injury, neither the institution nor the investigator can assume financial responsibility or liability for the expenses of treatment for such injury.
- By consenting to participate, you authorize the use of your bodily fluids and tissue samples for the research described above.
- Although the results of research, including your donated materials, may be patentable or have commercial value, you will have no legal or financial interest in any commercial development resulting from the research.

U.S. Dep't of Health & Human Services, Guidance on Exculpatory Language in Informed Consent, Aug. 19, 2011, https://www.hhs.gov/ohrp/regulations-and-policy/requests-for-comments/guidance-exculpatory-language/index.html.

5. *Newborns.* If you lived in Texas or Minnesota, would you consent to the use of your newborn's blood in research? Texas parents sued the state after discovering Texas officials had taken blood from newborns to test for genetic disorders without getting informed consent. Some samples were also given to federal law enforcement officials for research on DNA. One parent complained; " 'The nurses asked me if they could give my son a pacifier. They asked me if they could give him formula, . . . No one asked me if his DNA could be stored in a state database.' " Similar litigation arose in Minnesota. Amy Harmon, Dispute Highlights Risks in Use of Genetic Material, N.Y. Times, Apr. 22, 2010, at A17. Millions of blood samples were later destroyed as part of settlement agreements between outraged parents and the states. Do you agree with Javitt that the states lost valuable research specimens by not engaging in appropriate informed consent? Or do you think that states had a right to use unconsented newborn blood for research purposes? Do you think the state has a strong interest in attempting to detect new diseases early on? If you were the state, how would you argue to maintain the practice of obtaining newborns' blood for research purposes?

6. *Havasupai.* Members of the Native American Havasupai Tribe gave DNA samples to Arizona State University researchers to study diabetes, which occurs at high rates among members of the tribe. Researchers also used the samples to study schizophrenia and the tribe's geographical origins. How could informed consent have been protected in this situation? Did the Havasupai have the right to be informed that their DNA would be used for mental health and geographic origins research? Is your answer influenced by learning that the Havasupai oppose mental health research and that one of the researcher's articles, "suggesting that the tribe's ancestors had crossed the frozen Bering Sea to arrive in North America, flew in the face of the tribe's traditional stories that it had originated in the canyon and was assigned to be its guardian?" See Amy Harmon, Tribe Wins Fight to Limit Research of Its DNA, N.Y. Times, Apr. 22, 2010, at A1.

Although a geneticist involved in the research argued that she had permission to use the specimens for these studies, the university paid the tribe $700,000, returned the blood samples and gave other assistance to the Havasupai. Id. What lessons do you draw from this experience? Do you think the tribe had the right to restrict what research the university had its consent to perform?

7. *Restricting Further Donation.* It seems as if the court in *Catalona* prohibited the patients from restricting their biospecimen donation after it was donated by concluding that the donation was an inter vivos gift. How do you think this case would apply to egg donation contracts that allow the donor to restrict the intended parents' usage of the eggs (e.g., not to use them for research, not to donate to same-sex couples, to restrict the eggs to couples of certain religions)? Do you think the recipients should have the right to use the eggs as they see fit?

8. *The Best Standard.* Should individuals have a property or privacy right in their biospecimens? After reading this article, what rule would you propose for biospecimen research? Should human tissue be subject to research without consent? Subject to research without consent as long as it is unidentifiable? Available only if consent is given for biospecimens to be used in research? Available only if consent is given for biospecimens to be used in research specifically named in advance? Available only with consent and commercial compensation?

Practice Exercise: On the website, read the four different consent forms for the use of tissue research (titled Tissue A-D). Then assess the adequacy of the tissue protocols.

In 2011, the Department of Health and Human Services (HHS) issued an advance notice of proposed rulemaking (ANPRM) to request comment on how current regulations for protecting human subjects who participate in research might be modernized and revised to be more effective. On the subject of biospecimens,

> the ANPRM proposes requiring written consent for the research use of biospecimens, whether or not the specimens were initially collected for non-research purposes and notwithstanding whether they contain identifiable information. Such consent would generally "need not be study specific" and could include "open-ended future research." In other words, a participant would be presented with an "all or nothing" option to either refuse to permit any research use of his or her specimens, or to permit all uses, both those related to the study in which he or she is participating and any future studies. However, participation in a research study cannot be conditioned on a participant's agreement to "allow future open-ended research using a biospecimen."

Javitt, *supra*, at 426 (2013). What do you think of this standard? See id. at 434 ("[I]n light of what we know about the public's desire to have more nuanced choices regarding the use of their biospecimens, the ANPRM

arguably falls short in permitting 'open-ended' consent. More concerning, the ANPRM leaves unaddressed the "consent/donation" mismatch—the inherent unsuitability of a consent document to effect what is essentially a contractual (or quasi-contractual) transaction."). The new Common Rule continues to exempt such "secondary" research from consent requirements:

45 C.F.R. § 690.104 Exempt research

> (4) Secondary research for which consent is not required: Secondary research uses of identifiable private information or identifiable biospecimens, if at least one of the following criteria is met:
>
> > (i) The identifiable private information or identifiable biospecimens are publicly available;
> >
> > (ii) Information, which may include information about biospecimens, is recorded by the investigator in such a manner that the identity of the human subjects cannot readily be ascertained directly or through identifiers linked to the subjects, the investigator does not contact the subjects, and the investigator will not re-identify subjects;
> >
> > (iii) The research involves only information collection and analysis involving the investigator's use of identifiable health information when that use is regulated under 45 CFR parts 160 and 164, subparts A and E, for the purposes of "health care operations" or "research" as those terms are defined at 45 CFR 164.501 or for "public health activities and purposes" as described under 45 CFR 164.512(b); or
> >
> > (iv) The research is conducted by, or on behalf of, a Federal department or agency using government-generated or government-collected information obtained for nonresearch activities, if the research generates identifiable private information that is or will be maintained on information technology that is subject to and in compliance with section 208(b) of the E-Government Act of 2002, 44 U.S.C. 3501 note, if all of the identifiable private information collected, used, or generated as part of the activity will be maintained in systems of records subject to the Privacy Act of 1974, 5 U.S.C. 552a, and, if applicable, the information used in the research was collected subject to the Paperwork Reduction Act of 1995, 44 U.S.C. 3501 et seq.

Do you prefer Javitt's rule or the new Common Rule? Professor Javitt proposes one simple solution to the consent forms in these cases: one consent form would explain the research and a second, separate form would be a legal "donation agreement." Do you agree?

C. LOOKING AHEAD: MORE FINANCIAL OPPORTUNITIES

1. DESIGNER BABIES

23andMe is a company that sells home testing DNA kits to consumers. The company received a patent, #8,543,339, on a technology

that allows prospective parents to choose the traits of their offspring. Couples planning to have a baby together can test how their DNA would combine with each other or with possible sperm and egg donors. "What's unique about the patented technology is that it analyzes DNA from other individuals *together with* a person's own to identify 'a preferred donor' with whom 23andMe claims the person would be most likely to have a child with the traits that he or she preselects." Dov Fox, 23andMe's Designer Baby Patent, Huffington Post, Oct. 4, 2013, at http://www.huffingtonpost.com/dov-fox/23andmes-designer-baby-pa_b_4042165.html. Part of the controversy over the technology is that it not only allows parents to select against diseases, but also allows them to choose traits like hair and eye color, height and weight, and (possibly) intelligence and athleticism.

> **Go to** the website and look over 23andMe's patent. Look in particular at Figures 1–6 on pages 1–7, which explain how the technology works.

Should this technology be patented? Do you agree with Professor Fox that a moral element needs to be reintroduced into patent law, so that a patent does not have "utility" if it is injurious to society? Do you agree with him that Congress should add an "ethics representative" to the Patent Office so that it would be able to consider both the benefits and the harms of technology like this?

Duke's Professor Nita Farahany decided to check out what 23andMe would say about children she might have with her husband. She found out "that the child would have an 80% chance of bitter taste perception, no chance of being lactose intolerant, 100% chance of having wet earwax, 56% chance for brown or black eyes, 50% likelihood of sprinter-capable muscles, and little or no alcohol flush reaction." She said the results had "good entertainment value." She also said, "I believe that people should have access to information about themselves, and I think it's laudable that 23andMe has helped pave the way for people to better understand their genomes." Do you agree? Eliot Marshall, Company's "Designer Baby" Patent Divides Bioethicists, Science Mag., Oct. 5, 2013, https://www.sciencemag.org/news/2013/10/companys-designer-baby-patent-divides-bioethicists. For a fertility clinic's perspective on these changes, see Manuel Viotti et al., Estimating Demand for Germline Genome Editing: An In Vitro Fertilization Clinic Perspective, The CRISPR J., vol. 2, no. 5, 2019, https://pubmed.ncbi.nlm.nih.gov/31599685/.

2. CRISPR

Jennifer Doudna and Emmanuelle Charpentier received the Nobel Prize in Chemistry in 2020 for their work on CRISPR, (i.e., clusters of regularly interspaced short palindromic repeats). They "created a tool that can edit DNA, opening up the potential for curing genetic diseases, creating healthier babies, inventing new vaccines, and helping humans

to fight their own wars against viruses." Walter Isaacson, What Gene Editing Can Do for Humankind, Wall St. J., Feb. 19. 2021.

There was much caution about the proper and improper uses of CRISPR. A Chinese scientist, He Jiankui, used CRISPR on twin babies, Lulu and Nana, to edit a gene that influences the spread of AIDS. Professor Greely explains the difference between somatic cell lines and germline genome editing. Somatic cells are part of the body and editing of them lasts until the person dies. But germline cells can pass onto the next generation. This "possibility (not certainty) that the descendants' genes will be altered is what most upsets many people when it comes to editing the genes of early stage embryos." Henry T. Greely, CRISPR People: The Science and Ethics of Editing People 28 (2021). That is what upset people around the world when He broke some ethics rules when he created the twins. "He Jiankui, driven as far as I can tell by what Macbeth called 'vaulting ambition, which o'erleaps itself,' and aided by a serious lack of scruples, behaved terribly." Id. at 293. Do you agree? What can bioethical principles teach us about the proper use of CRISPR? How can CRISPR be used properly in the future?

The University of California, where Doudna is a professor, has been involved in a long patent battle with the Broad Institute, where Feng Zhang also did CRISPR research. California and Broad kept arguing about whose work was done first and whose patent was filed first. Both sides have won patents on different aspects of their work on CRISPR. Do you agree with Professor Greely that the "UC/Broad litigation is ridiculous. Truly, scores of millions, if not hundreds of millions, of dollars have been spent on this litigation. It has benefited the lawyers,. . .but it is hard to see it benefiting others." Id. at 42. How can CRISPR patents serves ethical interests?

3. NEXT GENERATION SEQUENCING (NGS)

New methods of DNA sequencing have started to replace the original Sanger sequencing described at the beginning of this chapter. NGS "describes a variety of laboratory methods that allow efficient determination of the precise order of nucleotides in a DNA sequence." David Kaufman et al., Clinical Integration of Next Generation Sequencing: A Policy Analysis, 42 J. of L. Med. & Ethics 5, 5 (2014). NGS is faster than earlier methods of genetic sequencing, opening up a wide range of possible clinical, prognostic, diagnostic and therapeutic uses. Id. NGS is fast because it does not "sequence the entire genome from end-to-end." Instead, it "employ[s] 'massively parallel' sequencing—meaning running thousands of sequencing reactions simultaneously." Id. at 10.

The speed of NGS increases the possibility that consumers will soon have access to Whole Genome Sequencing (WGS). Id. at 15. WGS identifies the complete DNA sequence of the genome, instead of focusing on individual gene tests like those involving BRCA1 and BRCA2, which

were involved in *Myriad*. Such testing could make much more genetic information available to consumers.

Professors Cook-Deegan & Chandrasekharan ask if use of these genome-analysis methods will be undermined by patent protection. Robert Cook-Deegan & Subhashini Chandrasekharan, Patents and Genome-Wide DNA Sequence Analysis: Is It Safe to Go into the Human Genome?, 42 J. of L. Med. & Ethics 42, 42 (2014). Should patents be allowed to block any WGS for consumers? Post-*Myriad*, can you think of any possible patents that would stand in the way of consumers gaining access to full genetic testing? What parts of WGS do you think can be patented?

Go to the website and learn how NGS sequencing works. Then review the ACMG guidelines for genome sequencing informed consent. Should parents consent to this procedure for their children?

What are the bioethical concerns about NGS? Is there any risk to allowing patients access to WGS? Should patients be asked to give specialized informed consent? See Saskia C. Sanderson et al., Opening the "black box" of informed consent appointments for genome sequencing: a multisite observational study, 21 Genetics in Medicine 1083 (2019), https://search-proquest-com.libproxy.lib.unc.edu/docview/2218972076?pq-origsite=summon. Should NGS change the types of genetic counseling patients receive? See Mina Yang & Jong-Won Kim, Principles of Genetic Counseling in the Era of Next-Generation Sequencing, 38 Ann. Lab. Med. 291 (2018), https://www-ncbi-nlm-nih-gov.libproxy.lib.unc.edu/pmc/articles/PMC5895857/?tool=pmcentrez&report=abstract.

4. VARIANTS OF UNCERTAIN SIGNIFICANCE

When scientists study genes, they can encounter mutations or variations. Sometimes, as in the case of BRCA1 and BRCA2, they can link variations to disease. In other circumstances, however, scientists simply do not know enough to determine if the variant is pathogenic or benign. These variants of uncertain significance (VUS) raise ethical problems for doctors and consumers, especially as more genetic testing, like WGS, is made available:

> A key challenge is that the clinical significance of a VUS result for disease risk is by definition unclear. This makes clinical management recommendations more complex, while also potentially creating anxiety or misunderstanding among patients. Further studies of the variant in question may lead to a VUS result being reclassified as either deleterious or not, raising policy and ethical questions about the duty to re-contact patients and who is ultimately responsible for this task. The methods of VUS classification and reclassification vary and are

> the subject of multiple international efforts, although there remain no universally accepted standards or methods for determining pathogenicity and reporting VUS results.

Jae Yeon Cheon, Jessica Mozersky & Robert Cook-Deegan, Variants of Uncertain Significance in BRCA: A Harbinger of Ethical and Policy Issues to Come?, 6 Genome Medicine 121 (2014); see also A.J. Clarke, Managing the Ethical Challenges of Next-Generation Sequencing in Genomic Medicine, 111 Br. Med. Bull. 17–30 (2014). Recall that in Chapter 2 we asked when researchers should disclose incidental findings—findings beyond the aim of the research study—to research subjects. Does the material you learned about genes and gene testing in this chapter convince you that incidental findings about genetics should be treated differently from other incidental findings?

> **Practice Exercise:** Draft an informed consent form that you would give to someone about to undergo BRCA1 and BRCA2 testing with possible VUS. Then go to the website and compare your forms with the information provided by Ambry Genetics. Do your recommendations match ACMG's?

While Myriad Genetics held the patent to BRCA1 and BRCA2, it kept a proprietary database of VUS associated with the cancer-related genes. Should this information have been shared with other scientists? Must it be shared with other scientists, post-*Myriad*?

Over time, some VUS are determined to be harmful. At what point should consumers be informed of the presence of VUS? Does it matter if the VUS occurs during BRCA testing or during WGS?

> **Practice Exercise:** What should Justin's parents do in the following situation? What should their doctor recommend?

> Justin, 6 months old, comes to the clinic for a developmental evaluation. His parents have no concerns about his progress, but are very concerned about the results of a CMA [chromosomal microarray] that was ordered shortly after birth because of a cleft palate and VSD [a hole in the wall separating the two chambers of the heart]. The CMA results show a small deletion that includes a gene involved in brain development, which is weakly linked with autism. The lab interprets this as a variant of unknown significance, stating that there is not currently enough information to determine whether it is benign or pathogenic.
>
> The Jackson Laboratory, Case Examples: Variant of Uncertain Significance (Justin), at https://www.jax.org/education-and-learning/clinical-and-continuing-education/cancer-resources/deciding-to-test/case-examples.

What follow-up do you anticipate between the doctor and Justin and his parents?

Mai Tran's gynecologist recommended that she have genetic testing because her family history showed breast cancer. Finding cancer-causing genetic variations can lead to all kinds of treatment for the patient. However, "many genetic findings are ambiguous, leaving doctors uncertain about whether a particular variant is truly dangerous." The more genes the test studies, the greater risk there is of getting inconclusive results, or VUS. Because the earliest gene sequencing was in White people, who also have more access to testing, members of racial minority groups are more likely to have VUS in their tests. Tran had a VUS in a gene associated with colon, uterine, and other cancers. Studies show that some doctors may inappropriately recommend surgery based on a VUS. What would you do in the midst of such testing? Christina Bennett, Ambiguous Genetic Test Results Can Be Unsettling. Worse, They Can Lead to Needless Surgeries, Wash. Post, Feb. 7, 2021, https://www.washingtonpost.com/health/genetic-tests-uncertain-results/2021/02/05/80a06d9a-65a2-11eb-8468-21bc48f07fe5_story.html.

> **Go to** the website to learn more about how a CMA works. After visiting the website, decide if Myriad does a good job explaining VUS.

In Chapter 7, we learn how the study of the brain—neuroscience—has impacted the practice of medicine and raised a new generation of bioethical questions.

CHAPTER 7

THE NEW FRONTIER: NEUROETHICS

Introduction. In Chapter 6, we focused on patents in the medical context. After understanding the Framers' intent for patents—to promote public knowledge and encourage invention—we questioned whether genetic material patents are and should be allowed. We looked at recent United States Supreme Court decisions on the issue, such as the *Myriad* decision. We then asked whether genetic materials are considered products of nature and what would it take to make genetic material patentable. We focused on the controversy surrounding genetic material, such as BRCA1 and BRCA2—a genetic mutation that correlates with an increased risk of breast cancer—and, also, stem cell genetic materials. After looking at the patentability of genetic materials, we shifted the lens to look at how research profits can affect medical research. We asked what the proper balance is between financially rewarding researchers for their hard work and making new technology available to patients. We examined the relationship between science and profit in studying genes.

In Chapter 7, we focus on the study of the brain, or neuroscience. As scientists have learned more specific details about how the brain works, bioethicists have struggled to understand these developments in light of traditional bioethical principles. Gradually, neuroethics has emerged as a subset of bioethics that focuses on the relationship between the brain and human behavior. The International Neuroethics Society describes the following differences and similarities between neuroethics and traditional bioethics:

> The brain makes us who we are. Therefore, there is a special case for ethics related to the brain and nervous systems. Bioethics covers ethical issues arising from general medicine and science. Neuroethics and bioethics overlap sometimes; for example, when seeking informed consent from people with cognitive impairments, who have difficulty understanding. Neuroethics covers a wide territory, for example:
>
> - How the brain creates the concept of personal responsibility;
> - Brain privacy, for example use of functional neuroimaging to obtain secrets or personal information;
> - The neural basis of morality, or what's called moral cognition;

- The neurobiology of decision making, and its connection to marketing, politics, or judicial rulings;
- Interventions, drugs, or devices that change thinking or personality.

Many aspects of our daily lives can be thought about more deeply in the context of advances in neuroscience. Some examples include:

- Drugs that alter the brain to treat children with learning disorders;
- Our sense of responsibility and justice in the courtroom;
- The moral status we confer on people with mental illnesses or addictive disorders

International Neuroethics Society, Frequently Asked Questions, at https://www.neuroethicssociety.org/f-a-q-.

Scientists have long been able to study the *structure* of the brain with a variety of technologies such as x-rays, CT (computed tomography) scanning and MRI (magnetic resonance imaging). Structural scans could provide courtroom evidence of how a person's brain was injured in a car accident or a criminal attack, or the damage caused by a stroke or tumor. More recently, scientists developed technologies that illustrate the *functioning* of the brain. See Owen D. Jones et al., Brain Imaging for Legal Thinkers: A Guide for the Perplexed, 2009 Stan. Tech. L. Rev. 5, 13 (2009). The *functioning* of the brain is revealed through different procedures, including PET scanning, EEG, MEG, and fMRI. In PET (positron emission tomography), radioactive tracers are injected into the subject and the increase and decrease in brain activity is recorded. Id. EEG (electroencephalography) and MEG (magnetoencephalography) apply sensors to the subject's head and record electromagnetic activity in the brain. Id. at 15. fMRI (functional magnetic resonance imaging) detects how the blood moves in the subject's head while he or she performs certain specific tasks. Id. at 16. As law professor Owen Jones explained, "The law at the moment exists in this gray zone where everyone acknowledges that both genetic and environmental factors could affect culpability,. . . But how do you know when, and how much?" Jon Schuppe, Blame my brain: A killer's bold defense gets a court hearing, NBC News, Apr. 27, 2019, https://www.nbcnews.com/news/us-news/blame-my-brain-killer-s-bold-defense-gets-court-hearing-n998676.

Go to the website to watch the videos and look at the pictures to understand how these tests work.

In recent years, neuroscience has been used more frequently in the courts. Professors Nita Farahany and Henry Greely discovered 2,800 cases where criminal defendants used neuroscience between 2005 and 2015. Only about 20% of the defendants got a positive result from the use of neuroscience. Eryn Brown, The brain, the criminal and the courts,

Knowable Magazine, Aug. 30, 2019, https://knowablemagazine.org/article/mind/2019/neuroscience-criminal-justice; Henry T. Greely and Nita A. Farahany, Neuroscience and the Criminal Justice System, 2:1 Annual Review of Criminology 451 (2019).

A significant influence by neuroscience on the law was first apparent in criminal law, which we examine in Section A. Scientists and lawyers asked whether neuroimaging could explain and identify criminal culpability and alter our basic assumptions about criminal justice. Neuroscience received even more attention after the Supreme Court appeared to be influenced by scientific studies of juveniles' brains when it ruled in Miller v. Alabama, 567 U.S. 460 (2012), that mandatory life without parole for those under the age of 18 at the time of their crimes violates the Eighth Amendment's prohibition on "cruel and unusual punishments." Id. at 465. Miller and other criminal cases led to more general questions about how to use neuroscience in the courtroom, a question that we examine in Section B. Finally, neuroscience has the potential to modify our thinking about tort law, death and dying, and other aspects of the law, as we learn in Section C.

A. CRIMINAL LAW LEADS THE WAY

According to Professor Jones, "neuroscientific evidence might aid law in at least seven (sometimes overlapping) ways:

1. Buttressing—by increasing juror confidence in a conclusion to which other, non-neuroscientific evidence already independently points (such as in the context of "diminished capacity" determinations);
2. Challenging—by calling into question or contradicting either other evidence in a case or a relevant legal assumption (such as those reflected in certain evidentiary rules);
3. Detecting—by identifying the existence of legally relevant facts (such as injuries, lies, or pain);
4. Sorting—by separating people into useful categories (such as those most likely to respond to drug rehabilitation);
5. Intervening—by providing new methods to achieve legal goals (such as through pharmacological interventions that would help to reduce recidivism);
6. Explaining—by illuminating decision pathways with information that may lead to more informed and less biased decisions (such as in the context of third-party punishment [TPP] decisions);
7. Predicting—by improving law's ability to estimate probabilities of future behavior (such as future violence)."

Owen D. Jones et al., Law and Neuroscience, 33 J. Neuroscience 17624 (2013). As Professor Jones has explained:

> Law and neuroscience seem strange bedfellows. But the engagement of law with neuroscientific evidence was inevitable. For one thing, the effectiveness of legal systems in regulating behavior and meting out justice often depends on weighing evidence about how and why a person behaved as he or she did. And these are things that neuroscience can sometimes illuminate. For another, lawyers are ethically bound to champion their clients' interests. So they remain alert for new, relevant, or potentially persuasive information, such as neuroscience may at times offer, that could help to explain or contextualize behavior of their clients.

Id. In this section, we study the role of neuroscience in criminal law, which has been the first field to make extensive use of neuroscientific insight. In the following death penalty case, the Supreme Court explicitly referred to scientific understanding of juvenile brains. As you read the case, ask yourself if the Court's reasoning is better explained by common sense or neuroscience.

Miller v. Alabama

United States Supreme Court, 2012.
567 U.S. 460, 132 S.Ct. 2455.

■ KAGAN, J., delivered the opinion of the Court, in which KENNEDY, GINSBURG, BREYER, and SOTOMAYOR, JJ., joined. BREYER, J., filed a concurring opinion, in which SOTOMAYOR, J., joined. ROBERTS, C.J., filed a dissenting opinion, in which SCALIA, THOMAS, and ALITO, JJ., joined. THOMAS, J., filed a dissenting opinion, in which SCALIA, J., joined. ALITO, J., filed a dissenting opinion, in which SCALIA, J., joined.

■ JUSTICE KAGAN delivered the opinion of the Court.

The two 14-year-old offenders in these cases were convicted of murder and sentenced to life imprisonment without the possibility of parole. In neither case did the sentencing authority have any discretion to impose a different punishment. State law mandated that each juvenile die in prison even if a judge or jury would have thought that his youth and its attendant characteristics, along with the nature of his crime, made a lesser sentence (for example, life *with* the possibility of parole) more appropriate. Such a scheme prevents those meting out punishment from considering a juvenile's "lessened culpability" and greater "capacity for change," *Graham v. Florida*, and runs afoul of our cases' requirement of individualized sentencing for defendants facing the most serious penalties. We therefore hold that mandatory life without parole for those under the age of 18 at the time of their crimes violates the Eighth Amendment's prohibition on "cruel and unusual punishments."

A

In November 1999, petitioner Kuntrell Jackson, then 14 years old, and two other boys decided to rob a video store. En route to the store, Jackson learned that one of the boys, Derrick Shields, was carrying a sawed-off shotgun in his coat sleeve. Jackson decided to stay outside when the two other boys entered the store. Inside, Shields pointed the gun at the store clerk, Laurie Troup, and demanded that she "give up the money." Troup refused. A few moments later, Jackson went into the store to find Shields continuing to demand money. At trial, the parties disputed whether Jackson warned Troup that "[w]e ain't playin'," or instead told his friends, "I thought you all was playin'." When Troup threatened to call the police, Shields shot and killed her. The three boys fled empty-handed.

Arkansas law gives prosecutors discretion to charge 14-year-olds as adults when they are alleged to have committed certain serious offenses. The prosecutor here exercised that authority by charging Jackson with capital felony murder and aggravated robbery. Jackson moved to transfer the case to juvenile court, but after considering the alleged facts of the crime, a psychiatrist's examination, and Jackson's juvenile arrest history (shoplifting and several incidents of car theft), the trial court denied the motion, and an appellate court affirmed. A jury later convicted Jackson of both crimes. Noting that "in view of [the] verdict, there's only one possible punishment," the judge sentenced Jackson to life without parole. Jackson did not challenge the sentence on appeal, and the Arkansas Supreme Court affirmed the convictions.

Following *Roper v. Simmons*, in which this Court invalidated the death penalty for all juvenile offenders under the age of 18, Jackson filed a state petition for habeas corpus. He argued, based on *Roper*'s reasoning, that a mandatory sentence of life without parole for a 14-year-old also violates the Eighth Amendment. The circuit court rejected that argument and granted the State's motion to dismiss. While that ruling was on appeal, this Court held in *Graham v. Florida* that life without parole violates the Eighth Amendment when imposed on juvenile nonhomicide offenders. After the parties filed briefs addressing that decision, the Arkansas Supreme Court affirmed the dismissal of Jackson's petition. The majority found that *Roper* and *Graham* were "narrowly tailored" to their contexts: "death-penalty cases involving a juvenile and life-imprisonment-without-parole cases for nonhomicide offenses involving a juvenile." Two justices dissented. They noted that Jackson was not the shooter and that "any evidence of intent to kill was severely lacking." And they argued that Jackson's mandatory sentence ran afoul of *Graham*'s admonition that " '[a]n offender's age is relevant to the Eighth Amendment, and criminal procedure laws that fail to take defendants' youthfulness into account at all would be flawed.' "

B

Like Jackson, petitioner Evan Miller was 14 years old at the time of his crime. Miller had by then been in and out of foster care because his mother suffered from alcoholism and drug addiction and his stepfather abused him. Miller, too, regularly used drugs and alcohol; and he had attempted suicide four times, the first when he was six years old.

One night in 2003, Miller was at home with a friend, Colby Smith, when a neighbor, Cole Cannon, came to make a drug deal with Miller's mother. The two boys followed Cannon back to his trailer, where all three smoked marijuana and played drinking games. When Cannon passed out, Miller stole his wallet, splitting about $300 with Smith. Miller then tried to put the wallet back in Cannon's pocket, but Cannon awoke and grabbed Miller by the throat. Smith hit Cannon with a nearby baseball bat, and once released, Miller grabbed the bat and repeatedly struck Cannon with it. Miller placed a sheet over Cannon's head, told him " 'I am God, I've come to take your life,' " and delivered one more blow. The boys then retreated to Miller's trailer, but soon decided to return to Cannon's to cover up evidence of their crime. Once there, they lit two fires. Cannon eventually died from his injuries and smoke inhalation.

Alabama law required that Miller initially be charged as a juvenile, but allowed the District Attorney to seek removal of the case to adult court. The D.A. did so, and the juvenile court agreed to the transfer after a hearing. Citing the nature of the crime, Miller's "mental maturity," and his prior juvenile offenses (truancy and "criminal mischief"), the Alabama Court of Criminal Appeals affirmed. The State accordingly charged Miller as an adult with murder in the course of arson. That crime (like capital murder in Arkansas) carries a mandatory minimum punishment of life without parole.

Relying in significant part on testimony from Smith, who had pleaded to a lesser offense, a jury found Miller guilty. He was therefore sentenced to life without the possibility of parole. The Alabama Court of Criminal Appeals affirmed, ruling that life without parole was "not overly harsh when compared to the crime" and that the mandatory nature of the sentencing scheme was permissible under the Eighth Amendment. The Alabama Supreme Court denied review.

We granted certiorari in both cases, and now reverse.

II

The Eighth Amendment's prohibition of cruel and unusual punishment "guarantees individuals the right not to be subjected to excessive sanctions." That right, we have explained, "flows from the basic 'precept of justice that punishment for crime should be graduated and proportioned' " to both the offender and the offense. As we noted the last time we considered life-without-parole sentences imposed on juveniles, "[t]he concept of proportionality is central to the Eighth Amendment." *Graham*, 560 U.S. at ___, 130 S. Ct. at 2021. And we view that concept

less through a historical prism than according to " 'the evolving standards of decency that mark the progress of a maturing society.' "

The cases before us implicate two strands of precedent reflecting our concern with proportionate punishment. The first has adopted categorical bans on sentencing practices based on mismatches between the culpability of a class of offenders and the severity of a penalty. So, for example, we have held that imposing the death penalty for nonhomicide crimes against individuals, or imposing it on mentally retarded defendants, violates the Eighth Amendment. Several of the cases in this group have specially focused on juvenile offenders, because of their lesser culpability. Thus, *Roper* held that the Eighth Amendment bars capital punishment for children, and *Graham* concluded that the Amendment also prohibits a sentence of life without the possibility of parole for a child who committed a nonhomicide offense. *Graham* further likened life without parole for juveniles to the death penalty itself, thereby evoking a second line of our precedents. In those cases, we have prohibited mandatory imposition of capital punishment, requiring that sentencing authorities consider the characteristics of a defendant and the details of his offense before sentencing him to death. Here, the confluence of these two lines of precedent leads to the conclusion that mandatory life-without-parole sentences for juveniles violate the Eighth Amendment.

To start with the first set of cases: *Roper* and *Graham* establish that children are constitutionally different from adults for purposes of sentencing. Because juveniles have diminished culpability and greater prospects for reform, we explained, "they are less deserving of the most severe punishments." Those cases relied on three significant gaps between juveniles and adults. First, children have a " 'lack of maturity and an underdeveloped sense of responsibility,' " leading to recklessness, impulsivity, and heedless risk-taking. Second, children "are more vulnerable . . . to negative influences and outside pressures," including from their family and peers; they have limited "contro[l] over their own environment" and lack the ability to extricate themselves from horrific, crime-producing settings. And third, a child's character is not as "well formed" as an adult's; his traits are "less fixed" and his actions less likely to be "evidence of irretrievabl[e] deprav[ity]."

Our decisions rested not only on common sense—on what "any parent knows"—but on science and social science as well. In *Roper*, we cited studies showing that " '[o]nly a relatively small proportion of adolescents' " who engage in illegal activity " 'develop entrenched patterns of problem behavior.' " *Roper*, 543 U.S. at 570, 125 S. Ct. 1183 (quoting Steinberg & Scott, Less Guilty by Reason of Adolescence: Developmental Immaturity, Diminished Responsibility, and the Juvenile Death Penalty, 58 Am. Psychologist 1009, 1014 (2003)). And in *Graham*, we noted that "developments in psychology and brain science continue to show fundamental differences between juvenile and adult minds"—for

example, in "parts of the brain involved in behavior control."[5] We reasoned that those findings—of transient rashness, proclivity for risk, and inability to assess consequences—both lessened a child's "moral culpability" and enhanced the prospect that, as the years go by and neurological development occurs, his " 'deficiencies will be reformed.' "

Roper and *Graham* emphasized that the distinctive attributes of youth diminish the penological justifications for imposing the harshest sentences on juvenile offenders, even when they commit terrible crimes. Because " '[t]he heart of the retribution rationale' " relates to an offender's blameworthiness, " 'the case for retribution is not as strong with a minor as with an adult.' " Nor can deterrence do the work in this context, because " 'the same characteristics that render juveniles less culpable than adults' "—their immaturity, recklessness, and impetuosity—make them less likely to consider potential punishment. Similarly, incapacitation could not support the life-without-parole sentence in *Graham*: Deciding that a "juvenile offender forever will be a danger to society" would require "mak[ing] a judgment that [he] is incorrigible"—but " 'incorrigibility is inconsistent with youth.' " And for the same reason, rehabilitation could not justify that sentence. Life without parole "forswears altogether the rehabilitative ideal." It reflects "an irrevocable judgment about [an offender's] value and place in society," at odds with a child's capacity for change.

Graham concluded from this analysis that life-without-parole sentences, like capital punishment, may violate the Eighth Amendment when imposed on children. To be sure, *Graham*'s flat ban on life without parole applied only to nonhomicide crimes, and the Court took care to distinguish those offenses from murder, based on both moral culpability and consequential harm. But none of what it said about children—about their distinctive (and transitory) mental traits and environmental vulnerabilities—is crime-specific. Those features are evident in the same way, and to the same degree, when (as in both cases here) a botched robbery turns into a killing. So *Graham*'s reasoning implicates any life-without-parole sentence imposed on a juvenile, even as its categorical bar relates only to nonhomicide offenses.

Most fundamentally, *Graham* insists that youth matters in determining the appropriateness of a lifetime of incarceration without the possibility of parole. In the circumstances there, juvenile status precluded a life-without-parole sentence, even though an adult could

[5] The evidence presented to us in these cases indicates that the science and social science supporting *Roper*'s and *Graham*'s conclusions have become even stronger. *See, e.g.*, Brief for American Psychological Association et al. as *Amici Curiae* 3 ("[A]n ever-growing body of research in developmental psychology and neuroscience continues to confirm and strengthen the Court's conclusions"); *id.* at 4 ("It is increasingly clear that adolescent brains are not yet fully mature in regions and systems related to higher-order executive functions such as impulse control, planning ahead, and risk avoidance"); Brief for J. Lawrence Aber et al. as *Amici Curiae* 12–28 (discussing post-*Graham* studies); *id.* at 26–27 ("Numerous studies post-*Graham* indicate that exposure to deviant peers leads to increased deviant behavior and is a consistent predictor of adolescent delinquency" (footnote omitted)).

receive it for a similar crime. And in other contexts as well, the characteristics of youth, and the way they weaken rationales for punishment, can render a life-without-parole sentence disproportionate. "An offender's age," we made clear in *Graham*, "is relevant to the Eighth Amendment," and so "criminal procedure laws that fail to take defendants' youthfulness into account at all would be flawed." THE CHIEF JUSTICE, concurring in the judgment, made a similar point. Although rejecting a categorical bar on life-without-parole sentences for juveniles, he acknowledged "*Roper*'s conclusion that juveniles are typically less culpable than adults," and accordingly wrote that "an offender's juvenile status can play a central role" in considering a sentence's proportionality.

But the mandatory penalty schemes at issue here prevent the sentencer from taking account of these central considerations. By removing youth from the balance—by subjecting a juvenile to the same life-without-parole sentence applicable to an adult—these laws prohibit a sentencing authority from assessing whether the law's harshest term of imprisonment proportionately punishes a juvenile offender. That contravenes *Graham*'s (and also *Roper*'s) foundational principle: that imposition of a State's most severe penalties on juvenile offenders cannot proceed as though they were not children.

And *Graham* makes plain these mandatory schemes' defects in another way: by likening life-without-parole sentences imposed on juveniles to the death penalty itself. Life-without-parole terms, the Court wrote, "share some characteristics with death sentences that are shared by no other sentences." Imprisoning an offender until he dies alters the remainder of his life "by a forfeiture that is irrevocable." And this lengthiest possible incarceration is an "especially harsh punishment for a juvenile," because he will almost inevitably serve "more years and a greater percentage of his life in prison than an adult offender." The penalty when imposed on a teenager, as compared with an older person, is therefore "the same . . . in name only." All of that suggested a distinctive set of legal rules: In part because we viewed this ultimate penalty for juveniles as akin to the death penalty, we treated it similarly to that most severe punishment. We imposed a categorical ban on the sentence's use, in a way unprecedented for a term of imprisonment. And the bar we adopted mirrored a proscription first established in the death penalty context—that the punishment cannot be imposed for any nonhomicide crimes against individuals.

That correspondence—*Graham*'s "[t]reat[ment] [of] juvenile life sentences as analogous to capital punishment," makes relevant here a second line of our precedents, demanding individualized sentencing when imposing the death penalty. In *Woodson*, we held that a statute mandating a death sentence for first-degree murder violated the Eighth Amendment. We thought the mandatory scheme flawed because it gave no significance to "the character and record of the individual offender or

the circumstances" of the offense, and "exclud[ed] from consideration . . . the possibility of compassionate or mitigating factors." Subsequent decisions have elaborated on the requirement that capital defendants have an opportunity to advance, and the judge or jury a chance to assess, any mitigating factors, so that the death penalty is reserved only for the most culpable defendants committing the most serious offenses.

Of special pertinence here, we insisted in these rulings that a sentencer have the ability to consider the "mitigating qualities of youth." Everything we said in *Roper* and *Graham* about that stage of life also appears in these decisions. As we observed, "youth is more than a chronological fact." It is a time of immaturity, irresponsibility, "impetuousness[,] and recklessness." It is a moment and "condition of life when a person may be most susceptible to influence and to psychological damage." And its "signature qualities" are all "transient." *Eddings* is especially on point. There, a 16-year-old shot a police officer point-blank and killed him. We invalidated his death sentence because the judge did not consider evidence of his neglectful and violent family background (including his mother's drug abuse and his father's physical abuse) and his emotional disturbance. We found that evidence "particularly relevant"—more so than it would have been in the case of an adult offender. We held: "[J]ust as the chronological age of a minor is itself a relevant mitigating factor of great weight, so must the background and mental and emotional development of a youthful defendant be duly considered" in assessing his culpability.

In light of *Graham*'s reasoning, these decisions too show the flaws of imposing mandatory life-without-parole sentences on juvenile homicide offenders. Such mandatory penalties, by their nature, preclude a sentencer from taking account of an offender's age and the wealth of characteristics and circumstances attendant to it. Under these schemes, every juvenile will receive the same sentence as every other—the 17-year-old and the 14-year-old, the shooter and the accomplice, the child from a stable household and the child from a chaotic and abusive one. And still worse, each juvenile (including these two 14-year-olds) will receive the same sentence as the vast majority of adults committing similar homicide offenses—but really, as *Graham* noted, a *greater* sentence than those adults will serve. In meting out the death penalty, the elision of all these differences would be strictly forbidden. And once again, *Graham* indicates that a similar rule should apply when a juvenile confronts a sentence of life (and death) in prison.

So *Graham* and *Roper* and our individualized sentencing cases alike teach that in imposing a State's harshest penalties, a sentencer misses too much if he treats every child as an adult. To recap: Mandatory life without parole for a juvenile precludes consideration of his chronological age and its hallmark features—among them, immaturity, impetuosity, and failure to appreciate risks and consequences. It prevents taking into account the family and home environment that surrounds him—and

from which he cannot usually extricate himself—no matter how brutal or dysfunctional. It neglects the circumstances of the homicide offense, including the extent of his participation in the conduct and the way familial and peer pressures may have affected him. Indeed, it ignores that he might have been charged and convicted of a lesser offense if not for incompetencies associated with youth—for example, his inability to deal with police officers or prosecutors (including on a plea agreement) or his incapacity to assist his own attorneys. And finally, this mandatory punishment disregards the possibility of rehabilitation even when the circumstances most suggest it.

Both cases before us illustrate the problem. Take Jackson's first. As noted earlier, Jackson did not fire the bullet that killed Laurie Troup; nor did the State argue that he intended her death. Jackson's conviction was instead based on an aiding-and-abetting theory; and the appellate court affirmed the verdict only because the jury could have believed that when Jackson entered the store, he warned Troup that "[w]e ain't playin'," rather than told his friends that "I thought you all was playing'." To be sure, Jackson learned on the way to the video store that his friend Shields was carrying a gun, but his age could well have affected his calculation of the risk that posed, as well as his willingness to walk away at that point. All these circumstances go to Jackson's culpability for the offense. See *Graham*, 560 U.S. at ___, 130 S.Ct. at 2027 ("[W]hen compared to an adult murderer, a juvenile offender who did not kill or intend to kill has a twice diminished moral culpability"). And so too does Jackson's family background and immersion in violence: Both his mother and his grandmother had previously shot other individuals. At the least, a sentencer should look at such facts before depriving a 14-year-old of any prospect of release from prison.

That is true also in Miller's case. No one can doubt that he and Smith committed a vicious murder. But they did it when high on drugs and alcohol consumed with the adult victim. And if ever a pathological background might have contributed to a 14-year-old's commission of a crime, it is here. Miller's stepfather physically abused him; his alcoholic and drug-addicted mother neglected him; he had been in and out of foster care as a result; and he had tried to kill himself four times, the first when he should have been in kindergarten. Nonetheless, Miller's past criminal history was limited—two instances of truancy and one of "second-degree criminal mischief." That Miller deserved severe punishment for killing Cole Cannon is beyond question. But once again, a sentencer needed to examine all these circumstances before concluding that life without any possibility of parole was the appropriate penalty.

We therefore hold that the Eighth Amendment forbids a sentencing scheme that mandates life in prison without possibility of parole for juvenile offenders. . . . Because that holding is sufficient to decide these cases, we do not consider Jackson's and Miller's alternative argument that the Eighth Amendment requires a categorical bar on life without

parole for juveniles, or at least for those 14 and younger. But given all we have said in *Roper*, *Graham*, and this decision about children's diminished culpability and heightened capacity for change, we think appropriate occasions for sentencing juveniles to this harshest possible penalty will be uncommon. That is especially so because of the great difficulty we noted in *Roper* and *Graham* of distinguishing at this early age between "the juvenile offender whose crime reflects unfortunate yet transient immaturity, and the rare juvenile offender whose crime reflects irreparable corruption." Although we do not foreclose a sentencer's ability to make that judgment in homicide cases, we require it to take into account how children are different, and how those differences counsel against irrevocably sentencing them to a lifetime in prison. . . .

We accordingly reverse the judgments of the Arkansas Supreme Court and Alabama Court of Criminal Appeals and remand the cases for further proceedings not inconsistent with this opinion.

It is so ordered.

■ JUSTICE BREYER, with whom JUSTICE SOTOMAYOR joins, concurring.

. . . Given *Graham's* reasoning, the kinds of homicide that can subject a juvenile offender to life without parole must exclude instances where the juvenile himself neither kills nor intends to kill the victim. Quite simply, if the juvenile either kills or intends to kill the victim, he lacks "twice diminished" responsibility. But where the juvenile neither kills nor intends to kill, both features emphasized in *Graham* as extenuating apply. The dissent itself here would permit life without parole for "juveniles who commit the worst types of murder," but that phrase does not readily fit the culpability of one who did not himself kill or intend to kill.

. . . Jackson simply went along with older boys to rob a video store. On the way, he became aware that a confederate had a gun. He initially stayed outside the store, and went in briefly, saying something like "We ain't playin'" or "'I thought you all was playin,'" before an older confederate shot and killed the store clerk. Crucially, the jury found him guilty of first-degree murder under a statute that permitted them to convict if, Jackson "attempted to commit or committed an aggravated robbery, and, in the course of that offense, he, or an accomplice, caused [the clerk's] death under circumstance manifesting extreme indifference to the value of human life." Thus, to be found guilty, Jackson did not need to kill the clerk (it is conceded he did not), nor did he need to have intent to kill or even "extreme indifference." As long as one of the teenage accomplices in the robbery acted with extreme indifference to the value of human life, Jackson could be convicted of capital murder.

The upshot is that Jackson, who did not kill the clerk, might not have intended to do so either. In that case, the Eighth Amendment simply forbids imposition of a life term without the possibility of parole. If, on remand, however, there is a finding that Jackson did intend to cause the

clerk's death, the question remains open whether the Eighth Amendment prohibits the imposition of life without parole upon a juvenile in those circumstances as well.

■ CHIEF JUSTICE ROBERTS, with whom JUSTICE SCALIA, JUSTICE THOMAS, and JUSTICE ALITO join, dissenting.

. . . The parties agree that nearly 2,500 prisoners are presently serving life sentences without the possibility of parole for murders they committed before the age of 18. The Court accepts that over 2,000 of those prisoners received that sentence because it was mandated by a legislature. And it recognizes that the Federal Government and most States impose such mandatory sentences. Put simply, if a 17-year-old is convicted of deliberately murdering an innocent victim, it is not "unusual" for the murderer to receive a mandatory sentence of life without parole. That reality should preclude finding that mandatory life imprisonment for juvenile killers violates the Eighth Amendment.

. . . In this case, there is little doubt about the direction of society's evolution: For most of the 20th century, American sentencing practices emphasized rehabilitation of the offender and the availability of parole. But by the 1980's, outcry against repeat offenders, broad disaffection with the rehabilitative model, and other factors led many legislatures to reduce or eliminate the possibility of parole, imposing longer sentences in order to punish criminals and prevent them from committing more crimes. And the parties agree that most States have changed their laws relatively recently to expose teenage murderers to mandatory life without parole.

. . . In any event, the Court's holding does not follow from *Roper* and *Graham*. Those cases undoubtedly stand for the proposition that teenagers are less mature, less responsible, and less fixed in their ways than adults—not that a Supreme Court case was needed to establish that. What they do not stand for, and do not even suggest, is that legislators—who also know that teenagers are different from adults—may not require life without parole for juveniles who commit the worst types of murder.

That *Graham* does not imply today's result could not be clearer. In barring life without parole for juvenile nonhomicide offenders, *Graham* stated that "[t]here is a line 'between homicide and other serious violent offenses against the individual.' " The whole point of drawing a line between one issue and another is to say that they are different and should be treated differently. In other words, the two are in different categories. Which *Graham* also said: "defendants who do not kill, intend to kill, or foresee that life will be taken are *categorically* less deserving of the most serious forms of punishment than are murderers." Of course, to be especially clear that what is said about one issue does not apply to another, one could say that the two issues cannot be compared. *Graham* said that too: "Serious nonhomicide crimes . . . cannot be compared to murder." A case that expressly puts an issue in a different category from

its own subject, draws a line between the two, and states that the two should not be compared, cannot fairly be said to control that issue.

Roper provides even less support for the Court's holding. In that case, the Court held that the death penalty could not be imposed for offenses committed by juveniles, no matter how serious their crimes. In doing so, *Roper* also set itself in a different category than this case, by expressly invoking "special" Eighth Amendment analysis for death penalty cases. But more importantly, *Roper* reasoned that the death penalty was not needed to deter juvenile murderers in part because "life imprisonment without the possibility of parole" was available. In a classic bait and switch, the Court now tells state legislatures that—*Roper*'s promise notwithstanding—they do not have power to guarantee that once someone commits a heinous murder, he will never do so again. It would be enough if today's decision proved Justice SCALIA's prescience in writing that *Roper*'s "reassurance . . . gives little comfort." To claim that *Roper* actually "leads to" revoking its own reassurance surely goes too far.

* * *

It is a great tragedy when a juvenile commits murder—most of all for the innocent victims. But also for the murderer, whose life has gone so wrong so early. And for society as well, which has lost one or more of its members to deliberate violence, and must harshly punish another. In recent years, our society has moved toward requiring that the murderer, his age notwithstanding, be imprisoned for the remainder of his life. Members of this Court may disagree with that choice. Perhaps science and policy suggest society should show greater mercy to young killers, giving them a greater chance to reform themselves at the risk that they will kill again. But that is not our decision to make. Neither the text of the Constitution nor our precedent prohibits legislatures from requiring that juvenile murderers be sentenced to life without parole. I respectfully dissent.

■ JUSTICE THOMAS, with whom JUSTICE SCALIA joins, dissenting.

The legislatures of Arkansas and Alabama, like those of 27 other jurisdictions, have determined that all offenders convicted of specified homicide offenses, whether juveniles or not, deserve a sentence of life in prison without the possibility of parole. Nothing in our Constitution authorizes this Court to supplant that choice.

[T]his Court's cases prohibiting mandatory capital sentencing schemes have no basis in the original understanding of the Eighth Amendment, and, thus, cannot justify a prohibition of sentencing schemes that mandate life-without-parole sentences for juveniles.

Because the Court's cases requiring individualized sentencing in the capital context are wrongly decided, they cannot serve as a valid foundation for the novel rule regarding mandatory life-without-parole sentences for juveniles that the Court announces today.

Today, the Court makes clear that, even though its decision leaves intact the discretionary imposition of life-without-parole sentences for juvenile homicide offenders, it "think[s] appropriate occasions for sentencing juveniles to [life without parole] will be uncommon." That statement may well cause trial judges to shy away from imposing life without parole sentences and embolden appellate judges to set them aside when they are imposed. And, when a future petitioner seeks a categorical ban on sentences of life without parole for juvenile homicide offenders, this Court will most assuredly look to the "actual sentencing practices" triggered by these cases. The Court has, thus, gone from "merely" divining the societal consensus of today to shaping the societal consensus of tomorrow.

Today's decision invalidates a constitutionally permissible sentencing system based on nothing more than the Court's belief that "its own sense of morality . . . pre-empts that of the people and their representatives." Because nothing in the Constitution grants the Court the authority it exercises today, I respectfully dissent.

■ JUSTICE ALITO, with whom JUSTICE SCALIA joins, dissenting.

[N]o one should be confused by the particulars of the two cases before us. The category of murderers that the Court delicately calls "children" (murderers under the age of 18) consists overwhelmingly of young men who are fast approaching the legal age of adulthood. Evan Miller and Kuntrell Jackson are anomalies; much more typical are murderers like Donald Roper, who committed a brutal thrill-killing just nine months shy of his 18th birthday.

Seventeen-year-olds commit a significant number of murders every year, and some of these crimes are incredibly brutal. Many of these murderers are at least as mature as the average 18-year-old. Congress and the legislatures of 43 States have concluded that at least some of these murderers should be sentenced to prison without parole, and 28 States and the Federal Government have decided that for some of these offenders life without parole should be mandatory. The majority of this Court now overrules these legislative judgments.

It is true that, at least for now, the Court apparently permits a trial judge to make an individualized decision that a particular minor convicted of murder should be sentenced to life without parole, but do not expect this possibility to last very long. The majority goes out of its way to express the view that the imposition of a sentence of life without parole on a "child" (*i.e.*, a murderer under the age of 18) should be uncommon. Having held in *Graham* that a trial judge with discretionary sentencing authority may not impose a sentence of life without parole on a minor who has committed a nonhomicide offense, the Justices in the majority may soon extend that holding to minors who commit murder. We will see.

Is such evidence more relevant in the case of juveniles, rather than adults? What about adults whose impairments stem from juvenile trauma, or whose conditions manifested themselves during childhood? Is Justice Sotomayor's dissent in the following case consistent with *Miller*?

Wessinger v. Vannoy

United States Supreme Court, 2018.
583 U.S. ___, 138 S.Ct. 952.

■ The petition for a writ of certiorari is denied.

■ JUSTICE SOTOMAYOR dissenting from the denial of certiorari.

Petitioner Todd Wessinger was sentenced to death by a jury that was never presented with significant mitigation evidence that may have convinced its members to spare his life. For instance, Wessinger suffers from a major neurocognitive disorder that compromises his decision-making abilities. As a child, he experienced a stroke in his left frontal lobe that affected how the left and right sides of his brain communicate. He also suffered from childhood seizures, and he has a hole in the area of his brain associated with executive functioning that resulted from some form of cerebrovascular illness.

The jury never considered this evidence at sentencing, or other mitigation about Wessinger's family history of poverty, alcoholism, and domestic violence, because Wessinger's trial counsel did not attempt to discover it. Wessinger's attorneys on postconviction review similarly failed to conduct any mitigation investigation in preparation for his state habeas petition.

The Court's denial of certiorari here belies the "bedrock principle in our justice system" that a defendant has a right to effective assistance of trial counsel, and undermines the protections this Court has recognized are necessary to protect that right.

Indeed, the investigation of mitigation evidence and its presentation at sentencing are crucial to maintaining the integrity of capital proceedings. The layers of ineffective assistance of counsel that Wessinger received constitute precisely the type of error that warrants relief under this Court's precedent. Yet, Wessinger will remain on death row without a jury ever considering the significant mitigation evidence that is now apparent. Because that outcome is contrary to precedent and deeply unjust and unfair, I dissent from the denial of certiorari.

Does the following case, *Madison*, add anything new to the Court's treatment of neuroscience? Does the status of mental disorders lead to the need for more neuroscience in the courts? How should a court determine if a prisoner is mentally incompetent?

Madison v. Alabama

United States Supreme Court, 2019.
586 U.S. ___, 139 S.Ct. 718.

■ JUSTICE KAGAN held that:

In this case, Vernon Madison argued that his memory loss and dementia entitled him to a stay of execution, but an Alabama court denied the relief. We now address two questions relating to the Eighth Amendment's bar, disputed below but not in this Court. First, does the Eighth Amendment forbid execution whenever a prisoner shows that a mental disorder has left him without any memory of committing his crime? We (and, now, the parties) think not, because a person lacking such a memory may still be able to form a rational understanding of the reasons for his death sentence. Second, does the Eighth Amendment apply similarly to a prisoner suffering from dementia as to one experiencing psychotic delusions? We (and, now, the parties) think so, because either condition may—or, then again, may not—impede the requisite comprehension of his punishment. The only issue left, on which the parties still disagree, is what those rulings mean for Madison's own execution. We direct that issue to the state court for further consideration in light of this opinion.

The only question left—and the only one on which the parties now disagree—is whether Madison's execution may go forward based on the state court's decision below. Madison's counsel says it cannot because that ruling was tainted by legal error—specifically, the idea that only delusions, and not dementia, can support a finding of mental incompetency. Alabama counters that the state court did not rely on that (concededly) incorrect view of the law. But we come away at the least unsure whether that is so—especially given Alabama's evidence and arguments in the state court.

■ JUSTICE ALITO, THOMAS & GORSUCH, dissenting.

What the Court has done in this case makes a mockery of our Rules.

Petitioner's counsel convinced the Court to stay his client's execution and to grant his petition for a writ of certiorari for the purpose of deciding a clear-cut constitutional question: Does the Eighth Amendment prohibit the execution of a murderer who cannot recall committing the murder for which the death sentence was imposed? The petition strenuously argued that executing such a person is unconstitutional.

After persuading the Court to grant review of this question, counsel abruptly changed course. Perhaps because he concluded (correctly) that petitioner was unlikely to prevail on the question raised in the petition, he conceded that the argument advanced in his petition was wrong, and he switched to an entirely different argument, namely, that the state court had rejected petitioner's claim that he is incompetent to be executed because the court erroneously thought that dementia, as opposed to other mental conditions, cannot provide a basis for such a claim.

This was not a question that the Court agreed to hear; indeed, there is no mention whatsoever of this argument in the petition—not even a hint. Nor is this question fairly included within those on which the Court granted review. On the contrary, it is an entirely discrete and independent question.

After this case was decided, Madison died in prison, so he was never executed by the state.

NOTES AND QUESTIONS

1. *The Influence of Neuroscience.* The Court originally invalidated the death penalty for juveniles under age 16 in Thompson v. Oklahoma, 487 U.S. 815, 823 (1988), on the basis that "[c]ontemporary standards of decency confirm our judgment that such a young person is not capable of acting with the degree of culpability that can justify the ultimate penalty." The Court did not refer to any scientific studies in reaching that conclusion, instead relying on developments in the state legislatures, which were gradually moving away from imposing the death penalty on juveniles. *Miller*, however, and to a lesser extent *Roper* and *Graham*, have been characterized as cases that rely on brain science or neuroscience to reach their conclusions about juvenile culpability. How important was science to Justice Kagan's opinion? Did science matter at all to the dissenting Justices? Do you agree with commentators who argue that neuroscience is a better basis for determinations of culpability than common sense or state legislation? See generally Laurence Steinberg, The Influence of Neuroscience on U.S. Supreme Court Decisions about Adolescents' Criminal Culpability, 14 Nature Rev. 513 (2013).

Do you agree with *Roper*'s explanation that there are three significant gaps between juveniles and adults: first, children have a " 'lack of maturity and an underdeveloped sense of responsibility,' " leading to recklessness, impulsivity, and heedless risk-taking; second, children "are more vulnerable . . . to negative influences and outside pressures," including from their family and peers; they have limited "contro[l] over their own environment" and lack the ability to extricate themselves from horrific, crime-producing settings' and third, a child's character is not as "well formed" as an adult's; his traits are "less fixed" and his actions less likely to be "evidence of irretrievabl[e] deprav[ity]"? Is the basis of your agreement or disagreement with this description common sense or neuroscience? Would you rather have the laws passed according to common sense or to neuroscience?

Do you agree with Professor Steinberg that there is good evidence the Court was influenced by neuroscience? Professor Steinberg argues: "[T]he only substantive change in the argument that adolescents are less mature than adults that had taken place between *Roper* and *Miller* involved an increased reliance on neuroscience. The period between these two cases was also characterized by growing coverage of research on adolescent brain development in the popular media." Id. at 517. If so, is this a good

development or a bad one? How would you describe the nature of that influence? Did the Justices rely on neuroscientific research? Did they displace legislative insight, as the dissent suggests? What do you think of Professor Steinberg's argument that neuroscience was useful because it "aligned with common sense and behavioural science":

> Although neuroscience appears to have influenced the Supreme Court's deliberations, it is important to recognize that the essential logic of these decisions is based primarily in a description of the ways in which adolescents' behaviour and thinking differs from that of adults, and only secondarily in differences in their brain structure and function. And that is as it should be. This way, the neuroscience complements and corroborates the behavioural science, but it does not make the behavioural findings any more real. In some regards, the most convincing evidence that adolescents are different from adults is what "any parent knows." Indeed, the neuroscientific evidence was probably persuasive to the Court not because it told us something new but precisely because it aligned with common sense and behavioural science.

Id. at 517–18.

2. *The Age-Crime Curve.* Crime studies identify an "age-crime curve," which remains the same across the crimes of robbery, burglary and rape, in which crime rates drop as people age. Generally, "individuals in their early 20s are more likely than either children or somewhat older adults to engage in risky behavior." Id. at 515. The same curve exists for age and risk-taking. Id. at 515–16. Does this evidence influence your assessment of *Miller*? Why shouldn't juveniles be punished more harshly than older individuals if they are more likely to commit crimes? Scientific studies also show that the connections between different parts of the brain become stronger as people age, and that this strength is "positively correlated with impulse control." Id. at 516. Does this information influence your assessment of *Miller*?

A Texas law review article argues that *Roper's* choice of 18 as the age for capital punishment should be changed to 21 because of the status of brains before 21. The "brains of people under twenty-one, unlike adults' brains but like teenagers' brains, are capable of triggering adult emotions but are not capable of managing or processing those emotions. . . .Specifically, recent neuroimaging studies show that the volume of white matter in the brain is relatively stable until around age twenty-one, when it begins to increase dramatically. That is important because white matter fibers transmit information between neurons, allowing different regions of the brain to communicate with each other. Additionally, increased white matter volume in the frontolimbic system—a part of the brain that is not fully developed until after age twenty-one—enables individuals to modulate anxiety, deal with fear, and become socially adept." John H. Blume et al., Death by Numbers: Why Evolving Standards Compel Extending Roper's Categorical Ban Against Executing Juveniles from Eighteen to Twenty-One, 98 Tex. L. Rev. 921, 930–32 (2020). Do you agree with the authors that people under age 21 are "less morally culpable" than older adults? Do you agree that the Court should change the death penalty age?

3. *Expert Witnesses.* American courts have used two different standards—named *Frye* and *Daubert* after the cases that developed those standards—to identify when expert witnesses may testify about scientific evidence. *Frye* was a D.C. Circuit case from 1923. Frye v. United States, 293 F. 1013 (D.C. Cir. 1923). The proposed testimony concerned an expert witness explaining an early effort at a lie detector, which sounds familiar in theory to using fMRI to detect lies:

> The test is described as the systolic blood pressure deception test. It is asserted that blood pressure is influenced by change in the emotions of the witness, and that the systolic blood pressure rises are brought about by nervous impulses sent to the sympathetic branch of the autonomic nervous system. Scientific experiments, it is claimed, have demonstrated that fear, rage, and pain always produce a rise of systolic blood pressure, and that conscious deception or falsehood, concealment of facts, or guilt of crime, accompanied by fear of detection when the person is under examination, raises the systolic blood pressure in a curve, which corresponds exactly to the struggle going on in the subject's mind, between fear and attempted control of that fear, as the examination touches the vital points in respect of which he is attempting to deceive the examiner.

Id. at 1013–14. The court ruled that expert testimony was permitted when the content did not "lie within the range of common experience or common knowledge" and was "sufficiently established to have gained general acceptance in the particular field in which it belongs." Id. at 1014.

Many states, including New York, continue to apply the *Frye* "general acceptance" standard in deciding whether to admit expert testimony. In 1993, however, in *Daubert* the Supreme Court acknowledged that Federal Rule of Evidence 702 had replaced the *Frye* standard for federal courts. Daubert v. Merrell Dow Pharm., Inc., 509 U.S. 579, 583 (1993). The facts involved expert witnesses who wanted to testify that Bendectin can cause birth defects. The Ninth Circuit had rejected the testimony because it was not "generally accepted" under *Frye*. Id. at 584.

The Supreme Court identified a "gatekeeper" role for trial judges to determine what evidence should be admissible. According to the current version of Rule 702:

> A witness who is qualified as an expert by knowledge, skill, experience, training, or education may testify in the form of an opinion or otherwise if:
>
> **(a)** the expert's scientific, technical, or other specialized knowledge will help the trier of fact to understand the evidence or to determine a fact in issue;
>
> **(b)** the testimony is based on sufficient facts or data;
>
> **(c)** the testimony is the product of reliable principles and methods; and

(d) the expert has reliably applied the principles and methods to the facts of the case.

Fed. R. Evid. 702. The Commentary to the Rules explains *Daubert*'s analysis to the expert testimony issue:

> *Daubert* set forth a non-exclusive checklist for trial courts to use in assessing the reliability of scientific expert testimony. The specific factors explicated by the *Daubert* Court are (1) whether the expert's technique or theory can be or has been tested—that is, whether the expert's theory can be challenged in some objective sense, or whether it is instead simply a subjective, conclusory approach that cannot reasonably be assessed for reliability; (2) whether the technique or theory has been subject to peer review and publication; (3) the known or potential rate of error of the technique or theory when applied; (4) the existence and maintenance of standards and controls; and (5) whether the technique or theory has been generally accepted in the scientific community.
>
> Fed. R. Evid. 702; see also *Daubert*, 509 U.S. at 593–95.

4. *What Neuroscience Contributes.* Science can provide a variety of images of the brain that could be used as evidence in criminal trials. The *structure* of the brain is evident in x-rays, CT (computed tomography) scanning and MRI (magnetic resonance imaging), which have long been used to show brain damage in tort lawsuits and other cases involving physical proof of injury. "These techniques . . . are used for information about how various parts of the body are structured. They can show whether structures are intact, and can reveal damage, atrophy, intrusions, and developmental anomalies." Owen D. Jones et al., Brain Imaging for Legal Thinkers: A Guide for the Perplexed, 2009 Stan. Tech. L. Rev. 5, 13 (2009). As you learned at the beginning of the chapter, the *functioning* of the brain is revealed through different procedures, including PET scanning, EEG, MEG, and fMRI.

> At its most basic, fMRI can be understood as a tool for learning which regions of the brain are working, how much, and for how long, during particular tasks. In much the same way that the body delivers more oxygen to muscles that are working harder, the body delivers more oxygen to brain regions that work harder. The fMRI technique measures blood oxygenation levels—within small cubic volumes of brain tissue known as "voxels"—as those levels change across time with the varying metabolic demands of active neurons. Changes in demand for oxygen are widely considered to be reliable proxies for inferring the fluctuating activity of the underlying neural tissue.

Id. at 17. What is the difference between a structural and functional brain image? Do you understand why two structural pictures taken a minute apart would not vary, but two functional pictures would? Id. at 30.

All scientific testimony must "rest[ ] on a reliable foundation and [be] relevant to the task at hand." Daubert v. Merrell Dow Pharmaceuticals, Inc., 509 U.S. 579, 597 (1993). Dr. Lorne Semrau, who holds a Ph.D. in clinical psychology, was prosecuted for health care fraud after he "upcoded" his bills,

namely assigned the wrong code for medical procedures so that he would be reimbursed more money for them by Medicare or Medicaid. One of Semrau's defenses was that "any improper billing was unintentional and despite his good faith attempts to be compliant [the wrong codes existed] because of the complicated and confusing nature of the codes." United States v. Semrau, 693 F.3d 510, 515 (6th Cir. 2012). Semrau offered fMRI testimony to prove he was truthful. Dr. Steven J. Laken planned to testify that certain regions of the brain are activated by deception and that fMRI scans of Semrau's brain could accurately depict whether Semrau was telling the truth. The tests were conducted in the following manner:

> Prior to the scheduled test date, Dr. Laken developed a set of twenty neutral questions and twenty control questions that would be asked during the scanning. The neutral questions—such as "Is today Tuesday?"—provided Dr. Laken with the "baseline" for the results to improve accuracy. The control questions—such as "Have you ever used illegal drugs?" and "Have you ever lied to a court?"—are included "just to fill up empty space" and do not directly contribute to the final analysis. Attorney Gordon and Dr. Laken co-developed Specific Incident Questions ("SIQs") directly relating to the upcoding and AIMS charges. The SIQs for the first scan included questions such as "Did you ever receive varying instructions or guidance regarding which codes to bill, including being told that 99312 would be the appropriate code to use instead of 90862?" and "Did you bill CPT Code 99312 to cheat or defraud Medicare?" The SIQs for the second scan included questions such as "Did you know that AIMS tests performed by psychiatrists [were] not a necessary service that could be separately billed?" The prosecution was not notified that Dr. Semrau was going to take the deception test and thus lacked an opportunity to submit its own questions to Dr. Laken for use during the test or to observe the testing procedures.

Id. at 518. The Sixth Circuit upheld the district court's refusal to admit the testimony because the "technology had not been fully examined in 'real world' settings" and the test results did "not purport to indicate whether Dr. Semrau was truthful about any single statement." Id. at 516.

In contrast, a Florida court allowed QEEG (quantitative electroencephalography) evidence to be submitted to the jury in the prosecution of Grady Nelson for the vicious stabbing of his wife and her two young children. Nelson was sentenced to life imprisonment instead of the death penalty. Jurors credited the brain science as influencing their understanding of Nelson's culpability. Owen D. Jones et al., Neuroscientists in Court, 14 Nature Rev. 730, 730 (2013). One juror said, "It turned my decision all the way around. The technology really swayed me. . . . After seeing the brain scans, I was convinced this guy had some sort of brain problem." Id. at 734. Does this example persuade you that brain scans should be used in all juvenile death penalty cases? In all death penalty cases? In all criminal cases? Would you expect the use of neuroimages to make jurors more likely to decide defendants are less responsible for their crimes and

more likely to reduce their sentences? See Michael J. Saks et al., The Impact of Neuroimages in the Sentencing Phase of Capital Trials 11 J. Empirical Legal Studs. 105 (2014).

Do you think fMRI results should be allowed in court to be used as a possible lie detector test as in the *Semrau* case? So far, courts have rejected the use of fMRI to show truthfulness or lying. William A. Woodruff, Evidence of Lies and Rules of Evidence: The Admissibility of fMRI-Based Expert Opinion of Witness Truthfulness, 16 N.C. J. L. & Tech. 105, 108–09 (2014). Proponents of fMRI lie detection argue that the brain uses more activity to lie than to tell the truth, and that this effort can be detected in the fMRI scan:

> The hypothesis underlying fMRI as a lie detector is that telling the truth is the natural or normal response of the brain and one would not expect to see increased activity over and above the normal background level of brain activity. Lying, however, requires the person to first recall the truth, then suppress the truth while creating a lie that might plausibly fit the objective facts, and finally, verbalize the falsehood. This increased neural activity demands more energy. To supply the energy demand, more oxygenated blood is directed to those regions of the brain processing the lie. This relative difference in energy demand, called the blood oxygenation level-dependent ("BOLD") differential by neuroscientists, is detectable by an fMRI scan. Comparing the BOLD differential between subjects known to be telling the truth with those deliberately lying allows researchers to hypothesize that an increased BOLD response in certain regions of the brain when the subject is answering questions is an indication of deception.

Id. at 109. fMRI differs from polygraphs, which measure physiological reactions to perceived stress. Id. at 119. Professor Jones has commented, "With the advent of fMRI, cognitive neuroscientists are examining whether brain-based lie detection is possible. Despite some very promising studies . . . the prospects for legal use remain almost entirely speculative." Owen D. Jones & Anthony D. Wagner, Law and Neuroscience: Progress, Promise, and Pitfalls in THE COGNITIVE NEUROSCIENCES (2019). Why would these neuroscientists have drawn this conclusion? Why is this use speculative?

5. *Neuroprediction.* What do you think about neuroprediction? Consider the question asked in the subtitle of this article, Andrew R. Calderon, A Dangerous Brain: Can Neuroscience Predict How Likely Someone Is to Commit Another Crime?, Aug. 14, 2019, https://www.themarshallproject.org/2018/08/14/a-dangerous-brain. Courts usually consider whether a defendant will be a future risk to society. Prof. Kent Kiehl has a test that uses brain age to measure future risk. Brain age considers how much gray matter is in the brain. By studying many brains, the scientists can usually predict who will be rearrested for the commission of another crime. Younger people are more likely to be rearrested. Should such neuroprediction now be used in court? Some scholars call neuroscience a " 'double-edged sword' that either unduly exonerates defendants or marks them as irredeemable future dangers." Others "argue that the science is

reliable enough to integrate with other risk assessments." Some say "the science of neuroprediction is not ready for prime time." Id. What do you think of neuroprediction?

6. *Judicial Interpretations of Miller*. After *Miller* was decided, Ackeem Riley, who was seventeen years and five months old at the time of his crime, was sentenced to life without parole by a trial judge in Connecticut, where the life without parole sentence was not mandatory. State v. Riley, 58 A.3d 304 (Ct. 2013). Riley and his friends had fired a gun toward a gang member and killed sixteen-year-old Troy Davis, who was in the area of the shooting. On appeal, Riley argued that *Miller* requires the sentencing judge "to take into account how children are different, and how those differences counsel against irrevocably sentencing them to a lifetime in prison," while the state argued *Miller* merely "afford[s] juvenile defendants the opportunity to present mitigating evidence." Id. at 313–14.

What do you think *Miller* requires? See id. at 314 ("*Miller* requires only the opportunity to present such evidence to a court permitted to consider it, and to impose a lesser sentence in its discretion"), but see id. at 317 (Borden, J., dissenting) ("[T]he sentencing court is required to take into account the differences, identified by that body of science, between the juvenile and the adult brains."). If you were a defense lawyer, what research would you do and what arguments would you present about a client like Riley? Would you make use of neuroscience in preparing your case? Are you influenced by the result in the Grady Nelson case, *supra* note 3?

According to the dissent in *Riley*, *Miller* requires the trial court to do two things: (1) take into account—by presentation from the state or the defendant, or both—the factors that distinguish the juvenile brain from the adult brain regarding the juvenile's diminished culpability and heightened capacity for change, and (2) take into account how those factors *counsel* against sentencing the juvenile irrevocably to die in prison. How would you do that? Would you rely on common sense? Behavioral science? Neuroscience?

7. *Blameworthiness.* Neuroscientist David Eagleman argues that blameworthiness is the wrong question in the criminal realm. Eagleman's book, *Incognito*, provides numerous instances of criminals who suffered from brain tumors and other brain disorders. David M. Eagleman, Incognito: The Secret Lives of the Brain (2011). According to Eagleman, "The lesson is clear: a slight change in the balance of brain chemistry can cause large changes in behavior. The behavior of the patient cannot be separated from his biology." Id. at 157. Thus we are mistaken to believe that "all adults possess the same capacity to make sound choices." Id. The condition of their brains determines their choices. This understanding is also part of the background to *Miller*:

> [F]indings of structural and functional differences between adolescent and adult brains that are plausibly linked to differences in individuals' ability to control their impulses and to stand up to peer pressure suggest that these aspects of adolescent immaturity are not merely reflective of juveniles' poor choices or different values but that they are at least partly due to factors that are not

> entirely under an individual's control, which makes immaturity a more convincing mitigator.

Steinberg, *supra,* at 517. If you accept Eagleman's premise, what should replace blameworthiness as the basis of the criminal justice system?

Eagleman recommends a "forward-looking legal system," which identifies the defendant's risk of reoffending and incarcerates based on that danger. Eagleman, *supra,* at 157. Would you trust neuroscience to develop such a system? A "forward-thinking legal system will parlay biological understanding into customized *rehabilitation*, viewing criminal behavior the way we understand other such medical conditions as epilepsy, schizophrenia, and depression—conditions that now allow the seeking and giving of help." Id. at 180. What do you think of a forward-looking, future dangerousness and rehabilitation-focused understanding of criminal law?

8. *Your New Criminal Justice System.* Think about the individuals described in this note. If you were to create a blameworthiness spectrum, where zero is not blameworthy and ten is completely blameworthy, where would each of these people fall on the spectrum? Do you take blameworthiness into account in your criminal justice system, or not?

a. *Whitman.* In 1966, Charles Whitman, after killing his wife and mother, took rifles to the top of the University of Texas Tower, where he fired shots across the campus for ninety-six minutes, killing sixteen and wounding numerous others. Before the shooting, the former marine had been puzzled by his health and thoughts, and requested an autopsy in his suicide note. The autopsy found a nickel-sized tumor, a glioblastoma, in his brain. Eagleman, Incognito, at 154–55.

b. *Alex.* After two decades of marriage and in a surprise to his wife, Alex began to show an excessive interest in child pornography. Doctors discovered a massive brain tumor in his orbitofrontal cortex. After removal of the tumor, Alex's interest in pornography waned. Six months later, the interest in child pornography returned and doctors found that a portion of the tumor remained in his brain. After that piece of tumor was removed, Alex displayed no more interest in pornography. Id.

c. *Benoit.* Chris Benoit, a professional wrestler, took steroids to improve his career. In a steroid rage he murdered his son and wife and then committed suicide. Id. at 175–76.

d. *Tiegreen.* Sixteen-year-old Christopher Tiegreen suffered severe head injuries when he flipped in his car several times, only six weeks after getting his driver's license. Before the accident, he had been a member of his high school's chorus and played soccer. After a month in a coma, Tiegreen awoke as a more violent person. When he was twenty-three years old he walked outside and violently attacked a woman and her twenty-month-old son. Kevin Davis, Brain Trials: Neuroscience Is Taking a Stand in the Courtroom, A.B.A. J., Nov. 1, 2012.

e. *Weinstein.* Sixty-five-year-old Herbert Weinstein, a New York advertising executive, strangled his wife and threw her out a twelfth-floor window after an argument about their children. Weinstein was discovered to have an arachnoid cyst on his brain, causing pressure on his temporal lobe. Id. We also know that Weinstein was a model prisoner for fourteen years and never performed any more violent attacks.

f. *Lotz.* 65-year-old Larry Lotz, a Vietnam vet, shot his wife four times after she scolded him for leaving a coffee pot on all day. They had been married 40 years. He then called 911 and said what he had done. She died at the hospital. His lawyer said Lotz had no reason to do this, and so argued that he suffered from PTSD and had early signs of Alzheimer's. The judge, however, rejected an insanity defense and found Lotz guilty of second-degree murder. Kevin Davis, Brain Matters: Millions have been invested in the emerging field of neurolaw, ABA Journal, Jun. 1, 2020, https://www.abajournal.com/magazine/article/millions-have-been-invested-in-the-emerging-field-of-neurolaw.-where-is-it-leading.

g. *Veterans.* What should happen to war veterans who suffer post-traumatic stress disorder (PTSD) and then commit violent crimes?

h. *Juveniles.* From *Miller* and the cases cited in *Miller*:

i. Kuntrell Jackson and Evan Miller.

ii. Fifteen-year-old William Wayne Thompson, with three older collaborators, participated in the murder of his brother-in-law. "The evidence disclosed that the victim had been shot twice, and that his throat, chest, and abdomen had been cut. He also had multiple bruises and a broken leg. His body had been chained to a concrete block and thrown into a river where it remained for almost four weeks." Thompson v. Oklahoma, 487 U.S. 815, 823 (1988).

iii. At age sixteen, Terrance Jamar Graham and friends tried to rob a restaurant and injured the manager during the attempt. Six months later, he participated in a home invasion, where they held the homeowner hostage and then left him locked in a closet. Graham's parents were crack cocaine addicts, and he started using alcohol at age nine and marijuana at age thirteen. Graham v. Florida, 560 U.S. 48 (2010).

iv. Seventeen-year-old Christopher Simmons decided he wanted to murder someone, and talked about his plan with friends. Simmons and friends entered Shirley Crook's home, bound her in duct tape, strapped her up with electrical wire, covered her head with a towel, and threw her into the Meramec River, where she drowned. He bragged about the crime to friends and then

confessed it to police. Roper v. Simmons, 543 U.S. 551 (2005).

i. *Wessinger and Madison.* What about Wessinger, who "suffers from a major neurocognitive disorder that compromises his decision-making abilities," or Madison, who is suffering from dementia?

9. *Neuroscience and Effective Assistance of Counsel.* Understanding that attorneys have a professional responsibility to investigate their cases, consider the following example of how neuroscience and professional responsibility intersect.

> Samuel Morgan was charged with two counts of murder and with aggravated kidnaping and rape. His lawyer, Lawrence Levin, met with members of Morgan's family shortly after Morgan was arrested. Morgan's mother and sister told Levin that Morgan suffered from seizures, which were due to a blow to the head that Morgan had suffered at age eight. Levin also learned from the family that Morgan takes seizure medication.
>
> Morgan was convicted of all charges and was eligible for the death penalty. During his opening statement at the aggravation-mitigation stage of the sentencing hearing, Levin told the court he would present evidence "regarding medical testimony as to the problems medically that the defendant has had and still suffers from." During the sentencing hearing, Levin stipulated to the admission into evidence of a 1978 presentence investigation report which noted that defendant suffered continuing seizures after receiving a blow to the head at age eight. Levin did no further investigation into Morgan's background.
>
> At the sentencing phase of the proceedings, Levin called Morgan's mother and sister to testify. Levin asked the mother whether the defendant had been hurt as a youngster and if the defendant "sometimes does things that he is not responsible for" when he fails to receive medical care or medication. Levin also asked the mother: "Since eight years old until today's date, has Morgan had problems as a result of the spot on his brain?" Finally, Levin inquired of Morgan's mother if she was aware that "unless Morgan takes his medication" he has "problems functioning."

People v. Morgan, 719 N.E.2d 681, 704–05 (Ill. 1999). Did Levin's conduct fall below an "objective standard of reasonableness" for an attorney? See Strickland v. Washington, 466 U.S. 668 (1984) (setting standards for constitutionally ineffective assistance of counsel). What investigation would you have counseled Levin to undertake? Can you think of any strategies or reasons why an attorney would choose to present a limited amount of evidence regarding mitigating circumstances?

Do you agree with Justice Sotomayor's dissent from denial of certiorari, arguing that Wessinger's lawyers should have investigated his seizures, stroke and possible neurocognitive disorder? Do you agree with the majority

or dissent in *Madison* about what the lawyers should have been allowed to argue? How does neuroscience make a lawyer more or less effective?

10. *Legislation.* Professor Shen explains that brain science has also started to appear in legislative discussions of juvenile culpability, but primarily on the side that "argues for lower mandatory sentences and against juvenile transfer to adult courts." Francis X. Shen, Legislating Neuroscience: The Case of Juvenile Justice, 46 Loy. L.A. L. Rev. 985, 996 (2014). He also finds that "lab neuroscience" and "lobbyist neuroscience" are two different things; "the rhetoric used by advocacy groups is more categorical than the measured approach suggested by the underlying research." Id. What should state legislatures do in light of the Supreme Court's cases about the brain and disease? Is it adequate for state legislators to change their laws so that juvenile life without parole is optional rather than mandatory? Do you agree that "neuroscience [should be] one—but not the only and not the primary—piece of evidence considered in the policy process"? Id. at 1016.

11. In a New Mexico case, lawyers for Anthony Blas Yepez asked to introduce evidence showing that Yepez has the MAOA gene, which gave him a genetic predisposition to violence. Because of the gene, they argued, he had not committed a murder intentionally. The trial court refused to admit the evidence about the gene. The appeals court affirmed, finding that although the trial court had erred in not admitting the evidence, the error was harmless. State v. Yepez, 428 P.3d 301 (N.M. App. 2018). The New Mexico Supreme Court granted review of the case, but refused to accept an amicus brief that argued, "First, we describe how MAOA studies based on the prior 'candidate-gene approach' are unreliable due to inherent flaws in the methodology, leading to inconsistencies in replication. Second, the general scientific consensus has emerged that the earlier MAOA studies (upon which the defense experts relied) are now an outdated method of studying psychiatric genetics. Third, to the extent that recent studies adopting the more rigorous genomewide association studies (GWAS) have attempted to replicate the earlier findings of MAOA candidate-gene studies, they have found no reliable correlation between MAOA and violence." Nita A. Farahany et al., Genetic Evidence, MAOA; State v. Yepez, 50:3 N. M. L. Rev. 469 (2020). Stanford law professor Henry Greely said " if he were a judge in Yepez's case, he probably would not allow the MAO-A evidence. 'It's not going as far as junk science, but it's close.' " Jon Schuppe, Blame my brain: A killer's bold defense gets a court hearing, NBC News, Apr. 27, 2019, https://www.nbcnews.com/news/us-news/blame-my-brain-killer-s-bold-defense-gets-court-hearing-n998676. What does this case tell you about science and how it should be used in the courts?

In the next section, we examine how scientific evidence about the brain can be used in the courtroom.

B. COURTROOM ISSUES

The process of remembering consists of three stages: acquisition—"the perception of the original event"; retention—

> "the period of time that passes between the event and the eventual recollection of a particular piece of information"; and retrieval—the "stage during which a person recalls stored information." At each of those stages, the information ultimately offered as "memory" can be distorted, contaminated and even falsely imagined. The witness does not perceive all that a videotape would disclose, but rather "get[s] the gist of things and constructs a "memory" on "bits of information . . . and what seems plausible." The witness does not encode all the information that a videotape does; memory rapidly and continuously decays; retained memory can be unknowingly contaminated by post-event information; [and] the witness's retrieval of stored "memory" can be impaired and distorted by a variety of factors, including suggestive interviewing and identification procedures conducted by law enforcement personnel.

State v. Henderson, 27 A.3d 872, 894–95 (N.J. 2011).

How good is your memory? Are you confident that if you were the subject of a crime, you would be able to recall the criminal's appearance and identify him or her after the attack was over?

Neuroscientists have taught us that our memories are not as good as we think they are. See Joyce W. Lacy & Craig E. L. Stark, The Neuroscience of Memory: Implications for the Courtroom, 14 Nature Rev. Neurosci. 649 (2013). Consider the following eight insights that neuroscientists have developed about memory. Do the scientists' findings match your common sense and experience?

Practice Exercise: It is time to test your memory skills. Go to the website and perform the Selective Attention Test. Then, perform the Whodunnit test and the Bomber on the Roof exercise. After taking the tests, do you feel confident in your memory and powers of observation?

1. Even highly trained subjects confront memory failure after stressful events. Soldiers trained to handle stress participated in a mock Prisoner of War Camp (POWC) during which an interrogator questioned them for thirty to forty minutes. Only a third of the participants were able to identify the interrogator afterwards. Two thirds identified the interrogator in a line-up even though the interrogator was not present in it. Id.

2. *Misinformation* can distort memories. Soldiers who were shown a photograph of someone not the interrogator before the identification session were more likely to falsely identify the interrogator. Id. Similarly, crime victims shown a photo of a non-perpetrator before identification can easily have their memory of the actual perpetrator distorted.

3. False memories can be implanted in people's minds so that they will remember, e.g., a hospital visit in their youth that never occurred. Id.

4. Memory can be influenced by questioning about the memory. "For example, when participants viewed footage of a car accident, the question 'How fast were the cars going when they *smashed* into each other?' elicited reports of 20 percent greater traveling speeds than the question 'How fast were the cars going when they *hit* each other?' despite the fact that participants in both conditions viewed the same footage. The former question was also more likely to elicit a false memory of broken glass at the site of the crash." Id. (emphasis added).

> **Practice Exercise:** Now, go back to the website and ask a friend or family member to administer the DRM Paradigm Test to you. Then test your memory for faces. How did you do? What did these tests teach you about your memory?

5. Feedback affects memory. Positive feedback from police officers about witness identification increases confidence, while negative feedback decreases it. Nonverbal feedback is also influential. Repeated questioning also increases witness confidence.

6. Confidence does not correspond to accuracy of memory. People who are most confident about their recollection often remember the least.

7. Time, age, and repetition change memories. Even witnesses' memories of the details of the September 11th terrorist attacks changed over time. Confidence in memory, however, did not decrease as the memories faded.

8. Mock jurors "fill in the gaps" by remembering testimony that did not occur in the actual case but that might be expected to occur in a criminal case.

Based on what you understand about memory, do you agree with how the Court of Appeals of New York handled the issue of eyewitness identification in the following cases?

People v. Abney

Court of Appeals of New York, 2009.
918 N.E.2d 486, 13 N.Y.3d 251.

■ READ, J.

Defendants in both of these cases unsuccessfully sought to introduce expert testimony on the reliability of eyewitness identification. The question for us to decide is whether, in light of our decisions in *People v. Lee*, 96 N.Y.2d 157, 726 N.Y.S.2d 361, 750 N.E.2d 63 (2001), *People v. Young*, 7 N.Y.3d 40, 817 N.Y.S.2d 576, 850 N.E.2d 623 (2006) and, especially, *People v. LeGrand*, 8 N.Y.3d 449, 835 N.Y.S.2d 523, 867 N.E.2d 374 (2007), the trial courts abused their discretion when they disallowed this testimony. We conclude that the trial judge in *Abney* abused his discretion, but that the trial judge in *Allen* did not.

I.
Abney
A. Facts and Trial

On June 2, 2005 at about 3:20 p.m., 13-year-old Farhana U., on her way home from school, was descending well-lit stairs into the subway station near the corner of Essex and Delancey Streets in Manhattan when a man whom she did not know approached her and asked for "some change." This man stood face-to-face with Farhana, about two feet away. She initially did not think he intended to harm her and was not afraid. Looking him squarely in the face, she said she had no change.

After Farhana "took a couple of steps forward," the stranger wheeled in front of her, placed a knife with a six-inch blade and "a big curve on the end" near her throat, and asked her "a couple of times" to hand over her necklace, a gold chain with a locket. As this man stood close by her, Farhana was "looking at his face"; she was "really scared" and "didn't know what to do." When Farhana refused his demand, screaming "No," he ripped the chain off her neck, and fled up the stairs. This entire encounter was fleeting.

Farhana continued down the stairs into the subway station and reported the robbery to a token clerk. At about 4:30 p.m., Detective Samuel DeJesus interviewed her at his desk in the transit station house at Columbus Circle. According to Detective DeJesus, Farhana seemed frightened; she told him that she had been robbed at knife-point by a stranger, a black man in his thirties who was over six feet tall, had "pinkish" lips, and wore a short-sleeved blue shirt and a blue bandana.

Farhana's physical description of the robber and how he carried out the crime prompted Detective DeJesus to suspect defendant Quentin Abney: he was familiar with defendant on account of his arrest for an earlier subway-related robbery. Telling Farhana that he would be "right back," the detective left his desk to put together an array of six photographs, including defendant's. When he returned, he told Farhana

that he "was going to show her a group of photos and, if she recognized anyone, to let [him] know which one and what number." Pointing out defendant's photograph, she responded, "that's him, number six."

On June 22, 2005, Detective Ernest Dorvil telephoned Farhana at her home to ask her to view a lineup. Upon arrival at the station house, she waited in an office with the door shut while the lineup was being put together. From the office, Farhana could not see defendant, who was in a "cell area" on the other side of the building, or any of the "fillers" selected to participate in the lineup. Once the lineup was assembled, Detective Dorvil escorted Farhana to the viewing room, where they were joined by another police officer and defendant's attorney. She identified defendant, in position number four (there were six men in the lineup); Farhana was "sure" that he was the man who had asked her for change and then robbed her at knife-point.

Defendant was arrested and charged with one count of robbery in the first degree. At the subsequent jury trial, Farhana testified on direct examination that the man who robbed her had a dark brown complexion, "puppy dog eyes," and "pinkish-purplish lips"; she did not remember whether he was wearing anything over his head, but thought his shirt was blue. Defense counsel cross-examined Detective DeJesus about the details of Farhana's initial description of the robber; Detective Dorvil about the lineup, eliciting testimony that he let Farhana know ahead of time that a suspect was included (which she contradicted, saying that the detective told her only that he wanted her to view "a couple of people"); and Farhana about the lineup and the appearance of the knife.

Defendant presented an alibi defense. . . .

The jury convicted defendant of first-degree robbery, and Supreme Court sentenced him as a persistent violent felony offender to a prison term of 20 years to life. He appealed.

B. Proffer of Expert Testimony

Before jury selection, defendant made a motion in limine to present expert testimony concerning "psychological factors of memory and perception that may affect the accuracy of eyewitness identifications." Specifically, he sought to call Dr. Solomon M. Fulero, who would "educat[e] the jurors on many counterintuitive findings that bear directly on the reliability of the identification evidence in [the] case," which were beyond the average juror's ken. Defendant identified 15 such factors: stress, exposure time, color perception under monochromatic light, event violence, cross-racial accuracy, similarity of lineup fillers, lineup instructions, rate of memory loss, postevent information, the wording of questions posed to an eyewitness, unconscious transference to the crime scene of someone seen in another situation or context, the witness's preexisting attitudes and expectations, simultaneous and sequential lineups, the lack of correlation of confidence and accuracy, and confidence

malleability. He specifically noted that the robbery was brief, the victim was under stress, and a weapon was used.

Supreme Court denied the motion as premature, with leave to renew at the close of the People's direct case. The trial judge observed that while he was aware that the People's case hinged on the eyewitness testimony of the 13-year-old victim "[a]t this [juncture] . . . [he], in the exercise of discretion, [did] not consider [the] case an appropriate one for an expert identification witness" for several reasons.

The trial judge reasoned that "[a]s a threshold matter," defendant's papers did not "appropriately narrow the scope of the expert's proposed testimony," which therefore threatened to turn into "a full-fledged seminar . . . which could lead to hours of academic discussion and speculation." Second, the proffered testimony about how police investigative techniques might influence a lineup identification was not relevant because the victim had previously picked out a photograph from an array, and so must have realized that a suspect would be included in the lineup. Third, two of the proposed subjects of testimony—postevent information and unconscious transference—"[had] not passed the Frye test" in other courts. Fourth, evidence about simultaneous versus sequential lineups was "unmanageable in a trial setting," because juries were "not experts on constitutional law and procedure and [could not] be educated about those topics during a trial."

Finally, the trial judge commented that "jurors know that, as a matter of common sense, a person's memory does fade as time passes." In his view, "[m]any" of defendant's concerns relative to the accuracy of Farhana's eyewitness identification could be adequately addressed by tailoring cross-examination and the jury charge. He indicated that defendant was "free to renew his motion at the close of the People's case, at which time he [should] narrow his proffer to the specific topics that he believes are relevant to the facts of this case."

After the People rested, defendant did, in fact, renew his motion, proposing a more limited range of subjects to be covered. Specifically, he asked to elicit expert testimony about the effect of event stress, exposure time, event violence and weapon focus, cross-racial identification, and lineup instructions, in addition to a new topic, double blind lineups. Defendant pointed out specific circumstances of his case to which the proposed testimony would be relevant. While acknowledging the trial judge's earlier ruling that witness confidence could be addressed through jury instructions, defendant specifically took exception to it.

The trial judge denied defendant's renewed motion on the ground that "having had the benefit of the witness' testimony," there was "nothing unique about [the] case . . . present[ing] issues that are beyond the ken of the ordinary juror." In his view, the relevant issues had been explored adequately during cross-examination, and could be argued in summation and covered in the jury charge.

C. Appellate Division

The Appellate Division, with two Justices dissenting, affirmed the judgment of conviction and sentence. . . .

Allen

A. Facts and Trial

At around 3:30 p.m. on March 10, 2004, two masked men barged into a busy barbershop in Queens, located across from the Woodside Housing Project. The mask worn by one of the men, who wielded what appeared to be a knife, left exposed the top portion of his face from his top lip to above his eyebrows. His accomplice (who has never been apprehended) displayed a gun and stated, "This is a holdup." The gunman grabbed Juan Almonte, one of the barbers, and pulled back the slide on his gun. He next struck the shop owner in the face with the gun; he chased down a barber who tried to escape to the basement, dragged him back, put a gun into his mouth, and rifled his pants pockets; he demanded money from another barber, who emptied his pockets of about $30 in tips.

The knife-wielding intruder asked Almonte for money, checked around his neck for a chain, tried to open an apparently locked drawer at his barber station, and then called out to the gunman, "It's time to go." The two robbers instructed everyone present to lie down on the floor. They fled the shop together, and someone called the police. This entire incident lasted only a few minutes.

Gabriel Bierd, a customer in the shop, quickly realized that the knife-wielding robber was defendant Gregory Allen, whom he encountered regularly in the neighborhood. Bierd had heard defendant's speaking voice several times during the previous six months, and he recognized him from both his "[b]ody type" and his voice.

When Sergeant Ronald Buell arrived at the barbershop to investigate the robbery, Bierd provided him with defendant's nicknames—"Junior" and "J.R."—and described him as a black male, about five feet, eight inches or five feet, nine inches tall. Bierd accompanied Sergeant Buell to the squad house, and looked through a "photo mug book" with 180 photographs, one to a page. Pedigree information was covered up. He picked out defendant's photograph (at page 64), identifying him as the knife-wielding robber. At Sergeant Buell's instruction, though, he looked through the remainder of the book. Buell then prepared a photographic array with six photographs, and Bierd selected defendant's. Sergeant Buell drove to the barbershop and showed this photographic array to Almonte, who likewise identified defendant as the knife-wielding robber.

Defendant was arrested at about 10:30 p.m. on the day of the robbery. He was charged with four counts of robbery in the first degree, two counts of attempted robbery in the first degree, two counts of robbery in the second degree, and three counts of attempted robbery in the second degree.

At defendant's trial, Bierd and Almonte recounted the robbery, and explained how they immediately recognized defendant as the knife-wielding robber. They testified to having picked defendant out in a lineup on July 7, 2004; they identified him in court.

Detective David Beutel testified that he arrested defendant on March 10, 2004 and, when he asked him his name, defendant replied that his nicknames were "Junior" and "J.R." Detective Beutel attempted to put together a lineup the next day, but defendant would not cooperate; he pulled his shirt over his head, got into the fetal position on a table, and refused to sit and hold up a number unless all the men in the lineup wore masks. Pursuant to court order, Detective Beutel finally organized a lineup on July 7, 2004, four months later. Bierd, Almonte and the barbershop's owner each viewed the lineup separately. Bierd and Almonte identified defendant as the knife-wielding robber; the shop owner did not recognize anyone.

Defendant called five defense witnesses. An investigator with the Legal Aid Society recounted her interview with Almonte, stating that he told her that he could see the skin around the knife-wielding robber's eyes and the bridge of his nose, and that his mask did not have a hole for the nose. Another investigator testified that he was present at the lineup on July 7, 2004, and that defendant's attorney asked for all the lineup participants to wear ski masks; a police officer testified that he recovered six latent prints from the door of the barbershop; and a detective testified that none of those prints matched defendant's. Finally, Danielle Allen, defendant's sister, told the jury that her brother had a scar on his nose as a result of a dog bite suffered in childhood, and that he had long had a scar on his cheek. Photographs showing these scars were admitted into evidence. Allen further explained that, at the time of the robbery, defendant was dating someone who lived in the Woodside Housing Project.

The jury convicted defendant of all the charges submitted to it (the trial judge dismissed three counts). On February 28, 2006, defendant was sentenced to concurrent, determinate prison terms of 15 years on each first-degree robbery conviction, 10 years on each attempted first-degree and second-degree robbery conviction, seven years on each attempted second-degree robbery conviction, and five years' postrelease supervision. He appealed.

B. Proffer of Expert Testimony

On July 14, 2005, defendant moved in limine to admit the expert testimony of Professor Steven Penrod regarding 17 "psychological factors of memory and perception that may affect the accuracy of eyewitness identifications." Attached to the motion was Dr. Penrod's curriculum vitae, a list of his publications, and a document written by Dr. Penrod discussing many of the factors about which he proposed to testify, but not how these factors were relevant to the case. This document mentioned unconscious transference only once, describing this phenomenon as when

"innocent persons seen in some other context can be mistakenly identified as having been seen at the crime or [where] a bystander at the scene is mistaken as the perpetrator."

The People opposed the motion on the ground that defendant had not demonstrated that the ability to assess the accuracy of the eyewitnesses' testimony was beyond the ken of the average juror, or that the psychological factors about which Dr. Penrod proposed to testify were relevant to this case, "particularly . . . where . . . defendant was known to one of the eyewitnesses [Bierd] after months of regular encounters." Further, the People argued that this case was distinguishable from the one-eyewitness identification cases relied upon by defendant. Here, there were two eyewitnesses who corroborated each other, and there was additional corroborative evidence, including defendant's refusal to participate in a lineup unless he and all the fillers wore masks. At the time, the People argued, defendant would have had no way to know that masks were involved in the robbery unless he was there when it took place.

Immediately before jury selection, defendant made additional arguments on the motion. According to defendant, the expert testimony would be "important" because the use of a gun made the robbery stressful, and Dr. Penrod would explain that high levels of stress could impair an identification. Additionally, Dr. Penrod would address "weapon focus," and the concept that there is "not necessarily a correlation between certainty and accuracy" of an eyewitness identification, although the "general public . . . thinks there is." Finally, defendant argued that Dr. Penrod's testimony on the subject of "unconscious transference" was relevant because the eyewitnesses claimed that they had seen defendant in the neighborhood before, and thus it was possible that they identified defendant because "he's the only one in the lineup that they've seen in the neighborhood."

The trial judge denied the motion, finding that "this is not an area in which an expert is at all helpful" because the proposed testimony involved matters of

> "common sense and life experience. . . . [T]he jury knows the longer you look at something the easier it is to remember . . . just like they know if a person is wearing a disguise, it makes it hard to recognize them. They don't need an expert to testify to these things."

He ruled that defendant should address the reliability of eyewitness identification during cross-examination and in summation.

After the People rested, defendant renewed his motion, reiterating his position that Dr. Penrod's testimony regarding unconscious transference was relevant because "statistics show that people are much more likely to identify someone they've seen before." The court denied the application, again deciding that the issue was a matter of common sense.

C. Appellate Division

The Appellate Division unanimously affirmed defendant's judgment of conviction and sentence because "the facts . . . [were] sufficiently distinct from those of [*LeGrand*] that . . . Supreme Court did not err in denying the defendant's request to adduce expert testimony regarding the reliability of eyewitness identification." The court emphasized defendant's confirmation that he used the nicknames given to the police by Bierd, and his knowledge that the robbers wore masks. Further, the court pointed out, two eyewitnesses identified defendant from a photographic array the day of the crime and then again, four months later, in a lineup; and one of the eyewitnesses had seen and heard defendant in the neighborhood regularly over a period of six months before the robbery. Defendant appealed, and a Judge of this Court granted his application for leave.

II.

In *Lee*, we held that expert testimony proffered on the issue of the reliability of eyewitness identification "is not admissible per se"; rather, "the decision whether to admit it rests in the sound discretion of the trial court," which should be guided by "whether the proffered expert testimony would aid a lay jury in reaching a verdict." We also noted that although "jurors may be familiar from their own experience with factors relevant to the reliability of eyewitness observation and identification, it cannot be said that psychological studies regarding the accuracy of an identification are within the ken of the typical juror." And finally, we recognized that because "expert testimony of this nature may involve scientific theories and techniques, a trial court may need to determine whether [it] is generally accepted by the relevant scientific community."

Applying these principles to the facts in *Lee*, we "[could] not say the trial court's denial of defendant's motion [to introduce expert testimony regarding the reliability of eyewitness identification] constituted an abuse of discretion." In reaching this conclusion, we observed that the trial judge entertained the defendant's motion during the People's case-in-chief, and so "was in a position to weigh the request against other relevant factors, such as the centrality of the identification issue and the existence of corroborating evidence." The crime in Lee was a carjacking, and the defendant was discovered driving the stolen vehicle, which corroborated the victim's identification of him as the carjacker.

Next came our decision in *Young*. . . . Calling the question a "close" one on the facts, we nonetheless decided there was no abuse of discretion. Young was a home invasion case, and we commented that if the trial had "turned entirely on an uncorroborated eyewitness identification, it might well have been an abuse of discretion to deny the jury the benefit of [the expert's] opinions." As it was, though, two of the defendant's female acquaintances were found to possess property stolen during the home invasion; neither of them could have been the robber (who was a male); and one of them said she got the property from the defendant. Under

these circumstances, we considered it "reasonable" for the trial judge to decide that the eyewitness's identification "was quite unlikely to be mistaken, and that [the expert's] testimony would be an unnecessary distraction for the jury.".

We most recently considered the admissibility of expert testimony on the reliability of eyewitness identification in *LeGrand*. There, we held that

> "where [a] case turns on the accuracy of eyewitness identifications and there is little or no corroborating evidence connecting the defendant to the crime, it is an abuse of discretion for a trial court to exclude expert testimony on the reliability of eyewitness identifications if that testimony is (1) relevant to the witness's identification of defendant, (2) based on principles that are generally accepted within the relevant scientific community, (3) proffered by a qualified expert and (4) on a topic beyond the ken of the average juror."

In *LeGrand*—unlike *Lee* and *Young*—there was no evidence other than eyewitness identifications to tie the defendant into the crime, the stabbing death of a livery cab driver in 1991. Further, the identifications on which the People's case depended were made nearly seven years after the crime, and the defendant was not convicted until 2002. In light of these facts, we decided that the trial judge abused his discretion when he disallowed expert testimony on those three factors where the defense expert's testimony at the *Frye* hearing "confirm[ed] that the principles upon which [he] based his conclusions [were] generally accepted by social scientists and psychologists working in the field": the correlation between confidence and accuracy, the effect of postevent information, and confidence malleability.

Finally, we noted in *LeGrand* that

> "[a]lthough the trend has been of late to more liberally admit such [expert] testimony—as recognized in *Lee* and *Young*—the admissibility of such evidence would also depend upon the existence of sufficient corroborating evidence to link defendant to the crime. In the event that sufficient corroborating evidence is found to exist, an exercise of discretion excluding eyewitness expert testimony would not be fatal to a jury verdict convicting defendant."

Applying our precedents in this area to the facts in *Abney* and *Allen*, we reach different answers to the question of whether the trial judge abused his discretion. While it was reasonable for the trial judge to deny defendant's pretrial motion in Abney as premature and overly broad, another outcome was called for when defendant renewed the motion at the close of the People's direct case. By that point, it was clear that there was no evidence other than Farhana's identification to connect defendant

to the crime, and she did not describe him as possessing any unusual or distinctive features or physical characteristics.

Defendant asked to elicit testimony from Dr. Fulero, who is a qualified expert on the subject of eyewitness identification research findings, about the following topics: the effect of event stress, exposure time, event violence and weapon focus, cross-racial identification, lineup instructions, double-blind lineups, and witness confidence. All but two of these subjects—lineup instructions and double-blind lineups—seem relevant to Farhana's identification of defendant, given the particular circumstances of the case. And as we stated in *LeGrand*, the principles related to witness confidence upon which Dr. Fulero proposed to testify are generally accepted within the relevant scientific community. They are also counterintuitive, which places them beyond the ken of the average juror.

Accordingly, the trial judge in *Abney* abused his discretion when he did not allow Dr. Fulero to testify on the subject of witness confidence. As for the remaining relevant proposed areas of expert testimony—the effect of event stress, exposure time, event violence and weapon focus, and cross-racial identification—the trial judge should have conducted a *Frye* hearing before making a decision on admissibility.

Finally, we do not consider the trial judge's error in *Abney* to have been harmless. While defendant's muddled alibi evidence was no doubt unhelpful to his cause with the jury, it is not overwhelmingly inculpatory either. And, of course, it is possible that defendant would not have pursued an alibi defense in the first place if Dr. Fulero had testified.

Contrariwise, we consider *Allen* to be more akin to *Lee* and *Young*. We are unwilling to second-guess the trial judge's exercise of discretion in Allen because the case did not depend exclusively on Bierd's eyewitness testimony—i.e., Allen is not a "case [that] turns on the accuracy of eyewitness identifications [where] there is little or no corroborating evidence connecting the defendant to the crime." Critically, Almonte independently identified defendant as the knife-wielding robber who searched him and stood nearby throughout the course of the robbery. And defendant was not a stranger to either Bierd or Almonte.

Accordingly, in *People v. Abney*, the order of the Appellate Division should be reversed and a new trial ordered; in *People v. Allen*, the order of the Appellate Division should be affirmed.

NOTES AND QUESTIONS

1. *Eyewitnesses and Scientific Evidence.* Scientific evidence has called into question the reliability of eyewitness testimony. Recall from Chapter 6 that we studied the structure of DNA as an essential component of every cell. DNA is also unique to each person. Scientists can test DNA—taken from a defendant's skin, saliva, semen, blood or hair—and determine with great

accuracy whether the defendant's DNA matches DNA left at the scene of a crime. Such testing can either exonerate or incriminate a defendant.

In Maryland in 1985, Kirk Bloodsworth was convicted of the murder and rape of a nine-year-old girl. Five eyewitnesses testified that they had seen Bloodsworth with the victim. Bloodsworth later became the first person exonerated by post-conviction DNA testing in a criminal case.

> Since the advent of forensic DNA analysis, a number of people convicted of crimes have been subsequently exonerated through DNA analysis of crime scene evidence that was not tested at the time of trial. Additionally, newer technologies have substantially increased the successful DNA analysis of aged, degraded, limited, or otherwise compromised biological evidence. As a result, crime scene samples once thought to be unsuitable for testing in the past may now yield DNA profiles. Moreover, samples that previously generated inconclusive DNA results may now be amenable to reanalysis using newer methods.

National Institute of Justice, Postconviction DNA Testing, Oct. 2, 2012, at http://www.nij.gov/topics/justice-system/wrongful-convictions/pages/dna-testing.aspx. Bloodsworth's release focused attention on the importance of the science of DNA testing and its availability in criminal trials. It also led to the recognition that "erroneous eyewitness testimony is the single largest cause of wrongful convictions in capital cases." Derek Simmonsen, Teach Your Jurors Well: Using Jury Instructions to Educate Jurors About Factors Affecting the Accuracy of Eyewitness Testimony, 70 Md. L. Rev. 1044 (2011). Is this a reason that DNA evidence should be collected and used as the main source of evidence in every case? A reason to abandon eyewitness testimony?

> **Go to** the website to see how DNA testing works. Then review a sample jury instruction adopted by New Jersey.

After reading *Abney*, do you think expert witnesses should be required at every trial to explain the flaws of eyewitness testimony? Or should experts be admitted only if they can offer "appreciable help" to the jury? Id. at 1045. Do you think that jury instructions are adequate to solve the problem? Would having a jury instruction like the one in New Jersey solve the problem of eyewitness identifications?

2. *Interviewing Eyewitnesses. Abney* and *Allen* demonstrate the risks of eyewitness testimony. Are there any procedures you can identify that would make eyewitness testimony more reliable? Neuroscientists Lacy and Stark provide numerous tips about how to interview eyewitnesses. See Joyce W. Lacy & Craig E. L. Stark, The Neuroscience of Memory: Implications for the Courtroom, 14 Nature Rev. Neurosci. 649 (2013). They recommend that a witness's level of confidence in her identification be recorded immediately after the identification, and before any post-identification feedback occurs.

Another technique is the "cognitive interview" (CI), which proceeds in the following stages:

> Interviewing should begin with a transfer of control to the witness, i.e. witnesses should be put at ease and made to feel comfortable. This is important in avoiding unintentional bias as witnesses may be easily manipulated by individuals of perceived power and authority, such as law enforcement. It is recommended that officers request the witness to mentally recreate the scene of the crime. This is based on research on context-dependent memory, which has shown that recall is better when it occurs in the same context as learning.
>
> Testimony ought to begin with an open-ended narrative; that is, witnesses should be encouraged to recall as much detail as possible, even if they recall events out of order or the details seem trivial. The interviewer should allow time for long pauses while the eyewitness thinks, relaxes, and gathers his or her thoughts. This approach contrasts with standard police interviews, in which a witness may often be interrupted and asked to report events in a specific order. Allowing witnesses to report events in their own order and at their own pace results in a more detailed and more accurate report. Witnesses should be asked to indicate when they are unsure and should be informed that they should not guess.
>
> After the free narrative, the interviewer can follow up with open-ended questions, keeping in mind that the wording of a question can lead to memory distortions (as discussed above). Indefinite articles should be used over definite articles. For example, asking whether the witness saw 'the gun' as opposed to 'a gun' implies that a gun was present. Lastly, it should be kept in mind that congruency among multiple eyewitness accounts does not necessarily entail greater accuracy as witnesses may communicate with each other and all are susceptible to the same memory errors.

Id. at 655–56. How confident are you in the CI? Should it be required in all police departments?

3. *Suspect Identification.* How would you conduct a line-up? Look across the room at a friend or family member. If you were to testify that the person you are looking at just committed a crime against you, who else should be in the line-up with your friend? Would the rest of the line-up be the same gender? The same race? The same height or weight? Wear the same clothes? What makes for a good line-up?

Stark and Lacy suggest the following:

> [E]ach line-up should only contain one suspect and the suspect should not stand out from the rest of the line-up. Fillers (other non-suspects in the line-up) should be selected on the basis of the eyewitness' description of the perpetrator. If an innocent suspect fits the description of the perpetrator more than the other people in the lineup, there is a higher likelihood that the suspect will be misidentified as the perpetrator. In a truly unbiased line-up, naive

> 'mock witnesses' who did not witness the crime should not select any one individual more frequently than the others.
>
> Although no line-up method can completely eliminate false identifications and increase the likelihood of a correct identification, some recommendations will reduce the number of misidentifications without substantially reducing the likelihood of a correct identification. The first is to warn witnesses that the true perpetrator may not be present in the line-up. Research has found that experimental witnesses have a tendency to select a suspect even if the actual target is not in the line-up. The instruction that the suspect may not be present in the line-up has substantially reduced the number of misidentifications, especially in line-ups in which the target was absent. Although the number of correct identifications were also reduced in these studies, this was only to a small degree. Secondly, sequential line-ups (in which the potential suspects are shown one after the other) tend to produce fewer false identifications than simultaneous line-ups (in which all potential suspects are shown together). This approach also reduces the number of correct identifications, but typically to only to a small degree.

Id. at 656.

Experts recommend that the administration of the line-up be either blind or double blind. "Double-blind administrators do not know who the actual suspect is. Blind administrators are aware of that information but shield themselves from knowing where the suspect is located in the lineup or photo array." State v. Henderson, 27 A.3d 872, 896 (N.J. 2011). Why do you think double blindness increases the reliability of the line-up? Do you think a composite—a sketch drawn by an artist to match a witness's description—would promote effective identification? See id. at 902 (some experts think composites are not effective because witnesses remember faces holistically and not feature-by-feature). "Quantitative and qualitative results suggest that the presence of neuroscience data in an expert report affects judges' perceptions of the quality, credibility, and scientificity (reliability, objectivity, scientific basis) of the report, and the persuasiveness of the evidence it provided. Moreover, this phenomenon was stronger in more experienced judges than in less experienced judges." Valerie Moulin et al., Judges' perceptions of expert reports: The effect of neuroscience evidence, 61 Journal of Law and Psychiatry 22 (Nov.-Dec. 2018). Does that conclusion affect your judgment about the use of neuroscience in the courtroom?

> **Go to** the website and review the rule that New Jersey adopted for recording eyewitness identifications. Did you follow a similar strategy when you proposed your procedures at the beginning of note 3?

Recall that in Section A we read about the case of Dr. Lorne Semrau, who was prosecuted for health care fraud after he "upcoded" his bills, assigning the wrong code for medical procedures so that he would be reimbursed more money for them by Medicare or Medicaid. One of Semrau's defenses was that "any improper billing was unintentional and despite his good faith attempts to be compliant [it was] because of the complicated and confusing nature of the codes." United States v. Semrau, 693 F.3d 510, 515 (6th Cir. 2012). Semrau offered fMRI testimony to prove he was truthful.

The magistrate judge in *Semrau* conducted a *Daubert* analysis to conclude that the fMRI testing was not admissible using the following analysis.

United States v. Semrau

United States District Court, W.D. Tennessee, Eastern Division, 2010.
No. 07–10074 Ml/P, 2010 WL 6845092.

AMENDED REPORT AND RECOMMENDATION

■ TU M. PHAM, UNITED STATES MAGISTRATE JUDGE.

B. Motion to Exclude Under Rule 702

The court's Rule 702 analysis begins with a determination of whether the witness is qualified by "knowledge, skill, experience, training, or education" to offer his or her opinion. This requirement has been treated liberally by the courts. Over the past several years, Dr. Laken has personally conducted research in the field of fMRI-based lie detection (including laboratory studies), is the inventor of the Cephos patent, has written articles in peer reviewed scientific journals on the subject, and regularly conducts fMRI-based lie detection tests on individuals through his company. The government did not challenge Dr. Laken's qualifications as an expert in its briefs or at the *Daubert* hearing. Thus, the court finds that Dr. Laken is preliminarily and generally qualified by his knowledge, skill, experience, training, and education to offer an opinion on fMRI-based lie detection in this case.

Although Dr. Laken is qualified to offer an opinion, the court nevertheless concludes that his testimony should be excluded because, at least at this early stage in its development, fMRI-based lie detection does not satisfy the requirements of Rule 702.

1. *Testing and Peer Review*

The first two *Daubert* factors are whether the theory or technique can be and has been tested and whether it has been subjected to peer review and publication The court finds that the underlying theories behind fMRI-based lie detection are capable of being tested, and at least in the laboratory setting, have been subjected to some level of testing. It also appears that the theories have been subjected to some peer review and publication, particularly within the last five years, as evidenced by

the articles co-authored by Dr. Laken, and the numerous peer reviewed articles by other researchers.

2. *The Known or Potential Rate of Error and the Existence and Maintenance of Standards*

The next *Daubert* factor is the known or potential rate of error and the existence and maintenance of standards controlling the technique's operation. Dr. Laken testified at the *Daubert* hearing that there are published known error rates. On the other hand, Dr. Imrey disputes the validity of the error rates because they are based on too small of a sample size. While it is unclear from the testimony what the error rates are or how valid they may be in the laboratory setting, there are no known error rates for fMRI-based lie detection outside the laboratory setting, i.e. in the "real-world" or "real-life" setting. In *Cordoba*, 194 F.3d 1053 (9th Cir. 1999), the court upheld the district court's rejection of the error rate testified to by the polygraph expert because the results of the tests were not transferable to real-life exams. . . . Here, like in *Cordoba*, the error rate of real-life fMRI-based lie detection is unknown. In *Mock Sabotage Crime*, Drs. Laken, Kozel, George, and Johnson, among others, discuss the factors that could affect the test results:

> . . . Three other issues that have yet to be addressed in the literature are time, motivation, and independence of deception behavior from investigator control. In terms of time, the deceptive event occurs shortly before scanning in most studies, while this likely will not be the case in many real life applications. Many studies entail little motivation or jeopardy at all, while the motivation (e.g. $50 for successful deception) or jeopardy (revealing personal autobiographical information) in other studies is not equivalent to what would be at stake in real applications. Because of ethical concerns, there are limits to the scenarios in which research subjects can participate. Current study questions range in valance from having deceptive responses regarding mundane daily events to the staged firing of a gun. Finally, and importantly, deceptive behavior is controlled in the laboratory setting. In all studies to date, the research team directs participants to deceive about a certain condition or choice of conditions. Despite creative designs, the behavior may resemble compliance with a cognitive task more than independent, volitional deception. Ultimately, validity using real cases where truth versus deception can be independently confirmed via other methods would be ideal. However, obtaining reasonable sample sizes and other logistics may hamper efficiency of such field testing.

The authors conclude by stating "Functional MRI is currently not ready to be used in real-world lie detection." . . .

Regarding the existence and maintenance of standards, Dr. Laken testified as to the protocols and controlling standards that he uses for his

own exams. Because the use of fMRI-based lie detection is still in its early stages of development, standards controlling the real-life application have not yet been established. Without such standards, a court cannot adequately evaluate the reliability of a particular lie detection examination. . . . The absence of real-life error rates and the lack of controlling standards in the industry for real-life exams are negative factors in the analysis of whether fMRI-based lie detection is scientifically valid.

3. *Whether the Theory or Method Has Been Generally Accepted by the Scientific Community*

The court next considers whether the theory or method has been generally accepted by the scientific community. . . . No doubt in part because of its recent development, fMRI-based lie detection has not yet been accepted by the scientific community. As noted above, experts in the field are of the opinion that fMRI "is currently not ready to be used in real-world lie detection."

In sum, the above-described application of the *Daubert* factors leads the court to conclude that Dr. Laken's testimony is inadmissible under Fed. R. Evid. 702.

Recall the *Abney* case, where the New York Court of Appeals determined that the trial judge had abused his discretion in failing to admit expert testimony on the reliability of eyewitness identification. In response to the high court's order, the trial court in New York conducted a *Frye* hearing to determine whether the defendant would be permitted to introduce at trial expert testimony on the reliability of eyewitness identification with respect to event stress, event violence, weapon focus, exposure time and cross-racial identification. In an unpublished subsequent opinion, the trial court made the following determination about the admissibility of the expert testimony in *Abney*. How did your experts differ from those presented in the actual case? Would the case have come out differently under *Daubert*?

People v. Abney

Supreme Court, New York County, New York, 2011.
31 Misc.3d 1231(A), 932 N.Y.S.2d 762 (Table).

Opinion

■ JILL KONVISER, J.

Pursuant to the ruling in *People v. Abney*, 13 N.Y.3d at 268, 889 N.Y.S.2d 890, 918 N.E.2d 486, this Court conducted a *Frye* hearing on September 17, 2010, September 20, 2010, November 12, 2010, and November 22, 2010. The purpose of the hearing was to determine whether the defendant would be permitted to introduce at trial expert testimony on the reliability of eyewitness identification with respect to

event stress, event violence, weapon focus, exposure time and cross-racial identification. The defendant called Dr. Nancy Franklin [an Associate Professor of Psychology at the State University of New York at Stony Brook] and the People called Dr. Barry Cooper [a clinical instructor in the Department of Psychology at the University of British Columbia, a contract psychologist with the Correctional Service of Canada, and a partner and the Director of Research and Development for the Pacific Alliance of Forensic Scientists and Practitioners]. This Court finds both credible. For the reasons that follow, the defendant's motion to elicit eyewitness expert testimony at trial is granted in part and denied in part. . . .

The *Frye* Hearing

Where, as here, a case turns on the accuracy of an eyewitness identification and there is little or no corroborating evidence connecting the defendant to the charged crime, a four part test must be satisfied before a defendant will be permitted to introduce at trial expert testimony on the reliability of eyewitness identification. Under this four part test, such expert testimony is admissible if it is: "(1) relevant to the witness' identification, (2) proffered by a qualified expert, (3) on a topic beyond the ken of the average juror and (4) based on principles that are generally accepted as reliable by the scientific community."

1. The Relevancy of the Proposed Testimony to the Witnesses's Identification

The defendant seeks to elicit expert testimony relative to the effect that event stress, weapon focus, exposure time, and cross-racial identification, have on the reliability of an eyewitness identification. . . . [T]his Court finds that expert testimony in these four areas would in fact be relevant to the identification testimony likely to be elicited during the retrial of this case.

. . . The first factor about which the defendant seeks to elicit expert eyewitness identification testimony is "event stress." Event stress stands for the proposition that a stressful event impairs the ability of a person to recognize an unfamiliar face accurately. As the allegations in this case show that the complainant was placed in a highly stressful situation as she was allegedly robbed in the subway at knife point by a complete stranger, the phenomenon of event stress is relevant to the circumstances under which the complainant identified the defendant.

The defendant also seeks to elicit expert testimony in the area of "weapon focus." Weapon focus "is the phenomenon which occurs when, during the course of a crime, a witness is exposed to a weapon, and the witness focuses his or her attention on the weapon and not on the perpetrator's face, which impairs the ability of the witness to make a subsequent identification of [a] perpetrator." In this case, a knife was used to commit the alleged robbery. As such, testimony with respect to

the weapon focus factor is relevant to the circumstances under which the complainant identified the defendant.

Expert testimony is also sought in the area of "event duration." Event duration, also known as "exposure duration" or "increased exposure time" refers to "the phenomenon that [the] longer a person is exposed to a face the more likely that person will make a correct identification at a later time." Likewise, it stands for the converse proposition that an identification is likely to be less accurate if the perpetrator is viewed only for a brief period of time. In this case, as the charged crime took only seconds to complete this Court finds that the phenomenon of event duration is relevant to the identification of the defendant.

Finally, the defendant seeks to elicit expert testimony in the area of "cross-racial identification." Cross-racial identification, also known as "own-race basis," is a "cognitive processing bias that people have that allows them to differentiate members of their own race better than they can differentiate faces of another race." As the parties have advised this Court that the complainant is of Asian/Indian descent and the defendant is of African-American descent, this Court finds that own-race bias is relevant to the complainant's identification of the defendant.

2. The Testimony Must Be Proffered by a Qualified Expert

This Court finds that the witness proffered by the defendant, Dr. Nancy Franklin, is an expert in the field of human memory and is adequately qualified to provide expert testimony in the areas of event stress, weapon focus, event duration and own-race bias.

Dr. Franklin received a Ph.D. in Psychology from Stanford University in 1989. At Stanford she specialized in the area of human cognition and memory and was a National Science Foundation graduate fellow. For the past 21 years she has been an Associate Professor of Psychology at the State University of New York at Stony Brook where she has received an impressive array of teaching awards and, until recently, was the head of the Psychology Department's "cognitive experimental area." Dr. Franklin lectures on the topic of memory and eyewitness identification and teaches a variety of psychology courses at Stony Brook, including a course in human memory focusing on eyewitness identification. Her primary area of research is dedicated to "false memory" and, in particular, the manner in which memory is affected by emotions, threats and anger. Dr. Franklin is currently conducting laboratory research and collecting data on cross-racial identification and on the effect anger and emotion have on the ability of a person to identify and process facial features.

A member of the Society for Applied Research in Memory and Cognition, the American Psychology Law Society, and the Psychonomic Society, Dr. Franklin is a peer reviewer for several scholarly journals, including the Journal of Memory and Language and the Journal of

Applied Cognitive Psychology and Cognitive Psychology, and has served on the editorial board of the Journal of Experimental Psychology: Learning Memory & Cognition. Dr. Franklin was a grant reviewer for the National Science Foundation and the Air Force Grants Office, has published numerous articles and book chapters in the area of cognition of memory, attends lectures and conferences on cognitive psychology, and keeps current regarding developments in the field of eyewitness identification by reading and studying applicable literature. Dr. Franklin has testified as an expert in the field of memory approximately fifteen times in New York County, Bronx County, Queens County and in Springfield, Massachusetts. She is listed as an eyewitness identification expert, specializing in eyewitness memory, identification and false memory, on the Verified Expert Roster of the Assigned Counsel Plan of the City of New York, of which this Court takes judicial notice. The Assigned Counsel Plan conducts background reviews of each expert on its roster, verifies the credentials of each expert and permits individuals to be included on the Verified Expert Roster only where he or she has met the Assigned Counsel Plan's minimum requirements.

This Court had the opportunity to see and hear Dr. Franklin testify over the course of three days during the *Frye* hearing. Her testimony, nearly three hundred transcript pages, makes plain that she is adequately qualified to testify as an expert in the areas of event stress, weapon focus, event duration and own-race bias. Dr. Franklin demonstrated a satisfactory familiarity and understanding of the research, theories, terminology and applications that underlie each of the four areas about which the defendant seeks to introduce expert testimony and is familiar with the extent to which each of these areas of study are accepted as reliable in the relevant scientific community.

Dr. Franklin is a long-tenured professor of cognitive psychology, teaches a university course on the subject of the reliability of eyewitness identification, lectures on memory and eyewitness identification, is familiar with the studies, research and articles dealing with each of the four areas about which she intends to testify, has been qualified on numerous other occasions as an expert, and is undeniably an expert in human memory, the very field upon which the criticisms of the reliability of eyewitness identifications are based. Thus, under the flexible and liberal standards applied to the qualifications of expert witnesses in New York, the People's claim that Dr. Franklin is not qualified to testify in the four areas proffered by the defense is rejected. Moreover, the People's argument with respect to Dr. Franklin's alleged lack of skill and expertise goes to the weight and not admissibility of her testimony and may be explored at trial by way of cross-examination.

Thus, in its discretion, this Court finds, based on Dr. Franklin's background, training and experience, as well as her *Frye* hearing testimony, that she is adequately qualified to testify as an expert in the

field of memory and to offer opinions with respect to the four areas about which the defendant seeks to elicit expert testimony.

This Court also finds that the People's expert, Dr. Barry Cooper, is a qualified expert in the field of eyewitness memory and forensic psychology. Dr. Cooper has a Doctorate of Forensic Psychology from the University of British Columbia, is a Clinical Instructor in the Department of Psychology at the University of British Columbia, is a contract psychologist for the Correctional Service of Canada, and is a partner and Director of Research and Development for the Pacific Alliance of Forensic Scientists and Practitioners, which "is a corporation that provides research, training and consultation services to various facets of the criminal justice system." Dr. Cooper is also a member of the American Psychology and Law Society, the Canadian Psychological Society, is a registrant of the College of Psychologists of British Columbia and has testified as an eyewitness memory expert on several occasions.

According to his hearing testimony and impressive curriculum vitae, Dr. Cooper has conducted research in the field of eyewitness memory "with victims and offenders of violent crime which directly relates to memory issues at trial," has conducted two field studies with respect to eyewitness memory, and has written about two dozen peer-reviewed publications in the field of eyewitness memory.

Based on Dr. Cooper's background, training and experience as well as his hearing testimony, which demonstrated his familiarity and understanding of the literature, research, methodology and techniques associated with eyewitness identification accuracy and reliability, Dr. Cooper is qualified to testify as an expert in the field of eyewitness memory and forensic psychology.

3. The Testimony Must be Beyond the Ken of the Average Juror

The Court of Appeals has held "[d]espite the fact that jurors may be familiar from their own experience with factors relevant to the reliability of eyewitness identification, it cannot be said that psychological studies regarding the accuracy of an identification are within the ken of the typical juror." [There is also] research demonstrating a number of common and widely held misconceptions on the subject among laypersons."

Based on this authority, this Court finds that the proposed testimony of Dr. Franklin and Dr. Cooper, which is premised upon "psychological studies regarding the accuracy of an identification," is beyond the ken of the average juror.

4. The Testimony Must be Based Upon Principles that are Generally Accepted as Reliable Within the Scientific Community.

"[U]nder *Frye*, the trial judge does not determine whether a novel scientific methodology is *actually* reliable. Rather, the judge determines whether most scientists in the field believe it to be reliable." Thus, "*Frye* is not concerned with the reliability of a certain expert's conclusions, but

instead, with whether the experts' deductions are based on principles that are sufficiently established to have gained general acceptance as reliable." . . .

The People, however, in what can be only characterized as an attempt to avoid the implications of *LeGrand* and the well-settled application of the *Frye* test in New York, argue that this Court is required not only to subject expert eyewitness reliability identification testimony to scrutiny greater than that which would be ordinarily applied to the evaluation of novel scientific evidence, but also to verify independently the validity of the scientific conclusions made by the defense expert. These arguments must be rejected. . . .

The People's argument that as a predicate to the admission of eyewitness identification expert testimony under *Frye* a finding must be made that the science underlying the proposed testimony has "a very high level of reliability, tantamount to . . . certainty" is based on a misreading. . . .

Equally without merit is the People's argument that even if the proposed eyewitness identification expert testimony passes muster under the *Frye* test, the foundational requirements for the admission of such evidence at trial require this court to verify independently the soundness and reliability of the expert's scientific conclusions. . . .

Thus, this Court will analyze the four proposed areas of expert testimony under the *Frye* test to determine whether each of them is generally accepted as reliable in the relevant scientific community. . . .

This Court's findings of fact and conclusions of law with respect to the admissibility under the *Frye* general acceptance test relative to the four proposed areas of eyewitness identification expert testimony are set forth below.

Dr. Franklin's *Frye* Hearing Testimony

Dr. Franklin testified that human memory does not operate like a video camera—it does not provide a person with a "perfect recording" of what transpired. Rather, as a person experiences an event he or she selectively encodes only certain pieces of what has been observed. As such, when recalling the observed event at a later time a person uses inferences, expectations, prior knowledge and what other people may have said about the event to fill in missing details. These factors can lead to a distorted memory of the observed event.

Dr. Franklin testified that there are "different rates of accuracy for different types of memories" and that memories for unfamiliar faces are "particularly bad." Indeed, Dr. Franklin testified that research has shown, that even under optimal conditions when a witness has an unobstructed view of an unfamiliar person of the same race in a well lit, violence free environment, the rate of misidentification, is about fifty percent.

According to Dr. Franklin, research in the eyewitness identification field is conducted in three ways—laboratory studies, field studies and, archival studies. The great majority of research is conducted through laboratory experiments, which involve the deliberate manipulation of one variable while keeping all others constant. The purpose of doing so is to enable researchers to assess the extent to which the manipulated variable may have influenced the result being studied. Moreover, as the true identity of the observed subject is known to the researchers in a laboratory setting, the manipulated variable's impact on an identification can be more definitively stated than in situations outside of the laboratory where the true identity of the subject is often unknown.

Field studies involve an analysis and study of actions that take place outside of the confines of the laboratory. She explained that field studies are generally conducted in two ways. One type of field study involves conducting experiments with confederates in a setting outside of the laboratory to determine whether a manipulated variable, such as stress or own-race bias, can effect [*sic*] the accuracy of an eyewitness identification. As an example of such a controlled field study, Dr. Franklin discussed John C. Brigham's 1982 convenience store field study that tested the ability of convenience store clerks to identify customers who had visited the store two hours earlier, and who were members of different races. A second type of field study involves the analysis of events outside of the laboratory where multiple variables may be at play and the true identity of the perpetrator may or may not be known. Dr. Franklin explained that such a situation may occur when a researcher interviews witnesses to an actual crime with respect to the circumstances under which an identification was made.

The third way in which eyewitness identification is researched is through archival studies.

Dr. Franklin explained that:

> [a]rchival studies don't involve an experiment or a researcher manipulating anything. What researchers do is go in and collect records, for example, from police departments, and then try to piece together comparisons for whether, for example, people were better at identifying members of their own race than members of another race, based on what you have from police records. The problem, of course, with archival studies is that witnesses are going to identify a suspect or not. We can never know whether they got the right answer the same way we can in a lab.

Dr. Franklin testified that the vast majority of research in the field of eyewitness identification is conducted in the laboratory. Field and archival studies are of limited utility and of marginal statistical importance as the sample sizes are generally small, the true identity of the perpetrator is not always known and the inability to isolate variables makes it difficult to determine whether a particular variable had an

effect on identification accuracy. By contrast, laboratory studies allow a hypothesis to be tested with a statistically significant number of subjects in an environment where the true identity of the perpetrator is known and variables can be isolated for the purpose of determining their effect on identification accuracy. Moreover, laboratory research permits scientists to test the veracity of their theories repeatedly under a variety of different scenarios and if the research results can be consistently replicated then there is a firm basis to believe that a particular variable's effect on the reliability of an eyewitness identification "is real."

Furthermore, while ethical constraints prohibit laboratory researchers from replicating the violence associated with actual crimes, Dr. Franklin testified that researchers, through the use of videos, photographs and other methods, have nonetheless been able to simulate variables such as stress or the presence of a weapon that are often experienced by individuals who observe an actual crime. By using the laboratory setting to isolate a particular variable's effect on the accuracy of an identification, researchers have determined that these variables, stress or the presence of a weapon, reduce the accuracy of eyewitness identifications, even though participants in these laboratory studies know that an actual real life crime is not unfolding before them. In fact, Dr. Franklin testified that the effect these variables have on the accuracy of an identification may be even greater in the real world as identification accuracy is impaired in the laboratory even though laboratory participants are obviously aware that they are merely participating in a study.

Dr. Franklin testified that the "vast majority" of scientists in the field believe that eyewitness identification laboratory research is applicable to real world events—such a proposition, she stated, is generally accepted in the scientific community. She explained that there is no significant debate in the scientific community with respect to the applicability of eyewitness identification laboratory research to identifications made by witnesses to actual crimes. Indeed, Dr. Franklin testified that only a "small handful" of her colleagues, such as Dr. Ebbe Ebbessen and Dr. John Yuille, believe that eyewitness identification laboratory research cannot be generalized to real world events.

Dr. Franklin testified that scientists in the field of eyewitness identification use a "sophisticated" statistical technique known as meta-analysis, which involves combining data generated from a large number of separate studies on a given topic in order to determine the reliability of a particular result or effect. Dr. Franklin explained that meta-analysis is "heavily relied on" and is "the gold standard in the scientific domain" as it is a statistical method by which data from a large number of different studies on a related topic is weighed in a particular manner so as to allow scientists "to make a single overarching statement" about whether an effect is indeed reliable. Thus, "instead of having several studies with a hundred subjects each, you may have a single meta-

analysis of 10,000 subjects contributing. That would allow you to have a very reliable stable effect if it's there to be found." She further explained that a person conducting a meta-analysis "casts a very wide net to look for all instances of studies that exist in the literature that meet those criteria," regardless of whether the studies demonstrate a particular effect, such as weapon focus. Dr. Franklin also testified that:

> [w]hat a meta-analysis provides is three important measures. One is overall reliability. So, that's a measure of does this phenomenon exist. That's really the most important thing a meta-analysis can tell you. It also gives you an estimate of overall effect size. So, that's direct and magnitude of effect. Then [the] third thing it does, which is really helpful in any scientific domain, is it gives you a number of failures to replicate that would need to be out there in order to overturn the meta-analysis conclusion.... [T]he techniques that are used are sophisticated involving pooling of data. If you take individual studies and you do basically a body count of how many found something, how many didn't find something, you can certainly do that when you are evaluating literature, and that's what you can do if you don't do meta-analysis. But it's sort of a blunt instrument for assessing the phenomenon you are interested in. What you want to do is look at pooled dated, weighted by number of observations that are contributing to get an overall proof of . . . what it is you are looking for [such as weapon focus or own-race bias, etc.]

Event Stress

Dr. Franklin testified that stress has a complex effect on memory [and] environment, a proposition that is generally accepted as reliable in the scientific community, according to Dr. Franklin.

According to Dr. Franklin, the general acceptance of this proposition is supported by the findings of a peer-reviewed 2004 meta-analysis . . . conclude[ing] that high levels of stress impair identification accuracy. The Deffenbacher meta-analysis showed that individuals in a low-stress environment were able to identify a perpetrator accurately in a target-present identification procedure 59 percent of the time while individuals in a high-stress environment were able to identify a perpetrator accurately in a target present identification procedure only 39 percent of the time.

Dr. Franklin testified that the event-stress phenomenon was also demonstrated in a peer-reviewed study conducted in 2004 by Yale University psychologist Dr. Charles A Morgan. . . . The study examined the eyewitness accuracy of more than 500 active-duty soldiers who were participants in a survival and interrogation training exercise. Morgan received permission to observe a military training exercise and then, at the conclusion of the exercise, tested the soldiers' ability to remember their interrogators.

Each soldier went through an initial period of food and sleep deprivation and tried to avoid being captured. All of the soldiers were eventually captured and subjected to a twelve hour period of confinement in separate cells. Following their confinement, the soldiers were subjected either to high or low-stress forty minute interrogations in well-lit rooms. In the high-stress interrogations the soldiers were exposed to extremely violent acts such as waterboarding or having a loaded gun placed to their heads. The low stress interrogations consisted of verbal confrontations. The next day, after the soldiers recovered from their food and sleep deprivation, identification procedures were conducted and they were asked to identify their interrogators. The soldiers who were interrogated in the low-stress environment were able to identify their interrogators accurately in a target-present identification procedure 62 percent of the time while those soldiers interrogated in the high-stress environment were able to identify their interrogators accurately in a target-present identification procedure only 30 percent of the time. Thus, Dr. Morgan concluded that extreme stress reduces eyewitness identification accuracy.

Dr. Franklin testified further that her conclusion that the event stress phenomenon is generally accepted as reliable in the scientific community is also supported by three additional studies.

Weapon Focus

The presence of a weapon impairs an eyewitness's ability to identify a perpetrator accurately, according to Dr. Franklin. Beginning in the 1970's, research has shown that when a weapon or an otherwise unusual object is present, a person's attention is drawn to the weapon or unusual object rather than to the facial characteristics of the person holding such weapon or object. Dr. Franklin testified that the weapon focus phenomenon is generally accepted as reliable in the scientific community. To support this proposition she relied on a 1992 peer reviewed meta-analysis. . . . The Steblay meta-analysis reviewed 19 laboratory studies that contained more than 2000 participants. Dr. Steblay concluded that a meta-analytic review of these studies showed that the presence of a weapon reduces identification accuracy. . . .

As further support for the general acceptance of the weapon focus phenomenon, Dr. Franklin referred to a 1987 study from Cutler, Penrod and Martens, which concluded that identification accuracy is decreased by the presence of a weapon. She also cited to an archival study by Professor Tim Valentine, which showed that the presence of a weapon "was significantly associated with witnesses being more likely to identify a foil."

Event Duration

Dr. Franklin testified that the amount of time that a witness has to view a perpetrator affects identification accuracy. Thus, "with longer exposure, you have a greater opportunity to lay down a stable memory"

and an identification tends to be more accurate. By contrast, an identification is likely to be less accurate if the perpetrator is viewed for only a brief period of time as such information cannot be properly encoded by the brain. While the event duration phenomenon may seem like common sense, Dr. Franklin testified that people tend to overestimate the amount of time they have viewed an event, especially when the viewing took place under stressful conditions.

Dr. Franklin explained that the event duration phenomenon, which is generally accepted as reliable in the scientific community, is supported by a 1986 peer reviewed meta-analysis from Shapiro and Penrod.

Own-Race Bias

Dr. Franklin testified that own-race bias is a cognitive process by which people are better at identifying members of their own race than members of another race. To support this proposition, Dr. Franklin cited to a peer reviewed 2001 meta-analysis from Meissner and Brigham, which reviewed data from "39 research articles, involving 91 independent samples and nearly 5,000 participants." The Meissner & Brigham meta-analysis concluded, *inter alia,* that a person was "1.56 times more likely to falsely identify a novel other-race face when compared with performance on own-race faces." The meta-analysis also concluded that a person was 2.2 times as likely to identify accurately an own-race face as opposed to the face of a person from another race.

Dr. Franklin testified that the overwhelming majority of the participants studied in the Brigham & Meissner meta-analysis were Caucasian and African-American. Dr. Franklin was not aware of any study that reviewed the extent to which the own-race bias phenomenon applied to persons of Asian/Indian descent, but as own-race bias has been found with every race that had been studied, Dr. Franklin opined that the own-race bias phenomenon extended to persons of Asian/Indian descent. She acknowledged that she was unable to point to any specific scientific studies to support her conclusion. Moreover, Dr. Franklin conceded that she did not know the extent to which the own-race basis phenomenon applied to persons of Asian/Indian descent.

Dr. Cooper's *Frye* Hearing Testimony

. . . While Dr. Cooper acknowledged that 99 percent of the research in the eyewitness identification field is conducted in the laboratory and that the phenomenon of event stress, weapon focus and own-race bias have been found to exist within the confines of the laboratory, he testified that there is a debate in the scientific community regarding the extent to which the results of eyewitness identification laboratory research are applicable to identifications made by eyewitnesses to actual crimes. Although a majority of the researchers in the field believe that laboratory research findings are transferable to identifications made by victims and witnesses to actual crimes, Dr. Cooper testified that he and other psychologists, including his mentor, John Yuille, do not believe that the

results of eyewitness identification laboratory research in areas of event stress, weapon focus and own-race bias can be applied to identifications made by eyewitnesses to actual crimes.

. . . Dr. Cooper explained that the laboratory studies conducted in the areas of events stress, weapon focus and own-race bias have "low external validity" in that they are conducted in controlled settings and, thus, do not account for the multiple variables that are often encountered by witnesses and victims to actual crimes. Thus, he noted that the accuracy of an identification made by a victim or witness to an actual crime could be affected by multiple simultaneously occurring variables such as: (1) the duration of the crime; (2) the lighting; (3) the opportunity the witness had to look at the perpetrator; (4) the distance between the perpetrator and the witness; (4) the stress associated with the event; (5) whether others, such as the witness's child, were present at the time of the event; (6) whether a weapon was present; (7) the number of times the witness spoke to others about the event; (8) the manner in which the witness was questioned "after the fact" regarding the event; (9), the nature of any identification procedure conducted in connection with the crime as well as other factors. By contrast, laboratory research takes place in a controlled environment where all but one of the variables are kept constant in order to assess whether the single manipulated variable impacts identification accuracy. As the victims of actual crime encounter multiple variables, the circumstances under which observations are made in the laboratory cannot be fairly compared to the conditions under which an actual crime is viewed.

Dr. Cooper further testified that psychologists have used laboratory research results to conclude that principles such as event stress or weapon focus are generally applicable to all eyewitness identifications. These laboratory findings, however, are based solely upon the answers given by the research subjects to questions regarding the single variable being studied. No effort is made to consider the individual background and characteristics of the observers, which are factors relevant to the accuracy of identifications made by eyewitnesses to actual crimes. . . .

Moreover, Dr. Cooper testified that laboratory research results are not transferable to real world events as the subjects of laboratory experiments—typically college students—are aware that they are participating in an experiment and not witnessing an actual crime. Thus, the laboratory research subjects are nothing more than uninvolved bystanders who are viewing events that are unimportant to them as opposed to actual violent crime victims who have had their physical well-being threatened and, presumably, have a greater interest in insuring that the perpetrator is correctly identified.

Dr. Cooper also testified that while event stress, weapon focus and own-race bias have been found to exist in the laboratory, field and archival research have not shown that these factors reduce identification accuracy. . . . Dr. Cooper testified that due to the inconsistencies between

the laboratory research and the field and archival studies, he is unable to render an opinion regarding whether event stress, weapon focus and own-race bias are generally accepted as reliable in the relevant scientific community.

Event Stress

With respect to event stress, Dr. Cooper testified that the field and archival studies are inconsistent with the laboratory findings that event stress has "a negative impact on memory." . . . Dr. Cooper testified that:

> John Yuille was one of the first to conduct a study of an actual eyewitness situation where people were interviewed by the police and then by the research team after the event. What they found was high rates of accuracy. 80 something percent accuracy for certain types of details that didn't decay significantly with the passage of time. These results were in stark contrast to the results of the laboratory. They tend to be wrong. When stress is high in terms of eyewitness memory then the other research, the results are complex, but the take home message for most of this research, stress doesn't necessarily have a negative impact on memory. Under certain situations people could have a detailed accurate memory when they are under certain levels of stress.

Moreover, while Dr. Cooper testified that the Morgan Study was a "fantastic study" that "elicited arousal levels that can't be examined in the control[led] circumstances of the laboratory" he noted that the results of that study were not transferable to real life events as the soldiers who participated in the Morgan Study knew that there were not actually prisoners of war and knew they would be returning to their families. He also maintained that the Morgan Study findings were not transferable to actual crimes as the study failed to disclose the manner by which the high and low stress conditions were imposed as such information had been deemed classified by the military.

Weapon Focus

Dr. Cooper also testified that field and archival studies have not shown that the presence of a weapon reduces identification accuracy. . . . Dr. Cooper testified that if a weapon focus effect did in fact exist in the real world it would occur only in "crimes of relatively short duration."

Own-Race Bias

Dr. Cooper testified that there is "mixed support" in the "real world" relative to the own-race bias phenomenon.

Dr. Cooper further explained that laboratory studies show that own-race bias has only a small impact on identification accuracy and that the methodology used in the laboratory to reach these conclusions relies heavily on showing undergraduate students pictures of "a number of different faces" from photographs as opposed to studying whether this

phenomenon is present in a mock eyewitness paradigm where the participants view a simulated crime. Due to these infirmities, the own-race bias laboratory research cannot be extrapolated to observations made by eyewitnesses to actual crimes. Moreover, Dr. Cooper noted that the laboratory research fails to account for the "contact hypothesis," which is premised on the notion that the own-race bias is not as strong with people who grew up in a diverse environment and were routinely exposed to members of other races. Finally, Dr. Cooper testified that the majority of laboratory research in the area of own-race bias had been conducted with African-Americans and Caucasians and he is unaware of any laboratory, field or archival research that has specifically studied whether the own-race bias phenomenon applies to identifications of African-Americans made by persons of Indian or Pakistani descent. In the absence of such research, Dr. Cooper testified that there is no scientific basis to conclude that the own-race bias phenomenon would apply in the circumstances set forth above.

Conclusions of Law

This Court finds the testimony given by Dr. Franklin and Dr. Cooper to be credible and makes the following conclusions of law with respect to the four factors that were the subject of the *Frye* hearing.

Event Stress

This Court finds that the defendant has met his burden of showing that the event stress phenomenon is generally accepted as reliable in the community of psychologists who study and conduct research in the eyewitness identification field. . . .

[The court in large part rejected Dr. Cooper's argument that laboratory tests could not transfer to real life.] In this case, Dr. Franklin's hearing testimony, the Deffenbacher meta-analysis, the Morgan Study, and the case law from New York and other parts of the country conclusively establish that the event stress phenomenon is generally accepted as reliable in the scientific community. Thus, the defendant may present expert testimony at trial with respect to the event stress phenomenon. The People, if they so choose, are free to call their own expert to rebut the defense expert's testimony.

Weapon Focus

This Court finds that the defendant has met his burden of proving that the weapon focus phenomenon is generally accepted as reliable in the relevant scientific community. . . .

Both Dr. Franklin and Dr. Cooper testified that the Steblay meta-analysis, which examined more than 2000 subjects, found that the presence of a weapon reduces eyewitness identification accuracy. . . .

This Court finds, based upon Dr. Franklin's testimony, the Steblay meta-analysis, the Kassin Survey results, the case law from New York and other parts of the country, and the additional studies and legal

writings with respect to the reliability of the weapon focus effect factor, that the defendant has met his burden under *Frye* of proving that the weapon focus effect is generally accepted as reliable in the scientific community. Thus, the defendant may present expert testimony at trial with respect to the weapon focus phenomenon. The People, if they so choose, are free to call their own expert to rebut the defense expert's testimony.

Event Duration

This court finds that the defendant has met his burden of proving that the event duration phenomenon is generally accepted as reliable in the relevant scientific community. . . .

The People do not seriously dispute the general acceptance of the event duration phenomenon. Rather, they argue that the defendant should be precluded from introducing such testimony as it is within the ken of the average juror. The Court of Appeals, however, has held that "despite the fact that jurors may be familiar from their own experience with factors relevant to the reliability of eyewitness observation and identification it cannot be said that psychological studies regarding the accuracy of an identification are within the ken of the typical juror[.]"

Accordingly, the event duration phenomenon is beyond the ken of the average juror. Moreover, as the defendant has established that this phenomenon is generally accepted as reliable under the *Frye* test, he will be permitted to introduce expert testimony with respect to event duration at trial.

Own-Race Bias

The defendant has failed to meet his burden of proving that it is generally accepted as reliable in the relevant scientific community that the own-race bias phenomenon applies to eyewitnesses identifications made by persons of Asian/Indian descent. Both Dr. Franklin and Dr. Cooper testified that the majority of research in the area of own-race bias concerns identifications made by persons of African-American and Caucasian descent. Indeed, Dr. Franklin testified that the overwhelming majority of the participants studied in the Brigham & Meissner meta-analysis, upon which the defendant principally relies in support of his claim that own-race bias phenomenon is generally accepted as reliable by the relevant scientific community, were Caucasian and African-American.

Dr. Franklin testified at the hearing that she was not aware of any study that reviewed the extent to which the own-race bias phenomenon applied to persons of Asian/Indian descent. While she opined that the own-race bias phenomenon extended to persons of Asian/Indian descent, she acknowledged that she was unable to point to any specific scientific studies to support such a conclusion. Dr. Cooper also testified that he was not aware of any scientific studies that had analyzed whether the own-race bias phenomenon applied to eyewitness identifications of African-

Americans made by persons of Asian/Indian/Pakistani descent. Due to the absence of any evidence showing that the own-race bias phenomenon applies to persons of Asian/Indian/Pakistani descent, the defendant has failed to meet his burden of proving that such a proposition is generally accepted as reliable in the relevant scientific community. Accordingly, the defendant's motion to introduce expert testimony with respect to the own-race bias phenomenon is denied.

Conclusion

The defendant's motion is granted in part and denied in part. The defendant's motion to introduce expert testimony at trial with respect to event stress, weapon focus, event duration, confidence malleability, the effect of post-event information on accuracy of identification, and the correlation between confidence and accuracy of identification is granted. The defendant's motion to introduce expert testimony at trial with respect to own-race bias is denied.

This constitutes the Decision and Order of the Court.

NOTES AND QUESTIONS

1. *The Experts.* How did you assess the experts, Dr. Franklin and Dr. Cooper? What did you think of their credentials? Did one expert seem more qualified than the other? What did you think of their testimony? Do you think the New York judge was influenced by the fact that one expert was from New York and the other from Canada? What was the most persuasive testimony that led to the admission of the event stress, weapon focus, and event duration testimony? Why was the own-race bias testimony excluded?

2. *What Is "Generally Accepted"?* In a Massachusetts case, Jeremy Gomes slashed Zachary Sevigny with a box cutter and was convicted of mayhem, assault and battery, and breaking and entering. Gomes asked for a jury instruction on eyewitness identification and human memory, which would tell the jury that:

> (1) human memory does not operate like a video recording that a person can replay to recall what happened; (2) a witness's level of confidence in an identification may not indicate its accuracy; (3) high levels of stress can reduce the likelihood of making an accurate identification; (4) information from other witnesses or outside sources can affect the reliability of an identification and inflate an eyewitness's confidence in the identification; and (5) viewing the same person in multiple identification procedures may increase the risk of misidentification.

Commonwealth v. Gomes, 22 N.E.3d 897, 903 (Mass. 2015). The trial court judge rejected the jury instruction because he thought the principles in the proposed instruction "were more appropriate for expert testimony or for closing argument." Id. at 904. Jurors are bound to follow jury instructions, which state the law; they may accept or reject the testimony of an expert witness. Id. at 907.

On appeal, the Supreme Judicial Court acknowledged its long-standing holding that "a principle concerning eyewitness identifications may become so generally accepted that, rather than have expert testimony on the point, a standard jury instruction stating that principle would be appropriate." Id. at 900. Gomes could not reach that standard because he had not provided "expert testimony, scholarly articles, or treatises" to show his argument was "generally accepted," and therefore his conviction was affirmed. Is that conclusion consistent with *Frye* and *Daubert*?

The Supreme Judicial Court, however, had just received a Study Group Report that it had commissioned on eyewitness testimony, and so used the case as an opportunity to review its standard for future jury instruction cases. Using the test that a principle is "generally accepted" enough to include in a jury instruction when "there is near consensus in the relevant scientific community adopting that principle," id. at 909, the court concluded that five scientific principles about eyewitness identification had reached near consensus. Can you guess which ones they were? See id. at 911–12 ("i. *Human memory does not function like a video recording but is a complex process that consists of three stages: acquisition, retention, and retrieval.* ii. *An eyewitness's expressed certainty in an identification, standing alone, may not indicate the accuracy of the identification, especially where the witness did not describe that level of certainty when the witness first made the identification.* iii. *High levels of stress can reduce an eyewitness's ability to make an accurate identification.* iv. *Information that is unrelated to the initial viewing of the event, which an eyewitness receives before or after making an identification, can influence the witness's later recollection of the memory or of the identification.* v. *A prior viewing of a suspect at an identification procedure may reduce the reliability of a subsequent identification procedure in which the same suspect is shown.*"). Do you agree that these principles are now "generally accepted"?

The Court also concluded future defendants could continue to present expert testimony about eyewitness testimony when necessary to their case. When do you think such expert testimony would be necessary? Why didn't the court apply the new instruction retroactively to Gomes?

3. *Due Process.* Barion Perry, an African-American male, was suspected of breaking into cars. Eyewitness Nubia Blandon saw Perry talking to police officers and identified him as the man she saw breaking into the cars. Later Blandon could not pick Perry from a photo array prepared by the police. Perry argued that introducing the eyewitness evidence into court violated due process because of the suggestive circumstances of Blandon's identification of Perry. The Supreme Court rejected that argument, concluding that due process is violated only "when the police have arranged suggestive circumstances leading the witness to identify a particular person as the perpetrator of a crime." Perry v. New Hampshire, 565 U.S. 228, 232 (2012). Does neuroscience persuade you to agree or disagree with the Court's conclusion? Does neuroscience persuade you that every use of eyewitness testimony violates due process?

Citing the empirical evidence on eyewitness identifications (which are "the single greatest cause of wrongful convictions in this country"),

dissenting Justice Sotomayor accused the majority of "adopt[ing] an artificially narrow conception of the dangers of suggestive identifications at a time when our concerns should have deepened." Id. at 264–65. Do you agree with the majority or the dissent? Should eyewitness identifications be rejected only when the police manipulate them, or in all circumstances in which scientists would doubt their validity? Do you expect that one day eyewitness testimony will be completely rejected as evidence in criminal cases?

4. *Looking Ahead.* What do you anticipate will be the most contested areas of expert testimony in neuroscience over the next twenty-five years?

C. LOOKING AHEAD: NEUROSCIENCE'S ROLE IN ALL AREAS OF THE LAW

1. MEASURING PAIN

Tort law allows injured plaintiffs to receive compensation for their bodily injury, pain and suffering and, in some circumstances, their emotional distress. Bodily injuries—broken arms and legs, and head injuries evident in x-rays and CT scans—have long been compensable. Tort law has often been ambivalent, however, about emotional distress, pain and suffering, and mental injury.

fMRI now offers the possibility of providing juries with brain scans claiming to identify when a person feels pain, compared to the typical, "On a scale from one to ten, how do you feel?" questioning. The technology could also be used by doctors to assess the condition of patients who suffer from chronic pain and to verify whether patients reporting pain are really suffering. Susannah Locke, The Pain Test: Doctors Have No Idea How Much Their Patients are Suffering: That's about to Change, Vox, Oct. 15, 2014, http://www.vox.com/2014/10/15/6895171/how-doctors-measure-pain-brain-scan-fmri; see also Adam J. Kolber, Will There Be A Neurolaw Revolution?, 89 Ind. L.J. 807 (2014) (discussing medical and legal possibilities if fMRI has 80 percent accuracy in figuring out whether a patient is in pain, the level of severity of that pain, possibility of emotional distress and if technology can identify "neuromarkers for chronic pain"); Tor D. Wager et al., An fMRI-Based Neurologic Signature of Physical Pain, 368 N. Engl. J. Med. 1388 (2013). However, in 2017, a

> **Go to** the website and read the summary of Dr. Wager's study of physical pain. How would you use his findings in the courtroom?

> **Practice Exercise:** What would you have to prove in order to use fMRI images in a tort case to prove damages? Make a list of things you would need to prove and make a list of things you would argue if you opposed the use of fMRI scans.

presidential task force of the International Association for the Study of Pain issued a Consensus Statement concluding that the use of brain imaging to support or dispute claims of chronic pain was not warranted. Karen D. Davis et al., Brain Imaging Tests for Chronic Pain: Medical, Legal and Ethical Issues and Recommendations, 13 Nature Rev. Neurology 624 (2017), https://www.nature.com/articles/nrneurol.2017.122.

The technology might also make it possible to figure out how severely injured criminal victims are. See Francis X. Shen, Sentencing Enhancement and the Crime Victim's Brain, 46 Loy. U. Chi. L.J. 405 (2014) (discussing possibilities of using brain scans to show mental injury and to then enhance criminal sentences based on mental injury).

2. MIND READING

Debate continues over the possibility that fMRI scans can be used to "read" people's minds. We know that fMRI can show blood flow and oxygen changes in the brain; can it tell what a person is thinking? Is it possible that one day the government could get a search warrant for your thoughts? See John Villasenor, Could the Government Get a Search Warrant for Your Thoughts?, Atlantic, July 26, 2013.

Under the Fifth Amendment, "no person . . . shall be compelled in any criminal case to be a witness against himself." Testimony is protected by the amendment, but physical evidence is not. Could the government eventually offer brain scans as physical evidence of a crime? Do you agree "[i]t would make little sense to provide constitutional protection to a suspected bank robber's refusal to answer a detective's question if the thoughts preceding the refusal—e.g., 'since I'm guilty, I'd better not answer this question'—are left unprotected. Stated another way, the right to remain silent would be meaningless if not accompanied by protection for the thinking required to exercise it"? Id.; see also Kiel Robert Brennan-Marquez, A Modest Defense of Mind-Reading, 15 Yale J. of L. & Tech. 214 (2013) (discussing whether brain scans would be testimonial or physical evidence under the Fifth Amendment).

What do you think about the prospect of hooking a criminal suspect up to an EEG and then showing her an object connected with the crime to see if her brain recognizes it? Usually a brain that recognizes an object will emit an electrical response. § 13:10 Brain evidence in court, Forensic DNA Evidence: Science and the Law. In India, police read details of the crime to a suspect and wait to see which areas of the brain light up. The brain scan evidence is admissible in court. Anand Giridharadas, India's Novel Use of Brain Scans in Court is Debated, N.Y. Times, Sept. 15, 2008, at A10. Do you anticipate such evidence being admitted into U.S. courtrooms?

Professor Kolber observes that DNA technology changed the possibilities of prosecuting individuals for past crimes. A person who

leaves her DNA at a crime scene can be prosecuted years later based on the DNA evidence. He raises the similar possibility that in the future fMRI could be used to judge whether a person had committed a crime in the past:

> The pedophilia research suggests that fMRI could someday be used to assess the likelihood that a person has committed or will commit a sex crime. The research on sexual orientation could potentially bear on the distribution of assets in a divorce or the way prisoners are segregated. Other neuroscientific research may uncover conscious or unconscious racial biases. People could be scanned for one purpose, say, to see how an advertising campaign affects their brains, while they inadvertently generate information that bears on their racial biases, sexual orientation, and other sexual preferences. One group of researchers recently demonstrated that the very simple electroencephalography (EEG) sensors in certain mass-market video games can already be used to make plausible inferences about gamers' private "information related to credit cards, PIN numbers, the persons known to the user, or the user's area of residence," and may enable more confident inferences as these sensors improve.

Adam J. Kolber, Will There Be A Neurolaw Revolution?, 89 Ind. L.J. 807, 838–39 (2014). What kind of privacy laws will we need in this new era?

The Supreme Court of India ruled that narco-analysis, the lie-detector test, and brain-mapping violated an individual's right against self-incrimination as well as her right to life and personal liberty. Selvi v. State of Karnataka. Narco-analysis means the defendants were given a truth serum, and then confessed. The lie detector measures physiological responses to questions, and brain-mapping the cognitive responses to questions. The defendants would have lost under the crime-control model, which emphasizes solving crimes, but they won under the due process model, which protects the rights of criminals. Gautam Bhatia, Privacy and the Criminal Process: Selvi v. State of Karnataka (April 22, 2018), https://ssrn.com/abstract=3166849. Would U.S. courts make a similar ruling? Should they?

3. A NEW YOU?

Individuals have long taken drugs to enhance their mental abilities. As we understand more about the brain, should individuals use new technology to enhance their mental abilities? Should we help crime witnesses testify better by boosting their memories? Are you entitled to a memory boost before you take the bar exam? See Owen D. Jones et al., Law and Neuroscience, 33 J. Neuroscience 17624 (2013).

Ritalin is frequently prescribed to help children who suffer from attention deficit hyperactivity disorder (ADHD) learn more and perform

better in school. Should it be prescribed to help a healthy child perform better on a standardized test? Should a doctor be legally prohibited or fined for doing so? Would it violate the bioethical principle of justice for healthy children to receive Ritalin? Is prescribing Ritalin any different from using caffeine to stay awake? See Presidential Commission for the Study of Bioethical Issues, Gray Matters: Topics at the Intersection of Neuroscience, Ethics, and Society, Vol. II 35 (March 2015). What bioethical principles should guide decisions about neural enhancement? See id. at 40 ("the importance of facilitating healthy development and wellbeing; respecting moral agency; informed consent to medical procedures and research; minimization of risk; public education and deliberation; equity and access across all demographic groups, and the reduction of disadvantage, suffering and stigma associated with neurological disorders.")

On the other side of personal improvement, brain research is discovering ways to help people reactivate their traumatic memories so that they can then block them. Other techniques could keep an unhappy memory from ever consolidating. How much time would you like to spend erasing or editing your personal memories? Michael Specter, Partial Recall: Can Neuroscience Help us Rewrite Our Most Traumatic Memories?, New Yorker, May 19, 2014, at 38. Would changing your memories change the person you are? Should potential witnesses in criminal cases be fined if they choose to erase their memories of the crime?

"When does the deterioration of your brain rob you of your identity, and when does it not?" How would you answer this question? Do you think Alzheimer's is the disease most likely to rob you of your identity because it takes away your memory? Would a neurodegenerative disease that took away your ability to walk or speak undermine your identity? A study in *Psychological Science* argues that the "single most powerful predictor of identity change was not disruption to memory—but rather disruption to the moral faculty." Thus the researchers considered frontotemporal dementia, which "obliterates executive function in the brain, impairing self-control and scrambling the moral compass . . . [leading to] antisocial outbursts, apathy, pathological lying, stealing and sexual infidelity," to be more destructive of identity than Alzheimer's, which affects memory, or ALS, which targets the motor system. "It is only when our grip on the moral universe loosens that our identity slips away with it." Nina Strohminger & Shaun Nichols, Your Brain, Your Disease, Your Self, N.Y. Times, Aug. 21, 2015, at A9. Do you agree? What capacities would you have to lose before your family or friends would conclude that you had lost your identity?

4. DEATH OR LIFE?

Technology has made it possible for scientists to study the brains of patients who may be in a non-responsive mental state, such as a

persistent vegetative state (PVS) or a minimally conscious state (MCS). Doctors can now ask patients questions and then see what responses arise on an fMRI. Such testing may provide a better indication of a patient's mental awareness than studying her physical responses to questions, e.g., by asking her to blink her eyes or shake her head. These discoveries can help medical professionals distinguish among the various non-responsive mental states to determine which patients have a higher likelihood of recovery. See Dalia B. Taylor, Communicating with Vegetative State Patients: The Role of Neuroimaging in American Disability Law, 66 Stan. L. Rev. 1451 (2014).

Neuroscientist Adrian Owen, for example, began his career by showing familiar faces to a patient in a coma. The part of the brain that recognizes familiar faces—the fusiform face area (FFA)—activated in response to the pictures. David Cyranoski, Neuroscience: The Mind Reader, Nature, Jun. 13, 2012, at http://www.nature.com/news/neuroscience-the-mind-reader–1.10816. Owen then developed techniques allowing PVS patients to answer yes or no to his questions. Owen thinks many diagnosed PVS patients—perhaps as many as one-fourth of them—are actually minimally conscious.

Go to the website and listen to the podcast describing Owen's work.

In one scenario, Owen asked patients first to imagine playing tennis, and then to remember walking through their house. Different areas of the brain would light up. Then he asked the patient to answer yes or no to his questions. If the answer was yes, the patient was supposed to think about tennis; if it was no, to think about their home. Then he would ask them specific questions: "Is your father's name Thomas? No. Is your father's name Alexander? Yes. Do you have any brothers? Yes. Do you have any sisters? No." Cyranoski, *infra*.

Practice Exercise: Imagine that parents like the Quinlans or the Cruzans decide to refuse artificial respiration, nutrition and hydration for a comatose daughter. A neuroscientist is ready to testify that the daughter can answer yes or no by imagining tennis and her house. If the hospital tries to comply with the parents' wishes, are they subject to a lawsuit under the ADA? How would the lawsuit turn out?

Some neuroscientists disagree with Owen, and believe that some patients can be responsive without being conscious. When would research like Owen's be allowed in court under *Frye* and *Daubert*?

> **Practice Exercise:** If, using Owen's technique, a patient who appeared to be in a PVS answered "yes" to the question "Do you want to die?" would the patient have a right to die? Argue both sides. How do you think the Supreme Court would rule in such a case?

The Americans with Disabilities Act (ADA) prohibits discrimination on the basis of disability. Disability is defined as "(a) a physical or mental impairment that substantially limits one or more major life activities of such individual; (b) a record of such an impairment; or (c) being regarded as having such an impairment." 42 U.S.C. § 12102(1) (2012). "An individual meets the requirement of 'being regarded as having such an impairment' if the individual establishes that he or she has been subjected to an action prohibited under this chapter because of an actual or perceived physical or mental impairment whether or not the impairment limits or is perceived to limit a major life activity." Id. § 12102(3)(A).

What would it take for patients with severe brain injury to receive the care that they need and are legally entitled to? How can we ensure that patients with the most severe injuries get the care they need? Can disabilities law help them? Megan S. Wright, Nina Varsava, Joel Ramirez, Kyle Edwards, Nathan Guevremont, & Tamar Ezer, Joseph J. Fins, Severe Brain Injury, Disability, and the Law: Achieving Justice for A Marginalized Population, 45 Fla. St. U. L. Rev. 313, 316 (2018).

5. SOLITARY CONFINEMENT AND THE DEATH PENALTY?

Should brain studies that show negative consequences of solitary confinement be used to stop solitary confinement in prisons? Studies show such confinement does psychological and neurological harm. Thousands of California prisoners were in solitary confinement, some for 10 and others for 20 years. Those prisoners eventually entered into a settlement with the state to limit solitary confinement to much rarer circumstances. President Obama then restricted solitary confinement in federal prisons. Ashker v. California, 2018 WL 3777168 (N.D. Ca. Aug. 9, 2018); Moheb Costandi, Using Neuroscience Evidence to Argue Against Solitary Confinement, Dana Foundation, Jan. 3, 2019, https://www.dana.org/article/using-neuroscience-evidence-to-argue-against-solitary-confinement/. How much should solitary confinement be limited?

How much should physicians participate in the death penalty? Is it an ethical violation for them to assist? Deborah W. Denno, Physician Participation in Lethal Injection, NEJM. Aug. 1, 2019, https://www.nejm.org/doi/full/10.1056/NEJMp1814786?query=neurology-neurosurgery. Why or why not?

6. WHAT IS THE PRACTICE OF MEDICINE?

Dr. Charles Binkley explains that Artificial Intelligence (AI) and Machine Learning (ML) now play a large part in the practice of medicine. Charles Binkley, The Physician's Conundrum: Assigning Moral Responsibility for Medical Artificial Intelligence and Machine Learning, Verdict, Feb. 8, 2021, https://verdict.justia.com/2021/02/08/the-physicians-conundrum. AI/ML are used to diagnose illness and to recommend treatments. Dr. Binkley explains that two ethical issues arise from this role. First, the reasoning behind AI/ML is complex enough that it is hard to explain; "the *why* behind a specific recommendation for an individual patient may not be possible to explain." Id. That means patients and physicians can face diagnoses and treatments "without any underlying reasoning." Id. Second, physicians share their agency with the technological systems. Although two human physicians can consult about their opinions, the physician and AI/ML cannot. Physicians may learn to defer to the technical opinion, and the technical decision may become the standard of care even if doctors disagree with it. The physician might override the system when it is wrong. . .or when it is correct. Such systems place new moral burdens on physicians while also providing great insight into patient well-being.

"As machine learning (ML) becomes more successful in the practice of medicine, medical malpractice cases will have to change. ML-generated medical diagnostics will have to become the standard of care. What would that do to a malpractice case?" A. Michael Froomkin et al., When AIs Outperform Doctors: Confronting the Challenges of A Tort-Induced over-Reliance on Machine Learning, 61 Ariz. L. Rev. 33, 33 (2019). What will the new malpractice case look like?

We hope you have a wonderful career practicing bioethics law.

INDEX

References are to Pages